D1448152

INTRODUCING SOCIOLINGUISTICS

SECOND EDITION

Rajend Mesthrie, Joan Swann,
Ana Deumert and William L. Leap

Edinburgh University Press

© Rajend Mesthrie, Joan Swann,
Ana Deumert and William L. Leap, 2000, 2009

Reprinted 2010, 2011, 2012, 2013

Edinburgh University Press
22 George Square, Edinburgh

www.euppublishing.com

First edition published by Edinburgh University Press in 2000.

Reprinted 2001, 2003, 2004

Typeset in Sabon and Gill Sans
by Servis Filmsetting Ltd, Stockport, Cheshire, and
printed and bound in Great Britain by
CPI Group (UK) Ltd, Croydon, CR0 4YY

A CIP record for this book is available from the British Library

ISBN 978 0 7486 3843 7 (hardback)
ISBN 978 0 7486 3844 4 (paperback)

The right of Rajend Mesthrie, Joan Swann, Ana Deumert and William L. Leap
to be identified as authors of this work has been asserted in accordance with the
Copyright, Designs and Patents Act 1988.

CONTENTS

LIST OF TABLES, MAPS AND FIGURES

List of Tables

List of Maps

List of Figures

ABBREVIATIONS

AAVE	African American Vernacular English
ASL	American Sign Language
BSL	British Sign Language
BUV	Berlin Urban Vernacular
CBA	cost-benefit analysis
EFL	English as a Foreign Language
ESL	English as a Second Language
IRE	initiation–response–evaluation
ISA	Ideological state apparatus
LANE	*Linguistic Atlas of New England*
LSI	*Linguistic Survey of India*
PSE	Pidgin Sign English
RP	Received Pronunciation
SASL	South African Sign Language
SED	*Survey of English Dialects*

ACKNOWLEDGEMENTS

Thanks are due to Rowan Mentis for polishing up the manuscript, Shirley Butcher and Laven Naidoo (Environmental and Geographical Sciences, University of Cape Town) and James Mills-Hicks for drawing the maps, Germain Kouame, David Fraser and Wendy Beck (University of Cape Town) for help with the illustrations. We would like to thank our students who have used the first edition in their studies and whose comments helped us in the preparation of this new edition. Grateful thanks are due to Carol Myers-Scotton for discussion and advice on the Markedness Model in code-switching.

We also thank many colleagues who took time to comment on their experience of the first edition: among others, Peter Bakker, John Baugh, Rakesh Bhatt, Jan Blommaert, Claire Cowie, Penny Eckert, Diana Eades, Mauro Fernández, Ernst Hakon Jahr, Hilary Janks, Rochelle Kapp, Paul Kerswill, Kay McCormick, Miriam Meyerhoff, Paul Roberge, Bernd Spolsky and Wim Vandebussche.

Thanks are due to Edinburgh University Press for their help and advice in preparing the second edition (and their patience), and to our co-publishers, John Benjamins.

Grateful acknowledgement is made to the following publishers and copyright-holders for permission to reproduce or modify a range of materials in this book that have been published elsewhere. Every effort has been made to trace copyright-holders; but if any have inadvertently been overlooked, the authors and publishers will be pleased to make the necessary arrangement at the first opportunity.

TABLES

Table 1.1 is from C. A. Ferguson (1950), 'Diglossia' in *Word* vol. 15, by permission of Linguistic Circle of New York; Table 3.1 is from W. Labov (1972), *Sociolinguistic Patterns*, by permission of University of

Pennsylvania Press; Table 3.2 is from P. Trudgill (1983a), *Sociolinguistics*, by permission of P. Trudgill, published by Penguin Books; Table 5.1 is from S. Gal (1979), *Language Shift*, by permission of Elsevier; Table 7.1 is from M. Haas (1944), 'Men's and women's speech in Koasati' in *Language* vol. 20 by permission of the Linguistics Society of America; Tables 8.1 and 8.2 are based on J. Fishman (1991), *Reversing Language Shift*, by permission of Multilingual Matters; the language statistics of South Africa in Chapter 12 are from *The People of South Africa: Population Census, 2001*, courtesy of the Department of Statistics, South Africa.

MAPS

Map 2.1 is based on G. A. Grierson (1927), *Linguistic Survey of India*, by permission of Low Price Publications; Map 2.2 is from H. Orton and N. Wright (1974), *A Word Geography of England*, by permission of Elsevier; Map 2.3 The lexical isogloss: *folk* vs *people* is from C. S. Upton and J. D. A. Widdowson (2006), *An Atlas of English Dialects* by permission of Taylor and Francis and the authors; Maps 2.4, 2.5 and 2.6 are based on P. Trudgill and J. K. Chambers (1980), *Dialectology* (2nd edn), by permission of Cambridge University Press and the authors; Map 4.1 is based on L. Milroy (1980), *Language and Social Networks*, by permission of Blackwell Publishers; Map 4.2 is based on N. Dittmar and P. Schlobinski (eds) (1988), *The Sociolinguistics of Urban Vernaculars*, by permission of Mouton de Gruyter publishers; Map 4.3 is from D. Crystal (1995), *The Cambridge Encyclopedia of the English Language*, by permission of the author and Cambridge University Press; Map 4.4 is from W. Labov et al. (2005) *The Phonological Atlas of North America*, by permission of Mouton de Gruyter; Map 5.1 is cited in N. A. Niedzielski and D. R. Preston (2000), *Folk Linguistics* by permission of Mouton de Gruyter; Map 5.2 is based on M. Brenzinger (1992), 'Patterns of language shift in east Africa', in R. K. Herbert (ed.), *Language and Society in Africa*, by permission of Witwatersrand University Press; Map 5.3 is from S. Gal (1979), *Language Shift*, by permission of Elsvier; Maps 9.2 and 9.3 are based on J. Arends, P. Muysken and N. Smith (eds) (1995), *Pidgins and Creoles: An Introduction*, by permission of John Benjamins Publishers.

ILLUSTRATIONS

Figure 1.1 is from Benjamin Lee Whorf (1956), *Language, Thought and Reality; Selected Writings of Benjamin Lee Whorf*, edited by John Carroll, by permission of MIT Press; Figure 1.2 is based on P. Trudgill

(1975), *Accent, Dialect and the School*, by permission of Edward Arnold Publishers and the author; Figure 2.1 is from D. Crystal (1995), *The Cambridge Encyclopedia of the English Language*, by permission of the author and Cambridge University Press; Figure 2.2 is based on K. M. Petyt (1980), *The Study of Dialect*, by permission of Andre Deutsch; Figures 3.3 and 3.4 are from W. Labov (1972a), *Sociolinguistic Patterns*, by permission of University of Pennsylvania Press; Figure 4.1 is from M. Chen (1972), 'The time dimension: contribution toward a theory of sound change', in *Foundations of Language* Vol. 8; Figure 4.2 is from J. Aitchison (1991), *Language Change: Progress or Decay?* (2nd edn), by permission of Cambridge University Press; Figure 4.3 is based on figures in W. Labov (1972a), *Sociolinguistic Patterns*, and J. Fowler (1986), 'The social stratification of (r) in New York City department stores, 24 years after Labov', unpublished MS, New York University; Figure 4.4 is from J. Coates (1993), *Women, Men and Language* (2nd edn), by permission of Pearson Education Limited; Figures 4.5 and 4.6 are from L. Milroy (1980), *Language and Social Networks*, by permission of Blackwell Publishers; Figure 4.7 is from N. Dittmar and P. Schlobinski (eds) (1988), *The Sociolinguistics of Urban Vernaculars*, by permission of Walter de Gruyter Publishers; Figures 4.8, 4.9 and 4.10 are from B. Horvath (1985), *Variation in Australian English: The Sociolects of Sydney*, by permission of Cambridge University Press and the author; Figures 4.12a and b are based respectively on W. Labov, 'The three dialects of English' and P. Eckert, 'Social polarization and the choice of linguistic variants', both in Eckert (ed.) (1991), *New Ways of Analyzing Sound Change*, by permission of Elsevier and the authors; Figures 4.13a and 4.13b are based on R. Lass and S. Wright (1986), 'Endogeny versus contact: "Afrikaans influence" on South African English', in *English World-Wide* vol. 7, by permission of the authors and John Benjamins Publishers; Figure 5.1 is from N. Coupland (1996), 'Hark, Hark the Lark: multiple voicing in DJ talk', in D. Graddol, D. Leith and J. Swann (eds) *English: History, Diversity and Change*, by permission of Taylor and Francis, and N. Coupland (2001), 'Language, situation, and the relational self: theorizing dialect style in sociolinguistics,' in P. Eckert and J. Rickford *Style and Sociolinguistic Variation* by permission of Cambridge University Press; Figure 6.1 is from J. Hill (1995), 'The voices of Don Gabriel: responsibility and self in a modern Mexicano narrative', in D. Tedlock and B. Mannheim (eds), *The Dialogic Emergence of Culture*, by permission of University of Illinois Press; Figure 7.1 is from B. Horvath (1985), *Variation in Australian English: The Sociolects of Sydney*, by permission of Cambridge University Press and the author; Figure 8.1 is drawn on the basis of data from K. H. Basso (1990), *Western Apache Language and Culture*, by permission of University of Arizona Press; Figure 9.1 is from W. R. O' Donnell and L. Todd (1980), *Variety in Contemporary English*, by permission of the authors; Figure 10.1 is from N. Fairclough (1992), *Discourse and Social Change*, by permission of Polity Press; Figure 10.2 is based on P. Bourdieu (1984), *Distinction: A Social Critique of the Judgement of Taste*, by permission of Taylor and Francis; Figure 10.3 is based on R. Jenkins (1992), *Pierre Bourdieu*, by permission of Taylor and Francis; Figure 12.2 is a photograph taken by M. Sebba; Figure 12.3 is from F. Coulmas (ed.) (1992), *Language and Economy*, by permission of Blackwell Publishers; Figure 12.4 is based on S. R. Ramsey (1987), *The Languages of China*, by permission of Princeton University Press; Figures 13.1, 13.3, 13.5 and 13.9 are from J. G. Kyle and B. Woll (eds) (1985), *Sign Language: The Study of Deaf People and Their Language*, by permission of Cambridge University Press and the editors; Figure 13.2 is from B. Bergman and L. Wallin (1991), 'Sign language research and the Deaf community', in S. Prillwitz and T. Vollhbaer (eds), *Sign Language Research and Application*, by permission of Signum Verlag; Figure 13.4 is from D. Crystal (ed.) (1987), *The Cambridge Encyclopedia of Language*, by permission of Cambridge University Press and the editor; Figure 13.6 is from C. Baker-Shenk and D. Cokely (1991), *American Sign Language: A Teacher's Resource Text on Grammar and Culture*, by permission of Gallaudet University Press; Figure 13.7 is from C. Penn (1992), 'The sociolinguistics of South African Sign Language', in R. K. Herbert (ed.), *Language and Society in Africa*, by permission of Witwatersrand University Press; Figure 13.8 is from T. Supalla (1991), 'Serial verb motion in ASL', in P. Siple and S. Fischer (eds), *Theoretical Issues in Sign Language Research*, by permission of University of Chicago Press; Figure 13.10 is from Timothy G. Reagan, 'The Deaf as a linguistic minority: educational considerations' in *Harvard Educational Review* vol. 55 (August 1985) by permission of the President and Fellows of Harvard College, and the author; Figure 13.11 is from Lucas et al. (2001b), *Sociolinguistic Variation in American Sign Language* by permission of Gallaudet University Press; Figure 13.12 is from A. J. Aramburo (1989), *The Sociolinguistics of the Black Community*, by permission of Elsevier; Figure 13.13 is based on a photograph supplied by The Bastion of the Deaf in Cape Town; Figures 13.14 and 13.15 are from W. A. Rudner and R. Butowsky (1981), 'Signs used in the Deaf gay community' in *Sign Language Studies* vol. 10, by courtesy of Gallaudet University Press;

CARTOONS

The cartoon on prescriptivism (Chapter 1) is from *English Today* vol. 6, by permission of the editor Tom McArthur, and the cartoonist, Doug Baker; the cartoon on US English (Chapter 1) is from D. Crystal (1988),

Rediscover Grammar, by permission of the author and the cartoonist, Edward McLachlan; The South African Truth Commission cartoon (Chapter 10) is by Zapiro, by permission of *The Sowetan* and Zapiro; the figure on Nazi Germany propaganda (Chapter 10) is from *Völkischer Beobachter* 1 May 1935; the cartoon sequence on teaching Xhosa (Chapter 12) is from K. Chisholm et al., *Xhosa: Let's Get Talking*, by permission of Karin Chisholm; the 'regular' cartoons (Chapters 1 and 5) are from *Dennis the Menace* (Hank Ketcham), and *Hagar the Horrible* (Dik Browne) (Chapter 11), both by permission of King Features Syndicate; *Garfield* (Jim Davies) (Chapter 2) by permission of Universal Press Syndicate; *BC* (Johnny Hart) (Chapter 3 and 10), *The Wizard of Id* (Brant Parker and Johnny Hart) (Chapters 1, 10 and 11) and *Andy Capp* (Chapter 4) by permission of Creators Syndicate.

TEXT

The extract from *Things Fall Apart* (Chapter 2) by Chinua Achebe (1962) is by permission of Heinemann Educational Publishers; the excerpt from *'Tis* (Chapter 2) by Frank McCourt (1999), is by permission of HarperCollins and the author; the excerpt from the poem, *Der Renner* by Hugo von Trimberg, is taken from S. Barbour and P. Stevenson (1990), *Variation in German: A Critical Approach to German Sociolinguistics*, by permission of Cambridge University Press; entry from the DARE webpage for Adam's housecat (Chapter 2) by permission of Harvard University Press; the poem 'Jack and Jill' (Chapter 2) is from *The Legal Guide to Mother Goose* by Don Sandburg, used by permission of Price, Stern & Sloan, a member of the Penguin Group (USA); the extracts of Guyanese speech (Chapter 3) are from J. Rickford (1987), *Dimensions of a Creole Continuum*, by permission of Stanford University Press; the extract 'banter in Belfast' (Chapter 4) is from L. Milroy (1980), *Language and Social Networks*, by permission of Blackwell Publishers; the transcripts of code-switching in Africa (Chapter 5) are from C. Myers-Scotton (1993), *Social Motivations for Code-switching: Evidence from Africa*, by permission of Oxford University Press; the example of Hungarian–German switching (Chapter 5) is from S. Gal (1979), *Language Shift*, by permission of Elsevier; the example of Chinese–English switching (Chapter 5) is from Li Wei (1998), 'Banana split? Variations in language choice and code-switching patterns of two groups of British-born Chinese in Tyneside', in R. Jacobson (ed.), *Codeswitching Worldwide*, by permission of Mouton de Gruyter; the re-transcription of Myers-Scotton (Chapter 5) is from P. Auer (1998), 'Introduction: Bilingual Conversation Revisited', in P. Auer (ed.) *Code-Switching in Conversation: Language, Interaction and Identity* by permission of Taylor and Francis; transcripts of language crossing (Chapter 5) are adapted from B. Rampton (1998), 'Language crossing and the redefinition of reality', in P. Auer (ed.) *Code-Switching in Conversation: Language, Interaction and Identity* by permission of Taylor and Francis; extract from Japanes rap lyrics (Chapter 5) is from A. Pennycook (2003), 'Global Englishes, Rip Slyme and performativity' in *Journal of Sociolinguistics* 7(4) by permission of Blackwell Publishers; the transcript of children's use of voice in narrative (Chapter 6) is from J. Maybin (1997), 'Story voices: the use of reported speech in 10–12-year-olds' spontaneous narratives', in L. Thompson (ed.), *Children Talking: The Development of Pragmatic Competence*, by permission of Multilingual Matters; evaluative comment on a child's story (Chapter 6) is from J. Maybin (2006) *Children's Voices: Talk, Knowledge and Identity* by permission of Palgrave Macmillan; the transcript of Mexicano narrative is from J. Hill (1995), 'The voices of Don Gabriel: responsibility and self in a modern Mexicano narrative', in D. Tedlock and B. Mannheim (eds), *The Dialogic Emergence of Culture*, by permission of University of Illinois Press; the transcript on women's cooperative talk (Chapter 6) is from J. Coates (1994), 'No gaps, lots of overlap: turn-taking patterns in the talk of women friends', in D. Graddol, J. Maybin and B. Stierer (eds), *Researching Language and Literacy in Social Context*, by permission of Multilingual Matters; the transcripts on doctor–patient talk (Chapter 6) are from P. A. Treichler et al. (1984), 'Problems and *problems*: power relationships in a medical encounter', in C. Kramarae, M. Schulz and W. M. O'Barr (eds), *Language and Power*, by permission of Sage Publishers, and from N. Fairclough (1992), *Discourse and Social Change,* by permission of Polity Press; bullet lists (Chapter 6) are from D. Eades (1996) 'Legal recognition of cultural differences in communication: the case of Robyn Kina', *Language and Communication* 16(3) by permission of Elsevier; the transcript of the job interview (Chapter 6) is from C. Roberts, E. Davies and T. Jupp (1992), *Language and Discrimination*, by permission of Pearson Education Limited; the examples of gender and politeness in Tzeltal (Chapter 7) are from P. Brown (1980), 'How and why are women more polite?: some evidence from a Mayan community', in S. McConnell-Ginet, R. Borker and N. Furman (eds), *Women and Language in Literature and Society*, by permission of Greenwood Publishing Group, Inc.; the transcript of doctor/ nurse talk (Chapter 7) is from J. Holmes (2006), *Gendered Talk at Work*, by permission of Blackwell Publishing; the two views on language death (Chapter 8) by K. Hale and P. Ladefoged (1992), are from *Language* vol. 68 by permission of the Linguistic Society of America; the rhyme 'This Little Pig' in Cameroon Pidgin and the extract from Guyanese Creole (Chapter 9) are from L. Todd (1984), *Modern Englishes: Pidgins and Creoles*, by permission of Taylor and Francis; the excerpt from the transcript of a Tok Pisin learner (Chapter 9) is from J. Holmes (1992), *An Introduction to Sociolinguistics*, by permission of Pearson Education Limited; the excerpt from the poem 'Listen Mr Oxford Don' (Chapter 9) is taken from J. Agard (1985), *Mangoes and Bullets*, by permission of Serpent's Tail Publishers; the example of the Guyanese Creole continuum (Chapter 9) is from W. R. O' Donnell and L. Todd (1980), *Variety in Contemporary English*, by permission of the authors; the excerpt on Indian English vocabulary (Chapter 9) is from the dictionary, *Sahibs, Nabobs and Boxwallahs* by I. Lewis (1991), by permission of Oxford University Press (New Delhi); the South African advertisements (Chapter 10) are from E. Bertlesen (1997), 'Ads and amnesia: black advertising in the new South Africa', in S. Nuttall and C. Coetzee (eds) *Negotiating the Past: The Making of Memory in South Africa*, by permission of the author; the transcript of caste discourse (Chapter 10) is from F. Southworth (1974), 'Linguistic masks for power: some relationships between semantic and social change' in *Anthropological Linguistics* vol. 16, by permission of Indiana University; the teacher–pupil transcripts (Chapter 11) are from William Leap (1993), *American Indian English*, G. Dorr-Bremme (1984) unpublished dissertation, and J. L. Solomon (1995), unpublished dissertation, courtesy of University of Utah Press, University of California (San Diego) and American University respectively; the excerpt from a scene involving teacher and child interaction is from a review of J. R. Dillard's 'Black English' by R. Fasold (1975) in *Language in Society* vol. 4 by permission of Cambridge University Press; the document on vernacular languages in education is by courtesy of UNESCO; the resolution on Ebonics is from the Internet (*The Linguist List*), by permission of the Linguistic Society of America; Constitutional Multilingualism, is an excerpt from the South African Constitution; excerpt on language marketing in Israel (Chapter 12) is from R. L. Cooper (1989), *Language Planning and Social Change*, by permission of Cambridge University Press; quotation about Chinese characters (Chapter 12) is from P. Chen (1996) 'Toward a phonographic writing system of Chinese: a case study in writing reform' in *IJSL* 122 by permission of Mouton de Gruyter; excerpt on role of elites in language planning (Chapter 12) is from R. L. Cooper (1989), *Language Planning and Social Change*, by permission of Cambridge University Press; excerpt on cost-efficiency of multilingual policies is from LoBianco (1996), *Language as an Economic Resource*, in Language Planning Report No. 5.1, Pretoria: Department of Arts, Culture, Science and Technology; the examples of Nynorsk/Bokmål (Chapter 12) are from Ivar Aasen (1859), quoted in E. Haugen (1968), 'Language planning in modern Norway', in J. A. Fishman (ed.) *Readings in the Sociology of Language*, by permission of Mouton de Gruyter; extract, *Equal Rights for Nynorsk* (Chapter 12) is from M. Oftedal, (1990), 'Is Nynorsk a minority language?', in Haugen et al. (eds), *Minority Languages Today*, rev. edn., by permission of Edinburgh University Press; excerpt on Constutional Multilingualism is from the South African Constitution (1996); the example of court translation (Chapter 12) is from N. C. Steytler (1993), 'Implementing language rights in court: the role of the court interpreter in South Africa', in K. Prinsloo et al. (eds), *Language, Law and Equality*, by permission of the University of South Africa; the excerpt on 'learning to speak' (Chapter 13) is from H. Lane (1984a), *When the Mind Hears*, by permission of Random House Publishers; the excerpts on the prestige of pidgin sign English and on situational switching in ASL (Chapter 13) are from B. Kannapell (1989), 'An examination of Deaf college students' attitudes toward ASL and English', and R. E. Johnson and C. Erting (1989) 'Ethnicity and socialization in a classroom for Deaf children' respectively, both in C. Lucas (ed.), *The Sociolinguistics of the Deaf Community*, by permission of Elsevier; the excerpt on non-standard signing (Chapter 13) is from J. C. Woodward (1976), 'Black southern signing', in *Language in Society* vol. 5, by permission of Cambridge University Press; the three quotations on language in Martha's Vineyard (Chapter 13) are from N. E. Groce (1985) *Everyone Here Spoke Sign Language: Hereditary Deafness on Martha's Vineyard*, by permission of Harvard University Press.

Despite exhaustive efforts, we have not been able to make contact with holders of copyright for the following extracts, and would be glad of any information to help us do so: the box on ploughing terms in Bihar (Chapter 1) from G. A. Grierson (1975 [1885]), *Bihar Peasant Life*, Cosmo Publishers; the extract from the short story 'Wa'er' (Chapter 3) by George Rew in the *Scots Magazine* (1990); examples of gendered pronouns in Japanese (Chapter 7) from S. Ide (1989), 'How and why do women speak more politely in Japanese' in *Studies in English and American Literature* vol. 24, Japan Women's University, repr. in S. Ide and N. H. McGloin (eds) (1990), *Aspects of Japanese Women's Language*, Kurosio Publishers; examples of gendered pronouns in Japanese (Chapter 7) from K. A. Reynolds (1986), 'Female speakers of Japanese in transition', in S. Bremner, N. Caskey and B. Moonwoman (eds), *Proceedings of the First Berkeley Women and Language Conference*, Berkeley Women and Language Group; the transcript of gender and power (Chapter 7) from C. West and D. H. Zimmerman (1983), 'Small insults: a study of interruptions in cross-sex conversation between unacquainted persons', in B. Thorne, C. Kramarae and N. Henley (eds), *Language, Gender and Society*, Newbury House; the profile of a slave ship (Chapter 9) based on E. Donnan (1965), *Documents Illustrative of the History of the Slave Trade to America*, vol. 2: *The Eighteenth Century*, Octagon Books; the poem 'Eden 22' (Chapter 9) by Mervin Mirapuri, Woodrose Publications, Singapore; Figure 12.1 is from W. Moritz (1978), *Das älteste Schulbuch in Südwestafrika/Namibia: H. C. Knudsen und die Namafibel*, John Meinert publishers; excerpts on 'deaf fakes' and sign language oppression (Chapter 13) from J. Harris (1995), *The Cultural Meaning of Deafness: Language, Identity and Power Relations*, Avebury Publishers.

NOTE TO READERS

We have aimed this book at readers who have little or no prior experience of linguistics. We have therefore tried to be as explicit as possible when using terms and conventions from linguistics, and have tried to keep them to a minimum. Such terms are explained in the Glossary. We have given in boldface (for example **register**) key concepts in sociolinguistics that readers should remember. Less important terms are given in quotation marks (for example 'relexicalisation').

Although we have kept them to a minimum, the use of phonetic symbols in Chapters 2 to 4 is unavoidable. We have given a rough indication of the pronunciations signalled by these symbols in the text. Since the principles of phonetic classification are vital to an understanding of the studies of accent in Chapters 2 to 4, we give a brief outline here, which you should use as a handy reference whenever symbols and terms pertaining to vowels occur in the text. A diagram of the vocal tract showing the main speech organs is given on the inside back cover of this book. For the purposes of this book the classification of consonants is less significant than that of vowels.

A vowel can be described by its position in two dimensions, depending on the position in the mouth of the highest point of the tongue. The two dimensions are 'front–central–back' and 'high–mid–low'. Figure A is a representation of the area of the mouth covered by these two dimensions.

Figure B represents in greater detail the characteristics of the basic vowels mentioned in this book. Alongside is a word in which each vowel in the chart occurs. The pronunciation of high-status speakers in southern England (for example newsreaders on the BBC World Service) is used as a model, except where indicated otherwise.

There are other properties that give rise to differences between vowels. One is that vowels may be produced with lips rounded or spread. This distinction gives rise to **rounded** and **unrounded** vowels. In Figure B, the rounded vowels are given in brackets. Another important distinction in many languages is that between **long** and **short** vowels, corresponding to

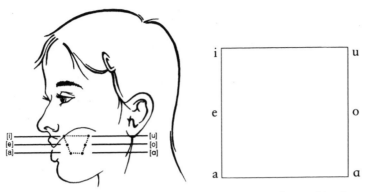

Figure A Sketch of tongue position for main vowels cited in the text

i: s<u>ea</u>t
ɪ   s<u>i</u>t
e   g<u>a</u>te (Northern English dialects)
ɛ   b<u>e</u>t
æ   b<u>a</u>t
a   p<u>a</u>th (Northern English)
ə   b<u>e</u>tt<u>er</u>
ɜ: b<u>ir</u>d
u: b<u>oo</u>t
ʊ   h<u>oo</u>d
ʌ   b<u>u</u>t
ɔ: c<u>a</u>ll
o   b<u>oa</u>t (Scottish English)
ɑ: p<u>a</u>rt
ɒ   h<u>o</u>t
ɣ   (pronounced like [o], with lips spread).

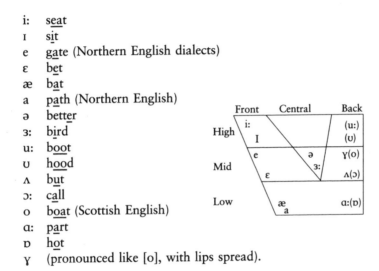

Figure B The vowel chart, showing position of main vowels cited in the text

the duration of the vowel. The colon symbol ':' is used to denote a long vowel: thus [e] is a short vowel, while [e:] is its long counterpart.

Diphthongs are combinations of vowels – for example [aɪ] denotes the vowel sound in the word *ride*, which is a combination of the vowels [a] and [ɪ].

Note the following linguistic conventions for representing sounds (taking 'p' as an example):

<p>   the spelling
[p]   the actual pronunciation
/p/   the **phoneme,** or abstract element as part of the sound system of a language
(p)   the **sociolinguistic variable.**

The need for these conventions is discussed in different parts of Chapters 2 to 4.

Finally, in citing words from other languages or dialects of English, italics are used for the actual word or phrase being cited, immediately followed by a rendition into written standard English in single inverted commas: thus, *kyat* 'cat' gives you a form in italics from a particular language (Caribbean Creole in this case) with its usual meaning in single inverted commas.

1
CLEARING THE GROUND: BASIC ISSUES, CONCEPTS AND APPROACHES

1.1 INTRODUCTION

This book is intended to introduce you to an important branch of language study, generally known as sociolinguistics. We assume that readers of this book are currently taking or are about to take an introductory course in linguistics. Accordingly, we start with a brief characterisation of the place of sociolinguistics within the overall discipline of linguistics.

'Language' and Linguistics

Linguistics may be somewhat blandly defined as the study of language. Such a characterisation leaves out the all-important formulation of how such study is to be conducted, and where exactly the boundaries of the term 'language' itself lie. Edward Sapir (1921: 7) in his influential book *Language*, which is still in print after 80 years, defined his subject matter as follows:

> Language is a purely human and non-instinctive method of communicating ideas, emotions, and desires by means of a system of voluntarily produced symbols. These symbols are, in the first instance, auditory and they are produced by the so-called 'organs of speech'.

Drawing on this characterisation, modern linguists (e.g. Ronald Wardhaugh, 1978: 3) conceive of language as a system of arbitrary vocal symbols used for human communication. This definition stresses that the basic building blocks of language are spoken words which combine sounds with meanings. The symbols are arbitrary in the sense that the link between the sound and the meaning system varies from language to language. There is no necessary connection between the form of a word and its meaning. For example, the term 'cat' in English refers to a particular animal by convention, not by a special connection between the sequence *c-a-t* and the animal. Of course, cats are referred to by other sound (or words) in other languages, for example *billī* in Hindi. An exception is formed by words which do reflect some property of the concept which they denote. In literary analysis, these are described as onomatopoeic, as in the word *buzz*, which to some extent mimics the sound made by bees (see the term 'icon' in the box below). The arbitrariness of linguistic symbols was stressed by the Swiss linguist, Ferdinand de Saussure, who differentiated between the 'signifier' (the word for a concept) and the 'signified' (the concept denoted by the word). These were two indistinguishable aspects of what he called the 'linguistic sign'.

Three types of signs distinguished by the US philosopher Charles Peirce in his general theory of communication systems

- A **symbol** involves an arbitrary relationship between sign and object, but which is understood as a convention, for example a green light as a traffic signal 'go'.
- An **index** involves a logical relation between sign and object (such as cause and effect), for example a weathercock, which stands for the wind but which is directly influenced by the wind direction.
- An **icon** involves a relationship whereby the sign replicates some characteristic of the object: for example a drawing of a cat replicates some features of the shape of a cat.

(cited in Noth 1990: 112–14)

At the time that Sapir was writing, not many linguists were familiar with the structure of sign languages used by hearing- and speech-impaired people. Rather than insisting that language has to be based on speech, linguists would today distinguish different modes of language: sign, speech, writing. Finally, the emphasis in the definition of language on *human* communication draws attention to differences between language and animal systems of communication. Research on the communicative systems of primates, bees and dolphins inculcates a great deal of respect among linguists for their abilities but also shows that their communicative systems are qualitatively different from the language capacity of humans. The ability to convey complex information about things that are not necessarily present, to discuss entities that do not necessarily exist and to use language to negotiate and plan is not found in the animal world (Hockett 1966). This is the sense in which Sapir, as cited above, took language to be non-instinctual. However, today many linguists, following Noam Chomsky (1965), prefer to see language as an instinct, in another sense – as a manifestation of an ability that is specific to humans. Aitchison (1976) has captured the differences and overlaps between humans and other animals in the title of her book characterising humankind as 'the articulate mammal'.[1]

Sociolinguistics' Antecedents

As the accompanying box indicates, different aspects of language have been in focus at different times in the history of linguistics. Interest in sociolinguistic issues was not excluded by the nineteenth-century historical linguists or by the structuralists of the twentieth century. The former belatedly took to the study of living dialects for the light that these could shed on changes that had taken place in the past, as was evident from ancient texts. There were two branches of what is now called sociolinguistics that had strong nineteenth-century antecedents: the study of rural dialects in Europe (discussed in Chapter 2) and the study of contact between languages that resulted in new 'mixed languages'. The work of Hugo Schuchardt (1882), Dirk Hesseling (1897) and Addison Van Name (1869–70) on contact between languages challenged some of the assumptions made by their contemporaries.

Key phases in linguistic study

- c.500 BC: Pānini and his followers in India produce oral treatises on phonetics and language structure. Later, independent traditions of language study develop in Europe.
- 1786: founding of modern linguistics, on the basis of a seminal speech by Sir William Jones concerning the relations between Sanskrit, Latin, Greek and other ancient languages. Linguistics enters a historical phase in which principles of language comparison and classification emerge.
- Early twentieth century: structuralism predominates in linguistics. 'Structuralists' like Ferdinand de Saussure in Europe and Leonard Bloomfield and others in the USA were concerned with internal systems of languages rather than with historical comparisons.
- 1957: Generative linguistics is founded with the publication of Noam Chomsky's *Syntactic Structures*. Linguistics shifts to a psycho-biological stage, with interest in the way in which children acquire languages on the basis of an abstract 'universal grammar' common to all languages.

In the USA, structuralists were motivated partly by the need to describe rapidly eroding American Indian languages in the early twentieth century before they became extinct. The work of scholars like Franz Boas, Leonard Bloomfield and Edward Sapir added a cultural or anthropological interest in languages. Via their acquaintance with the cultural patterns of societies that were novel to them, these scholars laid the foundation for studies of language, culture and cognition. Such an anthropological perspective of language was a forerunner to some branches of sociolinguistics, especially the ethnographical approach discussed in Chapter 6.

The term 'sociolinguistics' appears to have been first used in 1939 by T.C. Hodson in relation to language study in India (Le Page 1997: 19). It was later used – independently – in 1952 by Haver Currie, a poet and philosopher who noted the general absence of any consideration of the social from the linguistic research of his day. Significant works on sociolinguistics appearing after this date include Weinreich's influential *Languages in Contact* (a structural and social account of bilingualism) of 1953, Einar Haugen's two-volumed study of the social history of the Norwegian language in America (1953), and Joos (1962) on the dimensions of style.

Emphases in Current Sociolinguistics

Chomsky's emphasis in the 1960s on abstracting language away from everyday contexts ironically led to the distillation of a core area of sociolinguistics, opposed to his conception of language. In a frequently cited passage, Chomsky (1965: 3) characterised the focus of the linguist's attention on an idealised competence:

> Linguistic theory is concerned primarily with an ideal speaker-listener, in a completely homogeneous speech community, who knows its language perfectly and is unaffected by such grammatically irrelevant conditions as memory limitations, distractions, shifts of attention and interest, and errors (random or characteristic) in applying his knowledge of the language in actual performance.

While such an approach brought significant gains to the theory of syntax and phonology, many scholars felt that abstracting language away from the contexts in which it was spoken served limited ends which could not include an encompassing theory of human language. This period marked a break between sociolinguists with an interest in language use within human societies and followers of Chomsky's approach to language (with their interest in an idealised, non-social, psycholinguistic competence).[2] Whereas the Chomskyan framework focuses on structures that could be generated in language and by what means, the social approach tries to account for what can be said in a language, by whom, to whom, in whose presence, when and where, in what manner and under what social circumstances (Fishman 1971; Hymes 1971; Saville-Troike 1982: 8). For the latter group, the process of acquiring a language is not just a cognitive process involving the activation of a predisposition in the human brain; it is a social process as well, that only unfolds in social interaction. The child's role in acquiring its first language is not a socially passive one, but one which is sensitive to certain 'environmental' conditions, including the social identity of the different people with whom the child interacts.

Dell Hymes (1971) was the principal objector to the dominance of Chomsky's characterisation of what constituted the study of linguistic competence. He suggested that a child who might produce any sentence whatever without due regard to the social and linguistic context would be 'a social monster' (1974b: 75) who was likely to be institutionalised. Hymes coined the term 'communicative competence' to denote our ability to use language appropriately in different settings. Hymes' interest was not just in the production of sentences but also in characterizing the more social-bound aspects like when it is appropriate to talk and when to remain silent in different communities, rules for turn-taking, amount of simultaneous talk and so on. These topics are discussed in Chapter 6.

A distinction that persists (though it is not one that we particularly advocate) is that between the sociolinguistics (proper) and the sociology of language. Some scholars believe that the former is part of the terrain mapped out in linguistics, focusing on language in society for the light that social contexts throw upon language. For these scholars, the latter (sociology of language) is primarily a sub-part of sociology, which examines language use for its ultimate illumination of the nature of societies. Ralph Fasold (1984, 1990) has attempted to capture this formulation by writing two scholarly books, one devoted to *The Sociolinguistics of Society* and the other to *The Sociolinguistics of Language*. While we accept that there is some basis for such a partition, and something to be gained by it, in practice the boundaries between the two areas of study are so flexible as to merit one cover term. This book can be seen as a short introduction to both areas (which we consider *alter egos*, rather than a dichotomised pair) which for simplicity we label, unsurprisingly, *sociolinguistics*. Sometimes the distinction between the two orientations is expressed by the terms *macro-* and *micro-sociolinguistics*. As in other subjects, notably economics, macro-studies involve an examination of large-scale patterns relating to social structures (the focus is broad, as in the study of patterns of multilingualism in a country). Micro-studies examine finer patterns in context (for example, conversational structure or accents in a particular community).

1.2 RELATIONS BETWEEN LANGUAGE AND SOCIETY

A concern for the 'human communication' aspect within the definition of language implies attention to the way language is played out in societies in its full range of functions. Language is not just **denotational**, a term which refers to the process of conveying meaning, referring to ideas, events or entities that exist outside language. While using language primarily for this function, a speaker will inevitably give off signals concerning his or her social and personal background. Language is accordingly said to be indexical of one's social class, status, region of origin, gender, age group and so on. On the term 'index', see the box on page 2. In the sociolinguistic sense, this indexical aspect of language refers to certain features of speech (including accent), which indicate an individual's social group (or background); the use of these features is not exactly arbitrary since it signals that the individual has access to the lifestyles that are associated with that type of speech.

Chapters 2 to 4 will be concerned with the relationship between region of origin, age and – especially – social status and characteristic ways of using language. Many sociolinguists go one step further in characterising the way in which language is entwined with human existence. Susan Gal (1989: 347) argues that language not only reflects societal patterns and divisions but also sustains and reproduces them. Accent, for example, may reveal the social group to which a person belongs, but is also part of the definition of that social group. Ways of talking are not just a reflection of social organisation, but also form a practice that is one of social organisation's central parts. As such, they are implicated in power relations within societies, as we stress in Chapters 6 and 10.

The idea was once popular in anthropology that language and thought are more closely intertwined than is commonly believed. It is not just that language use is an outcome of thinking; but conversely, the way one thinks is influenced by the language one is 'born into'. Mind, according to this hypothesis, is in the grip of language. Edward Sapir and – especially – Benjamin Lee Whorf were led by their studies of American Indian languages in the early twentieth century to argue that speakers of certain languages may be led to different types of observations and different evaluations of externally similar phenomena. This claim came to be known as the Sapir–Whorf hypothesis. According to Whorf (1956: 213), 'we dissect nature along lines laid down by our native language'. Using a language forces us into habitual grooves of thinking: it is almost like putting on a special pair of glasses that heighten some aspects of the physical and mental world while dimming others. One example provided by Whorf concerns the distinction between nouns and verbs in Hopi (a language of Arizona) as opposed to English. The Hopi terms for 'lightning', 'wave', 'flame', 'meteor', 'puff of smoke' and 'pulsation' are all verbs, since events of necessarily brief duration fall into this category. The terms for 'cloud' and 'storm', on the other hand, are of just enough duration to qualify as nouns. Whorf (1956: 215) concludes that Hopi has a classification of events by duration type that is unfamiliar to speakers of European languages.

Another of Whorf's striking examples concerns tense and time. Whereas English dissects events according to their time of occurrence (relative to the act of speaking), Hopi expresses other categories in the verb, notably the kind of validity that the speaker intends the statement to have: is it a report of an event, an expectation of an event or a generalisation or law about events?

> The Hopi metaphysics does not raise the question whether the things in a distant village exist at the same present moment as those in one's own village, for it is frankly pragmatic on this score and says that any 'events' in the distant village can be compared to any events in one's own village only by an interval of magnitude that has both time and space forms in it. Events at a distance from the observer can only be known objectively when they are 'past' (i.e. posited in the objective) and the more distant, the more 'past' (the more worked upon from the subjective side). (Whorf 1956: 63)

The Sapir–Whorf hypothesis is a thought-provoking one that, in its strong form, suggests among other things that real translation between widely different languages is not possible. The hypothesis has proved impossible to test: how would one go about ascertaining that the perceptions of a Hopi speaker concerning the world are radically different from that of,

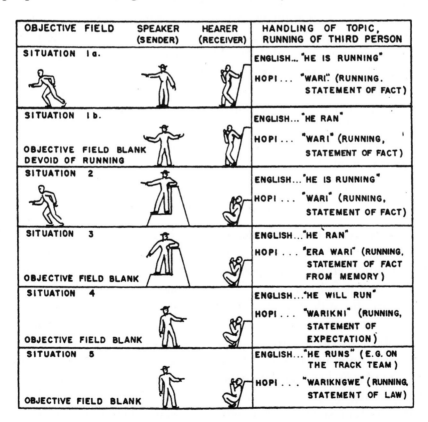

Figure 1.1   Contrasts between English and Hopi in expressing tense
(from Whorf 1956: 213)

say, a French speaker? Most linguists today insist that there are limits to which languages vary. In appealing to the notion of 'deep structure', Chomsky and his followers stress an underlying capacity for language that is common to humans. What seem to be radical differences in the grammatical structure of languages are held to operate 'on the surface', as mappings from an abstract and universal deep structure. Linguists feel safer in accepting a 'weak form' of the Sapir–Whorf hypothesis: that our language influences (rather than completely determines) our way of perceiving things. But language does not grip communities so strongly as to prevent at least some individuals from seeing things from different perspectives, from forming new thoughts and ideas. As Gillian Sankoff (1986: xxi) puts it, 'in the long term language is more dependent on the social world than the other way around . . . Language does facilitate social intercourse, but if the social situation is sufficiently compelling, language will bend.' Studies in the way that languages influence each other via borrowing and mixing are discussed in Chapters 8 and 9. The Sapir–Whorf hypothesis remains of considerable relevance to contemporary sociolinguistic debates, notably those about 'politically correct' language. These relate to issues like racism, sexism and discrimination against the aged, minorities and so on. Does the existence of a term like *the aged* predispose others to viewing people so described in a negative light? Would peoples' perceptions be different if no such word existed in English? Does a new term like *senior citizens* make the concept a more positive one? Those who believe that using new terms will change societal attitudes for the better are subscribing to a Whorfian view of the relation between language and thought. The use of euphemism and derogatory terms is discussed in Chapter 10 in the light of power imbalances in language.

'A Language' as a Social Construct

Up to now we have discussed *language* in the abstract, meaning the faculty of human communication in general terms. When we turn to *languages* as individual entities, the possession of specific societies, we run into problems of definition. It may come as a surprise to you that linguists are unable to offer a definition of what constitutes 'a language' in relation to overlapping entities like 'dialects'. For this reason, the term **variety** is a particularly useful one to avoid prejudging the issue of whether a given entity is (in popular terms) 'a language' or 'a dialect'. In many instances, the boundaries between languages are far from clear, especially where historical and geographical links are involved. Mutual intelligibility might seem a useful test of whether two varieties are distinct languages or not. In practice, however, it is almost always sociopolitical criteria that decide the status of a variety, rather than linguistic ones.

The case of Norwegian and Danish provides a clear illustration of the sociopolitical nature of the distinction between what counts as a language and what does not. For four centuries, Norway was ruled by Denmark. Danish was considered the official language, with Norwegian speech having dialect status (that is, it was considered a dialect of Danish). Upon political independence in 1814, Norwegian was declared an 'official language', distinct from Danish. The same has happened in what was formerly Yugoslavia, where for much of the twentieth century Serbian and Croatian did not have independent status but were officially considered as 'eastern' and 'western' varieties of the same language called Serbo-Croatian (or Croato-Serbian). These varieties did have independent status prior to the twentieth century, while being mutually intelligible as 'South Slavic' languages. Croatian, for example, had dictionaries, grammars and literary works. Centralisation began when the Kingdom of Serbs, Croats and Slovenes was formed (1918–29), yielding first to the Kingdom of Yugoslavia (1929–41) and then to Communist rule (1945–90). The bloody conflict that accompanied the break-up of the federation in the 1990s saw the formation of new states of Slovenia, Croatia, and Bosnia and Hercegovina. Not surprisingly, linguistic nationalism followed the new independence, with the differences between the varieties now being emphasised. Today Serbian, Croatian and Bosnian (a third variety

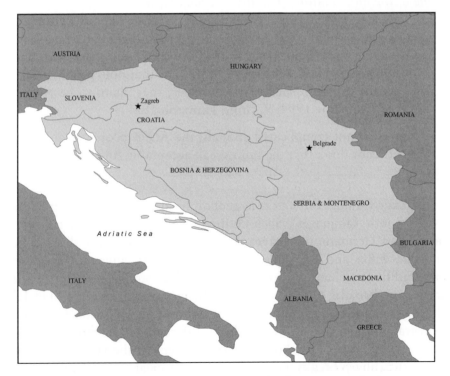

Map 1.1   New states arising from the former Yugoslavia

associated with Islam) are considered independent languages (see UCLA *Language Materials Project* 2007 on the internet).

In South Africa, Zulu and Xhosa have about 11 million and 8 million mother-tongue speakers respectively, making them the most spoken varieties in the country. In terms of their official status, social history and written forms they count as separate languages. Yet they are so similar in terms of their structure that mutual understanding is virtually guaranteed: anyone who speaks Zulu as a mother tongue understands Xhosa when first exposed to it and vice versa. Historical linguists classify the two varieties as part of a Nguni cluster, which includes Swati (or Swazi) and Ndebele (spoken in Zimbabwe and South Africa) as well. The term 'cluster' specifies that the varieties concerned are historically related, structurally similar and mutually intelligible. Whom is the sociolinguist to follow – the scientific linguists who posit one language cluster, or the communities themselves who see four distinct languages whose speakers are culturally and historically separate? (Swati is, for example, an official language of the kingdom of Swaziland.) Recent developments in South Africa's language policy are discussed in Chapter 12.

On the fuzzy boundaries between languages in Papua New Guinea, one of the most multilingual areas of the world
The language spoken in Bolo village is also from a linguist's point of view identical to Aria, but Aria speakers from other villages say it is not Aria. They say Bolo speakers really speak Mouk. However, the people of Salkei village, who speak Mouk, say that Bolo people speak Aria. As for the Bolo speakers themselves, they claim to be Anêm speakers. (Romaine 1994: 9, citing Thurston 1987)

[If this were not complicated enough, the Anêm people of another village do not think that the Bolo speak acceptable Anêm any more.]

Language varieties often exist as geographical continua, without natural divisions into 'languages'. Such continua have been claimed for North Indian and Germanic languages. In the Indian case (now divided into Pakistan, India and Bangladesh), several distinct languages exist with long traditions of literary production, including Sindhi, Kashmiri, Hindi, Rajasthani, Panjabi, Gujarati, Marathi, Bengali and others (see Map 1.2). These autonomous, regional languages do show sharp breaks in terms of their grammar, so that it is possible to differentiate one from the other. However, in terms of everyday, informal speech at the village level there are no such sharp breaks. Gumperz (1971: 7) speaks of a chain of mutually intelligible varieties from the Sind (in the north-west) to Assam (in the

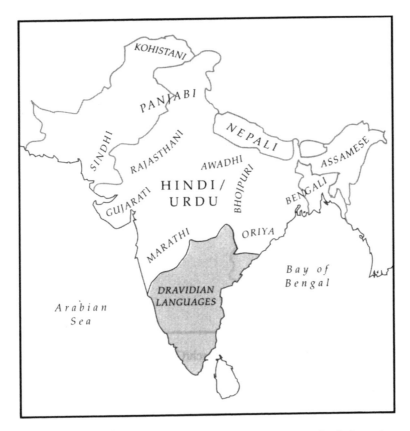

Map 1.2 The North Indian speech continuum (unshaded area)

north-east). It would thus be possible to traverse the subcontinent from the north-west to the north-east without discerning any radical differences in speech characteristics from one village to the next.

One result of the dichotomy between colloquial speech 'on the ground' and supra-regional, official languages is the difficulty linguists have in classifying border dialects: varieties that are sandwiched between two officially recognised languages. Very often it is not possible to assign such varieties to one rather than the other language, except in an arbitrary way:

> Dutch and German are known to be two distinct languages. However, at some places along the Dutch–German frontier the dialects spoken on either side of the border are extremely similar. If we chose to say that people on one side of the border speak German and those on the other Dutch, our choice is again based on social and political rather than linguistic factors. The point is further emphasized by the fact that the ability of speakers from either side of the border to understand each other will often be considerably greater than that of German speakers from this area to understand speakers of other German dialects from distant parts of Austria or Switzerland. (Trudgill 1983a: 15)

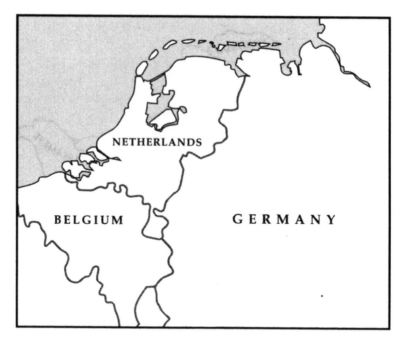

Map 1.3   The Dutch/German border

For further discussion of the West Germanic continuum in western Europe (made up of what are usually referred to as German, Dutch, Frisian and Flemish), see Trudgill and Chambers (1980: 6). We now turn to the issue of what forms of language are appropriate for sociolinguistic study.

1.3 PRESCRIPTIVISM

Description versus Prescription

A **descriptive** approach is one which studies and characterises the language of specific groups of people in a range of situations, without bringing any preconceived notions of correctness to the task, or favouring the language of one social group as somehow 'better' than those of others. One could attempt a description of the language of royalty in formal and informal situations, of mineworkers at work in Wales, and of street vendors in Cape Town in neutral terms, the way a scientist might describe the object of his or her study. By contrast, a **prescriptive** approach to language (or prescriptivism) is concerned with what might be termed 'linguistic etiquette'. In this section, we focus on English mainly, since the prescriptive tradition has been best documented for this language (for example Milroy and Milroy 1985a; Cameron 1995b). Prescriptivism is best exemplified by the traditional approach to the teaching of grammar in English schools. The

*'I am but the cleaner. It is he, Mr.
Gleason, to whom you should speak.'*

role of the language teacher is seen as upholding certain forms of language
as the norm to be emulated. Prescriptions are given covering different
aspects of language:

- Grammar: Don't end sentences with prepositions.
- Vocabulary: Don't say *cool*.
- Meaning: *Nice* only means 'finely nuanced', as in a nice *distinction*.
- Pronunciation: Don't pronounce the final *t* in *trait* (British English).

Prescriptive grammarians put forward a number of arguments in defense
of their preferences.

(1) *One form is more logical than another*. Prescriptivists believe that
language should obey certain principles of mathematics, notably the rule
that two negatives make a positive. The use of two negatives in a statement
like *I can't see no animals* is held to 'cancel each other out' and should
'really' mean *I can see animals*.

(2) *Appeal to classical forms*. Sometimes prescriptive grammarians back
up their judgments about correctness in modern languages by appealing
to the authority of classical languages. In the case of English, the language
sometimes held up as a model is Latin (in other parts of the world, languages
like Sanskrit, Classical Tamil and Classical Arabic are held up as similar
models). Although it had long declined as a spoken language and as a language of European diplomacy and education, Latin continued to be part of
educational curricula in Europe and elsewhere, and influenced many grammarians of the eighteenth century as to what should count as good English
usage. For example, when students are urged not to split the infinitive in

"YA NOTICE I DONT HARDLY SAY 'AIN'T' NO MORE?"

sentences like *Mary did her best to fully support Jill during her illness*, their teachers are paying homage to Latin, where split infinitives do not occur.

(3) *A preference for older forms of the language.* Prescriptivists are typically intolerant of innovations in language. This applies to new meanings, new synonyms and new syntactic constructions. For example, teachers and academics complain about the use of the word *hopefully* as a synonym for 'I hope/one hopes', preferring that it be used in its 'older' sense of 'in a manner full of hope'. For such a prescriptivist, *Hopefully they won't lose again* is unacceptable, but *She will speak hopefully of peace in the twenty-first century* is.

(4) *Injunction against the use of foreign words.* Some societies are intolerant of new words from foreign sources, sometimes for nationalistic reasons, at other times for fear of being swamped by neighboring languages or major world languages like English. A significant part of French prescriptivism, promulgated by L'Académie Française (The French Academy) and enacted by law, is devoted to ousting popular English words from the vocabulary: *le drugstore, le weekend, le dancing, le pop music* and so on. These efforts have not had much influence on the spoken language. English has for many centuries adopted and adapted words from other languages, and its speakers are today relatively liberal about accepting neologisms and borrowings. This was not always so. In the eighteenth century, which was a period of intense borrowing from French and coining of new words

based on Greek and Latin roots, the disparaging term 'inkhorn' was used to describe writers who used excessive foreign terms. Today some people in Britain still express reservations about 'Americanisms' in British English.

English words assimilated from other sources

cheese (Latin)	*royal* (French)	*opera* (Italian)
khaki (Hindi)	*algebra* (Arabic)	*mango* (Tamil)
chocolate (Aztec)	*glasnost* (Russian)	*zombie* (Kimbunda)

Colloquial Japanese words assimilated from English
hamu tosuto 'toasted ham sandwich'
apaato 'apartment'
pasokon 'personal computer'
kureemaru 'to do Kramers', that is to separate and fight over custody of children (based on the US film *Kramer versus Kramer*)

The Roots of English Prescriptivism

James Milroy and Lesley Milroy (1985) locate the origins of prescriptivism in what they call 'the Complaint Tradition', that is, a long-standing tradition of complaints about the adequacy of the English language compared to others. French had been the language of administration and education from the eleventh to the fourteenth century in England, after the Norman Conquest. From the fourteenth century on, when English took over from French as the language of education, misgivings were enunciated about the adequacy of English to the task. Complaints about the enormous amount of variation in regional varieties of English arose in this period that pre-dated the rise of a standard form of the language. Even after a standard form for writing emerged, writers continued focusing on the supposed inadequacies of English compared to classical languages like Latin and Greek and the more fashionable contemporary languages like French and Italian. This tradition reached its fruition in the eighteenth century, when writers and grammarians consciously set out their preferences about English usage in dictionaries and style manuals. Whereas previously variation in speech and writing was tolerated, the influence of writers like Jonathan Swift and dictionary-makers like Samuel Johnson gave authority to one kind of English over others.

Objections to Prescriptivism

In contrast to the prescriptive view of language, most linguists adhere to a position of 'linguistic equality' in asserting that all varieties of a language are valid systems with their own logic and conventions. Linguists point out that almost all the tenets of prescriptivism are based on the linguistic practices and preferences of the elites of a society, rather than on any natural or objective notion of correctness. We briefly review the typical responses of linguists to the prescriptive claims listed above:

(1) A view of the logic of language in strict mathematical terms is highly problematic. The work of syntacticians inspired by Chomsky has shown how complex the rules that generate a language can be. But they do not follow from elementary principles of mathematics, which have not been concerned with the nuances of natural language. If this were the case, then presumably using three negatives together would be unproblematic to the prescriptivist, since three negatives make a negative in mathematics. It should therefore be grammatical in Standard English to say *I don't want no spinach nohow*.

Double negatives are avoided in formal, middle-class speech and writing as a matter of convention rather than logic. With adjectival phrases, the rule is specifically suspended. *I am not unhappy with his suggestion* conveys the meaning 'neither quite happy (positive) nor quite unhappy (negative)'. Here, the two negatives (*not* and *un-*) refer to a neutral state. Double negation, which was standard in English up to the sixteenth century, is today used as a stylistic rule by people with a control of standard English to signify emphasis or rebellion. It is a popular device in English-language pop music, for example in the well-known song of rebellion of the 1960s by the Rolling Stones, 'I Can't Get No Satisfaction', the love song of the same period 'Ain't No Mountain High Enough' (sung by Marvin Gaye, composed by Ashford and Simpson), or a line from a song of the 1990s, 'Ain't no angel gonna greet me' (Bruce Springsteen: 'Streets of Philadelphia').[3]

(2) Regarding the appeal to classical languages, anti-prescriptivists point out that there is no strong reason to expect one language to match the mould of another, older (dead or, at best, embalmed) one. This view of linguistic independence is put provocatively by the US linguist Steven Pinker (1994: 374): 'Of course forcing modern speakers of English to not . . . whoops, not to . . . split an infinitive because it isn't done in Latin makes about as much sense as forcing modern residents of England to wear togas and laurels'.

(3) In response to the injunction 'older is better', linguists assert that languages are continually changing in subtle ways. New rules evolve and interact with older ones in subtle ways little appreciated by the guardians of traditional language. This is in fact shown by the example of new functions associated with *hopefully.* Pinker (1994: 381–3) suggests that not all English adverbs indicate the manner in which the actor performs the action. Rather, there are two classes of adverbs: sentence adverbs and

---

The first shall be last?

An example of 'linguistic etiquette' that prescriptivists often insist on is to put oneself last in coordinated phrases: thus *Mary, you and I* rather than *Me, you and Mary.* Yet the latter colloquial form follows a kind of linguistic logic in putting the first person (*I*), first; second person (*you*) next and third person (*he/she/it*) last. Philip Angermeyer and John Singler (2003) undertook a detailed descriptive study based on the actual usage of New Yorkers in a variety of spoken and written contexts. They found that the two sequences of coordination were not in fact equivalent, but carried nuances pertaining to politeness and formality. The rules in subject position can be broadly described as follows:

- Children first learn the basic (or vernacular) form 'Me and X' and use it in subject as well as object positions (*Me and Miriam are good friends. She gave the prize to me and Miriam.*)
- Schooling is mainly responsible for inculcating the standard rule of using 'X and I' in subject position and 'X and me' in object position (*Miriam and I are good friends. She gave the prize to Miriam and me*).
- However, many speakers have a third option of expressing politeness using 'X and I' in both subject and object positions (*Her and I are still sober and working together with God. She gave the prize to Miriam and I*).

There is thus some uncertainty as speakers waver between a need to use the standard (and formal) form 'X and me' and the polite 'X and I' in object position. Angermeyer and Singler's study shows that despite minor fluctuations, these three rules (for vernacular, standard and polite) have been stable in the history of English, citing examples from Shakespeare and Dickens through to modern celebrities, college graduates and political leaders.

verb-phrase adverbs. Sentence adverbs modify an entire sentence, stressing the speakers' attitude to the proposition being expressed, for example *frankly* in the sentence *Frankly, I don't give a damn*. Verb-phrase adverbs like *carefully*, on the other hand, modify the verb phrase only, as in *John carefully carried the kitten*. Although *hopefully* derives from a verb-phrase adverb, it has also been in use as a sentence adverb for at least sixty years. It is the latter function which is becoming more frequent. Pinker and others adhering to a descriptivist position thus challenge the idea that all change in a language reduces its preciseness or aesthetic value.

(4) Descriptive linguists point to the fact that all languages have adopted words from other sources. It is an essential part of language development. Many innovations serve to refer to new types of activities or to renovate and revivify aspects of language. An example comes from the modern use of *-bilia* to mean 'collectible things associated with the past', as in *rockabilia* ('rock music of the past') and *restorabilia* ('restored antiques'). This is a change from the original meaning of *-bilia*, from the Latin-based term *memorabilia*, where it was the root *memora* that meant 'memory' and the suffix *-bilia* simply denoted 'pertaining to'. What might to a prescriptivist seem an untenable change arising from an ignorance of Latin grammar is in another light a creative manipulation of language to serve new ends.

Further Debate – Is Prescriptivism Unavoidable?

It has long been the policy among linguists to ignore prescriptive judgements in their descriptions of language. There is a growing argument, however, that if their aim is to characterise the full range of language use and attitudes towards language, then sociolinguists cannot pretend that prescriptive ideas do not or should not exist. On the contrary, ideas about good and bad language are very influential in society. The British linguist, Deborah Cameron (1995b), coined the term 'verbal hygiene' for the practices born of the urge to improve or clean up language. Just as hygiene is necessary for good health, verbal hygiene is felt to be necessary for everyday language use. She points to the need to pay attention to the role of journalists, writers, editors and broadcasters in promoting an awareness of acceptable public forms of language.

A second pro-prescriptive argument is that even people who disapprove of the pedantry of traditional grammarians conform in their writing and formal speech to the conventions laid down by authorities of language such as editors. Critics sometimes censure sociolinguists for promoting a tolerance of dialect diversity while using the prestige dialect of their society themselves. According to this view, sociolinguists themselves are closet prescriptivists. They promote a view of non-standard language as the equal of standard language, but write textbooks in which double negatives and dangling participles are carefully weeded out. Moreover, they may penalise their own students for not writing in a formal, acceptable way. There thus seems to be no way of escaping from the existence and influence of language norms.

To some extent, prescriptivists and descriptivists have been talking at cross-purposes. The former are primarily concerned with improving public and formal language, the latter with describing colloquial speech (see section 1.5 below). A compromise position therefore seems possible – that variation in language is to be expected in informal speech, but that more formal contexts of use (like a public lecture) require shifts towards other, more educationally sanctioned, styles that minimise variation. This view emphasizes that some form of prescriptivism is necessary, for example in teaching a language to foreigners in classrooms, where the standard variety is the target. This might be termed a 'weak prescriptive' position. It holds that it is a necessary part of education to enable children to learn new styles of speaking and writing that are highly valued in particular societies. Mastering the standard form of a language involves making choices about what should count as appropriate usage in formal contexts.

However, most sociolinguists (see, for example, Trudgill 1975), would insist that the learning of standard English should not lead to a devaluation of the styles that students bring to schools with them. Mastery of formal standard English alone will not take foreign learners too far, unless their aims are to read and write without speaking. If the aim is to interact with speakers of English informally, then certain prescriptive principles might prove counter-productive. Cameron (1995b: 115) argues that '[t]here is nothing wrong in wanting standards of excellence in the use of language. Rather what is wrong is the narrow definition of excellence as mere superficial "correctness".' In keeping the debate about language standards at this superficial level, neither prescriptivist not descriptivist is entirely blameless.

Is Descriptivism Adequate?

The role of the linguist today goes beyond the academic description of language for its own sake, to be discussed with other academics at conferences. For one thing, sociolinguists are called upon as experts by governments in planning for education and governmental administration. In these matters, they are forced to make choices about the suitability of certain varieties of language and certain words and expressions within those varieties. Florian Coulmas (1989b: 178), a German linguist, argues that the stance of description for its own sake is inadequate:

> The scholar's serene detachment from the object of their studies is, however, in sharp conflict with the expectations of the speech community, as well as the actual needs of modern standard languages. What is a linguist good for when he

cannot give advice about good or bad language and refuses to make statements about what is good for our languages? Who else would be more qualified to make such statements?

This view holds that even if sociolinguists themselves prefer not to make prescriptive judgements, they should not ignore the fact that verbal hygiene is a part of the 'ecology of language' in most communities.

An important area where researchers have felt the need to go beyond descriptivism is sexism in language. Robin Lakoff's ironically titled book, *Language and Woman's Place* (1975), spawned a great deal of research into areas of language showing differences between men's and women's usage (discussed in Chapter 7). Such researchers were not content to describe or record gender differences in language, but helped to popularise the argument that languages could be sexist, that is, they could discriminate against women by presenting things from a male perspective. In Gal's terms language not only reflects inequalities that exist, but also helps to sustain and reproduce them unless challenged. We pick up this theme in Chapter 10, which analyses power inequalities in society and their bearing upon language.

Some examples of sexism in English claimed by Robin Lakoff (1975)

- Women are devalued in language, for example in slang terms like *chick or kitten,* or derogatory terms like *slut.*
- Words associated with women are not valued (for example, use of specific colour terms like *mauve* and *lavender*).
- A male perspective is the norm (for example, in terms like *he, man, mankind* for people in general).
- Expectations about femininity and ladylike speech force women into euphemisms or silence.

1.4   STANDARDISATION

Standardisation and the Standard Dialect

A discussion of prescriptivism goes hand in hand with the study of the rise of standard languages and their relation to other dialects. Garvin and Mathiot (1960: 783) defined a standardised language as a 'codified form of a language, accepted by, and serving as a model to, a larger speech community'. In other words, the standard form of a language is that dialect which is most often associated with specific subgroups (usually educated people or people having high status and authority within the society) and with specific functions serving a community that goes beyond that of its native speakers (for example writing, education, radio and television). The

term *codified* – based on Latin *codex* and English *code* – refers to the existence of explicit statements of the norms of a language, as in dictionaries
and grammars, especially concerning aspects of language use where some
variation exists among speakers. The definition of standardisation draws
attention to the social nature of the process. The popular conception that a
standard form of a language is automatically an 'original' or 'pure' form of
a language that pre-existed other dialects (which are 'deviations' from the
standard) is frequently incorrect. Standardisation occurs when a language
is put to a wider range of functions than previously – typically for the
spread of literacy, education, government and administration, and in the
expansion of the media. Successful standardisation involves the creation
(or acceptance) of a variety as the most prestigious one, on account of its
use by those who have status and power in the society.

> The power of a standard variety derives from historical accident and conven-
> tion. Parisian French, for example, is usually taken as the standard dialect of
> that language yet, if history had decreed that some other centre were to be
> the capital of France, then presumably its linguistic variety would now be the
> accepted standard. (J. R. Edwards 1979: 76)

In the Middle English period (roughly 1150 to 1500), there was arguably
no national literary standard English. While Chaucer wrote in the East
Midlands dialect (which included that of the city of London), other writers
used their own regional varieties. By the end of the fourteenth century,
a written standard had started to emerge, though it still contained some
variation. It is traditionally thought that standard English arose because
of the influence of an East Midlands 'triangle' bounded by three centres of
prestige: London, Oxford and Cambridge. This area was important for its
economic development (as a wealthy agricultural region and the centre of
the wool trade), its dense population, the social and political standing of
many of its citizens, and its centers of learning. David Crystal (1995: 110)
lists the following essential characteristics of modern standard English:

- It is historically based on one dialect among many, but now has special
  status, without a local base. It is largely (but not completely) neutral with
  respect to regional identity.
- Standard English is not a matter of pronunciation, rather of grammar,
  vocabulary and orthography.
- It carries most prestige within 'English-speaking' countries.
- It is a desirable educational target.
- Although widely understood, it is not widely spoken.

However, many points of disagreement exist among linguists as to the
exact provenance of the term 'standard English'. John Joseph (1987: 17)
believes that a standard language is not 'native' to anyone. It is a higher cultural endowment serving (formal) functions and has linguistic features that

cannot be mastered until after the period of normal first-language acquisition (that is, the age of four or five). Others disagree: for example, Michael Stubbs (1986: 87) argues that standard English is the native language of a particular social group – the educated middle classes. Whereas the former view places emphasis on vocabulary, including learned or technical terms and on complex (bookish) syntactic constructions, the latter view (subscribed to by most sociolinguists) concentrates on everyday, non-technical uses of language. For someone like Stubbs, the standard form of a language must, by virtue of having a community of native speakers, be divisible into formal and informal norms. Speakers of standard English, he argues, can be as casual, polite or rude as anyone else, and can use slang, swear and say things in bad taste or in bad style. This, of course, makes defining the features of a standard dialect much harder. Most English utterances can be easily classified (*I ain't seen them kids* is non-standard; *I haven't seen those kids* is standard though informal). However, there are some features which cannot be so easily categorised. Even among prescriptivists, there may be disagreements about the status of certain constructions. It makes sense to think of a gradient of 'standardness' in cases like the following:

> *The man what you saw.*
> *The man that you saw.*
> *The man who you saw.*
> *The man whom you saw.*

These four sentences exist on a scale from least standard to most standard. The first sentence is considered non-standard while the last one is considered standard in formal writing. The second and third sentences are intermediate in terms of standardness. Some editors, writers and teachers accept *that* and *who*, while others insist on restricting *that* to non-human referents and using *whom* as the only acceptable object pronoun for human referents. For historical reasons, we have focused on British English in order to stress the point that the rise of a standard form of a language is primarily a sociopolitical matter. The existence of a 'double standard' for English (in Britain and the USA) is an embarrassment to the prescriptivist and those who believe in the superiority of British standard English. In learning and teaching English, European and South Asian countries follow RP and British English norms, whereas South-east Asian and South American countries follow US English norms. Clearly US English is a dialect whose speakers had sufficient political and economic influence to have declared their social (and linguistic) independence. This did not occur without a tussle, however (see, for example, R. W. Bailey 1991: ch. 6). It is noteworthy that some constructions which have become non-standard in the course of British sociolinguistic history have remained standard in the USA. To this category belong syntactic constructions like the use of *for . . . to* verb complements as in *I would like for you to do this by tomorrow*, which counts as standard in the USA but not in Britain. US speakers tend to ask past-tense questions beginning with 'did', while people in Britain tend to favour 'have' (as alluded to in the accompanying cartoon). The same applies to features of verb morphology, as in *gotten* as past participle in the USA, *dove* as the past tense of *dive*, and past participle *snuck* in parts of the USA against *sneaked* in Britain. These reinforce the point that the standard forms of a language are based on pre-existing dialect usage, rather than dialect usage being necessarily a subsequent departure from a standard norm. Contrasting the British and US usage also serves as a reminder of the linguistic arbitrariness of what eventually counts as standard.

On RP

Crystal's characterisation of standard English excludes matters of pronunciation; in this view, it is not tied to any particular accent. However, the issue is not as simple as this. Theoretically, one can speak standard English with any accent, though in Britain, especially, these are seldom very localised accents – but rather modified regional accents. Nevertheless, there is one accent that has non-localised prestige and is something of a standard (or reference point) for teaching (British) English to foreigners. This is the accent used most frequently on British radio and television, known as Received Pronunciation (or RP), or sometimes as the Queen's English, Oxford English or BBC English. The 'received' part of RP refers to an old-fashioned use of the word for 'generally accepted'. RP was promoted in the public schools (i.e. exclusive fee-paying schools) of England and spread throughout the civil service of the British Empire and the armed forces. Crystal (1995: 365) notes that RP is not immune to change, as any examination of early BBC recordings will show. Further,

RP is no longer as widely used today as it was fifty years ago. It is still the
standard accent of the Royal family, Parliament, the Church of England, the
High Courts and other national institutions; but less than 3 per cent of the
British people speak it in a pure form now. Most educated people have developed an accent which is a mixture of RP and various regional characteristics –
'modified RP' . . .

Some scholars argue that accent *is* involved in notions of standardness.
Stubbs (1986: 88) points out that the fact that standard English only
occurs with 'milder regional accents' undermines the claim that phonetics
and phonology are not involved in people's ideas of standard English. He
observes that the very fact that there are such things as elocution lessons,
which focus on accent, means that people have an idea of what is and is
not standard in pronunciation. (See further Petyt 1980: 30–6.)

There is no US equivalent of RP – an accent that is considered the most
appropriate for education, broadcasting and so on, as Roger Lass (1987:
244) stresses:

> Every American can pretty much be identified as coming from someplace.
> Though there is a tendency for Americans with certain very marked regional
> accents to accommodate to a more widespread type under certain conditions:
> especially for Southerners and Northeasterners to adopt certain 'General
> American' features, such as being rhotic [pronouncing /r/ after vowels, as in the
> word *bird*]. This is particularly so in the media, where up till recently anyhow,
> new readers speaking southern standards for instance have tended to drop some
> very local features. It's worth noting that in the U.S. strong regionality is not
> negatively related to political success . . .

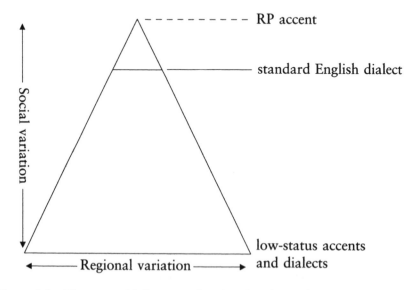

Figure 1.2   The pyramid diagram of regional and social variation in England
(based on Trudgill 1975: 21)

'General American' is a term that covers about two-thirds of the mother-tongue speakers of English whose accent is not recognisably local (Wells 1982: 118). It is the type of American English pronunciation that is taught to learners of English as a foreign language, and is to be found most commonly and with slight variation from Ohio to the mid-West and thence to the Pacific coast (Prator and Robinett 1972, cited by Wells, 1982: 118). More recent dialectological work in the US and Canada is discussed in Chapter 3.

Standardisation in Non-Western Settings

In many African centers, it was the advent of colonialism that brought literacy and standardisation. Missionaries attempted to target the maximally useful variety in which to convey the message of Christianity. This was often the variety used by the more prominent chieftains among whom they settled. In cases where the existing dialects did not have much significance outside their own localities, the choice was often arbitrary. In Southern Rhodesia (now Zimbabwe), the missionary-linguist C. M. Doke was called upon by the colonial authorities to make recommendations about the standardisation of a group of dialects (Korekore, Zezuru, Karanga, Ndau and Kalanga). Doke recommended that a unified literary language be created on the basis of two prominent varieties, Karanga and Zezuru. Whereas the grammar of the language, to be called Shona, would draw on these two varieties, the dictionary of Shona was to be as inclusive as possible, drawing on the other varieties too (Ansre 1971). This compromise along linguistic, social and demographic lines seems to have been moderately successful. People were expected to write Shona (the new standard) while continuing to speak one of the varieties that make up this language. However, since a large number of speakers who are prominent in the media originate from or around the capital, Harare, there are signs that the Zezuru variety is gaining the most prestige. At the same time, the educational authorities are experimenting with new methods that do not discourage children from writing in their own dialect of Shona (Batidzirai 1996). If this becomes a reality, it will no longer be true that 'Shona is the language which everyone writes and nobody speaks' (Ansre 1971: 691).

Such an attempt at blending together a standard (written) language was rare, however. Sometimes the elevation of one variety over another was based on factors like the region where the missionaries happened to be based. Ansre (1971: 687) provides the example of the Ewe language of Togo. The basic standard that arose in colonial times was based on the Anglo dialect, rather than its rival Anexo, because of the strength of the backing of the German government and German missionaries. While the standard was used in education and worship, economic factors have worked in a counter direction, favouring the Mina dialect (an offshoot of Anexo) in many parts of Togo.[4]

1.5   SPEECH VS WRITING

Compared to speech, writing is an invention that came late in human history and until recent times applied to a minority of languages. Even within literate societies, literacy was for a long time the preserve of the few. Children learn their first language as an oral entity by socialisation. Writing comes later (if at all) by conscious teaching.

Three linguists on the role of writing
Writing is not language, but merely a way of recording language by means of visible marks. (Bloomfield 1933: 21)

Language and writing are two distinct systems of signs; the second exists for the sole purpose of representing the first. The linguistic object is not both the written and the spoken forms of words; the spoken forms alone constitute the object. But the spoken word is so intimately bound to its written image that the latter manages to usurp the main role. People attach even more importance to the written image of a vocal sign than to the sign itself. A similar mistake would be in thinking that more can be learnt about someone by looking at his photograph than by viewing him directly. (Saussure 1959: 23–4, based on his lectures of 1907–11)

In linguistics it has become abundantly clear that writing is not just visible speech, but rather a mode of verbal communication in its own right . . . . It changes the nature of verbal communication as well as the speakers' attitude to, and awareness of, their language. Writing makes a society language-conscious . . . . Without writing modern societies cannot function . . . . Generally writing enlarges the functional potential of languages. (Coulmas 1989a: excerpted from pp. 12–14)

This **primacy of speech** over writing was stressed by structuralists like Bloomfield and Saussure. It led them to devise descriptions of linguistic structure without having to refer to spelling conventions and other visible marks like commas and full stops. Rather, they focused on the study of sounds and significant pauses (to which commas and full stops partly correspond). To a large extent, sociolinguists have followed suit in concentrating on the study of human interaction via speech. But as the third quote from Coulmas suggests, it is an oversight to exclude writing from the 'linguistic ecology' of modern societies. This book reports largely on speech-based research, and on sign language (in Chapter 13). The study of writing as a social practice is a relatively new interest in sociolinguistics (e.g. Street 1993, Blommaert 2005) which we have not been able to include, largely for reasons of space. Some inkling of the kinds of issues involved can be found in Chapter 11 on sociolinguistics and education. Furthermore, issues raised by Coulmas about modern communication, and the role of written language in societal modernisation are discussed in Chapter 12, on language planning and policy.

As we show in Chapter 3, many sociolinguists prefer to focus not just on speech, but on the more informal types of speech involving relaxed conversations between friends, peers and family members. These **vernacular** forms of language are the ones generally ignored in the classroom.

1.6   SOCIETIES AND SPEECH COMMUNITIES

Three Views of Society

In order to take the 'socio' side of the discipline of sociolinguistics seriously, we outline some of the major approaches to the study of human societies. This is, of course, a complex topic, as reference to any textbook of sociology will show. Within sociology there are three dominant theories of human society, and there is little agreement between adherents of these theories. Naturally, it is important for sociolinguists to be aware of their own working assumptions, for these will often determine the kinds of questions they raise and research about language. A coherent theory of language in society can only unfold within a particular theory of society. The three theories (or sets of ideas about how society works) that we shall outline here are **functionalism**, **Marxism** and **interactionism**.

Functionalism

This paradigm (or dominant theoretical perspective) was influential in western thought between the 1940s and mid-1960s. It pursued the view that a society may be understood as a system made up of functioning parts. To understand any part of society (for example the family or school), the part must be examined in relation to the society as a whole. Haralambos and Holborn (1991: 8) stress the analogy with biology: just as a biologist might examine a part of the human body such as the heart, in terms of its contribution to the maintenance of the human organism, the functionalist examines a part of society, such as the family, in terms of its contribution to the maintenance of the social system. The social system has certain basic needs (or functional prerequisites) which must be met if it is to survive (for example, food and shelter). The function of any part of society is its contribution to the maintenance of the overall whole. There is a certain degree of integration between the parts (social institutions) that make up the society. Functionalists argue that the order and stability which they see as essential for the maintenance of the social system are provided by 'value consensus', that is, agreement about values by members of society. In this view, two major occupations of the sociologist are the study of social subsystems and the value consensus that binds them together. Haralambos and Holborn (1991: 10) give the following example of value consensus:

> For example it can be argued that the value of materialism integrates many parts of the social structure in Western industrialized society. The economic system produces a large range of goods and ever increasing productivity is regarded as an important goal. The educational system is partly concerned with producing the skills and expertise to expand production and increase its efficiency. The family is an important unit of consumption with its steadily rising demand for consumer durables such as washing machines, videos and microwaves. The political system is partly concerned with improving material standards and raising productivity. To the extent that these parts of the social structure are based on the same values, they may be said to be integrated.

Concepts stressed within (but not exclusive to) this brand of sociology which are particularly useful to the student of sociolinguistics include: culture, socialisation, norms and values, and status and role.

- *Culture.* Although the popular sense of this word stresses 'high' culture (e.g. musical, literary and artistic achievements), in the technical sociological-anthropological sense the culture of a society refers to, 'the way of life of its members; the collection of ideas and habits which they learn, share and transmit from generation to generation' (Linton 1945: 203). Culture in this sense is a 'design for living', which defines appropriate or acceptable ways and forms of behavior within particular societies. In Chapter 5, we discuss research that shows that what counts as linguistically acceptable, desirable or highly valued behavior may vary from society to society.
- *Socialisation.* This refers to the process via which people learn the culture of their society. Primary socialisation takes place in childhood, usually within the family. The peer group (child's circle of playmates within and outside the home) is also an important reference group in transmitting social and linguistic behaviour.
- *Norms and values.* A norm is a 'specific guide to action which defines acceptable and appropriate behaviour in particular situations' (Haralambos and Holborn 1991: 5): think of dress codes at school, at home and at a party. In the course of socialisation, norms are inculcated by rewards (a sweet, a kind word) or punishments. Some norms become enacted in law to serve a larger society, for example a law forbidding nude bathing or in some societies the exposure of a woman's face in public. Values, on the

other hand, provide general guidelines as to qualities that are deemed to be good, desirable and of lasting worth. In many modern societies, the value placed on human life is a basic one, that determines norms of behaviour (standards of hygiene, settling of disputes, work-safety regulations and so on). Functionalist sociology proceeds from the premise that unless norms are shared, members of society would be unlikely to cooperate and work together. In this view, an ordered and stable society requires shared norms and common values. This has been the implicit assumption of much of sociolinguistic research.

- *Status and role.* Status refers to social positions that society assigns to its members (not just the high ones as in popular parlance). Such a status may be 'ascribed', that is, relatively fixed by birth, (for example one's gender status, or aristocratic titles in some societies), or it may be 'achieved'. The latter refers to statuses that result from some in society is accompanied by a number of norms which define how an individual occupying a particular status is expected to act. This group of norms is known as a 'role'. Social roles regulate and organise behaviour. In the course of a day, a person may play out several roles: that of teacher (at work), mother and wife (at home), client (with a bank), poet (at a leisure society) and so on. These roles are defined by their interactive nature: the role of doctor usually assumes the existence (if not the presence) of a patient; that of mother the existence of the child and so on. Each of these roles calls upon different forms of behaviour, including linguistic behaviour.

Status refers to differences between social groups in the social honour or prestige they are accorded by others. Status distinctions often vary independently of class divisions, and social honour may be either positive or negative. Positively privileged status groups include any groupings of people who have high prestige in a given social order. For instance doctors and lawyers have high prestige in a given social order . . . .

Possession of wealth normally tends to confer high status, but there are many exceptions. The term 'genteel poverty' refers to one example. In Britain, individuals from aristocratic families continue to enjoy considerable social esteem even when their fortunes have been lost. Conversely, 'new money' is often looked on with some scorn by the well-established wealthy.   (Giddens 1989: 212)

Marxism

Since the 1970s, Marxist approaches have become increasingly influential in sociology. Differing sharply from the functionalist belief that all social groups benefit if their society functions smoothly, Marxism stresses fundamental differences of interest between social groups. These differences ensure that conflict is a common and persistent feature of society, not just a temporary disturbance of the social order (as functionalists believe). Karl Marx (1818–83) stressed the economic basis of human organisation, which could be divided into two levels: a base (or infrastructure) and a superstructure. The base is determined by the forces of production (e.g. the raw materials and technology of a particular society) and the social relations of production (e.g. social relationships that people enter into – such as manager, worker – to produce goods). The other aspect of society, the superstructure, is made of the political, legal and educational institutions, which are not independent of the base but shaped by it. Marx believed that many societies contain basic contradictions that preclude them from existing permanently. These contradictions, involving the increasing exploitation of one group by another (for example, the exploitation of serfs by lords in feudal times), have to be resolved since a social system containing such contradictions cannot survive unchanged.

The concepts that Marxists emphasise in their studies include social class, exploitation and oppression, contradiction, conflict and change, and ideology and false consciousness. Class denotes a social group whose members share a similar relationship to the means of production. Essentially, in capitalist societies there is the ruling class which owns the means of production (e.g. land, raw materials) and the working class which must sell its labour power to earn a living. In a feudal society, the two main classes are distinguished relative to ownership of the land: the feudal nobility owns it and the landless serfs work it. 'Exploitation' is a technical term that stresses that the wealth produced by the labor power of workers is appropriated in the forms of profits by the ruling class. 'Ideology' within Marxist theory refers to the set of dominant ideas of an age: it emanates from the control of the ruling classes of the institutions of the superstructure. Such ideas serve ultimately to justify the power and privilege of the ruling class 'and conceal from all members of society the basis of exploitation and oppression on which their dominance rests' (Haralambos and Holborn 1991: 14). A clear example comes again from the feudal age in Europe when the dominant concepts were honour and loyalty, which appeared as the natural order and were celebrated in literature and implicit in superstructural institutions like the law courts and education. Similarly, according to many theorists, in the capitalist age exploitation is disguised by the ideology of equality and freedom, which appear to be not just sensible but natural and desirable. This, Marxists argue, conceals the reality that capitalism involves fundamentally unequal relationships: workers are not ultimately 'free' since they are forced to work in order to survive: all they can do is exchange one form of wage subordination for another.

Class versus caste societies

A caste system differs from a class-based society insofar as status and role are fixed from birth. This social system is found in countries like India and Senegal. The usually accepted attributes of caste in India are the following:

- *Endogamy.* Marriage is restricted to members of one's caste group.
- *Occupational specialisation.* Individual castes are associated with fixed occupations, inherited at birth.
- *Hierarchy.* There is a division of castes according to status, with the Brahman (or priest) at the top, and Shudras (working castes) at the bottom. Another group is considered 'outcaste'.
- *Hereditary membership.* One is born into a particular caste, and cannot change it despite individual merit.

However, the relative rigidity of caste society should not lead to an exaggeration of the flexibility of the class system, in which there are constraints on who has access to the best education, the most prestigious jobs and the most powerful positions. Societies which espouse freedom of opportunity were often built on a different set of principles. Analysts of class point to the historical system of racial capitalism built on slavery. This was a kind of colour-caste system that contributed to the growth of the southern US and European economies, which were subsequently able to denounce these principles.

Interactionism

A third school of thought within sociology, less influential than the previous two, adopts a bottom-up approach of examining small-scale encounters rather than large-scale social systems. It seeks to understand action between individuals. Haralambos and Holborn (1991: 15) emphasise that interactionism begins from the assumption that action is meaningful to those involved, and that those meanings are accordingly not fixed but created, developed, modified and changed within the actual process of interaction. Not only is the meaning of a social encounter a negotiated entity, but the individual develops a 'self-concept' (or idea of oneself) according to the interactive processes in which he or she participates, and according to the way he or she is evaluated therein. For the interactionist, social roles are not as clearly defined as within functional theory. Furthermore, interactionists argue that roles are often unclear, ambiguous or vague. This may provide actors with considerable room for negotiation, improvisation and creative action.

Much of sociolinguistics has proceeded implicitly from a functionalist perspective of society, though it must be said that the linguistic tends to overshadow the sociological. The latter is often considered useful largely for informal background information and orientation. In this book, we will focus on the major findings of such sociolinguistics but will be emphasising where and how they might fit together sociologically. Marxist approaches are not typically emphasised in the west, and, while we understand the scepticism with which Marxist/communist political practice has come to be viewed worldwide, from a scholarly point of view many of the insights emanating from sociolinguistics do fit the Marxist critique of social systems quite well. Some linguists like Norman Fairclough explicitly acknowledge their position as Marxist, and undertake sociolinguistic analyses of speech and writing based on a Marxist understanding of society. This line of research is discussed in Chapter 10, where we explore the linguistic ramifications of rule, control and power. Interactionism, which may not seem as substantial a sociological approach as the other two, has nevertheless inspired some important work in sociolinguistics which we introduce in Chapter 6. The development of language among children is best characterised in interactional terms. Languages are not products residing in grammars and dictionaries, but flexible interactive tools. There is accordingly an interplay between socialisation and language learning in early life. This interplay is stressed in the work of the British linguist, Michael Halliday (1978: 19), who describes the functions discernible in the pre-linguistic behaviour of infants (see box below). Since the school typically demands a more impersonal way of using language, interactionism forms a significant perspective in modern research on classroom language (see Chapter 11).

Outside Linguistics, an influential school of thought regarding culture in the modern world, *Postmodernism* can be seen as a combination of Marxism and Interactionism. This school of thought stresses identities as

---

The interactional functions of language in early infancy – Halliday (1978: 19)

1. *Instrumental* ('I want'): satisfying material needs.
2. *Regulatory* ('do as I tell you'): controlling the behavior of others.
3. *Interactional* ('me and you'): getting along with other people.
4. *Personal* ('here I come'): identifying and expressing the self.
5. *Heuristic* ('tell me why'): exploring the world outside and inside oneself.
6. *Imaginative* ('let's pretend'): creating a world of one's own.
7. *Informative* ('I've got something to tell you'): communicating new information.

fluid, multiple, fractured, unstable, contradictory and always open to possibilities of change. Few linguists endorse a fully chaotic view of language and culture, preferring to look for underlying regularities amid seeming flux. Still, there are times when a dynamic view of human behaviour is particularly appropriate, as when examining the expressive styles that young people experiment with and sometimes adopt.

Types of Societies/Types of Languages?

Societies may be classified in terms of their complexity, defined by their size, hierarchical organisation, economic structure, specialisation of tasks and interaction with other societies. It is important to note that there is no linguistic analogue to this. Languages cannot be arranged in a list from least to most complex. The structure of languages does not correlate with the complexity of the communities that typically use them. In terms of morphology, syntax and semantics, a language of an isolated mountain-bound community in the Himalayas is no less complex than any of the six world languages of the United Nations. The poet-cum-linguist, Edward Sapir (1921: 219), put it as follows: 'When it comes to linguistic form, Plato walks with the Macedonian swineherd, Confucius with the head-hunting savage of Assam'. Sapir's student Whorf, who, as we have seen, was intimately acquainted with the structure of Hopi and other Amerindian languages, was just as emphatic, if less poetic:

> The relatively few languages of the cultures which have attained to modern civilization promise to overspread the globe and cause the extinction of the hundreds of diverse exotic linguistic species, but it is idle to pretend that they represent any superiority of type. On the contrary, it takes but little real scientific study of pre-literate languages, especially those of America, to show how much more precise and finely elaborated is the system of relationships in many such tongues than is ours. (1956: 84)

A reverse argument is sometimes offered: people maintain that languages rich in inflections or in ways of combining basic grammatical units (morphemes) into words are perhaps too complex to function as languages of wider communication. Conversely, they suggest that the inflectional simplicity of English enables it to be effective as a language of international transactions. There are several things wrong with this argument. In the first place, the notion of complexity should not be limited to the morphology of a language. Modern linguistics emphasises the enormously complex organisation of all languages. One language might be morphologically 'simpler' on the surface, but a relatively simpler morphology (as with English) has to be made up in other components of the grammar: in the syntax and vocabulary. If we are to look for reasons for the spread of one language over another, the wrong place to start would be the structure of the language, as John Edwards (1995: 40) forcefully argues:

It is [. . .] clear, to the modern linguist at any rate, that these varieties [dominant languages] achieved widespread power and status because of the heightened fortunes of their users, and not because of any intrinsic linguistic qualities of the languages themselves. The most common elements here have to do with military, political and economic might, although there are also examples in which a more purely cultural status supports the *lingua franca* function. However, in this latter case, the cultural clout which lingers has generally grown from earlier associations with those more blatant features just mentioned. The muscle, in any case, which these languages have, derives from the fact that their original users control important commodities – wealth, dominance, learning – which others see as necessary for their own aspirations. The aphorism 'all roads lead to Rome' has linguistic meaning too.

This view is hard to assimilate within a functionalist and interactionist perspective. Edwards makes it clear that infrastructural factors ('military, political and economic might') and ideological factors ('cultural clout') are involved when a language becomes dominant over a wide area. By 'cultural clout', Edwards refers to factors like an established literature, a tradition of grammatical study of the language, and the high status of the language and its speakers.

Sapir, Whorf and descriptive linguists generally were at pains to stress that languages were in principle of equal complexity. This was a necessary step to guard against potential European and American ethnocentrism in linguistics and anthropology, and led to great advances in understanding language structure. Some sociolinguists argue that it is now time to recognise that if languages are all linguistically equal they are not all sociolinguistically equal. In this vein, Joseph (1987: 25–39) points to the effects of print literacy and standardisation in giving some forms of language and some languages an advantage over others, so that certain forms of language come to seem to be more important than others. Coulmas (1989b: 4) believes that the egalitarian perspective has led linguists to downplay the functions of language in society, in which all languages 'are clearly not equal'. (One such instance of an unequal function and position assigned to different languages within the same society is discussed in the next section.) However, it is not the case that some languages are better placed in an absolute sense to serve a range of sociolinguistic functions (for example, in formal speeches, writing or television) than others. Every language has the potential to add to its characteristic vocabulary and ways of speaking if new roles become necessary. Some languages have a superior technical vocabulary to that of others in certain spheres. This is a difference in actuality rather than in potential.

A rural technology: ploughing terms in nineteenth-century Bihar,
India

to plough	*har jot-*
first ploughing	*pahil cās*
second ploughing	*dokhār*
third ploughing	*tekhā*
land sown after a single ploughing	*bhokauā*
ploughing in the month of Magh of land to be sown in the next rainy season	*maghar jot-*
ploughing of millet when it is a foot high	*bidāh*
ploughing of a deliberately flooded rice field	*lewā*
ploughing with a plough having a new full-sized block	*nawṭha ke jot*
ploughing with a plough having a small worn block	*khinauri ke jot*
light re-ploughing to get rid of weeds and prepare for sowing of rice	*unāh*
small pieces of field which a plough is unable to touch	*pais*
cross-ploughing	*ārā*
ploughing in diminishing circuits	*caukeṭha*
centre plot round which bullocks have no room to turn	*badhār*
ploughing from corner to corner in small centre plot	*koniya jot*
ploughing of a crooked field	*ūnādyorhī jot*
ploughing along the length and breadth of a rectangular field	*sojhauā jot*
ploughing breadthways	*phānī*

(based on G. A. Grierson, *Bihar Peasant Life* 1975 [1885]: 171–4)

A bar over a vowel denotes a long pronunciation; a dot below a
consonant denotes a retroflex pronunciation (tongue tip curled backwards to strike the palate).

The Notion of 'Speech Community'

Traditionally, sociologists study societies in terms of categories like class,
ethnicity or regional and economic characteristics. 'Community' as typically
used in sociology suggests a dimension of shared knowledge, possessions or
behaviours. Linguists draw attention to another dimension of social organisation by using the term 'speech community'. Essentially, the term stresses

that language practices may be equally diagnostic of the social coherence of a group, and may be a more natural boundary for sociolinguistic study than, say, geographical cohesion alone. The term cannot be exactly equated with groups of people who speak the same language. Thus speakers of Spanish in Spain, Columbia and Texas do not form a speech community. (The term 'language community' is sometimes used to discuss the superset of speakers of the same language in different parts of the world.) Conversely, speaking different primary (or home) languages does not necessarily preclude people from belonging to the same speech community. In multilingual communities where more than one language is spoken by a majority of people, sufficient consensus about appropriate rules of speaking and interpreting linguistic behavior may arise for it to be considered one sociolinguistic unit (or speech community). This has been claimed, for example, of India, where a number of common sociolinguistic conventions have been found to underlie the great diversity of languages. Prabodh Pandit (1972) used the term 'sociolinguistic area' to describe this phenomenon.

Nevertheless, it must be admitted that 'speech community' is not precise enough to be considered a technical term. Even in linguistics, the emphases stressed by different scholars carry varied nuances, as Muriel Saville-Troike (1982: 17–18) emphasises:

1. Shared language use (Lyons 1970).
2. Frequency of interaction by a group of people (Bloomfield 1933; Hockett 1958; Gumperz 1962).
3. Shared rules of speaking and interpretations of speech performance (Hymes 1972).
4. Shared attitudes and values regarding language forms and language use (Labov 1972a).
5. Shared sociocultural understandings and presupposition regarding speech events (Sherzer 1977).

The core meaning that we might extract from these is that a speech community comprises people who are in habitual contact with each other by means of speech which involves either a shared language variety or shared ways of interpreting the different language varieties commonly used in the area. Peter Patrick (2002: 593) concludes his detailed survey of the complexities of the concept of speech community, with a more postmodern outlook:

> [Researchers] should not presume social cohesion or accept it to be an inevitable result of interaction; size and its effects should not be taken for granted; social theories, including class analyses, must be explicitly invoked, not accepted as givens; the speech community should not be taken for a unit of social analysis; and we ought not to assume that [they] exist as predefined entities waiting to be researched or identify them with folk notions, but see them as objects constituted anew by the researcher's gaze and the questions we ask.

1.7 MONOLINGUALISM AND MULTILINGUALISM

Many countries, especially in the west, attach special significance to the existence of one majority language per territory, adhering to an ethos of 'one state – one language'. Indeed, many of the states of Europe arose in a period of intense nationalism, with accompanying attempts to make national borders coterminous with language (and vice versa). The dominance of European powers in modern history has made this seem a desirable situation, if not an ideal one. The non-aligned sociolinguist would do well to bear in mind the essentially multilingual nature of most human societies, and that there are almost no countries in the world – even in western Europe – where everyone speaks, or identifies with, one language. In statistical terms, Grosjean (1982: vii) estimates that about half the world's population is bilingual. Romaine (1989b: 8) points out further that there about thirty times as many languages as there are countries. Even countries like France, Germany and England that are sometimes characterised as monolingual in fact have a vast array of languages within their borders. In France, for example, the following languages are still in use: French, Breton, Flemish, Occitan, Catalan, Basque, Alsatian and Corsican. There are also languages spoken in large numbers by more recent immigrants like Arabic from North Africa and Wolof from West Africa. In England, several Asian languages are used daily by some part of the population, for example Gujarati, Panjabi, Urdu and Hindi. In Germany, Turkish is prominent among the languages of immigrants and settled communities descended from immigrants.

In this book, 'bilingualism' will be used as a general term for the use of two or more languages in a society. The term thus subsumes the idea of 'multilingualism'. Many writers do the reverse using the term 'multilingualism' in the more general way (to mean the use of *two or more* languages). Neither usage is quite satisfactory, and the reader has to deduce whether in certain cases *multi-* means 'two' or *bi* means 'more than two'. In practice, with the aid of context however, there is little ambiguity. Some sociolinguists, however, prefer to restrict bilingualism to its literal sense of commanding two languages and multilingualism to more than two. This is the policy of the *International Journal of Multilingualism*, for example, which restricts its subject matter to the acquisition, use and theories regarding third or fourth languages (etc.) used by individuals, rather than second languages.

While bilingualism is common throughout the world, many schools have a policy that recognises (and replicates) the hierarchy of relations within a territory and in the world as a whole. Only a small proportion of the 5,000 or so languages of the world are used at high-school level as media of instruction, and still fewer at university level. Schools have often downplayed the value of the 'vernaculars' by minimising their use in classrooms or recognising them only as means of facilitating competence in the dominant language(s). Since the 1950s, and more especially since the 1970s, educationists have begun to recognise that multiculturalism and multilingualism are phenomena which should be encouraged, rather than treated as if they are transient. Sociolinguists are generally sympathetic to an approach that gives recognition to, and valorises, as many of a society's languages as possible. This is in keeping with a holistic approach that is sensitive to the needs of the children ('bottom up'), and not just the bureaucratic needs of the state ('top down'). These themes will be explored in Chapter 8, on language maintenance and shift, and Chapter 11, on education.

Diglossia – An Unequal Arrangement of Language Varieties

The term 'diglossia' was coined by the US linguist Charles Ferguson (1959) to denote a situation where two varieties of a language exist side by side throughout a speech community, with each being assigned a definite but non-overlapping role. Ferguson was interested in societies in which a classical form of a language (no longer spoken colloquially) was reserved for some functions like education, literature and public speeches, while a modern colloquial variety of the same language was used for other functions like domestic interaction. The community regards the classical form as superior, while the colloquial form tends to be taken for granted. Ferguson used the labels 'H' ('high') for the variety accorded social prestige and 'L' ('low') for the other variety. Ferguson stressed that these labels were meant for convenience of reference rather than as judgmental terms on his part. Arabic in many parts of the Middle East is the paradigm example of diglossia, with Classical Arabic being accorded public and prestigious roles while colloquial Arabic is used in other roles. Table 1.1 shows typical diglossic distributions of H and L in the societies that Ferguson studied.

Great importance is attached to using the right variety in the right situation. According to Ferguson, an outsider who learns to speak fluent, accurate L and then uses it in a formal speech is an object of ridicule. A member of the speech community who uses H in a purely conversational situation or in an informal activity like shopping is equally an object of ridicule. In a sense, this is verbal hygiene taken to an extreme, with one variety not deemed worthy of 'serious' use. Since the H form is learned via formal education, diglossia can be a means of excluding people from access to full participation in society. This might apply in some societies to women and the poorer sections of the populace (see for example, Jaakola 1976). Two varieties used in contemporary Greek society, Katharevousa ('H') and Dhimotiki ('L'), show the political tensions surrounding diglossia.

	H	L
Sermon in church or mosque	X	
Instruction to servants, waiters, workmen, clerks		X
Personal letter		X
Speech in parliament, political speech	X	
University lecture	X	
Conversation with family, friends, colleagues		X
News broadcast	X	
Radio 'soap opera'		X
Newspaper editorial, news story, caption on picture		X
Caption on political cartoon		X
Poetry	X	
Folk literature		X

Table 1.1 A typical diglossic distribution of language varieties
(Ferguson 1959: 329)

The H form is associated with the nineteenth-century upsurge in literature and the creation of a literary language based in part on older forms
of literary Greek. The L form is the colloquial variety as it has evolved
over the centuries. Katharevousa is strongly associated with religion and
'high' culture. Supporters of Dhimotiki feel that it can be used to a greater
extent in the public sphere in the interests of all citizens. There was serious
rioting in Greece in 1903 (when the New Testament was translated into
Dhimotiki). Even today, there is a political colouring to the preferences
for H or L. Under the liberal Greek government of the 1960s, a modified type of Dhimotiki (with elements from Katharevousa) was made the
language of schools and to a certain extent of newspapers. However, after
the coup of 1967, the military government decreed that Katharevousa be
used in the schools. The subsequent return of democracy to Greece saw a
restoration and strengthening of Dhimotiki (Trudgill 1983a: 115–16). In
other societies, like those of the Middle East or Tamil Nadu state in India,
the status of H (Classical Arabic and Classical Tamil respectively) is not
contested; it is felt to be the bearer of religion, culture and history, and a
symbol of unity.

Diglossia is different from a simple 'standard versus dialect' arrangement in other societies. First, the standard in non-diglossic societies is
typically a modern form spoken by some sectors of society from childhood. This is not the case with the H form in diglossia, which has to be
learned via formal education. Second, the relationship between standard
and dialect is typically a close one, and it is not always easy to draw the
line between the two. Again, in contrast the H and L forms of diglossia
have distinct grammars which are almost like those of different languages.
Whereas diglossia was meant to be a special concept limited to a few
communities, the standard–dialect dichotomy today applies to almost all

societies. One attempt at revising Ferguson's scheme, which has come to be known as 'Fishman's extension', places diglossia at the centre of any attempt to characterise societies in terms of their linguistic repertoires. Joshua Fishman (1967) argued that some societies show the kind of functional specialisation identified by Ferguson, where the roles of H and L were played by different languages, rather than two specially related forms of the same language. Fishman gave the example of Paraguay, where for the general population Spanish played the role of H while the indigenous language, Guarani, played the role of L. A similar situation holds for many African countries in which a colonial language like English or French is the H. Some critics feel that this extension dilutes Ferguson's original definition too greatly (for example Britto 1986: chs 2 and 3). However, in categorising societies by their language hierarchies, the parallels between 'narrow' (Ferguson's) diglossia and 'broad' (Fishman's extension) diglossia are of considerable interest. While some critics worried that broad diglossia more or less equated diglossia with bilingualism, Fishman (1967) pointed to the following relations between bilingualism and diglossia:

- Bilingualism without diglossia: e.g. German–English bilingualism in Germany.
- Bilingualism with diglossia: e.g. Guarani–Spanish bilingualism in Paraguay.
- Diglossia without bilingualism: e.g. Classical and colloquial Arabic in Egypt.
- Neither diglossia nor bilingualism: e.g. monolingual parts of the USA.

Fishman's extension thus gives an important way of categorising societies by their speech repertoires.

1.8   CONCLUSION

In this chapter, we have laid out the key issues that current sociolinguistics is concerned with. These issues, we have argued, go well beyond the lay perceptions about language that one encounters from time to time in letters to the press or in the prescriptive and literary focus on language that schools typically offer. Language is embedded in a social and historical context, and a full understanding of language can only be achieved by paying attention to those contexts. This applies equally to attitudes and judgements concerning language use as to the rise of standard forms of language. However societies and histories are not closed topics themselves but are subject to different analyses, as we have stressed in our accounts of functionalism, Marxism and interactionism. The sociolinguistic approach introduced in this chapter – especially the focus on speech rather than writing – serves as a background and an orientation towards appreciating the research presented in the rest of the book. Many of the issues raised in this opening chapter will be covered in greater detail in subsequent chapters.

Notes

1. The title is taken from a line in a poem by Ogden Nash.
2. Although for a long while William Labov, one of the most influential of socio-linguists, hoped that sociolinguistic studies could be made compatible with generative linguistics, the two branches of linguistics have gone their own ways, with interest in their own research problems.
3. On the history of *ain't* (another casualty of prescriptive sensibilities), see Joseph 1987: 127.
4. Anglo and Anexo are more usually written as – Aŋlɔ and Anexɔ.

2
REGIONAL DIALECTOLOGY

2.1 INTRODUCTION

Every two miles the water changes, and every four miles the speech. (North Indian proverb)

Swâben ir wörter spalten	Swabians split their words up
Die Franken ein teil si valtent	The Franks run them together
Die Baire si zerzerrent	The Bavarians tear them to pieces
Die Düringe si ûf sperrent	The Thuringians open them out

(excerpt from *Der Renner* by Hugo von Trimberg (1300), cited by Barbour and Stevenson 1990: 57–8)

The above extracts reveal an awareness common in many cultures that spoken forms of a language are not uniform entities, but may vary according to (respectively) the area people come from, or the social group they belong to. The way in which language varies systematically is one of the central concerns of sociolinguistics. There are three more ways in which a language may vary: according to context, time and the individual. Chapters 2 to 4 will discuss research on these types of variation, though the last has not been studied in any detail by sociolinguists. Within sociolinguistics, the focus falls more on the social group than on the individual, even though 'the uniqueness of individuals, arising out of differences in their memory, personality, intelligence, social background, and personal experience makes distinctiveness of style inevitable in everyone' (Crystal 1995: 3). The term 'idiolect' is sometimes used by linguists for an individual's distinctive way of speaking.

This chapter is concerned with **regional dialectology**, that is, the systematic study of how a language varies from one area to another. We survey the roots of dialect study in nineteenth-century Europe, and contrast monolingual dialectology in Europe with a survey carried out in India, a multilingual territory. We trace the decline of methods of traditional regional dialectology that focused mainly on rural areas in the second half

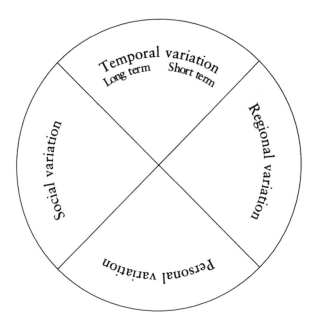

Figure 2.1   The dimensions of speech variation (from Crystal 1995: 3)

of the twentieth century, and cite newer studies that are interested in more modern themes like urbanization and labour movement and their effects on peoples' dialects. We also outline some aspects of language use that have eluded dialectologists thus far.

The term 'dialect' in sociolinguistics is used to describe the speech characteristic of a region (**regional dialect**) or of a group of people defined by social or occupational characteristics rather than by region alone (**social dialect**). Thus we may speak of the dialect of Cologne, the dialect of the upper classes of Boston, the dialect of farmworkers in south-east England and so on. Before discussing the concerns and methods of the approach to language that is known as regional dialectology, it is necessary to reiterate the key points mentioned in Chapter 1 concerning 'dialect' and related terms.

- In ordinary usage, the distinction between language and dialect is a political rather than a linguistic one. The way a speech continuum is cut up and labelled in the 'real world' is often based on political factors.
- Where the distinction between the two (language and dialect) is not significant for the analysis being done, linguists prefer to use the term 'variety'.
- Many linguists consider all dialects of a language to be equal, unless proven otherwise. That is, everyone's way of speaking is equally valid and capable of conveying fine nuances of meaning.
- Some linguists, however, believe that not all dialects are equal. In particular, the standard variety of a community may have the advantage over others

in matters like vocabulary development for more technical and formal purposes.

- The standard form of a language is a sociohistorical product rather than an entity that necessarily pre-dated other varieties of that language.
- Because of the above two considerations, it can be said that everyone speaks a dialect. However, the dialect of the most prestigious (and powerful) speakers on which the standard is based is seldom labelled a dialect by non-linguists.
- Accent is often part of the defining feature of a dialect, but may be separated from it.
- It is possible to speak the standard form of a language while using an accent associated with a particular region.

Two examples of dialect humor

Very often, small differences in language can serve large symbolic purposes, in marking off one group from another and sustaining social difference. This can be seen in the first excerpt from p. 102 of Chinua Achebe's novel *Things Fall Apart*, set in nineteenth-century Nigeria.

When they had all gathered, the white man began to speak to them. He spoke through an interpreter who was an Ibo man, though his dialect was different and harsh to the ears of Mbanta. Many people laughed at his dialect and the way he used words strangely. Instead of saying 'myself' he always said 'my buttocks'. But he was a man of commanding presence and the clansmen listened to him. He said he was one of them, as they could see from his colour and his language . . . 'Your buttocks understand our language,' said someone light-heartedly and the crowd laughed.

The second excerpt is from Frank McCourt's book, *'Tis*, dealing with an Irish immigrant's experience of US English.

If I had the money I could buy a torch and read till dawn. In America a torch is called a flashlight. A biscuit is called a cookie, a bun is a roll. Confectionery is pastry and minced meat is ground. Men wear pants instead of trousers and they'll even say this pant leg is shorter than the other which is silly. When I hear them say pant leg I feel like breathing faster. The lift is an elevator and if you want a WC or a lavatory you have to say bathroom even if there isn't a sign of a bath there. And no one dies in America, they pass away or they're deceased and when they die the body, which is called the remains, is taken to a funeral home where people just stand around and look at it and no one sings or tells a story or takes a drink and then it's taken away in a casket to be interred. They don't like saying coffin and they don't like saying buried. They never say graveyard. Cemetery sounds nicer.

2.2   A MULTILINGUAL PROJECT:

The Linguistic Survey of India

Sir George Grierson, a British magistrate resident in India for half a century and a trained Sanskritist and philologist, provided a classification of the languages of India (from 1894 onwards). He had been hired by the government of India to undertake a survey of north and central India, then containing 224 million people.[1] This task was all the more daunting as the India of the nineteenth century was a vast subcontinent that included what are now Pakistan and Bangladesh. Although the *Linguistic Survey of India* (or *LSI*) excluded the Dravidian-speaking parts of south India (which were being covered in another study), it did include languages belonging to historically different families (Austronesian, Sino-Tibetan and Indo-Aryan). The data collected included the following specimens of language:

- recital of a standard passage (the Biblical parable of the Prodigal Son) in a local village dialect, based on a version circulated in a widespread language like Hindi or Bengali;[2]
- an impromptu piece of folklore, prose or verse;
- translation of a list of 241 words and phrases.

Grierson used local government officials (district officers and their assistants) in different localities to write down specimens from suitable consultants in the local script and in Roman characters. On the basis of degrees of similarity across villages, Grierson grouped village speech into dialects and then dialects into languages. He posited the existence of 179 languages and 544 component dialects of these languages. The LSI included grammatical and historical descriptions and notes on local literature, in addition to descriptions of vocabulary items. Grierson's work is little cited outside the specialised field of Indian linguistics; but the scope of his work, its embedding in a multilingual context and its techniques make it deserving of wider recognition.

The LSI is significant in showing that the principles of dialectology remain largely the same, irrespective of whether the society is monolingual or multilingual. This is not surprising in view of the fact that there are no purely 'linguistic' ways of differentiating whether a variety is 'a language or a dialect'. With a dialect continuum especially, it is not always easy to conclude on dialectological grounds whether one or more languages is being spoken in a territory. Even if one works with a non-linguistic 'common-sense' notion of language based on historical criteria (e.g. political acceptance, standardisation and literary use), problems of demarcation remain, for just as one dialect *might* blend into another so too *might* one language blend into another. As Grierson puts it:

[Most] Indian languages gradually merge into each other and are not separated by hard and fast boundary lines. When such boundaries are spoken of, or are shown on a map, they must always be understood as conventional methods of showing definitely a state of things which is in its essence indefinite . . . (1927: 30–1) Although Assamese differs widely from Marathi, and a speaker of one would be entirely unintelligible to the other, a man could almost walk for twenty-eight hundred miles, from Dibrugarh to Bombay and thence to Dardistan, without being able to point to a single stage where he had passed through eight distinct tongues of the Indian Continent, Assamese, Bengali, Oriya, Marathi, Gujarati, Sindhi, Lahnda, and Kohistani . . . (1927: 141)

Just as dialects can be classified on the basis of key phonetic elements, languages can too. Map 2.1 shows Grierson's classification of north Indian languages based on the presence or absence of an /l/ in the past participle. Thus the words for 'beaten' in the shaded languages in Map 2.1 are as follows: Assamese *mār-il*, Bengali *mār-ila*, Bihari *mār-al*, Oriya and Marathi *mār-ilā*, Gujarati *mār-el*, Sindhi *mār-yalu*. On the other hand Hindi, which does not belong to this outer ring of north Indian languages, has *mar-a*.

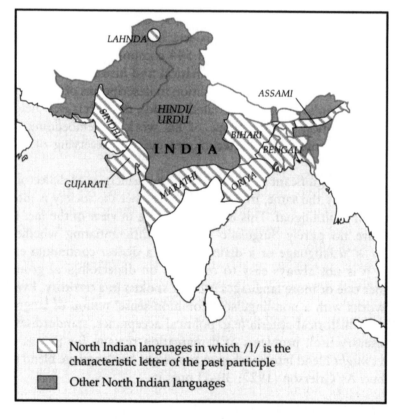

Map 2.1 North Indian languages of India which use an /l/ in the past participle (based on Grierson 1927: 140)

Although Grierson did not use phonetic transcriptions, he did compile gramophone recordings of some of the specimens in the survey. It is not surprising that many of Grierson's characterisations, labels and classifications should have been modified by more recent scholarship. But it is a tribute to his work that the *Linguistic Survey of India* still forms the baseline for historical-linguistic and sociolinguistic studies of the subcontinent.

2.3 MONOLINGUAL DIALECTOLOGY IN EUROPE

Initial interest in dialectology in Europe in the nineteenth century was a result of theories within historical linguistics, in particular the claim that 'sound laws are exceptionless'. For a long time, linguistics was chiefly concerned with the study of written texts, with a view to establishing which languages of the world were related, and to propose laws showing the phonetic correspondences between words of those languages. An example of a **sound law** is the correspondence identified by linguists between <bh>; in Sanskrit <b>; in Germanic languages and <f>; in Latin. (The angled brackets denote spellings.) Thus the word for 'brother' is *bhratar* in Sanskrit; *brothor* in Old English and *frater* in Latin. Linguists eventually turned their attention to sources that would supplement textual evidence and, they hoped, corroborate some of their theories. In particular they raised the possibility that dialect speech would preserve older and more regular forms than those of standard written forms of a language. The claim that sound laws were exceptionless turned out to be false; but it did serve as an impetus to the scholarly study of dialects. A second motivation for dialect research in the nineteenth and twentieth centuries was the feeling that rural speech was being rapidly eroded by the pressures of modernisation and urbanisation, especially in Europe. The need for surveys that would record as much of traditional rural dialect as possible was stressed. Dialectology began to proceed along independent lines, rather than being necessarily linked to historical studies. If anything, the model that began to play a more significant role was that of human geography, rather than history. Dialectology is therefore sometimes labelled 'linguistic geography' or 'geolinguistics'. Harold Orton and Nathalia Wright (1974: 21), two twentieth-century British practitioners of dialectology, describe their task as follows:

> A primary aim of linguistic geography is to reveal the occurrence and distribution of speech usages, especially those characteristic of particular regions. Their diffusion can be mapped clearly and simply. Close study of the resultant maps permits significant deductions to be drawn about the movements of those usages: whether, for example they are spreading or contracting, or whether, indeed, they have been partly supplanted by other features.

The following is a brief outline of the procedures associated with traditional dialectology (adapted from Petyt 1980: 49–51):

1. A preliminary investigation or pilot survey is often carried out, to gain some idea of the way usages vary over the area to be covered and to decide what sort of items are worthy of detailed investigation.

2a. A network of geographical localities where the fieldwork is to be conducted is decided upon. The number of such localities and the density of coverage is constrained by time, finances and number of fieldworkers, and possibly by the density of population in the area.

2b. A list of items to be investigated is drawn up in the format of a questionnaire. (Typical items are given in the box below.)

3. Fieldwork is then conducted. One or more trained investigators travel to the localities selected and make contact with people who they consider to be most suitable informants. Questionnaires are completed in the presence of the consultant. Since the 1950s, greater flexibility has been afforded by the advent of the tape recorder, as some parts of the interview can be recorded and transcribed later.

4. Data analysis is then undertaken. Lists are produced showing geographical patterns of distribution, usually with the aid of maps. Publication of lists and maps is a time-consuming and expensive undertaking which often occurs many years after the initial survey.

Some questions excerpted from the Survey of English Dialects (Orton and Wright 1974)
Vocabulary: e.g. *What do you call the thing you carry water in?* (Shows whether *pail* or *bucket* or some other item is used in an English-speaking area.)
Semantics: e.g. *People starve from hunger; what else can people starve from?* (cold in the north of England and Scotland.)
Grammar: e.g. *We say today it snowed; yesterday* it also — (The answer shows whether *snowed* or *snew* or some other form is the usual one.)

Some Pioneers of Dialectology

Georg Wenker, a German schoolteacher who tried to construct an accurate dialect map of Germany starting in 1876, and Jules Gilliéron, a French scholar who did a national dialectology survey in France in the 1880s, are acknowledged as pioneers of dialectology. Wenker carried out his investigation by post, contacting every village in Germany that had a school. His questionnaire comprised forty sentences having features of linguistic interest, which the local headmaster/teacher was asked to rephrase in the local dialect. The rather stilted nature of his approach can be seen in the very first sentence, *Im Winter fliegen die trocknen Blätter durch die Luft herum*: 'In winter the dry leaves fly around through the air'. Over 45,000 questionnaires were completed and returned (Barbour and Stevenson 1990: 62). The volume of data turned out to be more of a problem than a resource for the original aims of the project. Out of this research the *Sprachatlas des Deutschen Reichs* ('Language Atlas of the German Empire') was compiled, containing a series of maps each illustrating a single feature over north and central Germany. It was the first linguistic atlas ever produced, with the original hand-drawn version coming out in 1881.

Unlike Wenker, Gilliéron used on-the-spot investigation, rather than a postal survey. He employed a single fieldworker, Edmond Edmont, a greengrocer by trade and an amateur linguist trained in phonetics. Petyt (1980: 41) puts it as follows: 'Gilliéron bought Edmont a bicycle, and sent him pedalling off around 639 rural localities in France and the French-speaking parts of Belgium, Switzerland and Italy'. He chose one consultant per locality (occasionally two), usually a male aged between 15 and 85 years. The fieldwork was conducted between 1897 and 1901. Publication of the findings was relatively quick: thirteen volumes with 1,920 maps appeared between 1902 and 1910. Though his coverage was less comprehensive than Wenker's in terms of localities studied, Gilliéron's work provided the model for subsequent dialect surveys in Europe and America. In Britain, the *Survey of Scottish (English) Dialects* began in 1949, and the *Survey of English Dialects (SED)* was planned in the late 1940s and published between 1962 and 1971. There was no national survey in the USA, where dialectologists preferred to work more intensively on individual areas. The best-known early work of this nature is Hans Kurath's *Linguistic Atlas of New England*, published in three volumes between 1939 and 1943. More recent dialect work in the USA is discussed later in this chapter and in Chapters 3 and 4.

Drawing and Interpreting Dialect Maps

A key feature of dialectology is the **isogloss**: a line drawn on a map separating areas according to particular linguistic features.[3] These features can be items of vocabulary, sounds or relatively simple features of grammar. Isoglosses serve to mark off clearly areas in which a feature is found from those adjacent areas where it is not recorded or occurs only exceptionally, or together with another form. Map 2.2 shows an isogloss from the SED separating areas according to whether *brambles* or *blackberries* is the preferred term. Map 2.3 shows the distribution of *folk* vs *people* in the SED. Map 2.4 shows a famous isogloss separating the north of England from the south according to the vowel in the lexical set STRUT, CUP, LUCK. The term 'lexical set', which we use frequently in Chapters 2 and 3, was devised by John Wells (1982) as a convenient way of identifying vowel categories not by symbols, but by a set of words in which they occur. Although the vowel in a set like STRUT, CUP, LUCK may vary from one variety of English to another, within a given variety there is usually consistency within a set.[4] The lexical set is useful for students who do not have a background in phonetics, since it allows them to identify the sounds involved, even if the symbols for them are not known. Obviously, more advanced work in dialectology requires a good background in phonetics. To return to the isogloss in Map 2.4, to the north of the line the vowel is pronounced [ʊ] (the vowel sound in the word *book* in RP). To the south of the line it is pronounced [ʌ], which is the RP pronunciation as well. (The RP pronunciations are cited here

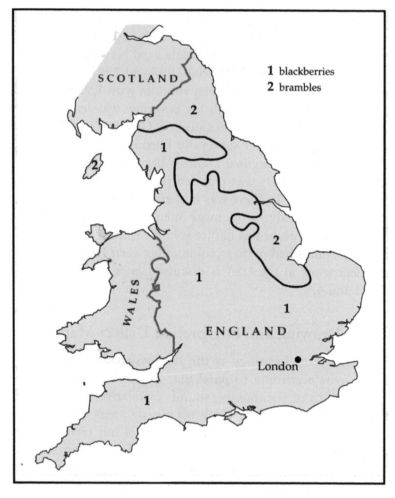

Map 2.2 The lexical isogloss: *blackberries* vs *brambles* (from Orton and Wright, *A Word Geography of England* 1974: 37)

as reference points that will help you to associate the phonetic symbols given with the sounds they represent. RP is useful since it is considered 'standard' by many people in Britain. Moreover, it is available internationally as a model on the BBC World Service.) Note that the RP vowel [a] in STRUT, CUP, LUCK, is the newer form. A. C. Gimson (1989: 110–11) dates this change to the seventeenth century, but stresses that the [ʌ] form finally emerged only in the early twentieth century and is arguably still undergoing modification.

Taken together, Maps 2.2, 2.3 and 2.4 show that isoglosses within one geographical area may exhibit quite different patterns. In detailed surveys, the geographical dispersion of words and sounds in particular words can be so disparate that dialectologists were led to claim that 'every word has its own particular history' (Jaberg 1908: 6). This hardly augured well for a theory of dialectology. However, some generalisations can be made from a reading of isogloss patterns.

Major dialect areas

If several isoglosses exhibit similar patterning (occurring close together, rather like a bundle), they are likely to represent a major dialect boundary.

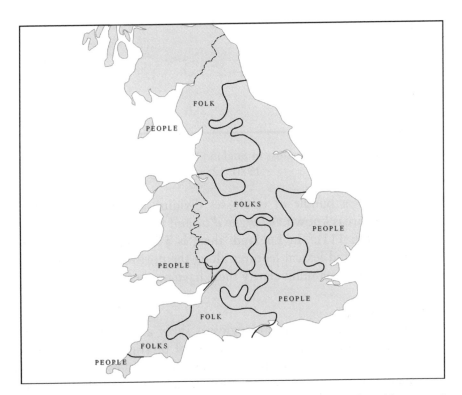

Map 2.3   The lexical isogloss: *folk* vs *people* (from Upton and Widdowson, *An Atlas of English Dialects* 2006: 84–5)

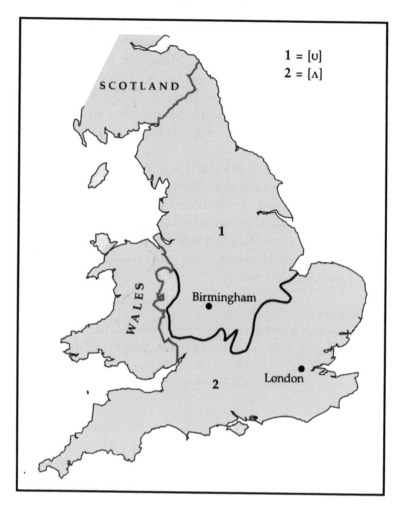

1 = [ʊ]
2 = [ʌ]

SCOTLAND

1

WALES

Birmingham

2   London

Map 2.4 The [ʊ] vs [ʌ] isogloss in England (based on Trudgill and Chambers 1980: 128)

Map 2.5 shows a bundle of isoglosses dividing France into two well-known dialect areas known as *langue d'oc* and *langue d'oïl* (Trudgill and Chambers 1980: 111).[5] In England, there is a bundle of isoglosses for several phonetic and lexical features along the north–south line depicted in Map 2.4, but to maintain clarity these have not been shown.

Centres of prestige

Concentric (or near-concentric) isoglosses show a pattern involving the spread of linguistic features from a centre of prestige (usually a city or town). Here the isoglosses resemble the ripples created by a stone thrown into a pond. Hence the term 'wave theory', for a branch of dialectology that attempted more dynamic representations than static isoglosses. The essential belief of its theorists (like Johannes Schmidt in the nineteenth century

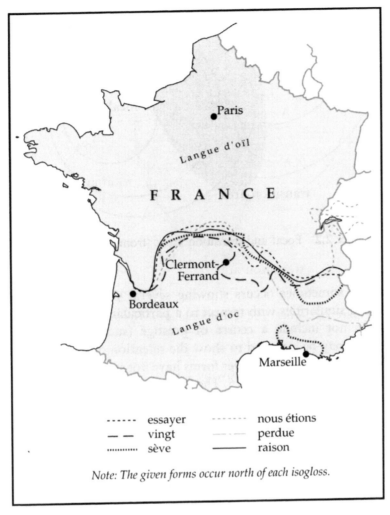

Note: The given forms occur north of each isogloss.

Map 2.5 A bundle of isoglosses that divide France into two (from Trudgill and Chambers 1980: 111)

and C. J. Bailey in the twentieth) was that linguistic innovations spread in wavelike fashion. In the idealised Figure 2.2, each circle represents the outer limit of a particular feature. While the concentric patterns are interpreted in particular ways by historical linguists, from the viewpoint of dialectology the most important point is that areas A and B are centres of prestige from which linguistic features (or innovations) spread outwards.

More recently, Peter Trudgill (1983a: 170–2) has suggested that the spread of innovations in modern societies occurs in other ways too. Certain sounds 'hop' from one influential urban centre to another, and only later spread outwards to the neighbouring rural areas, including the areas between the two centres. We discuss this theory further under Chapter 4 when discussing language change.

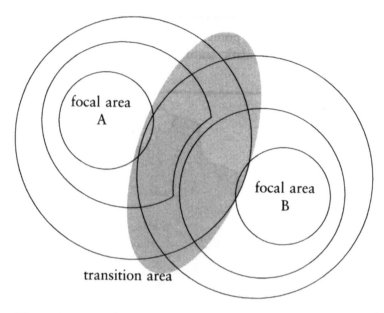

Figure 2.2   Focal and transitional areas (from Petyt 1980: 61)

Relic areas

A pattern sometimes occurs showing several small areas far apart exhibiting similarities with respect to a particular feature. Since these areas do not include a centre of prestige (such as a town), the isoglosses may be assumed to show the retention of old forms. They are relic areas into which newer forms have not spread. An example of a relic area is given in Map 2.6. The feature represented here is one we shall turn to frequently: the pronunciation of [r] after a vowel, or **postvocalic /r/**. 'Vocalic' is the linguistic term for vowels or vowel-like sounds. 'Postvocalic /r/ thus refers to the use of [r] after a vowel (e.g. *car*, *park*), but excludes the occurrence of [r] between vowels (e.g. *very*). Some writers prefer the term 'non-prevocalic /r/' instead of 'postvocalic /r/'. The three shaded areas indicate parts of England in which [r] still occurs after vowels (e.g. in words like *car*). The alternative pronunciation without [r] is more widespread and includes the prestigious centre of London. The shaded areas are therefore to be read as islands which the waves of sound change have not yet covered.

Transitional areas

Figure 2.2 also shows the possibility of a speech area developing which lacks sharply defined characteristics of its own, but shares characteristics with two or more adjacent areas. This is known as a 'transitional area'. We discuss an example which has come to be known as the Rhenish fan as a special case study below.

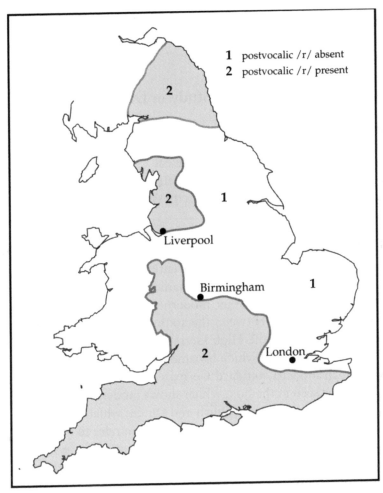

1 postvocalic /r/ absent
2 postvocalic /r/ present

2

2   1

Liverpool

Birmingham   1

2   London

Map 2.6 Isogloss for postvocalic /r/ in England (from Trudgill and Chambers 1980: 110)

Generally speaking, the patterning of isoglosses may be explained by geographical barriers which, especially in former times, kept speech communities from regular contact with each other: a deep river, a mountain range, a swamp and so on. The barriers may also be of a sociopolitical nature. People in a particular area may be subject to a particular set of political and social influences and accordingly develop a culture different from people in adjacent areas. They may, in the process, stabilise words and pronunciations that mark them as different from people from adjacent areas. On the whole, isoglosses are descriptive devices, which characterise the geographical dispersion of linguistic forms. As such, they have not really been central in the building of sociolinguistic theories. However, they do play an important role in developing an understanding of how the history of a language and the communities that use it is enmeshed with geographical and historical factors. A famous example of this is the bundle of isoglosses which has come to be known as the Rhenish fan.

The Rhenish Fan: A Case Study in Dialect Transition

The High German Sound Shift

English	pound/sleep	tide/eat	make/break
Dutch	pond/slapen	tijd/eten	maken/breken
German	Pfund/schlafen	Zeit/essen	machen/brechen

An interesting and well-known pattern of isoglosses shows variation in a transitional area in the northern Rhine region. These isoglosses represent a set of changes in pronunciation that differentiates contemporary standard German from other modern West Germanic languages (Dutch, Frisian, English, Afrikaans) and from other modern German dialects. This set of changes, which took place between the sixth to the eighth centuries AD, has come to be known as the **High German Sound Shift.** It affected the voiceless stops /p/, /t/ and /k/ which became fricatives in the south German dialects on which modern standard German was later based. The results of this shift can be seen in the box, which shows modern German forms as compared to related languages (English and Dutch) which were unaffected by the change. The terms 'High' and 'Low' German refer to the geographical location of the varieties, essentially the mountainous geography of the south ('High German') compared to the lowlands of the north ('Low German'). The variety spoken in the area intermediate to these two areas is known as 'Middle German'.

In Map 2.6, the main isogloss, called the 'Benrath line' after the town of Benrath, separates Low German from the other dialects. While Low German generally retains /p/, /t/ and /k/, the rest of the territory shows a differential response to the shift. In the latter area, different regions show the effects of the shift in different ways. Dialectologists use the following set of words to show how systematic this variation is: *ich, machen, Dorf, das, Apfel, Pfund, Kind*. This is the set of modern standard German words for 'I', 'make', 'village', 'the', 'apple', 'pound' and 'child' respectively. A second isogloss in Map 2.7, called the 'Germersheim line' after the town of Germersheim, separates the (High German) areas in the south, in which the sound shift has occurred in almost all words, from the Middle German area which has been only partly affected by the change. Only in Swiss German is word initial /k/ (as in *Kind*) pronounced as a fricative (*Chind*). The Middle German area is thus a transitional area between the Low German of the north and High German of the south.

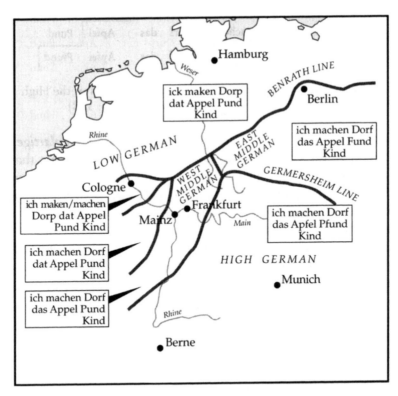

Map 2.7 The Rhenish fan

Within this Middle German territory, the greatest differentiation occurs in the west, that is, the northern Rhine region. Here the isoglosses branch out according to differences in the way the set of words is pronounced. This pattern has come to be called the Rhenish Fan (*Rheinischer Fächer*), since it resembles the folds of a fan. The differences between the areas in the folds of the fan can be read off from Map 2.7. They can also be read off from the stepwise formation in Table 2.1, in which the numbers represent subdialects of the fan. Line 3 in Table 2.1, for example, corresponds to usage in the Cologne area, while line 5 is that of the area around Mainz.

Theodor Frings (1950) interpreted the layered (*staffelartige*) distribution of the High German Sound Shift as evidence that the shift had originated in southern Germany and spread gradually northwards, losing its effect the further it moved from its area of origin. He drew upon political and cultural history to explain the location of the isoglosses within the fan. For example, the two isoglosses for *maken* vs *machen* and *Dorp* vs *Dorf* coincide with the old diocese of Cologne (Frings 1950: 6). However, it is unclear why the spread should have proceeded from south to north, as the territories in middle Germany were culturally and politically superior in the early Middle Ages. A spread from north to south would, therefore, have been more likely. Some dialectologists have accordingly suggested that a

Low German	1	ik	maken	Dorp	dat	Appel	Pund
	2	ich	maken	Dorp	dat	Appel	Pund
	3	ich	machen	Dorp	dat	Appel	Pund
Middle German	4	ich	machen	Dorf	dat	Appel	Pund
	5	ich	machen	Dorf	das	Appel	Pund
	6	ich	machen	Dorf	das	Apfel	Pund
High German	7	ich	machen	Dorf	das	Apfel	Pfund

Table 2.1 Dialect differences according to the effects of the High German
Sound Shift (from Romaine 1994: 138)

separate shift took place in the Middle German dialect area, independently
of developments in southern Germany (see Wells 1987: 427–8).

Criticisms of Traditional Dialectology

Critics of traditional dialect surveys point to severe flaws in conception and
execution. The first criticism is of the type of people interviewed. Dialect
surveys targeted native residents who were believed to speak the traditional
local dialect rather than a form contaminated by modern city dialects. These
were usually older people, often males (believed to speak local dialect more
consistently than women) who had not left their area for any length of time.
Trudgill and Chambers, who used the ironic acronym NORMs for this type
of informant (**N**on-mobile, **O**ld, **R**ural, **M**ale), conclude (1980: 35):

> However clear the motivation seems, it is nevertheless true that the narrow
> choice of informants in dialect geography is probably also the greatest single
> source of disaffection for it in recent times. Readers and researchers have ques-
> tioned the relevance of what seems to be a kind of linguistic archaeology. Young
> people who have been natives of a particular region for their entire lives have
> often been disturbed to discover that the speech recorded in field studies of their
> region is totally alien to anything that seems familiar to them. That discovery is
> not at all surprising when one considers that nowadays the greatest proportion
> of the population is mobile, younger, urban and female – in other words the
> diametrical opposite of NORMS.

That is, although traditional dialectology serves the important function of recording archaic speech, it is not representative of the speech of the areas studied.

The main focus of the traditional surveys fell on bits of language, rather than on speakers of a language. Language seems to have been considered as an organism having a life of its own, and individuals of interest 'only as a source of data for a given location, as human reference books rather than as members of complex social groups' (Barbour and Stevenson 1990: 74). That is, the methodology held little promise for a sociolinguistic theory of language.

From theoretical linguistics came the criticism that the approach to language itself was inadequate. Items studied were treated atomistically, as individual unrelated parts of language. This was in contrast to the emphasis in twentieth-century linguistics on language as a tightly-knit system, comprising abstract elements which derive their value from their contrast with other elements in the system. For example, maps drawn on the basis of isoglosses for vowel systems would be preferred by modern linguists to the isolated vowels on traditional dialect maps.

Social scientists (e.g. Glenna Pickford 1956) questioned the validity of the surveys, in terms of whether their survey methods were appropriate to the task set. They raised questions about the questionnaire design. For example, the extreme length of the questionnaires (sometimes requiring more than a day with the consultant) may lead to interviewer and interviewee 'fatigue bias' errors (especially if the consultant was old to begin with). Questions of fluctuations in fieldworkers' judgements of vowel quality have also dogged traditional dialectology.

Reservations like these about the treatment of crucial aspects of language variation led some dialectologists to turn their attention to social and urban dialects and to conduct their investigations along very different lines. In this they were assisted by the newer computer-based technologies not available to the pioneers of dialectology.

2.4   MODERN APPROACHES TO DIALECT

As noted above, traditional dialect study concerned itself with the differentiation of a language into dialects, and with older, rural speech forms which were often becoming obsolete. In contrast, modern studies focus on urban speech, often involving new speech forms arising from contact between speakers of different backgrounds.

Map 2.8 Places in Britain and Ireland cited in the text

The Border Dialect

Trudgill has been a pioneer in applying insights from modern sociolin-guistics to the study of geographical variation. One of the issues he has been interested in is the 'border dialect', that is how one variety within a

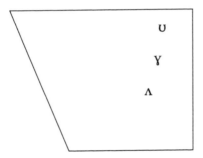

Figure 2.3 The vowels [ʊ], [ʌ] and [ɣ] on the vowel chart (See Note to Readers, pp. xxiii–xxv, for a general explanation of the principles underlying the vowel chart. Here [ʊ] is high, back and rounded; [ʌ] is mid, central and unrounded; [ɣ] is mid, back and unrounded.)

dialect continuum shades off into another. Traditional dialectology never adequately explored the linguistic behaviour of people living in the linguistic borderlands. By carefully re-examining the records of the SED (Survey of English Dialects), Trudgill and Chambers (1980: 132–42) posited two types of subvarieties or 'lects' characteristic of such areas: mixed and fudged lects. (The term 'lect' is widely used by linguists for smaller groupings within a dialect: one may speak of 'genderlects', 'ethnolects' or particular 'sociolects'). We use the example of the major ʊ/ʌ isogloss separating the northern dialects from the southern dialects of England (see Map 2.4). You will recall that there is a more or less clear-cut distinction where the north, has the older pronunciation [ʊ] in the lexical set STRUT, CUP, LUCK while the south has [ʌ] in this set. Trudgill and Chambers found some areas on the borderline of the isogloss which had mixed lects: that is, speakers used both [ʊ] and [ʌ]. They also found some areas where speakers produced an intermediate pronunciation between [ʊ] and [ʌ], phonetically [ɣ]. This sound is a 'fudge' (that is, a kind of compromise) since it is phonetically unrounded like [ʌ], but closer to [ʊ] in terms of vowel height, and intermediate between them in terms of backness.

David Britain (1997) has studied the border dialect area known as the Fens in England, a marshy area about 75 miles north of London and 50 miles west of Norwich. At one time, the sparse population lived on a few islands of higher ground. Only after the seventeenth century when the marshes were drained did the Fens become fertile, arable land attracting greater human habitation. The lack of communication between the eastern and western sides of the Fens before reclamation is reflected in the fact that this is still one of the major dialect transition zones in England. One of the features studied by Britain was the variation between east and west with respect to the diphthong [aɪ] (i.e. the vowel sound in the lexical set PRICE, WHITE, RIGHT). The eastern Fens have a centralised [əɪ], while the western Fens have [aɪ]. Britain describes an interesting compromise in the

Phonetic note

Diphthong: a vowel sound that is itself made up of two simple vowels. For example, the vowels [a:] and [ɪ] in combination give the diphthong [aɪ], as found in the set PRICE, WHITE, RIGHT.

Centralisation: the tongue position is relatively central compared to 'front' or 'back' positions.

The set [b, d, g, v, z etc.] is the set of voiced sounds, i.e. ones which are accompanied by vocal-cord vibration. This happens when the vocal cords (in the larynx) are close together and vibrate when air passes periodically through them.

The set [p, t, k, f, s etc.] is the set of voiceless sounds, i.e. ones produced without vocal-cord vibration. This happens when the vocal cords are kept apart momentarily.

The only vowel before which the diphthong [aɪ] occurs is the unstressed vowel [ə] as in *fire, liar, friar*.

This pattern of distribution (where a unit is pronounced in one way in certain environments and in another way in all other environments) is known technically as 'complementary distribution' in phonology.

central Fens, the part more recently opened to habitation. Here both pronunciations are found, but in a special pattern, determined by what kind of sound they are followed by. The centralised [əɪ] pronunciation occurs before voiceless consonants (like *p, t, k, f, s*), while [aɪ] occurs in other phonetic environments, namely before voiced consonants (like *b, d, g, v, z*) and before vowels. Britain argues that such 'fudging' occurred when newcomers tried to assimilate to the norms of more settled communities which were themselves divided in terms of pronunciation.

The Birth of New Dialects

The central image in traditional dialectology is that of diversification. Languages that were localised in centuries gone by gradually spread geographically and eventually diversified into dialects. Traditional dialectology ignored processes like urbanisation and colonisation. The invention of modern means of transport has resulted in intercontinental and internal movements of people that are quite different from those connected with

---

Historical note
Two notable areas outside the British Isles which retain the [əɪ] pronunciation are Martha's Vineyard in the USA (described in Chapter
3) and Canada.

---

traditional dialect formation. In this section, we briefly review two studies
of new dialect formation in territories that are far removed from the
original base of the dialects. These are sometimes labelled 'extraterritorial
varieties' or 'transplanted varieties'.

New Towns: The Milton Keynes Study

During the 1960s, the British government targeted several rural areas in
south-eastern England for industrial development. One of these areas was
Milton Keynes, a former village about fifty miles north-west of London,
which was designated a 'new town' in 1969. The rapid social and industrial
development of Milton Keynes led to the influx of large numbers of people
from other areas in the UK. New arrivals came mainly from London and
other parts of south-east England, northern England and Scotland. In this
new environment, speakers of a range of dialects came into direct and prolonged contact with each other. To investigate the linguistic outcomes of
this situation of dialect contact, Paul Kerswill and Anne Williams carried
out a developmental survey in the early 1990s (Kerswill 1996). They compared the speech of three groups of children (of ages 4, 8 and 12) with that
of their parents or caregivers. In all, forty-eight children and one parent or
caregiver per child were recorded on tape and video. From their detailed
analysis of ten phonetic features, the researchers showed that the accents
of the children neither closely resembled those of the nearby dialect area
nor showed any influence from their parents' speech. This process is called
dialect levelling in which the speech of a group of people (in this case children) converges towards a common norm, with extreme differences being
ironed out. Dialect levelling in Milton Keynes results from two different

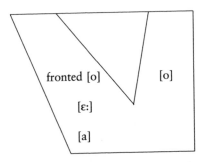

Figure 2.4 The vowels [o], fronted [o], [ɛ:] and [a] on the vowel chart

strategies: (1) linguistic features of the wider south-eastern area are adopted by the children; and (2) broad, regional variants are avoided and replaced by less localised sounds, including some RP-like vowel sounds.

One of the features investigated by Kerswill and Williams was the diphthong [oʊ] in the lexical set GOAT, HOME, GO. In the wider area of south-eastern England, the first vowel of this diphthong is being increasingly fronted. In Milton Keynes, the fronted pronunciation is found mainly among children, an example of strategy (1) above. The children's pronunciation of the word *boat*, for example, almost sounds like *bait* as pronounced in RP. The fronting of [oʊ] is part of the new dialect evolving in Milton Keynes. This dialect is relatively homogeneous, as the speech of children contains far less variation than that of the older generation.

As an example of the second dialect-levelling strategy, Kerswill and Williams refer to the pronunciation of the diphthong [oʊ] in the lexical set MOUTH, HOUSE, NOW. This sound has a range of regionally marked pronunciations in south-east England, ranging from [ɛ:] in broad London dialect to the RP-like [aʊ]. Adults in Milton Keynes use a range of broad, regionally marked variants, while children favour the less marked RP-like variants.

Tea Cakes in MK

I was at this canteen and placed in my order to the woman behind the counter. She looked a bit confused at my order, and to my surprise brought me a tray of cakes. I had ordered two cokes; she apparently thought I'd said 'tea cakes'.

(Young woman from Milton Keynes on being misunderstood by a northerner whose first language was also English. To hear *two* as *tea* suggests fronting of the [u:] vowel characteristic of young middle-class speakers of English worldwide. To hear *coke* as *cake* is an example of the fronting of the second element of the diphthong [əu].

Anecdote told to Anne Williams, researcher on the project on children's language in Milton Keynes.)

'Transplanted' Dialectology: The Eastern Hindi Diaspora

In the nineteenth century the British and other European governments sought to supply cheap labour to their various colonies throughout the world, by inducing Asians to emigrate as indentured workers. The term 'indenture' signifies the contract signed by workers tying them to a particular employer for a fixed number of years. In this way, over a million speakers of Asian

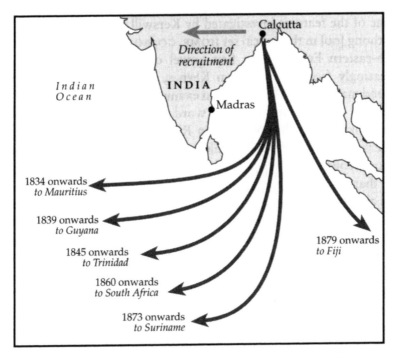

Map 2.9 Recruiting patterns and the eastern Hindi indentured diaspora of the nineteenth and early twentieth centuries

languages came to inhabit islands in the Caribbean (e.g. Trinidad, Jamaica), the Pacific (e.g. Hawaii, Fiji) and the Indian Ocean (Mauritius, Reunion) and mainland territories like South Africa, Guyana and Malaysia. We take as a brief example of new dialect formation in a 'transplanted' context the case of people from north India, speaking one or more of the varieties of the North Indian speech continuum (see sections 1.1 and 2.2). Recruitment of workers started out in the north-easterly parts (with Calcutta as a focal port for the shipment of the workers) and gradually moved westwards into the interior (see Map 2.9). Accordingly, it was speakers from the more eastern parts of the speech continuum who migrated. Their languages included Bhojpuri, Magahi and Awadhi, which may be loosely described as forms of 'eastern Hindi'. The earliest migrants were sent to Mauritius (1834); successive migrants went to Guyana (from 1839 onwards), Trinidad (1845), Natal (1860), Suriname (1873) and Fiji (1879).

Three salient processes occurred as speakers from a wide variety of related languages of north India communicated with each other and formed new identities in the new territories.

1. *Focusing:* that is, the stabilising of a new variety out of the wide range of antecedent varieties. This new variety tended to resemble Bhojpuri, a language of what are now the north-east Indian states of Bihar, Uttar Pradesh, Jharkhand and Uttarkhand.

Mauritius	*dekh-lak*	(1834)
Guyana	*dekh-le*	(1839)
Trinidad	*dekh-al*	(1845)
South Africa	*dekh-lak* or *dekh-las*	(1860)
Suriname	*dekh-is*	(1873)
Fiji	*dekh-is* or *dekh-ā*	(1879)

Table 2.2   The verb 'she saw' in transplanted varieties of eastern Hindi (times of initial migrations in brackets – based on Mesthrie 1992b: 72–6)

2. *Dialect mixing:* the new focused variety shows a blend of features from other dialects and languages of the north Indian speech continuum as well.
3. *Dialect levelling:* selection of some features from Bhojpuri and other varieties led to other features being lost. Only a small residue of alternate forms from different antecedent varieties survived: for example two alternate forms for 'she saw' are equally acceptable in South Africa (see Table 2.2).

These broad processes occurred, with slightly different results within each colonial territory, depending on the numbers of speakers of the various antecedent varieties. Mesthrie (1992b: 72–6) gives the example of forms that stabilised in the different colonies for the verb 'she saw' (i.e. third-person, singular, past, transitive verb):

Since the territories involved are not geographically adjacent, isoglosses cannot be drawn. However, a more abstract type of dialectology is possible, since there is a clustering of the varieties in Table 2.2 according to the initial time of immigrations. The first four territories show a past transitive form with *-l*, the last two do not. Mesthrie (1992b: 72–6) shows that the transplanted varieties which are more 'adjacent in time' (with respect to the initial migrations) are linguistically more similar. Mauritius has a type of Hindi that is the most 'eastern' in its linguistic characteristics, while the Hindi of Fiji has a more 'westerly' character. The territories between these two in Table 2.2 are intermediate in terms of their linguistic characteristics, especially in their verb suffixes. This, in turn, is a consequence of the recruitment patterns cited above. Recruiters in the employ of the British worked over a continuous geographical area in India, starting from the east near the port of Calcutta and proceeding westwards into the interior. Their activities are reflected in the fossilised dialect forms of varieties of Hindi that are far-flung in time and space.

Traditional Dialect in the Modern World

The study of traditional rural dialects has become increasingly divorced from the main concerns of linguists. Yet, despite the encroachment of the city, rural dialects are still in use in many parts of the world. One study of how traditional dialect survives in an urban setting is that of Caroline

McAfee (1983) on Scots. Based on questionnaires, her work provides a rich account of working-class Glasgow speech and of the extent to which traditional dialect survives in an industrialised world. Cities like Glasgow contain urban villages with strong community life and the corresponding ability to maintain traditional modes of speech, at least to some extent. Macafee concluded from her questionnaires that:

- Much use of the traditional vocabulary has given way to passive knowledge (that is, working class Glasgow speakers still understand older traditional dialect terms like *fernietickles* (for 'freckles'), but do not use them themselves).
- Knowledge of dialect forms has become more individual and idiosyncratic (suggesting gradual loss). For example one family remembered the word *peasewisp* (for 'a bundle or wisp of pea-straw') because *hair like a peasewisp* was a favourite saying of a grandfather.
- Many traditional dialect words survive only in metaphorical or idiomatic uses.
- Words that were once commonplace are now regarded as colourful or slang, on account of infrequent use, for example *brace* for 'mantelpiece'.
- Older speakers underestimate younger people's knowledge of the traditional dialect, probably because much of it has become passive.

These findings apply to vocabulary. For grammar and phonology, there is little difference between the norms of older and younger speakers: for example, both groups use terms like *hame* 'home' and *hoose* 'house'. Macafee's study suggests the importance of studying vocabulary separately and in a more probing way than done by modern dialectologists.

A sample entry from the DARE webpage for Adam's housecat

Adam's housecat n Also *Adam's cat, ~ house* chiefly S Atl, Gulf States See Map =Adam's off-ox 1.
1908 *DN* 3.285 eAL, wGA, *Adam's (house-)cat.* . . . "He wouldn't know me from Adam's house-cat." 1965–70 *DARE* (Qu. II26, . . "*I wouldn't know him from _____.*") 83 Infs, chiefly S Atl, Gulf States, Adam's housecat; LA25, OH90, VA69, 71, Adam's cat; AL10, Adam's house; FL48, A housecat, [corr to] Adam's housecat. [Of all Infs responding to the question, 26% had less than hs educ; of those giving these responses, 56% had less than hs educ.]

Abbreviations: S Atl: South Atlantic; eAL: East Alabama; wGA: west Georgia; Qu: Question; LA: Louisiana; OH: Ohio; VA: Virginia; FL: Florida; corr: corrected to.

In the US a project called DARE (*The Dictionary of American Regional English*) aims to document regionalisms, i.e. elements of US English that are not found everywhere in the country. These include words and phrases that vary from one area to another, and are learned at home rather than at school as part of oral rather than written culture. So far four volumes have been produced (from A to Sk) with a fifth and final volume to follow. DARE is based on face-to-face interviews with 2,777 people carried out in 1,002 communities throughout the country between 1965 and 1970. It also used print materials from letters, diaries, novels and newspapers.

2.5   MORE CHALLENGES FOR DIALECTOLOGISTS

Some prominent aspects of dialect identification either have not received sufficient attention within dialectology or have proved elusive when studied.

Prosody

Traditional dialectology has mostly concentrated on segmental units of sound (e.g. individual vowels and consonants) rather than continuous prosodic characteristics like rhythm, pitch, intonation and voice quality. The linguist Wolfgang Klein (1988: 147) claims that he can recognise a speaker of Berlin dialect 'after a few words', but finds it difficult even as a practising linguist to identify what it is that creates this perception of the 'flavour' of the dialect. He speculates that the specific 'flavour' may be a composite of features seldom studied by dialectologists: speech rate, pause structure and pitch range. Yet prosodic features are acquired first in childhood and are hence more deeply imprinted. For this reason, they are often retained when adults acquire a new language or a new dialect (for one such case study, involving a change from the Tsuruoka dialect of Japanese to the Tokyo standard with regard to prosody, see Chambers 2003: 213–16).

In many dialects of English, questions are formed by a change in the word order and by a high rising intonation contour (as in *Is Harriet coming over to dinner tonight?* or even *Harriet's coming over to dinner tonight?*). On the other hand, the statement *Harriet's coming over to dinner tonight* ends with a falling intonation. Gregory Guy et al. (1986) studied a phenomenon known as High Rise Terminals (HRT) or Australian Questioning Intonation (AQI).[6] This involves a new pattern of intonation for ordinary statements, with a rising intonation at the end of the statement, rather than the falling intonation expected of statements in many dialects of English. Guy et al. found that this pattern was a recent development, most common among teenagers, fulfilling the interactive function of enabling the speaker to check or confirm that the addressee is following the conversation. This type of variation in intonation pattern is only a small part of the prosodic characteristics of dialects that Klein had referred to. Phoneticians and sociolinguists have some way to go in characterising prosodic variation systematically, though new computer-based techniques make this more and more feasible.

Articulatory Setting

In addition to the movements of speech organs associated with the articulation of particular vowels or consonants, the organs of the vocal tract have certain preferred positions, which differ from those they have in a state of rest. The preferred shape (or general setting) of the vocal tract is known as the 'articulatory setting'. It may give a speech variety its characteristic 'colour' and is one of the ways in which dialects tend to be identified by lay people (for example, identifying a particular dialect as 'nasal').

Speaking of Scouse, the dialect spoken in Liverpool, the phonetician David Abercrombie (1967: 94–5) suggests that

> people can be found with adenoidal voice quality who do not have adenoids – they have learnt the quality from the large number of people who do have them, so that they conform to what, for that community, has become the norm. (Continuing velic closure, together with velarization, are the principal components needed for counterfeiting adenoidal voice quality.)[7]

G. Knowles (1978: 89) attributes the Scouse voice quality to the following:

> In Scouse, the centre of gravity of the tongue is brought backwards and upwards, the pillars of the fauces are narrowed, the pharynx is tightened and the larynx is displaced downwards. The lower jaw is typically held close to the upper jaw, and this position is maintained even for 'open' vowels.[8]

Articulatory settings and their relation to dialects present the same difficulties to researchers as the study of prosody. Phoneticians have not yet developed systematic descriptions of a range of possible articulatory settings that dialectologists can draw on. Descriptions of dialect articulation thus tend to be very specific, rather than comparative, for example Knowles (cited above) and Trudgill (1974: 185–8).

Discourse and Dialect

Ronald Macaulay (1991) has suggested that yet another area awaiting systematic exploration by sociolinguists is the possibility of locating dialects in everyday discourse. That is, dialectologists should pay attention to how the characteristic 'flavour' of a dialect may also reside in the special norms for interaction, special types of speech events that may be embedded within a conversation, and the use of elements whose function is to smoothen interaction and conversation. Macaulay attempted to characterise the dialect of English in Ayr, Scotland, by quantifying the use of **discourse particles** like *I mean, y' know, you ken, oh,* and so on. These particles serve to keep conversation flowing, and simultaneously give it a local and personal ('you and me') flavour. Perhaps more significant from the viewpoint of relating dialect and discourse are other norms of organising conversation and interaction. Such aspects of speech culture involve genres like narratives, children's language games, the use of riddles and proverbs in ordinary speech. Their potential in characterising dialect has still to be researched in detail. One of these which has been researched in detail – narratives – will be discussed in Chapter 6.

Register and Dialect

The term 'register' denotes variation in language according to the context in which it is being used. Different situations call for adjustments to the type of language used: for example, the type of language that an individual **uses** varies according to whether s/he is speaking to family members, addressing a public gathering, or discussing science with professional colleagues. Such variation contrasts with variation according to the **user**, that is, the regional background described in the first part of this chapter, and the social background of the user described in Chapter 3.

In this poem, the conventions of the legal register, are parodied by using them in a register where they do not apply (children's rhymes and stories)

> The party of the first part
> hereinafter known as Jack,
> and the party of the second
> part hereinafter known as Jill,
> ascended or caused to be
> ascended an elevation of
> undetermined height and
> degree of slope, hereinafter
> referred to as 'hill'.

(D. Sandburg, *The Legal Guide to Mother Goose*, 1978,
cited by Benson 1985)

Clear-cut registers involve the law (sometimes called 'legalese'), sports broadcasting and scientific discourse. However, the concept of register need not apply to specialised professions only, as Wallwork (1969: 110) makes clear:

Every time we insist on a letter which starts 'Dear Sir' ending with 'Yours faith-fully', rather than 'Yours affectionately', every time we tell a child not to use slang in an essay; every time we hesitate as to 'how best to put it' to the boss; every time we decide to telephone rather than to write, we are making decisions on the basis of the selection of the appropriate register for our purpose.

The significant point is that a register acquires its characteristics by convention, which people are then more or less obliged to use. Variation by person becomes minimal (except perhaps for accent). That is, the study of dialect without attention to contexts of language use makes traditional dialectology one-dimensional. Halliday et al. (1964) stressed three dimensions along which register may vary: field, tenor and mode.

> **Field:** nature of the topic around which the language activity is centred ('what is happening').
> **Tenor:** relations between people communicating ('who is taking part, and on what terms')
> **Mode:** medium employed ('is the language form spoken, written, signed etc.?')[9]

Halliday and Hasan (1985: 41) insist that registers are not marginal or special varieties of language, rather they cover the total range of language activity in a society:

> [R]egister is what you are speaking at the time, depending on what you are doing and the nature of the activity in which the language is functioning. So whereas, in principle at least, any individual might go through life speaking only one dialect (in modern complex societies this is increasingly unlikely; but it is theoretically possible, and it used to be the norm), it is not possible to go through life using only one register. The register reflects another aspect of the social order, that of social processes, the different types of social activity that people commonly engage in.

Register studies have not had as big an impact in dialect study as the authors had hoped, though some researchers have pursued a broader related area which has come to be known as genre theory, which we do not pursue in this book. The concept of register does however overlap with the concept of style, an aspect of language variation that we discuss in Chapters 3 and 6. Register and traditional dialect study have to a large extent been overtaken by interactional sociolinguistics, a branch which looks closely at conversational strategies employed by different groups of people when they communicate with each other (see Chapter 6).

2.6   CONCLUSION

In this chapter, we focused on studies of the geographical spread and diversification of speech. Some difficulties over the terms 'language' and 'dialect' were noted. The techniques of traditional dialectology were described, including the questionnaire-based survey. The analysis of survey data is usually presented by means of dialect maps, which show the distribution of key linguistic features via isoglosses. Dialect maps help linguists interpret certain patterns of usage: for example, where a new item originates from, and how it spreads. Patterns of isoglosses show whether an area is a focal area (a centre of linguistic prestige), a relic area or a transitional area. The *Linguistic Survey of India* shows that the techniques and results of dialectology are essentially the same for monolingual and multilingual surveys, provided that the latter involves a speech continuum (and not languages that belong to different families). This chapter points out the limitations of traditional dialectology in dealing with dynamic aspects of linguistic geography like the border dialect, the growth of new towns and transcontinental migrations. Aspects of language that seem salient in dialect identification, but which have still to be studied in detail by dialectologists, are identified: prosody, articulatory setting and discourse particles. Register is a feature of language use which cuts across dialect variation and also shows the limitations of a geographical focus alone.

A major shortcoming of this field as it has been traditionally practised is that it elevates regional characteristics above the social groupings that people fall into. Moreover, the field has traditionally been concerned with the forms of language that vary (accent, vocabulary, grammar), rather than the sociological functions fulfilled by such variation. Chapters 3 and 4 will look more closely at the social motivations for variation and change.

Notes

1. The south of India had a further 70 million then.
2. The idea of a Christian parable being used in India is odd, though it has to be said that the tale lent itself to very lively retellings. Grammatically, there was the added advantage of the tale involving three pronoun forms, three personal verb endings and a full range of tenses and noun cases.
3. 'Isogloss' is parallel to the terms 'isotherm' and 'isobar' in geography.
4. Wells (1982) calls this the STRUT vowel. We use three words per set to ensure that readers can identify the full set. Each set contains hundreds (even thousands) of words for which spellings may be inconsistent. Hence *monk*, *ton* and *country* belong to the STRUT set while *put* does not.
5. The terms were coined by a twelfth-century poet, Bernat d'Auriac, for varieties that used *oc* or *oïl* as the word for 'yes'.
6. The phenomenon also occurs in New Zealand, and is even suggested as having originated there rather than in Australia. It is also found in other parts of the English-speaking world including Canada, California and the southern USA. So the issue of origins is unclear.
7. Abercrombie tried to relate these to the health and physical conditions in the

poorer areas. This type of explanation linking accent with environment is rather dubious.

8. The speech organs referred to here are diagrammed in most introductory linguistic and phonetic texts, for example Ladefoged (1993). The anatomical term 'fauces' is more usually referred to as 'mouth cavity'.

9. The term 'mode' (coined by Spencer and Gregory 1964) replaced the term 'style' which Halliday et al. (1964) had used in their earlier work.

3
SOCIAL DIALECTOLOGY

3.1 INTRODUCTION

Prior to the early 1960s, dialectology had scored its main successes in studies of regional differentiation. Researchers had certainly been aware of linguistic distinctions of a social nature within a region, but had not developed systematic ways of describing them. This chapter, by contrast, takes as its central concern why different accents and ways of saying things should arise within the same community. Moreover, as the excerpt from the short story by George Rew shows, such differences can carry great social value. Speech can serve to mark the distinctiveness of people not just in terms of their region, but also in terms of their sex and social standing.

Class and divisions over accent
A prominent regional feature of many British varieties of English is the glottal stop, when certain sounds, notably /t/, are pronounced with a momentary closure of the glottis, producing words like *foo'ball*. Although heavily stigmatised in educational contexts, the sound is a stable one, if not on the increase. The opening excerpt from George Rew's short story 'Wa'er' (1990) vividly portrays class and regional divisions over accent:

'What is the more usual name for H_2O Ballantyne?'
I realise that the teacher has spoken my name. I look up to see Mr Houston's thin face peering expectantly at me through his thick round glasses. He is almost smirking with anticipation. Does he think I don't know the answer? Surely not! What has he planned for me, I wonder frantically.
'Wa'er' I answer confidently, in my distinctive Dundee accent.
Houston's smile grows slightly wider.
'Pardon?'

He puts a hand behind his ear and cocks his head.
'Wa'er' I say again, thinking perhaps I had mumbled the first time . . .
[After several repetitions and growing confusion] I look over and see
Caroline Paterson leaning toward me . . .
'James, it's water!' she whispers, and suddenly I understand I am not
speaking correctly, at least not in the opinion of Mr. Houston. He is
mocking my Dundee accent.

(As the story unfolds, the student defies the teacher's efforts to
'correct' his speech, and in the ensuing confrontation is, to his surprise, supported by the headmaster. Cited by Chambers 2003: 209.)

Earlier explanations of language variation within a dialect area fell into
one of two categories: dialect mixture and free variation. 'Dialect mixture'
implies the coexistence in one locality of two or more dialects, which
enables a speaker to draw on one dialect at one time, and on the other
dialect(s) on other occasions. 'Free variation' refers to the random use of
alternate forms within a particular dialect (for example, two pronunciations of *often*, with or without the /t/ sounded). The proponents of these
two views assumed that language is an abstract structure, and further that
the study of language excludes the choices that speakers make. William
Labov, a US linguist, argued, instead, that language involved 'structured
heterogeneity'. By this he meant the opposite: that language contained systematic variation which could be characterised and explained by patterns
of social differentiation within speech communities. This body of work
has come to be known by various names: variationist theory, the quantitative paradigm, urban dialectology, the Labovian school and secular
linguistics.[1]

3.2 PRINCIPLES AND METHODS IN VARIATIONIST SOCIOLINGUISTICS: THREE CASES STUDIES

Case Study 1: Children in New England

Labov was not the first to point to the interplay between social and linguistic determinants of certain linguistic alternations: John Fischer had
discussed the social implications of the use of *-in* versus *-ing* (e.g. whether
one said *fishin'* or *fishing*) in a village in New England in 1958. Fischer
noted that both forms of the present participle, *-in* and *-ing*, were being
used by twenty-one of the twenty-four children he observed. Rather than
dismissing it as random or free variation of little interest to linguists,
Fischer tried to correlate the use of the one form over the other with
specific characteristics of the children or of the speech situation. Girls,

for example, used more *-ing* than boys. 'Model' boys (i.e. ones whose habits were approved of by their teachers) used more *-ing* than 'typical' boys (those whose habits make them less favoured by their teachers). Fischer interviewed the children briefly in settings which ranged from relatively informal, to relatively formal, to the most formal involving classroom story recitation. One ten-year-old boy who was interviewed in all three situations showed more *-in* than *-ing* in the informal style, about the same number of occurrences of *-in* and *-ing* in the formal style, and almost no *-in* in the classroom story recital. Fischer (1958: 51) concluded: 'the choice between the *-ing* and the *-in* variants appear to be related to sex, class, personality (aggressive/cooperative), and mood (tense/relaxed) of the speaker, to the formality of the conversation and to the specific verb spoken'. Fischer thus approached the topic of variation in fairly sophisticated ways that foreshadowed much of the concerns of urban dialectology. In particular, his observation (1958: 52) that 'people adopt a variant not because it is easier to pronounce (which it most frequently is, but not always), but because it expresses how they feel about their relative status versus other conversants' remains a central tenet of variationist sociolinguistics.

Basic methods in variationist studies

1. Identify linguistic features that vary in a community (e.g. *-in* and *-ing*).
2. Gather data from the community by selecting a suitable sample of people.
3. Conduct an interview involving informal continuous speech as well as more formal dimensions of language use like reading out a passage aloud.
4. Analyse the data, noting the frequency of each relevant linguistic feature.
5. Select relevant social units like age groups, sex, social class.
6. Ascertain significant correlations between the social groups and particular speech.

Labov took some of Fischer's concerns further, creating an elaborate body of work which broke new ground in understanding language in its social context, accounting for linguistic change of the sort that had preoccupied historical linguists, and broadening the goals of linguistic theory. His book *Sociolinguistic Patterns* (1972a) is a foundational work within sociolinguistics.

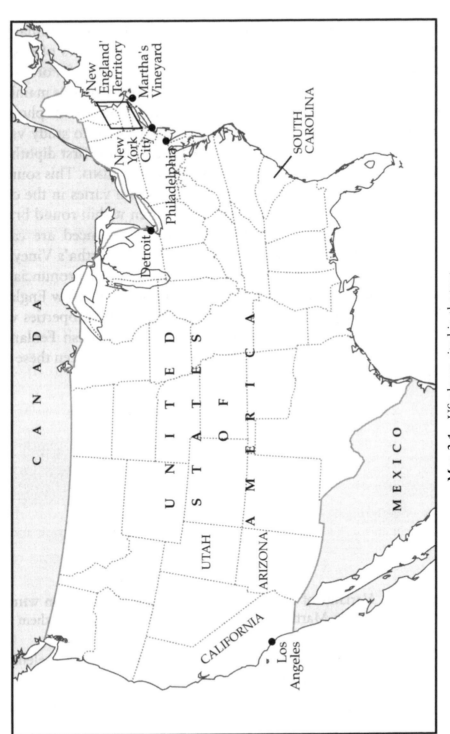

Map 3.1   US places cited in the text

Case Study 2: Martha's Vineyard

The island of Martha's Vineyard off the New England coast was the setting of Labov's study (1963) of the significance of social patterns in understanding language variation and change. The island is inhabited by a small number of Native Americans, larger numbers of descendants of old families of English stock, and people of Portuguese descent. Furthermore, it is overwhelmed by tourists from the mainland who come to stay in the summer. Among a range of phonetic characteristics of English on the island, Labov chose to study variations in the diphthongs [aɪ] and [aʊ]. We focus on the first diphthong only, which occurs in the lexical set PRICE, WHITE, RIGHT. This sound is called a **linguistic variable** since its pronunciation varies in the community. Linguistic variables like (aɪ) are written within round brackets. The different ways in which they are pronounced are called **variants**, and are written in square brackets. On Martha's Vineyard, the main variants of the variable (aɪ) were the [aɪ] pronunciation common in the surrounding mainland area known as 'New England' and a centralised pronunciation [əɪ], whose phonetic properties were described in section 2.4 (in connection with the English Fenlands.) There were four other pronunciations intermediate between these two variants. These are diagrammed in Figure 3.1.

Variables like (aɪ) fulfil three criteria that make them focal elements in the study of language in its social setting:

1. they are frequent enough in ordinary conversation to appear unsolicited in brief interviews;
2. they are structurally linked to other elements in the linguistic system – in this case, to the system of diphthongs in the dialect;[2]
3. they exhibit a complex and subtle pattern of stratification by social groupings.

Labov undertook sixty-nine tape-recorded interviews, during which variation along a number of dimensions including ethnicity, occupation and

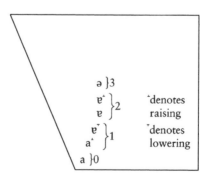

Figure 3.1   Variants of the first element /a/ in the diphthong in PRICE, WHITE, RIGHT, in Martha's Vineyard, and values assigned to them

Age in years	Index score for (aɪ)
75+	25
61–75	35
46–60	62
31–45	81
14–30	37

Table 3.1   Centralisation index for (aɪ) in Martha's Vineyard
(Labov 1972a)

geographical location became apparent.[3] In his analysis, Labov used a scoring system of 0 for [aɪ] and 3 for [əɪ]. The intermediate variants (see Figure 3.1) were assigned values of 1 or 2. The scoring system thus assigns zero to the pronunciation that is used by some Vineyarders, but which is more characteristic of the mainland USA. It assigns higher scores for pronunciations involving greater degrees of centralisation. Labov divided his interviewees into age groups which he felt showed significant differences in usage, and calculated the average scores per age group, expressed as an index. Scores may thus range from 0 to 300: the higher the score, the greater the use of typically centralised island variants rather than the general New England [aɪ]. These figures are given in Table 3.1. For short, Labov called this a 'centralisation index', that is, a measure of the degree to which different age groups used centralised pronunciations of the diphthongs.

Table 3.1 shows an interesting pattern by age. The index scores increase as one scans down the column, except for the last row: the 14–30 age group. This indicates that the 'island' way of pronouncing the diphthongs was generally on the increase: the younger the age group, the higher its score on the island variant (with the one exception). On the other hand, why should the 31–60 age group have relatively high scores for the 'island' variant, while the 61–75 and 14–30 age groups have roughly similar scores showing less use of the island variant?

Whereas Fischer's study (case study 1, above) had shown a consistent pattern of variation by sex and by other factors like 'acceptance of school norms', the Martha's Vineyard study shows ups and downs. By consulting older records of the dialect, in the *Linguistic Atlas of New England (LANE)* undertaken by Kurath et al. (1939–43), Labov argued that these ups and downs could be related to changes in speech norms over time in Martha's Vineyard as well as the rest of the USA. The centralised variant of (aɪ) was once the more usual one, going back to seventeenth-century England, and still recorded in moderate numbers in New England and Martha's Vineyard in the *LANE* records. In comparing *LANE* records with those of late twentieth-century Martha's Vineyard, it became evident that there had been an intervening drop in centralisation on the island, reflected in the low scores of the over-75 age group. That is, Martha's Vineyard was once in line with the rest of New England in showing a decline in centralisation; but the trend has been reversed, with younger people accentuating a pronunciation that was becoming less common in the speech of their elders.

In answering the question of why younger people of Martha's Vineyard seemed to be turning their backs on the older island and mainland trend in the USA, Labov cited social relationships between the relatively poor inhabitants of the island and the rich summer residents. A high degree of centralisation of (aɪ) is closely linked with strong resistance to the incursions of the summer people, which have to be tolerated for economic reasons. It is especially since around the Second World War that the social and economic pressures have brought on this resistance among younger groups. Using a pronunciation like [rəɪt] ('right') is a subconscious affirmation of belonging to the island and being one of its rightful owners (Labov 1963: 304). Or, as a subsequent commentator remarks, it has the same effect as wearing a t-shirt that says 'I'm not a tourist, I live here' (McMahon 1994: 242).

Although the oldest groups show reduced levels of centralisation, the one resistant group was a group of fishermen from a part of the island called Chilmark. Labov argues that the ways of these Chilmark fishermen – independent and stubborn defenders of the old way of living – served as a reference point for those of the younger generation throughout the island who might be seeking an identity opposed to that of the tourists. Finally, in answering the question of why the 14–30 age group does not exhibit the revived island-centralisation pattern, considerations regarding attitude and identity are again crucial. According to Labov's argument, these speakers do not feel the full stress experienced by the 30+ age groups, who had grown up in a declining economy, and who had made a more or less deliberate choice to remain on the island, or, having once sought work on the mainland, had elected to return to Martha's Vineyard. The youngest group, which included many high-school pupils, either harboured hopes of going to the mainland or had not yet made their choice. This indecision is unconsciously reflected in their indices for linguistic variables such as (aɪ).

More than any previous study, the analysis of diphthong variation in Martha's Vineyard showed the importance of studying the vernacular speech of individuals in its community setting. Labov used the term **vernacular** in this context to refer to the least self-conscious style of speech used by people in relaxed conversation with friends, peers and family members. Labov suggests that this is one's most natural style, whose grammar and phonetics is mastered at an early age via the influence of peer groups. The vernacular style represents informal speech oriented towards a local community. It may be modified in some ways during various stages of one's life, under the influence of more public-oriented interaction as in educational settings, media language and the influence of other social groups. Labov argues that the vernacular nevertheless remains the most basic style, one which can be studied with considerable reward from a variationist point of view. This is so since the vernacular is itself not devoid of variation: it may involve **inherent variation** – that is, alternate forms belonging to the same system acquired simultaneously, or nearly so, at an early age. The rules governing variation in the vernacular appear to be more regular than those operating in formal styles acquired in post-adolescent years. Each speaker has a vernacular style in at least one language: this may be the prestige dialect or a close version of it (as in the relatively few speakers whose vernacular is standard English) or, more usually, a non-standard variety. (The issue is clouded by arguments over the exact definition of 'standard English' – see the different views of the term 'standard' in section 1.4.)

Not all sociolinguists agree that the vernacular in this sense is basic, and that it should be the starting point of sociolinguistic analysis and a baseline for understanding other styles acquired by a speaker. They argue that all styles and registers are used in a complementary way by speakers and are equally deserving of sociolinguistic attention. A further problem pointed to by Ronald Macaulay (1988) is that the term 'vernacular' is used in two different senses by sociolinguists. In Labov's main formulation, it is the most informal speech style used by speakers. Another equally common meaning of the term refers to a non-standard variety that is characteristic of a particular region or social group. This sense can be found even in Labov's work, for example in his description of **African American Vernacular English** (formerly known as Black English, and sometimes referred to as *Ebonics*, on the insistence of many community leaders) as 'that relatively uniform grammar found in its most consistent form in the speech of Black youth from 8 to 19 years old who participate fully in the street culture of the inner cities' (1972b: xiii). It is quite usual for linguists to describe the vernacular of a city as a non-standard variety used by a majority of speakers, but not everyone.

Labov developed an empirical approach to the study of language that involved careful sampling of populations to ensure representativeness, fieldwork methods designed to elicit a range of styles from the least to the most formal, and analytic techniques based on the concept of the linguistic variable. The Martha's Vineyard study was a clear illustration of the interplay between linguistic and social factors in a relatively simple setting. The variation boiled down to a change in community norms per age group arising out of a stronger sense of 'us' (islanders) versus 'them' (mainlanders/tourists). In subsequent studies, Labov worked on more complex situations – large urban centres, and large populations with several ethnic groups and with rapid social change and mobility.

Case Study 3: Sociolinguistic Variation in New York City

One of Labov's most influential studies, published in 1966, showed essentially that if any two subgroups of New York City speakers are ranked on a scale of social stratification, they will be ranked in the same order by their differential use of certain linguistic variables. One of the most notable is the variable (r) after vowels in words such as *lark* or *bar*. English speakers in various parts of the world differ in the extent to which [r] is pronounced after vowels. RP for example is 'r-less', while Scots English is 'r-ful'.[4] To demonstrate that patterns of variation do exist for as large and complex a city as New York was an ambitious task, especially since earlier views held by linguists were discouraging:

> The pronunciation of a very large number of New Yorkers exhibits a pattern . . . that might most accurately be described as the complete absence of any pattern. Such speakers sometimes pronounce /r/ before a consonant or a pause and sometimes omit it, in a thoroughly haphazard pattern. (Alan Hubbell (1950), *The Pronunciation of English in New York City*, cited by Chambers 2003: 17)

Labov's hunch was that this was not true; that, as for Martha's Vineyard, seemingly fuzzy patterns of variability could be studied systematically and could contribute to linguists' knowledge of language and societal patterns. As a preparation for studying the speech habits of the city, Labov undertook a pilot survey, that is, a small-scale investigation meant to investigate the feasibility of a larger and more costly project. Labov's pilot study has become something of a classic in its own right.

The department store study

For his pilot survey Labov decided to study three sites, which he believed would show patterns of variation, typical of the city. His hypothesis was that the speech of salespeople at departmental stores would reflect, to a large extent, the norms of their typical customers. He then picked three large department stores in Manhattan:

- Saks Fifth Avenue: a high-status store near the centre of the high-fashion district.
- Macy's: a store regarded as middle-class and middle-priced.
- Klein's: a store selling cheaper items and catering for poorer customers.

By pretending to be a customer, Labov carried out a quick check of what items were found on the fourth floor of each store. He then asked the salespeople on different floors 'Excuse me, where are the women's shoes?' (or whatever item), knowing that the answer had to be 'fourth floor', a phrase containing two tokens of postvocalic [r]. (This term was introduced in section 2.3, as a shorthand way of describing the sound [r] after a vowel, though not between two vowels. Patterns of postvocalic [r] usage in England are depicted in Map 2.5.) By pretending to be hard of hearing and leaning forward with an 'excuse me?', he obtained two more tokens in more careful, stressed style as the salesperson repeated 'fourth floor'. On the fourth floor itself, Labov asked assistants, 'Excuse me, what floor is this?' As soon as he received these answers, Labov moved out of sight and wrote down the pronunciation and details like the sex, approximate age, and race of the sales assistant. Since these are large stores with numerous assistants, Labov was able to gather answers from 264 unwitting subjects. All in all, over 1,000 tokens of the variable (*r*) were collected (multiplying the number of speakers by four for the number of tokens) in a mere six-and-a-half hours, making this a remarkably successful (and amusing) pilot study.

Analysis of the data confirmed certain patterns of variation in the use of postvocalic /r/ according to linguistic context, speech style and social class associated with each store. Some 62 per cent of Saks' employees, 51 per cent of Macy's and 20 per cent of Klein's used [r] in at least one of the four tokens. In the more deliberate repetition, all groups show an increase in the use of [r], though interestingly it was the middle-status store's employees who showed the greatest increase. Labov commented (1972a: 52): 'It would seem that *r*-pronunciation is the norm at which a majority of Macy's employees aim, yet not the one they use most often'. The results were even more finely grained – for example, on the quieter and more expensive upper floors of the highest-ranking store, the percentage of [r] was much higher than amid the hustle and bustle of the ground floor.

The larger New York City study

The pilot study showed that, contrary to the views of linguists like Hubbell, /r/ in New York City could be studied systematically. One of the prerequisites of a full-scale study was to find a way of establishing a more representative sample of the city than its salespersons. In the full study, a proper sampling procedure was followed – the first time this had been done in linguistic fieldwork involving extensive interviews. It drew on an earlier sociological survey of the Lower East Side of New York City conducted by a sociological research group. The original survey used a random sample of 988 adult subjects representing a population of 100,000. Originally aiming to interview 195 of those respondents who had not moved house in the previous two years, Labov managed to reach 81 per cent of this target group. Interviews were conducted on an individual basis and involved four types of activity:

1. the main part, consisting of continuous speech in response to the interviewer's questions;
2. reading of a short passage;
3. reading lists of words containing instances of pertinent variables;
4. reading pairs of words involving key variables (for example the vowels in *God* and *guard*, which both have the vowel [a:] in New York City English).

Labov argued that moving from (1) to (4) corresponds to increasing formality and focus on language itself. Later on, at the stage of analysis, Labov divided sections of the continuous speech into the subcategories 'formal' and 'casual', depending on the interviewee's responses.

In grouping his speakers, Labov used a ten-point socioeconomic scale, devised earlier by the sociological research group. It was based on three equally weighted indicators of status: occupation of breadwinner, education of respondent and family income. On a ten-point scale, 0–1 was taken as lower class, 2–4 as working class, 5–8 as lower middle-class, and 9 as upper middle-class. It has become common practice to refer to the different groups by abbreviations like LWC (lower working-class), UWC (upper working-class), LMC (lower middle-class), UMC (upper middle-class), and so on. Labov's unusual term 'lower class' denotes people who are unemployed, or under-employed, homeless people and so on. Of the many variables examined by Labov, we focus on two: (th) and (r).

The variable (th) in New York City

The main variants of the (th) variable – that is, the initial sound in the lexical set THING, THICK, THIGH – are the general interdental fricative [θ] and less prestigious variants, the affricate [tθ] and dental stop [t̪] (so that *thing* and *thick* would sound more like *ting* and *tick*).

As with vowel variables, the differences between the variants of (th) are subtle and result from slight changes in tongue position vis-à-vis other articulators.

The [θ] pronunciation which is the form used in RP and other prestige varieties in the USA, Australia and other English-speaking territories, involves the tongue making fleeting and partial contact with the teeth of the upper jaw, with air flowing out under friction during the contact.

For [t̪], the tongue makes complete contact with the upper teeth, stopping the air flow momentarily.

As the symbol suggests, [tθ] involves a combination of the above two articulations, with the tongue making contact with the teeth and then releasing the air.

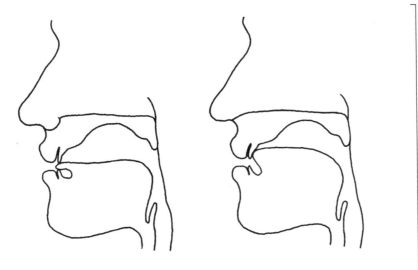

Figure 3.2 Tongue position for interdental fricative (left) and dental stop (right) variants of (th)

The variants [θ], [tθ] and [t̪] were assigned scores of 0, 1 and 2 respectively. Figure 3.3 shows the stratification of this variable according to class and style for eighty-one speakers. The vertical axis is a scale of average (th) index scores per socioeconomic group; while the horizontal axis represents the four contextual styles. The scores range from a possible 0 (for fricatives only) to 200 (for stops only). Figure 3.3 shows the following patterns:

- Style: There is consistent stylistic variation of the variable. The greatest occurrence of non-fricative forms is in casual speech for all groups, with decreasing frequency when moving through the more formal styles.
- Class: There is a stable pattern insofar as the graphs for each class are roughly parallel (apart from the equal LLMC and ULMC scores for casual speech).

Defining the (th) index in the way that Labov did yields the following relationship between social class and the (th) variable: an increase in social class or status groups is accompanied by decreasing index scores for (th). The variable may be characterised as **sharply stratified**, since there is a relatively large gap between the LC and WC scores as against the MC scores.

Postvocalic (r) in New York City

In his analysis of postvocalic (r) as used by the same speakers, Labov used a scoring system of 1 for use of [r] and 0 for its absence. The results of his analysis are shown in Figure 3.4, which has an additional category under 'style' involving **minimal pairs** of words. The term 'minimal pair' refers to the use of pairs of words which differ in only one sound, in this case by the

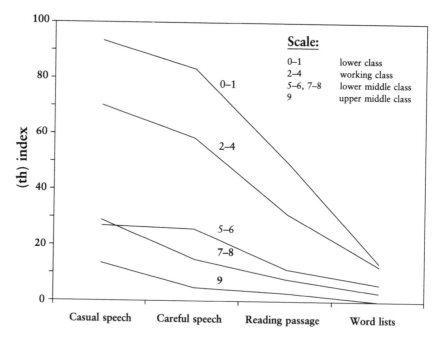

Figure 3.3　Social stratification of (th) in New York City (from Labov 1972a: 113)

presence or absence of postvocalic [r], for example *source* and *sauce* (in US English).

The New York study showed two aspects of sociolinguistic stratification: linguistic differentiation, and social evaluation. In terms of linguistic differentiation the patterning of (r) in Figure 3.4 shows the following tendencies:

- New Yorkers ranked on a hierarchical scale by non-linguistic criteria follow the same scale in (r) usage. There is **fine** rather than sharp stratification of the variable – that is, the divisions between the social classes are not as great as for (th).
- The differences between the groups are not categorical; that is, no group is characterised by the complete presence or absence of postvocalic [r].
- Nevertheless, at the level of casual speech, only the UMC shows a significant degree of r-pronunciation. The other groups range between 1 and 10 per cent on this variable. Thus, generally speaking, the pronunciation of postvocalic [r] functions as a marker of the highest-ranking status group.
- All groups show an increase when moving from informal to more formal styles. Thus the variable marks not only status but style as well.
- As one follows the progression towards more formal styles, the LMC shows a greater increase in the use of [r], until in word-list and minimal-pair styles they overtake the UMC averages.

Labov termed this last phenomenon **hypercorrection**. The LMC overshoots the mark and goes beyond the highest-status group in its tendency

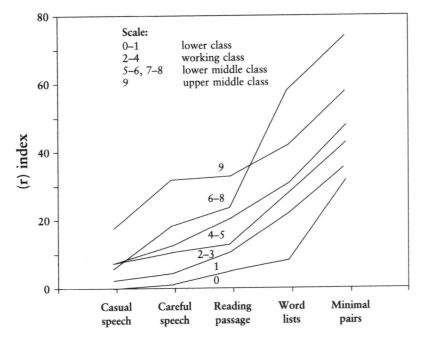

Figure 3.4   Social stratification of (r) in New York City (from Labov 1972a: 114)

to use the pronunciation considered correct and appropriate for formal styles. This is a consequence of the LMC's position in the class hierarchy, reflecting the wishes of its members to distance themselves from the working class and to become more like the upper middle class. In this sense, hypercorrection denotes the use of a particular variant beyond the target set by the prestige model. This crossover pattern differentiates the (r) variable from the stable (th) variable. Labov advances the hypothesis that this crossover pattern, coupled with differential scores in the various age groups (which we have not discussed here), is an indication of changing norms of pronunciation (see further Chapter 4).

Hypercorrection reveals a degree of **linguistic insecurity**: people who don't usually use a form in their casual speech try and improve on (or 'correct') their speech when it is being observed or evaluated. Social evaluation thus plays an important role in Labov's model. He used certain types of psychological tests to demonstrate his claim about linguistic insecurity. These were **subjective reaction tests**, modified from earlier tests devised by the psychologist Wallace Lambert. In one of the experiments, subjects were asked to rate a number of short excerpts on a scale of occupational suitability (that is, whether the speaker would be acceptable as a secretary, television personality, factory worker, and so on). The tape contained twenty-two sentences from five female readers in random order. Some of the sentences contained words with postvocalic (r), others had none. As these were taken from the reading passage, subjects were already familiar with the material. All subjects aged between 18 and 39 agreed in their tacit positive evaluation of [r] usage, irrespective of their own level of use of the variable. As part of the test, Labov played two versions of a sentence by the *same* speaker, one showing greater use of postvocalic (r) than the other. Labov used the label 'r-positive' for the following:

- attributing a sentence with some postvocalic [r] to a speaker with a higher occupational position than a sentence without any postvocalic [r].
- assigning a speaker to a higher occupational position for a sentence containing more postvocalic [r] than (unknowingly) for the same speaker on a sentence containing fewer realisations of postvocalic [r].

The percentage of 'r-positive' responses of subjects between the ages of 18 and 39 years was 100. Subjects aged over 40 showed a mixed reaction in their social evaluation; but the LMC speakers showed higher r-positive responses than the UMC. These led Labov to conclude that norms governing the use and perceptions of postvocalic [r] were undergoing some change. Such linguistic change is the subject of Chapter 4.

Three types of variables
- **Markers** are those variables like (r) and (th), which show stratification according to style and social class. All members react to them in a more or less uniform manner.
- **Indicators**, show differentiation by age or social group without being subject to style-shifting, and have little evaluative force in subjective- reaction tests. Only a linguistically trained observer is aware of indicators, for example the pronunciation of the vowels in *God* and *guard* (and similar sets of words) as the same in New York, and the use of 'positive anymore' in Midland USA (for example, *That's the way it is with planes anymore*). Positive anymore corresponds to 'still' or 'these days' in other dialects of English.
- **Stereotypes** are forms that are socially marked – that is, they are prominent in the linguistic awareness of speech communities, as in the case of 'h-dropping' in Cockney and other English dialects, or the stigmatisation of the *thoidy-thoid* street 'thirty-third street' pronunciation of New York speech. Judgements that bring about stereotypes are not necessarily phonetically accurate. The stigmatised New York City vowel, for example, is not the same as that in *toy*. *Bird* and *Boyd* are not pronounced the same in working-class New York dialect, though – influenced by comedians – outsiders might think so.

Labov suggested that generally members of the highest- and lowest-status groups tend not to change their pronunciation after it becomes fixed in adolescence; members of middle-status groups (UMC and LMC) may do so, because of their social aspirations. The linguistic insecurity of the LMC leads to especial fluctuation in formal speech contexts: hence Labov's claims about the consistency of vernacular speech over other styles. We noted earlier that these claims are specific to Labov's model of language. Sociolinguists with other perspectives do not see one style as more basic or consistent than others.

It is sometimes remarked that what linguists find socially significant in a variety are not what speakers themselves think important. The whole issue of speaker's evaluation is a complex one. Labov differentiated between different types of variables, depending on a speech community's consciousness of them (see accompanying box).

The issue of **prestige** is generally an important – and complicated – one in sociolinguistics. Labov distinguished between 'overt' and 'covert' prestige. **Overt prestige** refers to positive or negative assessments of variants (or of a speech variety) in accordance with the dominant norms of the public media, educational institutions and upper middle-class speech. In the New York City studies, interviewees who made the highest use of a stigmatised feature in their own natural speech showed the greatest tendency to stigmatize others for their use of the same form. On the other hand, the stability of working-class (WC) speech norms calls for other explanations, since these speakers did not, in fact, readily adopt middle-class (MC) norms. **Covert prestige** refers to this set of opposing values implicit in lower- and working-class lifestyles, which do not appear in conventional subjective-reaction tests. That is, WC speech is a mechanism for signalling adherence to local norms and values. In contrast to MC speech which reveals a concern for **status**, WC speech marks **solidarity**. (These themes are picked up in section 3.4 and in a different framework in Chapter 5.)

Generally, the New York study showed that socioeconomic differentiation cannot be ignored in studies of language structure. The character of (r) as a prestige feature within the linguistic system can only be gauged within the network of stylistic and social inequalities.

3.3 FIELDWORK METHODS IN VARIATIONIST SOCIOLINGUISTICS

Variationists stress the importance of the collection and analysis of a corpus that adequately represents the speech of members of the community under study. In practice, sociolinguistic surveys are based on anything from forty to 150 speakers. Samples going beyond 150 individuals tend to increase data-handling problems without a significant gain in analytic insights. Stressing the need to study the vernacular in its social context gives rise to what Labov termed the **observer's paradox**. That is, the vernacular, which the linguist wishes to observe closely, is the very style which speakers use when they are *not* being observed. This is akin to the 'experimenter effect' in other disciplines – that is, the need to ensure that the data which one collects are unaffected by the process of investigation. Labov has used a variety of techniques to get around the problem, the most favoured being the sociolinguistic interview. This involves a tape-recorded, personal interview lasting about an hour per person. The session is designed to be as informal as possible in an attempt to defuse the relative status of participants (usually middle-class researcher versus the 'subject'). Identification of the interviewer with the teaching profession would invariably typecast him or her as a prescriptivist and the one from whom information flows, rather than the other way around. The counter-strategy of the sociolinguistic interview is to emphasise the position of the interviewer as learner (about local ways and attitudes), and hence in a lower position of authority than the person to whom the interviewer is speaking. Interviewees are encouraged to talk about everyday topics of personal interest, and thus to take the lead during some parts of the interview. Successful topics often centre around childhood games, accusations of blame for things one may not have done, family, religion and, in some societies, dating and the opposite sex. The most famous topic centres around what has come to be known as the 'danger of death' question. Interviewees are asked to talk informally about their most frightening moment, when 'you thought you were in serious danger of being killed – where you thought to yourself, "This is it".' Speakers embarking on such a narration often become so involved in it as to be temporarily diverted from the act of being interviewed. Their speech consequently shows a definite shift away from formal style to the vernacular.

Labov stressed that interview speech should not be mistaken for intimate vernacular style. However, by using an empathetic approach and the right techniques, it brought one as close to the vernacular as was possible, while still obtaining large quantities of comparable and clear data. Among the cues that signify a relatively successful interview are modulations of voice production, including changes in tempo, pitch and volume, alterations in rate of breathing, and occasional laughter. Regarding fieldwork ethics, surreptitious recordings are generally considered undesirable. They breach the privacy of individuals as well as trust between interviewer and interviewee. Such deceit may negate good relations and trust necessary for long-term contact with a community. Linguists have found that even surreptitious recordings of friends have led to unhappiness.

The individual interview is not the only technique advocated by Labov, who has used a variety of other methods for other purposes. First,

---

On surreptitious recording of friends

The British linguist Jennifer Coates (whose research focuses on women's norms of conversation, rather than phonetic variation) presents the following account of her early lesson against 'candid' (or covert) recordings, even of a group of friends who met regularly:

> At this point I chose to tell the group that I had been recording them for nearly a year. I was staggered by their reaction: they were furious. In retrospect, I'm amazed by my own naivety. Recording people talking without their consent is a gross violation of their rights . . . (1996: 5)

---

participant observation of adolescent gangs in Harlem (New York City) by a group of fieldworkers formed an important database for a study of African American Vernacular English. The significance of adolescent gangs lies in the naturalness of these self-selected groups and the checks (conscious and subconscious) by members on any individual who produces non-vernacular forms not typical of the group, solely for the benefit of the tape recorder. Some sessions resembled a party rather than a discussion with outsiders. By using separate-track recordings in several group sessions, the researchers obtained clear, varied and voluminous data which informed their study of phonetic variables, syntax, narratives (storytelling modes) and adolescent street culture.

This approach was refined by Lesley and James Milroy in their studies in Belfast (see Chapter 4), and by Labov in long-term 'neighbourhood studies' in Philadelphia (starting in the 1970s). The neighbourhood studies were designed to obtain a large amount of linguistic and social data from individual neighbourhoods as social units. Participant observation in Philadelphia has allowed unlimited access to the linguistic competence of the central figures in individual networks, and group recordings which elicit close to vernacular styles. Included in the neighbourhood studies are systematic sociolinguistic interviews developed along the earlier New York City models. These remain the best source for comparable data on all members of a social network. Labov's later work thus moves away from an emphasis on a random sampling of a large community to judgement-sample selection of neighbourhoods for intensive study.

The second method involves rapid and anonymous surveys. In certain strategic locations, such surveys enable the study of a large number of people in a short space of time, provided that the social identity of the subjects is well defined by the situation. Labov's pilot study of (r) in New York department stores is a paradigm example.

The third method involves telephone surveys. In later work, Labov complemented the intensive but non-random neighbourhood studies by broader (and less detailed) representation using a telephone survey. Subjects chosen by a random sample participated in a fifteen-minute telephone interview, which included some spontaneous conversation, word lists and minimal pairs. The emphasis was on communication in Philadelphia, with reference mainly to telephone speech, and on special words and pronunciations in the Philadelphia dialect that might be sources of misunderstanding.

Finally, Labov has used a variety of field experiments to tackle specific problems. The subjective-evaluation test cited above is but one instance of these.

Assumptions of early variation theory
1. Society is hierarchically structured, like a ship or a layered cake.
2. Social class is basic to this structure; other categories like gender and ethnicity are also significant factors which cut across class stratification.
3. Social class can be characterised as a composite of several factors pertaining to education, income and so on.
4. Much variation in language correlates with this pre-determined hierarchy.
5. Style can be arranged on a single dimension from least to most formal, according to context.
6. Style shows a correlation with linguistic variants similar to that of social class.

3.4   A CLOSER LOOK AT STYLISTIC AND SOCIAL CATEGORIES

Influential as Labov's work was in the 1970s, almost all of its assumptions have been the subject of intense research and debate. In this section, we present research which has questioned, revised and extended some of these assumptions.

Style

Labov's account of style has been criticised for its one-dimensional nature. According to his account, styles can be arranged on a continuum, depending on the amount of attention people pay to the act of using language. The most natural style for Labov is the vernacular, during which a speaker is least conscious of the act of speaking. The least natural style in his model is the one which requires conscious attention to language, as mirrored in the word-list and reading-passage exercises. Later commentators (discussed in Chapter 5) argue that this conception of style does not really correspond

Five styles outlined by Joos (1959)
- **Intimate style** involves a great deal of shared knowledge and background in a private conversation between equals. 'Pillow talk' between partners is probably the best example of intimate style.
- **Casual style**, which is typical of informal speech between peers, includes ellipsis (or omission of certain grammatical elements) and slang between peers. (Joos's examples of ellipsis are *Friend of mine saw it*; *Coffee's cold.*)
- **Consultative style** is the norm for informal conversation between strangers. Slang and ellipsis might not be used to the extent that they are used in casual speech with a friend; but informal markers of rapport like *hmm, yes, I know* and informal linguistic elements like about, so, thing and so on may still abound.
- **Formal style** is determined more by the setting than by the person(s) interacting. Markers of formal English style include *whom, may I, for the purpose of* and so on. Some, but not all, of the language associated with formal style is school-based.
- **Frozen style** is a hyper-formal style designed to discourage friendly relations between participants.

with any aspect of speech. Reading words and passages cannot be claimed to be the same kind of activity as speaking. The latter is an interactive process between two or more participants. Labov had failed to build on an earlier account by Martin Joos (1959) which had outlined five styles, varying on a scale of formality from least to most formal (see accompanying box):

1. intimate; 2. casual; 3. consultative; 4. formal; 5. frozen.

Labov's field methods aimed to elicit as wide a range of styles as possible within the confines of the interview situation. Whereas the initial parts of an interview may show a consultative style, a successful interview gradually leads into casual style. The difference between a consultative style with an interviewer and an intimate style showed up dramatically in one of the interviews discussed by Labov (1972a: 89–90). Dolly (a pseudonym) was a friendly and relaxed interviewee whose speech in the interview may be characterised as consultative to casual. In a part of the interview pertaining to the meanings of certain words in the local dialect, she said: 'Smart? Well, I mean, when you use the word *intelligent* an' *smart*, I mean . . . you use it in the same sense? . . . [*Laughs*]: So some people are pretty witty – I mean – yet they're not so intelligent.'

Later the interview was interrupted by the telephone ringing, affording glimpses of Dolly's intimate to casual speech, which was radically different from even the most relaxed interview style.

> Huh? . . . Yeah, go down 'e(r)e to stay. This is. So you know what Carol Ann say? Listen at what Carol Ann say. Carol Ann say, 'An' then when papa die, we can come back' [*belly laugh*] . . . Ain't these chillun sump'm? [*falsetto*] . . . An' when papa die, can we come back?

Although it is rare for such an intimate style to appear in an interview, techniques like the 'danger of death' allow one to get relatively close to the most casual style. However, some sociolinguists (see Chapter 5 and 6) question whether speech styles can be adequately characterised without considering basic aspects of the speech context like the speakers, their relationship, communicative aims and the range of speech repertoires available in a community.

More on Class and Language

In Labov's formulation, classes can be delineated by means of a composite socioeconomic index. Classes tend to form a continuum, which correlates with scores for particular variables. On the whole, linguistic stratification mirrors social stratification. Labov argued that speech communities are in subconscious agreement about the relative values of different variants of a variable irrespective of their own scores for such a variable. This model of class is not without problems. In many instances, there appear to be more fundamental divisions over language than the New York City study suggests.

(a) Class differences in Norwich

An important study (published in 1974) that adopted Labov's approach to language research was undertaken by Peter Trudgill in the English city of Norwich. Like Labov, Trudgill aimed at describing the norms of a whole city via detailed interviews with a sample of its populace (in this case, fifty adults and ten schoolchildren). Trudgill analysed several linguistic variables pertaining to accent and grammar. We discuss two of these for the further light they shed on variation, social groupings and attitudes to language use. The first is an example of a grammatical variable: that is, it involves two or more alternative forms for the same grammatical unit. In Norwich as in some other parts of Britain, there are two alternative forms for the third-person singular present tense: *she sings, works, eats* and so on (the standard form) and *she sing, work, eat* and so on (the local dialect form without the -*s* inflection). Trudgill found that there was a correlation between social class and use of this variable. These findings are shown in Table 3.2.

In this table, the norms for casual speech are given for five classes that

MMC	100%
LMC	98%
UWC	30%
MWC	13%
LWC	3%

Table 3.2   The use of third-person singular *-s* in Norwich (Trudgill 1983a)

Trudgill delineates on the basis of a socioeconomic index constructed along similar lines to Labov's New York City. The figures represent use of the standard variant (-s). Like the example of New York City (th), this is a sharply stratified variable: there is a considerable gap between the norms for the middle classes and the working classes apparent from the figures for the LMC (98 per cent) as opposed to the group below, the UWC (30 per cent). In this regard, Norwich patterns are fairly typical of dialect grammar in England. The idea of shared norms and common evaluation does not seem to apply.

A more complex case involves the variable (oʊ) in Norwich, the vowel sound in the lexical set NOSE, ROAD, MOAN. There are a range of pronunciations for this sound, from the [oʊ] through [u:] to [ʊ]. Phonetically, the first sound is rather like (but not identical to) the RP vowel in the word *nose*, whereas the [u:] and [ʊ] are similar to (but again not exactly the same as) the RP vowels in the words *rude* and *put*. Trudgill found that the variant [U] was used only by the working class (although it was not the only variant they used). Furthermore, he found little difference between casual style and formal style, apart from the LMC, which does seem to exhibit 'correction' of their speech towards MMC norms in formal, reading-passage and word-list styles.

Like Labov, Trudgill used sociolinguistic interviews to collect speech samples. As part of these interviews, he used a self-evaluation test in which informants were asked how they usually pronounced words like these. In the prototype test in New York, people showed a distinct tendency to claim higher use of the prestige form than was evident in their interview speech. In Norwich, this was not necessarily the case. In particular, male informants were much more likely to under-report their use of the prestige variants (in favour of working-class norms). Female informants, on the other hand, had a tendency to over-report their use of prestige norms. This involves a kind of double wishful thinking: the men claimed to use the 'rougher' non-standard forms characteristic of some of their fellow workers more than they actually did, and the women reported using the standard prestige forms more than they actually did. Like Labov, Trudgill distinguished between overt and covert prestige attached to speech forms. Women in Norwich seem responsive to the overt prestige of the standard variety, while men seem more responsive to the covert prestige of localised Norwich speech. Although Labov had pointed to the existence of covert prestige in his New York study, he was unable to tap into it in evaluation tests. Trudgill conjectures that the difference in attitudes reflects differences in class-consciousness in the two countries – especially a lack of militant class-consciousness in the USA and the relative lack of 'embourgeoisement' of the British working class in the 1970s. Thus, while the study by Labov showed clear stratification by status in New York City over the variable (r), Trudgill's study emphasises the dimension of solidarity by men in Norwich as reflected in the variable (oʊ). Trudgill (1978: 194) describes this difference between status and solidarity in the two territories as follows:

> Levine and Crockett (1966) have demonstrated that in one American locality 'the community's march toward the national norm' is spear-headed by middle-aged MC women (and by the young). In Norwich, at least, there appears to be a considerable number of young WC men marching resolutely in the other direction.

(b) Class struggles in Cane Walk

John Rickford (1986) studied variation in a village in Guyana. This study supports Trudgill's idea that in some societies there are class divisions over language, rather than class continua and consensus. Rickford goes one step further than Trudgill in questioning whether the sociological model implicit in Labov's work is adequate to deal with this kind of variation. (Of the three sociological approaches to society discussed in section 1.6, of particular relevance here are functionalism and Marxism.) Cane Walk (a pseudonym for the village studied by Rickford) is still based along the lines of a colonial sugar-cane estate. The local stratification system involves three groups: (1) the 'senior staff', that is, the upper class whose members run the estate but live in exclusive areas elsewhere; (2) the 'estate class', made up of drivers, field-foremen, clerks, shopowners and skilled tradesmen who live close to the estate; and (3) the working class who, until the 1950s, had lived in inhospitable barracks on the estate and are still involved in cane-cutting, weeding, shovelling and so on. The roots of all three groups lie in the semi-forced migrations of indentured workers from India to the British and other colonies in the mid-nineteenth century. Although all three groups are bound by ethnicity and historical ties, Rickford argues that ethnicity is of far less importance here than class differences. The upper class and 'estate class' have 'life chances' that differ greatly from those of the workers who have far smaller and less stable incomes and very few opportunities for social and educational mobility. Samples of working-class and lower middle-class speech in Cane Walk are shown in the accompanying box.

Class division shows up in dramatic differences in language use. The vernacular of Cane Walk ranges from a **creole** form of English to a variety that is close to standard English. (Creoles and their relations to standard forms of European languages are discussed in Chapter 9.) Rickford analysed the degree to which the working-class and the 'estate class' drew upon nine subcategories of the singular pronoun forms – for example *I* versus *me* (for the first person). Working-class people in the survey used the standard

---

Working-class speech (Irene, a weeder in the cane fields)

Irene:	Mii bin smaal, bot mi in staat wok aredi wen di skiim kom – lang ting. mii staat wok fan twelv yeer.
Interviewer:	Twelv?
Irene:	Ye-es.
Interviewer:	How yu start so yong?
Irene:	Wel, akardinlii tu, yu noo lang ting, praiveeshan. Yu sii, mi modo an faado bin separeet, den mii – em – aftor mi sii ponishment staat, mii staat fu wok . . . mi goo op tu foot standard.

(Guyanese Creole is not generally written down, and Rickford here employs the common practice among linguists in using 'phonetic' spellings to give an indication of pronunciation. A version of the conversation in standard English is as follows: 'I was small but I had started to work already when the Housing Scheme came, a long time ago. I started to work at twelve years of age. (Twelve?) Yes. (How did you start so young?) Well, according to, you know how it was long ago, deprivation – You see, my mother and father had separated. Then I started – em – after I saw punishment starting, I started to work . . . I went up to fourth standard.')

Lower middle-class speech (Bonette, a senior civil servant)

| Bonette: | An ai tingk is wuz n ohfl weest ov taim, an wai ai tingk dee kep mii bak tu – am – rait it, iz biikoz ai felt di hedmaasto wohntid tu hav oz moch passiz oz posibl ogeens iz neem. Yu noo wot o miin? |

(This passage is essentially that of standard English apart from pronunciation, though in other excerpts Bonette draws upon some features of Creole grammar. In more conventional spelling, the passage reads: 'And I think it was an awful waste of time. And why I think they kept me back to – uhm – write it, is because I felt the headmaster wanted to have as many passes as possible against his name. You know what I mean?')

(Rickford 1987: 144–5, 192)

English variants only 18 per cent of the time, while the corresponding figure for the lower middle-class is 83 per cent. This basic difference extends to other areas of language use: accent and other grammatical and lexical features.

Rickford concludes (1986: 217–18):

> If we assume in functionalist terms that both groups share a common set of values about language and social mobility, we are hard put to explain this dramatic sociolinguistic difference, especially since their responses on a matched guise test indicate that both groups associate the most creole speech with the lowest status jobs and the most standard speech with the highest . . . . However, a separate question about whether speaking good English helps one to get ahead reveals sharp differences between the groups about the nature of the association between language and occupation. The estate class essentially share a functionalist view, seeing use of the standard variants as leading to increments of economic position, political power, and social status. For the [working-class] members, however, whose efforts to move upwards within the sugar estate hierarchy (and even outside of it) have rarely been successful, the social order is seen as too rigidly organised in favour of the haves for individual adjustments in language use by the have-nots to make much difference . . .

It is not the case – as is often assumed – that the working-class speakers don't use standard English because they cannot (through limited education, contact with standard speakers and so on). Rickford argues that many working-class speakers use creole rather than standard English as a matter of choice, as a revolutionary act emphasising social solidarity over individual self-advancement and communicating political militancy rather than accommodation.

(c) Class divisions among adolescents: Jocks and Burnouts in Detroit

Penelope Eckert (1989a) studied the sociolinguistic patterns of high school pupils in several high-schools in Detroit in the USA. The fieldwork technique which she used in one particular school is known as 'participant observation', since it involves observing people's behaviour while participating in their daily lives. Eckert noted the existence of two main groups of students: the first intends to continue its education at college level and cooperate in the adult-defined adolescent world of the school. Students in this group make the school their community and hence the basis of their social identity. The other group, made of students who intend to leave high school directly for the workplace, especially in blue-collar (i.e. largely manual) jobs, views the role of the school differently. While school is subconsciously viewed as a necessary qualification for employment, the extra-curricular activities on offer are not seen as good preparation for their next life stage. Instead, better opportunities are afforded by gaining familiarity with places likely to become their future workplace. This involves making contact with those who will aid them in the pursuit of employment. Students accordingly are forced to minimise their participation in school outside classes and to maximise their contacts in the local communities. The school's reward system, according to Eckert, precludes friendly coexistence between the two groups of students since 'it repays extracurricular activity with freedoms, recognition, and institutional status. The result is the ascendancy of one student category over the other, which elevates differences on their interests to the level of a primary social opposition' (1991: 216). This opposition is a familiar one in most US schools, and is explicitly recognised in names for the groups in different schools at different times, for example *Greasers* versus *Preppies*. In the Detroit schools that Eckert studied in the 1980s, the terms were *Jocks* for the group in the social ascendancy, and *Burnouts* for the 'alienated' group. (The labels refer to the association of Burnouts with drugs and the Jocks with sport.)[5]

Like Rickford, Eckert had used prior existing social groupings in the community being studied, rather than assuming a class continuum. Differences between the groups occur not just in career expectations and involvement in extra-curricular school activities, but also in symbolic forms of behaviour, dress and speech. Burnouts in the 1980s were wearing dark-coloured, rock-concert T-shirts while Jocks wore colourful and fashionable designer clothes. A third group exists within the school system which is sometimes explicitly labelled 'in-between'. However, according to Eckert, this third group does not have as strong an identity as the first two, and is in some ways defined by what it does not belong to.

Jocks and Burnouts have a lot to say about the way the other group speaks. Jocks consider the Burnouts' speech to be ungrammatical, full of obscenities and inarticulate; the Burnouts consider that the Jocks 'talk just like their parents' (Eckert 1991: 220). Eckert points out that while Burnouts of both sexes make regular use of obscenities in normal speech, male Jocks also use obscenities, but only in private interaction with other male Jocks. Jock girls avoid obscenities altogether. As for accent, there are similar trends: Burnouts adopt more local vernacular variants, while the Jocks remain more conservative in reproducing societally prestigious forms. Eckert (1988: 206) explains these in terms of pupils' ties with the city. The Burnouts see their future social roles as tied to the urban centre, while the Jocks are less motivated to adopt regional markers. Among the most salient of such markers that Eckert found were a backing of the vowel [e] so that in Burnout speech the vowel in BET, LED, BED sounds more like the vowel of BUT, BUD, CUT in adult, middle-class speech. (Some of the complex ongoing changes in the vowels of northern US cities like Detroit are discussed in Chapter 4.) That the difference in attitude towards a local identity results in subtle differences between Jocks' and Burnouts' speech is reminiscent in a broad sense of Labov's findings on Martha's Vineyard.

Eckert observes that the Jocks versus Burnouts split is not the same as the adult working-class/middle-class dichotomy, since some children of middle-class background become Burnouts and vice versa. On the whole, however, she shows that this is an adult class system in the making. The polarisation between students is surprising given the kind of stratification cited in other US Labovian studies. It may well be that linguistically speaking the job market in the USA transforms the high school polarity into a continuum. It is to the upper end of such a continuum that we turn in the final subsection on class.

The upper classes

The upper classes are often conspicuous by their absence in sociolinguistic surveys. Tables and diagrams compiled by Labov and Trudgill have as their upper limit the 'upper middle class'. There are two reasons for this: the smallness of the upper class as a group compared to the working class and middle class, and the inaccessibility of this group to outsiders. Until recently, linguists have had to rely on somewhat speculative accounts of upper-class linguistic mores. Fischer (1958: 52), in his account of variation between *-in* and *-ing*, referred in passing to 'the protracted pursuit of an elite by an envious mass and consequent "flight" of the elite'. He thus foreshadowed Labov's account of hypercorrection among the lower middle class. (Of course, the idea of an endless chase between elites and the lower middle class is not borne out in variation theory, since many linguistic variables are quite stable.) One indication of the 'flight' of the elite comes from the old debate in England about U and non-U language. The terms 'U' and 'non-U' were coined by the linguist Alan Ross (1959) for 'upper class' and 'non-upper class' respectively. Ross argued that the upper classes (i.e. the remnants of the old aristocracy) in Britain were distinguished solely by their language, rather than wealth and education as in former times. He differentiated between on the one hand 'gentlemen' and, on the other, 'persons who though not gentlemen, might at first sight appear or would wish to appear as such' (1959: 11). Examples of U and non-U language from the 1950s given by Ross were of the following sort:

> *greens* meaning 'vegetables' is non-U.
> *home* (*They've a lovely home*) is non-U; *house* (*They've a very nice house*) is U.
> *horse-riding* is non-U against U *riding*.

Ross's examples from accent, though impressionistic, are still worth quoting:

> U-speakers do not sound the *l* in *golf*, *Ralph* (which rhymes with *safe*), *solder*; some old fashioned U-speakers do not sound it in *falcon*, *Malvern*, either. Some

U-speakers pronounce *tyre* and *tar* identically (and so for many other words, such as *fire* – even going to the length of making *lion* rhyme with *barn*.

One scholar who has managed to penetrate the social and physical barriers associated with the upper class is Anthony Kroch. He provides an account of upper-class life in Philadelphia, whose norms are that of a hereditary elite. Unlike classes defined by sociologists or sociolinguists, the upper class is a self-recognised group whose members frequently meet face-to-face in social institutions of their own. According to Kroch (1996: 25) the upper class of Philadelphia is extremely self-conscious and demarcates itself sharply from the middle-class. Membership in this group is dependent on the following factors: wealth (inherited), colour (white), descent (Anglo-Saxon) and religion (Episcopalian, i.e. Church of England). There is a social register which lists members of this group.

Kroch gained access to this network via acquaintance with one member, and was able to carry out sociolinguistic interviews with several members. One interesting difference between these interviews and those carried out by Labov and Trudgill was that speakers became more relaxed when Kroch made it clear that his main interest was in their speech patterns rather than their social life. This contrasts greatly with lower middle-class insecurity about language. Kroch found that in terms of phonological variables there was not much difference between the upper class and the middle class:

> The properties that distinguish upper class speech are not phonemic but pro-sodic and lexical. They constitute what Hymes (1974[a]) calls a 'style' rather than a dialect. In particular, upper class speech is characterized by a drawling and laryngealized voice quality, and, contrastingly, by frequent use of emphatic accent patterns and of intensifying modifiers. (1996: 39)

Kroch comments further on the image of relaxation and ease projected by this type of speech. The use of intensifying modifiers (like *extremely*) and hyperbolic adjectives (like *outstanding*) and the prosodic stress patterns project self-assurance and an expectation of agreement from the listener. This sense of 'entitlement' (Coles 1977) is inculcated from childhood and maintained throughout life. As Coles defines it, entitlement is the socio-psychological correlate of power, status and wealth. It includes a sense of one's own importance and the expectation that one's views and wishes will be treated with respect. Members of the upper class project their sense of entitlement in all social and interpersonal interactions.

From Ross's examples on U and non-U in Britain and from Kroch's study, it appears that differences between the upper classes and the lower middle class are suggestive of a competition over status (see section 1.6 on the difference between 'status' and 'class' in strict sociological terms). On the other hand, there seems to be a bigger linguistic divide between the working and the middle classes, which seems a class division as opposed to differences over status. Much work has still to be done before any such conclusions about the links between language variation and class conflict can be firmly drawn. The centrality of class in sociology and in early sociolinguistics has been challenged by closer attention to gender as a primary category in social division.

Gender, Class and Language

It is seldom the case that class is the only sociological factor involved in language variation. There is a strong case for considering gender to be an equally significant (or more significant) factor. In Fischer's study in New England, girls were found to use more of the standard variant (-*ing*) than boys. Labov (1972a: 243) found that, in careful speech, women in New York City used fewer stigmatised forms than men. They were also more sensitive to prestigious variants. In formal speech, women were found to show greater style-shifting towards the prestige variants of their society than men. Labov believed that this was particularly a characteristic of lower middle-class women. He offered two tentative explanations for the difference in index scores between the sexes. He first raised the possibility that, as the ones generally more involved in taking care of children's development, women were more sensitive than men to what he called 'overt sociolinguistic values' (1972a: 243). A second, more 'symbolic' possibility that he offered was the following: 'The sexual differentiation of speakers is therefore not a product of physical factors alone . . . but rather an expressive posture which is socially more appropriate for one sex or the other' (1972a: 304). On Martha's Vineyard, for example, men were more 'close-mouthed' than women, and used more contracted areas of the vowel space in the mouth. This included a greater use of the centralised diphthongs discussed earlier. Labov comes close here to suggesting that linguistic variables don't just reflect different social categories, but are, in fact, involved in creating and maintaining a symbolic difference between the sexes.

In monitoring the (ing) variable among adults in Norwich, Trudgill (1974) came to a similar conclusion to Fischer: women use the standard variant to a greater extent than men. Trudgill put forth some possible explanations for this differentiation by gender, but as these have proved controversial and the basis for considerable debate in gender studies, we discuss them more fully in Chapter 7.

More recently, Eckert (1989b) has argued that there is no apparent reason to believe that gender alone will explain all the correlations with linguistic scores between men and women in a society. A more viable approach is one that combines gender and other categories like social class.

That is, a category like 'working class' may be too broad to account for the niceties of linguistic variation: working-class women may show crucial differences from working-class men. Similarly, 'male' versus 'female' may be too broad a division in itself, since gender – more than ever – is a fluid category admitting of various degrees of masculinity and femininity (see further Chapter 7 on these two categories).

Ethnicity and Dialect Variation

Another important factor that can upset the neat correlations between a speech community and its use of linguistic variables is ethnicity. Ethnic minorities may to some extent display the general patterns of the wider society but may also show significant differences. In his New York study, Labov (1972a: 118) made the following remarks about the city's Puerto Rican speech community:

> Puerto Rican speakers . . . show patterns of consonant cluster simplification which are different from those of both black and white New Yorkers. Clusters ending in *-rd* are simplified, and preconsonantal *r* is treated as a consonant: *a good car' game*. This does not fall within the range of variations open to other New Yorkers [who would say *a good card game*] . . .

Ethnic varieties such as Puerto Rican English in New York are called **ethnolects**. The factors that sustain an ethnolect are a sense of identity based on ancestry, religion and culture. Greater interaction within an ethnic group leads to differences from the dominant societal dialect or language. African American Vernacular English is ironically at one and the same time one of the more disparaged varieties of English in the classrooms of the USA and one of the best-studied by sociolinguists. We will use some of the vast research into this variety to illustrate the extent to which ethnic varieties (or ethnolects) may be polarised yet show degrees of overlap. As far as the postvocalic (r) and (th) variables studied by Labov are concerned, black speakers in New York showed the same patterns of stratification by class as other New Yorkers. Yet this is not true of certain other choices in vocabulary, grammar and pronunciation. Labov (1972b: 39–42) discusses the use of intervocalic (r) – the pronunciation of [r] between two vowels in words like *Carol, Paris, borrow* – in New York City. All white speakers that Labov interviewed showed 100 per cent use of intervocalic [r]. For this group, intervocalic (r) is not a variable. For black speakers, however, there is variation, with (r) either being pronounced as [r] or being merged with the following vowel. Loosely speaking, the latter form may be thought of as the dropping of intervocalic [r], sometimes represented by writers in spellings like *Ca'ol* and *Pa'is*. All black groups show variation irrespective of class. This is an example of language variation reflecting what Labov called 'ethnic

processes'. Labov's later work in Philadelphia stressed ongoing divergence between black and white speech (Labov and Harris 1986: 17), as witnessed in innovations like the use of -*s* as the marker of the past in narratives, rather than the traditional third person singular of the present tense:

> So, Verne was gonna go wif us. So I says, 'Shit, she don' gotta go, we go.' . . .

In such sentences, the -*s* in *says* seems to have become a general marker of the narrative past (also known as the conversational historical present). The construction is characteristic of many varieties of English: compare white middle-class US speech *Then she says* (followed by a quotation) *and then I say* (followed by a quotation). Whereas in such varieties the narrative past uses the same person-marking suffixes as the present tense, AAVE according to Labov and Harris (1986) is evolving a vernacular rule of zero (i.e. no suffix for all persons) for the present tense and *-s* for narrative past (in all persons). Labov and Harris (1986: 20) suggest that this divergence has to do with increasing ethnic segregation of blacks and whites in the USA. This applies more to working-class black communities than the middle classes. Not all linguists agree with this argument. Some argue that there is now greater cross-pollination of cultural and linguistic traits across race and ethnic barriers in the USA than in the past. Labov and Harris (1986: 22) respond that, whereas this might be true of the more obvious features like vocabulary and certain pronunciations, for more basic grammatical structures there is divergence: 'young black children from the inner city who must deal with the language of the classroom are faced with the task of understanding a form of language that is increasingly different from their own'. The disagreement seems to hinge around the issue we raised earlier about whether one style of language is more basic than another. In a sense, both parties are right: the vernacular varieties of white and black English (in the Labovian sense) might be diverging; yet at the same time there could well be convergence between non-vernacular styles of the two varieties.

Mismatches between home language and school language are discussed in Chapter 12. Labov's examples on ethnic differentiation call into question the view that he sometimes presents of New York as a community sharing norms of usage and agreeing about the social meaning of variability. The dialect divide between black and white in New York City portrayed by Labov and Harris seems more reminiscent of the basic divisions that Rickford studied in Cane Walk.

3.5 SOCIOLINGUISTICS ON TRIAL: AN APPLICATION OF URBAN DIALECTOLOGY

Language variation has often been studied 'for its own sake', treating language as the object of study. Yet such research may also have practical applications in various fields. In this concluding section, we illustrate the kind of contribution that variationists have made in courtrooms. Forensic linguistics is the name given to a branch of linguistics that is concerned with legal issues like voice identification, disputed authorship, anonymous letters and so on. The case that we use as an example here involved sociolinguistic testimony given on behalf of Paul Prinzivalli, an accused in a trial in Los Angeles in 1984. Prinzivalli, a cargo-handler for Pan American airlines, was alleged to have made bomb threats by telephone at Los Angeles airport. He was said to have a grudge against the company on account of its handling of shift schedules. Part of the threat was as follows:

> There's gonna be a bomb going off on the flight to LA . . . . It's in their luggage. Yes, and I hope you die with it and I hope you're on that.

An attorney for the defence asked Labov to contribute to the case on account of his experience with American dialects and in particular the dialect of New York City. On listening to a tape of Prinzivalli's own voice, Labov was sure that the bomb-threat caller and Prinzivalli were not the same person. His concern was how to convey his linguistic knowledge objectively to a judge, especially since Prinzivalli was known to be from New York and those who heard the bomb-threats thought the caller to be from that city as well. Labov, however, concluded that the caller's speech showed the features of the Boston area rather than New York. Together with colleagues from the University of Pennsylvania, Labov made detailed transcriptions of the two sets of recordings showing the differences in accent. In court he replayed the recordings through a loudspeaker which projected a clear and flat reproduction of the voices to all parts of the court-room. Several people who had thought that the two voices sounded similar were now struck by the differences that sound amplification projected. Labov pointed to specific and systematic differences between the two voices. The most significant of these differences between the two speakers was the way the vowels were pronounced in the sets LOT, COT, HOT and THOUGHT, CAUGHT, LAW respectively. In most English dialects these have distinct pronunciations, but in several US cities – including Boston – the vowels in these two lexical sets have merged. Thus in Boston *cot* rhymes with *caught* (see the Northern Cities Shift in section 4.5, and Map 4.4).

Labov was able to show that the bomb-threat caller had consistent merger in his pronunciation of the words *bomb* and *off*. On the other hand, Prinzivalli showed a distinction between these two words, which was typical of the New York region and the surrounding mid-Atlantic states. The last part of Labov's testimony involved measurements of the vowels of the two speakers via instrumental methods. This is a more objective means of presenting information than via auditory and perceptual means alone. The charts that Labov and his associates drew up, based on spectrograms (machine-drawn representations of the bands of energy released for vowels and consonants in speech), provided further testimony to subtle differences in the vowel systems of the defendant and the bomb-threat caller – for example in the way vowels were conditioned by following consonants.

On cross-examination, the prosecution asked whether a given speech sample could be identified as belonging to a given person. Labov pointed out that sociolinguists had less expertise in the identification of individuals than in the characteristics of speech communities. On the other hand, there are limits to the range of variation for any individual who belongs to the community. The question that naturally followed was whether an individual New Yorker could imitate the Boston dialect – that is, whether Prinzivalli could have disguised himself as a Bostonian. Labov's reply was that when people imitate or acquire other dialects they focus on the socially relevant features: certain new words and individual sounds. But they are not able to reproduce the intricacies of the vowel systems and the exact lexical sets that individual vowels are associated with in such systems:

> If it could be shown that the defendant had a long familiarity with the Boston dialect, and a great talent for imitation, then one could not rule out the possibility that he has done a perfect reproduction of the Boston system. But if so, he would have accomplished a feat that had not yet been reported for anyone else. (Labov 1988: 180)

The defendant was acquitted, since on the basis of the dialectological testimony there was a reasonable doubt that he had committed the crime. Prinzivalli was offered his job back at Pan American on condition that he did not sue for damages or back pay.

3.6   CONCLUSION

In this chapter, we introduced some of the aims, methods and approaches of variation theory. The central concept in this chapter is the linguistic variable. The variants of such a variable correlate with prominent social variables like class, gender, ethnicity and age groupings. They may also express different degrees of allegiance to a local identity. The majority of studies in the variationist tradition argue that society is stratified in terms of class, which is defined in terms of a socioeconomic index. Class stratification is mirrored by stylistic shifts towards the more prestigious linguistic variants in more formal contexts or contexts in which conscious attention is paid to language. Upward mobility among lower middle-class people and a concern for an increase in status is characterised in terms of hypercorrection in the use of certain variables. Ethnic and gender distinctions sometimes cut across class divisions so that the primary division for some variables may be along lines of ethnicity or gender. The prevailing model of class in variation theory is that of functionalism, involving shared norms, attitudes to, and evaluations of, language use by all classes. This model is called into question by some studies which argue that language shows up irreconcilable differences in some societies. Working-class speech in these instances expresses solidarity rather than a consciousness of status and upward mobility. The covert prestige of the vernacular is thus a counterbalancing force to the overt prestige of the standard variety.

Notes

1. The term 'secular' is meant to be opposed to the dominant ideas of Noam Chomsky which have become something of an orthodoxy in the USA. Labov has consistently argued that there cannot be a discipline of linguistics that is not social. 'Secular' also means 'long-lasting in time'. The rest of the terms are either transparent or will become clear in the course of this chapter.
2. Whereas the choice of a particular variant of a variable may sometimes depend purely on a linguistic context (i.e. usually the type of sound preceding or following the variable), the variables of greatest interest to sociolinguists are those which show social conditioning as well. (Hence the alternative term, 'sociolinguistic variable'.)
3. As with most linguistic variables, some of the variation is due not to social factors but to purely linguistic ones: centralisation was favoured in certain phonetic environments. Centralisation occurred most if the variable (aɪ) was followed by voiceless sounds like [t], [s], [p] or [f]. It was least favoured if the variable (aɪ) was followed by sounds like [l], [r], [m] or [n], which are phonetically liquids and nasals.
4. The usual phonetic terms corresponding to 'r-ful' and 'r-less' are 'rhotic' and 'non-rhotic'.
5. As Eckert points out, by no means all Burnouts actually use drugs.

4

LANGUAGE VARIATION AND CHANGE

4.1 INTRODUCTION

This chapter has two main focuses. First, it examines a key feature of the variationist school of linguistics – its interest in language change. Second, it presents new methodologies and analyses which have modified and extended the approaches developed by the Labovian school.

Language change

Here is the opening extract from the Lord's Prayer from different periods of English:

1. *Old English* (c.400 AD to c.1100): Fæder ure, þu þe art on heo-fonum, si þin nama gehalgod. To becume þin rice. (West Saxon text, end of tenth century, in W. B. Lockwood 1972: 132)
2. *Middle English* (c.1100 to c.1500): Fader oure þat is i heuen. blessid bi þi name to neuen. Come to us þi kingdome. (In C. Jones 1972)
3. *Early Modern English* (c.1500 to c.1800): Our father which art in heaven, hallowed be thy name. Thy kingdom come. (King James Bible)
4. *Modern English* (from c.1800): Our father who is in heaven, may your name be sacred. Let your kingdom come. (A modern rendition)

Note: Þ is an old symbol for *th*.

That languages can change dramatically over a long period of time can be seen from specimens of the 'same language' English, from its earliest written records to the present day. The specimens from the Bible provided in the above box are startlingly different, yet they belong to the same continuous tradition that is labelled 'English'. There are no sharp breaks between one phase of English and another: labels like 'old and 'middle' are ones used for convenience by scholars today. All speakers (and writers) would naturally have considered themselves to be using not just 'English', but a 'modern' type of English. Looking into the future, we can confidently predict that the colloquial English of the twenty-second century will be as different from present-day English as is the twentieth-first century from the eighteenth. As Jean Aitchison (1991: 76) poetically puts it, 'a change tends to sneak quietly into a language, like a seed, which enters the soil and germinates unseen. At some point it sprouts through the surface.' Historical linguists see it as a major challenge to chart out how and why such long-term and far-reaching changes occur. There are several reasons why the study of such change has become as much the business of sociolinguists as of historical linguists:

- Prescriptivism, the dominant ideology in language education, holds that changes in language norms occur to the detriment of the language, and are a result of sloppiness, laziness and a lack of attention to logic. Sociolinguists feel that there is thus a need for a more scholarly understanding of the processes of change and their social contexts.
- Sociolinguists have shown that variation and change in language go hand in hand. Changes within a speech community are preceded by linguistic variation. In Chapters 2 and 3 we showed how language variation occurs as a result of regional, social and stylistic differentiation. On the other hand, if a change occurs in one speech community and not in another, such change is the cause of variation between the two communities.
- Social groups within the same speech community may react differently to changes that are occurring, in terms of their attitudes and choices of variants.

4.2   MODELS OF LANGUAGE CHANGE

The main focus of this section will be on the way in which sound changes spread through a speech community. The main model which we consider here is the variationist model of change, which follows from the principles discussed in Chapter 3; we also consider complementary models regarding the way changes spread viz. (a) lexical diffusion and (b) the 'gravity' model.

Variationist Approaches to Change

In an important paper, Weinreich, Labov and Herzog (1968) showed that tracking down changes required close attention to the language system as well as the social system. All change is preceded by variation. This is not the same as saying that all variation leads to change. As an example of variation without change, we return to the example of *-in* and *-ing*. In Chapter 3, we discussed the seminal study of variation in the use of these variants in a New England setting by Fischer (1958). This variable (ing) has been found to have roughly similar social and stylistic patterns in many other parts of the English-speaking world: Norwich (Trudgill 1974), Ottawa (Woods 1991) and Australia (Horvath 1985). In none of these places does the variable seem to be undergoing change. In fact, the coexistence of *-in* and *-ing* is a highly stable feature of the history of English, going back to two different suffixes in Old English (c. AD 400 to c. 1100). These suffixes merged grammatically, but came to serve new functions indicating stylistic and social differences (Houston 1985). The stylistic and social stratification of (ing) in New England and Norwich were outlined in Chapter 3. Labov (1989) notes further how this variable (ing) is also stable in respect of the grammatical conditioning in three different continents where English is widely used. That is, in the USA, England and Australia, the variant *-in* occurs in the following environments in decreasing order of frequency:

- progressives and participles (e.g. *She is playing*)
- adjectives (e.g. *a flying fish*)
- gerunds (e.g. *Walking is good for health*)
- nouns (e.g. *ceiling, morning*).

When speakers produce *-in* rather than *-ing* it is most likely to be with participles like *playin'* rather than nouns like *ceilin'*. All of this suggests that the variation associated with (ing) has been stable since the early Middle English period at the social and the grammatical levels.

Linguists have a greater interest in variables undergoing change, as in the case of the centralising of diphthongs in Martha's Vineyard and in the spread of postvocalic (r) in New York City. By studying how variation triggers change in contemporary speech communities, sociolinguists have been able to make inferences about how similar changes must have occurred in past centuries. There is interest in how and why changes begin, what type of person or social group is likely to be an originator of change, and how new forms spread at the expense of older ones. Not all of these questions have been fully answered, though it is possible to outline the main steps in the model provided by Weinreich et al. (1968). Since the model has been principally concerned with sound change, our exemplification in the rest of this chapter is from studies of accent. In principle, with minor modification, the model could be used to describe long-term grammatical changes in a language.

1. The basis for linguistic change lies in the ever-present 'low-level' phonetic variability of ordinary speech. ('Low level' refers to minute phonetic differences between sounds which are often not noticed by members of the speech community.)

2. For reasons which appear arbitrary linguistically, a given phonetic variable (out of the many found in ordinary speech) becomes socially significant as a marker of group identification and stylistic level.

3. As a result of this sociolinguistic marking, the variable attains linguistic significance. ('Markers' were discussed in section 3.2.) That is, what was once purely phonetic variation becomes a linguistic variable of the sort discussed in section 3.4. While many linguistic variables are stable, in cases of language change one variant tends to be generalised or extended to new linguistic environments.

4. This 'new' variant may also be extended to new social groups.

5. The variant may eventually spread through the vocabulary system of the language and throughout the whole speech community (though opposing social processes might block the generalising of some rules).

6. The variant then becomes part of the community's repertoire: the sound change has been completed. (Adapted from Hock 1991: 648)

To make the outline more concrete, we exemplify it with the steps involved in the sound change involving centralised diphthongs in Martha's Vineyard, as outlined in section 3.2.

1. In the case of the diphthong /aɪ/, 'low-level variability' involves subtle variation in the articulation of the first element [a]. (In phonetic terms, this may be slightly fronted, backed, centralised, raised, rounded and so on.) The speech of the Chilmark fishermen contained certain 'older' centralised variants of this diphthong which had ceased to be used in most other parts of the island.

2. The variability becomes socially significant when a second social group (of young people identifying with the island), modelling itself on the first group, subconsciously adopts and exaggerates certain features, including the centralised Chilmark pronunciation of the diphthong.

3. The new speech feature gradually takes hold among the innovating group of younger people (30–45-year age group of English descent).

4. Centralisation spreads to other linguistic features, notably the first element of the diphthong [aʊ].

5. The new [əɪ] pronunciation becomes generalised as other social groups (e.g. other age and ethnic groups) model their speech on the innovating group.

Sociolinguists find it necessary to distinguish between two kinds of sound change: **changes from above** and **changes from below**. 'Above' and 'below' here refer simultaneously to levels of conscious awareness as well as position in the social hierarchy. 'Changes from above' involve new sounds introduced by the dominant social class. These are often consciously modelled on sounds used in other speech communities that have higher prestige. The increase in the use of postvocalic [r] in New York City is a change from above, whose impetus comes from the greater prestige of US speech varieties in which the variant is present. 'Changes from below' involve sounds that are originally part of the vernacular (in both senses of the word identified in Chapter 3), and which represent the phonetic processes that are based on articulatory process that make pronunciation easier. An example of such a process is the deletion of one consonant before another (e.g. in the pronunciation of /t/ in a phrase like *half-pas' five* or *trus' me*). Anthony Kroch (1978) has argued that changes from below are given full play in working-class dialects, whereas they are often arrested or suppressed by the middle class. There is also a gender effect in the implementation of sound change. In many studies involving change from above, including New York City (r), women have been found to be ahead of men in their scores for the 'new' variants. On the other hand, in changes from below, there seem to be more cases of men leading the change (Trudgill 1974: 95).

Lexical Diffusion

In addition to examining which groups are responsible for the initiation and spread of changes, linguists have been concerned with how a change spreads internally within the language. Lexical diffusion is the name of a theory that proposes that sound changes occur word by word. This theory evolved independently of the Labovian school, but it is complementary to and compatible with the interest of Weinreich et al. (1968) in long-term processes of change. The first hypothesis in lexical diffusion theory is that a sound change does not occur in all words or environments simultaneously. Rather, some environments are more conducive to the change (rather like the preference for postvocalic [r] at the end of words over the environment 'before a consonant'). Similarly, the change might be incorporated in some words before others. M. Chen (1972, 1976) analysed a number of sound changes that appear to have come about in this way. One is the loss of nasal consonants at the ends of words in French and the accompanying nasalisation of the vowel. This change resulted in the /n/ in a word like *bon* 'good' no longer being pronounced as a consonant; instead it was 'dropped' but not before leaving a nasalising effect on the vowel that preceded it. By a careful study of historical sources, Chen (1976) argued that this rule at first involved a few words, spread to others and then affected the entire vocabulary of French (see Figure 4.2).

A second hypothesis concerns the rate at which sound changes are effected in language. Chen proposed that the general rate of change in a language could be captured by an 'S-curve'. The idea behind an S-curve can be seen by reference to Figure 4.1. The horizontal axis measures intervals of time; the vertical axis measures the number of words in the language. Unlike a linear pattern, which would suggest a constant rate of change with an equal number of words being affected over equivalent units of time, the S-curve pattern suggests the following:

1. Initially the new pronunciation is to be found in a few common words. These are often words or groups of words important to a subgroup or subculture

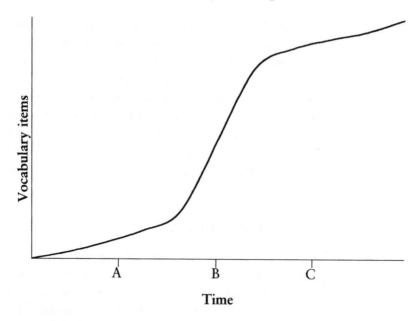

Figure 4.1   S-curve progression of sound change (from M. Chen 1972)

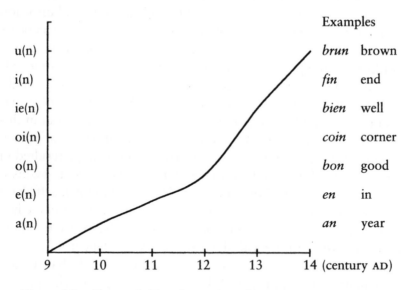

Figure 4.2   Change in French words ending in -*n* (from Aitchison 1991)

within the community. This is schematised as time phase A in the diagram, the period of innovation.

2. The change then spreads to other words at a relatively rapid rate, schematised by the steep rise in the curve over time phase B, the period of spread.

3. At the final stage, the rate of change slows down with the few last words to undergo the change at phase C, the completion of the change or period of maintenance

The Gravity Model

The model of lexical diffusion suggests how changes spread within a language. Dialectologists are also interested in how these changes spread across communities in a specific geographical area.

The 'gravity model' was proposed by Trudgill (1974) to describe the influence of bigger centres upon smaller ones. The analogy is taken from physics where bodies with larger mass exert a gravitational influence over smaller ones in their vicinity. Thus, though the moon is affected by the sun's mass, a greater influence is produced by the much closer Earth around which it therefore rotates. In Trudgill's model population size is analogous to mass in physics and geographical distance plays a similar role. Linguistic influence from one centre to the next is driven by proximity and population size. The equations provided by Trudgill are rather complex, and still subject to ongoing investigation. In the UK London is one centre of influence, whose norms spread out to larger cities and from there to smaller ones. Thus a town/city like Sunderland might be influenced by linguistic features from London, but only indirectly, since these would form a subset of forms that Sunderland shares with the neighbouring larger city, Newcastle. The model is complicated by issues of geographical boundaries and degrees of social contact.

Labov (2003), who prefers the term 'cascade model', shows how it works for the slightly easier case of the spread of new vocabulary. ('Cascade' suggests the flow of larger pools of water first upon smaller ones and from there to still smaller ones). Labov's example comes from variants for a sandwich made of cold cuts, cheese and garnish on a long roll, split in half: *subway, hero* and *hoagie*. Using advertisements in the yellow pages Labov showed how some of these terms diffused from a larger city to a smaller one. He focused particularly on the term *hoagie*, long favoured in Philadelphia. The term appears to have originated shortly after the First World War, when a variety of related spellings occur in the directories: *hoggie, hoogie, hoggie, hoagie*. By 1955 the most common spelling is *hoagie* and the term appears well established. In the neighbouring city of Pittsburgh *hoagie* makes an appearance in the directories in the early 1960s, a time when the more established term was *sub(marine)*. However, *hoagie* begins to take over and soon becomes the more common term. By what intermediate mechanisms do such terms spread? Labov argues that certain establishments in Philadelphia were providing the basic equipment needed to produce the sandwiches to neighbouring cities, and thus became associated with the product. The flow of influence was from the products of the bigger city to smaller ones. (Things later become more complicated by the appearance of the Subway chain of stores which independently promote the term *submarine* or *sub*.) The gravity model is not very easy to verify, since the subtleties of accent and human intentions, requiring sustained, long-term research, the kind of which we discussed in Chapter 3.

Sociolinguistic accounts of linguistic variability and social prestige are able to explain the far-reaching changes evident in the history of a language like English. As Crowley (1992: 215) puts it, English is the language of several large-scale societies that are socially stratified. Moreover, these societies are ones in which upward mobility is possible and people can aspire to reach greater social heights than those they were born into. Crowley points out further that not all societies are like this. In some countries, there is social stratification that is fixed: once born into a particular

---

Some studies of speaker agency in language change

Historical linguists have long tried to explain language change by examining a language as a structural system that carries its own predilection for change. Roger Lass (1997), for example, spoke provocatively of a "speaker-free linguistics". Sociolinguists, as we have seen, tend to foreground the social context and sociolinguistic differentiation instead. Current scholarship, in addition, stresses the role of ideas and beliefs about language (often termed 'language ideologies' or 'metalinguistic discourses'). Speaker agency is increasingly coming to be seen as an important, rather than marginal, factor in language change. Evidence is accumulating that speakers can and do make conscious changes to their languages and linguistic practices, often with the intention of building a linguistic identity that contrasts that those associated with other varieties:

- Donald Laycock (1982) gives the example of Uisai – a Papuan language – where speakers deliberately switched masculine and feminine gender agreement markers in order to make the local dialect more different from the dialects of neighbouring villages.
- Sarah Thomason (2001) reports that speakers of Ma'a (also called Mbugu) in Tanzania deliberately maintained pronunciations which marked their cultural distinctiveness and difference from the speakers of the surrounding Bantu languages.
- Don Kulick (1992) gives an example of a deliberate innovation from his field work in Papua New Guinea. At a local village meeting a conscious decision was taken by the villagers to change one central word; instead of the usual word for 'no', *bia*, a new word, *buɲe*, was to be introduced as a marker of local identity. The purpose of this change was to emphasise the village's difference from the surrounding villages whose residents used a similar form of speech.

group, there is little or no hope of moving out of it. The caste system of India is more or less like this, as is the division on the Pacific island of Tonga into commoners, nobility and royalty. Detailed sociolinguistic research on sound change in such traditional (non-industrialised) communities is still in its infancy (an example of such research is Lippi-Green 1989).

Real and Apparent Time

It is sometimes possible for linguists to undertake comparative studies over time to show the progress of a sound change. More often, it is not possible for reasons of finances and resources to do such long-term studies, especially since sound changes may take decades, and even centuries, to reach their conclusion. To overcome problems like these, it is quite common for linguists to undertake 'apparent-time' studies. A community is divided into age groups which are studied intensively for a short period to examine whether any differences occur. Where older age groups show low use of a variant while younger groups show increasingly greater use, we can *assume* that there is a change going on in 'real time'. (This was the procedure in the Martha's Vineyard study.) However, differences in language use between age groups are not always an indication of linguistic change. In the case of slang, for instance, an apparent-time comparison of two age groups (say above 30 years of age and below 30) might show that the younger group uses slang extensively while the other does not. To conclude from this that slang is on the increase in real time is not really warranted. Slang occurs in cycles generationally, with young people sweeping into it in adolescence and moving out of it as they grow older. The term 'age grading' is used to refer to such stable differences between age groups.

Like

Students at the University of Cape Town were asked in a first-year lecture on language change in 2007 to write down a linguistic feature which they thought distinguished their speech from that of their parents. Many of the students having English as their main language commented on the use of *like*. As one student put it: 'Words like *like* are, like, so overused . . . like'.

There are three long-standing uses of the word like in English:

- As a verb (*I like bananas*);
- As a comparative preposition (*He eats like a pig*).
- As a noun (*We will never experience the like again*).

There are three newer uses which are typically associated with young speakers, and which are diffusing worldwide across varieties of English:

- As a 'quotative' which introduces reported speech. Since *like* in this context is always used with the auxiliary verb to be it is also called the 'be like' form. (E.g. *I'm like why did you do that?*)
- As a hedge, that is, a mitigating device which lessens the impact of an utterance (*My parents like hate you*).
- As a discourse particle which is used to focus the hearer's attention and to sustain conversation (*I'm like really struggling with this assignment*).

Sociolinguists have been very interested in the origins and diffusion of *like*. These uses were first noted in the 1970s and in the US are associated with "Valley Girl speech" (i.e., the speech of teenage girls from San Fernando Valley in Los Angeles, as reflected in Frank Zappa's popular 1982 song *Valley Girl*).

Jennifer Dailey-O'Cain (2000) showed in an empirical study that the new uses of *like* are more common among younger speakers. She also found that it was used more by women; however, the gender differences were small and not statistically significant. Frequent use of *like* also affects the way people are perceived. Using the matched-guise technique, O'Cain found that older speakers who used *like* (with quotative, hedge and discourse functions) were evaluated as younger than they actually were. Speakers who made frequent use of *like* were also seen as more 'friendly', 'successful' and 'cheerful', but also as 'less intelligent' and 'less interesting'.

Sally Tagliamonte and Alex D'Arcy (2004) took a closer look at quotative *like* in Canadian English. Comparing interview data from 1995 with data from 2002–3, they found that the percentage of quotative *like* increased from 13 per cent to 58 per cent among those aged 18–28, thus reflecting rapid language change in real time. Gender had been found to be non-significant in 1995. By contrast in 2002–3 female speakers were found to use quotative *like* markedly more than male speakers. This shows that in linguistic change gender effects are not always visible from the outset, but can emerge as the change proceeds. Tagliamonte and D'Arcy doubt whether quotative *like* could be an example of age grading. They cite the work of Singler (2001), who showed that quotative *like* is also current among speakers well into their thirties. This indicates that we are probably dealing with an example of language change in progress, visible in real and apparent time.

Real-time Verification of Apparent-time Studies

Labov's study of the stratification of English in New York City was very much an apparent-time study, yet he used it to make broad inferences about the nature of sound change generally and the particularities of sound change in New York. To repeat this study and confirm his conclusions in real time would require an enormous amount of time and financial resources. However, it is not surprising that the shorter, easy-to-handle pilot study involving the three department stores has been replicated. Joy Fowler (1986) and Jeff Macdonald (1984) separately repeated the departmental store study, two decades after Labov, in an attempt to ascertain the extent of change in [r] usage in New York City. We focus on the work of Fowler, which managed to replicate Labov's methodology more closely than the other study. The only modification necessary was that, as Klein's (the low-price store) was no longer in operation, Fowler replaced this with May's, a store of similar size and with a similar clientele. Like Labov, Fowler counted the percentage of time that people produced postvocalic [r] in the utterance *fourth floor* (said twice as you might recall). As Figure 4.3 shows, in all three stores the figures for 1986 are higher than the 1962 figures. Change in real time *has* taken place. In particular, the following is observable in the follow-up study:

- The percentage of speakers who used 'all [r]' (i.e. [r] four times) increased in all three stores in real time.
- The greatest increase for 'all [r]' is shown at Saks, the highest-status store (though the overall increase is not very great).
- For 'some [r]' (i.e. use of postvocalic [r] in one, two or three of the four possible instances), all stores show a small increase.
- May's shows the greatest increase for use of 'some [r]', though again this increase is not very great.

Labov's (1994: 91) summary of this study is as follows:

> The precise replication of the Department Store Study shows that the sociolinguistic structure of the speech community is perhaps even more stable than anticipated. Under the pressure of the new *r*-pronouncing norm, New York City speech is changing slowly. Contrary to what I originally expected, the hypercorrect behaviour of the lower middle class, reflected in the pattern of Macy's employees, has not resulted in any sudden advance of *r*-pronunciation as a whole.

Two possibilities exist as to why change has not occurred in the intervening two decades to the extent predicted. The first possibility is that Labov's 'hypercorrection' hypothesis has not held up. That is, greater use by the lower middle class than the highest-status group in formal styles does not advance the change in progress appreciably. Hypercorrection as a feature of deliberate styles may not have a particularly great effect in change in vernacular norms. The second, and equally likely, possibility is that change in (r) usage is still at an early stage. In this view, the variant [r] is at the

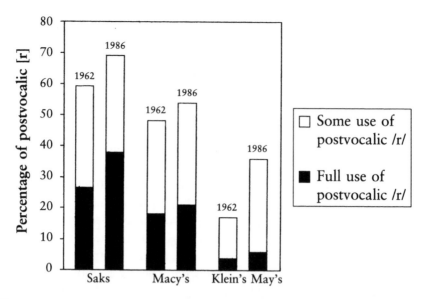

Figure 4.3 A real-time comparison between scores for postvocalic /r/ in New York City department stores in 1962 and 1986. Based on Labov (1972a) and J. Fowler (1986)

lowest segment of the S-curve of change, and a steep rise in [r] pronunciation in the next phase can be anticipated.

Forty years after Labov's groundbreaking study on Martha's Vineyard, two studies attempted to evaluate whether his predictions were borne out: viz. that there was change in progress over real time and that whilst initially structural in nature, this change was fuelled by a sense of social difference from the mainland. Interestingly the two studies, both deemed worthy of scholarly publication, came to different conclusions (Blake and Josey 2004; Pope et al. 2007). It is not our intention to focus *ad nauseam* on Labov's early studies, but the two follow-up studies assume great importance for testing the methods and conclusions of variationist sociolinguistics The first study came to conclude that the differences between island and mainland had been minimised in the intervening 40 years, and that centralisation of the diphthong (aɪ) was again receding, showing accommodation to mainland norms. The latter study, however, showed that centralised variants of both the (aɪ) and (au) diphthongs were on the increase in the ways predicted by Labov. It is too early to explain the conflicting results, but some pointers exist. First, the Blake and Josey study limited itself to the (aɪ) diphthong, whereas the second looked at both diphthongs, of which the 2nd had started to show greater centralisation than the 1st since in the 1960s. Had the first study looked at this variable (aɪ) it might have picked up some conflict in its results. Second, the Blake and Josey study was limited to one area of the island (Chilmark), whereas the second study covered all the areas of Labov's original fieldwork. It is possible that this skewed the results of the first study. Third, and most worryingly for the field, the role of the interviewer was a possible source of discrepancy. The first study involved a student from the mainland (Meredith Josey), working during the fieldwork in spring and early summer as an *au pair* for a family of long standing on the island and who relied to a large extent on their contacts. Was there accommodation to this mainlander having contacts with local families of high standing? The second study relied on a complete outsider as interviewer, a Scottish student (Jennifer Pope) who lived over, and undertook her interviews in, both winter and summer. Fourth, Blake and Josey undertook an acoustic analysis while Pope, Meyerhoff and Ladd carried out auditory analysis of the diphthongs. It is possible that this could be a source of discrepancy between the two studies. Guy Bailey (2002: xx) once remarked that replicating previous fieldwork was like stepping into the same river twice. It does look as though the Pope, Meyerhoff and Ladd study managed a more reliable stepping in, but another follow-up is needed to resolve the debate. At least both studies concur with Labov's insights into the link between variation and change on one hand and social factors on the other.

4.3   VERNACULAR MAINTENANCE AND CHANGE

Much research within the Labovian tradition has focused on the role played by the upwardly-mobile lower middle-class in processes of language change. It has been argued that most people will adopt linguistic variants which are associated with high social prestige while rejecting stigmatised, low-status variants. Despite the assumed social advantage of adopting such linguistic prestige forms, people in many inner cities and rural areas continue to maintain low-status variants in their speech. Sociolinguistic research has shown that the concept of social network is important for the understanding of such strategies of vernacular maintenance. Social networks were first used in a sociolinguistic study of Belfast which will be discussed in some detail in the following section.

Language and Social Networks: The Belfast Study

In their study of vernacular maintenance in Belfast, James and Lesley Milroy focused on three close-knit and relatively cohesive, lower working-class communities in Belfast, where vernacular use was common and widespread. Following Labov's study of vernacular use by black adolescents in Harlem (1972b), the Milroys formed the hypothesis that the use of vernacular forms is associated positively with the speaker's degree of integration into the community's **social network**. The concept of social network has been used successfully in anthropological research and refers to the informal and formal social relationships that individuals maintain with one another. Two criteria are particularly important for the description of networks: density and multiplexity. **Network density** refers to the number of connections or links in a network. In a low-density network, individuals usually know the central member but not each other (Figure 4.4.a). In a high-density network, the members of the network are known to each other and interact with each other regularly (Figure 4.4b).

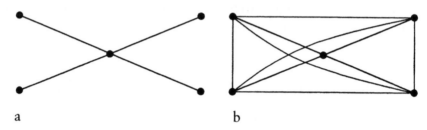

a   b

Figure 4.4 Low-density (a) and high-density (b) network structure (adapted from Coates 1993: 87–8) (dots represent individuals, lines represent the social links between individuals)

Multiplexity refers to the content of the network links. When individuals in a network are linked to each other in more than one function (co-employee, relative, friend, neighbour, member of the same sports club and so on), anthropologists speak of a multiplex network. A network in which the members are linked to each other in only one capacity (for example, co-employee) is called a uniplex network.

Dense and multiplex networks are typically found in rural villages and urban working-class areas. Such close-knit networks are also typical of the upper classes and the political elite, while the networks of the upwardly-mobile middle classes are characterised by uniplex ties and low network density (L. Milroy 1980: 179). Anthropological research since the 1950s has shown that dense and multiplex networks often act as norm-enforcement mechanisms, imposing all kinds of behavioural norms (dress, conduct, language use) on their members. The social and linguistic norms enforced are, however, not necessarily the prestige norms

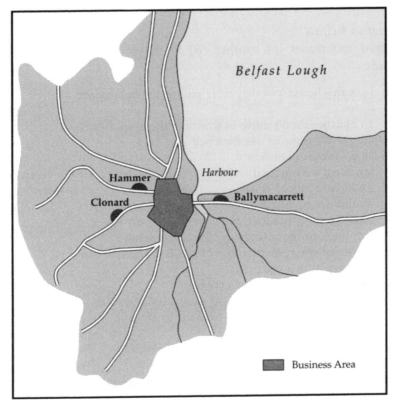

Map 4.1 Map of Belfast showing location of the inner-city areas studied by Milroy

of the wider society. Vernacular norms which symbolise solidarity with the other members of the network can equally be enforced by the local network.

Milroy carried out the fieldwork for the study during 1975–6 in three different working-class areas of Belfast: Ballymacarrett (East Belfast, Protestant), the Clonard (West Belfast, Catholic) and the Hammer (West Belfast, Protestant). All three areas were lower working-class communities and haunted by what Lesley Milroy has called 'social malaise[:] unemployment, sickness, juvenile crime, illegitimacy and premature death from disease' (1980: 72). Isolation from the mainstream, upwardly mobile society, however, fostered social solidarity. Hence dense, multiplex network patterns were found in all three communities. Male networks were particularly close in Ballymacarrett, where most men worked in the local shipyard and spent their work and leisure time almost exclusively in the local community. The Hammer and the Clonard, on the other hand, had lost their source of local employment with the decline of the linen industry. As a result, unemployment was high in both areas (between 35

Banter in Belfast

S (aged 19) teases his mother (B) in the presence of four of his friends.

B: I got this house 'cos they were pulling the bungalows
   down   (quiet)
S: ah but they didn't move us from out there/ so they
   didn't/ We came of our own bat   (louder)
B: ah we moves ourselves   (quiet)
S: squatted/ we squatted   (very loud)
B: we did not indeed squat   (even louder)
S: we did/ we squatted   (loud)
B: when you're a squatter you've no rent book/ I've a
   rent book to show anybody/ I've a rent book   (loud)
S: ah you're not a squatter now/ but when you first came
   here you were a squatter   (loud)
B: I've a rent book from the very first   (loud)
S: when you first came here you were a squatter/ 'cos
   I remember/ I had to climb over the yard wall
   and all   (S's friends laugh)
B: alright we had to get in that way (quiet)
S: squat (loud)
B: we didn't dear/ a squatter is someone that doesn't
   pay rent/ I've paid my rent book/ uh this about the
   third or fourth rent book I've got issued to me now   (quiet)
                                              (from Milroy 1980: 64–5)

[The symbol / is used to indicate a pause]

and 40 per cent), and local networks had been disrupted as ever more members of the community had to find employment outside the area.

An important concern of the research was how to gain access to the vernacular in its most natural form. The situation was complicated by the political and social conditions in Belfast, where outsiders to the community were usually viewed with suspicion. Milroy was able to enter the community as a 'friend of a friend', legitimately claiming ties with students who originated from the area. She was then able to meet further informants on the basis of the social networks associated with the initial contact. This fieldwork strategy, which is used widely in anthropology and sociology, is called **participant observation**, and implies that the researcher becomes part of the community which he or she is studying. Being neither an insider nor a real outsider to the community made it possible for Milroy to collect a variety of natural speech styles in different situational contexts without violating community norms of interaction (1980: 56). Instead of formally

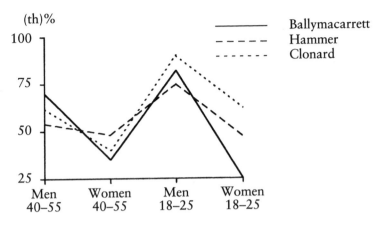

Figure 4.5 Frequency of deletion of (th) between vowels in Belfast
(L. Milroy 1980: 128)

conducting sociolinguistic interviews, Milroy was able to record natural conversations between the informants (see the box 'Banter in Belfast').

Milroy carried out a quantitative analysis of the data collected for forty-six speakers. The analysis showed that the use of several phonological variables was clearly stratified according to gender in the three working-class areas. The effect of gender on linguistic variation was most prominent for the voiced interdental fricative (th). In Belfast, vernacular (th) is often deleted between vowels (the word *mother*, for example, is pronounced [mɔər] in Belfast vernacular). Figure 4.5 shows that in both age groups (18–25 and 40–55 years) women used noticeably fewer vernacular variants than men. This pattern was most noticeable in the younger generation.

Although all informants were part of the local community in their area, there were differences between men and women regarding the degree of integration into the community network. To measure the integration of each informant into the social network of the community, Milroy (1980: 139–43) developed a six-point scale from 0–5 to indicate the degree of density and multiplexity of an individual's network (the so-called *Network Strength Scale* or NSS). According to Milroy's analysis, male network scores were notably higher than female scores, which implies that men had more and stronger ties to the local community than women. Of the three neighbourhoods, Ballymacarrett, where the pattern of gender stratification for (th) was most clearly marked, showed the closest relationship between gender and integration into the local network. In Ballymacarrett, men tended to be strongly integrated into the local community network. Most women on the other hand, worked outside the area, and their integration into the local network was therefore rather weak. Not only were the network patterns for men and women sharply different in Ballymacarrett, men's and women's activities were also separated and gender roles were

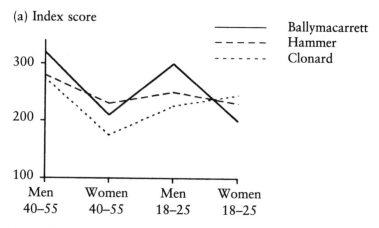

Figure 4.6 Backing of /a/ in three Belfast communities (L. Milroy 1980: 124)

clearly defined. The relationship between gender and integration into the network allowed Milroy to advance an explanation for the high degree of vernacular use by men when compared with women: men's higher levels of vernacular use were interpreted as a result of their stronger network ties. These stronger network ties acted as a norm-enforcement mechanism, supporting the use of local speech norms.

The link between integration into the network, gender and vernacular use also existed in the Clonard. On some linguistic variables, however, the situation was reversed for the younger generation, that is, young women showed greater use of certain vernacular variants than men. The graph given in Figure 4.6 represents the frequencies of vernacular forms for the vowel variable (a). In Belfast vernacular, the vowel (a) is typically pronounced as a back vowel. A five-point scale (ranging from 1 for tokens with [æ] to 5 for tokens with [ɔə] or [ɔˤ]) was used to measure the degree of vowel-backing.

Figure 4.6 shows that in the Clonard young women used backed variants of (a) at a particularly high level, even more frequently than young men from the Clonard.

Backing of /a/ is a relatively recent phenomenon and has been identified as a change in progress. It seems that the young Clonard women, who all work in a store outside the Clonard community, have adopted this innovation through their casual but regular interactions with customers from other localities of Belfast. Furthermore, because of social changes which took place in the area, young Clonard women had much stronger network ties than Clonard men. These strong local network ties then facilitated the spread and maintenance of the new vernacular variant within their own group. Milroy and Milroy have described the young women from Clonard as **early adopters**. Such early adopters of a linguistic change are typically closely integrated into the local network, but at the same time have regular but brief contacts with people from outside their social network. Linguistic **innovators,** on the other hand, were identified as marginal to the social group adopting the innovation, that is, they are linked to the network of the adopting group only by single, weak ties (Milroy and Milroy 1985b, 1992; see also Rogers 1995).

The Belfast study is an important contribution to the understanding of language change and language maintenance in a community. Language use, according to the Milroys, is influenced by both status and solidarity. Use of the standard language is associated with high social status, while the use of the vernacular indicates solidarity with local people, customs and norms. Vernacular use is typical in dense and multiplex network structures, which can be found in rural areas and the old urban working-class districts, where solidarity with the group encourages and demands the use of local, vernacular forms. While dense and multiplex networks function as a conservative force for the maintenance of the vernacular forms, a break-up of the traditional network patterns can initiate linguistic change (Milroy 1980: 162–3).

Dialect Loss and Maintenance in a Divided City: The Berlin Vernacular

The findings of the **Berlin Urban Vernacular (BUV)** project, which was carried out in the early 1980s under the leadership of Norbert Dittmar and Peter Schlobinski, give further support to Milroy's hypothesis of the strong relationship between vernacular maintenance and integration in a local community.

The political division of Germany into two separate states, the *Federal Republic of Germany* (FRG) in the west and the *German Democratic Republic* (GDR) in the east, was a direct result of Germany's defeat in the Second World War. The division was completed with the building of the Berlin Wall in 1961, which separated the territory of West Berlin from the eastern sector of the city. Only under specific conditions and limitations were West Berliners allowed to visit the eastern part of the city. East Berliners under the age of 65 years (62 years for women), on the other hand, were not allowed to visit the western part of the city at all. Social contact and communication was thus severely disrupted in the historical speech community of Berlin.

BUV (*Berlinerisch*) had received relatively little interest from traditional dialectologists, who saw it as a corrupted city slang, highly influenced by the German standard variety. Despite extensive linguistic influence from the standard variety, Low German dialect influence is still clearly visible in BUV. An important example is the retention of the Low German voiceless stops /p/, /t/, /k/ as opposed to the High German fricatives (see the examples

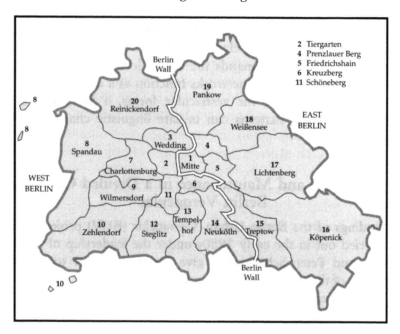

Map 4.2   Districts of Berlin (based on Dittmar et al. 1988a: 4)

given in the discussion of the Rhenish Fan in Chapter 2). These Low German relicts form a cluster of important linguistic variables in Berlin.

Three districts of Berlin were chosen for the data collection: the traditional working-class districts of Wedding (West Berlin) and Prenzlauer Berg (East Berlin), and Zehlendorf (West Berlin), a typical middle-class area.

The most important finding of the BUV project was that the pattern of linguistic variation reflected the political division of Berlin. While BUV variants had been maintained to a large extent in the East Berlin district of Prenzlauer Berg, a clear loss of typical BUV variants was observed in the affluent middle-class district of Zehlendorf. Speakers in the the West Berlin working-class area of Wedding were situated between the two extremes (see Figure 4.7).

Furthermore, research on speakers' attitudes showed that BUV was clearly stigmatised only in West Berlin, where it was seen as vulgar, working-class and an indicator of lack of education. The adjectives employed for the characterisation of BUV in West Berlin were, for example, *ordinär* (common), *vulgär* (vulgar), *schnoddrig* (brash) and *falsche Grammatik* (bad grammar), *tierischer Slang* (beastly slang), *Putzfrauensprache* (charwoman's language) (see Barbour and Stevenson 1990: 123; Schlobinski 1987). Standard German was generally seen as the legitimate prestige variety. In the East Berlin district of Prenzlauer Berg, on the other hand, BUV was not only commonly used but also perceived as highly prestigious. The stigmatised variety in East Berlin was Saxon, a German dialect spoken in a region south of Berlin.

An important reason for the stigmatisation of Saxon was that its speakers

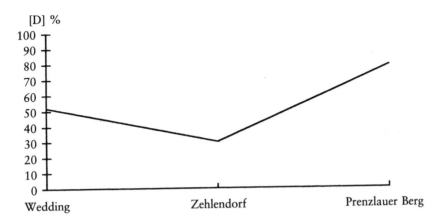

Figure 4.7   Dialect stratification in Berlin (Dittmar et al. 1988a: 17) (D denotes 'dialect index', i.e. the percentage of vernacular variants)

occupied many key political posts and positions in the repressive GDR government and administration. To some extent the use of BUV implied, therefore, resistance to the dominating language of the functionaries and the bureaucratic system of communism (Dittmar et al. 1988b: 33). Furthermore, though Wedding and Prenzlauer Berg are both traditional working-class districts, they have developed very differently since 1945. While Prenzlauer Berg has changed little and traditional social networks are still intact, Wedding has seen radical changes in the last forty years. The heavy influx of workers from West Germany and abroad has transformed the previously homogeneous population and caused a break-up of traditional networks.

The unification of Germany in 1990 led to wide-ranging social changes in the East, including the norms of language use. BUV use in East Berlin has

The stigmatisation of Saxon and Saxon-speaking people in East Berlin
Kommste inne Kaufhalle, ja, sprichste mit der Fleischabteilung, weil du da ( ) worden bist, EENE AUS SACHSEN, so 'ne sture und dämliche, von Tuten und Blasen keene Ahnung. Und, biste denn uf die Dame anjewie'n, wa, du fühlst dich als Berliner da irgendwie fremd, ja.

Translation:
Ya come into the department store, yeah, and talk with the women in the meat department 'cause you have been ( ), a woman from Saxony, a pig-headed and stupid one, doesn't know beans. And ya have to go to the woman, ya know? As a Berliner ya really feel like a stranger.
(Schlobinski 1987: 1,261)

declined considerably in the younger generation. However, some speakers refuse to assimilate and proudly insist on using *Berlinerisch*, even when talking to West Berliners. Many West Berliners seem to have little time for such strategies of linguistic identity maintenance, as the response of one West Berliner interviewed on television in 1992 shows: *die (Ostberliner) ha'm die Einheit jewollt und müssen sich nun unsren Jargon aneignen* 'the East Berliners wanted unity, so now they must learn to speak like us' (quoted in Schönfeld and Schlobinski 1995: 132).

4.4 NEW APPROACHES TO VARIATION AND CHANGE: THE NEED FOR INTEGRATION

In most of the sociolinguistic studies discussed so far, researchers have focused on the interplay between single units of pronunciation and the social meaning acquired within the community. Dissatisfied with this 'ato-mistic' approach, some researchers have focused instead on the interplay between different variables. They achieve this by using powerful statistical techniques which are able to consider several variables simultaneously, or by studying linguistic units as forming part of an integrated linguistic set whose members cannot be studied in isolation.

Patterns of Variation and Change in Sydney: A Case Study

To investigate the sociolinguistic patterns of variation and change in Australian English, the Sydney social dialect survey was carried out in the early 1980s under the leadership of Barbara Horvath (Horvath 1985). The study, which is in many ways indebted to Labov's work, contains important methodological innovations regarding the definition of what constitutes a speech community and the statistical procedures used for the analysis.

Since the end of the Second World War, Sydney has seen a massive influx of immigrants from non-English-speaking countries, mostly from Italy and Greece. Horvath, therefore, decided to include in her survey not only speakers from different social backgrounds, but also speakers of different ethnic origin: Anglos (Australians of English-speaking origin), Italians and Greeks. Including recent migrants into the study signalled that both native and non-native speakers of English were explicitly seen as being part of the Sydney speech community. This approach differs considerably from Labov's original definition of a speech community, which excluded non-native speakers (Labov 1966). The decision to include speakers from different ethnic groups also meant that ethnicity was included as an additional social variable, along-side the more conventional variables of age, gender and socioeconomic class.

A second important innovation of the study concerns the analytical methodology. Horvath used a multivariate statistical procedure called **principal components analysis**, which allowed her to consider in her final analysis more than twenty different linguistic variables simultaneously. Principal components analysis not only allows one to consider many different variables, but also helps to discover the structure of the relationships between the variables, that is, whether certain variables are correlated. Multivariate procedures are routinely used in many academic disciplines such as biology, zoology, medical sciences, social sciences, engineering and economics. In sociolinguistics, however, the use of these techniques has to date been sporadic. Researchers like Horvath have argued that instead of focusing on isolated variables, multivariate techniques allow the researcher to arrive at a closer understanding of linguistic **varieties** which can be seen as linguistic sets 'composed of many co-occurring features of phonology, morphology, syntax, and perhaps even discourse' (Horvath 1985: 153).

Traditionally, linguists have distinguished three sociolinguistic categories of Australian English: 'Cultivated', 'General' and 'Broad' Australian English. The inclusion of non-native speakers in the Sydney dialect survey, however, made it necessary to add two new categories: 'Accented' and 'Ethnic Broad' Australian English. 'Accented' refers to variants which are the direct result of transfer from the native language of the speaker. Such variants are generally not passed on to children and seem to have no influence on the development of the sound system of other varieties of Australian English. 'Ethnic Broad' consists of variants which have become ethnic markers of the English of immigrants and are frequently passed on intergenerationally. Five vowel variables (all diphthongs) were investigated in the study: (iy), (ey), (ow), (ay) and (aw).[1]

An investigation of the distribution of the different linguistic variants for these vowels showed the existence of a deep division within the Sydney speech community: a core speech community and a peripheral speech community were found to be clearly separated from each other. The periphery was characterised by the dominant use of vowel variants in the categories 'Accented' and 'Ethnic Broad'. All speakers in this peripheral group were adults of either Greek or Italian origin. Most of the members in this group were born outside Australia and had acquired English as a second language around the age of 20. On the other hand, 'Accented' and 'Ethnic Broad' variants were never used by members of the core speech community. An important non-linguistic characteristic of the core speech community was the disproportionate age distribution: ninety teenagers, but only forty adults were found in this group. While the teenagers came from all three ethnic groups, the adults in the core all belonged to the ethnic group 'Anglo'.

The ethnic and generational distribution of speakers across the core and the periphery allowed Horvath to describe the way in which migrants and non-native speakers enter into a speech community. This involved 'the formation of a peripheral community by the first generation, and then movement into the core speech community by the second generation' (1985: 178).

Horvath also showed that the core speech community could be divided further into four sociolects (i.e. social varieties). These four sociolects were characterised linguistically by quantitative but not categorical variation. In other words, speakers in the four groups used quantitatively varying mixes of Broad, General and Cultivated variants, but there was no group which never used a certain vowel variant, nor was there a group which used a certain type of variant exclusively. The general pattern from sociolect 1 to sociolect 4 shows a decrease of the 'Broad' and 'General' variants of the vowel variables and an increase of 'Cultivated' forms (Figure 4.8).

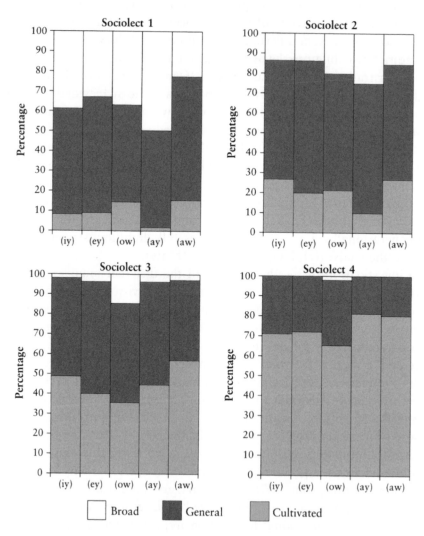

Figure 4.8   Distribution of the vowel variants across the four sociolects of the core speech community in Sydney (Horvath 1985: 77)

An investigation of the relationship between social variables and linguistic variation indicated that the four sociolects were primarily correlated with the social variables age and gender, while the effect of class was less pronounced. Figure 4.8 shows that the use of 'Broad' variants is most pronounced in sociolects one and two. Socially, the two sociolects are characterised by a high percentage of male speakers (over 60 per cent). Sociolects 3 and 4, on the other hand, are characterised by a high percentage of 'Cultivated' variants as well as a high percentage of female speakers.

Although gender and age stand out in the analysis, social class could also be shown to interact with linguistic variation in Sydney. In the linguistic continuum from sociolect 1 to sociolect 2, one sees a gradual increase of middle-class speakers and an equally gradual decrease of lower working-class speakers. This pattern parallels almost exactly the gradual increase of 'Cultivated' and the decrease of 'Broad' variants across the four sociolects. The percentage of upper working-class speakers across the sociolects, however, is more or less stable. See Figure 4.9.

The inclusion of different ethnic groups in the sample made it possible to examine the interaction of class, gender and ethnicity in Sydney. The pattern described above for the distribution of the three socioeconomic classes across the four sociolects was most visible for Anglo adults, but also for Anglo and Greek teenagers. For Italian teenagers, on the other hand, class played no role in the patterning of variation.

In 1965, Mitchell and Delbridge summarised the distribution of speakers across the three varieties of Australian English as follows: 'Broad' = 34 per cent, 'General' = 55 per cent and 'Cultivated' = 11 per cent. Based on the results of the Sydney dialect study Horvath modified the distribution of speakers for the early 1980s: 'Broad' (sociolect 1) = 13 per cent, 'General' (sociolects 2 and 3) = 81 per cent and 'Cultivated' (sociolect 4) = 6 per cent (Horvath 1985: 90). Furthermore, we have already mentioned the existence of generational differences: while adults were mainly found in sociolect 4, teenagers dominated in sociolects 2 and 3 where the General variants of the vowel variables were used most frequently. The differences between the distribution figures (1965 versus 1985), and the different linguistic behaviour of the two generations, can be interpreted as indicators of language change in progress. Speakers appear to have moved away from the two extremes of the Broad–General–Cultivated continuum and increasingly use vowel variables which are characteristic of General Australian English.

Barbara Horvath explained the twofold direction of language change in Sydney (from Broad to General and from Cultivated to General; Figure 4.10) with recent sociopolitical developments in Australia. Australian nationalism gained importance from the middle of the twentieth century. As a result, it became more and more acceptable to 'sound Australian',

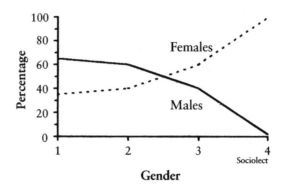

Gender

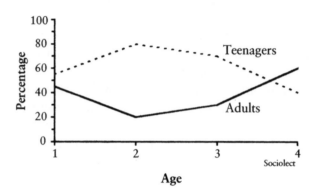

Age

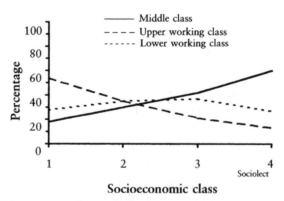

Socioeconomic class

Figure 4.9   Distribution of social characteristics across the three sociolects in Sydney (Horvath 1985: 79)

BROAD   ➡   GENERAL   ⬅   CULTIVATED

Figure 4.10   The direction of language change in Sydney

while 'Cultivated' variants were perceived as being too close to RP, and thus un-Australian. At the same time, many young, second-generation migrants avoided 'Ethnic Broad' and 'Broad' variants, using General variants instead. This was explained as a result of their desire to become part of Australian society and to distance themselves linguistically from their parents, who were part of the peripheral speech community.

However, second-generation migrants do not necessarily assimilate to Anglo norms in all contexts. First-generation migrants typically show variation patterns which are different from those of native speakers of the speech community (who have acquired the language from childhood). The situation is different for second-generation migrants, that is, those who arrive in the new country as young children (before the age of 7), or are born there. In the case of Australia, second-generation migrants acquire English (often, but not necessarily, alongside their heritage language) from childhood and are thus full members of the Australian-English speech community.

At the same time, they are also exposed to the second-language varieties of English of their parents' generation, and their identities continue to be shaped by their migrant background. While their language use is distinct from that of their parents, being clearly a variety of Australian English, it also shows – in specific contexts and with certain friends and acquaintances – reflexes of their ethnic identity and their early bilingual experiences in the home. The linguistic features used by these second-generation speakers in in-group interaction cannot necessarily be traced back to a single language. In Australia, this distinctly 'ethnic' language use is believed to have developed within **multi-ethnic adolescent peer groups** – consisting mostly of teenagers from Southern Europe (predominantly Italian and Greek) and the Middle East (predominantly Lebanese). This so-called 'ethnolect' of English is used primarily for identity display, reflecting the culturally hybrid identities of these speakers (situated between their cultural/linguistic heritage and the norms and traditions of the new society), and the communality of their experiences as non-Anglo (i.e. migrants from the UK, New Zealand or English-speaking South Africa do not take part in these identity formations).

As noticeable in the boxed extract, speakers themselves refer to this type of speech as 'Wogspeak' (or sometimes also 'Lebspeak', thus indicating the existence of a distinct Middle Eastern variety). Linguists such as Kiesling (2005) prefer the more neutral term 'New Australian English'. Although this variety is perceived as being distinctive, it is certainly not homogenous, and individual speakers use variants at different frequencies. A salient feature is the pronunciation of the suffix -er in words such as 'better' where it is pronounced in a more 'open' way, giving rise to variants such as [bɛra] (with variation in the /t/ as well). Other features include rounded front /u/, the voicing of voiceless stops (/p t k/), /th/ realized as /t/ and /d/ and the aspiration of /k/ (see Warren 1999; Clyne et al. 2000 for other features).

A pan-ethnic migrant variety
The Australian actor and comedian Simon Palomares, of Greek background, described the emergence of a pan-ethnic form of English on the Australian radio programme *Lingua Franca* (2004) as follows:

'We moved to Carlton in inner Melbourne, and it was like a migrant paradise. In Carlton in the '70s we weren't even ethnic, we were the dominant culture, everybody was from somewhere else, or if they weren't they didn't speak louder and slower to be understood. . . . It was here that the accent would have developed in an environment where we learned English from other migrants . . . . By and large, what we have is a Melbourne migrant accent that in some studies has already been branded as Wogspeak. Growing up in the inner city in Melbourne, our neighbours consisted mainly of Greeks, Italians, some Turks and later, Lebanese. And rather than each having their own accent, it was an accent that blended all into one new Australian accent. . . . It is an accent developed by kids whose English is not corrected at home, simply because English is not spoken at home, so a new set of organic rules have developed in the structure of speech . . . . Every now and then I still go to Lygon Street [a street in Melbourne's Italian quarter] to catch up with a schoolfriend of mine, and after a couple of minutes we always fall back into wogspeak, a collection of 'you knows', 'dis and dats', where elaborate words fall away to a subliminal understanding of our own language . . . . And it's not just an ethnic accent but also a class accent where us second-generation migrants regardless of education and success, tend to stay close to their original neighbourhoods. The closeness of these groups goes a long way to solidifying wogspeak as an established accent.

Stylised use of such ethnolects are common in public performances and media events with ethnicity as a dominant theme. In Australia, for example, there have been theatre shows and TV programmes such as *Wog Boys* and *Acropolis Now*. Similar phenomena – i.e. the emergence of a pan-ethnic variety distinct from native versions of a dominant language and the media appropriation of stylised forms of this ethnolect – have also been described for Sweden (Rinkeby Swedish – by Kotsinas 1988) and Germany (Auer 2003; Watzinger-Tharp 2004).

4.5 VOWELS SHIFTS: TOWARDS A HOLISTIC APPROACH TO DIALECT AND CHANGE

Current attempts to study clusters of features such as Horvath's Australian study are particularly promising in the area of vowel shifts. Vowel shifts are changes that operate across a whole set of vowels: for example, they

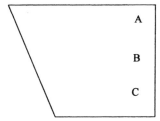

Stage 1: Showing three (back) vowels in a dialect.

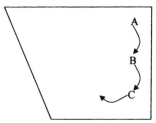

Stage 2: The chain shift. A moves towards B; B moves towards C;
C moves to centre (not necessarily in this order).

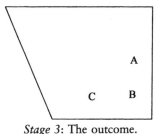

Stage 3: The outcome.

Figure 4.11   Sketch map of a hypothetical chain shift (dialects X
and Y)

may all be raised (in contrast to older dialects or the prestige dialects) or
lowered, fronted and so on. Such shifts are sometimes known as 'chain
shifts' because each change is related to the previous one, like the links of a
chain. The study of vowel shifts was pioneered by André Martinet (see e.g.
1952). Figure 4.11 shows a hypothetical chain shift, involving previously
similar dialects X and Y. After the chain shift dialect Y has vowels that are
consistently lower than those of dialect X. Martinet was particularly interested in the mechanisms of such vowel shifts. Was the shift set into motion
by the lowering of the high vowel (labelled 'A') which caused the other
vowels to be also lowered (a 'push chain'), or was it the low vowel (labelled
'C') which moved first, attracting the rest of the front vowels a step down
(a 'pull chain')? As a historical and structural linguist, Martinet's focus fell
on what types of chains were more common in the history of languages.
This structural interest in the types of shifts is shared by sociolinguists,
though it is not surprising that they should be equally concerned with

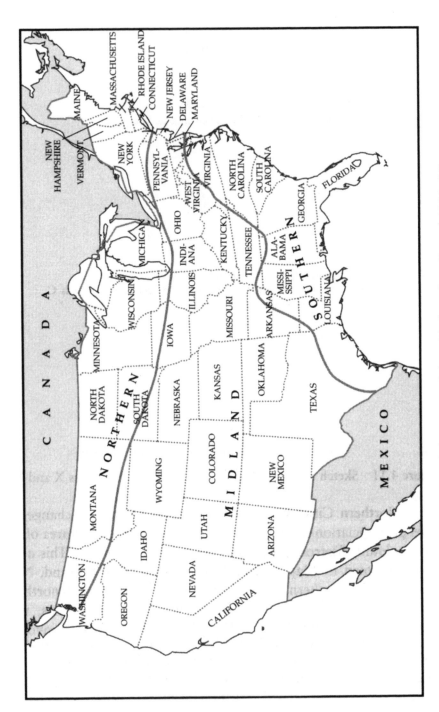

Map 4.3   The three dialect areas of the USA (based on Crystal 1995: 94)

their social differentiation within speech communities. Two vowel shifts in English dialects that are currently being studied by sociolinguists are the 'Northern Cities chain shift' and the 'Southern hemisphere shift'.

The Northern Cities Chain Shift refers to a series of changes in vowel pronunciation shown in cities of the northern dialect area of the USA, including Detroit, Chicago, Cleveland and Buffalo. This area, which is shown in Map 4.3, includes western New England, New York state, the northern parts of counties in Pennsylvania, northern Ohio, Indiana and Illinois, Michigan, Wisconsin and a less well-defined area extending westwards (Labov 1991). The shift involves six vowel sounds (phonemes) which may be heard as members of another phoneme by listeners from another dialect area, with some resultant confusion of meanings: *Ann* as *Ian*, *bit* as *bet*, *bet* as *bat* or *but*, *lunch* as *launch*, *talk* as *tock*, *locks* as *lax*. Labov's anecdote (1994: 185–6) about one unit of the chain shift might be helpful to those unfamiliar with the pronunciations involved:

> I first became acquainted with the Northern Cities Shift in 1968, during interviews in Chicago with a group of boys, 16–18 years old. One of them, Tony, introduced me to his friend [dʒæn]. Thinking that he had said 'Jan' I looked around for a girl. Then I realized that he was talking about his friend *John*.

The basic pattern of the shift in many cities is given in Figure 4.12a. In Detroit a complete rotation occurs with the backing of [ɛ] and [a] making

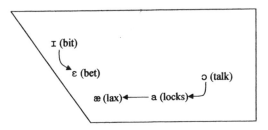

Figure 4.12a   Simplified sketch of the Northern Cities Chain Shift (based on Labov 1991: 17)

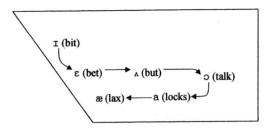

Figure 4.12b   Fuller Northern Cities Chain Shift in Detroit (based on Labov 1991: 15 and Eckert 1991: 222)

a full chain shift, as shown in Figure 4.12b. What is of particular interest to sociolinguists is the degree to which different groups participate in such shifts. For example, in her Detroit study (see section 3.4), Eckert found Burnouts to be well in advance of Jocks in their innovative use of [ɛ] and [a] and hence in their participation in the full Detroit shift. On the other hand, black speakers in the northern parts of the USA do not generally participate in the Northern Cities Chain Shift (Labov 1987: 72).

The **Southern Hemisphere shift** is the term used to describe another chain shift which occurs in South Africa and New Zealand (and partially in Australia), whose impetus lies in the influence of working-class British speech in these nineteenth-century colonies. Roger Lass and Susan Wright (1986) analysed the systematic shift which the short front-vowel series of South African English has undergone compared to other varieties like RP.

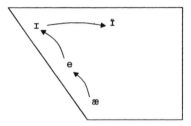

Figure 4.13a   The short front-vowel shift in South African English (based on Lass and Wright 1986)

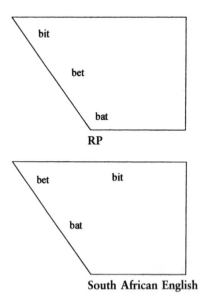

Figure 4.13b   Results of the shift: RP and South African front vowels compared, with reference to three key words

The two systems are geometrically related in the way depicted in Figure 4.13. Loosely speaking, the result of this shift is to make the South African pronunciation of a word like *bat* closer to RP *bet*; the South African pronunciation of *bet* sounds closer to RP *bit*; while the South African pronunciation of *bit* sounds intermediate between RP *bit* and the sequence *bVt* where V stands for the vowel in *hook*.

Speakers of English in these 'southern hemisphere' territories are classified by linguists as 'Cultivated', 'General' and 'Broad' according to a host of variables (Mitchell and Delbridge 1965). One of the key sets of variables is the vowel system which they typically use. In South Africa, 'cultivated' speakers use a vowel system close to RP without any vowel shift. 'Broad' speakers use the most advanced elements of the vowel shift.[2] The vast majority of first-language speakers of English have a vowel system that mediates between the two, showing some raising but not to the extent found in 'broad' South African English. It seems more feasible to analyse the vowels sociolinguistically as a set rather than isolating particular vowels for analysis. This is what L. W. Lanham and Carol Macdonald (1979) did when they tried to characterise typical white speakers of the different subvarieties:

Cultivated: Middle-class speakers having associations with England.

General: Middle-class speakers.

Broad: Mostly lower-middle or upper working class; identifying with the outdoors and sport; and significant contacts with Afrikaans-speakers, and hence partially influenced by Afrikaans norms.

Perception and Production Integrated: The Atlas of North American English

The culmination of twentieth-century work in regional dialectology is the *The Atlas of North American English* (Labov et al. 2006), primarily based at the University of Pennsylvania by Labov and his team of researchers. Previously known as the Phonological Atlas of North America, the project has been published as a large atlas with maps and text, with an accompanying CD that provides sound samples. It is the first national survey of the US and the first of English in North America. This project is informed by Labov's early work on social dialects and sound change as well as his more recent studies of vowel systems and of series of minute changes affecting entire vowel systems. Whereas Labov and other sociolinguists concentrated on intensive neighbourhood surveys in much of their work, the atlas is more broadly based, aiming to cover the whole of the US and Canada. Accordingly the methodology used was a telephone survey between 1992 and 1999 involving speakers born in urbanised areas with a population greater than 50,000. Interviews lasted between thirty and

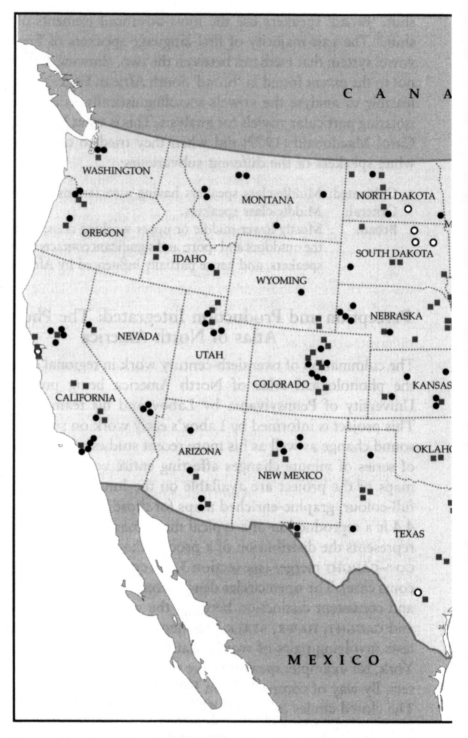

Map 4.4 Dialect map of the USA showing the merger of the vowels in COT and CAUGHT (from W. Labov et al. 2006)

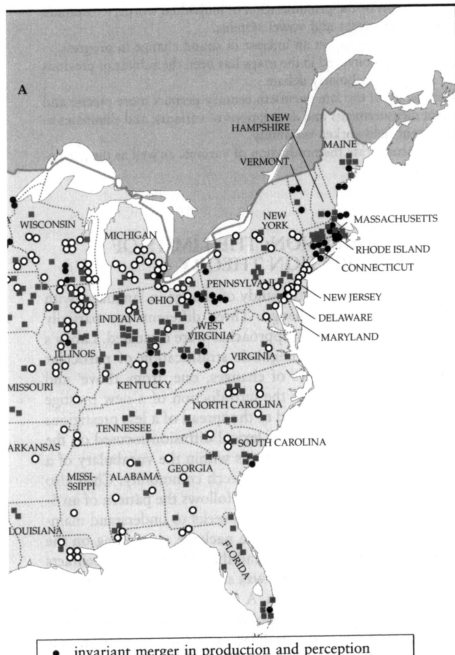

A

NEW HAMPSHIRE
MAINE
VERMONT
NEW YORK
MASSACHUSETTS
RHODE ISLAND
CONNECTICUT
NEW JERSEY
DELAWARE
MARYLAND
WISCONSIN
MICHIGAN
PENNSYLVANIA
OHIO
INDIANA
WEST VIRGINIA
VIRGINIA
ILLINOIS
KENTUCKY
MISSOURI
NORTH CAROLINA
TENNESSEE
ARKANSAS
SOUTH CAROLINA
MISSISSIPPI
ALABAMA
GEORGIA
LOUISIANA
FLORIDA

- • invariant merger in production and perception
- ○ invariant distinction in production and perception
- ■ variable

forty-five minutes and covered the kinds of topics discussed in Chapter 3, with much less emphasis on personal narratives and a greater focus on recent developments in the respondent's city and on specific lists of words and sentences (see Labov et al. 2006: 28–9). Map 4.4 is a reproduction of a typical map emanating from the project. It represents the distribution of a process that has come to be called the COT–CAUGHT merger (see section 3.5 in connection with the Prinzivalli court case). The open circles denote areas where speakers have a clear and consistent distinction between the vowels in LOT, COT, STOCK and THOUGHT, CAUGHT, HAWK. Furthermore, these speakers respond in tests involving pairs of words that the vowels are different. (In New York, for example, speakers have the vowels [ɑ:] and [ɔ:] in these two sets. By way of comparison, in RP these are [ɒ] and [ɔ:] respectively.) The closed circles in Map 4.4 denote areas where speakers have the same vowel in the COT–CAUGHT lexical sets, and where speakers say that the two vowels are the same in word-list tests. The black squares indicate areas where speakers show some variability or inconsistency. This work is a significant advance over traditional dialect surveys in several ways.

- Rather than displaying isolated and unrelated parts of language like vocabulary items or the pronunciation of individual words, it examines phonological processes and vowel systems.
- The maps are grounded in an interest in sound change in progress.
- The information conveyed in the maps has been the subject of previous intense study and scholarly debate.
- The technology of the early twenty-first century permits more precise and consistent acoustic measurements and descriptions of variants, and eliminates fieldworker variability to a large extent.
- The maps incorporate the production of variants as well as the perceptions of speakers.

4.6 CONCLUSION: THE LIMITS OF VARIATION THEORY

In this chapter, we focused on the study of change in language, with special emphasis on sound change. Several different but partially overlapping and complementary approaches were discussed. Labov's model stressed changes in the linguistic stratification of particular variables. He posited two types of changes, one 'from above' and another 'from below' to explain the introduction of a new prestige variant in a community as opposed to the spread of a less prestigious vernacular variant. Chen's model of lexical diffusion focused on the means by which a sound change spreads within the vocabulary of a particular speaker and/or a particular speech community. Chen also hypothesised that the rate of such change follows the pattern of an S-curve. Trudgill's 'gravity' model addressed the challenge of explaining how innovations spread in geographical space. Milroy's model of social networks seeks to understand maintenance and change as part of the same package, depending on the strengths of ties within a community and the nature of their contacts with outside groups. This approach was seen to apply in the dialect divide between East and West Berlin. A final concern of this chapter was the increasing emphasis in sociolinguistics on studying sets of variables (rather than isolated variables) in relation to societal patterns. In relation to this approach, the methodological innovations made by Horvath in her study of Australian English were cited. The study of ongoing vowel shifts in English in different parts of the world also relates to the attempt to study sets of related variables.

The study of linguistic variation has certainly revolutionised dialectology, historical linguistics and to a lesser extent other branches of linguistics. It has also been a defining feature of modern sociolinguistics. But there are some limits to its success. One is that the kind of variables identified as being the most salient in characterising a dialect are not necessarily the ones felt to be significant by lay people. Some of the general criticisms of traditional dialectology (see section 2.5) also apply to urban sociolinguistics. Notions like articulatory setting and intonation and rhythm remain a challenge to urban dialectology. A more general limitation is that its findings have to a large extent applied to western 'late capitalist' industrialised countries in which one language is dominant. There are not many large scale studies using variationist methods in countries in which the majority of people are multilingual or in countries with large rural populations. Linguists working in multilingual societies have found other types of variation to be more salient (Chapter 5). Another shortcoming of the paradigm is that it does not deal with language as an interactive process but focuses on the form of language and variation within the system. This has consequences for the way in which style (Chapter 6) and even gender (Chapter 7) are conceived in the model. The thesis that language reflects society rather than being caught up in societal organisation in more complex ways, is also a source of disaffection (Chapter 10).

Notes

1. Apart from the five vowel variables, Horvath also examined variation on five consonantal variables, the morpheme -*ing* and the intonational feature of high rising tone.
2. Lanham and Macdonald used different terminology, essentially corresponding to 'cultivated', 'general' and 'broad'.

5
LANGUAGE CHOICE AND CODE-SWITCHING

5.1 INTRODUCTION

The sociolinguistic studies discussed in Chapters 3 and 4 have been concerned with language variation in monolingual communities, or at least with variation within a single language in communities where more than one language is spoken. This chapter represents a change of focus. We look at language variation, and language use, in bi- and multilingual communities: at how bi-/multilingual speakers need to choose which language to use on any occasion, and at how speakers sometimes **code-switch**, that is switch back and forwards between languages, even during the same utterance.

A note on terminology
Most of the studies we shall discuss come from communities in which two or more languages are in daily use. We shall refer to these communities as *bilingual* (that is, the term 'bilingual' will be used here to avoid constant repetition of phrases such as 'bi- or multilingual'. Similarly, we shall sometimes use *language variety* as a neutral term when discussing general points that apply equally well to distinct languages or more closely related varieties (e.g. dialects or accents).

An assumption underlying much of the research discussed in this chapter relates to what has been termed the **indexicality** of language, or language varieties: the idea that language varieties are meaningful: they index, or point to a speaker's origin or of aspects of their social identity (for instance, their social class or ethnic group), but they also carry certain social values related to the speakers who use them and the contexts in which they are habitually used. Language varieties therefore constitute a meaning-making *resource* that may be drawn on in interaction with others. Section 5.2

below provides evidence from several studies of the meanings that may be attributed to different language varieties.

Later sections discuss patterns of language use, focusing mainly on bilingual communities but also drawing parallels with variable language use in monolingual settings. We look first at 'language choice' at a rather general level: to quote a highly influential researcher in the area, the pre-occupation here is with establishing 'who speaks what language to whom and when' (Fishman 1965). We then examine language use in specific contexts, looking at how, during the course of an interaction, speakers may adopt different language varieties or code-switch between varieties as a communicative strategy. Finally, we compare code-switching research with research on 'stylistic' variation in monolingual contexts such as those discussed in Chapters 3 and 4; we also review interpretations of speakers' variable language use that try to combine insights from research carried out in different contexts.

5.2   EVALUATION AND ACCOMMODATION: LANGUAGE VARIATION AS MEANINGFUL

A number of social psychological studies, carried out in both bi- and monolingual communities, have investigated how listeners respond to different language varieties. Many of these studies adopted a technique termed *matched guise*: the same speaker would be audio-recorded reading a passage in two or more different language varieties. The recordings were presented to listeners as coming from different speakers, and listeners were asked to evaluate each speaker along several dimensions. One of the original matched-guise studies was carried out in Canada by Wallace Lambert and his associates. Lambert et al. (1960) asked listeners to rate the same speaker reading out a passage in English and French and found that, in the late 1950s when this study was carried out, both French Canadian and English Canadian listeners rated the English guises more favourably than the French guises in several respects – in terms of both physical attributes (e.g. good looks) and mental/emotional traits (e.g. intelligence, dependability). French speakers were rated more highly in terms of sense of humour (by English Canadian listeners) and kindness and religiousness (by French Canadian listeners). These results have been added to and qualified in later studies, and attitudes themselves change over time (in Canada changing perceptions of French and English may be associated with the the increasing political mobilisation of French speakers in Quebec and surrounding areas that has taken place since the 1960s, and the development of policies to protect the French language – Heller 1992). However the main point which Lambert et al. established, that listeners are prepared to evaluate people on the basis of their language variety, has been found by several other researchers working in different contexts. Many early studies are reviewed in Giles and Powesland (1975).

Howard Giles himself carried out a series of studies of listeners' responses to British English accents (also reviewed in Giles and Powesland 1975). Giles found that a (male) speaker was rated as having higher social status when he adopted an RP accent than when he adopted a non-standard regional accent. When compared with certain regional accents (mild south Welsh, Somerset, northern English, Scottish-accented English), an RP speaker would also be rated more highly in terms of what Giles termed 'competence' (ambition, intelligence, self-confidence, determination and industriousness); on the other hand, in comparison with these regionally accented speakers, the RP speaker was given a lower rating for 'personal integrity' and 'social attractiveness' (seriousness, talkativeness, good-naturedness and sense of humour). Giles claimed that these positive associations could be a factor in the continuing maintenance of regional varieties of English. While these studies focused on British English accents, later studies report similar findings from other countries. For instance, Ball et al. (1989) report that speakers of 'cultivated Australian' are rated higher than speakers with 'broad' accents in terms of intelligence, competence, reliability, honesty and status; speakers with broad accents, however, are given higher ratings in terms of humorousness and talkativeness.

The matched-guise technique used in these studies was intended to hold constant factors other than the speaker's language variety that might affect how they were perceived (individual differences between speakers such as their voice quality, pitch of voice or rate of speaking might affect listeners' perceptions). The technique is rather artificial, however: particularly when a speaker imitates several language varieties, there is a danger of resorting to stereotypes which may, in turn, evoke stereotyped reactions. A later study carried out in Wales attempted to overcome this problem. Peter Garrett, Nikolas Coupland and Angie Williams (1999) elicited teachers' and teenagers' attitudes towards young male speakers who used different varieties of Welsh English. Listeners were asked to listen to extracts from narratives recounted by these speakers, and to rate speakers according to several characteristics, including whether they liked the person, how Welsh they sounded, how well they were likely to do at school. In this case, the researchers identified several factors that distinguished the speakers' performances (including the variety of English spoken, but also speed and quality of delivery, and the type of story being told). They used complex statistical techniques to relate these performance characteristics to the judgements made by listeners. Their analysis suggests that the way people evaluate speakers is likely to result from a combination of factors:

... we have evidence that social attractiveness, often said to be a recurrent accompaniment of 'nonstandard' dialects, may be achieved by quite different symbolic routes – and in our data, more importantly through innovative and humorous narrative-telling than by dialect alone. The data suggest that the dialect semiotic, while still powerfully active in some dimensions of self- and other-definition, works alongside other factors for young Welsh people, whose verbal performance styles have at least equal influence on social evaluations. (1999: 345)

The advantage of the approach adopted by Garrett et al. is that it allows systematic comparisons to be drawn between the potential effects, on listeners, of different speech characteristics. While Garrett et al. tried to use 'natural' extracts of speech, however, the process they adopted was still, necessarily, artificial, and this needs to be borne in mind in interpreting the findings. In addition to charges of artificiality, attitude tests have also been criticised on the grounds that they assume individuals hold a constant set of beliefs. In practice, the meanings attached to different language varieties are likely to be more ambiguous and to depend upon a range of contextual factors.[1]

Other researchers have used different means to elicit individuals' perceptions of language varieties. In a series of studies of **perceptual dialectology**, Dennis Preston asked informants in different areas of the USA to draw the location of regional varieties of US English on maps. Preston's informants' labelling of maps included value judgements of varieties, and he therefore investigated this systematically, asking the informants where the most, and least, 'correct' and 'pleasant' varieties of English were spoken. Map 5.1 below shows how informants in Michigan ranked different areas for 'correctness' (higher scores = ranked more highly in terms of correctness). Preston notes that the areas particularly associated with incorrectness, for these informants, were the South and New York City. By contrast, the informants gave their own state, Michigan, the highest score in terms of correctness (not all states demonstrated this level of linguistic confidence). For an overview of this work see Preston (1989) and, more briefly, Niedzielski and Preston (2000).

Later work by Preston and Nancy Niedzielski (2000) discusses these studies as an aspect of **folk linguistics** (a term sometimes used to refer to the beliefs about language expressed by ordinary people, as opposed to linguists). Niedzielski and Preston also report on a more recent project, concerned with the views people express in discussion about language. Interviews with informants in Michigan confirmed some of the beliefs expressed on dialect maps. In terms of regional variation, for instance, speakers identified 'North' and 'South' as the major American speech areas: northern speech was seen as more correct and southern speech as more incorrect or improper, associated with relatively poor education. Niedzielski and Preston investigated other dimensions of regional variation, as well as perceptions of social factors associated with language use such as ethnicity; status; style, slang, register and taboo; and gender (2000, Chapter 3).

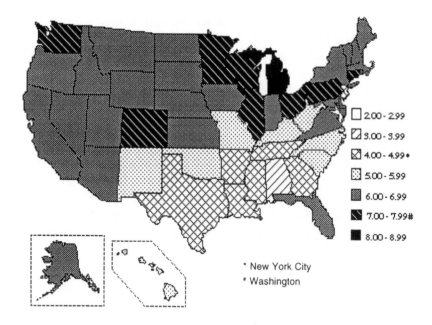

2.00 - 2.99
3.00 - 3.99
4.00 - 4.99*
5.00 - 5.99
6.00 - 6.99
7.00 - 7.99#
8.00 - 8.99

* New York City
# Washington

Map 5.1 Map of the USA showing Michigan informants' language 'correctness' ratings (cited Niedzielski and Preston 2000: 64)

Such evidence demonstrates that language varieties have a number of potential associations that may be drawn on by speakers and listeners. These associations are no doubt related to processes of language maintenance and change; at an individual level, they also help to explain why people vary the way they speak in interaction with others.

In addition to their studies of speech evaluation, Howard Giles and his associates have investigated such variation in the speech of individual speakers. Giles was particularly interested in how speakers changed the way they spoke according to the person they were talking to. This process was explained in terms of **speech accommodation theory** or, more broadly, **communication accommodation theory**. Giles argued that speakers accommodated to their interlocutor(s): they would tend to **converge** (adopt similar styles of speaking) when they wished to reduce the social distance between one another, and **diverge** (speak differently) when they wished to emphasise their distinctiveness or increase their social distance. An assumption underlying accounts of this process has been that convergence will be positively evaluated and divergence negatively evaluated. Speakers may converge or diverge along several different dimensions – choice of language in bilingual communities, use of certain accent or dialect features, and other vocal characteristics such as rate of speaking.

Many researchers have noted instances in which speakers accommodate

---

Accent accommodation

Speaker from the north-east of England, now living in the south-east:

> I don't think I've lost my accent altogether but when I do go back home and speak to my family I'm very much aware that I tend to slide across and speak in a sort of softer Northumbrian accent which is that of my mother [. . .] I've noticed in the local shops some of the staff have moved down from Newcastle, and when I find I'm talking to them I slip very quickly back into a northern accent and we joke about where we've come from, and it forms a common bond very quickly.

---

towards the speech of others. Peter Trudgill, whose work was discussed in Chapter 3, reanalysed some of his Norwich data, looking at his own speech in interviews with his informants. He found that his use of certain accent features closely mirrored that of his informants (Trudgill 1986). Similarly, Nikolas Coupland (1984) found that the accent of an assistant in a travel agency in Cardiff mirrored that of her customers so closely that it was almost as good an indicator of their social status as their own accent. Allan Bell (1984) found that newsreaders on New Zealand radio stations tailored their pronunciations to different audiences (depending on whether they were broadcasting on national radio or a local community station). Bell interpreted his findings in terms of what he refers to as **audience design** – the idea that speakers vary the way they speak primarily in response to an audience. This theory is broadly compatible with communication accommodation theory.

These and other studies provide support both for the existence of speech accommodation and for the usual interpretation of this process: that convergence will be positively evaluated, or be expected to be so, by listeners (that is, it was in Trudgill's, the Cardiff travel agent's and the New Zealand newsreaders' interest to be responded to favourably by their listeners). On other occasions, however, processes of accommodation and their interpretation are less straightforward. In a review of several aspects of speech accommodation, Howard Giles, Nikolas Coupland and Justine Coupland (1991) note that:

- Speakers do not necessarily accommodate to how their interlocutor actually speaks. Rather obviously, they may not be able to do so – speakers cannot simply imitate any language variety they come across. Furthermore, speakers sometimes converge towards how they expect their interlocutors to speak, rather than towards their actual speech.
- Several aspects of speakers' identities may affect patterns of accommodation: for instance, someone in a subordinate position may be more likely to converge towards a superior than vice versa.
- There are different motivations for convergence/divergence – it may be

necessary to maintain a distinctive identity without necessarily implying hostility towards the interlocutor (this may be the case, for instance, in interactions between teacher and pupil or doctor and patient).

- Listeners may not respond simply to the degree of convergence/divergence. In an early study carried out in Quebec, the major French-speaking area of Canada, Giles et al. (1973) looked at how English-speaking Canadians responded to a request made, in English, by a French Canadian. They found that the listeners responded more favourably to a request that seemed to require some effort on the part of the speaker – namely, that contained errors and disfluencies – than to a request made in French-accented but fluent English.

- Nor will convergence always be positively evaluated and divergence negatively evaluated – a speaker may be perceived as 'taking off' or ridiculing another's language variety, for instance.

Bell (2001), in a more recent reformulation of his theory of audience design, also places greater emphasis on speakers' need to position themselves in relation to a range of reference groups – 'our own ingroup and other groups, and our interlocutors' (p. 165), which will produce more complex communicative choices.

Accommodation theorists are interested in the specific motivations that may encourage individual speakers to adopt certain language varieties. 'Accommodation' is seen as a general phenomenon, applying in both monolingual and bilingual communities: speakers will accommodate using whatever linguistic resources are available to them. Other researchers have focused on the patterns of language choice made by groups of speakers, in this case mainly in bilingual communities, or communities in which distinct language varieties are used. It is to these studies that we turn below.

5.3 LANGUAGE CHOICE IN BILINGUAL COMMUNITIES

Who becomes bilingual in Africa? The simple answer is, almost everyone who is mobile, either in a socio-economic or a geographical sense. While there are monolinguals in Africa, the typical person speaks at least one language in addition to his/her first language, and persons living in urban areas often speak two or three additional languages. (Myers-Scotton 1993: 33)

Many studies of language use in bilingual communities have been concerned with the habitual language choices made by speakers. The term 'habitual' is important. In many cases, speakers could, in principle, use any of their languages in interaction with others, but in practice certain languages tend to be associated with certain contexts (with certain settings, topics, groups of interlocutors, and so on). In an early paper on language variation in bilingual settings, Joshua Fishman argued that, in cases of

'Gina is by lingual . . . that means she can say the same
thing twice, but you can only understand it once.'

stable bilingualism, '"Proper" usage dictates that only *one* of the theoretically coavailable languages or varieties *will* be chosen by particular classes
of *interlocutors* on particular kinds of *occasions* to discuss particular kinds
of *topics*' (Fishman 1972a: 437; Fishman's italics). 'Proper' usage seems to
refer to the usage that would be expected in particular contexts – in other
words, Fishman was concerned with establishing general patterns of language use, abstracted from the actual language choices made by individual
speakers (he termed this 'higher order societal patterning'). Fishman drew
on the concept of **domains** as a way of establishing such general regularities: he argued that, in stable bilingual communities, languages were associated with different domains of use.

While some aspects of Fishman's claims have been criticised (for
instance, the association between just one language and one domain does
not hold in some communities), several researchers have, like Fishman,
been concerned to establish patterns of language use at a general (societal
or community) level. Such research has often relied on large-scale surveys
investigating speakers' reports of their language use.

> *Domains of language use*
>
> Domains are defined, regardless of their number, in terms of *institutional contexts and their congruent behavioral co-occurrences. They attempt to summate the major clusters of interaction that occur in clusters of multilingual settings and involving clusters of interlocutors.* Domains enable us to understand that *language choice* and *topic*, appropriate though they may be for analyses of individual behavior at the level of face to face verbal encounters, are [. . .] related to widespread sociocultural norms and expectations. (Fishman 1972a: 441; Fishman's italics)
>
> Examples of domains could include the family, education, employment, friendship, government administration.

Carol Myers-Scotton (1993) reviews evidence from Africa – some of her own surveys carried out in the 1970s in Nigeria and Kenya, plus the work of other researchers. Myers-Scotton notes that, in Africa, the most common pattern of bilingualism is to use the speaker's own mother tongue plus an indigenous lingua franca, or an alien official language (such as English or French). For instance, a survey of 187 people living in Lagos, Nigeria, found that 95 per cent of the respondents spoke more than one language, and most of these spoke the same additional languages. Since Lagos is mainly a Yoruba-based city, 85 per cent of the non-Yoruba spoke Yoruba; in the case of the respondents as a whole, the main additional languages spoken were English (77 per cent) and pidgin English (74 per cent). Another survey carried out in Kenya found that the most common trilingual pattern was the speaker's mother tongue, Swahili and English (Myers-Scotton 1993: 36–7).

Evidence from urban communities in Africa suggests that patterns of language choice vary according to speakers' social backgrounds and the types of interaction in which they engage. Most urban Kenyans use their mother tongues at home or with others in the community from their own ethnic group. The mother tongue is important as a means of maintaining ethnic identity and in securing certain material advantages – for example, help from other members of the group in obtaining employment or other benefits. People at the top of the socioeconomic scale also use some English at home, particularly with their children to help them to do better at school. In Nairobi, speakers sometimes switch between their mother tongue, Swahili and English. This is particularly prevalent among children and young people, and a slang variety called Sheng has grown up in certain areas – a mix between Swahili and English.

At work, speakers may use their mother tongue with people from the same ethnic group, or Swahili with people from other groups. English is

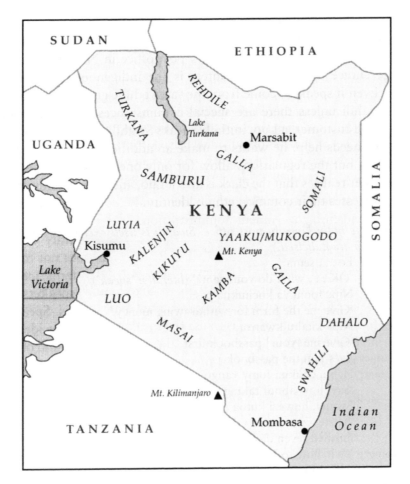

Map 5.2   East Africa and the languages cited in the text (adapted from
Brenzinger 1992)

used particularly in white-collar occupations. It may be used when communicating with superiors as an indicator of education and authority.
And its use among speakers who share a mother tongue may mark out a
relationship as one of the workplace. Outside work, Swahili and English
are used with people from other ethnic groups. Language choice is linked
to education: those who have been educated to secondary level more often
report some use of English, along with Swahili. English is also associated
with more formal, public interactions (Myers-Scotton 1993: 38–43).

   In bilingual communities, then, it is possible to identify certain broad
regularities or patterns of language use. This does not mean, however,
that individual speakers simply reflect these patterns. Insofar as a language
becomes associated with certain groups of speakers and contexts of use, it
will acquire important social meanings. Speakers may use the language to
convey information about their own identity and about the relationship

that obtains between themselves and others (or that they would like to obtain between themselves and others). This is demonstrated in the following example of a conversation in a post office in Nairobi. The usual language choice in service encounters is the indigenous lingua franca, Swahili. Even if speakers come from the same ethnic group, they will tend to use Swahili unless there are special circumstances. In the post-office example, the customer, a Luo, initially speaks Swahili then switches to Luo because he needs help: he wants to make an additional withdrawal from his account, but the regulations allow for only one withdrawal per week. The customer realises that the clerk is also a Luo, and the use of the mother tongue expresses their common ethnic identity.

> (*Setting: the main Nairobi post office. Swahili is used except for switches to Luo, which are italicised.*)
> Clerk: Ee . . . sema.
> 'OK . . . what do you want?' (*literally: 'speak'*)
> Customer: Nipe fomu ya kuchukua pesa.
> 'Give me the form for withdrawing money.'
> Clerk: Nipe kitabu kwanza.
> 'Give me [your] passbook first.'
> (Customer gives him the passbook.)
> Customer: Hebu, chukua fomy yangu.
> 'Say, how about taking my form.'
> Clerk: Bwana, huwezi kutoa pesa leo kwa sababu hujamaliza siku saba.
> 'Mister, you can't take out money today because you haven't yet finished seven days [since the last withdrawal].'
> Customer: (switching to Luo) *Konya an marach.*
> 'Help, I'm in trouble.'
> Clerk: (also speaking Luo now) *Anyalo kony, kik inuo kendo.*
> 'I can help you, but don't repeat it.'
>
> (Myers-Scotton 1993: 40)

Language choice can also be an uncertain matter. There is something of a tension, for instance, in the position of English in Kenya. English is an official language, along with Swahili. It is associated with high social status, but its use is also resented by those who see it as a threat to local languages and cultures. This tension is illustrated by the following two incidents recounted by a student at the University of Nairobi:

1. My brother was arrested by the police and sent to the chief for making beer without a license. He asked to be forgiven (in the local language) by the chief, who rejected the plea. I went to the chief's center where I found some policemen at the door. Nobody was allowed to enter. I spoke English to one of the policemen and said I wanted to see the chief. The police allowed me in. It was, I strongly believe, my English that gave me the honour to be allowed in. And it was my English, during my talk with the chief, that secured the release of my brother.

2. At a beer party near my home, two boys broke into talk in English. The reaction of the old men was bitter and they said, 'Who are those speaking English? Are they back-biting us? They are proud! Push them out.' Although the boys were not addressing the beer party as such, this was regarded as an insult.   (Myers-Scotton 1993: 30–1)

While the surveys above investigate language use across a range of domains, studies have also looked more closely at how different languages are drawn on within a single domain. Ingrid Piller (2001), for instance, in a study of newspaper and television advertising in Germany, noted that 70 per cent of her sample of television adverts used another language in addition to German, and that in 70 per cent of these bilingual adverts the second language was English (other languages included French and Italian). Second languages were associated with different positions in an advert. English was often found in voice-overs in television adverts and in slogans at the bottom of print adverts. Piller argues that English, here, connotes authority, often reinforced by colour and special fonts in print adverts or the use of a male voice-over and written text alongside speech in television adverts. For Piller, an important function of such bilingual advertising is the construction of a certain kind of reader – the main characteristics of this imagined reader include international orientation, future orientation, success orientation, sophistication and fun orientation (2001: 163–71).

Relationships between languages in bilingual communities may be relatively stable, but they may also change. A variety of social changes (migration, invasion and conquest, industrialisation) have been associated with a process termed **language shift**, in which the functions carried out by one language are taken over by another. Sometimes this shift threatens the viability of a language, and may even result in language death, as has been the case for some American Indian languages and some Aboriginal languages in Australia. (Chapter 12 will discuss formal language-planning measures that have been introduced to protect endangered languages.) In a now classic study, Susan Gal (1979) studied processes of language shift in Oberwart, a town in eastern Austria near the border with Hungary. Gal documents the transition of Oberwart from a peasant agricultural village in which the majority of the inhabitants were Hungarian speakers who were also bilingual in German, to a more ethnically diverse town, in which monolingual German speakers have become the majority and bilingual Hungarian speakers have begun to use German in a wider range of contexts. While Hungarian is associated with traditional peasant life, German is the language of waged work and has become associated with modernity and economic success:

It would not be too extreme to say that Hungarian spoken mostly by peasants and former peasants symbolizes the old ways of life, the old forms of prestige of the peasant community. These values are now being rejected by all but the oldest bilingual Oberwarters. In contrast, the educated upper class of Oberwart consists of German monolinguals. The world of schooling, of employment, and of material success is a totally German-speaking world. The language itself has come to symbolize the higher status of the worker and the prestige and money that can be acquired by wage work. While Hungarian is the language of the past and of the old, German is seen as the language of the future, of the young people who are most able to take advantage of the opportunities that Oberwarters feel exist in the German-speaking world.   (Gal 1979: 106)

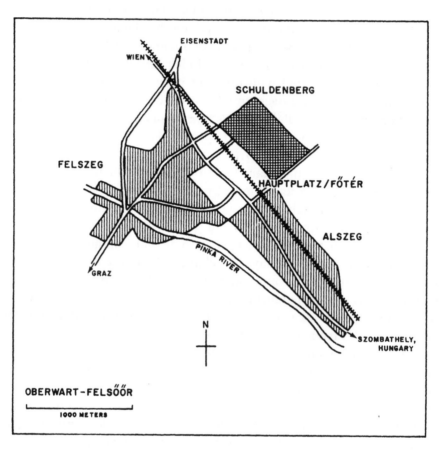

Map 5.3   Oberwart, showing the Felszeg area (Gal 1979: 28)

Notes

Hauptplatz (German) or Fötér (Hungarian) is the town centre, with numerous shops and banks, hotels, restaurants and cafés, a cinema and travel agency.

Schuldenberg (an ironic term in use among Oberwarters – *Schuld* = 'debt' and *Berg* = 'hill') is an area of private housing inhabited by fairly affluent people, overwhelmingly German-monolingual and newcomers to Oberwart.

Felszeg and Alszeg are the two older, Hungarian sections of the town; each of these is 'a peasant village in itself' with inns, grocery stores, a blacksmith and so on.

Of particular interest in Gal's study is her focus on the detailed processes by which shift occurs: the changes in the linguistic habits of individuals and groups of speakers and the motivations for these. Rather than relying on survey information, Gal spent a year in Oberwart carrying out **participant observation**: living as a member of the community while also observing people's language behaviour and recording examples of language use. Gal's work was based mainly in and around the Felszeg, one of the Hungarian sections of the town that was traditionally associated with peasant life. The speakers who served as her informants came from eight local households and their visitors. Gal interviewed members of her sample about their language use and their daily contacts with others in the community; she also observed their language use in different contexts; and she collected audio-recordings of her informants' speech. Initially, Gal used sociolinguistic interviews to elicit speech samples (building on methods devised by variationist sociolinguists such as Labov, discussed in Chapter 3). She elicited only a fairly narrow range of styles in this way, however. After she had spent some time in the community, she was able to collect naturally occurring conversations in a wide variety of settings, and much of her analysis of language use is based on these. Her study can be termed

---

An 'ethnographic' study of language shift

What is of interest to know is not whether industrialization, for instance, is correlated with language shift, but rather: By what intervening processes does industrialization, or any other social change, effect changes in the uses to which speakers put their languages in everyday interactions? How does the social change affect the communicative economy of the group? How does it change the evaluations of languages and the social statuses and meanings associated with them? How does it affect the communicative strategies of speakers so that individuals are motivated to change their choice of language in different contexts of social interaction – to reallocate their linguistic resources radically so that eventually they abandon one of their languages altogether?

An account that answers these questions would start with an ethnography of speaking and take seriously the sociolinguistic notion that, far from being anomolous, bilingual communities are salient instances of a universal phenomenon: the multiplicity and functional distinctiveness of language varieties in speech communities. It is within such a framework that language shift can be explained as a special instance of linguistic change.

(Gal 1979: 3–4)

ethnographic, in that she observed and tried to make sense of naturally occurring behaviour. In this respect, it contrasts both with survey studies of language choice in bilingual communities and with the relative 'artificiality' of data collection and analysis in many variationist studies.

Table 5.1 illustrates some of the findings from Gal's observations of bilingual speakers' use of Hungarian and German. Gal observed 68 of the speakers in her sample, 37 women and 31 men, noting when they used Hungarian, when German and when both languages. She found that the choice between Hungarian and German was associated with a speaker's age: older speakers used Hungarian across a wider range of contexts than younger speakers. For any one speaker, the most important factor influencing their choice of language was the interlocutor, the person being spoken to. Table 5.1 shows the language choices made by women speakers in interaction with different groups of interlocutors.

The data in Table 5.1 suggest that language choice is predictable: if one knows the age of a speaker, and the type of person they are talking to, one should be able to predict their choice of language with a reasonable degree of accuracy. Furthermore, there is a high degree of regularity in the pattern: while different speakers may use different languages with the same interlocutor, their choices are ordered in the same way – the further towards the right of the table one goes, the more frequently German is used. Gal argues that this ordering of interlocutors corresponds to an underlying dimension which she refers to as 'peasant' ↔ 'urban'/'Austrian': that is, the interlocutors to the right of the table are perceived as more 'urban' or 'Austrian' than those to the left. Predictably, this dimension is related to age: younger people are perceived as more 'urban' than older people; but other factors are also important: government officials are associated with 'urbanisation'/'Austrianness' regardless of their age, for instance. Gal argues that it is this factor that affects language choice: interlocutors more closely associated with 'urbanisation'/'Austrianness' will be spoken to more frequently in German. Given the effects of the interlocutor on a speaker's choice of language, it is not surprising that Gal also found that a speaker's social network – the different types of people with whom they habitually interacted – affected their overall tendency to use Hungarian or German (this finding can be related to research on social networks in monolingual communities, such as Lesley Milroy's Belfast study discussed in Chapter 4).

The difference between speakers of different ages lends support to Gal's claim that there is a process of language shift in Oberwart, with German making inroads into contexts formerly associated with Hungarian: you may remember from Chapter 4 that age differences have frequently been taken as indicators of linguistic change.

Other researchers have, like Gal, found a relationship between language choice and social networks. Li Wei, for instance, studied a very different

Number of speaker	Age of speaker	1	2	3	4	5	6	7	8	9	10	11	12	13
								Interlocutors						
1	14	H	G		G	G	G	G	G				—	
2	14	H	GH		G	G	G	G	G				—	
3	25	H	GH	GH	G		G	G	G	G	G	G	—	
4	15	H	GH		GH	GH	G	G	G				—	
5	13	H	GH		GH	—	G	GH					—	
6	13	H	H		GH	—	G	G	G				—	
7	27	—	H		GH	—	G	G	—			G	—	
8	3	—	H		GH	—	GH		—				—	
9	4	—	H		GH	—	GH	GH	—				—	
10	17	H	H		GH	—	—	GH	—	—			—	
11	39		H		GH	—	—	GH	G	G	G	—	—	
12	52	H	H	—	GH	—	GH	—	—	GH	G	G	—	G
13	23	—	H	GH	GH	—	—	GH	G		GH	G	—	
14	22	H	H		H	GH	GH	GH	—			G	—	
15	33	H	H	H	H	—	GH	—	—	H	GH	G	G	
16	35	H			H	—	GH	GH	—	GH	GH	G	—	
17	40	H			H	—	GH		—	GH	GH	G	—	
18	42	H			H	—	GH	GH	—	GH	GH	G	—	
19	43	H			H	—	—	—	—	GH	GH	G	—	
20	35	H	H		H	—	H	GH	H	H	GH	—	—	
21	40	H		H	GH	—	H	GH	H	H	G	—	—	
22	40	H		—	H	—	H	—	H	H	GH	—		G
23	50	H			H	—	H	H	GH		G	—	—	G
24	61	—		H		—	H	GH	—	GH	GH	—	—	G
25	54	H		H	H	H	H	H	—	H	GH	GH	—	—
26	55	H			H	—	H	H	—	H	GH	—	—	GH
27	61	H				—	H	H	—	H	GH	—	—	
28	59	H		H	H	H	H	H	H	H	GH	H	—	GH
29	50	H			H	H	H	H	—	—	H	GH	—	
30	50	H		H	H	—	H	H	—	H	H	GH	—	—
31	60	H		H		H	H	H	—	H	H	GH	GH	—
32	60	H				—	H	H	—	H	H	GH	—	GH
33	63	H				—	H	H	H	H	H	H	—	GH
34	64	H				—	H	—	—	H	H	H	—	GH
35	66	H				—	H	H	—		H	—	—	GH
36	68	H				H	—	—	H	H	H	H	—	H
37	71	H				—	H		H		H	H	—	

Interlocutors: (1) God; (2) grandparents and that generation; (3) black-market clients; (4) parents and that generation; (5) Calvinist minister; (6) age-mate pals, neighbours; (7) brothers and sisters; (8) salespeople; (9) spouse; (10) children and that generation; (11) non-relatives aged under 20; (12) government officials; (13) grandchildren and that generation.

Table 5.1 The choice of Hungarian or German by women speakers in Oberwart (Gal 1979: 102)

Note
In the cells, H = Hungarian; GH = German and Hungarian; G = German; a blank cell means that the category of interlocutor does not apply for that speaker; a dash means that there were insufficient observations to enable a judgement to be made; column 1, 'God', refers to the language of church services. This method of representing data is known as an 'implicational scale': the method is discussed more fully in Gal (1979: 101–4, 118–22).

community of bilingual speakers: British-born Chinese people living in the north-east of England, the children of those who had migrated to the region from the early 1960s. Some of the community came originally from Ap Chau, a small island near Hong Kong; others came from various parts of Hong Kong and from Guang Dong Province in mainland China. Li Wei (1998) found that, across the community as a whole, there was a language shift from Chinese (mainly Cantonese) monolingualism among the oldest generation, and also among some women in the middle generation, through to English-dominant bilingualism among the youngest (British-born) generation. However, patterns of language choice among the British-born speakers varied depending on the family's region of origin. Speakers whose families had come from Ap Chau seemed to have maintained their use of Chinese more than those from other regions: they reported their ability in Chinese at a higher level, and they used the language with a wider range of interlocutors in the Chinese community (like Gal, Li Wei uses an implicational scale to represent this pattern of choices). Li Wei relates this finding to social networks within the community: families from Ap Chau have a relatively high level of contact with others from the island. A major focus for such contact is the local evangelical church which provides opportunities for several social and cultural activities, including Chinese language lessons for British-born children.

Li Wei also discussed different types of code-switching in use among the Chinese community: switching between conversational turns (that is, when one speaker uses Chinese and another English), often found in interactions between speakers with different levels of ability and/or attitudes towards the two languages; switching within a speaking turn but at sentence boundaries; and switching between constituents in a sentence (often called 'intra-sentential code-switching'), as in the example below:

A: Yeo   hou   do   yeo CONTACT.
   Have very many have contact
   'We have many contacts.'
G: WE ALWAYS HAVE OPPORTUNITIES heu xig kei ta   dei
                                          will know that other
   fong gaowui di   yen.   Ngodei xixi
   place church POSS person. we   time
   dou KEEP IN CONTACT.
   always
   'We always have opportunities to get to know people from other churches.
   We always keep in contact.'

(Li Wei 1998: 165)

Note: Li Wei's transcript gives a literal translation beneath each Chinese utterance, then (in quotation marks) a more idiomatic translation of the whole speaking turn.

Li Wei argues that such mixed-code utterances constitute a 'distinctive linguistic mode', used particularly by young people from Ap Chau with other church members of a similar age.

Studies of language choice in bilingual communities have, then, demonstrated some regularities in the language used by different groups of speakers and in different contexts. They have also been able to document general trends in language use, for example processes of language shift, in which one language is replaced by another. (We discuss the phenomenon of language shift more fully in Chapter 8.) We suggested above that, while there is some degree of predictability in speakers' language choices, this does not mean that individual speakers simply *reflect* general, community-wide patterns: at an individual level, different languages or language varieties may serve as a resource that can be drawn on by speakers to communicative effect. Researchers such as Li Wei, Susan Gal and Carol Myers-Scotton have also been interested in the communicative strategies adopted by bilingual speakers in specific contexts, and in particular how code-switching between languages may be used strategically in interaction with others. We look further at examples of this in the following section.

5.4 CODE-SWITCHING IN BIDIALECTAL AND BILINGUAL COMMUNITIES

Carol Myers-Scotton (1993) comments that, until fairly recently, while it was known that bilingual speakers made choices between different languages – they used one language on certain occasions and another language on others – code-switching was not recognised as an object of serious study, and may even have been ignored by observers:

> To take a personal example, even though I was doing fieldwork intermittently from 1964–1973 on language use in African multilingual communities, I never recognized [code-switching] as a special phenomenon until 1972. Previously, I had obtained interview data on language use among urban workers in Kampala, Uganda and Lagos, Nigeria, and made extensive observations in multilingual communities. Workers had made statements such as, 'We sometimes mix languages when speaking with fellow-workers'. But [. . .] I interpreted 'we sometimes mix languages' to mean 'we use language X with such and such persons and language Y with other persons'. Even when I myself observed language in use, as I often did, I managed to 'ignore' codeswitching. (Myers-Scotton 1993: 48)

Since Myers-Scotton's early experiences, code-switching has come to represent a significant strand of research within sociolinguistics. Research has focused on the the relationship between code-switching and social identity as well as on the interactional functions of code-switching. We give examples of both of these below.

Code-switching and identity

Myers-Scotton sets the beginnings of the current interest in code-switching at 1972, around the time of the publication of a highly influential study of a bidialectal community in Norway, carried out by Jan-Petter Blom and John Gumperz (1972, rev. edn 1986). Blom and Gumperz's study looked at language use in the village of Hemnesberget, in northern Norway. Two language varieties were used in Hemnesberget: Ranamål, a local dialect, and Bokmål, the standard variety. (You will see in Chapter 12 that Norway has two standard varieties, Bokmål and Nynorsk, but Blom and Gumperz note that only Bokmål was used in this part of Norway at the time they carried out their study.)

Ranamål and Bokmål are linguistically similar, but were thought of by local speakers as distinct entities. Furthermore, their distinctive features were maintained, largely because of the different social functions they fulfilled. Ranamål symbolised local cultural identity: it was associated with home, family and friends, and more generally with locally based activities and relationships. Bokmål, on the other hand, was associated with formal education and with 'official transactions, religion and the mass media' (p. 411); it was also used by those (often non-locals) who occupied high social status in the community. The two varieties were, then, used on different occasions and by different speakers, but Blom and Gumperz also show how speakers could switch from one to the other during the same social event. In a community administration office, for instance, clerks would use Bokmål or Ranamål phrases depending on whether they were talking about official or unofficial matters; and local residents would speak with a clerk in Ranamål to enquire about family affairs then switch to Bokmål for the 'business' part of the transaction.

This communicative use of code-switching to convey certain social meanings has since been studied by many researchers working in bilingual communities all over the world. In her study of language use in Oberwart, Susan Gal (1979) found that, in those contexts in which speakers could use either Hungarian or German, they sometimes switched between languages, and such switches often conveyed a particular meaning associated with the habitual use of the two languages in the community. For instance, in an argument conducted in Hungarian, a switch to German might give extra force: it could end the argument, serving as a last word that was not to be outdone. In the example below, a mother has called to collect her daughter, looked after by the child's grandparents during the day. The girl has been misbehaving and when her mother calls she is tired. The grandfather sympathises with her as she whines and cries:

1. Grandfather:	Szëginke.
	Poor little one.
2. Grandmother:	Udz ne jáccá ha má ámus vadzs!
	Don't fool around like that if you're sleepy!
3. Mother:	àcs csek ej ju pofont!
	Just give her a good slap.
4. Grandmother:	Hodzsne.
	Oh sure.
5. Grandfather:	(*to child*) Ju hocs e te mamád nincs itthun
	It's a good thing your mother is not home (all day)
6.	mer igën sok pofont kapná tülö.
	because you'd get an awful lot of slaps from her.
7. Mother:	**Jo, oadnuŋ mus sajn!**
	You bet, there has to be order!
8. Grandmother:	Rossz is! e mëdzs cüpüt vennyi osztán et nenit
	She sure is bad! We go to buy shoes and she
9.	ju mëgrugdzsa aki mëgprobágassa melik
	gives the lady a good kick, the lady trying to
10.	pásszul neki. Szíp ë leán.
	fit her with shoes. Some nice little girl.

(Gal 1979: 113)

Note: these are Gal's transcription and spelling conventions; Hungarian is in plain text and German in bold. The mother switches to German in line 7 (transcribed phonetically in the extract) to justify her choice of methods.

In lines 5 and 6, the grandfather appears to be addressing the child but is indirectly commenting on the mother's recommendation to give her a good slap. The mother switches to German in line 7 to justify her choice of methods. Gal argues that the argument here revolves round a clash of values symbolised by the two languages (the traditional, lax method of child-rearing associated with the peasant community as opposed to more modern, strict discipline). The mother's switch to German marks the end of the interaction between herself and the grandfather – it ends the argument. The grandfather says nothing for several rounds of talk, and nothing more at all about slapping.

While many arguments are ended by a switch to German, German need not be used in this way:

> The point is not that a switch to German is always used to express anger, to indicate the last and most effective increase in a show of anger in an escalating disagreement, or to win an argument. It is not. The point is, rather, that if a speaker wants to, switching to German at a particular point in an argument can accomplish these communicative purposes. (Gal 1979: 117)

Gal points out that switches to German can fulfil other functions – for instance, they can express expertise or knowledgeability when a speaker is giving an opinion. This suggests that the meaning of individual switches needs to be interpreted in context.

One of the most comprehensive accounts of social motivations for code-switching comes from Carol Myers-Scotton's work in Africa. Section 5.3 illustrated the functions fulfilled by different languages in Nairobi, one of the contexts studied by Myers-Scotton. Myers-Scotton argues that, when used in interaction, these languages convey certain meanings about the speaker, and also index certain rights and obligations that speakers wish to obtain between themselves and others.

Other code-switching researchers, including Susan Gal, have distinguished between 'unmarked' language choices, in which the language used is one that would be expected in that context, and 'marked' choices, in which the language used would not normally be expected. Marked choices may function as attempts to redefine aspects of the context, or the relationship between speakers. Myers-Scotton has developed this idea into what she terms a *markedness model* of conversational code-switching. She distinguishes between four code-switching patterns prevalent in her African data: code-switching as a series of unmarked choices between different languages; code-switching itself as an unmarked choice; codeswitching as a marked choice; and code-switching as an exploratory choice.

Code-switching may be associated with a series of unmarked choices when aspects of the context such as a change in topic or in the person addressed make a different language variety more appropriate. In the following example, a visitor to a company speaks with the security guard in Swahili, the usual language for such interactions between strangers. When the security guard discovers the visitor comes from his own ethnic group, he switches to their joint ethnic language, Luyia, which indexes their common identity and marks the relationship as one between 'ethnic brethren' rather than strangers. When another visitor approaches, the security guard switches back to Swahili to address him.

(*Setting: entrance to the IBM Nairobi head office. The visitor, from the Luyia area of Western Kenya, approaches and is addressed by the security guard. Swahili is in plain text and Luyia in italics.*)

Guard:	Unataka kumwona nani?
	'Whom do you want to see?'
Visitor:	Ningependa kumwona Solomon I—.
	'I would like to see Solomon I—.'
Guard:	Unamjua kweli? Tunaye Solomon A—. Nadhani ndio yule.
	'Do you really know him? We have a Solomon A—. I think that's the one [you mean]'.
Visitor:	Yule anayetoka Tiriki – yaani Mluyia.
	'That one who comes from Tiriki – that is a Luyia person.'
Guard:	*Solomon menuyu wakhumanya vulahi?*
	'Will Solomon know you?'
Visitor:	*Yivi mulole umuvolere ndi Shem L— venyanga khukhulola.*
	'You see him and tell him Shem L— wants to see you.'

Guard: *Yikhala yalia ulindi.*
              'Sit here and wait.'
Another visitor (just appearing): Bwana K— yuko hapa?
              'Is Mr K_ here?'
Guard (to this visitor): Ndio yuko – anafanya kazi saa hii. Hawezi
kuiacha mpaka iwe imekwisha. Kwa hivyo utaketi hapa mpaka
              aje. Utangoja kwa dakika kama kumi tano hivi.
              'Yes, he's here – he is doing something right now. He can't leave
              until he finishes. Therefore you will wait here until he comes. You
              will wait about five or ten minutes.'
(Guard goes to look for Solomon A—.)

(Myers-Scotton 1993: 88)

Code-switching itself may also be an unmarked choice. In this case, no meaning need be attached to any particular switch: it is the use of both languages together that is meaningful, drawing on the associations of both languages and indexing dual identities. Li Wei's example, cited above, of young people in the north-east of England switching between Chinese and English, would be an example of code-switching as an unmarked choice. Myers-Scotton notes that in her African data such switching often involves an indigenous language and English. In the following example, three young men switch between Swahili and English.

(*Part of a conversation recorded at a shopping centre near a housing estate in Nairobi. Swahili is in plain text and switches to English are italicised.*)

L.   Mbona hawa *workers* wa East African Power and Lighting wakenda
      strike, hata wengine nasikia washawekwa *cell*.
      'And why on earth did those East African Power and Lighting workers
      strike, even I've heard some have been already put in cells [in jail].'
K.   Ujue watu wengine ni *funny* sana. Wa-na-*claim* ati mishahara yao iko *low*
      sana. Tena wanasema eti hawapewi *housing allowance*.
      'You know, some people are very funny. They are claiming that their salaries
      are very low. They also say – eh – they are not given housing allowances.'
M.   Mimi huwa nawafikiria lakini wao huwa na *reasonable salary*.
      'As for me, I used to think, but they have a reasonable salary.'
K.   Hujajua watu wengi *on this world* hawawezi kutoesheka. Anasema
      anataka hiki akipewa a-na-*demand* kingine.
      'Don't you know yet that some people on this world [sic] can't be satis-
      fied. He says he wants this and when he is given [it], he demands another
      [thing].'
L.   . . . Kwani ni ngumu sana ku-*train* wengine? Si ni kupata *lessons* kidogo
      tu halafu waanze kazi?
      ' . . . Why it is difficult to train others? Isn't it just to get a few lessons and
      then they should start work?'

(Myers-Scotton 1993: 118–19)

Myers-Scotton comments that these men come from different ethnic groups and probably do not know one another's ethnic languages, so they need to use a lingua franca. They could use just Swahili, which has some prestige as an 'urban' language, and which also has the virtue of being 'indigenous'. However, English also has some appeal: it is associated with upward mobility, it is the language of the international community and it is used in the international mass media, which may make it particularly appealing to these young people:

> The young men . . . are not satisfied with either the identity associated with speaking English alone or that associated with speaking . . . Swahili alone when they converse with each other. Rather, they see the rewards in indexing both identities for themselves. They solve the problem of making a choice by evolving a pattern of switching between the two languages. Thus, [code-switching] itself becomes their unmarked choice for making salient simultaneously two or more positively evaluated identities. (Myers-Scotton 1993: 122)

In contrast to code-switching as an unmarked choice, codeswitching is marked when it does not conform to expected patterns. Myers-Scotton suggests that it means: 'Put aside any presumptions you have based on societal norms for these circumstances. I want your view of me, or of our relationship, to be otherwise' (p. 131). Marked switching may be used to increase social distance, or to express authority, as in the example below where a salaried worker on a visit to his home village switches from the local language, Lwidakho, to Swahili and then English when talking to a farmer who wants to borrow money. In the transcript, Swahili and English are indicated; otherwise, Lwidakho is used:

Farmer:	(Lwidakho) Khu inzi khuli menyi hanu inzala-
	'As I live here, I have hunger-'
Worker:	(interrupting) (Swahili) *Njaa gani?*
	'What kind of hunger?'
Farmer:	Yenya khunzirila hanu –
	'It wants to kill me here –'
Worker:	(interrupting again, with more force) (Swahili) *Njaa gani?*
	(What kind of hunger?)
Farmer:	Vana veru –
	'Our children –' (said as an appeal to others as brothers)
Worker:	(Swahili) *Nakuuliza, njaa gani?*
	'I ask you, what kind of hunger?'
Farmer:	Inzala ya mapesa, kambuli.
	'Hunger for money; I don't have any'
Worker:	(English) *You have got a land.*
	(Swahili) *Una shamba.*
	'You have land [farm].'
	(Lwidakho) Uli nu mulimi.
	'You have land [farm]'
Farmer:	. . . mwana mweru –
	' . . . my brother –'
Worker:	. . . mbula tsisendi.

'I don't have money'
(English) *Can't you see how I am heavily loaded?*

(Myers-Scotton 1993: 82–3)

Myers-Scotton notes that this exchange takes place in a rural bar. The farmer speaks Lwidakho and perhaps a little Swahili. The worker comes from the same area, but is working in an urban centre away from home. Until this point, the entire conversation has been in Lwidakho, which would be the unmarked choice in this context. Swahili and English are marked choices. Myers-Scotton comments that they are no doubt used here because of their association with authority, but that, importantly, their usage also has a shock value because this departs from the expected.

Finally, code-switching may have an exploratory function when the unmarked choice is uncertain – for instance, when little is known about an interlocutor's social identity, or when there is a 'clash of norms', as in the following example where a local businessman meets up with a former classmate, now a university student and home for a visit. In this case, three languages are used: Kikuyu (in plain text), Swahili (also in plain text, but indicated) and English (in italics). Myers-Scotton comments that Kikuyu, or perhaps Kikuyu/Swahili, would be the unmarked choice.

K1: *How are you Mr Karanja?*
K2: *Fine*, niguka.
     'Fine, I've just arrived.'
K1: *Well, please, let's take one bottle*, ga (Swahili) kuondoa *dust* wa *thought*.
     'Well, please, let's take one bottle, a little to remove the dust from our thoughts.'
K2: (Swahili) sawa.
     'Fine.'
K1: (to bar waiter): (Swahili) Lete *scotch on the rock* hapa.
     'Bring scotch on the rocks here.'
Waiter: (Swahili) Nini?
     'What?' (The waiter has no idea what K1 has in mind. This is a rural bar.)
K1: *Hear him! Tusker beer warm.*
     'Listen to him! Some warm Tusker beer.'
K2: *How are things?*
     'How are things?'
K1: Ti muno. *Why were you rioting in the Nairobi campus?*
     'Not bad. Why were you rioting in the Nairobi campus?'
K2: No maundu ma kimucii.
     'Just matters of home.'
K1: *Even if the country cannot do without you* gu-*stone cars* ti wega.
     'Even if the country cannot do without you, to stone cars is not good.'

(Myers-Scotton 1993: 143)

This example is exploratory, according to Myers-Scotton, because the businessman seems uncertain how to relate to the student, his former class-mate. He tries English, a marked choice in this local bar, as well as some

Kikuyu and Swahili. He ends up by using English inappropriately, and more frequently than his companion, who, as a university student, would have more familiarity with the language.

An important point to note in these examples is that all these choices are socially significant – unmarked choices are as meaningful as marked choices, indexing certain types of social relations between speakers. Studies of the social motivations for code-switching, such as those discussed above, suggest the following:

- Bilingual code-switching is meaningful: it fulfils certain functions in an interaction.
- A speaker's choice of language has to do with maintaining, or negotiating, a certain type of social identity in relation to others; code-switching between languages allows speakers (simultaneous) access to *different* social identities.
- Particular switches may be meaningful (e.g. Gal's example of a young woman switching from Hungarian to German, or Myers-Scotton's example of a security guard switching from Swahili to Luyia); but also, the act of code-switching itself may be meaningful (e.g. Li Wei's example of young people switching between Chinese and English, or Myers-Scotton's example of young people switching between Swahili and English).
- Code-switching may be an unmarked, or expected choice, or a marked, or unexpected choice; in this latter case, it may function as an attempt to initiate a change to relationships.
- Code-switching is useful in cases of uncertainty about relationships: it allows speakers to feel their way and negotiate identities in relation to others.

These points take us back to a concept with which we began this chapter – the idea of the indexicality of language. Code-switching research, however, suggests that language use does not simply reflect social meanings, associated with particular contexts of use, but serves to reproduce, or sometimes challenge or renegotiate social relations, and recreate or redefine particular contexts.

Code-switching and conversation management

While the social motivations for code-switching, and the association between switching and speakers' and listeners' social and cultural identities, have been a major interest in sociolinguistic approaches to code-switching, researchers have also been interested in how code-switching functions as an aspect of conversation management. Peter Auer (1998) draws on a **conversation analysis** framework to analyse the local, interactional functions of code-switching. A major interest of conversation analysisis is in the sequential organisation of conversation, and how this is managed by participants. Auer illustrates what he sees as the value of this approach in a re-analysis of one of Myers-Scotton's examples of marked switching, cited above (pp. 168–9). Auer retranscribes the conversation translated into English, with 'interactional activities' indicated in a right hand column. Lwidakho is in plain text, Swahili in italics and English in bold:

1	Farmer:	As I live here, I have hunger –	indirect request
2	Worker:	(interrupting:)	
		What kind of hunger?	clarification request
3	Farmer:	It wants to kill me here –	elaboration
4	Worker:	(interrupting again, with more force:)	clarification
		What kind of hunger?	request/2nd attempt
5	Farmer:	Our children –	indirect request/2nd
		(said as an appeal to others, as	
		brothers)	attempt
6	Worker:	*I ask you, what kind of hunger?*	clarification request/3rd
			attempt
7	Farmer:	Hunger for money; I don't have any	answer
8	Worker:	**You have got a land.**	indirect decline
9		*You have land [farm]*	indirect decline/2nd version
10		You have land [farm]	indirect decline/3rd version
11	Farmer:	. . . my brother –	indirect request/3rd attempt
12	Worker:	. . . I don't have money	direct decline
13		**Can't you see how I am heavily loaded?**	

(Auer 1998: 10–11)

Auer argues that the worker, at line 2, profits from the farmer's initial indirect request – in asking for clarification, he neither declines nor complies with the farmer's request. The farmer, however, does not answer the worker's question, but elaborates on his previous statement (line 3). The worker repeats his request (line 4) but again, this is not answered by the farmer (line 5). The worker repeats his request for a third time (line 6) and this time receives an answer from the farmer. From lines 1 to 6, Auer suggests, the two speakers are out of tune with one another – in conversation analytical terms, they are operating with two different sequential structures. After the farmer's answer (line 7), his initial request is still 'open', and the worker is under pressure to respond to this. The worker repeats his response in three languages – this adds emphasis, but also the worker is gradually converging on the farmer's preferred language, Lwidakho. Auer suggests that this convergence towards the farmer's language may mitigate his decline of the farmer's request. When the farmer begins a further indirect request, the worker declines this in Lwidakho then English – i.e. declining both the request and the commonality assumed by use of the farmer's language. Auer comments on this analysis:

> Close attention to conversational structure and sequential development can [. . .] lead to a deeper understanding of this piece of interaction. They cast a very different light on the interactional meaning of language choice and language alternation, since it can be shown that the worker accommodates with his language choice the farmer, exactly at the point where the sequence reaches its climax. (Auer 1998: 12)

Auer notes that this does not exclude the possibility of linking 'microscopic aspects of conversational organisation' to wider structures and meanings (e.g. the broader meanings of different language varieties), but rather grounds any broader claims in the local detail of interactions.

Auer's re-analysis is contested by Myers-Scotton (2008, personal communication). Her counter-argument emphasises the social meanings of language varieties. She suggests also that conversations are cognitive as well as social performances: 'speakers hold in their minds metarepresentations of the likely social consequences of their linguistic enactments of their personal goals. Thus, speakers weigh not just what they say, but how they say it.' In the extract above, because the preceding talk has been in Lwidakho, the shift to Swahili stands out – it deserves notice. Although the farmer is a speaker of Lwidakho (perhaps with some limited Swahili), he will understand the pragmatic import of a shift to Swahili and, later, English. As discussed above (p. 168), in this rural context, where everyone speaks Lwidakho as a first language, using Swahili or English may be a way of negotiating social distance between participants. Myers-Scotton comments:

> I argue that it is the marked use of English and Swahili that is the core of what the worker attempts to accomplish interactionally: he wishes to distance himself from the farmer. When the worker says in line 2 (in Swahili) *njaa gani* 'what kind of hunger?' and repeats it in line 4, and then in a modified form in line 6, these are not clarification requests, as Auer interprets them. At the utterance level, these are confrontational rejections in the guise of pseudo-questions. To deviate from the farmer's use of Lwidakho breaks the sequential development; to frame them in Swahili is to treat the farmer as a stranger, not an ethnic brother. English, which appears in lines 8 and 13, is even less expected because of its associations with authority and formality. Of course such associations can and do change; they are dynamic and depend on the setting and how a particular linguistic variety is used in the 'here and now' and over time.
>
>   Also, it is hard to argue that the worker's use of Lwidakho [line 10] is a way to mitigate declining a request when he has been so explicit in placing distance between the two of them by using Swahili and English, which bestow 'outgroupness' on their relationship. Auer identifies the climax as line 12 in which the farmer uses Lwidakho for a more direct rejection of the farmer's request, but this is not the climax. The climax is the worker's attempt at closure in line 13. With its interpersonal emphasis (*Can't you see how I am heavily loaded?*), this line trumps any semblance of line 12 as converging mitigation. In effect, line 13 questions the farmer's good sense and/or his unwillingness to recognize the reality of the worker's situation. And it is done in English.
>
> (Myers-Scotton 2008: personal communication)

Whereas Auer focuses on the detail of the sequential structure of the interaction, Myers-Scotton's analysis suggests that such interactions can be better understood by considering the participants' likely awareness of community norms and linguistic practices.

In this case a 'conversation analysis' and a 'social' interpretation are in conflict: Auer's analysis provides an alternative interpretation to Myers-Scotton's; Myers-Scotton argues that Auer has misinterpreted the interaction. But it is possible to combine a focus on sequential structure and social meaning. For instance, in the example of conversational data from Gal's study in Oberwart, cited above (pp. 164–5), the choice of Hungarian or German is associated with different sets of social values. But the mother's switch to German in line 7 also brings a particular conversational episode to a close and silences the grandfather. Similarly, a switch to a different code may mark the beginning of a new conversational topic, or a new interactional frame (e.g. indicating that a comment is to be taken humorously or ironically).

For a critical review of code-switching research, including Myers-Scotton's markedness model and Auer's conversational approach, see Woolard (2004).

Language crossing, or styling the other

In this section we turn to research on code-switching that provides evidence of highly complex relationships between language and social identity, including practices that problematise straightforward associations between language varieties and the social groups that speakers belong to. One of these practices is a type of code-switching termed **language crossing** (Rampton 1998, 2005). Ben Rampton identifies crossing as the adoption of a language variety that isn't generally thought to 'belong' to the speaker. In a later formulation he refers also to 'styling the other': 'ways in which people use language and dialect in discursive practices to appropriate, explore, reproduce or challenge influential images and stereotypes of groups that they *don't* themselves (straightforwardly) belong to' (Rampton 1999: 421 – Rampton's italics). These concepts have been applied by several other researchers.

The idea of crossing derives from a study Rampton carried out with speakers from different ethnic backgrounds who were members of adolescent friendship groups in the South Midlands of England. Among these informants he noticed instances of different types of crossing: the use of Panjabi by speakers of Anglo and African Caribbean descent; the use of Creole by speakers of Anglo and south Asian descent; and the use of what he termed stylised Asian English by all three groups. In using these varieties, speakers were not actually claiming membership of particular ethnic groups (e.g. a white Anglo speaker using Creole was not laying claim to an African Caribbean identity), and nor were speakers actively deconstructing ethnic boundaries. However Rampton argues that, in foregrounding inherited ethnicity, crossing at least partly destabilised this.

Rampton notes also that the young people he studied had differing alignments with the varieties they used. This is illustrated in two contrasting extracts below showing speakers crossing into, respectively, Creole and stylised Asian English.

The first extract begins with a brief tussle, as two boys, Asif and Alan, seek to undermine the authority of their teacher, Ms Jameson. After Ms Jameson finally leaves the room, Asif uses Creole as a form of subversive critique. Rampton notes here that Creole cannot always be distinguished from the local multiracial vernacular, and that Asif's pronunciation of *that* in *dat's sad man* (line 12) is ambiguous. However, the vowel in *not* and the stretched [l] in his first *lunch* (marked in bold in the transcript) are more clearly Creole influenced.

Participants: Asif (15, male, Pakistani descent, wearing the radio-microphone), Alan (15, male, Anglo descent), Ms Jameson (25+, female, Anglo descent), and in the background, Mr Chambers (25+, male, Anglo descent).
Setting: 1987. Asif and Alan are in detention for Ms Jameson, who was herself a little late for it. She is explaining why she didn't arrive on time, and now she wants to go and fetch her lunch.

```
 1  MS J     I had to go and see the headmaster
    ASIF     why
    MS J     (    ) (.) none of your business
    ALAN     a- about us (    )
 5  MS J     no I'll be [back
    ASIF                [hey how can you see the headmaster when
             he was in dinner (.)
    MS J     ((quietly)) that's precisely why I didn't see him
    ASIF     what (.)
10  MS J     I'll be back in a second with my lunch [(    )
    ASIF                                            [NO ((loud tut))
             dat's sad man (.) (I'll b    )
             I [had to miss my play right I've gotta go
    ALAN       [(    with mine    )
15           (2.5) ((Ms J must now have left the room))
    ASIF     ((Creole influenced)) ll unch (.) you don't need no
             lunch [not'n grow anyway ((laughs))
    ALAN           [((laughs))
    ASIF     have you eat your lunch Alan
```
                                        (Adapted from Rampton 1998: 295)

In the seond extract, Sukhbir uses his normal vernacular in telling off some younger pupils as they run past the school bike sheds. When this has no effect, his friend Mohan switches to stylised Asian English. Rampton argues that Asian English has negative associations here – in this case, it attributes reduced competence, and perhaps irresponsibility, to the younger pupils.

Participants and setting: At the start of the school year, Mohan (15 years old, male, Indian descent, wearing radio-microphone), Jagdish (15 years old, male, Indian descent) and Sukhbir (15 years old, male, Indian descent) are in the bicycle sheds looking at bicycles at the start of the new academic year. Some new pupils run past them.

Sukhbir	STOP RUNNING AROUND YOU GAYS (.)
Sukhbir	[((laughs))
Mohan	((using a strong Indian accent for the words in bold:))
	[EH (.) **THIS IS NOT MIDD(LE SCHOOL)** no more (1.0) this is a respective (2.0)
Anon	(school)
Mohan	school (.) yes (.) took the words out of my mouth (4.5)

(Adapted from Rampton 1998: 297)

Note the following transcription conventions:

Square brackets mark the beginning of overlapping speech;
(school) – an uncertain transcription
((laughs)) – 'stage directions' or comments
CAPITALS – loud enunciation
bold – instance of crossing of interest
(.) – pause of less than one second
(1.0) – timed pause (approximate length of pause in seconds)

Rampton comments on these and other extracts that, when crossing into Creole, speakers often seemed to identify with the voice they were taking on:

Creole was much more extensively integrated into multiracial peer group recreation than either stylised Asian English or Panjabi . . . it was used much more by members of ethnic out-groups [i.e. other ethnic groups]. Creole symbolised an excitement and an excellence in youth culture that many adolescents aspired to, and it was even referred to as 'future language' (1998: 304–5).

This contrasted particularly with stylised Asian English, a variety associated with limited linguistic and cultural competence. Interviews and other evidence suggested this represented 'a stage of historical transition that most adolescents felt they were leaving behind, and in one way or another [Asian English] consistently symbolised distance from the main currents of adolescent life' (1998: 305). Stylised Asian English was often used, not in relation to the speaker's own identity, but, as in the example above, in relation to an identity attributed to the person addressed.

Rampton relates these differing alignments to ideas about language developed by the Russian literary theorist Mikhail Bakhtin, and particularly to

Bakhtin, voice and double-voicing

For Bakhtin, all language involves speaking through the 'voices' of others (i.e. speakers draw on utterances, and their associated meanings, that are continually recycled and re-articulated, so that words carry with them the 'taste' of other speakers and other contexts). 'Double-voicing' means that an utterance carries two sets of meanings, or 'semantic intentions'. This occurs when a speaker '[inserts] a new semantic intention into a discourse which already has, and which retains, an intention of its own. [. . .] In one discourse, two semantic intentions appear, two voices' (1984 [1929]: 189). An example might be someone telling a story and quoting another speaker in such a way that (e.g. by adopting a particular tone of voice) the narrator's viewpoint is evident behind that of the quoted speaker. Bakhtin identifies two types of double-voicing: 'uni-directional double-voicing', where the meanings or semantic intentions are consistent; and 'vari-directional double-voicing', where the speaker introduces a semantic intention directly opposed to the original one. An example of the latter might be political satire, or quoting someone ironically. These ideas are particularly relevant to language crossing, which involves taking on voices associated with other speakers, and demonstrating different levels of alignment with these voices.

Bakhtin's notion of **double voicing** (see above). In Bakhtinian terms, Creole crossing would normally be an instance of 'uni-directional double voicing', in which speakers demonstrate positive alignment with a voice they are taking on. Stylised Asian English, by contrast, would correspond to 'vari-directional double-voicing' in which speakers distance themselves from a particular voice – in the example above, attributing its negative associations to others.

Similar ideas about language and identity are drawn on by Alastair Pennycook in a study of English and globalisation, with a particular focus on English and other languages in rap or hip hop. Pennycook (2003) argues that work on global Englishes, while it may reflect a range of intellectual and political standpoints, tends to operate with a relatively fixed conception of language and identity (see also Chapter 9 on this point). Research that focuses, alternatively, on English as an agent of western linguistic imperialism, or more positively on the diversity of 'world Englishes', fails to engage with how people may use English in more complex ways, and to a range of effects. He takes, as examples, extracts from Japanese hip-hop lyrics, such as the following from the rappers Rip Slyme. In this case Pennycook's analysis is of written lyrics rather than a live performance:

Lyrics	Transliteration and translation
Yo Bringing That. Yo Bring Your Style	*Transliteration and translation*
	Yo Bringing That, Yo Bring Your Style
人類最後のフリーキーサイド	Jinrui saigo no fruiikiisaido
	Yo Bringing That, Yo Bring Your Style
	The last freaky side of the human race

(Pennycook 2003: 515)

The first line here may be seen as a form of styling the other in Rampton's terms. *Yo* is a term commonly used in hip-hop slang, originating in African-American Vernacular English. It is therefore evidence of borrowing from US rappers. The use of English is also common in Japanese music. However, in this case the English is juxtaposed with Japanese that is itself mixed. Pennycook points out that, in the second line, the first part of the phrase uses Japanese Kanji script (for 'human race' and 'last'); while the second part uses Katakana (adopted generally for the transcription of non-Japanese words) and Hiragana (used mainly for Japanese morphemes and grammatical items). *Furiikiisaido* represents an English-based word with Japanese morphology.

Pennycook notes that English is not, here, being used for international communication. Rather, it is part of the rappers' identity repertoires, indexing certain cultural affiliations: 'While Rip Slyme is clearly heavily influenced by global rap, it seems problematic to exclude the possibility that this Japanese rap is simultaneously global and, at the same time, expressive of Japanese language and culture. Japanese rap in English is part of Japanese language and culture' (p. 517). Pennycook draws on contemporary models of language and identity that see language use not as representing pre-existing identities but as (re)creating identities in the act of speaking or performing. In this sense, it is not the case that Rip Slyme is representing a pre-existing Japanese culture and identity through their use of language. Rather, these and other lyrics are instances of the use of language 'to perform, invent and (re)fashion identities across borders' (pp. 528–9). Such ideas about identity are consistent with Rampton's suggestion that crossing may act to destabilise ethnic boundaries. They are also associated with contemporary research on language and gender, and are discussed further in Chapter 7.

5.5 CODE-SWITCHING AND STYLE-SHIFTING

Code-switching studies are interested in the language use of individual speakers and how this is associated with certain aspects of speaker identities, and the contexts in which conversations take place. They have this in common with research on 'stylistic variation' in monolingual communities discussed in Chapters 3 and 4. The research methods adopted, however, are

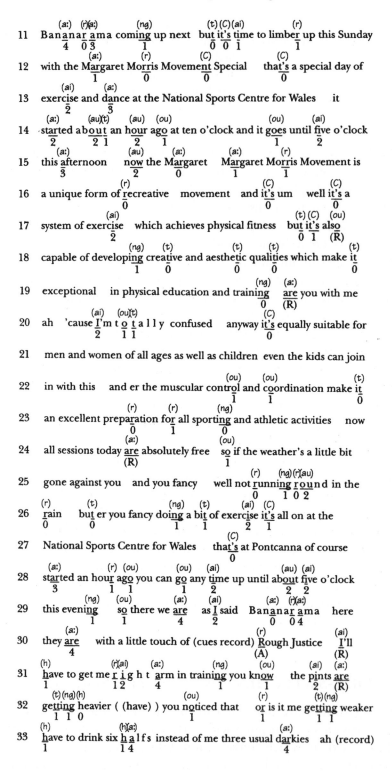

Figure 5.1   Extracts from a radio DJ's speech (Coupland 2001: 205)

Note: In the extracts, sociolinguistic variables are underlined; the variable itself is given above the line; and its value (i.e. how standard or non-standard it is) is indicated below the line. The following variables have only two possible scores – 0 = standard, and 1 = non-standard:

(C)   – a consonant cluster
(t)   – the pronunciation of /t/ between vowels
(r)   – the pronunciation of /r/ before vowels
(ou)   – the pronunciation of the first part of the diphthong in *so*
(ng)   – the pronunciation of the *-ing* ending as either '-ing' or '-in'
(h)   – the presence or absence of /h/ at the beginning of a word

For one vowel variable in the extract it was possible to range pronunciations along a 3-point scale, from 0 = standard to 2 = non-standard:

(ai)   – the pronunciation of the first part of the dipthong in *I* and *-ise*

In the case of another vowel variable a wider range of pronunciations was distinguished, from 0 = standard to 4 = maximally non-standard:

(a:)   – the pronunciation of the vowel in *are* and *arm*

radically different. The code-switching studies discussed above have tried to understand speakers' switching behaviour in context and from this to arrive at some generalisations about code-switching patterns: the approach adopted is broadly **qualitative**. By contrast, studies of stylistic variation have tended to adopt a **quantitative** approach, investigating potential correlations between sociolinguistic variables, social groups and speaking contexts.   Something very like a code-switching approach has however also been used to investigate variable language use amongst monolingual speakers. Nikolas Coupland (1985, 2001) analysed the speech of a disc jockey (DJ) on Radio Cardiff, in Wales. The DJ used several local Cardiff pronunciations in his speech. Coupland argues that it is possible to analyse the DJ's speech by using traditional variationist techniques: identifying a number of sociolinguistic variables and, for each one, totalling the DJ's use of different variants. However, this simply demonstrates the obvious: that the DJ's speech is generally very non-standard.

Like most speakers, the DJ's use of different pronunciations is not uniform: he uses many local Cardiff pronunciations, but he also uses some more standard pronunciations, and these seem to be associated with different contexts. While, in one sense, the DJ is always talking in the same context – his own local radio programme – it is possible to identify certain 'micro-contexts': different communicative activities such as making public announcements, reading out letters, introducing records and being funny. The DJ seems to adopt more or less standard features as he shifts between these micro-contexts: for instance, he tends to use more standard pronunciations when publicising the show or making a formal announce-ment, and more Cardiff pronunciations when talking about local events or making jokes about his own competence, as in Figure 5.1.

In Figure 5.1, the DJ is making an announcement about a local dance/ fitness event. This is probably based on written information, and contains a preponderance of standard pronunciations. He then switches to more non-standard forms in a humorous aside ('are you with me ah 'cause I'm totally confused'); later he uses several non-standard pronunciations – in this case in a humorous reference to drinking the local beer. However, the DJ varies not just between more and less standard speech: he also introduces other varieties, such as the American 'yeah' to introduce certain records – a form of crossing, or styling the other, in Rampton's terms. Furthermore, the meaning of the DJ's switches need to be interpreted in context – the introduction of American features seems to be playful, parodying his DJ patter; the use of local Cardiff forms may signal self-deprecating humour in a reference to himself but social solidarity in a reference to local cultural history. Finally, the contexts themselves can sometimes only be identified by an appeal to the DJ's speaking style. Coupland refers to the DJ as 'the orchestrator of contexts' (2001: 208): his speech does not simply reflect contexts, it also creates them. Studies of style shifting, such as Coupland's Cardiff study, while they show similarities with research on bilingual code-switching, also contrast markedly with variationist studies of (mono-lingual) stylistic variation.   Variationist studies may give the impression that individual speakers simply reflect wider social divisions and particular speaking contexts – that their language use is determined by factors such as their social class, ethnic group or the formality of a situation. In fact the position adopted by variationist researchers is not necessarily quite so determinist as this: Labov and Trudgill, for instance, argued that speak-ers were, in part, responding to the overt or covert prestige of different language varieties. Accommodation theorists such as Howard Giles and his associates (discussed in section 5.2) have given greater emphasis to the creativity involved in language behaviour, focusing on speakers' use of different language varieties to express solidarity with or social distance from their interlocutors. The code-switching and style-shifting studies dis-cussed in section 5.4 and earlier in this section have, similarly, highlighted creativity in speaker's language choices, seeing speakers as using different language varieties strategically as a means of negotiating, maintaining or redefining communicative contexts and sets of social relationships.

Many variationist studies have interpreted 'stylistic' variation in terms of the degree of attention paid to speech. Labov and Trudgill associated the increased use of vernacular pronunciations in personal anecdotes with lack of attention: speakers, they argued, paid less attention to their speech when narrating events in which they had some personal involve-ment than when reading from formal texts or word lists (see Chapter 3). Code-switching and style-shifting studies, with their evidence of speakers selecting different varieties as appropriate, do not seem consistent with a straightforward interpretation in terms of the degree of attention paid to speech, and Susan Gal has explicitly questioned this interpretation on the basis of her work in Oberwart. The varieties of Hungarian spoken in Oberwart ranged from the local dialect to standard Hungarian. Speakers interviewed by Gal in Hungarian often maintained their use of the standard variety even when giving highly emotional accounts. Gal herself was not local, and spoke standard Hungarian. She argues that in this case, when talking to a relative outsider and a 'standard' speaker, speakers probably saw the standard variety as appropriate for conveying personal involvement and emotion: local Hungarian conveyed peasant status, and this might serve as a distraction. Gal suggests that different norms could obtain in New York, where the interviewer might be perceived as a person for whom the vernacular was more meaningful in conveying emotional involvement.

Whereas variationist studies of speaking style have often seen this as varying along a single continuum from formal to informal, code-switching and style-shifting studies suggest that speakers' variable language use is more complex, probably operating along several dimensions. We mentioned that Susan Gal's bilingual speakers in Oberwart had access not only to two languages but also to different styles in those languages; Carol Myers-Scotton showed that speakers in Africa may switch between three different languages in conversation; Ben Rampton and Alastair Pennycook illustrated complex patterns of speakers 'styling the other'; and Nikolas Coupland, in his analysis of the Cardiff DJ's speech, found that the DJ introduced features from several language varieties, and that the meaning of the same features was not consistent but depended on how these were used in context. However, while Coupland's focus is on moment-by-moment variability in the DJ's speech, he also sees links between such local, contextualised behaviour and larger-scale quantitative studies such as those discussed in Chapter 3:

> Individuals within what we conventionally recognize to be meaningful social categories enact dialect personas with sufficient uniformity for survey researchers to detect numerical patterns of stratification. [. . .] It is in relation to group norms that stylistic variation becomes meaningful; it is through individual stylistic choices that group norms are produced and reproduced.
>
> (2001: 198)

Similarly, Penelope Eckert, whose study of Belton High was referred to in Chapter 3, sees quantitative patterns in language variation as reflecting speakers' local, contextualised stylistic choices (Eckert 2000).

5.6 CONCLUSION

Chapter 5 has focused, in the main, on language variation in bilingual communities, but we have also drawn some comparisons with monolingual 'stylistic' variation. We have suggested that language varieties (different languages in bilingual communities or accents and dialects in monolingual communities) are meaningful, and that they therefore constitute a resource that can be drawn on by speakers. We have looked at how researchers have identified patterns of language choice, and 'language shift', in bilingual communities; and at how they have investigated individual speakers 'code-switching' between two or more languages in different contexts. We have suggested that evidence of code-switching in bilingual communities is compatible with qualitative approaches to monolingual style shifting and that, in combination, these might lead one to question some interpretations of speakers' variable language use that emanate from early variationist research: for instance, the reliance on a single dimension of 'stylistic' variation (from more to less formal), and on a single interpretation of 'speaking style' that depends on the degree of attention paid to speech.

While some studies discussed in this chapter (such as those that attempt to establish general patterns in language choice) have adopted a quantitative approach, most can broadly be described as qualitative, focusing on the interpretation of language in context and viewing individual speakers' language choices as a communicative strategy. Qualitative approaches represent an important tradition within sociolinguistics: we look at this further in Chapter 6.

Note

1. Some evidence from social and discursive psychology suggests that the same individual may express different, even conflicting views about social phenomena on different occasions. Discursive psychology shifts the focus from individual attitudes to the particular ways of speaking or 'interpretative repertoires' people may draw on in talking about social phenomena (Potter and Wetherell 1987; see also Edley 2001). This principle, applied to language, would suggest that a range of 'repertoires' are in circulation about particular language varieties. These are not necessarily consistent. For instance, the same variety may be seen both as 'authentic' and serious, connoting positive local values, and as humorous, connoting more negatively stereotypical values. Individuals may draw on combinations of these 'repertoires' in talking about varieties. This is a potentially interesting line of enquiry, but empirical research is still needed to show how the process would operate with respect to language variation.

6
LANGUAGE IN INTERACTION

6.1   INTRODUCTION

This chapter examines how speakers use language in interaction with others, an area of sociolinguistic study that draws on research traditions such as **interactional sociolinguistics**, the **ethnography of speaking, ethnography of communication,** or **linguistic ethnography.** We looked at some aspects of this in Chapter 5, in examining how speakers vary their use of accents, dialects or languages to communicative effect. Other aspects of language use have also been of interest to sociolinguists, however: the way people talk to one another – how they hold conversations, tell stories, make jokes, argue or tease one another – will vary in different cultural contexts. Studies of these phenomena frequently adopt a qualitative approach to the study of language, drawing on anthropological or ethnographic methods of research.

'Interactional sociolinguistics' is associated particularly with the foundational work of John Gumperz (1982a, 1982b), whose study of code-switching in Norway you met in Chapter 5. It is also used more broadly, however, for qualitative sociolinguistic research on language in interaction. The development of ethnographic approaches owes much to Dell Hymes, whose notion of communicative competence was discussed in Chapter 1 (pp. 4–5): Hymes was concerned to establish models of the interaction between language and social life, or 'the multiple relations between linguistic means and social meaning' (1972: 39), and advocated, as a starting point, detailed ethnographic accounts of the distinctive 'ways of speaking' evident in different communities.

Several empirical studies have attempted to document different ways of speaking: a glance through early collections reveals titles such as 'Culture patterning of speech behaviour in Burundi' (Albert 1972), '"To give up on words": silence in Western Apache culture' (Basso 1972), or 'How to ask for a drink in Subanun' (Frake 1964). There has also been a focus on how speaking practices pattern within a community (such as the identification

'Doing ethnography'

'Doing ethnography' in another culture involves first and foremost field work, including observing, asking questions, participating in group activities, and testing the validity of one's perceptions against the intuitions of natives. Research design must allow an openness to categories and modes of thought and behavior which may not have been anticipated by the investigator. The ethnographer of communication cannot even presuppose what a speech community other than his own may consider to be 'language', or who or what may 'speak' it: 'language' for the Ojibwa includes thunder; dogs among the Navajo are said to understand Navajo; the Maori regard musical instruments as able to speak; and drums and shells are channels through which supernatural forces are believed to speak to members of the Afro-Cuban Lucumí religious cult.

Ethnography by no means requires investigating only 'others': one's own speech community may be profitably studied as well. Here, however, discovering patterned behavior which operates largely unconsciously for the native investigator presents quite different problems for 'objectivity'. One of the best means by which to gain understanding of one's own 'ways of speaking' is to compare and contrast these ways with others, a process that can reveal that many of the communicative practices assumed to be 'natural' or 'logical' are in fact as culturally unique and conventional as the language code itself. A valuable by-product which emerges from this process is an essential feature of all ethnography: a deeper understanding of cultural relativism.

(extract from Muriel Saville-Troike (2003), *The Ethnography of Communication*, pp. 3–4)

of differences between high- or low-status speakers, or between children and adults, or between the types of language used in different contexts). While such studies cover a wide range of topics, and represent different research interests, they tend to have certain features in common:

- a focus on the analysis of naturally occurring speech;
- an emphasis on the context in which speech is produced;
- an interest in the meanings or functions of language, not just in the distribution of different language forms;
- (a related point) an interest in the role of language in managing relationships between speakers;
- the adoption of qualitative, rather than quantitative, methods of analysis (while some studies may use a mixture of methods, the emphasis is still broadly qualitative).

In these respects, interactional studies contrast with much of the variationist research discussed in Chapters 3 and 4.

Many studies, particularly early studies, have been descriptive, but researchers have also adopted a critical perspective in the study of language in interaction. Power has been identified as an important dimension in many (some would say most) interactions, and researchers have demonstrated how language may be used to negotiate highly unequal relationships between speakers, or groups of speakers. Some researchers have taken a more interventionist stance, drawing on sociolinguistic evidence to argue for changes to speaking practices in certain social contexts.

In the remainder of this chapter, we discuss some (highly selective) examples of research on language in interaction, in an attempt to give a 'flavour' of the field. We look first at patterns of speaking and silence within different communities; then at the structure and use of narratives, or personal stories, and the organisation of everyday conversation; we examine how language may formally 'encode' relationships between different speakers; and finally how certain language practices may serve to establish and maintain unequal relationships. As part of this last topic, we also look at the application of sociolinguistic analysis in a number of institutional contexts.

6.2   SPEAKING AND SILENCE

Within linguistics, silence has traditionally been ignored except for its boundary-marking function, delimiting the beginning and end of utterances. The tradition has been to define it negatively – as merely the absence of speech. (Saville-Troike 1985: 3)

While formal linguistics may have paid scant regard to silence, other disciplines that have informed sociolinguistics have recognised the importance of studying silence as an aspect of human communication. Anthropologists, for instance, have studied patterns of speaking and silence and how these vary in different communities. Of interest here is when, in a particular community, it is deemed appropriate to speak, and when to be silent. The focus is not on silence as an *absence* of speech, but as something that has communicative meaning alongside speech.

In a relatively early study, K. H. Basso (1972) studied speaking and silence in the South Athapaskan (Apache) settlement of Cibecue in east-central Arizona. Basso found that people were silent with one another on several occasions, such as when meeting strangers, when meeting children who had returned from boarding school and when beginning courting. A common feature of these occasions was that relationships between speakers were ambiguous or uncertain in some way. He gives one example of a meeting between strangers, two men working with others in a cattle round-up crew. Basso's informant, quoted below, was also a member of the crew:

> One time I was with A, B and X down at the Gleason Flat working cattle. That man, X, was from East Fork (a community nearly forty miles from Cibecue) where B's wife was from. But he didn't know A, never knew him before, I guess. First day, I worked with X. At night, when we were camped, we talked with B, but X and A didn't say anything to each other. Same way, second day. Same way, third. Then, at night on fourth day, we were sitting by the 1fire. Still, X and A didn't talk. Then A said: 'Well, I know there is a stranger to me here, but I've been watching him and I know he is alright.' After that, X and A talked a lot . . . . Those two men didn't know each other, so they took it easy at first. (cited Basso 1972: 72)

Basso comments that, in cases such as this, it is not common practice to introduce strangers to one another. Eventually, strangers will begin to talk, but it would not be appropriate to rush this. Other cultures might expect different behaviour under such circumstances – formal introductions, for instance, or strangers engaging in 'small talk' to get to know one another. Such cultural differences may give rise to misunderstandings – Basso points out that silence among communities such as the Athapaskans has sometimes been taken by others as indicating 'lack of personal warmth'.

Finnish proverbs and sayings on silence

Listen a lot, speak little
One word is enough to make a lot of trouble
One mouth, two ears
A barking dog does not catch a hare
A fool speaks a lot, a wise man thinks instead
Brevity makes a good psalm
One word is as good as nine

(cited in Lehtonen and Sajavaara 1985: 193)

Several studies have reported on 'silent' cultures, such as other Native American groups, Inuit and Finns. Perhaps because of the relative loquacity of the (western-influenced) research community, silent behaviour is often seen as remarkable – as something that needs to be explained. It is also occasionally seen as undesirable. Jaakko Lehtonen and Kari Sajavaara relate the acceptance of silence among Finns to traditional living conditions, where people lived in separate houses (rather than villages) and there was little scope for social interaction. They comment that increased international contact may bring about changes to the Finnish culture: 'if the result is a more communicative Finn, the development is certainly not for the worse' (1985: 200). In a later paper, however, Sajavaara and Lehtonen (1997) also comment on the danger of judging behaviour such as silence according to inappropriate (outsider) cultural norms.

By way of contrast, Gregory Nwoye (1985) discusses the role of silence as a marked form of behaviour among the Igbo people in Nigeria. The Igbo place great importance on the art of speaking: greetings are highly elaborate and protracted, even among total strangers. Nwoye argues that the Igbo are characterised by 'ebullient loquacity'. In this context, silence is an important form of behaviour, meaningful because it contrasts with the more talkative norm. It is used as 'a means of managing highly-charged situations and relationships' (p. 191): in the comfort of bereaved friends, to reject a proposal of marriage and in certain ritual contexts, such as sacrifices.

Deborah Tannen (1985) discusses the characteristics of a 'New York Jewish' style of speaking, which she claims derives from an effort to avoid silence. Tannen's study contrasts with the studies mentioned above in that it is based, not on observation of general patterns of behaviour, but on a detailed examination of a long conversation that she recorded, then transcribed and analysed. The conversation took place during a Thanksgiving dinner involving six people: three New Yorkers of Jewish background (of whom Tannen was one), two Californians of non-Jewish background and one person from England (with one Jewish parent). During the dinner, the New Yorkers did most of the talking and were felt by other participants to have 'dominated' the conversation. The features that characterised their conversation included:

1. Fast rate of speech
2. Fast rate of turn-taking
3. Persistence – if a turn is not acknowledged, try try again
4. Marked shifts in pitch
5. Marked shifts in amplitude
6. Preference for storytelling
7. Preference for personal stories
8. Tolerance of, preference for simultaneous speech
9. Abrupt topic-shifting (Tannen 1985: 102).

Tannen suggests that the New Yorkers would have been uncomfortable with silence in this context – they throw out topics to fill up the conversational space, but are not offended if what they say is ignored. The non-New Yorkers may have been operating to a different set of rules, according to which people spoke less but expected what they said to be attended to. Tannen interprets her own research (and other research on speaking and silence mentioned above) in terms of **politeness theory**: silence, she argues, is often a form of negative politeness – not imposing on others. This can occur in any culture, but would be unmarked in cultures such

Politeness theory

Penelope Brown and Stephen Levinson's model of **politeness** is based on the notion of **face**. 'Face' refers to a person's public self-image: it is derived, in part, from the everyday use of the term in expressions such as 'losing face'. Brown and Levinson distinguish two aspects of face: 'positive face', the desire for appreciation and approval by others; and 'negative face', the desire not to be imposed on by others. In interacting, speakers need to balance a concern for other people's face with a desire to protect their own.

Speakers will draw on politeness strategies as a means of paying attention to another person's face and avoiding 'face-threatening acts': 'positive politeness' strategies involve the expression of friendliness or approval (an example might be explictly including someone in a conversation); 'negative politeness' strategies involve not imposing on others or threatening their face (an example might be phrasing a request indirectly: 'Could you possibly close the door?').

The actual expression of politeness will depend upon several factors:

- Concerns about face may be overridden: for instance, in cases of danger or great urgency, speakers may be less inclined to bother about indirect requests.
- Some impositions are regarded as greater than others. A request that is felt to be a considerable imposition may require greater attention to (negative) politeness than a minor favour.
- Relationships between people (or, more precisely, how theseare perceived in context) are highly important. In certain contexts, for instance, a speaker in a powerful position may feel able to impose upon others in a less powerful position.
- The kinds of politeness strategies that are felt to be appropriate will also vary in different cultures.

This model of politeness is discussed in Brown and Levinson (1987). The notion of face comes from earlier work by Goffman (1967). There are several more recent critical reviews of politeness theory, e.g. Eelen (2001). Politeness theory has also been drawn on, sometimes critically, in studies of language and gender – see Chapter 7.

as the Athapaskans and Finns. Silence may also, however, be perceived as an absence of positive politeness, by not satisfying the needs of others for attention and involvement. This is likely to be the case in relatively loquacious groups such as the Igbo and the New Yorkers studied by Tannen.

Tannen argues, like Basso (above), that such differences between speakers can give rise to misunderstanding, or miscommunication, and also to negative evaluations of speakers by others whose behaviour differs. Mainstream Americans, for instance, are likely to have negative perceptions of the speaking style of American Indians (with its greater tolerance of silence) *and* the speaking style of New York Jewish people (with its faster pace than the 'mainstream' style).

The studies discussed in this section draw attention to differences in speaking practices between different groups: they emphasise that not everyone interacts in the same way, and that differences often have a cultural basis. A shortcoming of this kind of work is that what is seen as being in need of explanation is behaviour that is marked – that differs from a perceived (and not always fully acknowledged) norm. There is a danger, then, in exoticising certain forms of behaviour. Such work also involves making generalisations about societies and cultures: it may in part rely on, and contribute to, stereotypes about human behaviour.

While the studies discussed above focused on silence (or loquacity) as a characteristic of certain groups of speakers, silence may also be studied as an aspect of any interaction. For instance, in a study of reference to death in consultations between doctors and elderly patients and their families, Nikolas Coupland and Justine Coupland (1997) note that orientations to the quality of life and to death are 'core aspects' of these interactions, but that 'these orientations are systematically oblique, tentative and often mitigated' (1997: 145). In talking with others we tend to present certain versions of events, and certain topics or viewpoints may be foregrounded, played down, or 'silenced'. Silence, in the sense of pauses in speaking, is also an aspect of conversation management. Brief pauses, for instance, may help to structure speaking turns, and longer pauses, even of a second or two, may be interactionally meaningful. The use of pauses, or gaps in speaking, also varies across cultures – a topic we refer to in section 6.4.

6.3 NARRATIVES

Many ethnographically oriented researchers have been interested in the role of **narratives**, or stories, in interaction. Narratives, in this sense, refer not just to more formal storytelling performances but also to the routine accounts of incidents and events that permeate everyday conversation. Some researchers have been interested in the content of narratives: these may represent the only descriptions, or the most accessible descriptions, of certain events and so provide valuable sources of information for anthropologists and social historians. Language researchers have often focused on aspects of narrative form, or structure, and on the role of narrative in encoding descriptions of life experiences.

In telling a story, narrators need to make certain choices – about the inclusion of certain episodes, the description of people and events, and in many communities the use of one (or more) language varieties rather than others, as well as choices between different linguistic forms and structures. Narratives cannot be regarded simply as neutral, factual accounts: they are always representations, constructed by the narrator to make a certain point. The choices made in narrating a story allow narrators to represent themselves in a certain light, and to evaluate other people and events in the story.

You may remember from Chapter 3 that William Labov, in his studies of the language of New York City, elicited narratives of personal experience from his informants. Chapter 3 discussed the 'danger of death' narratives that were designed to elicit samples of vernacular speech, but Labov also collected stories on other topics – for instance fights (in response to the question 'Were you ever involved in a fight with a guy bigger than you?', with a follow-up prompt of 'What happened?'). In an important and pioneering essay, Labov (1972b) analysed the characteristics of narratives collected from informants in south central Harlem. He argues that at its most basic, a narrative may contain simply a series of 'narrative clauses', presented in the order in which the events described actually took place, as in the following brief example of a pre-adolescent narrative:

a This boy punched me
b and I punched him
c and the teacher came in
d and stopped the fight.
                      (Labov 1972b: 361)

While it is possible for accounts to be ordered differently, Labov claims that, in practice, the narrative structure always reflects the actual temporal sequence of events. This claim seems to hold for personal narratives, at least in 'western', English-speaking contexts, but other structures sometimes occur: Allan Bell, for instance, has demonstrated that contemporary newspaper stories have a different narrative structure (Bell 1991).

Narratives may contain additional elements: Labov argues that a fully formed narrative may include the following:

- *Abstract*, which summarises the events to come or offers a preliminary assessment of the significance of those events.
- *Orientation*, which identifies the setting, characters and other background and contextual details relevant to the narrative.
- *Complicating action*, a series of narrative clauses, as illustrated above – the basic details of the storyline.
- *Evaluation(s)*, which indicate the point of the story, or the reason(s) why the

Selling Tiny

The [following] story, from my interview with Karen (11 years) and her friend Helen (10), demonstrates the structural pattern identified by Labov and how it becomes adapted within a specific conversational context. It also shows the way in which the evaluative functions of stories are explored through the characters' voices and through links with the surrounding conversation. Karen had been telling me about all the animals she used to have at home, 'three different houses ago', as she put it. At various times the family had thirty-six dogs, parrots, cockateels, budgies, ferrets, rabbits, cats, hamsters, and guinea-pigs. Karen explained that they moved house because her parents split up and divorced, but then got back together again (although they had not legally remarried). The conversation moved back to the family pets, and I asked Karen if both her parents liked animals.

Janet:	Are they both keen on animals?
Karen:	Well my dad isn't that keen, my mum is. [A] We used to have this little dog called Tiny and my dad sold her. [O] Well we were going to try and get rid of some of our dogs, one day a man come and he said, he (*dad*) was showing him all the other dogs and he didn't show him Tiny [C] and he goes, 'Who lives in that kennel there?' and he (*dad*) goes, 'Oh, that's my wife's dog, Tiny' and he took one look at her and he said, 'I'll have her, yes,' he goes, 'I want her' and my dad goes, 'Er, alright'. So he sold it. Just before the man went I went into my house and I goes, 'Mum, Dad's sold Tiny!' and she just burst into tears and so I come running up going, 'Dad, if you sell Tiny Mum will never talk to you ever again!'. [R] He goes, 'Sorry, you can't sell (*buy*) that' and I took off, rushed into the house with Tiny and my mum just, her face, she was crying her eyes out, as soon as she saw her, she goes, 'Give me her here now' [r] and when he come in she goes, 'You horrible thing, I never, told you I'd never sell Tiny as long as I live!' And then
Helen:	/As long as it's lived as well
Karen:	[c] And then my dad let one of the dogs out, well he let Tiny out and he thought this other dog would be playful with her, and she killed it.

(Maybin 1997: 38–9)

Transcription key
Comments in italics within parentheses clarify unclear references.
/ indicates where another speaker interrupts or cuts in.
Letters in square brackets indicate Labov's structural elements: [A] = abstract; [O] = orientation; [C] = complicating action; [R] = resolution; [r] = alternative resolution; [c] = coda.

speaker thinks the story is worth (re)telling. Such material may occur at the end, but may also be included at any point within the narrative.

- *Result* or *resolution*, which resolves the story.
- *Coda*, which signals the end of the narrative and may bridge the gap between the narrative and the present time.

The box illustrates these elements. The example comes from research on children's language carried out by a British researcher, Janet Maybin (see also Maybin 2006).

Labov was particularly interested in the 'evaluation' elements evident in his corpus of narratives: he illustrated several techniques narrators could use to demonstrate the point of their story or to show how they wanted certain events to be interpreted. These included stepping outside the story to comment on it ('But it really was quite terrific', 'But it was quite an experience'); attributing certain feelings to a protagonist in the story ('that night the manager, Lloyd Burrows, said, "You better pack up and get out because that son of a bitch never forgives anything once he gets it in his head"'); or using certain linguistic devices like repetition or quantifiers (such as *all* in 'he had cuts all over') to intensify parts of the story. Maybin takes these ideas further. She argues that naturally occurring narratives are not 'self-contained' like those elicited by Labov: they depend for their interpretation on links that can be made with other stories, conversations from other contexts and the relationship between conversationalists. Karen's story about Tiny is, at one level, a response to Maybin's question on whether her parents are equally keen on animals: Karen's father is less keen than her mother, as demonstrated by his willingness to sell Tiny. But Maybin argues that the story also develops previous comments Karen has made about her parents' divorce. It is about the relationship between Karen's parents, and about her own role in the family:

> Rather than providing a definitive evaluative comment on an event, I would suggest that Karen's story is just one of many conversational narratives through which she visits and revisits the puzzle of her parents' relationship and of their different evaluative perspectives, and explores her own role in the family. The story's function and meaning for Karen, and probably also for Helen, are related not just to its immediate context in the interview conversation with me, but also to other conversations and other contexts where Karen has told stories with a similar theme. (Maybin 2006: 133)

Central to Karen's portrayal of her parents are the different voices she gives them: her father gruff and matter-of-fact, her mother hysterical and tearful. As narrator, Karen is not simply quoting characters in a story, but representing these in particular ways. The slightly exaggerated representation of her mother's voice suggests to Maybin a certain detachment: that Karen is both representing her mother's feelings and distancing herself from them. Maybin's use of the term 'voice' here comes from the work of the Russian theorist Mikhail Bakhtin, referred to in Chapter 5. The different meanings reflected in Karen's reporting of her mother's speech (her mother's feelings, and Karen's distancing herself from these) would be an instance of 'double voicing' in Bahktin's terms (see p. 176). Bakhtin's work has been influential in narrative analysis. Maybin draws on his ideas to suggest that the use of different voices allows Karen to try out and evaluate different positions – in this case she can explore both her father's and her mother's perspectives as well as commenting on these through her representation of the voices.

Other researchers have explored the role of different voices in personal narratives. Jane Hill (1995) presents a close analysis of a lengthy narrative collected from Don Gabriel, an elderly resident of San Lorenzo Almecatla, a small town located five miles north of the city of Puebla, in the Republic of Mexico. In this narrative, Don Gabriel tells the story of the murder of his son some eight or nine years earlier. To tell this story, Don Gabriel also has to describe his son's role in the coming of a passenger bus-service to their village, attempts by the bus service promoters to embezzle money from the village treasury (for which the son was responsible), the son's refusal to be party to the embezzlement, the son's journey to Puebla to confront the promoters, the anonymous letter advising Don Gabriel of the son's murder, Don Gabriel's journey to Puebla, the attempts by others to deny knowledge of the murder and to cover up the crime, Don Gabriel's discovery of his son's body, attempts by the police to recast the son's death as a justifiable homicide, and the burial of the son without the knowledge of his family.

In addition to different voices, Don Gabriel uses two languages in his story: Mexicano (Nahuatl) and Spanish. The use of these languages interacts with the voice system. The story is told mainly in Mexicano, Don Gabriel's first language and the language of the local town, which also represents traditional peasant values. But Don Gabriel needs to resort to Spanish to discuss aspects of his son's financial dealings and the motive for his murder. Spanish is the language of the city and of the capitalist notion of 'business for profit' which, argues Hill, is 'antithetical to the values of reciprocity and community solidarity that people in towns like Almecatla hold sacred' (p. 108). The alternation between Mexicano and Spanish therefore represents a clash of cultural values. In the story Spanish terms are distanced from Don Gabriel: they are assigned mainly to the voices of other characters and, within the system of self-laminations, to the voice of the neutral narrator (Hill argues that this voice is 'farthest from the moral center of this part of the voice system', p. 133).

Narratives may seem like monologues, in that one person is talking for most, if not all of the time, but Hill's analysis, like Maybin's, would suggest

261	>\Ah pues, <ayamo tlen 'huehcah lo 'mismo.] P	Ah well, not long ago it was the same thing.] P
262	> Ce nomu' chacho máyor ni'can 'chanti.] N	My oldest son who lives here.] N
263	Lo 'mismo] N	The same thing] N
264	de que 'nemi ica in . borra'chera como] N	that some one going around . drunk as] N
265	te quiti] N	he was working] N
266	(spits) quibalacea'rohqueh.] N	they shot him.] N
267	>Ccalaqui'lihqueh tres 'tiros, 'ya me'rito.] N,T	They put three bullets into him, just like that.] N,T
268	>Pero onimavi'varoh.] N	But I survived.] N
269	Pues, este, \oyec sano hasta axan.] P	Well uh, he was healthy until now.] P
270	\Oyec sano.] P	He was healthy.] P
271	\Nada más \cosa de 'neh, nopersonali'dad.] P	It's just a personal thing, a personal matter.] P
272	Quihtoz aquinonon, " 'Algún accidente?"] P, INT	If somebody should ask, 'Some accident?] P
273	\Amo . . . 'Amo 'amo.] P	No . . . No, no.] P

Figure 6.1   Coda from a narrative by Don Gabriel (Hill 1995: 108)

Transcription note

This coda marks the end of the narrative and a return to the present: in line 272, 'Some accident?' takes the listener back to an initial question asked by Hill (to check whether Don Gabriel had suffered any accidents in his life) which elicited the entire story.

   Transcription conventions include:

] = units of the 'voice system'.

Letters after each bracket indicate the particular voice: P = evaluator voice; N = narrator voice; T = intonational modification of the voice: high-pitched, voice breaks; INT = unglossed in the original but probably signifies interviewer voice.

. . . = noticeably long pauses.

Other symbols represent detailed pitch and intonational features.

that they are **dialogic**. Both researchers emphasise the importance of the interaction between different voices within the narrative, and the cultural values represented by these. A more general point is that any utterance may be seen as, in part, a response to previous utterances from the same or earlier texts, and a forerunner of later utterances: to return to Bakhtin, no speaker is 'the first speaker, the one who disturbs the eternal silence of the universe' (1986: 69). Maybin argues that the children's narratives which she analysed could themselves be seen as turns in a 'long conversation', carried on over time and in different contexts as the children revisited themes and ideas that were important to them, exploring these from different perspectives. Finally, the immediate audience plays an important part in any narrative: a narrative may be elicited by something said by another speaker; the narrator will take account of (even silent) listeners in deciding how to tell a story; and listeners may also contribute directly to a narrative, as when Helen prompts Karen in 'Selling Tiny'. Sometimes listeners may play a more active role, acting as a 'co-narrator'. Neal Norrick found this was a common pattern in family narratives, where family members recounted well-known, shared narratives. Such co-narration served to ratify family membership, producing 'shared memories, feelings and values' (1997: 207).

The next section looks more closely at the detail of interactions, or conversations, and how these are organised: how speakers take turns in conversation; how they carry out certain conversational activities, such as requesting and giving information; and how they negotiate relationships with one another as they talk.

6.4   CONVERSATION MANAGEMENT

One of the starting points for many studies of **conversational turn-taking** has been a seminal paper written by Harvey Sacks, Emanuel Schegloff and Gail Jefferson in 1974. Sacks et al. focused on what they saw as a problem for those engaged in ordinary, spontaneous conversations: since the order of turn-taking was not pre-specified (as it might be in a ceremony or a debate), and turns could be of any length, how did speakers know when a current turn was about to end and they could begin speaking? How did successive speakers coordinate their conversational efforts so that the talk flowed smoothly?

Sacks et al. argued that, in any turn, there were **transition relevance places**: points where an utterance was potentially complete. These were signalled by syntactic cues, and also by intonation (in face-to-face conversation, non verbal behaviour such as gaze and gesture would also be important; but the precise nature of turn completion cues is not discussed in detail in this early paper). At each transition relevance place, it was possible for the current speaker to select another speaker, or for another speaker to 'self-select' and begin talking. If this did not happen, the current speaker could continue talking. This model of turn-taking suggests that, normally, only one person speaks at a time; that any gaps between successive turns are very brief; and that overlapping speech is minimal, and normally located around transition relevance places.

Sacks et al.'s model has been further elaborated and refined. Of particular relevance here, however, are studies that look at variability in turn-taking. These suggest that the model is too narrow and, probably, culturally specific. Jaakko Lehtonen and Kari Sajavaara's account of speaking and silence in Finland (mentioned in section 6.2) notes that longer gaps are allowed between speaking turns among Finnish speakers than among speakers in the USA or Sweden. The acceptability of gaps between turns differs in different contexts, however: these are shorter in informal situations with strangers, but may be longer either in more intimate conversations, or when discussing abstract topics involving some reflection. Lehtonen and Sajavaara's comments are based on intuition and personal impression, rather than empirical study. They also point to the existence of stereotypes about different groups of speakers. The Häme people from the south-western areas of Central Finland, for instance, are reputed to be particularly slow of speech. Lehtonen and Sajavaara quote an anecdote from the Folklore Archives of the Finnish Literary Society: 'Two Häme brothers were on their way to work in the morning. One says, "It is here that I lost my knife." Coming back home in the evening, the other asks, "Your knife, did you say?"' (cited in Lehtonen and Sajavaara 1985: 98).

One feature that contributes to the organisation of conversation is the use of **minimal responses** (sometimes also called 'backchannel' signals): words such as (in English) *mmh*, *yeah* and *right*, that are generally analysed, not as speaking turns in their own right, but as conversational support provided by listeners, indicating their involvement in the conversation. Lehtonen and Sajavaara suggest these are used less frequently by Finnish speakers than by speakers of Central European languages, or speakers of English in Britain or the USA. Too frequent use is, in fact, considered typical of drunken behaviour. Finns use many non-verbal signals (such as head-nods and gaze) to indicate their involvement: Lehtonen and Sajavaara comment (p. 196) that '[t]he typical Finn is a "silent" listener'.

Different turn-taking patterns have been reported from other cultural contexts. Overlapping speech, for instance, is common among many groups of speakers (in Sacks et al.'s model, although brief overlaps were predicted, long sequences of overlapping speech were treated as errors or violations, in need of repair). Reisman (1974) reported that public talk among villagers in Antigua was characterised by simultaneous speech. And in Deborah Tannen's study of the Thanksgiving dinner conversation, she found that her New York speakers very frequently overlapped other speakers' turns.

Jennifer Coates, a British researcher, has also questioned the universality of the 'one person at a time' model proposed by Sacks et al. Coates transcribed and analysed a large corpus of informal talk between British women friends. In her analysis of this data, she found it difficult to sustain the notion of an individually constructed speaking turn: turns seemed rather to be jointly constructed between speakers. Coates' transcription methods emphasise this, bracketing together speakers who contribute to a joint turn as in the example of A, C and D below:

(A, C and D '*struggle to define a concept they can't name* (Schadenfreude)':

⎧ D: it's sort of pleasure
⎨ C: a perverse pleasure=
⎩ A: =in their

⎧ C: =yeah
⎩ A   downfall=

(Coates 1994: 181)

Overlapping speech was also very common among this sample of speakers:

(*C, D and E are discussing child abuse*)

C: I mean in order to accept that idea you're

⎧ C: having to.   ⎡ completely
⎨ E: mhm. completely review your ⎣ view of your
⎩ D: yes

⎧ C: change ⎤ your view of your husband=
⎨ E: husband⎦ =   = that's right
⎨ B: = yes
⎩ A: yeah   mhm

(Coates 1994: 182)

Transcription key
{ long brackets group speakers together, and indicate that the contributions from these speakers should be read as a jointly constructed speaking turn;
[ ] square brackets indicate the start and end of overlapping speech;
= an equals sign indicates that there is no perceptible pause between one speaker stopping and the next beginning.

In this case, E completes the utterance begun by C; C herself overlaps this completion, echoing E's words; A, B and D provide supportive 'minimal responses' (*yes, yeah* and *mhm*).

Coates sees this kind of talk as highly cooperative, and suggests it is more common among female speakers. In an analysis of informal talk among men (Coates 1997), she found patterns that corresponded more closely to the 'one person at a time' model proposed by Sacks et al. (Gender differences in talk are discussed further in Chapter 7.)

Sacks et al.'s model of turn-taking also seems to assume that talk is fairly democratically organised – that all participants have the right to contribute at transition relevance places. However, a variety of social and cultural factors will affect how speakers contribute to an interaction. We shall look at some examples of 'asymmetrical' talk in section 6.6 below.

We have focused, so far, on turn-taking patterns and how these have been found to differ between different groups of speakers. Other aspects of conversational style are also used variably among different social groups: forms of greeting, for instance; making requests; getting and giving information. We shall illustrate these more general features of conversational style from work carried out by Diana Eades among Aboriginal English speakers in Australia (reported in several papers, including Eades 1988 and 1991). There are formal linguistic differences between some varieties of Aboriginal English and standard Australian English (e.g. differences in pronunciation and grammar). However, Eades argues that, even where Aboriginal English speakers use more standard grammatical forms, their language may differ in important ways from the language used by white Australians. Eades was interested, in particular, in the relative 'indirectness' of Aboriginal speakers, in contrast to the more direct speech of white Australians.

Eades found that there were several constraints on the use of direct questions in Aboriginal English. Questions could be used to seek 'orientation information', such as clarification of a topic or checking on the time or place of an event. In this case, the question was frequently in statement form with rising intonation: 'You were at the pub?' or 'Janey came home?' (rather than 'Were you at the pub?' or 'Did Janey come home?'). Eades argues that such questions are an example of 'indirectness' because the speaker is presenting known or supposed information for the listener to confirm or deny.

This strategy was more evident in seeking substantial information (such as important personal details, or a full account of an event), when it was rare for questions to be used at all. More usually, the person seeking information would contribute some knowledge of their own about the topic. This would be followed by a silence. The required information need not be given immediately: sometimes it was not given for several days. Similarly, Aboriginal speakers tended not to make direct requests; nor did they directly question a person's motives or reasons for doing something; personal opinions tended to be expressed cautiously. Eades relates these communicative practices to Aboriginal people's lifestyles. She notes that Aboriginal social life is very public, conducted in the view of others. Furthermore, because Aboriginal people have commitments to an extended family network, most aspects of their lives are shared with several relatives. Personal privacy is regarded as important, but this is maintained interactionally, through speaking styles that do not impose on others. Although Eades does not draw explicitly on politeness theory in her work, the Aboriginal speaking styles which she discusses would probably count as negative politeness in Brown and Levinson's model (discussed in section 6.2).

The use of different interactional styles by Aboriginal and white Australian speakers can lead to communication problems. In contexts such as meetings and university tutorials, Aboriginal speakers may be offended by the forceful opinions expressed by white speakers; white speakers, on the other hand, may become frustrated by the indirect and roundabout style adopted by Aboriginal speakers. Aboriginal speakers may try to accommodate to different speaking styles, but this can also lead to communication problems. An example discussed by Eades is the use of 'gratuitous concurrence', where a term such as *yes* is used, not necessarily to signal agreement, but to facilitate the ongoing interaction or hasten its conclusion. This may lead to misunderstandings in interaction with white Australians, and there can be serious consequences in institutional settings where direct questioning is used, such as police interviews, law courts, employment interviews, medical consultations, classrooms and government consultations. (We discuss below some practical applications of Eades' research in Australian court cases.)

6.5   ENCODING RELATIONSHIPS

While the examples of research discussed so far have focused on the different ways in which conversations are structured, it has also been apparent that such differences give rise to conversational outcomes: to positive or negative perceptions of different speakers, or groups of speakers, for instance. In speaking in a particular way, a speaker is saying something about the kind of person they are, and constructing a certain kind of relationship with others. In engaging in conversation, speakers are necessarily doing a certain amount of 'identity work', through their use of conversational style as well as their use of a particular accent, dialect or language.

Sometimes, relationships between speakers and listeners are explicitly encoded in language. In many languages, speakers can signal their relative status through the use of certain forms of address: in English, these would include terms such as *madam*; a title plus second name (*Dr Jones, Ms Bennett*); a first name (e.g. *Margaret*); a term of endearment (*love, honey*). Speakers of certain languages need to select appropriate pronoun forms depending on their relationship with the person they are addressing or talking about: French, like many European languages, distinguishes between different forms of the second-person pronoun *you* (the forms *tu* and *vous* are associated with, among other things, familiarity or social distance). The use of such **T and V pronouns** is discussed further in Chapter 10. Some languages, such as Javanese (Errington 1988) and Japanese (Ide and Yoshido 1999; Tsujimura 2007 Ch. 7) have more elaborate **honorific** systems that express different levels of politeness or respect for the person addressed or referred to. The use of such forms is not fixed or static: usage may shift as relationships change, and may even vary in different contexts depending on which aspect of a relationship needs to be emphasised.

An example of this complexity can be seen in a study by Alessandro Duranti (1992) of the use of Samoan 'respect' vocabulary. In Samoan, there is a set of words called *upu fa'aaloalo* ('respectful words'), that are distinguished from more ordinary 'common' terms. Respectful words describe individuals and groups, and some of their actions, attributes and possessions. They are used to address or refer to those with high social status: titled people, including chiefs and orators. The term 'come', for instance, has three forms:

sau (common)   afio mai (used for chiefs)   maliu mai (used for orators).

In the example below, a high chief, Salanoa, uses the term 'maliu mai' to refer to a senior orator who has just arrived at an event:

Salanoa: ia 'o le **maliu mai** laa o le Makua
(so the senior orator has **arrived**)

(Duranti 1992: 84)

While the use of such terms does, as their name suggests, signal respect, Duranti argues that their function is actually more varied than this. He found that respectful words were sometimes used of people who were not entitled to them, whereas those who were entitled to them did not always receive them. This was partly a question of context: respectful words were more closely associated with formal or public events. But usage could be inconsistent: on one occasion different terms, one respectful and the other common, might be used of the same individual. Duranti relates this variable usage to the Samoan notion of personal identity, which he argues is less fixed than in 'western' traditions: people are seen as composite personae with different 'sides' which may be highlighted or downplayed. The choice between common or respectful words, he suggests, can be used to highlight different aspects of the identity of the person addressed or referred to. Rather than simply reflecting pre-established social relations, such terms construct variable relationships between the speaker and the person being talked to or about.

Duranti relates his interpretation to politeness theory (summarised above, in section 6.2). But he also questions aspects of Brown and Levinson's model of politeness. In Brown and Levinson's model, showing respect for another would be a form of negative politeness: by signalling the higher status and power of a listener, a speaker is diffusing any potentially face-threatening acts. They are making it clear that they are not able to make any impositions upon the listener. Duranti, however, argues that respectful terms may well constitute an imposition, by reminding a listener of the obligations of their position. He gives the example of a senior orator who questioned Duranti's note-taking when he was carrying out fieldwork. A chief replied to the orator:

'o a kou **vagaga** aa ma **saugoaga** lea ua kusikusi uma lava e le kama
(it's your **speech** [i.e. of the orators] and the **speech** [of the chiefs] that the boy has been writing down word by word)

By using respectful words to refer to the speeches of the orators and chiefs, and also the term 'boy' to refer to the researcher, the speaker is emphasising the relative power of the orator, and implying that a man in his position need not take any notice of the researcher's work: 'What could a "boy" do to such a powerful man? He (that is, I) could only take notes and learn from the old man's high eloquence' (Duranti 1992: 92).

6.6 ASYMMETRICAL TALK

We have emphasised throughout this chapter the role of talk in negotiating relationships between speakers. Such relationships are frequently unequal, or **asymmetrical**, in that one speaker, or group of speakers, is in a more powerful position than others. This may be evident in the use of status-related terms, such as those discussed in the previous section, but it will also affect the overall organisation of an interaction and the different speaking styles adopted by participants. Many researchers with an interest in this topic have focused on institutional contexts (such as hospitals and clinics, schools and colleges, police stations and law courts, workplaces). Speakers in such contexts may have different formal statuses (doctor/patient, teacher/student, barrister/witness, employer/employee) which affect their participation in interactions: they may be expected to have greater or fewer interactional 'rights' depending on their relative status. Cultural differences in interactional style, which we mentioned earlier, will also be important in such contexts, intersecting with status to affect both the conduct of interactions and their outcomes.

Analyses of doctor–patient talk have often shown how such talk both reflects and maintains unequal power relations between participants (e.g. Cicourel 1981, 1985; Fischer and Todd 1983). An interesting variant on this theme comes from a US study by Paula Treichler, Richard Frankel, Cheris Kramarae, Kathleen Zoppi and Howard Beckman. Treichler et al. (1984) discuss two successive interactions, one between a doctor and a patient and the other between a medical student and the same patient. Both interactions were recorded as part of a medical training programme.

The transcript below is a brief extract from near the beginning of the first of these interactions. The doctor has introduced the medical student who will sit in on the consultation, and at the point where the extract begins he switches topic to focus on the patient's symptoms. The doctor asks several questions to elicit information from the patient. He notes down some of this information while the patient talks. The patient provides brief responses to the doctor's questions:

> Dr: Great. So *how* you doing today Joseph
> Pt: Not too good doct//or

	Dr:	Not too good. I see you kinda hangin' your head low there.
	Pt:	Yeah.
	Dr:	Must be somethin' up (.) or down I should say. Are you feelin' down?
	Pt:	Yeah
	Dr:	What are you feelin' down *about* (0.7)
	Pt:	Stomach problems, back problems, *side* problems.

[086

'2/9/82'	Dr:	*Problems* problems
	Pt:	Problems and *problems*

090]

	Dr:	Hum. What's:: we- what's goin' on with your stomach. Are you still uh- havin' pains in your stomach?
	Pt:	Yeah it's- can't hold no *food* water
	Dr:	How 'bout uh-:: are you- y' still throwin' up?
	Pt:	Oh yes.
	Dr:	Hmh
	(2.0)	

[105

'Still N&V'	Pt:	Nervous tensions (.) can't sleep.

111]

	Pt:	.hhh
	Dr:	I see. An::d so this has be::en since December you've been havin' this (0.2) this nausea =
	Pt:	= Oh. yeah =
	Dr:	= and stuff. [. . .]

(Treichler et al. 1984: 81–2)

Transcription key

The first (left-hand) column shows notes made by the doctor; 'N & V' = nausea and vomiting.

In the second column, Dr = doctor; Pt = patient.

In the third column:

- punctuation indicates intonation not grammar: a full stop indicates sharply falling intonation; a question mark sharply rising intonation; a comma indicates slightly rising or slightly falling intonation;
- stressed syllables are italicised (e.g. *how*);
- double slashes (e.g. doct//or) indicate an overlap: that the next speaker's turn begins at this point;
- (.) and (0.7) indicate pauses (numbers indicate tenths of a second);
- square brackets with numbers [086, 090] indicate the start and finish of the doctor's note-taking; the numbers indicate elapsed time in tenths of a second;
- 'What's:: we-' – colons indicate prolongation of the preceding syllable (each colon represents one tenth of a second); a hyphen indicates that the previous syllable has been cut off;
- '.hhh' signals an inhalation.

This pattern continues through most of the interview: the doctor's questions control the pattern of turn-taking and determine the overall course of the interaction – when the patient speaks, which topics are raised, elaborated or downplayed – and it is the doctor's notes that would constitute the final record if this had not been recorded for research and training purposes. At one point, encouraged by the doctor, the patient says rather more, explaining that he suffered an injury some time ago which left him unable to work. He is now worried because his social security payments are to be cut. The doctor acknowledges this but returns to what he sees as the current problem – the patient's biomedical condition. Treichler et al point out that the training programme the doctor is involved in attempts to integrate 'psychosocial' information within a medical framework, but the doctor clearly finds it hard to do this. Other analyses (e.g. Mishler 1984) have pointed to a struggle between different 'voices' in doctor–patient consultations: the doctor continually asserts a 'medical' voice, whereas the patient frequently mixes this with the voice of the 'lifeworld' or everyday experience.

When the medical student is left to talk to the patient, he begins by saying he is 'curious' about the pain felt by the patient. Thereafter, his interactional style is different from the doctor's: after asking a question he is willing to leave quite long pauses; and he gives minimal responses such as *uh huh* and *yeah*, encouraging the patient to say more. The transcript below provides a brief example of this style: the medical student has discovered the patient gets confused and asks him to elaborate on this.

MS: Uh huh. Confusion. [looks at pt] Tell me a little more about your
confusion.
[7 sec]
Pt: Get angry. (U) [vocalises, moves right hand] (U) violent intentions. (?)
MS: Yeah
Pt: [looks at MS] I have killed before and I could do it again – easy.
MS: Uh huh.
Pt: And I know that the court won't hold this against me cause I got a
mental case – brain damage [moving hands – slumps]
MS: I see. So that was since you – since 1968?
Pt: Yes
MS: Um hmm. I see.

(Treichler et al. 1984: 88)

Transcription key
The first column is blank as no notes are recorded by the medical student at this point.
In the second column, MS = medical student; Pt = patient.
In the third column, conventions are as in the transcript above, plus:
relevant non-verbal information is given in brackets: [looks at MS].

By continuing to encourage the patient to talk, the medical student discovers that he is seeing a psychiatrist, that he has been in an alcoholic detoxification and rehabilitation programme and that he regularly takes Thorazine, a drug he feels may have a bearing on his stomach problems. Treichler et al. comment that this information was not previously known, but is relevant to the patient's treatment.

There are clearly differences in status between the doctor, the medical student and the patient which will affect how each of them approaches the consultation as well as how they are responded to by other participants. But it is also probably relevant that the doctor and the medical student are both white, whereas the patient is black; and that the patient is dependent on social security. While Treichler et al. are concerned particularly with the implications of professional status, several other social and contextual factors will affect the conduct of this and other medical interactions. In a different study, Candace West (1984) looked at the extent to which doctors and patients interrupted one another. West was able to compare consultations between female and male doctors and female and male patients, and found that use of interrruptions was related to gender as well as to participants' status as a doctor or patient. Male doctors used interruptions more than their patients (whether female or male). They frequently interrupted with a further question before the patient had finished answering the previous one, and this allowed them to control the direction of the interview. Female doctors, on the other hand, received more interruptions, particularly from male patients. On the basis of this evidence, West suggests that gender may take precedence over professional status in determining the conduct of medical interactions (gender differences in language are discussed further in Chapter 7).

Norman Fairclough (1992) discusses changing practices in medical interactions, relating these to more widespread social change. The transcript below shows an extract from a consultation between a female patient and a male doctor which bears little resemblance to the interactions analysed by Treichler et al. or West:

```
      P:  but she really has been very unfair to me . got⌈no
      D:                                                 ⌊hm
      P:  respect for me at⌈all and I think . that's one of the reasons
      D:                   ⌊hm
  5   P:  why I drank s⌈o much you know – a nd em
      D:              ⌊hm          ⌈hm   hm⌈hm  are you
          you back are you back on it have you started drinking
          ⌈again
      P:  ⌊no
 10   D:  oh you haven't (uncle⌈ar . . .)
      P:                       ⌊no. but em one thing that the
          lady on the Tuesday said to me was that . if my mother
          did turn me out of the⌈house which she thinks she
      D:                        ⌊yes                      hm
```

```
15  P:   may do . coz . she doesn't like the way I've been she has
         turned me o⌈ut befo⌈re . and em. she said that .
    D:            ⌊hm    ⌊hm
    P:   I could she thought that it might be possible to me for
         me to go to a council⌈flat
20  D:                        ⌊right yes
```

(Fairclough 1992: 145)

Transcription key
Full stops mark short pauses, a dash marks a longer pause;
square brackets show overlapping speech;
unclear material is in parentheses.

Fairclough discusses a striking feature of this interaction: the absence of question/answer sequences directed by the doctor. Turn-taking seems to be more collaboratively managed between doctor and patient, and it is the patient who raises and switches topics. Both doctor and patient seem to accept a mixture of 'medical' and 'lifeworld' voices. Fairclough relates the doctor's strategy to politeness theory: for instance, the doctor's question (lines 6–7) is uttered rapidly, quietly and with some hesitation, which minimises its face-threatening potential. The doctor does not surrender interactional control to the patient – he controls the beginning and end of the interaction (not shown in this extract) and he does elicit medical information (for example, about the patient's drinking). This is achieved, however, by the use of more mitigated forms. Fairclough suggests that this alternative medical interaction is a blend between two genres: a 'standard' medical interview (such as the example from Treichler et al. cited above) and counselling. This, he argues, coincides with a more widespread shift towards informal conversational practices in several institutional contexts:

> doctors in this sort of medical interview appear to be rejecting the elitism, formality, and distance of the medical scientist figure in favour of a (frequently simulated) 'nice', 'ordinary' person, a 'good listener'. This accords with general shifts in dominant cultural values in our society, which devalue professional elitism and set a high value on informality, naturalness, and normalness. (Fairclough 1992: 147)

The analysis of asymmetrical talk adds to our understanding of how interactions work, both in terms of conversation management (for example, the management of turn-taking) and of how participants negotiate (potentially changing) relationships with one another. Such analysis, particularly when carried out in institutional contexts, may also have an applied focus. Treichler et al. were part of an interdisciplinary team that included language analysts and health workers; they were concerned with the practical implications of their work and with the development of intervention programmes that would benefit all participants in medical encounters. Insofar as their work led to changes in interactional practice, it may well have brought about a more conversational style such as that recorded in another (later) context by Fairclough. This interventionist approach bears some resemblance to Diana Eades' work on Australian Aboriginal language use, discussed earlier. Much of Eades' work has been concerned with the application of sociolinguistic analysis in legal contexts.

Eades (1996) discusses an Australian court case for which she provided sociolinguistic evidence. The case concerned Robyn Kina, an Aboriginal woman convicted of the murder of the man she lived with. A later appeal found that Kina had acted in self-defence against a man who was repeatedly violent towards her and the conviction was overturned. It was at this appeal that Eades provided evidence. Kina had not been called to give evidence at her original trial, and her lawyers noted that they had difficulties taking instructions from her. They did not therefore discover that she had acted under provocation. This became clear only later, when Kina was interviewed for two TV documentaries about victims of domestic violence who kill their spouses in self-defence. It was Kina's interviews on these documentaries that led to the instigation of a successful appeal.

The question Eades needed to address (along with two other expert witnesses, a psychiatrist and a social worker) was why Kina had talked to TV journalists about her self-defence, whereas her original lawyers had not obtained this information. After reviewing documents relating to the case, and talking to Kina and her counsellor, Eades concluded that Kina was communicating in an Aboriginal way. Her lawyers could not communicate in this way, and were also unaware that the communication difficulties they experienced were the result of cultural differences. On the other hand, the TV journalists and Kina's counsellor employed similar strategies to those evident in Aboriginal ways of communicating. Eades refers to features of Aboriginal communication such as those discussed above (pp. 197–9) – e.g. the avoidance of direct questions to elicit substantial information, and the use of silence, waiting till people were ready to give information. She argues that interviews with Kina's lawyers would have been problematical in several ways:

- A one-sided interview which was basically structured by a large number of questions would have been difficult for her to participate in successfully.
- In particular, she would have found it extremely difficult to provide information about embarrassing personal details in the context of a one-sided interview.
- She would have responded to questions with silence. [. . .] [S]uch silence is often wrongly interpreted by an interviewer as unwillingness to answer, or lack of relevant knowledge, or agreement with a proposition.
- As information is seen as part of a relationship, every time that Kina's legal counsel changed (i.e. three times after the committal hearing and before the trial) she would have felt the need to develop a new relationship with the new solicitor before much significant information could be 'given away'. It

appears that little ground was made in developing such a relationship with any of the solicitors who worked with her leading up to her trial.

(Eades 1996: 218)

By contrast, the interviews for the TV programmes were more consistent with Aboriginal ways of finding out information:

- The interviewer took the time to establish some sort of relationship with Kina before conducting the TV interview.
- The interviews provided the opportunity for Kina to give several uninterrupted narrative accounts in telling different parts of her story.
- Unlike the lawyer interviews, the TV interviews were primarily concerned with hearing Kina's story. Having no need to structure the information, the journalists used prompts to encourage her to say what she wanted to say. In contrast, in the lawyer interview, the lawyer needs to find out about certain aspects which are determined to be legally relevant.

(Adapted from Eades 1996: 222)

Eades' evidence was accepted by the appeal court along with other evidence. Other consequences of the case were that the legal aid office that had originally represented Kina organised workshops for its staff on cross-cultural communication. The Attorney-General at the time also publicly recognised the need to be sensitive to problems of cross-cultural communication.

Eades' work on the Kina case is an example of **forensic linguistics**, the use of expert linguistic evidence in criminal investigations (you saw another example of this in the work of William Labov, discussed in Chapter 4). In this case, the evidence was presented in support of a person who had already been convicted, but there are various ways in which sociolinguistic evidence might inform legal systems. For instance, Eades also produced a handbook advising legal professionals on communicating with Aboriginal speakers (Eades 1992). This contained sections on, for instance, asking questions and understanding Aboriginal answers. Eades (2004) notes that this was launched with considerable publicity, it was reported to be used in law schools and in offices of Aboriginal Legal Services and other lawyers who work with Aboriginal clients. It has also been cited in legal judgements and drawn on in reports from the Queensland Criminal Justice Commission (the state in which it was produced.)

Despite the apparent success of such sociolinguistic interventions, in a later review Eades (2004) argues that there are shortcomings in interventions that rely solely on promoting an understanding of cultural differences in communication. She advocates the adoption of a **critical sociolinguistics** approach that recognises issues of power and inequality. Eades cites another legal case, known as the Pinkenba case, in which police officers were tried for picking up three Aboriginal boys aged 12, 13 and 14 who were wandering round a shopping mall. The boys were not charged with any offence, but were driven to Pinkenba, an area 14 kilometres out of town, and left to find their own way home. The boys were witnesses for the prosecution during the initial committal hearing, but were unable to maintain a consistent story under cross-examination from defence lawyers. Charges against the police officers were therefore dropped. In one specific instance, one young man, under aggressive questioning about whether he knew he did not have to accompany the police officers, answered *yeh*, thus contradicting an earlier response. Eades interprets this as an instance of 'gratuitous concurrence' (see pp. 198–9 above), rather than an agreement with the proposition of the lawyer's question. Eades notes that the defence lawyers in the case had copies of the *Handbook*, and argues that they were able to use this knowledge to manipulate Aboriginal ways of speaking and subvert witnesses' attempts to communicate.

Eades argues that in order to understand this and similar events we need to go beyond sociolinguistic analysis of 'power in the discourse' (i.e. in the cross-examination) to take into account broader structural inequalities within society, and within the judicial system ('power behind the discourse') which have led to the historical domination of Aboriginal people. For Eades, the cross-examination only makes sense in relation to structures in which Aboriginal people are routinely criminalised:

> It was not just that the police took the boys for a ride in circumstances where it is ludicrous to claim they could have exercised their legal right to refuse. But the whole criminal justice system worked to legitimize the actions of the police officers. (2004: 507)

This is not to see such structural inequalities as immutable constraints. Rather, power is something that needs to be worked at and that may also be resisted. In this case, resistance took place not in the courtroom, but in complaints that led to charges being brought in the first place, and street protests following the dropping of these charges. Eades notes that her continuing work on this case seeks to investigate:

> . . . the mechanisms of power involved in the relationships between Aboriginal people and the criminal justice system. Sociolinguistic micro-analysis of courtroom cross-examination is central to this investigation, as is the analysis of the wider power struggles that involve the criminalisation of Aboriginal young people and the naturalisation of police control over them, as well as Aboriginal resistance to such processes. (2004: 507–8)

There is further discussion of critical approaches in Chapter 10.

Celia Roberts, Evelyn Davies and Tom Jupp were concerned, like Diana Eades, with the outcomes of communication differences between different cultural groups – in this case, in the workplace. Roberts et al. (1992) discuss several aspects of language and discrimination in the workplace, drawing on their involvement in the Industrial Language Training Service, an organisation which provided training in English as a second/additional language for ethnic-minority workers in Britain during the 1970s and 1980s. The ILT also trained supervisors, union stewards and others to help them improve their communication skills in multi-ethnic settings. An important part of the service's work was the sociolinguistic analysis of language, which both grew out of and fed back into practice. Roberts et al. point out that multi-ethnic workplaces were often sites of overt racism and abuse. Interactional discrimination, however, could also be rather more subtle.

Roberts et al. draw on a number of theoretical and analytical perspectives in examining workplace communication, including pioneering research by John Gumperz and his associates on interethnic communication (for example, Gumperz 1982a, 1982b). They identify several linguistic factors, such as differences in intonation patterns, that sometimes led to misunderstandings between workers and supervisors or managers, and that could affect the way workers were evaluated in contexts such as job interviews. They argue, however, that in order to understand communication in the workplace there is a need to go beyond a purely linguistic analysis.

When groups of people who do not share a common language come together, there is clearly a danger of misunderstanding or 'miscommunication'. One might expect this to be resolved by effective language training. However, Roberts et al. show that the position of ethnic-minority workers was not substantially changed by language training: those who could communicate in English still occupied low-paid, frequently unpleasant jobs, and their relations with employers did not significantly improve. The data collected and analysed by ILT trainers showed evidence of the continuing disadvantages faced by ethnic-minority workers, frequently based on cultural assumptions that were not shared between workers and managers or supervisors. The transcript below, for instance, shows a brief extract from a job interview: the applicant, B, is Asian with near-native-speaker competence in English. He is being interviewed by N for a job as a driver/conductor with a transport company.

N: . . . What do you think L— Buses is going to offer you that R— don't offer you?

B: Well, quite a lot of things, for example like um . . . Christmas bonus.

N: Uh huh.

B: So many things, holidays and all that. Well, we get holidays in R— but you er . . . get here more holidays than you get in R— (laughs).

N: All right. OK . . . Before you actually went to R— four years ago you were in Africa.

B: Yes.

N: And that was where, Kenya?

B: No, Malawi.

N: Malawi, and you were doing what there?

B: We had our own business there. I was working in a shop, it's a grocery shop.

N: What made you decide to sell up and come to England?

B: Well um you know it's just like what happened in Uganda (PHONE) could happen there, come to this country you know and settle myself.

N: Did you find it easy to settle here?

B: Not quite, I was alone here, I had no relations and nobody . . .

N: You came over totally cold, nowhere to go . . .

B: Yes.

N: Nowhere to live.

B: I was looked after by the government. I'm alright now.

N: OK. You've been driving for two and a half years.

B: Yes.

N: You obviously don't drive in the job you're doing. What sort of driving experience have you had?

B: In this country?

N: Um hum.

B: I've got um light goods vehicle driving licence and I've . . . I don't think done nothing wrong.

N: What sort of vehicles have you driven?

B: Well, Cortinas.

N: Basically car experience rather than vans or anything larger . . .

B: Yes.

(Roberts et al. 1992: 44–5)

Roberts et al. point out that, in asking what the prospective job will offer the applicant, the interviewer, N, expects him to talk about the relevance of his experience and abilities, or about the challenges the job will provide. The applicant, B, however, interprets the question literally and talks about bonuses and holidays. When asked about his driving experience, his answer may appear defensive (in many countries interviews are seen as a test, designed to probe weaknesses and catch interviewees out, and this may explain B's caution). It is likely, therefore, that B was unsuccessful in this interview because he failed to recognise the purpose of the interviewer's questions: he did not have any difficulty with their surface meaning. This raises the question of whether workers should be trained to change culturally specific behaviour and adopt practices with which they may feel uncomfortable, such as 'selling' themselves to prospective employers. The ILT's decision to offer training to all those involved in multi-ethnic workplaces – workers, supervisors and managers – represented a commitment to more widespread institutional change:

> The task was to change the communicative environment of a workplace and to redefine the bureaucratic processes of access so that they took account of cultural and linguistic diversity. It would clearly be unjust if those with the least communicative power in Britain were expected to bring about these changes.

Training focussed only on black workers would assume an assimilationist or, at best, integrationist approach. Training for white and black workers and managers was a commitment to a pluralist approach, to effecting change where power – or at least some power – lay. (Roberts et al. 1992: 10)

6.7 CONCLUSION

In analysing language in interaction, sociolinguists have been concerned not simply with the forms of language but with how these are used to communicative effect in particular cultural contexts. This emphasis extends and sometimes challenges ideas about language use that underpinned research discussed in earlier chapters. While most sociolinguistic research takes account of something called 'context', for instance, what this means in practice varies considerably between different sociolinguistic approaches. In the case of interactional sociolinguistics, 'context' refers to naturally occurring contexts of use, rather than different contexts constructed by the researcher. Researchers such as Duranti, in his study of Samoan respect vocabulary, have shown how detailed micro-analysis, relating terms and expressions to their use by particular speakers, in particular settings, to particular effect can provide a fuller understanding of sociolinguistic phenomena. In their research into language in the workplace, Roberts et al. argued that they needed a broad view of context, to take into account not just the immediate setting and participants (e.g. candidate and interviewer in a job interview) but also the wider context in which participants lived and worked. This wider context would affect the cultural knowledge and experiences which people brought with them into an interaction, as well as the specific strategies which they used to interpret and take part in the interaction. Language use is not simply a response to a particular context, however. In speaking in a certain way speakers may help to construct contexts (e.g. as relatively formal or informal). This idea of context as partly constructed in discourse was also evident in studies of code-switching and style-shifting discussed in Chapter 5.

Sociolinguistic research has been concerned to document the language use of different social groups, often drawing contrasts between members of different social classes, age groups, ethnic and other groups. A danger with this approach is that it may give rise to a rather fixed notion of social identity: in practice, speakers' allegiances are likely to be more fluid and variable. Interactional sociolinguistic studies (those discussed in Chapter 5 as well as this chapter) show speakers expressing different aspects of their identity and negotiating relationships with others as they talk – in speaking at all (or in remaining silent), in using certain interactional styles, in addressing or referring to others in certain ways. Even relationships that seem to be relatively fixed, such as doctor–patient relationships, are maintained (and may be redefined) in routine encounters. Power often plays an important part in relations between people, a factor that has been recognised by several studies discussed in this chapter.

Many studies of interaction have investigated contexts in which speakers from different cultural backgrounds, and with different cultural understandings, come into contact. There has often been a focus on factors that contribute to 'miscommunication': misperceptions of speakers (as in Basso's contention that Athapaskan speakers were felt to lack 'personal warmth', or Eades' reference to frustration in encounters between Aboriginal and white Australian speakers); or misunderstandings of what people mean (as in Roberts et al.'s account of a job interview) – in each case, because of differences in interactional style. The term 'miscommunication' is, however, problematical. It may imply a certain neutrality – that misunderstandings simply happen and that all speakers are equally affected by them. In practice, some speakers will be affected more than others. Power is likely to be a factor here, affecting who is seen as incompetent, or whose understandings prevail. Studies of 'miscommunication' in institutional contexts suggest that there may be serious consequences for those in less powerful positions: differences in interactional style may affect whether a defendant or a witness is believed in a court of law, or whether an applicant gets or keeps a job. Researchers concerned with such issues often aim, not simply to analyse and interpret language in interaction, but also to have an effect on speaking practices. Eades and Roberts et al., for instance, demonstrate an explicit commitment to social justice, and intend their work to be of immediate practical relevance.

Many topics addressed in this chapter will be followed up in later ones. Issues in gender and interaction, referred to briefly here, are discussed more fully in Chapter 7. The relationship between language and power is the main focus of Chapter 10. And Chapter 12 discusses the involvement of sociolinguists in policy-making, in this case at national level.

7

GENDER AND LANGUAGE USE

7.1 INTRODUCTION

The idea that women and men use language differently has a long history within 'folklinguistics', a term used by some researchers to refer to sets of popular beliefs about language (see Chapter 5). In terms of systematic empirical investigation, there are several interesting early studies (for example, anthropologically oriented accounts of 'women's and men's language' dating from the 1920s, 1930s and 1940s), but the growth of language and gender as a major research area began later, around the beginning of the 1970s. While the initial focus of research was on generalised gender differences, more recent studies have taken greater account of context, attempting to provide a more contextualised and nuanced account of how speakers may draw on language (and other communicative systems) to negotiate gender, along with other aspects of identity. This shift in sociolinguistic research is associated with more general developments in gender theory.

As an area, language and gender has been characterised by interdisciplinarity, with valuable contributions from anthropology, various forms of discourse analysis, education, literary theory, media studies, social psychology, sociology, women's studies and lesbian and gay studies as well as sociolinguistics more narrowly defined. Many, or more probably most, contributors to the field have been feminists, and there has been an emphasis both on the development of theory and on more practical concerns. Language and gender is a topic that is of interest in its own right; it is also important because of what it can add to our understanding of language and how it works, and to the sociolinguistic study of language.

This chapter considers aspects of language and gender that are most closely related to sociolinguistic issues identified in previous chapters. In particular, we focus on spoken rather than written language and on studies that examine language structures and how these are used (in contrast, say, to social psychological studies that have looked at the *content* of spoken interaction, relating the expression of people's beliefs and attitudes to the social construction of gender). The issue of sexism, or sexist 'bias' in language, is considered later, in Chapter 10. The further reading suggestions on p. 445 indicate work in other traditions that may be followed up by interested readers.

We adopt a broadly historical approach across the chapter, looking first at studies of distinctive female and male forms in certain languages, then at variationist studies (building on the discussion of language variation in Chapters 2–5), at interactional studies (building on the discussion of language in interaction in Chapter 6), and finally at examples of more recent 'contextualised' studies. We also try to give a sense of some of the debates that have characterised, and continue to characterise, this highly dynamic research area.

7.2   WOMEN'S AND MEN'S LANGUAGES

The men have a great many expressions peculiar to them, which the women understand but never pronounce themselves. On the other hand, the women have words and phrases which the men never use, or they would be laughed to scorn. Thus it happens that in their conversations it often seems as if the women had another language than the men. (Rochefort 1665, cited Jespersen 1922: 237)

Rochefort was writing about the language of the Carib Indians, from the Lesser Antilles in the West Indies. He tells a local story – that the Caribs had killed all the male members of the Arawak tribe who used to inhabit the islands, and married the Arawak women. These women had retained their own language and passed this on to their daughters. Their sons, however, learned the language of their Carib fathers.

The story of the 'separate languages' spoken by the Caribs naturally aroused a great deal of interest, but the female and male varieties seem to have been less distinct than Rochefort thought. The linguist Otto Jespersen re-examined Rochefort's data and found that only about one tenth of the vocabulary items showed distinct female and male forms.

Linguists studying several languages have found evidence of 'sex-exclusive' language forms, that is, cases in which an obligatory grammatical distinction is made between female and male speakers. Some early evidence of this comes from linguistic descriptions of Native American languages. For instance, Mary Haas (1944), in a study of Koasati, found differences in verb forms which are shown in Table 7.1.

The different forms recorded by Haas were more common in older speakers – such differences seemed to be dying out among younger ones.

Similar findings have been reported from studies of other Native American

Female form	*Male form*	*Meaning*
lakawčĭn	lakawčî·s	don't lift it!
lakawwîl	lakawwís	I am lifting it
lakáwwilit	lakáwwilič	I lifted it
		(Haas 1944: 143–4)

Table 7.1   Female and male verb forms in Koasati

Note: These spellings are Haas's attempts to represent pronunciation accurately.

languages – (for example, by Sapir 1929) and of languages spoken in other countries – see Trudgill (1983a) for a brief review. Early commentators on these linguistic distinctions tended to see them as indexical of social practices and beliefs. Language functioned as a kind of social mirror, reflecting important social distinctions. Writing in 1944, Furfey argued that the existence of different female and male forms of language meant that speakers were conscious of women and men as different categories of human beings. Furthermore, he added:

> at least at some period in the history of language, this distinction must have been regarded as being of a certain consequence; for it would seem to be a general truth that the great categories of grammar are not based on distinctions regarded by the speakers as trivial. (Furfey 1944: 222)

A language that has given rise to some debate about the incidence of female and male forms is Japanese. Gender differentiation is said to occur in several features of Japanese phonology, grammar and lexis (for examples of different uses of pronoun forms, see the box). The overall impression given is that women are relatively 'polite, gentle, soft-spoken, non-assertive and empathetic' (Okamoto 1995: 298). Gendered language forms are said to reflect the different roles and statuses of women and men (for instance, women's relative powerlessness). However, several empirical studies suggest that there is actually considerable variability in the use of gendered forms. Age is an important factor, with older women using 'feminine' forms more frequently than younger women. There are also geographical variations, with some researchers arguing that feminine speech is associated particularly with urban areas. Shigeko Okamoto comments that (1995: 309):

> 'Japanese women's language' is a construct based largely on the speech style of traditional women in the middle and upper-middle classes in Tokyo, corresponding to the 'ideal feminine' variety in *Yamanote kotoba* [refined' language variety spoken in Yamanote, the 'hillside' region in Tokyo].

Okamoto and Shibamoto Smith (eds) (2004) include a range of contemporary studies of gendered language use in Japanese.

Two accounts of gendered pronoun forms in Japanese
The repertoires of personal pronouns of men and women are different as follows:

	Men's speech	Women's speech
First person (I)		
Formal	watakusi	watakusi
	watasi	atakusi*
Plain	boku	watasi
		atasi*
Deprecatory	ore	Ø
Second person (you)		
Formal	anata	anata
Plain	kimi	anata
	anta*	anta*
Deprecatory	omae	Ø
	kisama	

(*marks variants of a social dialect)

Two kinds of differences are noted here. First, a difference in levels of formality can be observed. The level of formality of *watasi* is formal for men but plain for women and that of *anata* is formal for men but plain or formal for women. This means that women are required to use more formal forms. . . . Second, we notice pronouns of deprecatory level: ore, *omae* and *kisama* in men's speech but none in women's speech. There is no deprecatory word in women's speech.

This use of more formal forms is a display of deferent attitude . . . . The avoidance of deprecatory level is a display of good demeanor. Thus, categorical differences in the repertoire of personal pronouns lead to women's automatic expression of deference and demeanor. This makes women's speech sound politer. (Ide 1989/1990: 73–4)

It has been noted that the use of *boku* 'I' (Male) by junior high school girls has recently become quite common in Tokyo. Girls who were interviewed in a TV programme explain that they cannot compete with boys in classes, in games or in fights with *watasi*, 'I' (Female) [. . .] The use of *boku* and other expressions in the male speech domain by young female speakers has escalated to a larger area and to older groups of speakers. However, since they know that *boku*-language is not acceptable in the society outside schools, they use *watasi*-language in talking to 'members of the society'. In other words, as school girls they are bilinguals who have two distinct codes, *boku*-language and *watasi*-language. They select a code according to the situation.

(Reynolds 1986/1990: 140)

Rosalie Finlayson (1995) discusses the practice of *hlonipha* (or *isihlo-nipho sabafazi*: 'women's language of respect') in southern African languages. Finlayson's examples come from speakers of Xhosa in South Africa. Hlonipha refers to the avoidance, by married women, of any syllables that occur in the names of their in-laws – particularly the father-in-law, mother-in-law, father-in-law's brothers and their wives and father-in-law's sisters. There are a number of linguistic processes that women may employ to avoid uttering these syllables: they may delete consonants, replace one consonant by another, replace a word by another that is semantically related, use a paraphrase or, increasingly among younger women, borrow a word from English or Afrikaans. If a new bride had a male in-law whose name was *Bheki* or *Bhengu*, for instance, she would need to avoid the syllable *bhe-* in words such as *i-bhekile* ('a tin can'). She might choose one of the following forms as an alternative:

> *i-ekile* (consonant deletion)
> *i-wekile* (consonant substitution)
> *ikonkxa* (synonym, meaning 'a case or tin in which preserves are kept')
> *isikhelelo* (paraphrase, meaning 'something that can be used for drawing liquid').
> *Note:* Prefixes like *i-* which denote the class to which a noun belongs, are exempt from hlonipha.

The practice of hlonipha is reinforced by the extended family that a young woman would traditionally marry into. Hlonipha is associated with other forms of respect for senior, particularly male, relatives. The young woman would need to avoid senior members of the household physically, and would usually avoid areas of the homestead frequented by men. It is suggested that such forms of avoidance – linguistic and nonlinguistic – are respectful because they ensure that someone who is a relative stranger in the household, and who also enjoys low status, does not draw attention to herself (uttering someone's name would direct their attention towards the speaker).

Finlayson notes that hlonipha is less common in urban communities, where there is usually less direct involvement with in-laws. Some urban women claim still to practise hlonipha, but in this case they are often relying on a core vocabulary of known hlonipha words rather than avoiding the syllables of their in-laws' names. On the other hand, there are still cases in which a young woman leads a 'dual life', working in an urban environment where she would not use hlonipha but switching into this variety on her return home in the evening.

Hlonipha clearly establishes a distinction between female and male speakers, but like Japanese women's language it has also been associated with women's relative powerlessness, particularly in traditional societies. It is argued that hlonipha reflects women's inferior social status but also that, as a daily practice, it upholds traditional status differentials.

The use of hlonipha, and of women's and men's language use in Japanese and Koasati, illustrates several ideas that will recur throughout this chapter:

- Language may have a direct relationship with gender (as in the case of the exclusively female and male forms in Koasati), but language forms generally have a range of associations (for instance with status and power) which may in turn be related to gender. This corresponds to a well-known distinction made by Elinor Ochs (1992) between direct and (more commonly) indirect 'indexing' of gender in language use.
- A related point: research on gender and language use has traditionally been concerned with *differences* between female and male speakers, but also with issues of *power* and *dominance*. There has sometimes been a tension between 'difference' and 'dominance' positions in research.
- Interpretations of gendered language use have seen this as reflecting (pre-existing) social distinctions, but also as actively maintaining these.
- Terms such as 'women's language' and 'men's language' imply homogeneity among women and men; more recently, however, researchers have emphasised diversity between women, and between men, as social groups.

7.3   VARIATIONIST STUDIES: QUANTIFYING GENDER

Gender and Social Stratification

Many studies of language variation and change, including the urban 'stratification' studies discussed in Chapters 3 and 4, have found evidence of gender differences in the populations surveyed. William Labov, in his study of New York City, and Peter Trudgill, in his study of Norwich, in England, found that within each social class group, and across each stylistic context studied, their female informants tended to use more 'prestige' or high-status language features, and their male informants more vernacular language features. This finding has been replicated in several studies carried out, particularly in 'western' and often English-speaking contexts (e.g. Macaulay 1978; Shuy 1970; Wolfram 1969). As with other findings from stratification studies, such gender differences represent a statistical tendency. It is not the case that there are distinct 'female' and 'male' forms: both women and men were found to use 'prestige' pronunciations, but, all other things being equal, women tended to use more of these than men.

You may remember from Chapter 3 that Trudgill also suggested there was a relationship between gender and linguistic change in his Norwich study. In a later review of this issue that takes account of his own research and work by other researchers such as Labov, Trudgill (1983a) argues that men tend to lead language change when this involves new vernacular forms, but that women lead change towards new prestige forms. He gives two main interpretations for these findings: first, that women use more prestige forms because they are more status-conscious, and so more aware of the social significance of language; and second, that working-class speech has connotations of masculinity (and associated qualities such as 'toughness') which make it more appealing to men.[1] Early studies of gender as an aspect of social stratification raised several methodological issues.

Sampling: women, men and social class

Many studies took class as their primary social division, making comparisons between women and men in the same social class. Men were allocated to a social class on the basis of a number of factors (in the case of Trudgill's study, these included occupation, education, salary and housing locality). Women were usually allocated to a social class on the basis of their husband's or father's class position, rather than in their own right. More recently, researchers have pointed to problems in this approach: it is by no means obvious that women always occupy the same class position as their husbands or fathers, and there are also problems in the criteria used to allocate people to social classes. Deborah Cameron (1992: 64) points out that if the family is used as the unit of classification and wives and husbands are allocated to class groups on the basis of economic criteria, wives would occupy a lower social position than their husbands; but if one used education and type of occupation as criteria, many women, especially wives of working-class men, would come out above their husbands. This could affect the results of variationist studies in which women were found to use more prestige language features than men from 'the same' social class groups.

The sociolinguistic interview

You saw in Chapter 5 that the relative artificiality of sociolinguistic interviews, along with the construction of different stylistic contexts, could be seen as problematic, and this has implications for research on language and gender. The conduct of sociolinguistic interviews (characteristics of the interviewer, the questions asked, where the interviews take place, what participants perceive to be the purpose of different speaking tasks) will affect the speech of informants and may affect female and male informants differently.

Interpreting gender differences

Of the two main interpretations we mentioned above, Trudgill's claim about women's 'status-consciousness' has been the subject of some criticism and would not now be generally accepted, mainly because of the absence of convincing independent evidence that women actually are more status-conscious than men. There is, on the other hand, some evidence for the association of working-class speech with masculinity. You saw in Chapter 3 (section 3.4) that Trudgill administered 'self-evaluation' tests to his informants, which showed that many women 'over-reported' their use of prestige language forms (i.e. claimed they used prestige forms when they didn't), whereas many men 'under-reported' their use of such forms (i.e. claimed they used vernacular forms when they actually used more prestige forms). Trudgill suggested that the 'covert prestige' enjoyed by vernacular speech appealed more to male than to female speakers. Other research has offered support to an association between working-class speech and masculinity, and middle-class speech and femininity. For instance, J. R. Edwards (1979b) asked listeners to evaluate the speech of children, finding that working-class girls were sometimes mis-identified as boys and middle-class boys as girls, and also that middle-class voices were perceived as higher, smoother and more feminine and working-class voices as lower, rougher and more masculine. (For more detailed critical discussion of stratification studies see, for instance, Cameron 1992; Coates 1993; and Graddol and Swann 1989.)

Stratification studies such as those carried out by Labov and Trudgill were concerned to identify 'sociolinguistic patterns' within a speech community. Informants were selected on the basis of their membership of pre-specified social groups, and systematic comparisons were made between the speech of these groups across different speaking styles. The main 'gender' finding that emerged from such work – that women use more 'prestige' and men more 'vernacular' features of speech – is a highly general one. Other approaches to language variation discussed in Chapters 3 and 4 have provided more detailed insights into the relationship between language and gender and have caused this initial finding to be modified in several respects. We turn below to approaches focusing on social network theory, and more generally on differences in women's and men's lifestyles and patterns of interaction.

Gender and Lifestyle/Patterns of Interaction

In her study of vernacular speech in three working-class communities in Belfast (mentioned in Chapter 4), Lesley Milroy (1980) found gender differences in the expected direction with men, overall, using more vernacular forms of language than women. But this general finding obscured important differences between the communities: gender differences were particularly strong in Ballymacarrett, but they were less extreme in the Hammer. In the Clonard, the expected pattern obtained among older speakers, but this was reversed among younger speakers. You may remember from Chapter 4 that Milroy's main focus was on how close-knit social

networks could act to maintain vernacular varieties. She argued that differences in social networks in the three communities could help explain
differences in women's and men's speech. In Ballymacarrett, for instance,
the men had particularly strong local ties, whereas many women worked
outside the community; the population of the Hammer was being dis-
persed to other areas of the city and this process disrupted their interaction
patterns; in the Clonard, there was high male unemployment with men
moving over a fairly wide area, whereas many younger women worked
together and had close ties within the local community.

Milroy's work receives some support from a US study carried out by
Patricia Nichols. Nichols (1979) studied the speech of a rural Black community living on an island in South Carolina. Within this community,
there was a continuum of speech varieties ranging from an English-related
Creole through a form of 'Black vernacular English' to a regional standard English. On the island, young and middle-aged women were leading a
change towards more standard speech, whereas young men in particular
retained more Creole features. Older women and men had similar speaking
styles on the island, but in a nearby mainland community older women
retained more Creole features than older men. Nichols relates her findings
to differences in lifestyle within the communities. The island community
had at one time been fairly self-contained. At the time of Nichols' study,
people did travel off the island but women and men had different patterns of contact. Men rarely had college training: they tended to work in
the construction industry, often alongside other island men. Women had
traditionally found domestic work, but more recently they had begun to
work in commerce, or in some cases as teachers; several young women had
college training. On the mainland, older women were employed locally
in domestic work or seasonal farm work. Older men held labouring jobs
locally or in nearby towns, but they tended to travel further afield than
older women and to have more non-local contacts.

Milroy and Nichols emphasised employment patterns in interpreting
language variation among the communities they studied, but other factors
may also be important. In a study carried out in a village in South Wales,
Beth Thomas (1988) found that women's use of a vernacular pronunciation feature in Welsh was associated with their attendance at particular
chapels, and with the roles they took on in these chapels. While there are
some differences between these three studies – for instance, Milroy and
Thomas drew on the theory of social networks, a concept not referred to
explicitly by Nichols – their overall approach, and their findings, are consistent. Such research suggests that, in order to understand gender differences in language it is important to look at women's and men's lifestyles in
different communities: whom they interact with, and what might motivate
them to adopt certain varieties.

Evidence of language use in bilingual communities has lent support to this approach. Susan Gal, in her study of an Austrian peasant community bilingual in Hungarian and German (discussed in Chapter 5), found that young women in the community tended to prefer to speak German. She argues that this is because they did not wish to be associated with peasant life: their lives would be affected by the type of person they married, and they would work harder and under worse conditions as a peasant wife than as a worker's wife. Gal also discovered that peasant men had begun to find wives outside the village – usually monolingual German speakers. Both local young women and incoming women, therefore, were helping to promote the language shift in the community towards the use of German (Gal 1978, 1979).

Gender and Acts of Identity

An interesting finding to emerge from Lesley Milroy's Belfast study was that sometimes women and men used different linguistic variables to express their integration into the local community (section 4.3). For some variables (such as (a), the vowel in *hat*, and (th), the consonant in the middle of *mother*), there was an association between high network scores and vernacular pronunciation for both women and men (in the case of these two variables the association was stronger for women); on the other hand, only men with high network scores used more vernacular pronunciations of the variable (u) (the vowel in *pull*). One might suggest that, in this latter case, the vernacular pronunciation was a sign both of integration into the community and of masculinity.

Penelope Eckert's study of 'Jocks' and 'Burnouts' in a high school in Detroit, which you met in Chapter 3, provides further evidence of an association between gender and other aspects of a speaker's identity. Eckert found an interaction between gender, social status as a Jock or a Burnout and urban–suburban orientation. In the case of one variable ((ay) – the vowel in *fight*), boys were leading in the use of an urban vernacular pronunciation, but Burnout girls were also leading Jock girls. By contrast, in the case of another variable ((æ) – the vowel in *bad*), girls were leading in the use of a suburban vernacular pronunciation, but Jock boys were also leading Burnout boys. Eckert comments that there seems to be a complex association between, on the one hand, masculinity, Burnout affiliation and urban-ness and, on the other hand, femininity, Jock affiliation and suburban-ness. However, this does not obtain for all variables: in the case of the variable (uh) – the vowel in *cut* – there is a more straightforward relationship between urban and Burnout affiliations (these and other patterns are discussed in Eckert 1998 and, more briefly, 2006).

Barbara Horvath's use of principal components analysis in her study of language variation in Sydney (see Chapter 4) allowed her to examine the association between different speaker characteristics, and how these were related to language use. She found, for instance, that certain vowel variables were used by the 'Anglo' teenagers in her sample to signal gender differences, although they were not used in this way by Italian or Greek teenagers. Horvath also reanalysed some of Labov's New York data, to show how certain differences in pronunciation which he had interpreted in terms of social class could, in fact, be better accounted for in terms of gender (Horvath's re-analysis is illustrated in Figure 7.1).

Labov discussed the spread of the different pronunciations across social-class groups. Horvath, however, added four horizontal groupings, separating speakers who used more, or fewer, fricative pronunciations. When these groups are examined, it is apparent that groups 1 and 2 (more frequent use of fricatives) contain many more female than male speakers, and that groups 3 and 4 (more frequent use of stops) contain more male than female speakers. In a later paper, Lesley Milroy (1992) offers a similar reinterpretation of some features of Tyneside vernacular speech which, she suggests, are better thought of as a male norm than as a working-class norm.

Milroy, Eckert and Horvath have been critical of the tendency, in Labovian stratification studies, to take class as the primary social division. Milroy comments that this has contributed little to our understanding of gender differentiated language, or of how gender interacts with social class: 'a rather depressing conclusion to emerge from scrutiny of more than twenty years of work in the Labovian tradition' (1992: 165). Milroy argues that gender and class should be differentiated in sociolinguistic research. She suggests there is a 'division of labour' in the use of sociolinguistic variables: some variables may 'double up', marking out both class and gender; others may, primarily, mark gender *or* class *or*, of course, other sociocultural characteristics. The argument here has something in common with the idea of language use as an 'act of identity' (Le Page and Tabouret-Keller 1985) in which speakers select certain ways of speaking so as to be like groups with which they wish to identify, or unlike groups from which they wish to distance themselves.

Unlike the accounts of 'women's and men's languages' discussed in section 7.2, variationist studies have always been concerned with statistical tendencies – the tendency of women to speak in one way and men in another. Nevertheless, studies carried out in the Labovian 'social stratification' mode have often interpreted gender differences in language in terms of characteristics which seemed to be inherent in women or men – women's status-consciousness, for instance, or men's attraction to the covert prestige of working-class speech. In contrast to this, more recent studies have emphasised women's and men's lifestyles and interaction patterns – factors

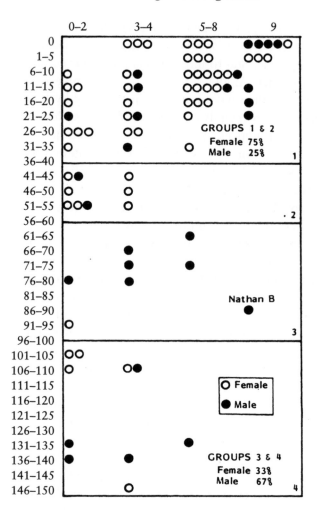

Figure 7.1 A reanalysis of Labov's (1966) findings for the variable (dh) in New York City (Horvath 1985: 65)

Note

Figure 7.1 shows the distribution of the variable (dh) (the first consonant in *then*) in one speaking style: careful speech, associated with formal interviews. Individual speakers are represented by circles. They are grouped in columns according to their social class (1–2 = lower class, 3–4 = working class, 5–8 = lower middle class, 9 = upper middle class).

(dh) may be pronounced in its standard, fricative form [ð], or more like a stop [d]. Speakers towards the top of Figure 7.1 use more [ð] pronunciations (a score of 0 would mean that only [d] pronunciations were used by that speaker); speakers towards the bottom of the figure use more [d] pronunciations (a score of 200 would mean that only [d] pronunciations were used by the speaker).

which may explain not only differences between women and men but also differences that occur between groups of women and between groups of men. In this case, language use is being linked to some sort of social or interactional practice which is, in turn, related to gender. Some studies have also investigated the complex associations of linguistic variables both with gender and with other aspects of a speaker's identity. Overall, language varieties are probably best seen as related to gender both directly (when there is a strong association between, for instance, a particular pronunciation feature and female or male speakers) and indirectly (when features of language are associated with certain attributes or practices that are, themselves, gendered). For an overview of language and gender from a variationist perspective, see Romaine (2003).

7.4 GENDER IN INTERACTION: 'DEFICIT', 'DOMINANCE' AND 'DIFFERENCE'

An important strand of language and gender research has focused on how female and male speakers interact with one another, in a variety of contexts ranging from informal conversations to more formal meetings, interviews, seminars and so on. There is a substantial body of evidence that women and men, and girls and boys interact, to some extent, in different ways. Such differences as occur have often been thought to disadvantage female speakers in mixed-sex interaction. This area of language and gender is one that has a number of practical as well as theoretical implications: within education, for instance, there have been concerns about potential inequalities in classroom talk (Swann 2003). Some research has also focused on potential misunderstandings said to arise from gender differences in communication – a point we return to below.

There are links between studies of gender and talk discussed in this section and the studies of spoken interaction discussed in Chapter 6. In both cases, researchers have been interested in how talk between people is organised; in differences in conversational style between different social and cultural groups; and in conversational outcomes – what speakers accomplish during the course of routine interactions. In this section, we review briefly the results of empirical studies carried out since the early 1970s, which have provided evidence of female and male conversational styles. The bulk of this work has been carried out among speakers of English in 'western' contexts such as the USA, the UK and New Zealand. We then examine some areas of debate that have grown out of this research.

Empirical studies of gender and talk have documented several specific features of conversational style that are said to differentiate between female and male speakers. Examples of these are:

Amount of talk: male speakers have been found to talk more than females, particularly in formal or public contexts.
Interruptions: male speakers interrupt female speakers more than vice versa.

Conversational support: female speakers more frequently use features that provide support and encouragement for other speakers, for example 'minimal responses' such as *mmh* and *yeah*.

tentativeness: there are claims that female speakers use features that make their speech appear tentative and uncertain, such as 'hedges' that weaken the force of an utterance ('I think maybe . . .', 'sort of', 'you know') and certain types of 'tag questions' (questions tagged on to statements, such as ('It's so hot, isn't it?').

Compliments: a wider range of compliments may be addressed to women than to men, and women also tend to pay more compliments.

(For more detailed discussion of this and other evidence from earlier studies, see Coates 1993; Crawford 1995; Graddol and Swann 1989; Holmes 1995.)

Such empirical studies show *tendencies*: they suggest that women tend to speak in one way and men in another. Clearly not all women, or all men, talk in the same way, and the way people talk also differs considerably in different contexts. These are points to which we return below. Overall, however, findings such as those listed have given rise to a number of general claims. One long-running area of debate has concerned whether female and male styles are better interpreted in terms of cultural differences between the sexes, or in terms of the relative power of female and male speakers.

Robin Lakoff (1975) claimed that women use a number of language features that, collectively, indicate uncertainty and hesitancy. These features, argued Lakoff, deny women the opportunity to express themselves strongly, and make what they are talking about appear trivial. Lakoff's claims have been associated with a **deficit** model of women's language use – she seemed to be suggesting that the way women speak is inadequate in several respects. She related these claims to social inequalities between women and men, arguing that women's speaking style denied them access to power (1975: 7). Lakoff's claims were based on informal observations and her own intuitions about language use. They have given rise to considerable debate, and have been investigated in several empirical studies, some of which we refer to below. Lakoff herself has revisited these early ideas in a later publication based on her work (Lakoff 2004).

In an early study of interruption patterns that has now become something of a classic, Don Zimmerman and Candace West (1975) found that more interruptions occurred in mixed-sex than in single-sex conversations; and that virtually all the 'mixed-sex' interruptions were perpetrated by men. Zimmerman and West's approach differed from that of Lakoff in that it was based on an empirical study of conversation. They also focused, not on women's inadequacy, but on men's oppressive speaking behaviour. Zimmerman and West saw interruption as a violation of a speaker's right to complete their turn. In interrupting women, they argued, men are denying women's equal status as conversational partners. Zimmerman and West's work has been associated with a **dominance** position on women's and men's language. They related local interactional behaviour to the greater degree of power more generally available to men: 'there are definite and patterned ways in which the power and dominance enjoyed by men in other contexts are exercised in their conversational interaction with women' (1975: 105). Zimmerman and West followed up their research in several later papers. The illustrations of interruptions shown in the box were cited in a study published in 1983.

Interpretations in terms of power or dominance have been common among other researchers. In an analysis of conversations between couples, Pamela Fishman (1983) found that women gave more conversational support than men. They expressed interest in their partner's conversational topic, and made more frequent use of minimal responses such as *mmh*, *yeah* and *right*, indicating their involvement. Topics raised by men therefore had a greater chance of success (of being elaborated upon and pursued) than those raised by women. Fishman saw women's conversational supportiveness as an 'expected' characteristic of being female: women are expected to keep conversation going. But she also related her interpretation to power. Power, she argued, is 'a human accomplishment, situated in everyday interaction' (p. 89). It is partly through interaction that the hierarchical relations between women and men are constructed and maintained.

An alternative explanation of women's and men's language use derives from the work of Daniel Maltz and Ruth Borker (1982). Maltz and Borker argued that women and men constitute different 'gender subcultures'. They learn the rules of 'friendly interaction' as children when a great deal of interaction takes place in single-sex peer groups. Certain linguistic features are used to signal membership of their own gender group, and to distinguish themselves from the contrasting group. These linguistic features come to have slightly different meanings within the two gender subcultures. For example, in the case of female speakers, minimal responses simply indicate attention – that speakers are listening to the conversation. For male speakers, however, they indicate agreement with the point being made. It is not surprising, therefore, that female speakers should use them more than male speakers. Such differences in conversational style, however, frequently give rise to misunderstandings when women and men communicate with one another. (Maltz and Borker's work is closely related to research on misunderstandings in 'interethnic' communication, discussed in Chapter 6.)

This **cultural difference** explanation has been further developed by the US linguist Deborah Tannen in several publications, including her popular but controversial book *You Just Don't Understand: Women and Men in*

Interruptions as 'intrusions' in conversation

Example A

    Female: Both really (#) it just strikes me as too 1984ish y'know to sow
               your seed or whatever (#) an' then have it develop miles away
               not caring i⌈f   ⌉
    Male: ⌊Now : :⌋ it may be something uh quite different (#)
               you can't make judgements like that without all the facts being
               at your disposal

Example B

    Female: So uh you really can't bitch when you've got all those on the
               same day (4.2) but I uh asked my physics professor if I couldn't
               chan⌈ge that⌉
    Male: ⌊Don't ⌋ touch that
    (1.2)
    Female: What?
    (#)
    Male: I've got everything jus' how I want it in that notebook (#) you'll
             screw it up leafin' through it like that.

                                (West and Zimmerman 1983: 105)

Transcription conventions

Spellings are as in the original transcript;

(#) = a brief pause of about a second that it wasn't possible to discriminate precisely;

(4.2) = a timed pause (4.2 seconds);

Square brackets indicate the extent of overlapping speech.

West and Zimmerman observe that here the interrupted speakers drop out and the interrupters use 'the usurped turns to pursue their own agendas' (p. 105).

Conversation (1990). Tannen argues that 'women speak and hear a language of connection and intimacy, while men speak and hear a language of status and independence' (1990: 42). Understanding these differences will help people communicate better with one another. Tannen claims, for instance, that men may feel interrupted by women who overlap their speech with words of agreement and support; on the other hand, women are irritated by men who interrupt to change the conversational topic. It's important, in such cases, to understand that women and men are trying to do different things as they talk:

> Men who approach conversation as a contest are likely to expend effort not to support the other's talk, but to lead the conversation in another direction, perhaps one in which they can take center stage by telling a story or joke or

displaying knowledge. But in doing so, they expect their conversational partners to mount resistance. Women who yield to these efforts do not do so because they are weak or insecure or deferential but because they have little experience in deflecting attempts to grab the conversational wheel. They see steering the conversation in a different direction not as a move in a game, but as a violation of the rules of the game. (Tannen 1990: 215)

The British linguist Jennifer Coates has also been concerned primarily with differences in women's and men's speech, but her approach is different from Tannen's. Coates' position is more explicitly a feminist one: she argues that interpretations of women's and men's speech that relate this primarily to power and male dominance have given rise to a rather negative view of female speaking styles. One of her aims has been to 'revalue' women's talk: 'Early work on women's language had labelled it as "tentative" or "powerless". More recently, and in reaction to this, there has been a move to value women's talk more positively, using terms such as "co-operative"' (Coates 1988: 95).

Much of Coates' work has focused on informal conversation in all-female groups (see Coates 1996; in an interesting further study she also contrasts this with talk in all-male groups – Coates 1997). Her account of women's talk is highly positive. She found that the conversations she analysed were characterised by cooperation, with women concerned to support one another's contributions rather than compete for the floor. (Chapter 6 includes two of Coates' examples of turn-taking among female speakers, which illustrates this cooperative principle – see pp. 198–9.)

Coates provides a useful corrective to the 'deficit' view of women's speech proposed by Lakoff and also to some work in the 'dominance' tradition which, while not suggesting that women's speech was deficient, did imply that it was relatively ineffective. Setting a high value on women's talk, however, and illustrating this with examples from all-female groups, cannot actually refute the claim that women are routinely disadvantaged in interaction with men.

The cultural difference position, and particularly the popular work of Deborah Tannen, has attracted more general criticism. Critics such as Aki Uchida (1992) and Senta Troemel-Ploetz (1991) do not deny that speaking styles associated with women may be valuable in their own right. They are, however, critical of the focus on miscommunication in interactions between female and male speakers. They argue that interpretations based on miscommunication ignore the power dimension in relations between women and men; they ignore the evidence, from a number of studies, that men's 'different' speaking styles allow them to dominate in mixed-sex interaction. Troemel-Ploetz argues that, in her attempt to avoid any negative assessment of men's speaking styles, Tannen is, effectively, cementing patriarchy (p. 150).

Deborah Cameron (1995a, 1995b) is also concerned about the absence of a power dimension in work that takes a cultural difference position. She traces the roots of this to one of the principles that underlie much of modern linguistics: that different language varieties are equal in linguistic terms, and it is wrong to label some varieties as inferior. This relativist position is, she argues, misplaced in relation to language and gender: the relationship between women and men is complementary but unequal, and simply understanding (or even celebrating) difference is to leave this unchallenged. Cameron suggests that this position is untenable particularly for feminist researchers: 'Feminism is not about celebrating the skills required of women by our present arrangements, but about changing those arrangements root and branch. Feminism must question sexual divisions of labour in every sphere of life' (1995b: 198). While critiques of popular accounts of gender differences in language, such as Tannen's work on miscommunication, tend to be published in academic books and journals, Cameron (2007) presents a more popular account, attempting to dispel 'myths' about women's and men's language for a more general audience. Cameron argues that myths matter – for instance, they may affect career opportunities and other life chances. Sociolinguistic evidence is drawn on here as a form of social intervention designed to encourage – and enable – people to question popular stereotypes.

7.5   GENDER AND POLITENESS

Some researchers have drawn on politeness theory to interpret women's and men's language use. Robin Lakoff had argued that part of women's social role was that of 'arbiter of morality, judge of manners' (1975: 52), and this encouraged them to be linguistically polite. One of the most influential early accounts of gender and politeness, however, comes from research carried out by Penelope Brown in Tenejapa, a Mayan community in Mexico. Brown (1980) draws on the model of politeness she developed with Stephen Levinson (discussed in Chapter 6) in which politeness is described as showing concern for people's 'face', and two types of politeness are distinguished: positive politeness, which has to do with the expression of warmth or friendliness towards others; and negative politeness, which has to do with not imposing on others, or threatening their face. She found that women in the Tenejapan community used the extremes of positive and negative politeness, while men spoke more 'matter-of-factly'. Furthermore, women had certain characteristic styles of politeness. There were also characteristically masculine styles, such as 'sexy joking' and a preaching or declaiming style. Brown relates these findings to the social positions of women and men in Tenejapan society – women's relative powerlessness, for instance, their vulnerability in relation to men and their need to protect their reputations. In a later paper, Brown (1990) places greater emphasis on the importance of context, showing how the female protagonists in a court case are able to engage in angry confrontation, flouting the norms of language behaviour.

Politeness theory has been drawn on in the interpretation of women's linguistic deference in Japanese, and it seems consistent with linguistic behaviour in other contexts – for instance the use of hlonipha in African languages. A study of (English) language use in New Zealand, carried out by Janet Holmes, was also informed by politeness theory. Holmes argues that '[w]omen's utterances show evidence of concern for the feelings of the people they are talking to more often and more explicitly than men's do' (1995: 6). She relates this claim to several aspects of women's and men's language use, including the conversational features listed earlier (pp. 225–6). Part of her discussion focuses on hedges, including tag questions.

Historically, tag questions have been controversial in language and gender research. While Robin Lakoff claimed they were used by women more than by men, empirical support for this has not been consistent.

Some early studies (e.g. Baumann 1979; Dubois and Crouch 1975) found, contrary to expectations, that tag questions occurred as often in male as in female speech. A later study did find more of Lakoff's features,

---

Some examples of politeness among female speakers of Tzeltal in Tenejapa

1. Use of irony as a positive politeness strategy (stressing shared assumptions and interpretations between speaker and listener):
   Tzeltal: *mak* yu'wan ma ja'uk ya'wil!
   Literally: *Perhaps* because *maybe* it's not so, *as it were, you see.*
   Implicating: Isn't that just how it is?
   Tzeltal: ja' yu'un ma ya *nix* xlaj jtak'intik yu'une, yakubeli.
   Literally: It's because our money *just* doesn't get used up because of drunkenness.
   Implicating: It *does* get used up!
2. Use of hedging and understatement as a negative politeness strategy (the expression of strong feelings might be seen as an imposition on the person addressed):
   Tzeltal: ya nix jmel ko'tantik yu'un ts'in *mak*.
   Literally: I just really am sad then because of it perhaps.
   Tzeltal: *puersa* k'exlal ts'in *mak*!
   Literally: She's *really* embarrassed then *maybe*!
   (Compare English: She's really a bit upset!)

   (Brown 1980; repr. in Coates 1998: 90, 92)

including tag questions, among female speakers (Preisler 1986). These different findings may be due, in part, to differences in research methods (e.g. different ways of identifying and coding tag questions). A more fundamental problem, however, relates to the interpretation of tag questions – the functions they are said to carry out in conversation.

Lakoff argued that women frequently used tag questions where they were reluctant to state a proposition baldly: 'The way prices are rising is horrendous, isn't it?' (1975: 16). (She acknowledged that tag questions also had other functions.)

Holmes looked more closely at the functions of tag questions, and identified two main differences between women's and men's language use: women used more 'facilitative' tags, inviting the addressee to contribute to the conversation (e.g. 'You've got a new job, Tom, haven't you?'). Men, on the other hand, used more 'epistemic modal' tags, expressing uncertainty about the information conveyed (e.g. 'Fay Weldon's lecture is at eight isn't it?').

Holmes argues that facilitative tags express positive politeness, showing concern for the listener. Women's greater use of these suggested they were more positively polite than men. Other features investigated by Holmes could also be interpreted in terms of women's greater politeness – particularly positive politeness.

In discussing associations between gender (or other social categories) and language use, it seems important to take into account the kinds of functions utterances fulfil. Holmes conceded out, however, that identifying such functions is not straightforward. This is borne out by a study of tag questions in a corpus of British conversational data, carried out by Deborah Cameron, Fiona McAlinden and Kathy O'Leary (1988). Cameron et al.'s findings were not identical to those of Holmes. A more important point, however, was the difficulty faced by the researchers in identifying different types of tag questions. Tags such as 'You were missing last week/ weren't you' (Cameron et al. 1988: 82) request information about which the speaker is uncertain, so should be classified as 'epistemic modal'. But Cameron et al. felt that in this case the tag also served to mitigate or softened the speaker's request (a 'softening tag', in Holmes' terms). It was not, therefore, always possible to allocate tag questions unambiguously to one category or another.

These findings alert us to a problem that has dogged research in language and gender (as well as other areas of sociolinguistics) and that has sometimes been termed the 'form/function' problem. Chapter 6 mentioned that 'interaction' studies tended to be interested not simply in the distribution of linguistic forms, but in the meanings or functions which those forms took on in specific contexts. Early studies of language and gender identified language *forms* that were used differently by women and men, but the model of language that underpinned such analyses was, at least by implication, a *functional* one. It was of little interest, for instance, that men's speech overlapped women's to a certain extent: what was of interest was that this was said to constitute an interruption, an (undesirable) incursion into an ongoing speaking turn. It rapidly became clear, however, that it was not possible simply to 'read off' functions from linguistic forms: Jennifer Coates argues that, in her all-female conversations, overlapping speech is a form of cooperation between speakers.

The evidence we have referred to from tag question studies takes this one step further. It is not just that forms may have different functions. Cameron et al. argue that utterances are usually multifunctional – they carry out more than one function simultaneously.

Holmes also expresses caution in relation to general claims about 'women's speaking styles': speaking styles will be affected by context and by what is being talked about (both of which may, in turn, be related to gender). She is cautious, furthermore, about relating her politeness interpretations to power, at least in any straightforward way: she points out that many features analysed as 'powerless' when they are seen as 'women's style' (e.g. hedges and other linguistic markers of tentativeness) could be analysed quite differently in other groups of speakers (e.g. as caution or restraint when used by academics). This suggests, she argues, that 'women's subordinate societal status may account not so much for the way women talk, as for the way their talk is perceived and interpreted' (1995: 111).

7.6 CONTEXTUALISED APPROACHES: PERFORMANCE AND PERFORMATIVITY

Changing Conceptions of 'Language' and 'Gender'

The points made above about the multifunctionality of utterances, and the need to interpret language use in context are in line with a more general shift in language and gender research, dating from around the 1990s. Sometimes termed a postmodern shift, or turn (Cameron 2005; Swann 2002), this has to do with a refocusing of research along several dimensions:

- an increasing emphasis on the fluidity, and context-specificity of language functions or meanings;
- a view of gender itself as relatively fluid and variable;
- a preoccupation with the interactional 'performance' of gender.

On the first point, language functions, or meanings are seen as not simply 'in the language', but as negotiated between speakers. On any one occasion, utterances are multifunctional and sometimes ambiguous. Ambiguity itself may be an interactional resource, played on by speakers and listeners. These points relate particularly to the affective or interpersonal aspects of language, which have been of particular concern to language and gender researchers. They are relevant not just to studies of interaction, or talk, such as those discussed in the previous two sections, but to studies of language varieties. If the meanings of tag questions and overlapping speech are highly context-dependent, so too are the meanings of particular accent or dialect features. Linguistic features may be drawn on to particular effect in particular contexts. Certain features may be drawn on ironically, playfully or subversively. Charting the distribution of linguistic features across different social groups or contexts may conceal differences in the way they are actually used, or what they mean in specific contexts. (Nikolas Coupland's 1985 study of a Cardiff DJ's speech, discussed in Chapter 5, addressed this issue in relation to accent features.)

On the second point, gender too is seen as relatively fluid. It may be salient in some contexts but not others. It is also seen not as an independent category, but as embedded in other social categories (race, class, sexuality etc), in turn embedded (and reproduced) within structures of power, authority and inequality.

Finally, recent research has tended to focus on gender not as a prior category that affects how people speak, but as something that is performed, or brought into being in the act of speaking. This is often theorised in terms of **performativity**. Within linguistics, the term 'performativity' derives from speech act theory (particularly the work of J. L. Austin (1962) and John Searle (1969)) – a view of language as a form of action. Austin termed certain utterances performative in that they perform an action simply by virtue of being uttered (for instance, saying 'I promise to pay you' constitutes the act of promising). He came to realise, however, that all language performed an action (even a statement such as 'It's raining heavily' performs the act of stating). All language may, therefore, be regarded as performative. The concept of performativity was adopted by the feminist philosopher Judith Butler in her work on the enactment of gender. Butler saw gender as being produced and 'created through sustained social performances' (1990: 141), rather than as a fixed attribute of a person. Gender, she argued, is: 'the repeated stylization of the body, a set of repeated acts within a rigid regulatory frame that congeal over time to produce the appearance of substance, of a natural kind of being' (Butler 1990: 33). In influential work drawing on these ideas, Deborah Cameron has argued that speech is part of the stylisation process:

> The 'performative' model sheds an interesting light on the phenomenon of gendered speech. Speech too is a 'repeated stylization of the body'; the 'masculine' or 'feminine' styles of talking identified by researchers might be thought

of as the 'congealed' results of repeated acts of social actors who are striving to constitute themselves as 'proper' men and women. Whereas sociolinguistics traditionally assumes that people talk the way they do because of who they (already) are, the postmodernist approach suggests that people are who they are because of (among other things) the way they talk.

(Cameron 1997: 49)

These ideas about performativity, combined with the relatively fluid and contextualised conceptions of language and gender referred to above, paint a highly complex picture in which aspects of gender may be played up or played down in particular interactions, negotiated, sustained or subverted in the act of speaking. Such processes have been a focus of attention, to varying degrees, in a range of empirical studies of language and gender.

Contextualised Approaches in Empirical Research

Janet Holmes, whose work on politeness we referred to above, emphasises the complex nature of 'gendered talk' in a recent study of language in the workplace. Her focus is on 'how women and men negotiate their gender identities as well as their professional roles in everyday workplace talk' (2006: 1). Both women and men, she argues, draw on a range of communicative strategies, including the adoption of speaking styles that are conventionally seen as feminine and masculine, selecting these strategies in response to particular interactional contexts. In the following example, for instance, a male doctor adopts what Holmes sees as a feminine style, and a female nurse responds in a masculine style.

> Context: Doctor to nurse in the nurse's station of a hospital ward. There is another nurse present who is eating her lunch.
> 1. Doc: [softly]: there's another um: + thing that I would like to ask for
> 2. Nur: what's that
> 3. Doc: somewhere in delivery suite or at Ward 11
> 4. er there are those plastic er read containers for ++ for blood tests
> 5. I need I need beside the the line there's a plastic end for this . . .
> 6. [*some discussion between all three about what exactly is needed and*
> 7. *where one might be*]
> 8. Doc: yeah so er we + could you just could we maybe have one
> 9. from er ward eleven oh this stuff er +
> 10. Nur: well you go down to ward eleven and get it
> 11. cos I don't want to have to
>
> (Holmes 2006: 163)

Note: + = a pause of up to one second

Holmes notes that in this case the doctor uses several hedges, hesitations and repetitions, finally switching from a relatively direct request (*could you*) to a more indirect *could we maybe have one* – features that would conventionally be seen as feminine. The nurse, on the other hand, uses much more direct, unmitigated speech (conventionally masculine) in her response to the doctor at line 11. For Holmes, this exchange challenges expectations of gendered speech, as well as expectations resulting from professional status: how one might expect a nurse to respond to a doctor. More relevant here are the particular context of utterance, and other aspects of the speakers' identities: 'the nurse's age, seniority and medical experience, compared to the relative inexperience of the young intern' (2006: 164).

Some particularly interesting, and influential insights on the linguistic performance of identity have come from studies of language, gender and **sexuality**. 'Sexuality' in this case refers not just to to sexual orientation but also sexual identity and sexual desire (the balance varies in different studies). For instance, Rusty Barrett (1999) has studied the language of African American drag queens, focussing on how, in their performances, they adopt stereotypical 'white women's' language but also code-switch between this and other varieties to index variously their identities as drag queens, African Americans and gay men. Similarly, Kira Hall (1995) studied the language of telephone sex workers – women (and one man) who create a fantasy persona for the sexual gratification of male callers. She found that this is achieved by the adoption of a stereotypically feminine speaking style that has much in common with the kind of powerless language associated with female speakers in earlier studies – although in this case the women are deliberately manipulating a gendered style, and Hall argues that they felt in control of the interaction. The attribution of powerlessness, then, is at least open to question in this context. Niko Besnier (2003) looked at the language use of *fakaleitī*, transgendered male speakers in Tonga who are said to 'act like women'. *Fakaleitī* frequently switch between Tongan and English, although their competence in English is limited. English is associated here with prestige, modernity and contact with the external world, and also with contemporary femininity: with women's aspirations towards upward mobility and freedom from traditional constraints – in all cases qualities that *fakaleitī* do not actually possess. Besnier demonstrates how speakers draw on these multiple meanings strategically within specific contexts – sometimes humorously or playfully – in the negotiation of fakaleiti identity.

The studies above, like other work discussed in this chapter, are concerned with the social meanings that may be attributed to certain language forms (e.g. dialect features, the use of particular languages, or conversational structures), even where these meanings are complex and variable. In a study of 'gay men's English', however, William Leap (1996) argues that this cannot be defined simply in terms of a set of structural features:

the significance of such features 'lies in their connections to other forms of social practice – in this case, to the social practices that define and delimit gay experience in US society' (1996: xii). Leap emphasises the variability of gay language use:

> I am interested in the stereotypic varieties of Gay English: for example, the catty, bitchy dialogue associated with Matt Crowley's *Boys in the Band*; the self-absorbing linguistic play during 'cruising'; and the code words that confirm gay identity during informal conversations between strangers in public places. But I am also interested in gay men's use of English when they have a quiet evening at home with close friends or interact with colleagues and friends, gay and straight, on the job, at a restaurant, or in a shopping mall. (1996: xi)

The following example of Leap's data comes from a crowded bookstore-café in Dupont Circle, in what is sometimes termed Washington DC's 'gay ghetto'. A is a prospective customer, enquiring about a table for a mixed-gender group, and B is acting as the café's *maître d'hôte* for the evening:

```
 1 A:  Table for five – how long do we wait?
 2 B:  Table for five [Pauses, consults list] About one hour.
 3 A:  One hour. [Consults with group] Nope, can't do it. That
 4       is too long.
 5 B:  Try the Mocha House. They might not be too crowded
 6       tonight.
 7 A:  Yeah, OK, we can go there. But you people are more
 8       fun.
 9 B:  Well, I don't know about that. [While he says this, moves
10       head to side, drops voice level, gives trace of smile]
11 A:  Yeah, you're right. [Establishes direct contact
12       with maître d'] Maybe the Mocha House is more fun,
13       but I still like your dessert drinks here.
14 B:  [Not breaking eye contact] Well, you'll just have to
15       come back and try us again sometime.
```

(Leap 1996: 2)

Note: This extract is transcribed from fieldnotes made by Leap at the time.

Leap comments that the opening of the conversation (lines 1–4) could occur in any similar café or restaurant encounter. Two further episodes (B's recommendation of an alternative restaurant in lines 5–6 and A's expression of preference for the present café in lines 7–8 and 11–13) may also seem gender-neutral, but Leap contends that they are rich in gay-centred, gendered messages. The Mocha House, for instance, is some distance from the present café, but is known as a popular meeting place for gay men. If speaker A were gay, and familiar with the area, he would recognise this and listen for further gay-centred messages. On the other hand, the Mocha House is also frequented by heterosexual customers, so speaker A would not need to interpret the utterance as gay-centred. In fact, A shows no immediate evidence of making this interpretation, but he does comment that 'you people are more fun', an expression Leap regards as ambiguous. B's statement, and non-verbal behaviour, build on this. A acknowledges that the Mocha House may be more fun, but offers a further reason for preferring the present café – he likes their dessert drinks (lines 12–13). Leap regards this reference as more overtly sexual ('dessert often provides a prelude to other activities'). He comments:

> This combination of verbal and nonverbal statements was much more forceful than any of the other statements in the text and provided the basis for the more elaborate and somewhat more gay-explicit version of 'please come again' that the maître d' used as his closing remark. (p. 4)

We mentioned earlier that many studies concerned with the distribution of language features among women and men have seen language not simply as reflecting gender divisions but also as helping to construct these. Qualitative, contextualised studies, such as Holmes' workplace study, Barret's study of drag queens, Hall's study of telephone sex workers, Besnier's study of Fakaleiti in Tonga, and the example of café discourse from Leap's study of gay men's English attempt to capture such constructions 'on the hoof' – to examine gender as a process, something that is 'done' by particular speakers in specific contexts (alongside other processes, such as power, that are associated with gender). 'Doing gender' may be a complex business, as people shift between different positions and stances. The borders between femininity and masculinity are not always secure; and there are differences in how femininity and masculinity are experienced by different people. Leap's study also draws attention to the complex nature of word and utterance meaning, in an attempt to document the covert expression of gendered meanings in language which might otherwise appear to be unremarkable.

Continuing Challenges and Debates

Studies that emphasise the local, qualitative exploration of gender provide limited scope for, and have limited interest in the establishment of generalisations about larger patterns in language use. Researchers often make an explicit contrast between such work and earlier studies in which gender was seen as a prior category that affected language use.

In a review of current developments in language and gender within sociolinguistics, Swann and Maybin (2008) argue that contextualised approaches to language and gender have become mainstream, but that, in their turn, they face a number of challenges:

a) The focus on the local, contextualised playing out of gender plays down, and sometimes explicitly rejects, earlier assumptions about gender as a prior category – something that speakers *have*, rather than what they *do*. However clearly gender is not done afresh in each interaction. Speakers necessarily bring with them a 'gendered potential' – the sedimentation of accrued prior experience, of prior genderings – and this may be drawn on (performed, renegotiated, contested, subverted or of course ignored) in response to particular interactional contingencies. In this sense, gender may legitimately be seen as both a prior category (something that one has) *and* a contextualised practice (something one does, that bolsters, subverts, etc. the category).

b) In order to interpret an interaction in terms of gender, i.e. to see the relevance of gender within an interaction, researchers themselves must have some prior conception of this. In practice, contemporary 'local' research is often framed by, and thus dependent upon, patterns identified in earlier research, even when it seeks to qualify these. [For instance, Barrett and Hall drew on prior conceptions of 'women's language' in their studies, while acknowledging the ideological status of this concept; and Holmes drew on established beliefs about feminine and masculine speaking styles.]

c) A particular challenge for researchers working with complex models of identity and identification is how to untangle the maze of interconnections between the aspects of language and gender in which they are interested, and other multiple dimensions of people's social practice.

d) A focus on the particularities of specific interactions may lead researchers to miss broader connections with other contexts. Alongside these particularities there will also be continuities with others; such continuities form the stuff of general, even quantifiable patterns that may, in principle, be identified in research.

e) It is also debatable how far research on situated language use does actually restrict itself to local relevance. Researchers usually wish to do more than address isolated and disconnected particularities. There is a danger, however, in moving towards more generalisable claims without adequate methodological warrants.

(Adapted from Swann and Maybin 2008: 25–6)

Some researchers have discussed the potential of a combination of methodological approaches – for instance, the quantitative documentation of broad, general patterns along with more qualitative exploration of local practices that both contribute and form exceptions to such patterns (e.g. Holmes 1996; Swann 2002). In this case, quantitative examination of inter-group differences may complement qualitative approaches within the same study, or it may contribute to a backdrop of general claims that inform more local, qualitative research. Alternatively, qualitative ethnographic observation and interviews may inform and help to substantiate quantitative claims about differences between social groups, and about language change (see e.g. work by Eckert, discussed earlier in this chapter and in previous chapters).

7.7   CONCLUSION

We mentioned earlier (section 7.1) that language and gender can be regarded as an interdisciplinary field of study, covering several different aspects of (written and spoken) language. We have focused here on studies that are relevant to other areas of sociolinguistics, and particularly to 'variationist' and 'interactional' research. Many issues have emerged that echo concerns and interests discussed in earlier chapters. Within variationist research, for instance, there has been a development from studies that identified general 'gender patterns' in the distribution of linguistic features towards more recent preoccupations with fairly complex sociolinguistic patternings and factors that might explain these. While variationist approaches have tended to involve quantitative methods (they are referred to in some reviews of language and gender as 'the quantitative paradigm'), studies of gender and interaction have adopted both quantitative and qualitative methods (with an increasing emphasis on qualitative, 'contextualised' approaches). Across the field as a whole, researchers have come to challenge straightforward 'binary' gender distinctions and to emphasise diversity among women and among men. Nor is gender seen simply as a fixed, a priori category related to language use but as something that is refashioned, in various ways, in the course of everyday language use. This parallels current interests in other areas of (particularly) interactional sociolinguistics, which focus on the moment-by-moment construction of speakers' identities. Set against this, we have seen above that there is also (continuing) debate about the potential value of combining insights from qualitative and quantitative approaches.

Gendered language use inevitably raises issues of power and inequality between women and men (though some approaches, for example cultural difference approaches, have downplayed the importance of power; and more recent, contextualised approaches would emphasise that power is not fixed and monolithic but fairly complex, negotiated and on some occasions contested). There has always been a high level of commitment among researchers, many of whom are concerned not just to provide a 'neutral' interpretation of language behaviour but also to challenge inequalities in language use. Such commitment is at odds with any view of sociolinguistic researchers as impartial observers of language, but many would argue that, at any rate, complete neutrality is impossible to attain: the values held by researchers will affect what they choose to observe and investigate, how they carry out their research and how they interpret their findings. Previous chapters have shown that sociolinguists regularly take a stand on language issues, and that many have intervened in areas such as education and forensic linguistics. Some researchers have explicitly rejected impartiality and choose to 'declare their interests' rather than hide these behind a screen of objectivity. Such issues are discussed further in relation to sociolinguistic contributions to language policy and practice (Chapters 11 and 12), and language and power (Chapter 10).

Notes

1. Trudgill (1983b) has discussed other interpretations, but still seems to favour the two we refer to. Deborah James (1996) also discusses a wide range of interpretations.
2. Holmes defines 'epistemic' as follows: 'Epistemic forms indicate the extent of the speaker's confidence in the truth of the proposition expressed in the utterance' (1995: 113).

8
LANGUAGE CONTACT 1: MAINTENANCE, SHIFT AND DEATH

8.1 INTRODUCTION

The next two chapters are concerned with the subfield of sociolinguistics known as language contact. This subfield is essentially concerned with the outcomes for speakers and their languages when new languages are introduced into a speech community. Language contact sometimes occurs when there is increased social interaction between people from neighbouring territories who have traditionally spoken different languages. But, more frequently, it is initiated by the spread of languages of power and prestige via conquest and colonisation. This chapter briefly focuses on how languages are adapted under these circumstances, especially on the ways in which contact between cultures affects the languages in contact. We then turn to the conditions under which communities are able to maintain their languages in the face of societal change. Some aspects of the topic have been discussed earlier, for example contacts between dialects in monolingual settings. Furthermore, interactional miscommunications that occur in multilingual societies were discussed in Chapter 6. And code-switching, described in detail in Chapter 5, is a phenomenon arising out of language contact *par excellence*. Particular attention in this chapter is given to the circumstances under which a bilingual community gradually gives up one language in favour of another. As a case study of such phenomena, we survey, in some detail, the conditions surrounding bilingualism among native Americans in the last few centuries, as a background to the position of one community, the northern Ute, today. The theme of contact will be continued in Chapter 9 by examining the rise of new forms of communication under extreme kinds of pressure, especially in the era of slavery and in the postcolonial world.

8.2 CONTACT AND BORROWING

Language contact has traditionally been a subfield of historical linguistics, concentrating on changes in language that are due to 'external' influence from other languages, rather than with 'internal' change. One concern of language-contact studies that overlaps with the discipline of historical linguistics is the nature of **borrowing**. 'Borrowing' is a technical term for the incorporation of an item from one language into another. These items could be (in terms of decreasing order of frequency) words, grammatical elements or sounds.

English borrowings from Xhosa and Zulu in South Africa
(The Zulu and Xhosa originals are given in parentheses)

dagha	'mud or mortar used in building'	(*udaka*)
donga	'a dry watercourse, gully'	(*udonga*)
sangoma	'a traditional healer or herbalist'	(*isangoma*)
indaba	'an important protracted meeting'	(*indaba*)
imbizo	'a national conference of the Zulu people'	(*imbizo*)

In section 1.2, we gave examples of borrowings in international English from a variety of sources and of Japanese borrowings from English. Borrowing is different from code-switching, which assumes a mastery of two or more languages and the use of a wide range of rules of the languages being switched. By contrast, borrowing usually involves the adaptation of a word into the phonetic and grammatical system of the other language. Furthermore, the borrowing of a word does not presuppose a knowledge of the language from which it is taken. English speakers in South Africa who use words like *donga* and *dagha* might not actually speak Zulu or Xhosa. The term 'borrowing' does not have the sense of impermanence and single ownership evident in its everyday meaning. Once borrowed, a word like *donga* becomes a part of the borrowing language: there is no intention of returning it! On the other hand, the word is also likely to remain part of the 'donor' language. Speakers might not actually be aware of the 'borrowed' status of a word, especially if it is assimilated into the pronunciation system of their language. Many English-speaking South Africans are surprised to learn that *donga* and *dagha* are not English in origin.

Sociolinguists are more interested in the cultural aspect of borrowings, since the process of borrowing is also a process of learning and acculturation. Anthropological linguists consider language a highly flexible instrument which registers changes in a community more than any other element of culture (Basso 1967: 471). English in South Africa has adopted a great many words from African languages and Afrikaans to describe the local landscape and customs. African languages have, in turn, assimilated a great many terms from English, to do with Christianity, technology and modernity. In the modern world, the power and prestige of English and its associated Anglo-American technology have penetrated a large section of the globe. Terms relating to long-distance travel, domestic appliances, computers, television and other forms of communication occur as borrowings from English in language after language. Some examples from modern colloquial Xhosa are given in the box.

Modern Xhosa borrowing	*English source*
ibhayiskile	bicycle
ithivi/ithelivhijini	TV/television
irediyo	radio
ikompyuta	computer
imoto	motor-car
iteksi	taxi
ividiyo	video

(The prefix *i-* shows adaptation to the Xhosa system of nouns.)

Some cultures may try to resist such incursions from languages which have terms for advanced technology. Casagrande (1954) gives some examples from Comanche, a language of the south-west USA, whose speakers have had to adapt to Spanish and English in the last two centuries. Some terms are indeed borrowed from Spanish and English, but there is a counter-tendency whereby speakers use the grammatical resources of Comanche to express new entities. Thus the word for bicycle noted by Casagrande is *na-taʔ-ʔai-ki-ʔ*, which translates literally as 'thing to make oneself go with the feet' (ʔ denotes a glottal stop, while the hyphen is used to separate grammatical elements). Likewise, the term for 'lemon', introduced in the colonial era, is not simply taken over from Spanish or English but has a variety of descriptions, some of which may be composed on the spot. One such invention noted by Casagrande is *ʔohapltiʔa-taka-sikikimatl* which translates as 'orange's brother, tastes sour'. A more systematic example of resistance to borrowing comes from the southern Athapaskan-speaking Western Apache, studied by the US anthropological linguist Keith Basso. Basso documented the way in which an entire set of words pertaining to the human body in southern Athapaskan was extended to cover a conspicuous item of material culture introduced by whites – the motor vehicle. Basso obtained his data from five male Apaches who were over 45 years of age and spoke very little English.

In addition to the terms for the external parts of the motor vehicle, fine distinctions are also made for the internal parts. Thus the electrical wiring

> All were present on Fort Apache between the years of 1930 to 1935, when Apaches first began to purchase and drive pick-up trucks. Unlike many younger Apaches, who are bilingual, my informants were totally unfamiliar with English labels for automobile parts. This is not to say that the use of extended anatomical terms is confined to members of the older generation. To the contrary, this terminology is part of every Apache's basic vocabulary and is commonly resorted to in daily conversation. Long before an Apache child learns that a truck has a battery, he knows it has a 'liver'. (Basso 1967: 472)

is described as 'veins' in southern Athapaskan, the distributor as 'heart', the radiator as 'lung', the fuel tank as 'stomach' and so forth. Resisting or embracing words from another language can be broadly linked to language attitudes. Community leaders from a culture dominated by another often express the fear of their language being swamped by terminology from a more dominant language like English. However, sociolinguists seldom find a direct relation between borrowing and the demise of a language. To some extent, borrowing can instead be seen as an adaptive strategy undertaken by speakers to enrich certain registers of a language, rather than having to switch to the new language for that register. Linguists point out that the history of English – hardly a declining language – is replete with periods of intense borrowing. The main phase during which borrowings from Latin, Greek and French changed the vocabulary system of English drastically was 1500 to 1700. For threatened languages of subordinate status in the modern world, however, there is little room for complacency about the incursions of a dominant language.

8.3 LANGUAGE MAINTENANCE, SHIFT AND DEATH

The term 'language shift' was first used by Uriel Weinreich (1968 [1953]: 68) to denote the change from the 'habitual use of one language to that of another'. The terms 'maintenance' and 'shift' were consolidated in a pioneering article by Joshua Fishman in 1964. **Language maintenance** denotes the continuing use of a language in the face of competition from a regionally and socially more powerful language. The opposite of this term, **language shift**, denotes the replacement of one language by another as the primary means of communication and socialisation within a community. The term **language death** is used when that community is the last one (in the world) to use that language. Studies of language maintenance efforts

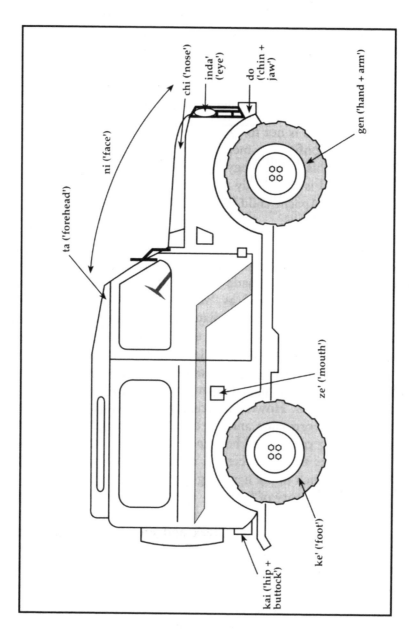

Figure 8.1 A selection of Western Apache anatomical terms used for parts of motor vehicles (based on Basso 1990:17)

can be found in Kloss (1966) and Fishman (1966). Two notable classics in the field of language shift are Nancy Dorian's case study (1981) of the demise of Gaelic in north-east Scotland and Susan Gal's study (1979) of the shift from Hungarian to German in a community in Oberwart, Austria. The latter was described in Chapter 5.

The extinction of Cornish in England in the eighteenth century is an example of language death as well as shift (to English).[1] The demise of an immigrant language like Norwegian in the USA (studied in detail by Einar Haugen (1953)) exemplifies shift without death, since the language still survives in its original setting in Norway. Language death without shift is exemplified by the fate of Tasmanian, whose speakers were almost entirely wiped out just seventy-three years after the first contacts with British settlers in 1803.

Last speakers of a language

- Ishi was the last speaker of Yahi and last survivor of the Yahi people of Northern California. He was taken to the University of California in 1911. He spoke faultless Yahi and only learnt to communicate in English in his last years.   (Swadesh 1948)
- Truganini, the last speaker of Tasmanian, is said to have died with her own language intact, and with no knowledge of English, save for a few borrowings that had already been incorporated into Tasmanian.   (Swadesh 1948)
- Nell Mandrell was the last speaker of Manx, once spoken throughout Isle of Man. He died in 1974.   (Nettle and Romaine 2000:2)
- Tefvik Esenc was a farmer from the farm village of Haci Osman in Turkey. When he died his gravestone carried the inscription he had composed: 'This is the grave of Tefvik Esenc. He was the last person able to speak the language they call Ubykh.' His three sons were unable to converse with their father in this native language as they had shifted to Turkish.   (Nettle and Romaine 2000: 1–2)

Although languages like Latin, Ancient Greek and Sanskrit are often referred to as dead languages, this use of the term is not common in socio-linguistics. Languages like these gradually evolved by continuous transmission from one generation to the next, and spread into regional dialects which gave rise to autonomous and eventually standardised speech forms. At no stage was there a sharp break from one colloquial speech system to another. Latin 'lives' as modern French, Spanish, Portuguese, Italian and Romanian. On the other hand, it is accurate to speak of the death of ancient European languages like Pictish, Etruscan and Gothic.

Hebrew provides the unusual example of a language which did 'die' (that is, it had ceased to be the medium of everyday conversation of Jewish people) but was revived with considerable effort in the late nineteenth and early twentieth century (see further Blanc 1968, Spolsky and Shohamy 1999: 1–24).

Four types of language death

- **Gradual death:** involves gradual replacement of one language by another (that is, it also involves language shift), for example replacement of Gaelic by English in parts of Scotland.
- **Sudden death:** rapid extinction of a language, without an intervening period of bilingualism. The last speaker is monolingual in the dying language, as in the case of Tasmanian.
- **Radical death:** due to severe political repression, a community may opt, out of self-defence, to stop speaking their language. The last speakers are thus fluent in the dying language, but don't actually use it or transmit it to their children. For example, the massacre of thousands of Indians in El Salvador in 1932 led the surviving speakers of Cacaopera and Lenca to stop speaking these languages, as a survival strategy so as not to be identified as Indians.
- **'Bottom-to-top' death:** a language ceases to be used as a medium of conversation, but may survive in special use like religion or folk songs. For example, (Southeastern) Tzeltal is dying in Mexico, with only a few older speakers in scattered villages, but survives in the register of prayer.

(based on Campbell and Muntzel 1989)

Causes of Shift

For a large number of cases involving indigenous languages in Australia and the Americas, the causes of shift and death are clear. Once-viable and autonomous speech communities were either destroyed or deprived of their traditional land and resettled with other groups who did not always share the same language. Nettle and Romaine (2000) propose that where an indigenous group retains control of its traditional habitat and way of life, language maintenance is likely. Thus the areas where languages are most abundant are in the tropics, where small scale economies can be built around a rich, local ecosystem. The reality, however, is that the world's indigenous peoples and their languages are dying out or being assimilated into modern civilization because their habitats are being destroyed (2000: 47–8). The authors cite the European settlement into different parts of the world as the intrusion of a whole ecosystem into the domain of another. By contrast where local communities have control over local resources, they are much more likely to conserve them.

> This is not because traditional peoples have some mysterious essence that keeps them in harmony with nature [. . .] as some romantic portrayals of indigenous people imply. It is for the more practical reason that it is the traditional people who will have to stay around in the environment and make their living there [than outside developers]. (Nettle and Romaine 2000: 160)

Eventual reorientation to a new, westernised society further weakened traditional forms of the surviving languages among the young.

Turning to other situations involving urbanisation and immigration, the cause of shift is more complex. It is one of the few points of agreement in studies of minority and immigrant languages that there is no single set of factors that can be used to predict the outcome of language-maintenance efforts. Causes of shift are generally multiple and interrelated. Kloss (1966) has pointed out that many of the factors may even cut both ways. Thus, none of the following factors on their own can be used to predict the ability of a language to survive: (1) absence or presence of higher education in the dominated language; (2) relatively large or relatively small numbers of speakers of the dominated language; (3) greater similarity or greater dissimilarity between groups speaking the dominant and dominated languages respectively; and (4) positive or hostile attitudes of the dominant group to the minority.

In his review of the field, Fishman (1972b) emphasises the ambivalence of generalisations that might seem to have common-sense validity. Thus, language maintenance is not necessarily a function of strict adherence to group membership or strong feelings of nationalism. Urban dwellers are not necessarily more prone to language shift than rural dwellers. It is not always the case that the more prestigious language displaces the less prestigious one. Women may be in the rearguard of shift in some instances, men in others.

Nevertheless, some linguists have pointed (after the fact) to specific factors that have, in practice, caused the decline of certain languages. These factors can be grouped as follows: economic changes, status, demography, and institutional support (Giles et al. 1977; Appel and Muysken 1987: 32–45).

Economic factors
Economic changes are by far the most salient of the factors leading to shift, though the relation is neither necessary nor sufficient. The juxtaposition of different speech communities is frequently brought about by invasion, seeking of refuge, immigration of workers, or trade. All of these (except,

perhaps, for some instances of refuge) have an underlying economic motive. In many countries, modernisation, industrialisation and urbanisation often lead to bilingualism in a vernacular language and a more widespread regional language associated with the economy. In conjunction with other factors (discussed below), these may lead to shift.

Bedwyr Jones (1990) traces the beginnings of language shift in Wales to the late fifteenth century. Although there had been extensive contact and conflict between English and Welsh prior to this time, the period saw the creation of a Welsh upper ruling class which became increasingly anglicised as it grew more and more drawn to the social, economic and cultural sphere of London. The second phase in the decline of Welsh involved the immigration of English-speakers into the coalfields of south-east Wales in the second half of the eighteenth century. With respect to Scottish Gaelic, Derick Thomson (1990) argues that the exodus of people from the Scottish Highlands in search of work in English-speaking areas in the nineteenth century was a key factor in its eventual decline. Economic factors thus counteracted the efforts of the Gaelic Schools Society to foster stable Gaelic–English bilingualism.

Less commonly, economic changes can positively affect a threatened language. Frederik Paulsen (1990) describes the case of the Ferring dialect of Frisian spoken on the North Sea islands of Föhr and Amrum. After the decline of traditional herring-fishing, a school was founded in the sixteenth century to teach navigation skills to boys, who subsequently found employment in the new Dutch overseas shipping companies. Speaking Ferring was an advantage, and immigrants had to learn it if they wished to become members of this closed seafaring community. This was one of the main factors enhancing maintenance of a previously threatened language.

Demographic factors

Numbers of speakers do have a bearing on successful language maintenance: it might seem obvious that the smaller the size of a community, the stronger the threat of language shift and death. However, it is not possible to specify a 'critical mass' of speakers necessary for the survival of a language. Matthias Brenzinger et al. (1991) cite the case of Bayso, an Eastern Cushitic language of southern Ethiopia, which has resisted language replacement for 1,000 years although the number of its speakers has always been small (in the region of 500 in 1990).

Apart from absolute numbers, or proportions of speakers of dominated language to dominating language, the distribution of speakers is of some significance. Enforced or *de facto* segregation of immigrant communities would appear to offer better chances of language maintenance, all other things being equal. Wen Lang Li (1982) found that third-generation Chinese

Americans residing in Chinese-dominant neighbourhoods ('Chinatowns') were less likely to have adopted English as their mother tongue than their age-mates outside the Chinatowns. For an immigrant group, endogamy (i.e. marriage restricted to within the group) will also improve chances of a family language being transmitted to offspring.

Institutional support

The use of a minority language in education, religion, the media or administration may assist attempts to bolster its position. But, for minorities, this can only be done at great cost. There are limits to the extent to which a non-dominant immigrant language (or, more usually, languages) can be used in schools. A major asymmetry exists between use of a minority language in educational settings (associated with formal and standard norms of a language) and the hyper-colloquial and localised use characteristic of a language in its dying stages.

German was once a prominent language of the USA, not far behind English at the time of independence. Since then, it has declined as a colloquial language, with most speakers eventually shifting to English. German is, however, maintained until the present day among Old Order Amish and Mennonite communities in Pennsylvania, whose religious beliefs preclude them from participating in modern ways of dress, behaviour and speech. The institution of religion is the most significant factor here, though other factors like endogamy and resistance to economic and social change, may also play a contributory role.

Status

Some writers consider a group's self-esteem and the status of their language (oral or written, vehicle for sacred texts, major regional language elsewhere in the world, and so on) to play a role in maintenance or shift. These are not entirely separate from economic and class factors, however. Thus, Arabic is a high-status language in the Middle East, but not in Europe, where it is mainly connected with immigrant working-class speakers and refugees.

Aditi Mukherjee (1996) undertook a study of maintenance patterns of Panjabi and Bengali in Delhi. The presence of these languages in Delhi is largely due to the relocation of Hindus from East and West Pakistan (now known as Bangladesh and Pakistan respectively) since the late 1940s. Bengali is being maintained in more domains than is Panjabi in Delhi. An important reason for the differential pattern of maintenance is the higher status that Bengalis accord their language, especially for literary and cultural traditions, compared to the majority language of Delhi, Hindi. In contrast, Panjabis in Delhi accord their language a lower literary and cultural status than Hindi.

The Course of Shift

A shift from one language to another cannot be effected without an intervening period of bilingualism in the 'shifting' community. In the initial phases of the relationship, the languages may show specific distribution patterns over specific domains. More public and formal domains may, by force of circumstances, be allotted to the dominant societal language, with more informal and personal domains like the home allotted to the minority language. Language shift involves the progressive redistribution of the languages over these domains, with the home, religion, folk songs and tales usually being the last bastions of survival for the dominated language.

Many shifts involve more than one minority language, whose positions are weakened not only by the dominant language but also by each other. Immigrant communities from different areas of origin may develop close associations in the workplace and neighbourhood, which demand the use of a lingua franca. The most expedient, or least divisive, choice is often the dominant societal language. A similar ethos among different Native American groups in the USA, and Aboriginal groups in Australia forced into reservations, has accelerated the pace at which English developed as a lingua franca, often to the detriment of the indigenous languages.

One of us, William Leap, cautioned in 1981 that there were no instances, historical or contemporary, where a Native American community has intentionally allowed ancestral language fluency to disappear (see the case study in section 8.5). Although this would appear to be the general norm worldwide, there have been a few claims of shift having been deliberately hastened by members of the speech community. Eidheim (1969) discusses the case of the Saami fjord community which aspires to full participation in public life, as defined by Norwegians. Many families have taken the drastic decision of preventing their children from learning Saami. Matthias Brenzinger (1992) describes the conscious decision made by the Yaaku of East Africa in the 1930s to give up their language in the face of social, economic and linguistic pressure from the dominant Maasai. After adopting the value system of the pastoralists, the Yaaku considered the Maasai lifestyle and their language to be superior and to have higher prestige than their own 'hunter-gatherer' language. They discouraged the use of the old language even within their own community, insisting that the Yaaku language 'with its semantic emphasis on hunting was unfit for a cattle-breeding society' (1992: 302).

Speaker Competence in Language Shift

The shrinkage of domains in the course of shift is paralleled by receding competence in successive generations of the shifting community. Speakers of a language that is in its last stages may exhibit a range of competence in the outgoing language from full command to zero. Such speakers have been characterised as 'young fluent speakers', 'passive bilinguals' and 'semi-speakers' (Dorian 1981).

- **Young fluent speakers** are those who have native command of the ancestral language, but who show subtle deviations from the norms of fluent, older speakers.
- **Passive bilinguals** are able to understand the ancestral language (even down to its finest nuances), but are unable to use the language in productive speech.
- **Semi-speakers** are those whose ability to speak the ancestral language is flawed, but who continue using it in certain contexts in an imperfect way.

Dorian describes the semi-speakers of Gaelic in east Sutherland, Scotland, as having relatively halting delivery, speaking in short bursts, and exhibiting linguistic deviations of which older speakers are mostly aware. On the other hand, they are able to build sentences and alter them productively. This competence distinguishes them from the passive bilinguals. Dorian attributes the existence of semi-speakers (rather than young fluent speakers or passive bilinguals) in east Sutherland to a combination of the following factors:

- Late birth order in a large, relatively language-loyal family. In such a family the eldest might emerge as a fluent speaker, whereas the last two or three children may emerge as semi-speakers. Although their parents might continue addressing the last two or three children in Gaelic, the influence of elder siblings who bring back English from the school and playground is stronger.
- Strong attachment to one or more grandparents (most often a grandmother), who usually use far more Gaelic than one's parents. Less commonly, it is the influence of aunts and parents that encourages the semi-speaker phenomenon.
- Temporary absence from the community often fosters a reawakening of loyalty to the dominated language, which may result in 'semi-speech' if there are fellow exiles who share those feelings.
- An inquisitive and gregarious personality might also lead some young people to participate in conversations with elders in Gaelic. Such outgoing individuals actively wish to conduct conversations in the preferred language of the other party, despite the possible stigma of their own errors.

Gender and Shift

Domain, social network and gender prove to be crucial concepts in understanding the way in which speakers shift or resist shift from one language to another economically more powerful one. The influential study by Gal (1979) showed in detail how the patterns of language use change according to these variables. The details of this study were given in Chapter 5, where the stress lay on the 'code choices' that people make as societal circumstances change. You will recall that people in Oberwart increasingly use German in situations that were formerly reserved for Hungarian, until the religious domain ('talking to God') was the last one in which Hungarian survived as the main choice of code. In addition to domain, social networks are significant indications of code choices and the increasing shift to German.

On the whole, Gal found that two factors correlated most strongly with a choice of one language over the other: age of the individual and the 'peasantness' of his or her network. The latter reflects the status of a person's social contacts (whether traditional peasant or associated with the new working class) correlating more accurately with language choice than whether individuals themselves were of peasant or worker status. This seems a strong vindication of the social network approach in sociolinguistics.

Gal showed that women's behaviour in this regard showed a significant difference from that of men. Women were less constrained than men in letting their current social network determine the choice of Hungarian or German. Rather, they were in advance of men in their choice of German. Gal argues that rejection of the use of local Hungarian was part of the rejection by younger women of peasant status and peasant life generally. Hungarian had become the symbol of peasant status and a particularly hard life for wives who had to do much of the agricultural drudge work and the domestic chores. Many young men shared such a view of the life choices ahead of them. However, the possibility of a young man taking over the family farm could bring some advantages over wage labour, such as independence. On the other hand, women 'do not want to be peasants; they do not present themselves as peasants in speech' (1978: 13). That is, a young woman of Oberwart prefers to marry a wage labourer (who would be associated with German, even though he might be of peasant Hungarian stock). This leaves young men with peasant networks or a peasant lifestyle with no choice of an endogamous marriage; they are forced to marry women from outside Oberwart, where there is less stigma against a peasant marriage. Such marriages hasten the process of language shift, since the women from outside villages are German-speaking, and children of such marriages become monolingual.

Gender and matrimonial relations seem to play a significant part in a number of other language-shift situations. One such case involves the Yaaku of Kenya, in the Brenzinger study cited previously. Why did the Yaaku give up their language (consciously if the sources are to be believed) in favour of the Maasai language? After the more dominant group of Maasai moved into the traditional area of the Yaaku, there was a gradual decline in endogamy among the Yaaku. Whereas traditionally Yaaku girls received beehives as wedding gifts (i.e. bridewealth), when they began marrying Maasai men they received livestock instead. Soon Yaaku parents began demanding this from Yaaku men as well, necessitating a traumatic change in lifestyle for younger Yaaku men. They had to acquire cattle by serving as herders for the Maasai. This brought them closer to the Maasai in lifestyle, since pastoralism (keeping cattle) involved a more sedentary lifestyle than hunting and gathering. Marriage between Yaaku men and Maasai women then became a possibility. As in the Oberwart case, the children of such marriages became monolingual in the dominant language. Although the details are not as clear, the Yaaku case does show significant parallels with Oberwart.

It would be a mistake to see women as the innovators in all cases of language shift. There are cases where gender does not seem to be involved, as in Mukherjee's study (1996) of the language choices among Panjabi and Bengali immigrants in New Delhi. There are also cases where men are in advance of women. It is popularly believed that this is a result of women being restricted to more domestic roles (especially in immigrant communities), while men are first exposed to the domain of external work. Sometimes the explanations run a lot deeper. R. K. Herbert (1992) discusses a case of language shift in the Ingwavuma district of northern Zululand (now KwaZulu-Natal) among Thonga immigrants from Mozambique in contact with the dominant Zulu majority. Men adopted the Zulu language noticeably earlier than the women. This is how an anthropologist, Walter Feldgate (1982: 23), described the situation in the late 1960s:

> The linguistic situation among the Tembe-Thonga is very interesting. Despite the varying ethnic origins of the people, the languages spoken are exclusively Zulu and Thonga, with Zulu being predominantly the language of the men, and Thonga the language of the women. On the South African side of the border men never speak Thonga, whereas on the Mozambique side, while Zulu remains the dominant language of the men, they are not reluctant to speak Thonga as is the case in South Africa. On both sides of the border women speak Thonga almost exclusively. It is not at all uncommon to find men addressing women in Zulu and the women answering them in Thonga.

By the 1990s, many women had shifted to Zulu too, but in contrast to the men they speak a noticeably Thonga-influenced Zulu. This is an unwillingness to adopt Zulu completely, rather than an inability to learn. In understanding the differences in language choice and use, considerations of women's lower status in Zulu society than in Thonga society are crucial. Herbert (1992: 13) argues as follows:

> Although the issue is particularly complex, the reluctance of women to shift to Zulu may be associated with a somewhat better status allocated to women within Thonga groups than within Zulu groups. The realignment of identity includes a strengthening of male power and status at many levels of organisation; a move which women do not readily embrace.

8.4   THE LINGUISTICS OF OBSOLESCENCE

Linguists have been interested in the patterns characteristic of dying languages. In dying languages, vocabulary is relatively restricted, inflections are simplified or generalised, and grammatical rules that move phrases from one characteristic position to another (as in forming English questions, for example) are rare. Some scholars have asked whether dying languages resemble pidgins, simplified languages arising from contact between two or more different languages, as we discuss in Chapter 9. This does not appear to be the case, since dying languages do not show a tendency to uniformity in word order. Nor are there any reports of the kind of wholesale breakdown of grammatical structure in dying languages that one finds in pidgins. In connection with dying East Sutherland Gaelic, Dorian maintains that word order is unchanged, subordinate clauses are formed with ease, and certain categories which have marginal or indirect semantic significance persist. Dorian's (1978) characterisation of the morphology of East Sutherland Gaelic will be taken as a brief exemplification of the linguistics of language obsolescence. Among the ways of forming the plural of nouns in the traditional dialect of area are the following:

- adding suffixes like *-en* to some nouns
- changing the final consonant of a word
- irregular formations (e.g. *te* 'house' (sg) versus *tror* 'houses')
- internal vowel change (e.g. *mak* 'son' (sg) versus *mik* 'sons').[2]

There are yet other ways of forming the plural of specific nouns, involving combinations of the above processes. Semi-speaker speech shows certain trends like the notable rise in the use of suffixes, especially the use of a 'favoured' suffix by individuals. This leads to a simplification of the original grammar of Gaelic. However, a great deal of the original complexity remains. All the processes listed above are in use among semi-speakers, though to a lesser extent than among fluent speakers. Dorian (1978: 608) concludes that 'East Sutherland Gaelic may be said to be dying, at least with regard to noun plurals and gerunds (or verbal nouns), with its morphological boots on'.

8.5   A CASE STUDY: LANGUAGE CONTACT, MAINTENANCE AND SHIFT AMONG NATIVE AMERICANS

American Indian languages offer fertile ground for understanding language maintenance and language shift from the perspective of the dispossessed. More than 200 American Indian languages are still spoken in the USA and Canada, in spite of 400 years of Euro-American internal colonialism. This statistic serves as a reminder that speakers are often able to act on deeply-felt commitments to language maintenance even when facing pressures of assimilation and threats of cultural genocide. At the same time, the fact that more than 500 Native languages were spoken in North America at the time of the European 'discovery' of the 'new world' in the fifteenth century is a warning that language shift, and even language death, may occur in spite of the strengths of speaker commitments. In fact, a careful study of American Indian language histories reveals that maintenance and shift are usually part of larger 'package' of linguistic and social processes which shape the conditions of language contact and its sociolinguistic outcomes. Moreover, maintenance and shift may not be the only linguistic responses which emerge within contact settings: new languages can be acquired. In some instances, new language varieties may even be created – without disrupting existing linguistic resources, language fluencies or language loyalties.

The following case study of how maintenance, shift and other socio-linguistic options have been played out at several different points in American Indian language-contact history is based on William Leap's book *American Indian English* (1993). Leap discusses the following episodes in that history:

- inter-tribal contact;
- European linguistic colonialism;
- new simplified or mixed lingua francas;
- English-language schooling.

Indigenous Language Diversity and Tribal Multilingualism

American Indian languages are not in any sense a single or unified linguistic grouping, and may be classified on linguistic grounds not only as separate languages but sometimes as unrelated families of languages. Prior to the first European contact, there was Indian language diversity within every area of Native North America. That is, Indian tribes whose members spoke related languages were living next to Tribes speaking languages that were entirely different. 'Tribe' is a specialised term in anthropology that does not have any of the disparaging overtones that it sometimes has in popular usage. In a tribal society, kinship relations (membership in family, lineage, band or clan) and task-specific associations (work groups, governing councils, ceremonial and secret societies) provide the basis for social organisation. Together, kinship ties and membership in associations create sets of interlocking ties which make sure that everyone in the tribe is 'related', directly or indirectly, to everyone else. Thus, the education of each member of the tribe is of personal interest to the tribal membership as a whole. Initiation ceremonies and other rites of passage give public, formal expression to this broad and collective interest. In this chapter, we refer to 'Tribes' with a capital letter as the term used by Native American

people themselves. Inter-tribal communication for trade, political negotiation or other purposes would then involve one or more of the strategies in
the following three paragraphs.

Members of different Tribes talked to their neighbours in their own
ancestral languages if both languages were members of the same linguistic
family. This was the case for Northern Ute and Chemehuevi (Southern
Numic languages from the Great Basin), for Isleta and Taos (Tiwa languages from north-central New Mexico), and for Choctaw and Chickasaw
(Muskogean languages from the US Southeast). Communication in
these instances assumed that people were willing to adjust expectations
about grammar and discourse, so that they could interpret correctly the
neighbour's language choices. Speakers learned how to make these interpretations either by observing conversations and developing their own

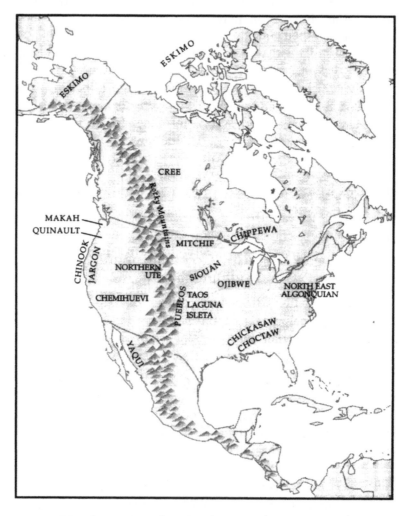

Map 8.1   Map of Native American languages cited

sense of the relevant points of contrast, or by seeking training from more experienced speakers of their language. Older speakers (aged over 65) of Northern Ute, Isleta, and Choctaw regularly include anecdotes to this end when telling stories about their childhood.

If neighbouring languages were not closely related, as was the case for Isleta (Tanoan) and Laguna (Keresan) pueblos in central New Mexico, Makah (Wakashan) and Quinault (Coastal Salish) on the Washington coast, or the Iroquois and Algonquian Tribes in the north-east, Tribes learned the language(s) of their neighbours and developed criteria to determine which Tribe's language was the appropriate means of conversation in any speech setting. The decisions were not the same in all cases. Among the Eastern pueblos, for example, hosts commonly spoke with guests in the guests' ancestral language; for Tribes on the Northwest coast, guests (or, at least, the spokesperson(s) for that party) were expected to talk with their hosts in the language of the host community.

Tribal leaders designated one of the languages widely spoken in the region to serve as their code for inter-tribal communication, and Tribes not already familiar with that language learned enough to be able to use it for such purposes. This appears to have been the case for Choctaw/ Chickasaw, which became a lingua franca for the Tribes of southern Alabama, Mississippi and Louisiana who were not already speakers of closely related languages and, in some instances, for Tribes which were part of the same language tradition. This designation of one language as a regional *lingua franca* for all of the region's Tribes pre-dates the emergence of the Cree confederacy and the beginnings of Spanish and French colonisation (Crawford 1978: 7–8, 30–2). This practice was thus not tied to tribal expansion or colonialism.

European Linguistic Colonialism and Tribal Multilingualism

European colonisation affected every facet of Tribal life in Native North America, including ancestral language skills and communication strategies. Whether the conditions of contact involved trade, political negotiation, open hostility or some combination of those conditions, the coming of the Europeans forced Tribes to develop means of communicating – as well as resisting communication – with non-Indian outsiders as well as with other Tribes.

The introduction of European languages to the Tribes was closely linked to conditions of contact, and Tribal acceptance of European language skills varied accordingly. In a now-classic study of American Indian language acculturation, Dozier (1956) shows how differences between Jesuit and Franciscan approaches to missionisation in the Spanish-controlled US south-west produced entirely different patterns of Spanish-Indian-language pluralism. The Yaqui used Spanish extensively in the presence of Spanish-speaking missionaries and colonists, whereas the Pueblos refused to speak Spanish in the presence of non-Indians, even after they became fluent in that language.

Where conditions of colonial rule were less extreme, some Indian languages began to be spoken more widely under European influence and patronage. For example, Taylor (1981: 178) writes:

> It is certain that Ojibwa became a lingua franca thanks to its use by the fur companies, whose employees were often native speakers of some Ojibwe dialect (Chippewa, Algonkin, Saulteaux) and whose local officials, as often as not, had Ojibwa wives.

Mobilian, which was already an established means of inter-tribal communication in southern Alabama, Mississippi and eastern Louisiana, became the French and Spanish colonists' code-of-choice for French and Spanish communication with those Tribes. Through this process, Mobilian acquired new vocabulary but also a more simplified sentence syntax.

The interpreters

Until the publication of Frances Karttunen's book *Between Worlds* interpreters had seldom been given their due in the history of the world. Though frequently portrayed in the colonial sources as useful but passive intermediaries, they were much more than that. An interpreter was not simply a vehicle for translating the surface structures of one language into those of another. He or she was concerned with communication as well as negotiation. Karttunen describes three female interpreters who played a larger-than-life role in the conquest of North America:

- Doña Maria (*La Malinche*), who interpreted for Cortés in the conquest of Mexico.
- Sacajawea, who accompanied Lewis and Clark on their pioneering expedition into the US interior.
- Sarah Winnemuca, a US army scout and lobbyist for the Northern Paiutes in Washington.

In the course of their employment they had learned the languages of these strangers and they had some understanding of what the men believed and how they behaved. This knowledge made them powerful brokers between their employers and their peoples, but it located them on the periphery of their home communities, where they were regarded with suspicion. (Karttunen 1994: 79)

New Linguistic Codes

New speech forms also emerged in some of these contact settings, through a synthesis of European and Indian language grammars and rules of discourse. Some examples of these are given in Chapter 9, since they more appropriately fall under the category of 'pidgin'. Two other non-indigenous language traditions contributed to language diversity among the Tribes during the colonial period and westward expansion which followed it. Both traditions had particularly powerful effects on the knowledge of English which was taking shape in Indian country during this period. First were the varieties of non-standard English which were one of the antecedents to today's African American Vernacular English. These codes were introduced into the Indian south-east in the early years of the seventeenth century as a result of the slave trade and the commercial ties between the Southern colonists and the Caribbean. Forms of AAVE spread from the south-east into the west due to several factors:

- inter-Tribal slave trading, whose networks moved Blacks from the Atlantic coast toward the Mississippi valley and beyond;
- Tribal willingness to extend sanctuary to escaped slaves (usually these were not Tribes involved in slave-trading);
- voluntary migration by recently freed former slaves into Indian country, when looking to establish homesteads in 'unclaimed' territory;
- interaction between Tribes (and their members) and the 'Buffalo Soldiers' – units of Black soldiers stationed at strategic military posts throughout the west during the US–Indian military conflicts of the later nineteenth century and during the years after those conflicts.

Each of these arrangements placed speakers of some form(s) of African-American English into close contact with Tribal communities or with particular segments of those communities. In some cases, contact became a basis for long-term relationships between these parties, though more often connections were less enduring.

The 'gold rush' of 1849 brought over 60,000 Chinese people to California as mine or railroad workers. Some of them eventually started businesses on or near Indian settlements, necessitating the development of a lingua franca. This was the so-called 'Chinese pidgin' (English), which together with Chinese languages also had important influences over some of the Indian English language traditions in the US Southwest.

English-language Schooling and Tribal Multilingualism

By the 1860s, when railroad construction began in earnest in the American west, English had already become the primary language of the non-Indians living east of the Mississippi river and in the eastern areas of the Great Plains. English had joined French, Spanish and the various ancestral languages (and, in some cases, had replaced those codes) as language(s) of daily experience for Tribes in the eastern and north-central states. Also by this time, English-speaking traders, missionaries, military personnel, railroad and mine workers, freedmen and -women, and other settlers had moved into the plains, the Southwest and the Northwest coast (areas explored and colonised by persons from other European-language traditions). Tribes whose previous encounters with English had been limited now interacted with speakers of English on an increasingly regular basis.

While Tribes may have had access to English during the second half of the nineteenth century, the Tribal familiarity with English which emerged during this period did not permeate the Tribal speech communities. Nor did familiarity with English displace ancestral language skills or disrupt Tribal strategies for multilingual communication in this period.

Young people's language skills were even less likely to be affected by the (limited) presence of English in their home or Tribal communities. Certainly, young Indian people became more aware of English during the second half of the nineteenth century. Because conversations with English-speaking non-Indians took place in public settings, young people had opportunities to observe how Tribal leaders or their delegates used English and other languages to exchange ideas, bargain and reach consensus on particular issues. But these discussions were between adults and hence not open to the participation of young people. Hearing adults using English in these settings did not necessarily prompt young people to develop proficiency in English on their own.

As a result, even as late as the 1860s, when speakers of English were beginning to settle all across the west, schoolteachers working in the on-reservation mission schools in the American west reported that their students came to school unfamiliar with English. Up to the 1890s, administrators in on-reservation schools favoured using the students' ancestral language as the language for initial instruction, since their students' English skills were not sufficiently developed to enable their participation in English. US-based Indian education 'authorities' raised strong objections to such proposals, setting the stage for English-only arts instruction. Consequently, a neglect of ancestral language development became the main feature of the US government's policy in Indian education in the late nineteenth century, and has continued to be so since that time. The government's justification for this policy was deceptively simple: if the Tribes were not providing opportunities for Indian students to learn English in home and community settings, then the schools had to create opportunities for English-language learning. By the end of the nineteenth century, the off-reservation boarding-school programme had become the federal government's policy-of-choice to this end.

American Indian English and Tribal Multilingualism in the Twentieth Century

The language-learning experiences in the Indian boarding schools were successful in promoting American Indian students' development of English-language fluency. Importantly, the English which Indian students acquired in boarding-school settings, and which they brought home to their Tribal speech communities, was not necessarily the English which school language policies wanted them to acquire. While classroom-based language instruction certainly had an effect on Indian student language skills, of greater importance were the language-learning experiences open to Indian students outside of the classroom – in the dormitories and dining halls, on the sports field, during practical work details. In these settings, fellow students, and not the school faculty, were the sources and role models for English-language education. What the students learned, and took home with them when they left the boarding schools, was the prototype of today's American Indian English(es) – varieties of English which are heavily influenced by the details of ancestral language grammars, rules of discourse and text-making practices (Leap 1978, 1993). Under this arrangement, English was no longer a language known and used by a limited number of individuals in the tribal speech community, as had been the case for so many of the Tribes in previous years. Student recollections of the rigours of English-only boarding-school policies, as well as the practical benefits stemming from English fluency within the classroom, gave returning students reasons to transmit English skills to younger members of the Tribe who were likely to be sent to the boarding schools.

Indian English also began to gain value in its own right within the Tribal speech communities. This gave community members reasons to acquire Indian English fluency – even if they had been fortunate enough to gain control over more standardised varieties of English in other settings. Among other things, the ancestral language base underlying each Indian English variety gave its speakers ways to communicate in ancestral language terms even though they were talking to outsiders. Such Indian-affirming English codes became especially valuable in face-to-face conversations with non-Indians who had gained access to 'on-reservation' lands.

An enrichment of English to take on community nuances can be seen in a number of native American Indian English varieties studied by Leap (1993). As an illustration, we focus on the northern Ute reservation of north-eastern Utah (see Map 8.1). Leap's emphasis on English as one of several codes that blended into the repertoires of communities which were traditionally multilingual and which developed coherent strategies for communication with outside groups is particularly apt for the northern Ute. Domains like on-reservation administration, education, religion, shopping trips and visits outside the reservation and outside employment bring Ute people into contact with other members of their Tribe, with Indians from other Tribes, and with outsiders.

There are six distinct language traditions within the northern Ute reservation's speech community, each of which provides its speakers with a range of varieties, styles and registers which are relevant to the speakers' everyday experiences. Leap identifies three types of northern Ute varieties which are used on the reservation, and a great deal of personal variation, since distinctiveness in the speech of individuals is highly valued. At the beginning of the twentieth century, one or more of these varieties of Ute served as the 'first language' for Ute families on this reservation. For most persons in the oldest age groups today, some form of Ute has remained the primary language. At the end of the twentieth century, however, fewer than 44 per cent of Ute adults, and fewer than 20 per cent of the Ute children under 18, could speak the Ute language 'adequately or better'. Furthermore, Ute remains the primary language for domestic conversation in fewer than 40 per cent of the on-reservation households.

Leap also identifies three types of English on the reservation. The most regularly used in community life is Ute English, which, much as in the case of the Tribe's ancestral language, is really a cluster of language varieties which vary widely across speakers, bands and communities. All of these varieties share certain details of pronunciation, sentence structure, classifications of meanings and speaking styles which closely parallel distinguishing features of Ute language grammar; in a sense, to speak Ute English is almost like speaking the Ute language in a form which non-Indians will understand. In spite of these close ties with the ancestral language, speakers of Ute English do not need to be speakers of Ute. Indeed, the 'first language' for many Ute people, particularly those under 21, is now Ute English, with Ute language skills learned later in life, if at all.

Two other language varieties that coexist with Ute English are Basin English and standard English. Basin English resembles, in part, other varieties of non-standard English found throughout the US south-west, but there are certain features of pronunciation which are specific to this area (the so-called Uintah Basin) of north-eastern Utah. In many instances, speakers of Basin English are non-Indian, and often they have been residents of this area for several generations. However, speakers who have moved into the area more recently also learn Basin English because it provides ways to establish connections with their non-Indian neighbours. Ute people recognise the distinctiveness of Basin English, and some refer to it as 'cowboy English', phonetically [kboi+Ingls], using a Ute pronunciation rule to reshape the syllable structure of the first English word.

Opportunities for speaking standard English in these settings have to compete with the widespread use of Ute English (among Utes) and Basin

English (among non-Indians) which already occur there. Standard English is closely associated with schooling and with the language of instruction in the classroom.

From this detailed case study, it can be seen that American Indian speech communities have never been single-language communities. Language pluralism was the dominant theme in the language histories of the Tribes long before the beginning of European colonisation. Colonisation simply extended and further diversified those multilingual practices. In this sense, the presence in today's American Indian speech communities of distinctively Indian varieties of English, more standardised varieties of English, as well as one or more varieties of the Tribe's ancestral language(s) are the latest expression in the Tribe's commitments to maintain ancestral language fluencies by incorporating the linguistic traditions of others into their own language resources and making additional adjustments (or 'adaptations') in their existing linguistic resources. This is why, although the overall picture concerning Native American languages includes the extinction of communities and their languages, the desire and capacity for language maintenance among others should not be underestimated. Linguists are increasingly aware that they have a role to play in helping communities safeguard their linguistic traditions while confronting the realities of the twenty-first-century global village. It is to this theme that we now turn.

8.6   SAVING ENDANGERED LANGUAGES

It is estimated that in the period 1490–1990 about half of the world's languages ceased to be spoken. Of the surviving 5,000 to 6,000 languages in the world today, many are themselves in various stages of obsolescence, struggling to hold their own not only as first languages but also as second languages. The linguist Michael Krauss (1992: 7) has argued that unless something is done now, the present century 'will see either the death or the doom of 90% of mankind's languages'. However, one scholar (Brenzinger 1992) is of the opinion that for East Africa, at least, language shift and death are not necessarily more frequent today than before – they have been side-effects of migrations and expansions of ethnic groups over the last 5,000 years.

In the early twenty-first century, Aboriginal languages of Australia are greatly in decline. It is estimated that of the 200 languages of precolonial Australia, fewer than 50 had viable communities in which children were able to speak the language in c.2000. Furthermore, only 18 of these languages have at least 500 speakers. In the USA, the fate of Amerindian languages is not much better. Even Navajo, felt to be one of the most resilient of the American Indian languages of the 1980s, is currently in decline, with monolingual speakers aging and declining in number. Benally and Viri (2005: 94) put it as follows:

> There are 85,555 Navajo individuals between the age of 24 and 54 years of age. Roughly speaking, those over 40 are more likely to have less proficiency, with the majority of those 30 years and younger more likely to have no proficiency in Navajo language. And incidently they are now the parent generation

In Europe, the Celtic languages (Welsh, Gaelic, Breton) struggle to survive against English and French. In Southern Africa, languages of the Khoi and San families have been the victims of shift and death. Generally, minority languages on the African continent have given way to other, more powerful or prestigious African languages rather than to languages of European colonialism.

Two views on language death
Safeguarding diversity and cultural wealth
The last fluent user of Damin [spoken by initiated men among the Lardil people of Mornington Island in North Queensland, Australia] passed away several years ago. The destruction of this intellectual treasure was carried out, for the most part, by people who were not aware of its existence, coming as they did from a culture in which wealth is physical and visible. Damin was not visible for them, and as far as they were concerned, the Lardil people had no wealth, apart from their land. (Hale 1992:40)

Community views of progress in dominant languages
As a linguist I am of course saddened by the vast amount of linguistic and cultural knowledge that is disappearing, and I am delighted that the National Science Foundation has sponsored our UCLA research, in which we try to record for posterity the phonetic structures of some of the languages that will not be around much longer. But it is not for me to assess the virtues of programmes for language preservation versus those of competitive programmes for tuberculosis eradication, which may also need government funds . . .

Last summer I was working on Dahalo, a rapidly dying Cushitic language, spoken by a few hundred people in a rural district of Kenya. I asked one of our consultants whether his teen-aged sons spoke Dahalo. 'No,' he said. 'They can still hear it, but they cannot speak it. They speak only Swahili.' He was smiling when he said it, and did not seem to regret it. He was proud that his sons had been to school, and knew things that he did not. Who am I to say that he was wrong?

(Ladefoged 1992: 810–11)

Some important cases of symbiotic cooperation between linguists and local communities are discussed in the journal *Language* (vol. 68). A number of interest groups have been formed with the intention of protecting dying languages or at least recording as much as possible of their structure, vocabulary an cultural norms. These include the Endangered Languages Committee of the Linguistic Society of America, and endangered languages projects and foundations in Germany, France, Australia, the UK and elsewhere.

A Model for Reversing Language Shift

A firm believer in the need to reverse the trend towards the domination of minority languages is Joshua Fishman, who has argued that 'there is no language for which nothing at all can be done' (1991: 12). He devised an eight-point scale which characterises different stages of shift and the extent to which a particular language is endangered. The GIDS (*Graded Intergenerational Disruption Scale*) is rather like the Richter Scale in geology in that it measures and reflects different degrees of sociolinguistic disruption and disarray. In his formulation, 'X-ish' is the language being lost, 'Y-ish' the language which is spreading; 'X-men' (*sic*) are the people for whom X-ish was (or still is) a community language, 'Y-men' the people associated with the dominant language.

Corresponding to this diagnosis is Fishman's scheme for reversing

Stage 8: Most vestigial users of X-ish are socially isolated old people, and X-ish needs to be reassembled from their mouths and memories and taught to demographically unconcentrated adults.
Stage 7: Most users of X-ish are a socially and ethnolinguistically active population but they are beyond childbearing age.
Stage 6: The attainment of intergenerational informal oracy and its demographic concentration and institutional reinforcement.
Stage 5: X-ish literacy in home, school and community, but without taking on extracommunal reinforcement of such literacy.
Stage 4: X-ish in lower education that meets the requirements of compulsory education laws.
Stage 3: use of X-ish in the lower work sphere (outside of the X-ish neighbourhood/community) involving interaction between X-men and Y-men.
Stage 2: X-ish in lower governmental services and mass media but not in the higher spheres of either.
Stage 1: some use of X-ish in higher-level educational, occupational, governmental and media efforts (but without the additional safety provided by political independence).

Table 8.1 The GIDS (Graded Intergenerational Disruption Scale) (based on Fishman 1991: 87–107)

1. Education, work sphere, mass media and governmental operations at higher and nationwide levels.
2. Local/regional mass media and governmental services.
3. The local/regional (i.e. non-neighbourhood) work sphere, both among X-men and among Y-men.
4b. Public schools for X-ish children, offering some instruction via X-ish, but substantially under Y-ish curricular and staffing control.
4a. Schools in lieu of compulsory education and substantially under X-ish curricular and staffing control.
   II. *RLS to transcend diglossia, subsequent to its attainment*

5. Schools for literary acquisition, for the old and for the young, and not in lieu of compulsory education.
6. The intergenerational and demographically concentrated home–family–neighbourhood: the basis of mother-tongue transmission.
7. Cultural interaction in X-ish primarily involving the community-based older generation.
8. Reconstructing Xish and adult acquisition of XSL.
   I. *RLS to attain diglossia*

Table 8.2   A programme for reversing language shift (based on Fishman 1991: 395)

language shift, which involves specific activities needed at each point of the GIDS scale, if language shift is to be reversed. The aim of his programme is to eventually ensure continuous intergenerational transmission of dominated languages as spoken vernaculars, not just for special purposes like reading, religious recitation and so on. Table 8.2, like Table 8.1, is meant to be read from the bottom up.

Stage 8 is meant to facilitate the revival of a language no longer used as a colloquial language of a community. This requires the efforts of committed community members who might have a passive knowledge of the language, and of linguists. The society dedicated to the revival of Cornish in England is currently at this stage. So too are some First Nations communities of Canada like the Huron, who are working with linguists to salvage whatever they can (via written grammars and documents) of their ancestral language, which no community member knows well any more. Maarten Mous found surviving speakers of Yaaku in north central Kenya, whose language was previously believed to be extinct (see the discussion under 'Gender and Shift' in section 8.3). Members of the Yaaku community now hope to revive the language, as sociopolitical conditions are less antagonistic to pre-modern hunter-gatherer peoples and there is now the possibility of communal ground rights for the Yaaku people of the forest. Based on his fieldwork and interaction with semi-speakers and rememberers, and three fluent speakers each aged around 100 years, Mous (2005) is cautious about prospects for revival of the 'pure' Yaaku of former times that some revivalists wish for. Rather, he proposes the more pragmatic approach of increasing the number of Yaaku words whilst retaining the grammar that most community members are fluent in, viz. Maasai. It remains to be seen how community leaders react to such an effort. Successive stages in Fishman's scheme (starting with stage 8 in Table 8.2) are meant to foster the dominated language in more and more contexts, to enable its survival in the first instance as a language of the home (in a diglossic relation to the societally dominant language). The second part of his scheme involves more assertive demands and plans for use of the dominated language in wider domains in direct competition with 'Y-ish'.

Fishman has pinpointed a clear way of diagnosing stages of shift, and of ways of reviving, consolidating or spreading a dominated language at different stages of shift. But the model is not unproblematic. In stressing the need for a dominated group to develop its own schools, spheres of work, playgroups and so on, it seems to carry segregative tendencies which run counter to more pluralist ideals in many modern societies. The model also seems to presume clear differences and unambiguous attitudes concerning in-group versus out-group identities. Modern sociology stresses, instead, the fluidity of the concept of identity – that people may have multiple identities which are deployed in different situations, and themselves open to further modification (see Chapters 5–7). On the other hand, the primacy of ethnicity in many conflict-ridden parts of Europe and Africa would suggest that there is a place for the application of the model in some societies.

8.7 CONCLUSION

The study of language shift and death is one which affects linguists directly, since languages provide the database of their subject. Sociolinguists are, however, more concerned with communities of speakers rather than the structure of their language for its own sake. Of course, syntactic and phonological expertise is required if one wishes to record endangered languages for the purpose of helping communities maintain their languages in the face of more powerful ones. Yet, as Fishman's model makes clear, language endangerment is a question of power politics rather than linguistic structure. More linguists are needed in the twenty-first century who are prepared to work closely with minoritised communities so as make clear the choices before them and the consequences of such choices. (We return to this issue in the context of the use of minority languages in education in Chapter 12.)

In this chapter, we discussed instances of borrowing and what they reveal about cultural contact. The main theme of this chapter was, however, language maintenance and shift. The phenomenon of language death was also outlined. Some linguists identify four different types of language death, depending on the sociohistorical circumstances a speech community faces. Although maintenance and shift cannot be predicted from prevailing circumstances, four factors play a crucial role: economics, status, demography and institutional support. Dorian's work on characterising the repertoires of a community undergoing language shift was highlighted, especially her description of the 'semi-speaker'. Not all dying languages exhibit the semi-speaker phenomenon. A case study of American Indian language contacts with each other and with European languages shows the operation of maintenance and incipient shift from the community's perspectives. Though the northern Ute community prizes fluency in their traditional languages, the power of English can be seen in the way it is increasing among younger community members. However, as is frequent in cases of language shift, the English spoken on the northern Ute reservation reflects a continuity in speech norms. In a sense, English on the reservation is an 'Indian language' fulfilling both modern and traditional ways of speaking. Projects in many parts of the world that aim to document dying languages and possibly help some communities to maintain their languages were outlined in this chapter. In this regard, the programme proposed by Fishman to reverse language shift is particularly relevant. Such programmes intended to assist speakers of endangered languages illustrate the need to go beyond prescriptivism and descriptivism, as we discussed in Chapter 1.

Notes

1. There is, however, a society dedicated to reviving Cornish as a spoken language.
2. These spellings are simplifications of the system that Dorian used: *t* and *k* should be read as aspirated consonants and *o* as a long vowel.

9
LANGUAGE CONTACT 2: PIDGINS, CREOLES AND 'NEW ENGLISHES'

9.1 INTRODUCTION

In this chapter, the theme of language contact is continued. We first present an extreme kind of contact which results in new languages. Under slavery especially, large numbers of people were able neither to maintain their ancestral languages nor to shift to the colonial language. Instead, they created new languages (**pidgins** and **creoles**) that were only partly based on the languages around them. We survey the circumstances in which such languages arise, with a special focus on the era of slavery. This chapter is also concerned with the structure of these languages and their similarities in different parts of the world. We examine the major explanations put forward by sociolinguists for such similarities. The kind of contact, under slavery especially, that gave rise to pidgins and creoles is contrasted with the acquisition and spread of languages of power and prestige under colonialism, especially varieties that have come to be called '**New Englishes**'.

9.2 PIDGINS AND CREOLES

This small swine he been go for market
This small swine he been stay for house
This small swine he been chop soup withi fufu
This small swine he no been chop no nothing
And this small swine he been go wee, wee sotei for house.[1]
(Glosses: *chop* 'to eat or drink'
fufu 'boiled balls of cassava, yams and plantain'
sotei 'until')

This version of 'This Little Piggy' recited by a speaker in Cameroon may seem highly unusual from the viewpoint of the conventions of ordinary written English. Yet sociolinguists, some of whom spend their working lives studying such forms of speech, conclude that they are systems in their own right, with their own linguistic norms. For example, *been* is consistently used as a marker of the past tense of the verb that follows it in the above nursery rhyme. The technical term for the language exemplified here is **pidgin**; the example is from Cameroon Pidgin English given by Loreto Todd (1984: 275). The discipline of pidgin and creole studies, sometimes called **creolistics**, essentially deals with new codes arising from the (involuntary) realignment of people who once were part of separate linguistic traditions.

Pidgins arise when groups of people who do not speak a common language come into contact with each other. (Some theorists, like Keith Whinnom (1971), argued that the creation of a pidgin depends on contact between speakers of three or more mutually unintelligible languages.) The need for the rapid development of a means of communication results in a relatively simple type of language which may draw on the languages of the groups involved. The formation of a pidgin differs from the process of 'second-language acquisition', during which one of the first languages of a group is gradually learned by others. Pidgins by contrast are not necessarily 'targeted' at one of the pre-existing languages, since the main aim of speakers is to enable communication, rather than to learn another language. In terms of structure, they do not bear close resemblance to any of the languages in contact, though they draw vocabulary items from these languages.

The term 'pidgin' thus denotes a simple form of language showing signs of language mixing, which no one speaks as their first language. Nevertheless, pidgins develop their own rules and norms of usage. The creolist Peter Mühlhausler (1986: 5) offers the following comprehensive definition:

> Pidgins are examples of partially targeted or non-targeted second-language learning, developing from simpler to more complex systems as communicative requirements become more demanding. Pidgin languages by definition have no native speakers, they are social rather than individual solutions, and hence are characterized by norms of acceptability.

In practice, matters can be a bit more complicated. Researchers find it useful to differentiate between pidgins in terms of how complex their grammatical structures are (for example, in tense formation, singular/plural distinctions and so on). In turn, these differences relate to the functions which a pidgin fulfils.

- A **jargon** (or **pre-pidgin**) has relatively unstable structure, draws on a limited vocabulary and is frequently augmented by gestures.
- A **stable pidgin** (usually just labelled 'pidgin', and to which Mühlhausler's definition best applies) is one which has a recognisable structure and fairly developed vocabulary, but which is in practice limited to a few domains (for example, the workplace, a marketplace and so on).

- An **expanded pidgin** is one which has developed a level of sophistication of structure and vocabulary as a consequence of being used in many contexts, including interpersonal and domestic settings, as well as some formal uses like public speeches or political pamphlets.
- **Creoles** are languages which developed out of pidgins to become the first language of a speech community. Pidgins and creoles arise out of a diversity of circumstances, including certain types of trade, some situations of war and large-scale movements of people. We shall sample some of these below. However, as the majority of creoles are spoken in former slave-holding societies, it is necessary to give a fairly detailed account of this form of labour.

A narrative from Guyanese Creole
Maanin suun abi bina gu bakdam said fu gye waata pan di swiit waata trench kaaz abi na bin gat non stan paip a iisteet dem taim. Mi bina tek di tuu big bookit fram bakpaat abi hows an mi lil sisii di nada pinii wan. Abi giit owt kwik taim an ron, ron, ron sutee abi miit kaaz nof badii an dem bai an gyal piknii bin ga fo dip waata an ker am ahows fo dem muuma mek dem tii.

[Translation: Early in the morning we used to go to the back of the estate to get water from the sweet water trench because we didn't have any standpipes on the estate in those days. I used to take the two big buckets from behind our house, and my little sister the other little one. We used to get out quickly because many people and their boys and girls used to have to dip water and take it home for their mother to make their breakfast.]

(from Todd 1984: 59–60)

Historical Background

Although slavery has existed since antiquity and in many parts of the world, our focus will be on New World slavery (that is, forced movement of African slaves to the Caribbean, the southern USA and South America). This was a consequence of the period of colonisation when European powers conquered vast territories throughout the world, from small islands to whole continents. Few parts of the world were uninhabited during this time (Mauritius and St Helena, small islands in the Indian Ocean and the Atlantic respectively, being exceptions).

In the seventeenth century, Europeans established settler colonies in the New World in order to develop plantations for crops like tea and tobacco. Many indigenous peoples of the Caribbean (for example the Carib Indians) resisted attempts by the European colonists to enslave

The roots of language contact, imposition and spread
By 1500 enough had been done for the business of exploration and
new enterprise to be attacked confidently . . . . Confident in the
possession of the true religion, Europeans were impatient and con-
temptuous of the values and achievements of the civilizations they
disturbed. The result was always uncomfortable and often brutal.
It is also true that religious zeal could blur easily into less avowable
motives. As the greatest Spanish historian of the American conquests
put it when describing why he and his colleagues had gone to the
Indies, they thought 'to serve God and his Majesty, to give light to
those who sat in darkness and to grow rich as all men desire to do'.
   Greed quickly led to the abuse of power, to domination and exploitation by force.   (Roberts 1976: 656)

them, and were often decimated in the process. Those who survived
often fell prey to European diseases. The principal form of economic
organisation, the plantation, involved the use of imported labour on a
massive scale under the control of small numbers of European masters.
The development of slavery as an institution went hand in hand with
early capitalism and the development of the plantation economies in
various parts of the world, which were meant to serve European markets.
Operating from the seventeenth to about the middle of the nineteenth
century, New World slavery was almost certainly one of the most inhu-
mane institutions of all times.

The Sale Triangle

The system into which slavery was incorporated involved a triangular
system of importation (Europe – Africa – 'New World'). The following
summary is based on the section on early modern plantation slavery which
is part of a more general entry in the *New Encyclopaedia Britannica* entitled
'servitude' (1986: 225–38). Ships set off from ports like Liverpool, Bristol,
Amsterdam and Bordeaux for the west coast of Africa. They carried liquor,
firearms, cotton goods and trinkets that were exchanged for slaves brought
from the African interior to one of the numerous slave factories (or trading
posts) along the Gulf of Guinea (which became known as 'the slave coast').
The majority of slaves originated from west Africa in the area bounded by
the Senegal River in the north and Angola in the south. They came from a
variety of ethnic and linguistic backgrounds, including those of the Wolof,
Malinke, Fulani, Akan, Yoruba, Ibo, Hausa and Mandinka. Slaves experienced the horrors of being captured in their homes or while travelling, of

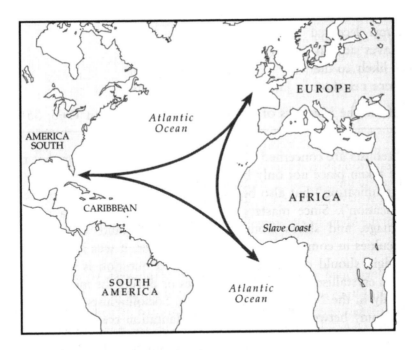

Map 9.1 The Sale Triangle

being marched on the long journey to the coast in chains, and often having to await a ship at collection posts for many months.

Then began the middle passage, a journey of at least three months from Africa towards the West Indies or other New World colonies. Closely packed in the hulls to save space, often chained to prevent rebellion or suicide, provided with inadequate food, water, sanitation and ventilation, about 20 per cent of slaves died *en route* to the colonies. In the New World slaves would either be taken to prospective employers directly or be kept in stockades to await a purchase. The third leg of the sale triangle involved the return to Europe of ships laden with New World products: sugar, tea, tobacco, indigo, coffee, and so on. One of the main items was molasses, from which rum was distilled and used for the purchase of more slaves on the next trip.

Creolists are concerned with the type of communication that must have taken place not only between slave master and slave ('vertical communication') but also between slave and slave ('horizontal communication'). Since masters and slaves did not share a common language, and slaves from different areas would also have had difficulties in communicating with each other, it was inevitable that a pidgin should develop. One unresolved question is whether this pidgin crystallised in the slave factories or during the middle passage or only in the New World plantations. Sociolinguists now accept a dichotomy between **fort creoles** and **plantation creoles**. The

Profile of a slave ship

Name of ship:	Zong
Left São Tomé island	6 September 1781
Slaves on board	440
White crew	17
Arrived in Jamaica	27 November 1781
Slaves deceased	60
Crew deceased	7
Slaves sick on arrival and likely to die	greater than 60
Price per slave in Jamaica	20–40 pounds.

(from the Memoirs of Granville-Sharp, in Donnan 1965: 555)

former developed at the fortified posts along the west African coast, where European forces held slaves until the arrival of the next slave ship (Arends 1995: 16). Guinea Coast Creole English, according to Hancock (1986), is one such fort creole. Plantation creoles, which are more numerous, evolved in the New World colonies, under the dominance of different European languages. These languages are called **superstrate** languages, since they were socially dominant, in contrast with the **substrate** languages of the slaves. The term 'substrate' denotes the subordinate position of the slaves and their languages. Some examples of plantation creoles and how they are traditionally classified follow:

Language	Where spoken	Superstrate
Jamaican Creole	Jamaica	English
Negerhollands	Virgin Islands	Dutch
Haitian Creole	Haiti	French
Papiamento	Netherlands Antilles	Spanish
Angolar	São Tomé	Portuguese

It is a matter of debate whether the process of pidginisation happened anew with each voyage, or whether sailors on the basis of their experience passed down the rudiments of a pidgin to enslaved people. Was a Portuguese pidgin the first pidgin to develop in this context, since the Portuguese were frequently the earliest of the New World colonisers and slave traders? Answers to these questions are not easily resolved, since such pidgins have long become extinct or have evolved into creoles. But linguists are increasingly tracking down and piecing together fragmentary accounts in old documents that shed light on one hypothesis or another.

Slaves were consigned to a variety of tasks in the New World: in mines, in ports and generally in heavy manual labour. Sometimes they were trained in various trades or served in domestic employment. But it is the

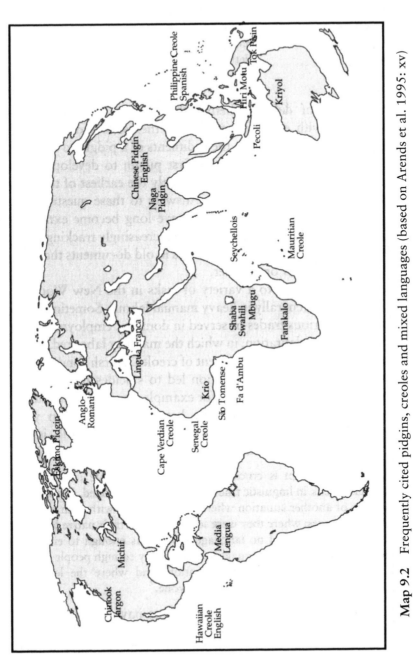

Map 9.2   Frequently cited pidgins, creoles and mixed languages (based on Arends et al. 1995: xv)

study of the plantation, in which the majority laboured, which is the most crucial for the development of creoles. Harsh conditions of work, social instability and alienation led to suicides or premature death of many slaves. In Suriname, for example, the life expectancy of a slave after arrival was somewhere between five and ten years (Arends 1995: 17). If plantation life was socially traumatic, it was equally linguistically traumatic, as Sankoff (1979: 24) summarises:

> The plantation system is crucial because it was unique in creating a catastrophic break in linguistic tradition that is unparalleled. It is difficult to conceive of another situation where people arrived with such a variety of native languages; where they were so cut off from their native language groups; where the size of no language group was enough to ensure its survival; where no second language was shared by enough people to serve as a useful vehicle of intercommunication; and where the legitimate language was inaccessible to almost everyone.[2]

Under these conditions, a pidgin is assumed to have evolved for both vertical and horizontal communication, drawing on elements from various languages including several African languages and the dominant European language. At one time, linguists believed that planters had a deliberate policy of enforcing linguistic segregation (that is, of keeping apart slaves from the same geographical area in Africa) in order to avoid the threat of insurrection. This would have intensified the slaves' need for a lingua franca. However, recent historical work suggests that this was neither a practical policy nor a commonly employed one.

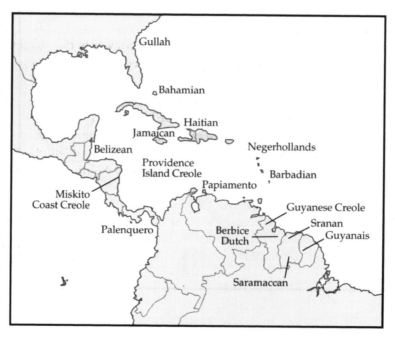

Map 9.3   Frequently cited Caribbean creoles (based on Arends et al. 1995: xv)

In time, the slaves' pidgin would develop into a creole. Exactly how this happened is still the subject of intense research and debate in creolistics, as we discuss below. We first present other settings in which pidgins have been known to develop.

Trade

Pidgins may develop in certain types of trading activities where several linguistic groups of people are involved and interpreters are initially unavailable. Naga Pidgin is a contemporary pidgin of the mountain regions of north-east India, spoken by people in Nagaland and Arunachal Pradesh. It seems to have originated as a market language in Assam in the nineteenth century among the Naga people. It is based on Assami (or Assamese), an Indo-European language of Assam, whereas the Naga people speak Tibeto-Burmese languages which are historically unrelated to Assami. Today the pidgin serves as a linking language (or lingua franca) between people who have about twenty-nine distinct languages among them (Sreedhar 1974). It is being creolised among small groups like the Kacharis in the town of Dimapur, and among the children of interethnic marriages.

European settlement

The movement of settlers from Europe to places where the indigenous population had not been decimated or moved into reservations, and where a slave population did not form the labour force (e.g. Papua New Guinea, China, India, East Africa), necessitated the learning of the indigenous languages (e.g. of Hindi in North India and Swahili in East Africa). Sometimes pidgins developed especially where contacts between Europeans and indigenous people were restricted to the domain of employment. Fanakalo is a stable pidgin, spoken in parts of South Africa, which probably originated from contacts between English people and Afrikaners with Zulus in the province of Natal in the mid-nineteenth century (Mesthrie 1989). Its vocabulary is drawn mainly from Zulu and to a lesser extent from English and Afrikaans. The structure of Fanakalo, however, seems closer to English than any other language. This stable pidgin, which later proved useful in the highly multilingual mines of South Africa, shows no sign of creolising.

War

American wars in Asia (Japan, Korea, Vietnam and Thailand) since the end of the Second World War have resulted in a marginal, unstable jargon or pre-pidgin called Bamboo English. It seems to have been a simplified form of English, with many words taken from local languages (Schumann 1974).

Labour migration
Within a colonised country, people belonging to different areas or different ethnic groups might be drawn into the work sphere without being overtly forced. Such accelerated contact might necessitate a quick means of communication, giving rise to pidgins. This has happened in many of the Pacific Islands, where a form of pidgin English developed, for example Tok Pisin in the island of Papua New Guinea. Some linguists believe that industrial pidgins have come into being in western and Middle Eastern centres which have attracted a large, multinational workforce in recent times (see the box on *Gastarbeiterdeutsch* below). Whether these are pidgins or forms of second-language acquisition that resemble pidgins is not clear.

Pidgins in North America
Pidgins and other lingua francas abounded in North America in the era of European colonisation. These are outlined in Leap (1993). Modern international idioms like *No can do* and *Long time no see* are probably derived from such pidgins.

- Michif, an Algonquian-French-based code originally spoken by Chippewa and Cree peoples living in Canada, and still used today by communities in North Dakota and in Canada.
- a French-Siouan code, used for purposes of economic exchange by French traders and Tribes living west of the Great Lakes area and across the plains long before non-Indian settlements appeared in those areas.
- an Algonquian-English pidgin used by the Tribes on the north-eastern coast.
- an Indian-Spanish language, Chileño, used by Tribes from California to Puget Sound.
- Chinook jargon, whose grammar made use of linguistic processes common to any number of languages, indigenous and European, rather than from a single language source.
- 'Trader Eskimo', which shows connections to Danish and English as well as evidence of indigenous language grammatical processes.
- Chinese pidgin English was also used in some parts of the west (see section 8.5). Browne (1868: 390) reports the following exchange spoken by a Paiute tax-collector to a Chinese worker:

> Me Piute cappen. Me kill plenty Melican man. Dis' my lan'.
> You payee me, John. No payee me, gottom me killee you.

(see further Map 8.1)

9.3 PIDGIN STRUCTURES AND THEORIES OF THEIR ORIGIN

Pidgins are not always comparable, since they come in varying degrees of complexity. In the following outline we shall focus, for convenience, on stable pidgins rather than pre-pidgins or expanded pidgins. Compared to 'full' languages, pidgins do have certain characteristics that make them easier to master. Fanakalo pidgin, for example, used to be taught to employees in some South African mines in about three weeks.

Pidgin Vocabulary

The size of the vocabulary of a pidgin is necessarily small, though there are some striking processes that enable its basic roots to be extended semantically. That is, pidgins make maximal use of minimal resources. John Holm (1988: 73) and Loreto Todd (1994: 3,178) identify some of the characteristics of pidgin vocabularies as follows.

(i) Polysemy
Many pidgin words are polysemous, that is, capable of expressing several meanings, which are mostly clear or clarifiable in context. Some examples follow from Cameroon Pidgin English, a variety that has its origins in Africa during the era of slavery:

shado	'shadow, soul, reflection'
bif	'meat, animal'
water	'water, lake, river, spring, tear'
belly	'stomach, seat of emotions'.

(ii) Multifunctionality
A single word may be put to a variety of basic grammatical uses in a pidgin. Thus in Tok Pisin a word like *sik* functions as both noun and adjective: *mi sik* 'I am sick' (adj.); *em i gat bigpela sik* 'he has got a terrible disease' (Romaine 1988: 38). Such multifunctionality may be carried over into a creole, as is shown with the word *sik* in Sranan, a creole English of Suriname. In this language, *sik* may be used as noun and adjective (as in the Tok Pisin examples), but also as intransitive verb ('to be ill') and as transitive (or causative) verb ('to make someone ill').

(iii) Circumlocution
Concepts that are expressed as basic words in 'full' languages are often expressed by circumlocution (or paraphrase) in pidgins. In the following set of examples showing circumlocution in Tok Pisin, a key element is the use of the superstrate verb *belong* as a preposition meaning 'of':

gras bilong fes	'beard'
gras bilong hed	'hair'
gras bilong ai	'eyebrow'
wara bilong skin	'sweat'
pinga bilong lek	'toe'
pela bilong op bottle	'bottle opener'

(Glosses: *gras* < *grass*; *fes* < *face*; *bilong* < *belong*; *ai* < *eye*; *pela* < *fellow*; *op* < *open*; *pinga* < *finger*; *lek* < *leg*; *hed* < *head*. Note that the symbol < means 'based on or derived from'.)

(iv) Compounding

Abstractions may be indicated by compounding in pidgins, as in the following Tok Pisin forms:

big maus	'conceited' (literally 'big mouth')
drai bun	'tough, toughness' (literally 'dry bone')
tu bel	'in two minds, doubting' (literally 'two belly').

Compounding may also be used systematically to denote gender of nouns:

hos man	'stallion'
hos meri	'mare'
paul man	'rooster'
paul meri	'hen'

(Glosses: *hos* < *horse*; *paul* < *fowl*; *man* < *man*; *meri* < *Mary* (= 'female').

Grammatical Structure

Pidgins are more often described in terms of what structures they lack, than in terms of the presence of features they share. For example, pidgins have very few suffixes and grammatical markers of categories that are mandatory in the 'input' languages. Tense often has to be inferred from context in many pidgins, or is expressed by temporal adverbs like *before, today, later, by-and-by* and *already*. In the following example from Chinese Pidgin English (Bakker 1995: 37), past tense is marked by the adverb *before*. (It is the normal convention when presenting sentences from a language other than English to supply first a line of word-by-word equivalents, with key grammatical elements in capitals. This is followed by a rendering into idiomatic English within parentheses.)

| Before | my | sellum | for ten dollar |
| PAST | ISG | sell | for ten dollars |

('I sold it for ten dollars')

The use of adverbial elements to indicate tense is especially common in pidgins that draw on a European language as the main source of

Past-tense markers in some English-based pidgins	
Hawaiian Pidgin English	*pau* (from Hawaiian *pau*)
Tok Pisin	*pinis* (from English *finished*)
Cameroon Pidgin English	*don* (from English *done*)
Cameroon Pidgin English	*bin* (from English *been*)
Chinese Pidgin English	*before* (from English *before*)

vocabulary. Some stable pidgins like Fanakalo of South Africa, by contrast, show the presence of several verb suffixes:

-ile (past tense):	e.g. *dlala* 'to play' vs *dlalile* 'played'
-isa (causative):	e.g. *enza* 'to do' vs *enzisa* 'cause to be done'
-wa (passive):	e.g. *pheka* 'to cook' vs *phekwa* 'is cooked'.

On the whole, though, the grammatical marking in Fanakalo is fairly simple in comparison to its main source language, Zulu.

Jeff Siegel (1996) analyses some pidgin structures, showing that they could be more complex than similar structures in the superstrate language. He studied the pronoun system of Bislama, a pidgin language spoken in the South Pacific country of Vanuatu. Bislama does not make distinctions in gender in pronouns, and may thus appear to be simpler than English (with its gender forms *he, she, it*) in this regard. However, two important distinctions not made in English are to be found in Bislama. We concentrate on one of these distinctions, that between 'inclusive' and 'exclusive' pronouns. In Bislama there is a first-person pronoun, *yumi*, meaning 'we or us, including you'. This contrasts with the exclusive pronoun *mifala*, which means 'we or us, not including you'. Thus in a sentence like *Fred invited us to the party*, Bislama grammar makes it explicit whether the listener is included in the invitation (*yumi*) or not (*mifala*). This complexity is characteristic of extended, rather than restricted, pidgins.

Theories of the Origins of Pidgins

Several theories have been put forward to account for the similarities between pidgins that have developed in various places and at different times. These can be broadly grouped into three types: (1) monogenetic theories; (2) theories of independent parallel development; and (3) theories of linguistic universals.

Monogenesis

This was a theory that had considerable support in the 1960s, claiming that pidgins that drew on a European language for a large part of their vocabulary (namely, a majority of the world's pidgins) were ultimately

Gastarbeiterdeutsch: pidgin or 'second language'?

The simplified German spoken by migrant workers of different nationalities, including Turkish, Greek, Serbian and Croatian nationals, in Germany has been described by some linguists as an industrial pidgin. In Germany, the migrant workers are called *Gastarbeiter*, 'guest workers'. The term *Gastarbeiterdeutsch* (Guest Worker German) accordingly is used by linguists for this variety. *Gastarbeiterdeutsch* shows a number of features typical of pidgin languages, such as grammatical simplification and vocabulary reduction. Other researchers have, however, argued that the social setting in which this variety of German exists differs in important ways from the sociocultural context of differs in important ways from the sociocultural context of pidgin languages. Most importantly, exposure to the superstrate language (standard or dialectal German) exists via a variety of means (communication with German-speaking colleagues and officials, TV and radio). Furthermore, as Blackshire-Belay (1993) points out, *Gastarbeiterdeutsch* shows more inflectional morphology than commonly reported for pidgin languages. Her research has shown, for example, that several different verb forms are used besides the infinitive form (V-*en*).

1. infinitive
   ich gehen Geschäft
   I GO SHOP
2. second-person singular
   bringst du meine Lotto auch
   BRING YOU MY LOTTERY NUMBERS TOO
3. third-person singular
   eine Dusche funtioniert nur an Freitag
   SHOWER FUNCTION ONLY ON FRIDAY
4. stem
   weil die Klima pass nix meine Bruda
   BECAUSE CLIMATE AGREE NOT MY BROTHER

This indicates that Gastarbeiterdeutsch is better classified as a second-language variety that is gradually getting closer to German, rather than a pidgin.

derived from pidgin Portuguese. Scholars who put forward this theory (for example, Keith Whinnom 1956; Taylor 1961) stressed the fact that the Portuguese were the earliest explorers or colonisers of many parts of the world, setting up the first bases for trade and slave labour. The pidgin form of Portuguese was itself believed to be connected to Sabir or Lingua

Franca. This was the link language between Muslims and Christians in Europe which has been recorded from the fourteenth century onwards, but which probably came into being as early as AD 1000 (den Besten et al. 1995: 88). According to this theory, the Portuguese pidgin formed the structural basis for later pidgins that were modelled on it but which replaced its vocabulary by words from other European languages. This process of changing the vocabulary of a language while retaining its essential structure is known as **relexification**. There are at least two hypotheses about how such a relexification would have occurred. One hypothesis is that slaves learnt the Portuguese pidgin on the African coast in the forts, slave factories or on board ship, and took this to the plantations of the New World. Later, this pidgin would have been adapted to the vocabulary of the dominant language of the plantation (that is, it would have been relexified). An alternative (but related) theory is that it was the sailors who carried the pidgin Portuguese to various territories and adapted it lexically to the dominant language of particular ports. Slaves would thus be exposed to the relexified version of this pidgin in the African ports. In support of this theory, scholars like Hancock (1976) point to the existence of a nautical element in many pidgins and creoles.

Some nautical terms in pidgins and creoles
Krio (an English creole of west Africa; Hancock 1976)

gjali	'kitchen' (<*galley*)
bambotgjal	'prostitute' (<*bum-boat girl*)
kjapsaj	'overturn' (used of any vehicle or appliance) (<*capsize*)

Cameroon Pidgin English (Todd 1990: 31)

hib	'to push or lift' (<*heave*)
manawa	'a wasp' (<*man o' war*)
jam	'to be stalemated' (<*jam*)
kapsait	'to overturn or spill' (<*capsize*)

Independent parallel development

Other scholars believe that pidginisation and creolisation occurred in different places and at different times, but under parallel circumstances which produced similar outcomes. For one thing, the dominant European languages were not dissimilar in structure. Moreover, many of the languages of the slaves taken to the Atlantic colonies belong to the same group of languages which linguists classify as 'West African'. In the Pacific, the substrates came largely from the Austronesian family (to which belong a variety of languages like Malay, Maori, Filipino, Javanese and so on).

Adherents of this theory suggest that there were broad parallels between the superstrate languages, within the group of substrate languages, and also in the circumstances of language learning.

Scholars differ over matters of detail, however. Some stress the importance of the European input while others see a greater role for the African or Austronesian substrate languages. Furthermore, the role of simplification strategies by the slavers is disputed. Scholars like Bloomfield (1933: 472) thought that Europeans, convinced of their own superiority, would have 'talked down' to the slaves. In this way, they may have prevented meaningful access to the 'real' superstrate language. This simplified and frequently condescending way of talking to non-native speakers is known as 'foreigner talk'. Bloomfield suggested that the condescension also included baby talk – that is, speaking to slaves as if they were children[3] The words that sailors and masters heard from the mouths of slaves (which either echoed the foreigner or baby talk of the slavers or were genuine manifestations of early second-language learning) would have been interpreted as further evidence of their inability to learn a European language. Given these far from optimal conditions of language learning, the theory holds that it is hardly surprising that no more than a rudimentary form of communication – a pidgin – evolved. While some elements of this theory are valid, the general model of language learning that it presupposes – that languages are learned mainly by imitation – is not supported today.

Young visitor to Papua New Guinea
When I first heard Pidgin English I just thought it was baby talk. I thought anyone can do that. It had words like *liklik* for 'little' and *cranky* for 'wrong' and *nogut* for 'bad'. It just made me laugh. Then I began to realise it wasn't as easy as I'd thought. People kept correcting me when I tried, and they got annoyed if I didn't take it seriously. I soon learned better.

(cited by Holmes 1992: 93)

Of the two theories discussed thus far, the idea of independent parallel development receives the wider support, since many scholars find it hard to believe that a process that happened once could not have occurred more frequently in very similar circumstances. Note that both theories are restricted to European-based pidgins. They do not apply in cases like Naga Pidgin and Fanakalo where the languages supplying the vocabulary are non-European (Assami and Zulu respectively). Yet scholars see many broad similarities between these pidgins and those of the Atlantic and Pacific areas. A third type of explanation is therefore necessary.

Linguistic universals

A third approach attempts to clarify the similarities underlying all pidgins, irrespective of the particularities of the situation that gave rise to them. It stresses instead the inherent linguistic skills of all humans. It is thus more of a psycholinguistic than a strictly sociolinguistic account. Todd (1994: 3, 180) puts it thus:

> Africans, Americans, Asians, Europeans, and Polynesians would have used their innate linguistic abilities to create simple communication systems which could be elaborated by having recourse to their mother tongues or to the linguistic common denominators which are thought to underlie all human languages . . . . It is . . . likely that speakers, in contact situations, simplify their languages in particular ways.

In appealing to the dominant theory within current linguistics – that language learning is accomplished because of the innate linguistic abilities of humans – Todd's account contrasts with the emphasis on faulty imitation in the baby-talk/foreigner-talk accounts cited above.

9.4   CREOLE STRUCTURES AND THEORIES OF THEIR ORIGIN

Creolisation involves expansion of a pre-existing pidgin. A creole community needs a language to cover all aspects of its existence, not just words related to a specific domain like trade or work. Vocabulary may be expanded by using words from the substrates and (especially) from the superstrate or by innovative combinations of already existing words. More complex phonological rules develop than may be found in pidgins. The most fascinating part of creolisation, however, is the reorganisation of the grammar that includes the development of a coherent verbal system with tense and related categories marked explicitly, and the development of complex clauses that include embedding of subordinate clauses. In short, creolisation turns a pidgin into a fully-fledged language, essentially indistinguishable from non-creole languages in its grammatical and semantic capacity.

Theories of Creolisation

The bioprogramme

An important theorist in studies of creolisation is Derek Bickerton, whose **bioprogramme** theory has stimulated a great deal of research and debate. Bickerton stressed that although creoles were to some extent derived from pidgins, the two types of language were totally different. Pidginisation is second-language learning with restricted input, while creolisation was first-language learning with restricted input. The term 'input' refers to the

Intertwined languages

Language intertwining . . . should be taken to be a type of language genesis different from cases like creolization or pidginization, and also from lexical borrowing and language shift. Language intertwining is a process which creates new languages which have roughly the following characteristics: 'An intertwined language is one which has lexical morphemes from one language and grammatical morphemes from another'. (Bakker and Muysken 1995: 41–2)

Media Lengua is an example of such a language, spoken in Ecuador. Virtually all its lexical elements are of Spanish origin, while the grammar is almost identical to Quecha, an indigenous language. It is spoken by people whose parents are Indians who spoke only Quecha. Media Lengua involves a case of code-mixing that has become solidified, rather than a cycle of pidginisation and creolisation. (Examples of this phenomenon, with short texts, are given in Bakker and Muysken.)

range of expressions from the target language that a learner is exposed to. Learning a restricted pidgin as part of one's secondary linguistic repertoire posed no problem for an individual's social and linguistic development, since the individual could still rely on the first language for communication within his or her own speech community.

To Bickerton's way of thinking, in a multilingual environment where the only widely used language among adults was a rudimentary pidgin, children were faced with a crucial problem of language acquisition. Drawing on some of Chomsky's (1965) ideas, Bickerton (1981) argued that children have an abstract, innate capacity for language (a kind of linguistic blueprint) which would be fleshed out and fine-tuned by the dominant language(s) they are exposed to from birth. But if there was no first language easily available (as in a plantation situation where a number of African languages and a European superstrate language existed, but were not as frequently used as the pidgin), acquisition would have to take a different path. Since the pidgin was not an adequate model from which the child could use its abstract 'language capacity' to deduce a full set of rules, the language capacity (or bioprogramme) would essentially 'create its own language'. Actual words are not provided by the bioprogramme, but abstract syntactic and semantic structures are. The structure of a creole at the time of its formation was, according to Bickerton, therefore largely that of the human blueprint for language, with words from the languages present in the child's environment 'plugged' onto the abstract structures provided by the blueprint.

In a non-creolising situation, the abstract grammar is set (or reset) according to the rules that can be deduced from the dominant language(s) of the environment. In a creolising situation, the abstract grammar is played out in a relatively 'pure' form. In keeping with the claims of Chomskyan linguistics, Bickerton assumed that children are the ones who played a major role in creolisation, since adults have passed the stage where their capacity for language was active.

> Creolisation illustrates the human capacity to 'create' language. Far from being an imitation of their parents' pidgin, a first generation creole can be structurally quite different. I have observed first generation creole speakers of Tok Pisin in Papua New Guinea who spoke a language that was so different from their parents' pidgin that the latter could not follow the creole when spoken by the children among themselves. When communicating with their parents these children switched to the former's less developed variety. (Mühlhausler 1991: 160)

A major part of Bickerton's argument was that the creoles he had studied were all similar in structure, irrespective of the diversity of languages that went into their making. He set out a list of twelve grammatical structures that he believed to be common to creoles, but not to non-creoles. These were therefore likely candidates for the 'natural' grammar contained in the bioprogramme. Three such features are outlined below: multiple negation, the zero copula and 'serial verb' constructions. A fourth (reduplication) has been added here, though it was not one of Bickerton's original twelve features.

(i) Multiple negation
Creole languages prefer a system that marks negation in as many 'slots' in a sentence as possible. This contrasts with rules in languages like (standard) English which usually mark negation only once in a sentence. The example below is from Guyanese Creole (Bickerton 1981: 66).

Non dog na   bite non kyat
No   dog NEG bite no   cat
('No dog bit a cat')

(ii) Zero copula
The term 'copula' refers to the verb *be* in its many forms (*am, is, are, was, were*) before an adjective, preposition or noun. In the sentence *She is tall*, the copula *is* precedes the adjective *tall*. However, in the sentence *She is playing*, the verb *is* is classified as an auxiliary, not a copula. Creole languages do not generally use a copula. This is particularly true of adjectival contexts, as in the following Jamaican Creole sentence:

```
di        kaafi      kuol
the       coffee     cold
('The coffee is cold').
```

(iii) Reduplication

In expanded pidgins and Creoles, the repetition of a root may be used productively to add meanings related to intensity, plurality, duration and frequency. Some examples follow from Cameroon Pidgin English (Todd 1984: 134):

fain 'lovely'	*fain fain* 'really lovely'
big 'big'	*big big* 'very big'
bos 'boast'	*bos bos* 'to be continually boasting'
tok 'talk'	*tok tok* 'to talk all the time, prolonged talk'
memba 'remember'	*memba memba* 'recollections'.

Bakker (2003) emphasises that reduplication is rare in most pidgins, but occurs more commonly in expanded pidgins (and Creoles).

(iv) Serial verbs

The term 'serial verb' refers to a sequence of two or more verbs (without conjunctions) having the same subject. The examples below (cited by Holm 1988: 183–90) will show that one of the verbs frequently fulfils a role played by elements other than verbs in the European superstrate languages.

Gullah Creole English (spoken on the islands adjacent to the south east coastline of the USA, especially along South Carolina and Georgia) has a serial verb construction in which the verb *pas* (based on English *pass*) functions as a comparative element:

```
I     tol    pas    mi
He    tall   pass   me
('He's taller than me').
```

In African American Vernacular English, serial *say* may function as a complement marker:

They told me say they couldn't get it.
('They told me **that** they couldn't get it').

In Ndjuka, an English-based creole of eastern Suriname, the second of a pair of serial verbs may function as what counts as a preposition in the superstrate languages.

```
A     teki    nefi    koti    a      meti.
he    took    knife   cut     the    meat
('He cut the meat with a knife').
```

Bickerton argued that the above three constructions (and more) were part of a natural bioprogramme grammar. His general theory has been the subject of considerable empirical research and debate. Critics of the theory lodge the following objections:

- The view that children alone are the main agents of creolisation has not been proven. Evidence from two pidgins that are currently becoming a primary language (Tok Pisin and Cameroon Pidgin English) shows that adults are as much involved as children (Jourdan 1991).[4] This calls into question the extent to which the innate language capacity, which is believed to fade after childhood, can be said to control the creolising process.
- Many of the features that Bickerton identifies as creole universals are probably due to the influence of specific African languages that were once used in the New World. Serial verbs, for example, can with justification be considered to be of African origin (Sebba 1984). It is significant that these features are not common in creoles and extended pidgins of the Pacific area, precisely those areas which did not involve slavery out of Africa.
- The sharp break between pidgin and creole believed to have occurred widely in the plantations has not been demonstrated. Studies from Tok Pisin show an intermediate variety (an extended pidgin phase) between the original pidgin and the creole. This does not mean that there are no differences between 'pidgin' and 'expanded pidgin' varieties of Tok Pisin; however, such differences seem to be better explained by other accounts of creolisation to which we now turn.

Gradualism: an alternate account of creolisation

An alternative to the bioprogramme hypothesis is provided by what are called **gradualist** accounts. Many scholars hold that the case of Tok Pisin is not unique; that the processes of gradual creolisation of an expanded pidgin that had been a significant mode of communication for several generations may have occurred elsewhere in the past. Under these circumstances, children and adults would have been simultaneously involved in the gradual process of transforming the pidgin into a creole. The two types of language would have coexisted for a time. More than that, the need to create a successful mode of communication for a wide range of functions was the chief determinant of the types of forms which gradually developed and stabilised in the creole. Gradualists find no need to posit the workings of a 'linguistic blueprint'. Out of the demands of communication, grammatical forms gradually developed and stabilised. This view is put most succinctly by Philip Baker (1995); see following box.

Baker specialises in the study of Mauritian Creole, a language derived from contact between French, African languages and – to a lesser extent – Asian languages on the island of Mauritius. Historical data from Mauritian and other creoles suggests that specific grammatical constructions evolved slowly. An example provided by Baker concerns the first time that specific auxiliary verbs of Mauritian Creole appear in historical documents. Prior to the early nineteenth century, combinations

One common thread running through all the . . . different accounts of how Creole languages were formed is failure. People tried to acquire a European language and failed, or they tried to maintain their traditional language and failed. Either way, Creole languages were the result of failure. This is not my personal view. I hold that all Creoles and all pidgins are, initially at least, successful solutions to problems of human intercommunication. (Baker 1995: 6)

[Slaves] were slowly creating a new language. Their collective motivation for doing so was their desire to communicate with people who did not speak their own language (1995:12) . . . Thereafter they gradually elaborated their creation unless or until changing circumstances deprived it of its usefulness or desirability. (Baker 1995: 13)

of auxiliary verbs like *ete* (denoting the simple past), *fini* (denoting completion of action), *fek* (denoting the immediate completion of action) and *va* (denoting the future) are not to be found. At that time, each auxiliary occurs only with a main verb. Combinations of these auxiliaries started to appear after 1816, with *te* (a modified form of *ete*) as the first element and any of the other three (*fek*, *va*, *fini*) as the second element. These combinations enabled new meanings like *te* plus *va* denoting 'future in the past' (rather like the English auxiliary *would* in the phrase *He said he would tell the truth*). Crucial to the gradualist argument is the great period of time over which the grammatical rule that enables *te* to combine with other auxiliaries unfolds. First combinations of *te* with these auxiliaries occur in 1816 with *fini*, in 1855 with *va* and in 1878 with *fek*. The bioprogramme hypothesis suggests that there should be a jump from a simple system to a complex one during the period of creolisation. Baker's data show the opposite: compound verb forms appear slowly over more than one generation (for example, there is a sixty-year gap between *te* + *fini* and *te* + *fek*). Gradualist accounts of creolisation are generally persuasive, though they are often dependent on fragmentary bits of evidence for their proof.

Decreolisation

Sometimes changes in social circumstances permit Creole speakers greater access to the superstrate language. The structure of the creole may then begin to change in contact with the superstrate. This change has come to be termed **decreolisation**. In the history of slave-holding societies, decreolisation was not very common. The class relations between descendants of slaves and the descendants of slave masters was a rigid one that persisted for centuries. Furthermore, education in the superstrate language

A current controversy in Creole studies – the 'exceptionalism' debate

Many linguists below see Creoles as a class apart, in terms of their history and characteristic structures (*a* and *b* below). This position has been strongly critiqued by others who see such an 'exceptionalist' position as overstating the differences between creoles and other varieties which show the effects of contact and borrowing (*c* and *d* below), and lending itself (inadvertently) to the propagation of racist conclusions by non-linguists.

(a) What happened in [the formation of Hawaiian Creole English] was a jump from protolanguage to language in a single generation. Moreover, the grammar of the language that resulted bore the closest resemblance not to grammars of the languages of Hawaii's immigrants; nor to that of Hawaiian, the indigenous language, nor to that of English, the politically dominant language; but rather to the grammars of other Creole languages that had come into existence in other parts of the world (Bickerton 1990: 119).

(b) Creoles, then, are mixed languages of a sort. However, more specifically, they combine pidginized elements from the creators' and the dominant group's languages and then expand this into a true language. The expansion is accomplished largely through refashionings already in the pidgin, this directed in part by universal 'default' constructions that older human languages have often drifted away from. (McWhorter 2002: 159)

(c) Creole vernaculars are not outcomes of abnormal, unusual, or unnatural developments in language evolution. Rather, they make more evident restructuring processes that must have taken place in the evolution of other languages. (Mufwene 2001: 192).

(d) The broken transmission and linguistic fossils dogmas are robustly disconfirmed by a range of comparative data and empirical and theoretical observations . . . Haitian Creole's structural patterns appear not to instantiate the sort of extraordinary break in transmission that would set the genesis of Haitian Creole from other instances of language change via language contact [of African languages with French]. (DeGraff 2003: 379, 398)

(Glosses: *protolanguage* = 'simple forms of language like pidgins and those claimed to predate the evolution of human languages today'; *Broken transmission* = 'situation when pre-existing languages are not passed on from one generation to the next') was not widespread until the twentieth century. Another factor inhibiting decreolisation was the fact that the original superstrate may have been replaced by other official European languages. This was a consequence of rivalry and conquest among the European powers, which lasted for centuries. In Mauritius for example, the first colonisers were the Dutch (from 1638), and then the French (from 1715), under whose slave policies a French-based creole developed in the eighteenth century. The British took over the island in 1810 adding English as a co-superstrate language. After independence in 1968, English remained as the official language, making the possibility of decreolisation unlikely. Rather, a kind of diglossia (or triglossia) pertains between Creole on the one hand and French and English on the other.

In societies where decreolisation has been possible, there is a wide range of linguistic varieties between the creole and the superstrate language. Linguists identify three central systems within this variety: the basilect, acrolect and mesolect.

- **Basilect** refers to the 'deep' creole which is furthest removed from the lexifier language: the two forms represent different linguistic systems which are usually mutually unintelligible.
- **Acrolect** denotes a variety spoken by some members of the creole community which is essentially the same as the superstrate language, except perhaps for accent and one or two grammatical differences.
- **Mesolect** represents a variety which is intermediate between these two poles (though in practice a mesolect is so fluid as to warrant the identification of further subvarieties such as upper, lower and mid-mesolect).

In a decreolising community such as Guyana, studied by Bickerton (1975), speakers may be located on various points of the continuum between basilect and acrolect, in terms of their usual vernacular usage. However, speakers shift between the various lects according to topic, style, addressee, situation and so on. This shifting is of particular significance, since speakers may then deploy different grammatical structures (not just stylistic alternatives of essentially the same structures). The example in Figure 9.1 shows the continuum between Guyanese Creole and the English acrolect, between which a series of mesolectal forms occur (O'Donnell and Todd 1980: 52).

Recreolisation

The opposite of decreolisation is a process whereby the acrolectal and upper-mesolectal varieties start to become more, rather than less, creole-like. The social conditions for this reversal are the opposite of those favouring decreolisation: social mobility is stifled in some ways. Fiona Wright (1984) studied the norms of black adolescents in Britain, whose

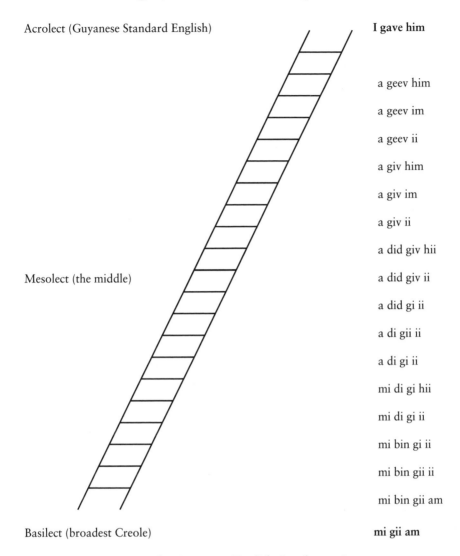

Acrolect (Guyanese Standard English)

I gave him

a geev him

a geev im

a geev ii

a giv him

a giv im

a giv ii

a did giv hii

Mesolect (the middle)

a did giv ii

a did gi ii

a di gii ii

a di gi ii

mi di gi hii

mi di gi ii

mi bin gi ii

mi bin gii ii

mi bin gii am

Basilect (broadest Creole)

mi gii am

Figure 9.1 The Guyanese English Creole continuum

parents had immigrated from various parts of the Caribbean. These adolescents spoke the local English dialect of their area, and a form of creole which had undergone decreolisation in their parents' generation. However, an increase in basilectal creole constructions occurs among adolescents, which Wright calls **recreolisation**. This phenomenon has been noted in several parts of England. Life in England has not brought the social mobility (or the decreolisation) that the original immigrants might have expected for their children. White youths who are part of a social network of primarily black youths may even speak the creole fluently (Sebba 1997: 226).

Excerpt from 'Listen Mr Oxford Don' by John Agard

Me not no Oxford don
me a simple immigrant
from Clapham Common
I didn't graduate
I immigrate
   But listen Mr Oxford don
I'm a man on de run
and a man on de run
is a dangerous one
   I ent have no gun
I ent have no knife
but mugging de Queen's English
is the story of my life
   I don't need no axe
to split/up you syntax
I don't need no hammer
to mash/up you grammar
   . . .

This excerpt draws from the variety called 'London Jamaican'

9.5 LANGUAGE SPREAD AND 'NEW' VARIETIES OF ENGLISH

Slavery was officially abolished in 1834, but this did not signal the end of large-scale contacts between Europeans and Africans. The nineteenth century saw the growth of imperialism as European powers tried to carve up the rest of world as their possessions. This brought superstrate languages like French, Portuguese, German and – above all else – English into a much more prominent position in Asia and Africa than before. The case of New World Spanish is notably different: South American territories had been colonised much earlier, and attained their independence much earlier.

The linguistic results of colonial contact included some 'indigenous' pidgins, having vocabulary from local languages rather than from a European superstrate (for example Fanakalo in South Africa, Sango in the Central African Republic). Such pidgins arose especially in the context of menial positions that local people were expected to serve (as house-servants, bearers and so on). The children of Europeans often learned an indigenous language of the colony, and quite often acted as interpreters between their parents and the local people. However, local people were expected to adopt the language of the colonists for official purposes. The term 'language spread' is sometimes used to describe the process whereby 'the uses or

---

The European scramble for the world

Colony	Superstrate language	Year of colonisation	Year of independence
India	English	1858	1947
Mozambique	Portuguese	c.1900	1975
Algeria	French	c.1830	1962
Singapore	English	1819	1965
Kenya	English	1886	1963
Senegal	French	c.1854	1960
Congo	French	1885	1960

(based on Barraclough 1982)

The dates denote the approximate or official periods of colonisation. In practice, European powers had already been present in the territories concerned for many decades, and sometimes (as in India) for centuries.

---

the users of a language increase' (Cooper 1982: vii). In modern times this phenomenon applies to languages like English, French, Swahili, Russian, Spanish and many others. In eras gone by, it applied to Sanskrit, Arabic, Latin and so on. 'Language spread' is a rather apolitical way of describing what is often the result of a process of language imposition by a greater colonial power, creating new linguistic relations in particular territories.

While the era of colonisation of Africa and Asia by European powers ended in the mid-twentieth century, their linguistic effects are still felt in the now-independent territories. With the redrawing of group borders after independence came a new sense of nationhood between groups of people who previously had little substantial contact with each other. Conversely, in some cases the postcolonial era ushered in a rejection of nationhood and fragmentation and wars between groups of people who had been artificially drawn together within the same colonial borders. In the case of those who accepted a new sense of nationhood, **lingua francas** that would enhance national communication became necessary. Modern lingua francas in various parts of the world include English, French, Swahili and Hindi. Every pidgin is a lingua franca, but clearly not every lingua franca is a pidgin. The dilemmas of choosing a national language in postcolonial contexts will be discussed in Chapter 11. In this section, the key sociolinguistic issues concerning new forms of English in different parts of the world will be outlined. The focus is partly on English for its own sake – as the language that has 'spread' the most in the modern world and received the most sociolinguistic attention. At a more general level, the discussion should be taken as an example of the sociolinguistic outcomes of the spread of languages of power and prestige.

Defining Characteristics of 'New' Varieties of English

Platt et al. (1984) used the term 'New English' for a variety that satisfies the following criteria:

- It has developed in an area where English is not spoken as a first language by a large number of people.
- It has developed through the education system rather than being acquired initially as a language of the home.
- It is used for a range of functions (e.g. as an inter-group language, in parliament, in official communication, in the media).
- It has become 'indigenised' by adopting words from local culture and 'nativised' by stabilising some structural features associated with local languages and/or the language-learning process.

There are some problems with this characterisation, notably in its narrowness. The definition excludes, for example, the English of Aboriginal Australians on the grounds of there being a majority of first-language speakers in the country. Critics also point out that the term 'New' is misleading since English in India has a longer history than in Australia and New Zealand, yet the latter are not considered 'New Englishes'. There are even more serious theoretical objections which we discuss below.

These varieties have continued to play an important (if controversial) role in the 'new' nations after they gained their independence. In these countries, English is frequently used in government, administration and education, sometimes together with other indigenous languages. Apart from such formal usage, English may also be used for internal communication among people who do not share a common language (especially among an educated elite). This is the situation in countries like India, Sri Lanka, the Philippines, Nigeria and Ghana. The category 'ESL' (English as a Second Language) is used by linguists in reference to such territories. It contrasts with the category 'EFL' (English as a Foreign Language), where English plays a more restricted role internally and is not generally a medium of instruction in schools. Furthermore, while New English countries typically have a distinct body of literature in English, EFL countries do not.

Some scholars (e.g. Platt et al. 1984) argue that just as creoles exist as a broad class of languages with a well-defined set of sociohistorical and linguistic characteristics, so too do New Englishes. They cite a few similarities that are widespread in the New Englishes.

Copy pronouns

Platt et al. (1984: 120) provide the following examples of a construction commonly employed in the new Englishes:

East African English: *My daughter, she is attending the University of Nairobi.*
Bangladesh: *People, they don't have that sort of belief now.*

Fiji: *Most Indians, they know English.*
Singapore: *But the grandsons, they know to speak Malay.*

In this construction, the first noun phrase of the clause is repeated (or 'copied') as a pronoun, especially where some sense of contrast or emphasis is intended. Although pronoun copying is a regular feature of colloquial L1 English, it is believed to be used more frequently and in a wider range of registers in the New Englishes. (L1 is the abbreviation linguists use for a person's first language; L2 for a person's second language and so on.)

Invariant tags
This construction was described in section 7.2, on women's language. It involves the addition of a tag which has a clearly defined grammatical relationship with the subject and verb phrase of the main clause. Consider the sentence *The Sri Lankan girl has won, hasn't she?* Here the main clause has the subject *the Sri Lankan girl*, which is replaced by the pronoun *she* in the tag. The main-clause verb phrase has an auxiliary *has*, which is repeated in the tag in its negative form, *hasn't*. Now consider the sentence *The Sri Lankans won again, didn't they?* Here the subject *the Sri Lankans* is again replaced by a pronoun (*they*). This time the main sentence doesn't have an auxiliary verb. Whenever this happens, there is a rule in varieties like British and American English which adds the auxiliary verb *did* in the tag, again in a negative form.[5]

The rule for tag formation is thus more complex than may appear to the adult native speaker of English, who learned it unconsciously as a child. Many New Englishes have evolved a rule that has just one invariant form of the tag (like *no, not so, isn't it*) which avoids the complexities of the rules illustrated above. The following examples are from Platt et al. (1984: 129):

West African English: *He loves you, **isn't it**/He loves you, **not so**?*
Sri Lanka: *Upili returned the book, **isn't it**?*
India: *He is going there, **isn't it**?*

Such a rule was probably devised unconsciously by the first generation of learners of English in individual colonies and passed on to succeeding generations, thus becoming the norm.

Double marking of clauses
Another characteristic of second-language acquisition that has stabilised in the New Englishes is the need to make relations between clauses as explicit as possible. In 'adversative' clauses, for example, this often entails using a conjunction in both clauses rather than once only. Adversative clauses are ones beginning with *but, though* or *although* – that is, the one clause bears an oppositional relation to the meaning of the other clause. The examples

from Williams (1987) show that some new Englishes mark adversatives more explicitly than in L1 English:

West Africa: **Although** you are away, **but** you do not forget.
India: **Though** the farmer works hard, **but** he cannot produce enough.

Not all New English features involve the stabilisation of strategies of second-language acquisition. Each variety shows specific indigenisation in its features of vocabulary and accent. By retaining (and thus sharing) some features from the indigenous languages of the territory, New Englishes blend into their sociocultural context. For example, English in India has a set of retroflex consonants, formed with the tongue curled backwards to strike the hard palate (instead of alveolar stops) in words like *ten* and *die*, which seems quite prominent to outsiders. (For example, it was a stock piece of the British comedian Peter Sellers' imitation of Indian English.) On the other hand, this pronunciation of English is unremarkable within India, since it blends with the sound patterns of the Indian languages. While this process has traditionally been cast in a negative light as 'interference' (a technical term in second-language acquisition studies), from a sociolinguistic perspective this is better characterised as 'enrichment'.

Droog [19C. Kan. *drūg.*] Name given to hill-forts in Karnataka. [Thomas and William Daniell, *Oriental Scenery* (1801).]

Drumstick [19C.] 'The colloquial Anglo-Indian name (in the Madras Presidency) for the long slender pods of the fast-growing *Moringa oleifera*, the **Horse Radish Tree** of Bengal.' [YB: Haafner, *Voyages* (1811).]

Dub (sb. vb) [18C. Tel. *dabba.*] A small copper coin, value 20 **Cash**. Slang: 'to *dub* up', 'to pay on the nail'. [*OED* & YB; *Lives of the Lindsays* (1781: ed. 1849), iii.]

Dubash, dobash [17C. fr. H. *dōbāshī*, 'man of two languages'.] An interpreter. In mercantile houses, the broker transacting business with Indians and corresponding to the Calcutta **Banyan**. In Gujarat reputed to act like Bunyan's Mr Two Tongues. Also *dūbāshī, dōbāshī*. See **Topass, Truchman**. [*OED* & YB; *Eng. Fact. in India* (1618-1669).]

Dubba, dubber [18C. H. *dabbah*; Mahr. *dabara*; Guj. *dabaro.*] A bag made of buffalo hide 'used for holding and transporting **Ghee** or oil'. [YB & *OED*; *Eng. Fact. in India* (1618-1669).]

Dubbawalla [20C. Mar. *dubba-* or *dabara-wala.*] In Bombay and elsewhere one who delivers food in **Tiffin Carriers** from houses to offices. See **Khana** & **Coolie**. [*CIWIE.*]

Figure 9.2 Excerpt from a dictionary of Indian English (from Lewis 1991: 105)

Three views on English in India

1. *English in India is a special variety*

The non-native varieties function in societal, linguistic and cultural networks that are distinctly different from those of America and Britain. Since English is used for intercultural interaction across languages in South Asia and Africa, the result has been a slow process of acculturation; which one might label, for example, South Asianisation or Africanisation. This is an inevitable linguistic process, which has applied earlier to Latin, Sanskrit, and various other languages. It is a process that is impossible to stop, but perhaps difficult for purists to accept. (Kachru 1986: 120)

2. *English in India is no different from English in England, the USA or elsewhere*

English, like any other language, has several varieties, each defined by the praxis of those who can be said to share it; and English, like other languages (including Latin and Sanskrit in the past) has varieties in more than one national or geographical unit. Why should this fact give warrant to a two-way classification of the varieties involved? (Singh 1995: 283)

3. *English in India is still an alien language*

If English as a language of identity was really moving in, one would expect its elite users in India to adjust their address habits to metropolitan norms, with the upwardly mobile strata . . . following suit. That expectation is not met. We conclude that English is not 'one of us', but an important presence that one must be polite to; and Auntie is the way we express our politeness in our current social conjuncture; so the term 'Auntie Tongue' best expresses what English is to its users in India. (Dasgupta 1993: 201)

Controversies in New English Studies

Braj Kachru pays particular attention to the ways in which English in India has become part of the sociocultural context of the country. He provides examples from vocabulary, syntax and discourse conventions which illustrate this process. He coined the term **nativisation** for the process of turning a once-foreign language into a local language with local nuances. A nativised language is not a 'native' language, which by definition is learned as a first language.

This view is disputed by Rajendra Singh (1995), who doubts that there are any significant differences between new Englishes and the English of territories where it is widely spoken as a first language. The difference in status, he argues, is due to an over-literal interpretation of historical patterns and processes. From a purely linguistic viewpoint, no-one has demonstrated that there are qualitative differences in the structures of new Englishes and others. All varieties of English have their characteristic words, phrases and accents: 'new' Englishes can be analysed and characterised by the same dialectological principles discussed in Chapter 2. Singh argues that there has been a failure to give due weight to the fact that native Englishes (those varieties of English learnt as a first language) are spoken largely by monolinguals, while areas where New Englishes flourish are multilingual. There is no need to accord a variety special status on the grounds that it is acquired only in childhood, as is the case in monolingual settings. Singh insists that in multilingual settings there is no particular reason to expect that all languages will be acquired at home, or that the sequence in which one acquires one's languages should lead to the privileging of one over another.

A third argument somehow manages to disagree with both viewpoints put forward thus far! For Probal Dasgupta (1993), English in India does not penetrate into deeper cultural levels of Indian life in the way that other Indian languages do. To characterise it as 'nativised', as Kachru does, is therefore inaccurate. But so too is any assertion that it has equal status with, say, British or American English. Dasgupta metaphorically refers to English as an 'auntie' language, drawing on a term used by Indian schoolchildren for the mothers of their friends. For their 'real' aunts, these children use a kinship term like Hindi *mausi* 'mother's sister', *maami* 'mother's brother's wife', *kaaki* 'father's brother's wife' or *phua* 'father's sister'. Dasgupta's point is that English has not really penetrated into, or ever been capable of entering, certain cultural domains. Like the children to their 'aunties', Indians have outwardly paid homage to English, and at the same time kept it at a distance.

This debate is an ongoing one in a number of formerly colonised countries, with implications for their educational and linguistic policies.

Variation within New Englishes

One reason why New Englishes might well repay being studied as a separate group is that they are typically made up of a continuum of subvarieties, rather like that of a creole in contact with its superstrate. At one end of this continuum, New Englishes have forms close to the L1 English of the former colonisers in terms of structure and pragmatics and to a lesser extent accent. At the other end is a variety that shows the greatest divergence from L1 norms, being essentially a 'fossilised' form originally characteristic of users who had limited opportunities of learning and using the colonial language. Still other varieties show intermediate levels of approximation

A *poem in Singapore English mesolect, 'Eden 22', by Mervin Mirapuri*

> i send an invitation
> come
> we dig together
> you came
> but doorman say
> no digging here
> your host
> he grows beard
> his club illegal
> but car waiting
> to take madam
> to cultural festival
> with nice
> nice person

(quoted by Platt 1983: 403)

to target language norms and L1 proficiency. Platt (1975) has suggested that these subvarieties be labelled in the same way as the main points of a post-creole continuum: **basilect, mesolect** and **acrolect**.

Many New English speakers develop an ability to shift up and down the continuum (though not all speakers get close to the acrolect). This ability depends on speaker variables (including education level, motivation and exposure to English) and situational variables (like degree of formality, topic, type of interlocutor). The acrolect obviously carries overt prestige in formal and educational contexts, and in conversation with L1 speakers. Although the basilect shares little of this overt prestige and is usually suppressed or discouraged in educational contexts, it carries degrees of covert prestige as the more appropriate variety in informal contexts. These are also the contexts in which the vernacular form of the L1 is the most appropriate code between people from the same language group.

One of us, Rajend Mesthrie (1992a: 219), gives an example of such downshifting by the security guard at a South African airport, who speaks a variety that linguists label 'South African Indian English'. Encountering a passenger from the same socioethnic background, he asked *You haven' got anything to declare?* In avoiding the more usual bureaucratic formula, *Do you have anything to declare?*, the speaker showed 'downshifting' to a mesolectal variety which shows several differences from the acrolectal sentence:

- in using *got* instead of *have*
- in using a negative form of the question rather than a positive form

- in avoiding the auxiliary verb *do*
- in signalling a question by a intonation rather than changing the word order to *haven't you got?*

By downshifting in this way, the guard was tacitly affirming some solidarity while still performing his duties. (A similar example in a multilingual context is described by Myers-Scotton – see Chapter 5.) However, there are limits to 'dropping down' in New Englishes. As Chew (1995: 165) observes in another context, 'it is unlikely that a Singaporean would mistake an educated English speaker speaking informally for an uneducated speaker'.

The question of what are the most appropriate norms in New English territories is still the subject of considerable debate among sociolinguists. Unlike territories where a creole is spoken, no-one proposes that basilectal norms are appropriate for formal educational use in 'New English' territories. However, many believe that acrolectal and upper-mesolectal forms showing degrees of nativisation are appropriate in this context. The ESL/EFL (English as a second/foreign language) industry turns out materials that draw on standard British or standard American norms. Some scholars argue that these norms are less appropriate in many New English contexts, since the aim of speakers in these territories is to communicate with other L2 speakers of English, rather than with L1 English-speakers. Kachru and other scholars believe that a degree of linguistic independence is possible and advocate the acceptance of a new set of standard forms based on the norms of the New English of a specific area. However, the same scholars concede that the attitudes of speakers are somewhat ambiguous. As Kachru (1992b: 60) observes,

> The non-native speakers themselves have not been able to accept what may be termed the 'ecological validity' of their *nativized* or *local* Englishes. One would have expected such acceptance, given the acculturation and linguistic nativization of the new varieties. On the other hand, the non-native models of English (such as RP or General American) are not accepted without reservations. There is thus a case of linguistic schizophrenia . . .

Globalisation and the Further Expansion of English

A model that is now widely used in place of the ENL–EFL–ESL trichotomy is the 'Three Circles Model' of Braj Kachru (1988). He uses the term 'World Englishes' to cover the sum total of Englishes on the planet, and conceptualises them as belonging to one of three circles: the 'Inner Circle' of territories where English is the dominant mother tongue (the UK, USA, Canada, Australia etc.), the 'Outer Circle' of territories to which the language spread via colonialism, and the 'Expanding Circle' to which the language has spread via globalisation, without there being significant numbers of English-speaking settlers. The last two circles are roughly synonymous with ESL and EFL respectively. In linguistic terms, Kachru characterises the Inner Circle as 'norm-providing', since it exerts influences on the other circles via teaching resources and literary materials. He sees the Outer Circle as 'norm-developing', i.e. different territories are in the process of developing and gradually accepting some of their own linguistic norms. He characterises the Expanding Circle as 'norm-dependent', since English is usually used for external communication with other nations, and there is no tradition of using English for literary purposes. For the Expanding Circle there has been no one defining encounter with British or American rule. English is restricted to being a subject studied in the classroom and an important means of international communication, and interaction with tourists. This sense of the 'global connectivity' afforded by English to the Outer Circle is effectively captured in a Microsoft commercial on French television (Martin 2002: 11) in the accompanying box:

Written online English-language 'chat' in Microsoft commercial for French audiences (from Martin 2002: 11)

A: Hi! I'm Francois.
B: Hey, Francois. Hi Bill, Hi Kimoko.
C: What's it like in Paris now?
A: It's Spring. The tourists are blooming.
B: Same here. What's going on in Russia?
D: Confusion, political upheaval, the usual.
C: I'm in Indonesia.
E. I'm in Newark.
A. That's nice.

(Note that the crisp simple language used and the play on *blooming* is effective as advertising copy, but need not reflect actual EFL norms.)

The notion of an expanding circle is particularly apt in the twenty-first century, with English becoming increasingly important in places like China, Japan and Europe. Under pressures of a globalising economics and culture the demand for English is so great that numerous Outer Circle countries are currently lowering the age at which English is introduced to primary schoolchildren. The notion of 'English as a foreign language' is accordingly no longer apt in some countries. Berg et al. (2001) argue that rather than being EFL, English has become a 'second first-language' in Sweden. Although Swedish is used in some 'H' functions, it is already subordinate to English as a means of communication with other countries of the European Union.

Globalisation and the increasing use of English as its vehicle has meant that Outer Circle countries face certain common changes and challenges. These include cultural erosion in the face of Western technology and commercialism and the possible decline and loss of local languages in the long term. Paradoxically, English is the main medium via which the cultures of India, China and Brazil (to name three new global economic players) become known to the rest of the world.

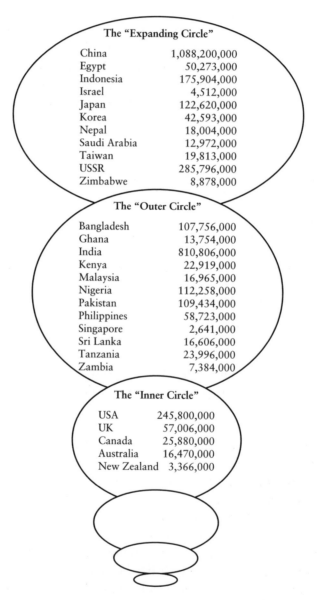

The "Expanding Circle"

China	1,088,200,000
Egypt	50,273,000
Indonesia	175,904,000
Israel	4,512,000
Japan	122,620,000
Korea	42,593,000
Nepal	18,004,000
Saudi Arabia	12,972,000
Taiwan	19,813,000
USSR	285,796,000
Zimbabwe	8,878,000

The "Outer Circle"

Bangladesh	107,756,000
Ghana	13,754,000
India	810,806,000
Kenya	22,919,000
Malaysia	16,965,000
Nigeria	112,258,000
Pakistan	109,434,000
Philippines	58,723,000
Singapore	2,641,000
Sri Lanka	16,606,000
Tanzania	23,996,000
Zambia	7,384,000

The "Inner Circle"

USA	245,800,000
UK	57,006,000
Canada	25,880,000
Australia	16,470,000
New Zealand	3,366,000

Figure 9.3 Braj Kachru's Circles model of World Englishes (from Kachru 1988: 5)

9.6 CONCLUSION

In this chapter, we focused on two types of language contact, one whose outcome was new languages (pidgins and creoles), the other which produced distinct (but non-creolised) forms of a colonial language. Some of the more prominent features of pidgins were described, especially with respect to the structure of their vocabularies. The process by which pidgins turn into creoles, called creolisation, is still the subject of intense debate, centring around Bickerton's bioprogramme hypothesis. Less controversial are aspects of the pidgin–creole cycle involving decreolisation or recreolisation.

Pidgins and creoles are no longer seen as linguistic curiosities and debased forms of European languages. There is nothing in the structure or semantic capacity of creoles, and even expanded pidgins, that precludes them from being used in formal domains, including education, administration and government. Tok Pisin, for example, is one of the three official languages of Papua New Guinea (the others being English and Hiri Motu, an indigenous pidgin). Since independence in 1975, Tok Pisin has been the preferred language of the House of Assembly, though English is the official medium of communication (Romaine 1989a: 6).

This chapter has also focused on 'New English' varieties that arose in different parts of the colonised world. They differ from pidgins and creoles in that the degree of restructuring which they show is not as great. Yet, paradoxically, this has made these 'New Englishes' less obvious candidates for official recognition as languages in their own right. They remain to a large extent dependent on the norms set by the metropolis (London, Washington and so on). Themes hinted at in this chapter concerning power in, and via language and the choice of languages for education, development and nationhood form the basis of the next three chapters. Pidgins and creoles raise many questions about the relation between community language and school language. The development of pidgins and creoles for the purposes of writing and use in education systems goes hand in hand with the economic and social development of communities. Themes arising from these considerations are picked up in the next three chapters on power, education and language planning respectively.

Notes

1. In this initial example, English spellings have been used in writing down this rhyme. As the examples in the rest of the chapter show, sociolinguists prefer a more 'phonetic' spelling system for pidgins.
2. Sankoff's term 'legitimate' is perhaps better understood as the dominant language, that is, the one 'legitimated' by the ruling Europeans.

3. In linguistics, 'baby talk' denotes the way adults talk to children, while the language of very young children is simply called 'child language'.
4. This evidence seems to conflict with that of Mühlhausler quoted above. A synthesis of these opposing views is possible: while adults are involved in creolisation in some cases, they may not always be. On the other hand, children seem to be always involved in the process.
5. In this simplified form of the rule, we have ignored changes according to the tense of the main verb or its polarity (that is, whether it is positive or negative).

10
CRITICAL SOCIOLINGUISTICS: APPROACHES TO LANGUAGE AND POWER

10.1 INTRODUCTION

To date, there is no comprehensive theory of sociolinguistics that attempts to provide an account of language and society that ties in the rich but diverse findings and approaches of the sort discussed in this book. One book carrying the title *Sociolinguistic Theory* (Chambers 2003) limits itself to synthesising and explaining the findings of a single branch of the subject, variation theory (discussed in Chapters 2–4 above). The author sees variation theory as the core area of sociolinguistics and pushes other topics into the disciplines of sociology (e.g. bilingualism, the use of honorifics) and political science (e.g. language planning). This is a rather extreme position which paradoxically tries to exclude as much of the social as possible from the realm of 'sociolinguistics'.

It is not surprising that, with such restrictions, even the account of language variation that Chambers gives is one-sided. Essentially, the theory propounded within this view of sociolinguistics is that language reflects society, as witnessed by the close correlations between aspects of language and social hierarchies (see Chapter 3). Chambers (2003: 250) argues further that language variation follows a biological instinct concerned with establishing and maintaining a social identity: 'we must mark ourselves as belonging to the territory, and one of the most convincing markers is by speaking like the people who live there'. Differences that exist are to a large extent explainable in terms of status and gender differences among speakers.

Critics of the 'language reflects society' position in sociolinguistics point to the following:

- Society and language are so closely intertwined that society cannot be said to be 'out there' independent of a language whose task it is to reflect it. As Roger Fowler (1985: 62) puts it, 'language is a reality-creating social practice'.
- Rather than reflecting society, there is a sense in which language misrepresents (or distorts) the key social relations within a community.

The school of sociolinguistics that stress this more 'problematised' view of language has come to be known as **'critical linguistics'** and more recently **'critical discourse analysis'**. The title of this chapter is meant as a cover term for these two approaches as well as that of others, for example the work on symbolic power by Bourdieu in section 10.6. One of the chief concerns of a critical sociolinguistic approach is the analysis of samples of language to reveal the way language creates, sustains and replicates fundamental inequalities in societies. This approach is much more open to insights from sociology concerning social organisation, inequality, power and conflict. Such a conflict model of society is not a point of departure that the majority of sociolinguists are comfortable with. This stems partly from their own political beliefs. A second reason is that sociolinguists, especially variationists, find it less easy to 'operationalise' (that is, to analyse and rework) sociolinguistic data within the framework of a critical sociology than within consensus models of society.

   We therefore begin this chapter with a study that is accepted by both 'critical' and 'non-critical' linguists, insofar as it examines in detail a phenomenon of everyday speech in many societies that shows the effects of power. Thereafter, we summarise the key approaches to power in modern sociology. Efforts to harness such approaches in sociolinguistics are then presented, especially that of the British linguist, Norman Fairclough. Examples from within this framework – critical discourse analysis – are presented, mainly in terms of the analysis of media language. A case study of propaganda and powerful language in Nazi Germany is presented. Thereafter, we consider cases of resistance to such powerful language. Finally, we discuss the main ideas in a model of domination by the use of language and other symbols espoused by the French theorist, Pierre Bourdieu.

10.2   POWER

Face and Power in Sociolinguistics

The use of honorifics, especially the second-person pronoun forms, was discussed in Chapter 6. Many languages of medieval Europe had two forms for the second-person pronouns for example French *tu* and *vous*, which forms the basis for the distinction between 'T and V' forms in sociolinguistics. In explaining the dynamics of this pronoun distinction, R. Brown and Gilman (1960) explicitly referred to 'power'. They defined this as the ability of one individual to control the behaviour of another: 'Power is a relationship between at least two persons, and it is non-reciprocal in the sense that both cannot have power in the same area of behaviour' (1960: 255). This non-reciprocal relationship showed up in language:

superiors used T and received V. The terms 'superior' and 'inferior' are of course defined with reference to societal bases of power (the state, church, army, wealth, the family), but also to other factors like age, gender and physical strength. As noted in Chapter 6 this distinction applies in many modern languages, in pronoun distinctions, use of honorific suffixes, titles and so on.

According to Brown and Gilman, an independent distinction developed in Europe which made the system of signalling relative power more complicated. The outcome of this change was to associate reciprocal T with solidarity and reciprocal V with non-solidarity in most modern European languages that have the T/V distinction. Brown and Gilman defined solidarity in terms of personal relationships and degree of friendliness. Essentially, this means that differences of power and status are less likely to determine the choice of T or V. Rather, it is whether relations of solidarity hold between the participants. When relations are (or become) 'solidary', T is usually exchanged irrespective of status. Where relations are not solidary, V is exchanged. However, it cannot be assumed that the linguistic expression of power and status has been completely diminished in favour of the variable of solidarity in western Europe. Some theorists argue that power has been somewhat redistributed and diffused, but also to some extent disguised. Despite the western distaste for the face-to-face expression of differential status, residues of the old power hierarchy exist in, for example, the right to initiate reciprocal T (where reciprocal V might have been previously appropriate) in a relationship between two acquaintances. This right still belongs to the more powerful interlocutor. Relative status and power might still be signalled by related linguistic phenomena like the terms of address in British English (*madam*, *sir*, *your ladyship* and so on).

The discussion of 'politeness' in Chapter 6, especially P. Brown and Levinson's discussion of the notion of 'face' and 'face needs', connects with the more modern use of T and V in Europe. The degree of politeness in interaction between speakers according to Brown and Levinson (1987: 15, 74–80) is dependent on three factors:

- social distance between speaker and addressee;
- the relative power of the one over the other;
- the degree of imposition associated with the interaction (in terms, for example, of goods or services required).

Surprisingly, Chambers (2003: 9) explicitly excludes pronoun choice and related variation from the realms of sociolinguistic theory. This is mainly due to the variationist school's stress on the vernacular, that is, on 'equal encounters' between speakers (for example in relaxed peer-group styles). On the other hand, critical linguists take the opposite view, stressing the insights for sociolinguistics that 'unequal encounters' offer. Pronouns, names, titles and address forms are particularly clear and well-defined subsystems of language that reveal asymmetries of power or solidarity between individuals (and the institutions they might represent). But they are not atypical of the way language is generally intertwined with social institutions and social inequality. Critical sociolinguistics goes a stage further than Brown and Gilman, and Brown and Levinson, in pursuing not just power, politeness and face *in* discourse but the power *behind* the discourse as well.

Power in Sociology

One of the best-known accounts of the concept of power is arguably that of Max Weber (1947), who regarded power as the fundamental concept in relations of inequality. In general terms, power denotes the probability of persons or groups carrying out their will even when opposed by others. Weber argued that classes, status groups and political parties are all involved in the distribution of power. Power is based on access to resources which might include economic resources, as well as physical force like that of the military. Successful rule involves the legitimisation and acceptance of power. This legitimisation involves the conversion of power to 'bases of authority' (for example a monarchy, a legal system, an educational system). David Lockwood (1973: 270) notes that power is often a latent force, involving not just the capacity to realise one's end in a situation of conflict, but also the potential to prevent opposition from arising in the first place. Power in this view is best realised if the actor can manipulate situations so as to prevent the need for coming to the point of decision at all. Antonio Gramsci (1971) drew a distinction between **rule**, where the exercise of power is obvious or known, and **hegemony**, where the exercise of power is so disguised as to involve rule with the consent of the governed. These aspects of power surface in language studies in various degrees. At the macro level, they are involved in matters like language imposition and spread (see Chapter 9). Some of the theorists cited in the rest of this chapter argue that even at the micro level of language structure and use, the effects of power turn up in more areas than is generally acknowledged in linguistics.

10.3   CRITICAL DISCOURSE ANALYSIS

Norman Fairclough, who extended the work of earlier critical linguists like R. Fowler et al. (1979), is the central proponent of an approach that ties in analysis of samples of language (or 'texts') with a 'conflict' understanding of society. Fairclough (1989: 3) points out that not only are sociolinguists reliant on sociological theory, but also that there is a 'linguistic turn' in late twentieth-century and subsequent social theory. Such a reciprocal relationship has developed not just because language is the primary medium of social control and power, but because it has grown dramatically in terms of the diversity of functions to which it is applied in modern society. For Fairclough, ideology is pervasively present in language, and the ideological nature of language should therefore be one of the major themes of modern social science. Fairclough was particularly interested in the ideological complexities of certain language functions in politics, news broadcasting, advertising and so on.

Critical discourse analysts draw on language theorists and sociologists whose writings are rather abstruse and not well known in mainstream linguistics. We therefore present some of their key ideas that relate to language before presenting Fairclough's model of language use.

Ideology and Ideological State Apparatuses

In sociology, two related uses of the term 'ideology' occur. The first refers to the systems of ideas, beliefs, speech and cultural practices that operate to the advantage of a particular social group. Classical Marxist scholars view ideology as a system of ideas and practices that disguise (or distort) the social, economic and political relations between dominant and dominated classes. As noted in Chapter 1, in the original model of social organisation, Marx and Engels analysed ideology as part of the superstructure rather than the economic base. The neo-Marxists whose ideas we present here, on the other hand, see ideology as more fundamental, stressing the dynamic relation between the base–superstructure–ideology triangle.

Louis Althusser (1971) stressed the relative autonomy of ideology from the economic base, and the significant role played by ideologies in reproducing or changing economic and political relations. Althusser also put forward the view that ideology works through putting (his term is usually translated as 'interpellating') individuals into 'subject positions'. The ambiguity of the word 'subject' here captures both claims about ideology – the illusion it creates of active and free human agents (e.g. the subject in a sentence) – and the relationship of being subject or subordinate to some power (e.g. the Queen's subjects). Ideological processes take place within various organisations and institutions such as the church, the legal system, the family and, most of all, the educational system. Althusser terms these **ideological state apparatuses** (in short, ISAs). Nicos Poulantzas (1973) went further in dividing the state system into a repressive apparatus (army, police, tribunals and sometimes even a government and its administration) and an ideological apparatus (church, political parties, unions, schools, mass media and the family). The latter is concerned with the promotion and naturalisation of certain values and beliefs rather than the use of force.

Signs of Struggle

More explicitly embedded in linguistics is V. N. Voloshinov's characterisation of ideology via language. Voloshinov was a Soviet scholar prominent in the 1920s, whom many analysts believe to have been actually Mikhail Bakhtin, forced to adopt a pseudonym to publicise his unorthodox ideas. (We continue to refer to their works separately, since not everyone agrees that the two authors are in fact one person.) Central to Voloshinov's work is a critique of the purely structural emphasis placed by Saussure upon the fundamental unit of language, the sign. As we noted in Chapter 1, Saussure's important insight was that the linguistic sign (a combination of signifier and signified) was arbitrary. The 'signifier' spelt *d-o-g* clearly has no inherent link with the concept 'dog' that it names. The same object (or 'signified') could be called something else (like *inja* in Zulu, *chien* in French). The relationship between a 'concept' and the 'word for it' (Saussure's work makes it clear that these notions are themselves problematic) is not a necessary one. Rather, it is agreed upon by a kind of social contract within a speech community. Saussure's characterisation of society was a general and abstract one, without any particular interest in subgroups within. For critical linguists who take seriously social arrangements and divisions within a society, the notion of language as a system of socially neutral signs is implausible.

In contrast to Saussure, Voloshinov and Bakhtin stressed the ideological nature of the sign. For Voloshinov (1973: 21, originally written in 1929), 'the forms of signs are conditioned above all by the social organization of the participants involved and also by the immediate conditions of their interaction'. Furthermore, 'sign becomes an arena of the class struggle' (1973: 23). In other words, the linguistic sign is open to different orientations and evaluations in the social world. Though Voloshinov's interest was in class inequalities, his formulation can be extended to other struggles over language and struggles within language, like those of gender and minority rights. This is what Bakhtin (1981) referred to as 'heteroglossia' – the coexistence and interplay between several 'voices' or linguistic and social orientations in a speech utterance. Bakhtin suggests that this multiple orientation (or open-endedness of language) is opposed by dominant classes, in whose interests it is to downplay the 'polyphonic' semantic and social possibilities of the sign. Instead, dominant classes try to make the sign 'uniaccentual'.[1] Bakhtin's view emphasises that we enter into human consciousness and social consciousness via our learning of language. To have a subjectivity, to be human, is to have first entered via language into dialogue with others. The 'self' is therefore social since it is a collection of various roles, made up of what he terms 'languages' or 'voices' spoken by others. This 'construction' of the self via language has been neglected in sociolinguistics, despite the agreement that speaking involves making 'acts of identity' (see Chapter 5). It is, however, a theme that is being explored with some success in current social psychology – see J. Potter and Wetherell (1987).

Discourse and Decentred Subjects

The notion of power being diffused, concealed or buried by the effects of ideology, and therefore requiring an 'archaeology' of its own, leads us to a brief characterisation of one of the more important modern thinkers on the subject, Michel Foucault. Foucault is not as influential a figure in linguistics as he is in a variety of disciplines including literary theory and psychology. His work – notwithstanding his difficult style and sometimes obscure approach to a number of topics – has influenced critical linguists. For Foucault, power 'is everywhere', it is not a commodity that can be acquired but exists in all kinds of relations including the political, economic and educational arenas. In his early work, Foucault pursued 'the constitution of the subject', a theme Althusser had brought up in connection with the effects of ideology. The individual subject (i.e. human being), according to Foucault, was not imbued with a unique consciousness or personality; rather, she or he was an 'empty entity', the intersection point of a number of 'discourses'.

The term 'discourse' is used in many different senses in the social sciences. In structural linguistics, 'discourse' denotes continuous speech beyond the level of the sentence. 'Discourse analysis' of this sort (e.g. G. Brown and Yule 1983) involves a grammatical approach to the topic, examining linguistic relations across sentences in connected speech. There is interest, for example, in certain elements which act mainly as links between sentences. For example, in the sentence *Well, I know that*, the word *well* links with a previous statement and cannot in this usage act as an initiator of discourse itself.

A second meaning of 'discourse' concerns what might be called 'conversational management'. In describing rules for turn-taking and similar interactive phenomena, this type of discourse analysis is more person-oriented than the structural approach (see Chapter 6).

'Discourse' in social theory is a rather more slippery concept, denoting different ways of structuring areas of knowledge and social practices. Discourses are manifested in particular ways of using language and other symbolic systems like visual images. They may be thought of as systems of rules implicated in specific kinds of power relations which make it possible for certain statements and ways of thinking to occur at particular times and places in history. According to James Gee (1990: xix), they are 'ways of behaving, interacting, valuing, thinking, believing, speaking, and often reading and writing that are accepted as instantiations of particular roles by specific groups of people'. Foucault (1972) discusses the example of 'the discourse of medicine'. Excluded from the medical discourse of the west for a long time, but now beginning to become prominent, are alternative 'discourses' like those of homoeopathy and acupuncture. Likewise, the discourse of economics (growth, wealth and development) excluded the space for environmental discourses until the late twentieth century.

Foucault's notion of speaking subjects being 'empty entities' stands in stark contrast to more humanist approaches which see people as individuals having a full 'command' over language. The implication of Foucault's approach is that, to understand the self (or speaking subject), researchers have to study language and discourse. For some critical theorists, there is a sense in which language speaks through people! Potter and Wetherell (1987: 109) comment on this position from a perspective within social psychology that has come to be called 'social constructivism' (or the social construction of identity):

> In this tradition people become fixed in position through the range of linguistic practices available to them to make sense. The use of a particular discourse which contains a particular organisation of the self not only allows one to warrant and justify one's actions . . . [as an individual being], it also maintains power relations and patterns of domination and subordination. In constructing the self in one way, other constructions are excluded, hence to use a common phrase found in this tradition, the creation of one kind of self or subjectivity in discourse also creates a particular kind of subjection.

Few sociolinguists would go all the way in accepting Foucault's idea of completely decentred human subjects. The idea that language controls consciousness amounts to a Whorfian view, which we argued in Chapter 1 to be unconvincing in its 'strong' form. Consciousness-raising is itself a viable activity, as feminist and black consciousness movements have shown. That is, discourses are themselves unstable and subject to changes; competing discourses can be found within the same society. It is difficult to comprehend, despite Foucault, how discourses originate without some kind of human agency. It is nevertheless easier to accept that once discourses arise, they may 'flourish' via acceptance by an individual child or adult subject.

In his later work, Foucault shifted to the view that individuals are constituted not by discourse but by relations of power, which forms the ultimate principle of social reality (Sarup 1993: 73). Power does not operate in a purely top-down approach, with those 'in' power exerting forms of coercion or restraint upon uncompliant subjects. Rather, complex differential power relationships extend to every aspect of our social, cultural and political lives involving different and often contradictory 'subject positions'. As in Gramsci's notion of hegemony, power is secured not so much by the threat of punishments as by the internalisation of the norms and values implied by the prevailing discourses within the social order.

Foucault placed less emphasis on the ISAs than Althusser had. He believed that power is much more diffuse than in Althusser's model, and that the state can only function on the basis of other already existing power networks, like the family, other kinship groups, specialised knowledge and so on. Just as hegemonic practice is often inseparable from what seems attractive and desirable, for Foucault what is 'socially useful' is always in some ways involved in 'power-serving' purposes. For example, power has become a ubiquitous property of the knowledge and technologies that shape modern institutions in the expanding global economy.

Fairclough brings a more linguistic dimension to the study of discourse than evident in Foucault's work. Figure 10.1 shows Fairclough's three-layered model of discourse, which presents discourse as simultaneously involving three dimensions:

1. a language text, which may be spoken, written or signed;
2. discourse practice (involving text production and text interpretation);
3. sociocultural practice (involving wider social and political relations).

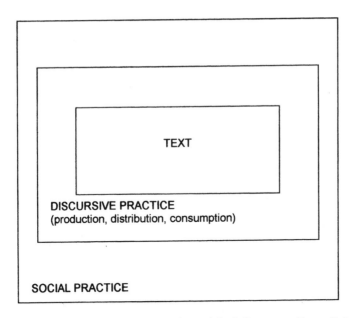

Figure 10.1   A three-dimensional model of discourse (from Fairclough 1992: 73)

To illustrate the three dimensions of this model, we take the example of an interaction between marital partners:

- **Text** – characteristics of the speech exchange in terms of conversational properties like turn-taking, narrative or argument structure, politeness phenomena, specific characteristics of the grammar and accent (including speech accommodation as described in Chapter 5).

- **Discourse practice** – what are the discourse types that are being employed in the interaction (e.g. 'pillow talk', 'small talk', 'argument', 'academic or political discussion' and so on); how does this exchange fit in with the above 'genres' or speech events; is more than one genre drawn upon?
- **Social practice** – how does this exchange derive from, reinforce or challenge expected relations between marital partners, the family as an institution and gender relations in the broader society?

Building on Foucault (1981), Fairclough introduces the concept of an 'order of discourse' which relates discourse practices to what might be termed 'the social order'. Not all types of discourse are equally validated in different social and institutional settings. There is often a hierarchy of acceptability. Fairclough (1989: 30) provides the example of the role of conversation as a discourse type. For example, conversation has no 'on-stage' role in legal proceedings, but it may have a significant 'off-stage' role in informal bargaining between opposing lawyers. In education, on the other hand, conversation may have approved roles not only between classes and during breaks, but also as a form of approved activity within some lessons. The role of conversation on television is again quite different. Particular social settings and institutions may thus have different preferred 'orders of discourse'. To a large extent, these institutions are defined by their particular order of discourses. The historical shift in many societies from more explicit to more implicit exercise of power means that common-sense notions of language practices (for example in the classroom, or in lawyers' or doctors' rooms) become important in sustaining and reproducing power relations. Fairclough stresses a critical approach to language interaction known as 'critical language awareness'.

10.4   CRITICAL LANGUAGE AWARENESS IN ACTION

Analyses within the field of critical discourse analysis often focus on texts drawn from the media: television and newspaper reporting, advertising, and so on. In the rest of this section, we illustrate Fairclough's view that ideology is promulgated not just by some ISAs but via language itself, in three areas: the media, advertising and propaganda. Each of these areas is worthy of full-length study in its own right, from a variety of perspectives. At high school, students are often given a basic training in analysing the ways in which short texts belonging to these genres are used with persuasive (or 'emotive') effect, and to counter this with a critical awareness. Critical linguists go one step further in looking more closely at the social forces behind the linguistic persuasion.

Newspaper Reporting

Foucault's idea of a decentred human subject placed at the centre of competing discourses applies to the generalised addressee which is the target of media discourse. Fairclough (1989: 49) suggests that media discourse has built into it a subject position for an 'ideal subject', and actual viewers, listeners or readers have to negotiate a relationship with this idealised subject. John Downing (1980: 179) has said of the media that 'their power lies . . . in their capacity to shape public feeling while appearing only to express it'. Fairclough gives the example of two ways in which an event like redundancies in the car industry may be reported: *Thousands are out of work* as against *Company directors have sacked thousands of workers*. The first sentence represents the matter as a state of affairs, without an overt agent, while the second puts the matter more bluntly with a full *subject–transitive verb–object* sequence. Text analysis thus serves to show how a systematic selection among alternative sentence types represents unemployment as a condition for which no-one is responsible, or alternatively as the consequence of specific agents. Fairclough (1989: 52) argues that it is a form of power 'to constrain *content*: to favour certain interpretations and 'wordings' of events, while excluding others . . . . It is a form of hidden power, for the favoured interpretations and wordings are those of the power holders in our society, though they appear to be just those of the newspaper.'

Such a deconstruction of media texts by an 'expert' is not beyond criticism. Henry Widdowson (1995) points to the rather closed methods of approach taken by CDA. He stresses that texts can be read in different ways at different times and under different circumstances. Fairclough's approach, on the other hand, appears to be an 'imposed' analysis, with the analyst speaking "from above" for the average consumer, rather than attempting a bottom-up approach favoured in sociolinguistics. Until tests are undertaken of the responses of individual readers to the language and content of newspaper reports, the analyses remain subjective. As Fairclough (1992: 89) himself notes elsewhere, studies in the way the media is received by audiences (e.g. Morley 1980) show that people can sometimes be immune to the effects of the ideologies supposedly in the texts. Blommaert (2005) notes three problems with CDA. First, the analysis rests too strongly on the grammatical effects in the texts themselves. As Blommaert (2005: 35) puts it, focusing on texts alone means that 'analysis stops as soon as the discourse has been produced – while [. . .] a lot happens to language users long after they have shut their mouths'. Second, CDA claims universal validity for its approach, whilst focusing almost entirely on western contexts, which Blommaert characterises as 'highly integrated, Late Modern, post-industrial, densely semioticised First-World societies'

(2005: 35). Third, Blommaert finds a lack of attention to historical factors in CDA. If the interest is in issues of power, then synchronic analysis of texts (focusing on one moment of time) will not provide an adequate analysis of how power comes into place.

Ads as an Example of Discourse

Advertising discourse is an inescapable element of the modern media. Critical discourse analysts see the consumption practices and aspirations promoted by ads as part of the process of forming group and individual identities among 'subjects' in westernised societies. Even in societies where the capacity to buy is limited, the desire for commodities is enhanced via the influence of mass advertising and exposure to western films and magazines.

Ads are identifiable as 'texts' by features like 'code-play' and 'cohesion'. By 'code-play' is meant the frequent use of puns, rhymes, alliteration, parallel statements and other poetic devices. 'Cohesion' refers to the link between sentences in forming a unit like a paragraph or stanza formed by some of these forms of code-play. Advertisements also involve outrageous exaggeration (usually relating to the quality of product) and occasional euphemism (usually relating to the customer). Cars are never *second-hand*, they are *pre-owned*; detergents no longer come in *small*, *medium* and *large* sizes, but in *standard*, *large* and *extra-large*; potential customers are never *choosy*, they are *discerning*. Because ads are usually entertaining, their exaggerations seem excusable and natural to the genre (that is, naturalised within the register). Yet many analysts of the genre find the same 'licence' allowed to advertisers as to politicians and media producers, to inculcate what Lord Acton called 'the atmosphere of accredited mendacity' (Hughes 1988: 8–9).

Ads show two further characteristics: they are often parasitic (being dependent upon other discourses) and opportunistic (seizing upon whatever powerful idiom is available). Fairclough analyses such features as a more general property of 'intertextuality', where one text draws upon, appropriates or comments ironically on another. The notion of intertextuality ultimately relates to Bakhtin's characterisation of the polyphony inherent in language use. Eve Bertelsen (1997) shows how the discourses associated with the dismantling of apartheid in South Africa in the mid-1990s were soon displaced and appropriated by other discourses:

> *Foschini* (fashion house): You've won your freedom. Now use it. Get a Foschini's credit card today.
> *Black Like Me* ('hair relaxer' product): I've made my choice. Perfect Choice. Black like me. Embracing black dignity and beauty. Giving you freedom of choice. (*Spoken in alternate ads by two prominent Black media personalities.*)
> *Weigh-less* (slimming company): Changing the Shape of the Nation.

Intertextuality is evident here in the way the discourse of political struggle is incorporated into commercial texts. Such a competition between discourses is itself a feature of key moments in social change. Democracy is being redefined as individual freedom, especially the freedom to consume. Whereas the first post-apartheid government was elected on the democratic ideal of 'A better life for all. Working together for jobs, peace and freedom', advertisers effectively erased in their ads the 'all' and 'together' which had rendered the slogan democratic. Rather, they promoted the individualised, middle-class, consumer subject.

A Mobile Army of Metaphors: Language of the Super-powerful

Related to the theme of the shaping of ideology via language is the degree of control and persuasion implicit in media language representing governments, especially the superpowers of today. Again the theme has a pedigree outside sociolinguistics, in media studies, discourse analysis, literary studies, sociology and even other branches of linguistics like semantics. In his book *Language: The Loaded Weapon* (1980), Dwight Bolinger identified three characteristic processes of the semantics of the powerful:

- **euphemism** (downplaying one's own aggression);
- **dysphemism** (exaggerating the bad qualities of one's opponents);
- **mystification** (the use of jargon to conceal certain activities).

On the left: generals during the apartheid era now denying the meaning of their instructions. On the right: their operatives who carried out their instructions.

These processes applied to the 'marketing' by the US media of the Vietnam War in the 1960s. Bolinger discusses cases of mystification (*termination with prejudice* = 'assassination', *defoliate* = 'bombing of countryside'), euphemism (*involvement* = 'invasion', *pacification* = 'bombing of civilians'), and dysphemism (*terrorist* = 'enemy soldier'). The examples are from Bolinger (1980: 132) and Hughes (1988: 220–2).

Similar examples can be found from proponents of almost any political philosophy. The same strategies were employed in the discourse of the former communist bloc, with its derogation of *bourgeois imperialism* and *capitalist lackeys*. As a case study of the language of dictatorship, we turn to Nazi Germany (1933–45).

Propaganda in Nazi Germany

On coming to power, in 1933 the Nazi Party (*National Socialist German Workers' Party* – NSDAP) pursued a policy of *Gleichschaltung*, literally 'putting everyone in the same gear'. This policy attempted to transform all aspects of German life according to an anti-semitic and nationalistic ideology. A centralised *Ministry of Information and Propaganda* was set up in 1933 under the leadership of Joseph Goebbels. The ministry quickly gained control over the German mass media, especially press, radio and film. Several studies have shown how ordinary, everyday terms became vehicles for Nazi ideology (e.g. Ehlich 1989).

The major support base for the National Socialists came from the middle classes and the agrarian sector. The urban working classes traditionally voted for the communist and socialist parties, and were particularly resistant to the promises and ideology of National Socialism (Peukert 1987). To include the industrial workforce into the 'national community' (*Volksgemeinschaft*), the Nazis crushed possible opposition from the labour movement. They also used their propaganda machinery to win the support of the workers, which was seen as important for political stability and economic productivity. Part of this propaganda strategy was the semantic manipulation of the terms 'worker' and 'work', which became soaked with National Socialist ideology.[2]

Nazi propagandists used the words 'German' and 'worker' as synonyms: all Germans were defined as being workers. Intellectual workers (*Arbeiter der Stirn*, i.e. workers of the mind) and physical workers (*Arbeiter der Faust*, i.e. workers of the fist) together formed 'the German nation'. The National Socialist ideology of a racially pure and socially harmonious national community (*Volksgemeinschaft*) became thus linked directly to the concept of 'worker'.

The Nazi interpretation of 'worker' and 'work' was directly linked to the party's racist and anti-semitic ideology. Only Germans were identified as 'workers', and 'work' as a positive and productive activity was seen as the domain of German nationals. 'Jewish work', on the other hand, was defined not as work, but as robbery and money-grabbing. The 'honest, national worker' was juxtaposed not only against the 'Jewish thief' but also against the denationalised German worker (*Asphaltprolet*, *Großstadtprolet*), who had been alienated from the national community by Jewish-Marxist agitation. A third category juxtaposed against the 'German worker' were anti-social 'idlers' and 'loafers' (*Arbeitsscheue*, *Arbeitsbummelanten*, literally 'work-shy people, slow-poke workers'). They were seen as being guilty of destroying the productivity and economic/political success of Germany. While coercion was used to deal with Jews and idlers, persuasion and propaganda were the tools for the mobilisation of the working class.

Emotional language, creation of associations and connotations, repetition and simplification of reality are the key elements of propaganda. Most popular were constructions using terms such as honour and nobility. 'Labour ennobles' (*Arbeit adelt*) was a popular slogan repeated day in and day out in radio, film and press. Other constructions connected the area of work to the area of war: 'Soldier of work' (*Soldat der Arbeit*), 'Armies of workers' (*Arbeitsarmeen*) and 'German Labour Front' (*Deutsche Arbeitsfront*) (Seidel and Seidel-Slotty 1961). A third group of expressions connected work with religion, as in the expression 'sacredness of work for the community' (*Heiligtum der Arbeit für die Gemeinschaft*). The slogans and phrases discussed here were endlessly repeated in the media, which led to what has been termed **lexical hardening** (Ehlich 1989): that is, the word 'worker' became directly and positively associated with contexts of war, honesty, honour and religion.

The art of propaganda
Adolf Hitler summarised the art of propaganda in *Mein Kampf* as:

> Its [propaganda's] effect for the most part must be aimed at the emotions and only to a very limited degree at the so-called intellect . . . all effective propaganda must be limited to a very few points and must harp on these slogans until the last member of the public understands what you want him to understand by your slogan.
> (quoted in Pratkanis and Aronson 1991: 250–1)

Despite such large-scale propaganda, the working class remained, on the whole, distrustful of National Socialism. Everyday life didn't match up to the national utopia proclaimed by the party. Although he was honoured and glorified, the German worker was still poor and, in fact, getting poorer. The longer the regime lasted, the less people believed in its utopian slogans (Peukert 1987). Thus, although the Nazis aimed at

Holzschnitt von Josef Weiß, München

„Es gibt nur einen Adel, den Adel der Arbeit"

Adolf Hitler

'There exists only one type of nobility, and that is the nobility of work'
(Völkischer Beobachter, 1 May 1935)

the total control of public language, they did not succeed in their linguistic *Gleichschaltung*. Carnival speakers in the Rhine region regularly poked fun at the word creations and manipulations of the Ministry for Information and Propaganda. Resistance to official politics and language use is also evident in the popularity of political jokes, whose existence was a serious concern for the Nazi Party (Zenter 1983). The Jewish literary critic-cum-linguist, Victor Klemperer, who survived the Holocaust, argued that such strategies of resistance were a typical reaction to overt political and linguistic oppression.

> The Lingua Tertii Imperii (the language of the Third Reich) was a prison language (a language of both, the prison officers and the prisoners) and to the languages of prisons belong inevitably (as acts of self-defence) words of pretence, confusing ambiguities, the counterfeiting, and so on. (Klemperer 1975: 89, translated by A. Deumert)

10.5   RESISTANCE TO POWERFUL LANGUAGE

The analyses in the previous section have two characteristics in common: (i) they concentrate largely on language of the media, that is, language that does not involve personal interaction; and (ii) they make assumptions about how the language of mass communication is 'received' by the audience (or 'addressees'). Some studies of interactive, spoken norms make it clear that the language of the powerful is not swallowed whole by the less powerful.

The Weapons of the Weak

One scholar who has examined the everyday norms of the politically dispossessed in terms of resistance is James Scott. His book *Weapons of the Weak* (1985) is a classic in the wider field of political science, but has important lessons that are often overlooked by the sociolinguist. Wherever there is power (and Foucault thinks it is everywhere), there is resistance as well. Resistance, like domination, need not be a calculated, conscious and readily visible mode of operation. Like domination, the most effective forms of resistance in daily life (barring periods of war or revolution) may well be those that are transmitted as something else. Based on a study of the antagonisms and interactions between peasants and landlords in Sedarka, a pseudonym for a village in a rural part of Malaysia, Scott's emphasis differs from that of Gramsci and Althusser in stressing not consent, complicity and 'false consciousness' but resistance and the memory of previous repression. Scott finds it necessary to distinguish between the 'onstage' behaviour of the peasants (i.e. their 'face' when dealing with the local landlord elites) and their 'offstage' behaviour (when they interact among themselves away from the immediate influence of the elites). Linguistically, this shows up in a number of ways, including features of speech style and manner, naming practices and proverbs, though Scott's examples are mainly from the realm of meaning and naming practices.

It was once common practice, before the advent of mechanisation when peasant labour was necessary and desired, for the rich farming landowners to keep on the good side of the peasants. This was done by giving wages in advance, gifts and invitations to feasts. In the symbolic realm, landowners would describe their own behaviour as 'assistance', 'help', 'kindness' and 'sympathy'. With a change to mechanisation, relations between landlords and peasants changed and peasant labour became devalued. Changing linguistic practice was part of the deterioration in social relations. Scott differentiates between the 'onstage' or public use of language by peasants within earshot of the rich and their 'offstage' behaviour in the privacy of the peasant dwelling area. The rich of Sedarka described themselves as barely managing, while the poor describe them as *kaya* 'rich', almost without exception. The poor do not use this word onstage; but offstage they lose no time in calling a spade a spade. The vocabulary of the rich is characterised by euphemisms concerning their status, while the discourse of the dominated contains an element of onstage censorship. Both processes are part of the discourse generated by, and constitutive of, class struggle. Scott cites further examples involving nicknames for two members of the elite, who in public are called *Haji Kadir* and *Haji Pak*. These are respectful names made up of the title *Haji* implying the holiness of one who has made a pilgrimage to Mecca, followed by their proper names. The common offstage names used by the peasants for these persons are *Kadir Ceti* and *Haji Broom*, irreverent and censorious names based on *Ceti*, a non-Muslim moneylender associated with usury, and on the English word *broom*, implying a single vigorous sweeping action in 'cleaning out the poor'. In Sedarka, semantics itself has become subject to a kind of social relativity. That is, the 'meaning' of key terms may well differ according to the class position of the speaker. The tussle over naming in Sedarka exemplifies Voloshinov's view of the sign as an arena of struggle.

It is no longer enough that the descendants of slaves, chartists and suffragettes should be permitted to speak: they are not content to speak in their master's voices, according to conventions laid down within traditions that excluded them. Indeed the new advocates of what has come to be called 'political correctness' are putting pressure on the masters to change their own tune. (Cameron 1995b: 26)

Political Correctness, Power and Resistance

Some studies suggest that power is not so easily subverted. There are cases where semantic changes, far from being simple reflections of social change, might actually serve to conceal a lack of meaningful change. Franklin Southworth (1974) reports on a field study he undertook with a team of researchers in certain south Indian villages. Of several examples provided by Southworth pertaining to changes in caste practices and caste terminology and the semantics of power, we concentrate on one: the use of terms for former 'outcastes' in a village in the state of Tamil Nadu. (Caste was briefly characterised in section 1.6.) The older term *paraiyan* denoted a member of an 'untouchable' caste, the lowest in the societal system. The more acceptable term became *arijan*, based on a term introduced in the twentieth century by Mahatma Gandhi, *harijan* 'God's people'. Caste reforms aimed at improving the status of 'untouchables'. Southworth describes an interview with an ex-president of a village, during which three labourers (formerly *paraiyan*) approached. Up to that point, the discussion had centred on caste and social life in the village. While the interview was in progress, the wife of the ex-president made some remarks to the labourers (as asides). These remarks did not disturb the interview, but turned up quite clearly on the tape:

Interviewer: Who are these three people? Where are they from?
Ex-president: Harijans, from this place itself.
Interviewer: What do you mean, 'Harijans'?
Wife (in background): The name is Paraiyan.
Ex-president: Oh, they are in the colony.
Interviewer: In the *cheri*? [dwelling place for former 'outcastes']
Ex-president: One should not call it the 'cheri', they say.
Wife (in background): Yes, one may say [i.e. there is nothing wrong with calling it that].
[Original interview in Tamil]

This is an interesting text, with its polyphony of voices (including interviewer talk), its silences (the labourers are excluded from speaking) and the tussle over signs. These major concerns of Voloshinov and Bakhtin are now increasingly popular in literary analysis. The ex-president employs euphemism, which seems to come easily to him as a village official aware of the government's policy. Furthermore, he is accustomed to talking with outsiders and people of high status. His wife seems to be more concerned with the status quo within the village. She counters her partner's tendency to euphemism by plain speaking within earshot of the labourers. The use of fancy words by her partner, she suggests, is only for the benefit of the visitors. In most village contexts, Southworth argues, the emergence of the term *arijan* involves a new semantic distinction, giving the speaker the choice between an insulting term and a respectful term. *Arijan* lacks the stigma of the term *paraiyan*, but the status connotations linger. The new term thus becomes the polite way of connoting disrespect. The intention of Gandhi and his followers in India's independence movement had been to bring about social change in the long term. This social change was initiated by programmes of caste reform, by trying to change people's attitudes and by semantic changes. Until those changes put into motion are realised fully (no easy task), the use of terms like *arijan* can be subverted to mask the nature of power relations and conceal the extent of socioeconomic differences within the society.

Southworth's analysis has been vindicated by the appearance of a new term in the 1990s in Indian political discourse, *dalit*, which political movements led by members of the lower castes use in preference to *harijan*. They argue that the latter term is a ruling-class euphemism drawn from religious teaching and therefore evokes a hierarchy created by God. In popular usage it has also become somewhat patronizing. The new term *dalit*, which literally means 'oppressed, down-trodden', is meant to challenge ruling-class hegemony by pointing to human rather than divine causes. The Tamil Nadu study with its tussles over semantics creates problems for the simple view cited in section 10.1 that 'language reflects society'.

Anti-language

Another example of resistance to powerful language comes from Halliday's study of the language of oppositional subcultures within a society. Halliday coined the term 'anti-society' for a group of people who reveal their oppositional status to a dominant society by several means, including their use of language. He uses the term 'anti-language' for the special language of this group. The clearest example of an anti-society is the underworld, which in many countries is organised like a society though showing direct antagonism to it. Other counter-cultures of relevance here are the hippy movements of the west in the 1960s and Rastafarian culture, which have a voluntary 'drop-out' status in relation to the mainstream and a culture and language that challenge the assumptions of the dominant.

Halliday uses the term 'relexicalisation' to denote the replacement of old words for new in the anti-language, especially in areas of vocabulary crucial to the identity of the anti-society. In Elizabethan England, a vast population of criminals, which made a living off the wealth of the established society, relied on its own lexicon called 'pelting speech', with relexicalisations like *laws* for 'strategies of theft', *lift* for 'one who steals a package' and *marker* for 'one to whom a package is handed'. Anti-languages are not just relexicalised in some areas of vocabulary, they are 'over-lexicalised'. Halliday cites an account by Mallik (1972) of the underworld language of Calcutta, which contains, for example, twenty-one words for 'bomb', forty-one for 'police' and so on.

Halliday (1978: 175) argues further that an anti-language is 'a metaphor for an everyday language; and this metaphorical reality appears all the way up and down the system. There are phonological metaphors, grammatical metaphors and semantic metaphors.' An example of such a metaphor is the inversion of the world, symbolised by the inversion of elements within words in the Calcutta underworld anti-language: for example, *kodan* for *dokan* 'shop' (showing exchange of consonants), *karca* for *cakar* 'servant' (showing syllable inversion) and soon on. The cumulative effect of these inversions is of verbal display, humour as well as resistance and rebellion. At the same time, they ensure secrecy. Anti-languages have similarities with other forms of sublanguages, for example teenage slang, CB (Citizen's Band radio) language and children's games involving use of intrusive syllables (e.g. Pig Latin) or inversion. There are also similarities with certain social dialects, which seem to carry a great deal of oppositional culture in them, notably African American Vernacular English. There is probably a continuum between these types of speech. Going back to Poulantzas's distinction between repressive and ideological state apparatuses, it would seem that anti-languages are a response to the repressive apparatus, while the other forms on the continuum signify rebellion against the ideological apparatus. Teenage slang, for example, is a response to the ideological state apparatus, essentially the confines of language norms of school, family and adults. The term 'antilanguage' should not be taken too literally – they are essentially lexical-substems, rather than independent language systems with a grammar of their own.

Debates about Sexism: Successful Resistance?

Perhaps the most overt and, arguably, successful opposition to power in dominant or standard forms of language has come from research on language and gender. Feminist researchers have identified areas of language structure and use that favour a male perspective and are demeaning of

women. Some claims in this regard by Robin Lakoff were outlined in Chapter 1. Examples include the male-as-norm phenomenon evident in certain English structures, while a marked form is used for the female (*manager–manageress*; *waiter–waitress*), and the use of *man* and *he* as the generic form for all people. (*Man is never satisfied. He is always seeking new ways of bringing up his children.*) Feminists drew analogies between such usage and more obviously patriarchical practices like women adopting the surnames of their husbands. Since the 1970s, there has been a tussle over the signs of language between the proponents of change and the guardians of tradition. Dale Spender (1990: 153) makes claims like the following in her forceful book *Man Made Language*:

> By promoting the use of the symbol *man* at the expense of *woman* it is clear that the visibility and primacy of males is supported. We learn to see the male as the worthier, more comprehensive and superior sex as we divide and organise the world along these lines.

Though this line of argument met with some support and sympathy from male academics, male reaction was often stridently protective of the status quo. Arguments in defence of *man* and other usages drew on notions of correctness, aesthetics and tradition. These were not always based on historical fact: for example, scholars pointed out that use of plural forms like *they* for generic *he* was once common in English, with examples found in Shakespeare and other writers. Sometimes opposition to feminism and language reform came in the form of jokes that exaggerated feminists' claims, with forms like *personhole* and *persondate* for *manhole* and *mandate*. Susan Romaine (1994: 125) ironically characterises language reform from the conservatives' position as 'a msguided attempt to change

---

Using 'man' to mean both the male human and all humans is unnecessarily confusing. The word 'man' should only be applied to males. If some of those who make up the other half of the population are under discussion as well, then the terms 'people', 'humans' or 'humanity' are available and unambiguous. Other alternatives are:

man-hour	work-hour
manpower	workforce
man-made	artificial, synthetic
man-to-man	person-to-person
prehistoric man	prehistoric people
man a post	fill a post
. . .	

If the sex of a person being discussed is unknown or could be female or male, use: *she or he; she/he; (s)he*. Alternatively, the plural offers a non-sexist pronoun, or the pronoun may be unnecessary:

Man and his universe	Humans and their universe
	Humans and the universe

(excerpts from the (British) National Union of Journalists guidelines 1982, cited by Graddol and Swann 1989: 101, 107)

herstory?' Sometimes the reaction was neither objective nor reasoned. 'Spokespersons of the world – get lost!' read one extract from the British newspaper, the *Guardian* (7 February 1983), cited by Graddol and Swann (1989: 103).

Debates over gender perspectives and biases in language support the views of theorists cited earlier, concerning hegemony, denaturalising ideology, and understanding 'femininity' as a discourse. While being made to seem socially useful and aesthetically clear, traditional English usage with its gender loading is often implicated in power-serving purposes. That the non-sexist movement in language has met with some success can be seen from guidelines concerning appropriate usage now common in the west.

Changing language alone is not the intention of gender research, rather it is to effectively change societal arrangements over gender. According to Cameron (1995a: 197), 'ultimately it is men who have the power (in public and private life) whereas women have only responsibility'. Contesting sexism in language is a part of a larger struggle. Cameron (1995a: 199) points to possible changes in management styles that might be genuinely empowering of females:

> What is happening, at least in theory, is a shift in the culture of Anglo-American corporate capitalism away from traditional (aggressive, competitive and individualistic) interactional norms and towards a new management style stressing flexibility, teamwork and collaborative problem-solving, which is thought to be better suited to changing global economic conditions. Some companies attempting to promote the new values have begun to practise linguistic intervention aimed at 'feminizing' the interactional styles of *male* employers (Graddol and Swann 1989); while in women's magazines there has been a vogue for features celebrating 'female management styles' as an idea whose time has come.

Critical linguistics focuses largely on written texts and oral media language. It favours the analysis of 'linguistic signs' at the level of the word and 'turns of phrase'. It is interested in the form as well as the content of such signs. These preoccupations make critical linguistics and critical discourse analysis appear to be adjacent fields to, rather than subfields of, sociolinguistics, where the main focus is on spoken interaction, accent and the form and function (but seldom the content) of linguistic utterances. But the theoretical focus on ideology, hegemony and resistance does raise issues that sociolinguistics cannot continue to avoid. Questions like which social group is dominant in public speech and writing, which groups are merely 'represented' and by what means, do form part of a larger ecology of language use and human communication, into which particular branches of sociolinguistics fit. In the rest of this chapter, we examine the work of a sociologist and cultural critic whose ideas bridge the gap between critical linguistics and general sociolinguistics.

10.6   SOCIOLINGUISTICS AND SYMBOLIC POWER: THE WORK OF PIERRE BOURDIEU

Pierre Bourdieu worked in much the same critical sociological tradition as the others we have drawn on in this chapter. Unlike them, he goes beyond discourse analysis to address a range of concerns of modern sociolinguistics. Although he was not a linguist, his work in politics, culture, education and language offers a base that a unified sociolinguistic theory could be built on.

Symbolic Domination

For Bourdieu, every linguistic interaction, however personal and insignificant it may appear, bears the traces of the social structure that it both expresses and helps to reproduce. Sociolinguistic competence accordingly goes beyond formulations of grammatical and communicative competence (see section 1.1). It includes the right to speak, to make oneself heard, believed, obeyed and so on. The philosopher J. L. Austin (1962) drew attention to utterances that are only appropriate within a specific context: *I hereby sentence you to six months' hard labour* presupposes a judge in court, invested with the authority to pass judgement over someone being tried. Here the act of speaking coincides with the act of passing sentence. Word and authority coincide. Bourdieu argues that the efficacy of 'performative' utterances like these is not to be found in language or in a special context, but is inseparable from the existence of an institution which gives meaning to the utterance. These institutions are not always physical ones; they may include any social relations between speaker and listener. Therefore, in his words, 'what speaks is not the utterance, the language, but the whole social person' (1977b: 653).

Two key aspects of Bourdieu's thinking are the ideas of a communicative economy and of symbolic power. The model of human communication that he evoked is a systematic analogy of the discipline of economics, stressing that communication is a part of the economics of everyday living. At the same time, the practices people think of as 'economic' (e.g. buying and selling of goods) are part of a wider category of social practices, which pertain to everyday existence. In his way of thinking about language use, Bourdieu was concerned with the economics of linguistic exchanges: that is, what are the elements of exchange, on what markets are they exchanged, what is their value, what are the linguistic investments that are made, what profit can they yield and what capital accumulates? Such questions suggest an interplay between global and local histories in the linguistic habits of individual speech communities.

Bourdieu outlines four types of resources or 'capital' available to human beings:

- economic capital (wealth in the form of cash and assets);
- cultural capital (forms of knowledge, skill and education);
- social capital (resources based on connections and group membership);
- symbolic capital (accumulated prestige, honour).

Individuals are distributed in the social space according to (1) the total amount of capital they possess, (2) the composition of their capital and (3) their trajectory in the social space. The last concept, characterising how a person's initial capital is transformed throughout his or her life history, is described in Figure 10.2. The top-left corner is made up of occupations associated with high cultural capital but low economic capital; the top-right corner is made of the opposite (high economic capital but low cultural capital); the bottom section involves occupations with low cultural and economic capital; the top-centre with high cultural and economic capital. Bourdieu's model characterises people's class position in terms of their relative positions within the social space, and not in an absolute way.

For Bourdieu, linguistic interactions between speakers (in terms of content and, more so, style) depend largely on the social relation between the speakers. This relation is the same as their respective standing in the social space schematised in Figure 10.2. Interactions take place within a 'linguistic market'. The latter term demarcates the specific structured space

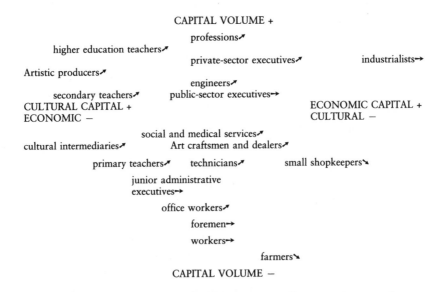

Figure 10.2   Occupations in social space according to volume and types of capital. Trajectories (i.e. how initial capital is likely to be transformed throughout life histories) are indicated by arrows (adopted and simplified from Bourdieu 1984: 128–9)[3]

in which people interact via language. Examples of such a market include the education system, the labour market, 'high society', government and ordinary daily interactions between people. Favoured patterns of language (style, discourse, accents) are conceived of as symbolic assets which can receive different values depending on the market in which they are offered. This notion is similar to Fairclough's account of an 'order of discourse'.

For Bourdieu, power is essentially the capacity to mobilise the authority accumulated within a market. Such power is seldom exercised as overt physical force. Rather, it is transmuted into a symbolic form and thereby endowed with a legitimacy it would not otherwise have (Thompson 1991: 23). Power is then exercised through symbolic exchanges. Control of the 'symbolic marketplace' is a central part of the exercise of all social power. '**Symbolic domination**' is a favourite phrase of Bourdieu's which refers to the process whereby the ruling-class is able to impose its norms as the sole legitimate competence on the formal linguistic markets (education, the bureaucracy, 'high' society). This dominance is described as symbolic rather than purely linguistic, since other facets of ruling class life (modes of dress, forms of transport, leisure activities) come to seem desirable and the norm to aspire to. The properties of the linguistic market endow linguistic products with a certain value. Within specific markets, certain 'products' have greater value than others. Part of socialisation involves learning how to produce expressions which are highly valued on the markets concerned. However, opportunities for learning a range of styles of speaking are not equally distributed in a society. The competences that have the most value are those that are most unequally distributed. A clear example is the small number of people who command the prestige accent of their society, for example RP in England. Other examples include people who command the 'high' variety in situations of diglossia, those who have access to functional literacy in some societies, those who have a command of an academic or literary style or those proficient in certain oratorical styles.

A precondition for symbolic domination is that those who are subjected to power believe in the legitimacy of those who wield it. Power thus always involves a 'misrecognition'. Although control of this 'legitimated' variety is differentially distributed in stratified societies, those who do not command the standard are led to accept its authority, 'correctness', its persuasive powers and right to be obeyed (Gal 1989: 353). For Bourdieu, this is a misrecognition of the standard form of a language, since it is not in an absolute sense more 'correct' than other varities. Symbolic domination results in euphemisation which Bourdieu's editor, J. B. Thompson (1991: 19–20), characterises as follows:

> All linguistic expressions are, to some extent, 'euphemized' – they are modi-
> fied by a certain kind of *censorship*, which stems from the structure of the
> market, but which is transformed into *self-censorship* through the process of

anticipation. Viewed from this perspective phenomena of politeness and tact-fulness, of choosing the right word for the right occasion are not exceptional phenomena . . . . Tact is nothing other than the capacity of a speaker to assess market conditions accurately and to produce linguistic expressions which are appropriate to them, expressions which are suitably euphemized.

Earlier in this chapter, we drew attention to the role that the power distance between speakers plays in Brown and Levinson's account of politeness. The mastery of the rules of politeness, especially the ability to fine-tune one's language according to the interlocutor and other aspects of the context, presupposes a (subconscious) acknowledgement of the sociopolitical hierarchy. In Bourdieu's (1977a: 95) typically provocative words, 'the concessions of politeness are always political concessions'. His characterisation of the euphemism necessary in all linguistic interaction is exemplified in Scott's study of the everyday language between rich and poor in Sedarka.

The final concept that Bourdieu proposes in his analysis of language within a theory of social practice is that of the **habitus** (or 'system of habits'). The term is an old one in rhetoric, which Bourdieu adapts to denote a system of durable, transposable 'dispositions', arising from the conditions of existence of a particular class or group in society. The closer the relative position of individuals in the social space, the more likely is their participation in a shared class habitus. As Figure 10.3 shows, the habitus is the link between 'objective' material conditions for class and 'subjective' dimensions of class and status formed by group and individual lifestyles. The 'dispositions' that make up a habitus include the way one walks, speaks, acts, eats and so on. They are acquired through a gradual process of inculcation that is socially differentiated and comes to denote a style of living. The habitus becomes almost 'inscribed' in the characteristic body postures arising from early discipline: 'sit up straight', 'don't talk with your mouth full' and so on. Developing out of this is a characteristic style of articulation that becomes associated with particular groups.

Figure 10.3   Class, habitus and class formation (based on Jenkins 1992: 142)

This aspect of Bourdieu's model has much in common with Bernstein's account of the differences between the working-class and middle-class life described in Chapter 12.

One advantage of Bourdieu's general theory is that it is capable of characterising microlinguistic variation as well as macrolinguistic situations. We exemplify this briefly with respect to the spread of French in France and of English in postcolonial Africa, and by examining how findings in linguistic variation (Chapter 3) are compatible with the broader sociological framework offered by Bourdieu.

Unifying a Linguistic Market: Two Case Studies

French

Frequently, standardised languages serving the state are legitimated by veiling the conflictual processes involved in their rise. Bourdieu draws on the work of Ferdinand Brunot on the history of the French language to illustrate the unification of the French linguistic market. The existence of a standard French language which is dominant over the entire state is a relatively recent phenomenon. In medieval times, what is now the standard form coexisted with other dialects, all of which were used for ordinary writing and literary contexts. From the fourteenth century onwards, in the central provinces of the *pays d'oïl* (i.e. Champagne, Normandy, Anjou, Berry – see section 2.3 and Map 2.5), the French dialect emanating from Paris began to gain ground and started to have the status and function of an official language. The other dialects thus underwent a 'devaluation' in becoming restricted to largely oral purposes. Whereas the word 'patois' previously meant 'incomprehensible speech', it now came to mean 'corrupted and coarse speech, such as that of the common people'. Included in this characterisation were the dialects and varieties that once had the status of independent languages.

In the *langue d'oc* (see section 2.3 and Map 2.5) regions of southern France, the Parisian dialect did not take hold until the sixteenth century, and the local dialects continued to be used for local texts. A situation of bilingualism arose: members of the peasantry and lower classes spoke only the local dialect, while the aristocracy, bourgeoisie and petty bourgeoisie had access to the official language as well. State linguistic unification arose with the Revolution of 1789. It was to the advantage of the new rulers to promote the official language as the language of the entire nation, since it gave the local bourgeoisie of priests and doctors as well as teachers a monopoly over politics and communication. Bourdieu warns against a simplistic view that linguistic unification was contingent upon the technical needs of communication between the different parts of the territory, especially between Paris and the provinces. He also dismisses the equally simplistic view that sees it in terms of raw power, as the direct product of a state centralism determined to crush 'local characteristics'. Rather, 'the conflict between the French of the revolutionary intelligentsia and the dialects or *patois* was a struggle for symbolic power in which what was at stake was the *formation* and *re-formation* of mental structures' (1991: 48). That is, the new language of authority which arose was eventually 'legitimated' by the expansion of the education system and the bureaucracy. This was a language with its new political vocabulary, terms of address and reference, metaphors, euphemisms and other representations of the social world linked to the interests of the new bourgeoisie. According to Bourdieu, these were inexpressible in the local idioms shaped by the specific interests of peasant groups.

The French case is by no means unique, and key features like state formation, capitalism and class formation apply to a wide range of standard or state languages of western Europe. In other parts of the world, a multilingual situation was restructured by colonisation and the market assumptions of the European colonisers.

English in Nigeria

Abiodun Goke-Pariola (1993) characterises the sociolinguistic situation in postcolonial Nigeria in terms of Bourdieu's framework. The process of colonisation (in the nineteenth century) involved, among other things, the integration of a new linguistic market. Prior to this, over 400 independent groups spoke a variety of often mutually unintelligible languages, with no single over-arching lingua franca. English was a principal tool in the process of colonisation. With its associations of military, technological and educational superiority, it forced a restructuring of the linguistic market. To speak English was in itself a form of power, and local persons who acquired a knowledge of the language increased their own power dramatically. Education in English became the main means of acquiring the new form of cultural capital. In many parts of the country, people resisted attempts to use the indigenous languages in schools. However, as access to higher education was limited, a new elite class was created of local people who acquired the requisite cultural capital associated with English. With the restructuring of the colonial linguistic market came a new linguistic habitus, which included behaving and sounding as much like the ruling class as possible. The most salient of these habits, typical of the new elites, is stereotyped even today in Nigeria and elsewhere in Africa as 'speaking through the nose'. This appears to refer not to the phonetic feature of nasality as such but to the adoption of intonation patterns, stress rhythms and a linguistic demeanour associated with speech of the former colonial elite. Goke-Pariola argues that because the colonial linguistic market works to the advantage of the new postcolonial ruling elite, it shows no sign of being dismantled. This analysis holds for territories like India and Sri Lanka, where a similar situation of stratified diversity occurs, with English – as the language legitimated by the former rulers – still proving difficult to dislodge.

Linguistic Variation and the Economics of Linguistic Exchanges

Bourdieu offers a reading of variationist sociolinguists discussed in Chapter 3, using his notions of symbolic domination, linguistic market, habitus and euphemisation. He takes as an example the language use of an elderly woman from a small town in Béarn (a province of south-western France), where a local dialect, Béarnais, is spoken. She first used a 'patois French' to a young female shopkeeper in the town, who was originally from a larger town in Béarn, and who might not have understood the local dialect. The next moment, she spoke in Béarnais to a woman of the town of the same age as herself, who was originally from the villages. Later, she used a French that was strongly 'corrected' to a minor town official. Finally, she spoke in Béarnais to a roadworker in the town, who was originally from the villages and about her age.

Such a versatility in code choice and style-shifting is commonplace in many parts of the world. From a micro- or interactional perspective, factors such as age, personal repertoire of interlocutors, relative status, topic, rights and obligations and accommodation are involved here. Bourdieu stresses a broader perspective – the integration of speakers into a larger political economy. A speaker's assessment of the 'market conditions', and the anticipation of the likely reception of his or her linguistic products, serve as an internalised constraint on his or her speech choices. Bourdieu implies that the natural code for the town should be Béarnais, but it is not *legitimated* in all contexts. Thus, at one and the same time, the woman's linguistic behaviour shows skill and versatility, as well as the effects of symbolic domination. The theory of symbolic domination would appear to explain instances of class divisions in language as well as competition over status (see section 3.4). In the dominant classes of New York City – the upper and upper middle class of Labov (1966) – is evident the linguistic behaviour of those whose habitus has become the embodiment of the norm. Bourdieu stresses the 'relaxation in tension' in the use of language by this class. This relaxation provides evidence of a relation to the linguistic market that can only be acquired thorough prolonged and 'precocious' familiarity with markets that are characterised by a high level of control. By 'control' he means attention to the forms and formalities of the prestige code, as well as more general 'practices' like avoidance of error and exaggeration, and keeping a distance from one's utterances rather than 'surrendering without restraint or censorship to their expressive impulse' (Bourdieu 1991: 85). This contrasts with what Bourdieu characterises as the lower middle class's unhappy relations to their own linguistic productions. This linguistic insecurity is most evident in hypercorrection, which Bourdieu (1991: 13) interprets as 'inscribed in the logic of pretension which leads the petits bourgeois [lower middle class] to attempt to appropriate prematurely, at the cost of constant tension, the properties of those who are dominant'. This is a rather strong (and judgemental) characterisation of a class divided against itself linguistically, whose members seek at the cost of constant anxiety to produce linguistic expressions that bear the highest yield on the market (in terms of prestige at least). These expressions bear the mark of a habitus other than their own.

As far as gender variation is concerned, Bourdieu (1991: 83) accepts Labov's characterisation of women being more prone than men to linguistic insecurity. Bourdieu summarises the position as follows. In societies where the traditional division of labour between the sexes still holds, women can only seek social mobility through symbolic production and consumption, and are consequently even more inclined to invest in the acquisition of the 'legitimated' competences. That is, deprived of other forms of capital (and of power), women are thrown into the accumulation of symbolic capital. This account may not seem very different from Trudgill's (1974: 93–5) explanation of the differences between male and female speech in western societies noted in Chapters 4 and 6. However, it escapes the criticism that Trudgill's analysis tends to assess women's language from the viewpoint of male language as the norm. In terms of Bourdieu's thinking, it is not that male language is somehow more 'normal', but that as the language of the dominant group it is legitimated and assumes symbolic domination of the linguistic market. Eckert (1989b) argues that femininity (with its linguistic manifestations of a quiet and relatively high-pitched voice, politeness and cooperative talk) is a mitigation or even a denial of male power. These 'feminine' kinds of behaviour are avoided by men at the lower end of the socioeconomic scale, for whom female competition in the workplace is a bigger threat than for other classes. By contrast, what is called 'effeminacy', involving among other things the rejection of overt power, is more prevalent among upper-class males. This is paradoxically the group that exercises the greatest global power (via an ultimate appropriation of the labour power of others). Eckert's argument that class and gender interact in complex ways linguistically is compatible with Bourdieu's characterisation of the habitus and of social trajectories.

Bourdieu portrays the working class as alienated from the mechanisms of the linguistic market. In Chapter 3, we reviewed studies showing a polarisation between the working-class varieties and the legitimated varieties in Norwich (Trudgill 1974), Guyana (Rickford 1986) and Detroit (Eckert 1989a). In Bourdieu's thinking, members of dominated groups are unable to exercise the liberties of plain speaking in formal linguistic markets, where they are forced to use a language or style that they are unaccustomed to. Otherwise, they might enforce a kind of self-censorship and escape into abstention or silence. Again, this echoes a theme in Bernstein's early writing (1974) concerning the exclusion of working-class codes in contexts like education which require an elaborated code. Bourdieu's generalisation on class language faces some of the same criticisms that were raised by linguists in the 1960s against Bernstein's work (see Chapter 11). Both theorists seem to undervalue the structure and function of working-class vernaculars. From his integrated societal perspective, Bourdieu (1991: 71) characterises the contexts in which the vernacular thrives as relatively insignificant:

> [T]he unification of the market is never so complete as to prevent dominated individuals from finding, in the space provided by private life, among friends, markets where the laws of price formation which apply to more formal markets are suspended . . . . Despite this, the formal law, which is thus provisionally suspended rather than truly transgressed, remains valid, and it re-imposes itself on dominated individuals once they leave the unregulated areas where they can be outspoken . . .

This analysis partly fits Scott's account of onstage and offstage behaviour of peasants in Sedarka. But there are some differences of emphasis. Bourdieu's suggestion here that the speech forms of the dominated in the private sphere are a temporary relaxation from the tensions of the linguistic market contrasts with Scott's argument that onstage and offstage behaviour are equally part of consciousness. In the private sphere, domination gives way to symbolic resistance. This resistance is a symbolic undermining of the self-awarded status of the rich by a variety of linguistic and other means, including the invention of nicknames. There are several aspects of Bourdieu's model that can be questioned. In matters of specific detail, we have already suggested that he undervalues the possibilities of resistance to symbolic domination. Second, many sociolinguists would question whether economic and political exchanges are the key aspect of language and whether 'free speech' and vernacular usage (in both senses of the term identified in Chapter 4) are the exception rather than the rule. In terms of Bourdieu's economic model, the vernacular would count as 'free' in the other sense of 'being exchanged without any cost or charge'. The model does not add much to the study of the vernacular, except to point to its relation to other modes of speech in the 'symbolic economy'. The dimension of power is emphasised in Bourdieu's work at the expense of the dimension of solidarity.

10.7 CONCLUSION

This chapter has been concerned with the work of scholars who follow Marx in taking a critical approach to the study of society, and hence to language. They see inequality and hence the potential for conflict in all aspects of society. As a background, we cited the work of Althusser and Foucault on ideology and discourse. More specifically, linguistic insights were drawn from the characterisation of the linguistic sign by Voloshinov and Bakhtin. Their argument that the potential for domination and resistance is implicit in the linguistic sign was illustrated by studies of phenomena such as class inequality in Sedarka, caste change in South India, the anti-language of the underworld in Elizabethan England and struggles over gender in the west. The main models in the chapter are those of Fairclough and Bourdieu. Fairclough developed a three-layered model of critical discourse analysis involving text, discursive practice and social practice. His emphasis falls particularly on how the ideological effects of texts (written and spoken) are produced. He advocates a critical language awareness of the media in particular. Bourdieu's model of symbolic domination draws upon a wider notion of class than one involving economic capital alone. Key notions in his account of language and inequality are the linguistic market, the habitus and euphemisation.

One might question whether the approach to language by power theorists cited in this chapter leads to an inflexible account of all speech interactions. Are relationships between people and their social roles more dynamic than the account of the different types of capital they possess? Brown and Levinson (1987: 79) warn against an over-deterministic account of power in accounting for speech phenomena like politeness. A person from a lower caste in south India might approach a Brahman for ritual services with great deference. But the roles might be reversed if the person belonging to the lower caste is a government official, from whom the Brahman requires assistance. In the modern world, people's roles have become multidimensional, and human communication more flexible than any theory has been able to capture. Still, the work discussed in this chapter, particularly that of Bourdieu, provides the beginnings of a framework against which many, if not all, of the broader phenomena associated with language in society, and society in language, can be analysed.

Notes

1. Bakhtin's terminology contrasts 'polyphony' with 'monophony'; Voloshinov contrasts the 'multiaccentual' nature of the sign as against the drive to make it 'uniaccentual'. We have selected the terms 'polyphony' versus 'uniaccentual' here.

2. The examples given here come from different sources: mainly from articles in the National Socialist newspaper *Völkischer Beobachter* (1933–9), but also from speeches by Adolf Hitler and Joseph Goebbels, as well as from the examples listed in Seidel and Seidel-Slotty (1961) and Klemperer (1975).

3. Note that Bourdieu does not illustrate in any detail how symbolic and social captial (i.e. those forms of capital which are linked to Weber's notion of 'status') are involved in the construction of class locations. Although he identifies all four forms of capital as constitutive of the locations in the social space in most of his writings on class, he only uses the notions of economic and cultural captial in the empirical study of consumption patterns in France. In a footnote to an empirical study of consumption patterns in France, however he remarks: 'A fuller presentation of the fundamental principles of this construction, i.e. the theory of the different sorts of capital, their specific properties and the laws of conversion between these different forms of social energy, which is simultaneously a theory of the classes and class fractions defined by possession of a given volume and structure of capital, is reserved for another book, so as not to overcomplicate the present analysis' (1984 [1979]: 572, n. 17).

11

SOCIOLINGUISTICS AND EDUCATION

11.1 INTRODUCTION

Educational sociolinguistics is the subfield of sociolinguistics dealing with relationships between language and education. Most research in this subfield has examined these relationships within classroom settings, though recent interests in informal education, community-centred instruction and media/distance education raise interesting questions about language and education relationships outside of the schools.

We begin by offering brief definitions of education and schooling, and by showing how language, broadly defined, is important to the teaching and learning experiences which occur in school settings. Particularly important here for sociolinguists are the differences between language use in the classroom and language use commonly found in the students' homes and communities. Educational linguists are concerned with describing these differences, often drawing on the ethnographic traditions discussed in Chapter 6. Sociological explanations for differences in characteristic habits of pupils from different social backgrounds have also proved of relevance to educational sociolinguistics. In this chapter, we cite studies which are concerned with tracing the effects of the language of the home on classroom-based teaching and learning experience, and vice versa. The writings of Basil Bernstein are central to this theme. In the final section, we examine debates for and against using localised languages of the home as languages of education. We list proposals favouring this innovation put forward by a committee of specialists. In relation to this debate, we examine the work of James Cummins, which is concerned with finding an effective policy in bilingual education for minority and immigrant children. Two case studies documenting parental concerns about language and their involvement in developing new programmes of bilingual education conclude this chapter.

11.2 TEACHING, LEARNING AND SCHOOLING

In every society, there is information which members of the society need to know, and skills which they need to acquire, in order to meet the responsibilities and obligations of citizenship. Education refers to the teaching and learning activities through which members of a society gain access to this information and to these skills. Often, the teaching and learning is supervised by older members of a society and conducted for the benefit of the society's younger members, a process which some researchers term 'child socialisation'. But teaching and learning also unfolds within generations, as well as between them. And for some topics for example, computer literacy – adults are just as likely to be learners as well as teachers. In tribal societies, education includes the training given to young people to prepare them for 'initiation' or other ceremonies marking their transition from childhood to adulthood. (See section 8.5 on the definition of the term 'tribe'.) Education also includes the observation and imitation of artisans and other skilled persons as they carry out their crafts. Community-wide storytelling, gossip and public debate, too, form a part of teaching and learning. Moreover, outside of particular forms of initiation conducted in private, secret locations, education in tribal societies takes place in public settings. The information made available in public settings to some learners is potentially available to all. In state societies, the transfer of information and skills also takes place throughout the community. However, the 'official' responsibility for education is assigned to particular social institutions – most notably, the school – and not left in the hands of individuals. What people learn in these settings may or may not be consistent with what they learn at home or elsewhere in the community. These home/school language and cultural differences are one of the sources of classroom-related educational problems, and are a topic of great interest for educationally focused sociolinguistics research.

Classroom Language

The site for much research in educational linguistics has been the classroom. Sociolinguists have used audio- and videotape recordings, surveys and interviews with students, parents, teachers and other school personnel.

They have also relied on ethnographic observations to gain insights into the language use which helps to shape educational experiences in these settings. In this section, we present three segments of teacher–student conversations which show some types of data collected through this research and the insights which they offer.

1. 'Dividing by nine'

William Leap (1993) discusses language use in a third-grade classroom on the northern Ute reservation (see section 8.5 for a background to this community). The teacher was born in the US Midwest and moved to north-eastern Utah as an adult. She is a native speaker of the standard English spoken in the Midwest and speaks no Ute. Frank, the student, is an 8-year-old member of the Ute Indian Tribe. He was born on the reservation and grew up in a home where the Ute language was regularly spoken by grandparents and other elders. He does not speak Ute himself, but is a native speaker of the distinctive variety of English used throughout the reservation. The conversation comes from a discussion of long-division problems which the teacher had written on the board. After working through several of the problems herself, she began asking individual students to solve other problems in the set. The problem she gave Frank was to divide 85 by 9. He worked with the problem but could not give a correct answer. The segment begins as the teacher tries to help him find a solution.

1. *Teacher:* What is nine times nine?
2. *Frank:* Ninety.
3. *Teacher:* No, that is too big. We know that nine times nine is
4. eighty-one. What is nine times nine?
5. *Frank:* Eighty-one.
6. *Teacher:* Eighty-one. You know that nine times nine is eighty-one. Can you get a
7. nine out of here (*motions to the 90*
8. *on the board*)?
9. *Frank:* Yes.
10. *Teacher:* OK, if we take nine out of here, what do we have?
11. *Frank:* Eighty-one.
12. *Teacher:* What about eighty-three divided by nine?
13. *Frank:* (*without hesitation*) Ten.
14. *Teacher:* (*with irritation*) Ten?

(Leap 1993: 219)

2. 'Old Ironsides'

The setting for the second example, taken from Cazden (1988), is an elementary-school classroom in a San Diego (California) public school. The segment begins during 'show and tell' time, when, at the teacher's request, the student (Nancy) began to describe a recent family outing.

1. *Nancy:* I went to Old Ironsides at the ocean. [*Nancy explains*
2. *that Old Ironsides is a boat and that it's old.*] We also spent
3. our dollars and we went to another big shop.
4. *Teacher:* Mm. 'N what did you learn about Old Ironsides?
5. *Nancy:* [*Brief description of the furnishings and the guides'*
6. *costumes*] I also went to a fancy restaurant.
7. *Teacher:* Haha. Very good.
8. *Nancy:* And I had a hamburger, french fries, lettuce and a –
9. *Teacher:* [*interrupts*] OK. All right what's – Arthur has been
10. waiting and then Paula, OK?

(Dorr-Bremme 1984, as reported in Cazden 1988: 16)

3. 'Letter to a pen-pal'

Solomon (1995) reports the following conversation in a combined fourth/fifth grade classroom in a bilingual (English and Spanish) public school in Washington, DC. The teacher is a Hispanic woman, who was born in Venezuela. She is fluent in English and Spanish. The student, Roberto, comes from a working-class Hispanic family, which emigrated to the DC area from El Salvador several years before Roberto was born. He is a first-language speaker of Spanish, and is learning English as a second language through the ESL (English as a Second Language) programme at this school. The extract centres around the activity of replying for the first time to pen-pals from a neighbouring school. Students were busy writing replies to questions like 'where do you live?' and 'do you have a pet?' The teacher noticed that Roberto was answering his pen-pal's questions with one- or two-word replies, and not with complete sentences. The segment begins with her response to this practice:

1. *Teacher:* OK, now, here's the problem. This letter goes back to
2. [the pen-pal], right? If you answer the questions here – like
3. you put 'No dog' or 'yes', she won't know the answer to this
4. question because it's not on this letter. You need to answer
5. her letter. Do you understand? OK. So what we need to do is we
6. need to change these into sentences so she'll know the answers
7. to these questions.

[*The student goes back to work. Several minutes later, the teacher returns and the exchange continues*]

8. *Teacher* [*looking over Roberto's letter*]: Good. OK, and what
9. do you put at the end of your sentence? 'Do you have pets at
10. home?' And you wrote what?
11. *Roberto:* Yes, a [*unclear*].
12. *Teacher:* Yes.
13. *Roberto:* A monkey.
14. *Teacher:* OK, why don't you explain that to her.
15. *Roberto:* I said, 'Yes, a [*unclear*].'
16. *Teacher:* So what sentence are you going to write?

17. *Roberto:* 'Yes, I do.'
18. *Teacher:* 'I do', what?
19. *Roberto:* 'I do have . . .'
20. *Teacher:* 'Have . . .' have what?
21. *Roberto:* 'A dog.'
22. *Teacher:* OK, you can tell her that. [*Teacher writes the desired*
23. *sentence and reads it aloud*:] 'I have a dog in [*unclear*].'
24. What goes at the end? OK, now you said you have a dog and two
25. cats, and then you put 'no dog'. Do you know why you put that?
26. *Roberto:* [*unclear*]
27. *Teacher:* All right, the important thing is that you understand
28. that when you're writing back to your pen pal you have to
29. answer the questions in your letter, right? . . . OK, what I'd
30. like you to do now, then, is go to your final copy. [*activity*
31. *continues*]

(source: Solomon 1995: 58–9)

Educational linguists use examples like the three above to show that class-room-based teaching and learning is heavily dependent on language. While teachers may use visual aids and other resources to help them present new information to students, **teacher talk** is a primary means of classroom instruction, while listening, answering and question-asking are typically expected of pupils. Also important are the many forms of written language which can be found in the classroom, ranging from writing on the board to library books and other resource materials. Because it is so important to teaching and learning activities, language is heavily regulated in the class-room. Teachers are the primary speakers in the classroom, and teacher talk is almost always the primary language register in use. Thus, teacher talk makes up eight of the fourteen lines in example (1) and twenty-three of the thirty-one lines in (3). On the other hand, student talk in those conversa-tions makes up only five and seven lines, respectively. Teacher talk occurs less frequently in example (2), but it still dominates the conversation in that example in ways we discuss below. Moreover, teacher talk unfolds in lengthy and complex constructions, while student talk is composed of smaller and more topically focused phrases and, in some instances, only single-word replies.

Besides being the primary speaker in classroom conversations, teachers also maintain tight control over the conversations – even when they are not speaking. Teachers determine the topics for discussion in classroom conversations and they control each student's 'right to speak' on those topics. They also regulate the amount of time each speaker can spend in discussion. In example (2), Nancy gives an eager response to the teacher's call for a description of a recent family outing. Her comments suggest that the exciting part of her outing was not the visit to the warship (*Old Ironsides*), but the visit to the gift shop, the big store and the fancy restaurant. The points that she wanted to discuss do not conform to the teacher's expectations about a suitable student response. Hence in line 4, the teacher disregards the comments about shopping, and tries to return Nancy's attention to the warship. In line 7, in what looks like an attempt to discourage the less suitable themes, the teacher initiates 'closure' on Nancy's narrative: *Haha Very good*. When Nancy fails to comply with this attempt at closure to talk about the restaurant (line 8), the teacher reasserts control over the speech event (lines 9–10). Nancy's participation, is terminated when the teacher extends the right to speak to two other students who will presumably fulfil her expectations about the task at hand.

Conflicting definitions of the assignment's purpose also structures the teacher's response to the student's use of written language in example (3). Roberto writes to his pen-pal as if he is in face-to-face contact with a close friend. But as the teacher's comments make clear, Roberto's reply is expected to satisfy classroom expectations about written language. Written communication is less context-dependent, involving a great deal of repetition and redundancy. Thus whereas an answer to a question like *Do you have any pets?* requires a fragment answer in oral communication (*Yes, a dog and a cat*), the pupil still has to learn the rather different conventions of the written code (*You asked whether I have any pets. Actually, I have a dog and a cat*). The disjuncture between home and school language will be explored further in section 11.3.

Structure and Culture in Classroom Conversation

One of the earliest findings in analyses of classroom language was that teacher-student exchanges were not randomly constructed, but were organised in terms of a three-part sequence. Mehan (1979) called this an 'IRE' sequence (short for 'initiation – response – evaluation'). The sequence occurs as follows:

- initiation of the sequence by the teacher, often in the form of a request for information directed at one or more of the students;
- response to the teacher's request from one of the students;
- evaluation of the student's reply by the teacher, often accompanied by a request for information or other initiation of the next IRE sequence.

Example (1) can be easily analysed in terms of an underlying IRE structure. Line 1 contains the teacher's initiation, line 2 the student's reply, and lines 3–4 an evaluation (*No, that is too big*) as well as the initiation for the next IRE sequence (*What is nine times nine?*). Line 5 contains Frank's reply to the second initiation. Lines 6–7 contain the teacher's evaluation (*Eighty-one. You know that nine times nine is eighty-one*), as well as the initiation for the next IRE sequence (*Can you get a nine out of here?*). And so on. Subsequent research (discussed in Mehan 1979 and Cazden 1988) has shown that while IRE sequences may be the backbone of classroom communication, they rarely unfold so neatly. For example, IRE sequences are not completely independent of each other. Instead, several teacher initiations and student responses may occur before the teacher provides evaluation. Students as well as teachers may initiate IRE sequences, and may also offer forms of evaluation to each other and to the teacher. Students as well as teachers may rework the 'function' of particular statements within the sequence, so that the regulatory effects of 'initiation', 'response' and 'evaluation' may become tempered by other, equally important, social and cultural messages. For example, Frank does not try to move outside of the IRE sequencing which governed the teacher–student turn-taking in example (1). He does not use his (limited) opportunities for speaking to shift discussion into a format which is less tightly regulated. He does not disrupt the sequencing by offering additional remarks. Instead, he willingly follows the teacher's lead by replying directly to her initiation, and allows the teacher to evaluate his statements and to initiate further replies. He works hard to cooperate with the conversational expectations and requirements which are structuring this exchange. In this sense, Frank's cooperation with the teaching/learning task at hand is quite different from Nancy's repeated attempts (example 2) to shift discussion away from the visit to the warship (the topic of interest to the teacher) and towards topics of greater personal concern.

Leap (1993) draws attention to the differences between the expectations of home and school regarding interaction. The prominent turn-taking feature in example (1), as in other instances of classroom English, is question-asking and -answering, and the IRE framework underlying it. However, question-asking in Ute English (as in the Ute language itself), depends on an entirely different set of sociolinguistic assumptions. Asking a question in Ute English is as much an affirmation that the person being addressed knows the answer as it is a request for information. Accordingly, once an Ute English speaker is asked a question, the speaker is virtually obliged to respond to it. What the speaker says in reply to a question is not nearly as important as is the fact that the speaker meet his/her linguistic and cultural obligations by saying something. This is evident in Frank's ready (and mathematically incorrect) responses to the teacher's questions. They reflect his familiarity with the requirements of IRE structure, as well as his use of Ute English rules of question-answering, this creating of his own style of in-class participation. An appreciation by the teacher that Frank is being cooperative should make it easier to help him master the mechanics of division in the long run.

11.3 DISADVANTAGE AND CLASSROOM LANGUAGE

Differences between classroom language and home/community language and cultural tradition are one of the most widely cited explanations for classroom-related language difficulties experienced by pupils. Susan Philips (1972, 1983) studied the differences between assumptions governing speech and silence found in (Indian) homes and in the (non-Indian-controlled) public schools on the Warm Springs reservation. Warm Springs children learn early in life that speaking is an adult privilege; children are expected to listen quietly to adult conversations, and to learn from what they hear. Once children reach adulthood, they will have acquired enough information to have things worth saying, and will, in turn, provide verbal lessons for the next generation of younger listeners.

In classroom settings, the social meanings associated with silence are read quite differently by teachers and other school personnel. Here, a child's silence signals the failure to complete homework assignments, to pay attention to class discussion, or to be an active and participatory learner in other ways. The likelihood of conflicts between intended and received messages is enormous under these circumstances. And as Philips' research shows, the school success of Warm Springs students is seriously short-changed by those conflicts.

Shirley Brice Heath (1983) found similar differences between language use in classroom versus home/community in her studies of the 'ways with words' in rural South Carolina. Heath conducted extensive observations of home language use within middle-class white, working-class white and working-class black communities. Then she went into the local elementary schools, to see whether these patterns of home language use prepared students for successful school experiences. Middle-class white parents spend much time reading stories aloud and discussing story-events with their pre-school children. Heath argues that middle-class white children are therefore not surprised by the question-asking, revoicing and other features of teacher talk and respond enthusiastically to its demands.

Working-class white parents also spend time reading stories, but are more likely to read *to* their children than to read *with* them. Reading is largely a one-sided speech event, with parents presenting the story and children absorbing it. Thus, Heath argues, working-class white students come to school less familiar with the question-centred language of teaching and learning which teachers use in the classroom. While they can provide accurate retellings of a storyline, they are less comfortable giving their own opinions or making predictions based on such material.

Working-class black parents do not spend time in reading stories, or in any other one-to-one linguistic exchange. However, they encourage children to think and speak for themselves, and are delighted when children do so in public settings. Heath finds that such preparation transfers into the classroom with some difficulty. Teachers are not willing to reinforce such outspokenness, and are often distressed at the amount of talk which working-class black students introduce into the classroom. Both points undermine teachers' claims of control over language and create conflicts between students and teacher which may never be resolved.

Philips' and Heath's explanations for home/school language differences are tightly focused around differences between the home and school cultures. This 'cultural relativist' stance was not characteristic of educationists in the 1960s and early 1970s, who saw linguistic and cultural deficits in the performance of working-class and minority children at schools. In the next section, we examine the approach to language problems in the classroom from such a 'deficit' perspective.

Elaborated and Restricted Codes

Basil Bernstein, a British sociologist who was an influential figure in education in the 1960s and 1970s, is generally considered as the main protagonist of the deficit approach. Bernstein's writings are numerous (including the four-volume collection *Class, Codes and Control*), and show a development of ideas. It is accordingly not easy to summarise his work, as some of his later ideas are at odds with his earlier writings. Bernstein recognises that students from different economic and social backgrounds respond differently to educational experiences in the classroom. He explains these differences by focusing on the close connections between language learning and socialisation. For Bernstein, the language which speakers use within a particular social setting expresses what speakers can say as well as what people can do within that setting. Unavoidably, language is closely linked to the speakers' location within the social structure. By learning a language relevant to their social position, speakers learn the requirements and restrictions which regulate behaviour within that social position. According to Bernstein, two different kinds of language may thus emerge, which he called **restricted** and **elaborated codes**. An elaborated code is closely associated with the opportunities open to middle-class people. Bernstein characterised this as a code (or 'orientation') which provides its speakers with precise, highly creative and richly expressive linguistic descriptions. He argued that speakers who make use of elaborated codes have access to a wide range of syntactic and semantic alternatives, which encourage them to utilise these options in imaginative and unpredictable fashions. By contrast, the restricted code provides its speakers with a much more limited range of linguistic options. Speakers who make use of a restricted code often leave much of their commentary without elaboration, if not entirely unsaid. The restricted code is associated with the working class and other marginalised groups who have little access to a range of opportunities within society.

Bernstein claimed that a restricted code uses minimal linguistic resources: sentences are usually short, linkages between sentences are repetitive and predictable (*and then*, *so*, *next*), adjectives and adverbs are infrequent and undetailed. Consequently, speakers using restricted code constantly seek confirmation for their statements (*you see*, *you know*) from other participants in the conversation. Overall, where an elaborated code is a language of expressive and explicit statement, a restricted code is a language of highly implicit meanings. Bernstein argued that working-class culture in Britain in the 1960s and 1970s relied on solidarity, shared understandings, fixed-role relationships between people and the authority of parents. Such factors tended to favour greater use of a restricted code. (Examples of a restricted code would include Roberto's responses to the teacher's questions in example (2), and so would his answers to his pen-pal's questions. In both cases, Roberto frames his responses in terms of terse, clipped, almost telegraphic statements. He does not elaborate on his remarks, or do anything else to move the discussion beyond the minimal expectations of the question.) Bernstein saw middle-class family life as less authoritarian than its working-class counterpart. In socialising their children, middle-class parents stressed talking about things rather than doing them silently. Their children were able to use language to articulate decontextualised ideas to a greater extent than working-class children. In a paper written in 1960, Bernstein observes:

> one mode [of speech], associated with the middle-class, points to the possibilities within a complex conceptual hierarchy for the organization of experience, the other, associated with the lower working-class, progressively limits the type of stimuli to which the child learns to respond. (1960: 276, cited by J. R. Edwards 1979a: 35)

For Bernstein, the elaborated code was explicit and expressive, and showed the ability to organise experience conceptually. To this end, it favoured complex sentences and a large vocabulary drawing upon all parts of speech.

Bernstein's work has received divergent responses. In the USA, it was associated with a 'deficit hypothesis' which held that the reason why working-class and minority children did badly at school was that their language was deficient. These children were held to be victims of 'verbal deprivation'. As a result, compensatory education came into being, attempting to 'teach language' to such children who were believed not to have any language (e.g. Bereiter and Engelmann 1966).[1] In the USA, there was a racial tinge to the argument for compensatory education (as the accompanying box illustrates).

Scene from a film showing a programme developed by a team of educationists for children
A film showing the corrective program developed by a team of educational psychologists for children alleged to have these language deficiencies was screened for linguists at the 1973 Linguistic Institute in Ann Arbor, Michigan. It contained the following sequence:

> Earnest White teacher, leaning forward, holding a coffee cup: 'This-is-not-a-spoon.'
> Little Black girl, softly: 'Dis not no 'poon.'
> White teacher, leaning farther forward, raising her voice: 'No, This-is-not-a-spoon.'
> Black child, softly: 'Dis not a 'poon.'
> White teacher, frustrated: 'This-is-not-a-spoon.'
> Child, exasperated: 'Well, dass a cup!'

The reaction of the linguists, after they had finished applauding and cheering for the child, was a mixture of amusement, incredulity, and anger.

(Fasold 1975: 202–3)

Many sociolinguists, especially those familiar with the varieties spoken by minorities, rejected the assumptions about the inferiority of African-American Vernacular English and other varieties that commanded little social prestige. In two famous papers entitled 'The logic of nonstandard English' (1969a), and 'Contraction, deletion and inherent variability of the English copula' (1969b) Labov attempted to refute the notion of language deprivation among minorities. The most convincing part of his argument involved a demonstration that absence of the verb *be* (also known as the 'copula'; see section 9.3) in AAVE in many contexts where standard English required it was not due to any difference in logic (or lack of logic, as the deficit theorists believed).[2] Rather, on close inspection it turned out to be surprisingly parallel to the standard English rule. The mechanics of Labov's argument are provided separately in the box below.

Sociolinguists criticise Bernstein for the lack of examples evident in his writings. They argue that, without detailed exemplification, aspects of

The logic of non-standard English: the verb 'to be' in AAVE
(based on Labov (1969b))
Labov noted contexts in which the deletion of 'copula' *be* (and its variants like is and are) is frequent in AAVE. In the following examples, a dash denotes the absence of the verb *be*, and an asterisk denotes a sentence that is not permissible in a particular variety.

<u>Sentences in which AAVE allows deletion of the verb be</u>

Noun phrase	She — the first one started us off.
Predicate adjective	He — fast in everything he do.
Locative	You — out the tape.
Negative	But everybody – not black.
Participle	He just feel like he – getting cripple up *from* arthritis.

Rather than treat these sentences as ungrammatical, Labov pointed out that they correspond to sentences that in standard American English (SAE) permit the copula to be contracted (e.g. SAE: *She's the first one who started us off*). He also pointed out that there were sentences in which AAVE did not allow deletion. These were precisely the sentences in which the equivalent in SAE did not allow contraction, as the following examples show:

<u>Sentences in which AAVE disallows deletion of the verb be</u>

SAE	AAVE
Final position in a sentence	
*He's as nice as he says he's	*He's as nice as he says he —.
*How beautiful you're!	*How beautiful you —.
Are you going? *Yes I'm	Are you going? *Yes I —.
An unstressed following word	
*Who's it?	*Who — it?
*What's it?	*What — it?

Thus wherever SAE permits **contraction**, AAVE permits **deletion**. Where SAE disallows contraction, AAVE disallows deletion. The strong parallels between the two dialects with respect to the contexts of contraction and deletion thus suggest that they are governed by the same logic. Difference in linguistic structure between one social dialect and another does not imply a cognitive difference.

his work border on the stereotypical. Labov's demonstration of the logic underlying the deletion of the verb *be* dispelled the idea that the black child was non-verbal or linguistically deprived. Yet there is still a feeling that, in rejecting all aspects of Bernstein's theory, sociolinguists may have thrown out the baby with the bathwater (see e.g. Halliday 1969). Many children still experience difficulties in bridging the gap between the variety spoken within their community and the variety demanded by the school, despite the demonstrations of underlying similarity. As the examples of classroom language in this chapter show, power, regulation and control are embodied in teacher–student communication and are central to students' success or failure in the classroom. Bernstein's work does address these issues and could just as well suggest a different practical application from that made by the deficit theorists. As Trudgill (1975: 69–70) argues, it is likely that the problem lies not with the child from a working-class or minority background, but with the expectations of schools. Trudgill suggests that schools should be flexible enough to adapt to the needs of the child. Interpreted in this way, Bernstein's ideas could be used to suggest that it is not the child who should be made to change, but the school system itself. Efforts in this direction are described later in this chapter.

One scholar who has kept some of Bernstein's sociological insights is Pierre Bourdieu. His idea of a 'habitus' (see 10.6) draws essentially on the distinction between restricted and elaborated code. He conceives of linguistic practices as forms of capital which provide speakers with access to desired positions in the labour market. This aspect of Bourdieu's model has much in common with Bernstein's account of the differences between working-class and middle-class life. However, Bourdieu does not share Bernstein's earlier proposal that it is a restricted code which disadvantages children of the working class in educational settings. Rather, Bourdieu sees education as part of the process of symbolic domination of the working class. He views the school as the primary site through which members of society acquire the forms of linguistic capital which mediate their experiences within the labour market. Bourdieu argues that schools are sites of 'social reproduction' – that is, they serve to consolidate class and gender differences and constrain the opportunities available to students later in life. This argument can be criticised for being too mechanical and for overlooking the ways in which people can act to overcome certain inequalities.

Still, like Heath, Bernstein and other researchers, Bourdieu's arguments remind us that classroom language cannot be understood outside of a broader analysis of social opportunity and social control. Those connections are particularly important for sociolinguists interested in finding ways to improve student language skills and, thereby, increase their opportunities for successful educational experiences.

11.4   DIALECT AND LANGUAGE CHOICE IN THE CLASSROOM

In most parts of the world, education had for a long time been the preserve of the few ('elites'). The choice of which language or dialect to use to teach children (or 'medium of instruction') reflected the interests of these elites. By the late twentieth century, that position had changed considerably. In countries that are monolingual, the choice of a medium of instruction might seem uncontroversial, though there were times in Europe when a classical language (Latin) was preferred over German, French, English and other European languages. In those European countries in which one language dominates, an important issue is the relationship between the standard and regional dialects in education (see, for example Cheshire et al. 1989). In multilingual communities, deciding which language or languages to use as media of instruction is the central issue. Under colonial rule in Africa and Asia, languages like English and French were often selected as the medium of instruction in schools. Upon independence, countries like Kenya and Tanzania had to weigh up the benefits of retaining the coloniser's language against choosing indigenous languages. Possibilities of social and educational change arose via new choices of the language of instruction. These possibilities are raised in a document compiled by UNESCO (United Nations Educational, Scientific and Cultural Organisation).

UNESCO commissioned a committee of specialists in 1951 to study and report on the issue of which languages could be used in education worldwide. The report of the committee came out in 1953, and is still the basis for any discussion of the topic. The recommendations of the committee are given in the accompanying box. Page references in this section are to the version of the document reprinted in Fishman (1968).

The report was particularly concerned with the extent to which the home languages of a community could be introduced as a medium of instruction in schools. This concern was linked to the development of formal education in poorer countries where material resources were limited. The 1950s were a time of social change when the policies of colonisation and imperialism were being questioned, as well as elitism in educational policy. The committee used the term 'vernacular' in a way that challenged the disparaging sense which it then had. In colonial parlance, a 'vernacular' was any local language, contrasting with the language of colonial administration. The committee defined a vernacular instead as

> a language which is the mother tongue of a group which is socially or politically dominated by another group speaking a different language. We do not consider the language of a minority in one country as a vernacular if it is an official language in another country. (Fishman 1968: 689–90)

The Use of Vernacular Languages in Education
(A summary of the report of the Unesco Meeting of Specialists held in 1951; see UNESCO 1953)

1. The mother tongue is a person's natural means of self-expression, and one of his first needs is to develop his power of self-expression to the full.

2. Every pupil should begin his formal education in his mother tongue.

3. There is nothing in the structure of any language which precludes it from becoming a vehicle of modern civilization.

4. No language is inadequate to meet the needs of the child's first months in school.

5. The problems of providing an adequate supply of schoolbooks and other educational materials should be specially studied by UNESCO.

6. If the mother tongue is adequate in all respects to serve as the vehicle of university and higher education, it should be so used.

7. In other cases, the mother tongue should be used as far as the supply of books and materials permits.

8. If each class in a school contains children from several language groups, and it is impossible to regroup the children, the teacher's first task must be to teach all pupils enough of one language to make it possible to use that language as the medium of instruction.

9. A *lingua franca* is not an adequate substitute for the mother tongue unless the children are familiar with it before coming to school.

10. Adult illiterates should make their first steps to literacy through their mother tongue, passing on to a second language if they so desire and are able.

11. Educational authorities should aim at persuading an unwilling public to accept education through the mother tongue, and should not force it.

12. Literacy can only be maintained if there is an adequate supply of reading material, for adolescents and adults as well as for school children, and for entertainment as well as for study.

13. If a child's mother tongue is not the official language of his country, or is not a world language, he needs to learn a second language.

14. It is possible to acquire a good knowledge of a second language without using it as the medium of instruction for general subjects.
15. During the child's first or second year at school, the second language may be introduced orally as a subject or for general subjects.
16. The amount of the second language should be increased gradually and if it has to become the medium of instruction, it should not do so until the pupils are sufficiently familiar with it.
17. Efficient modern techniques should be used in teaching the mother tongue and a foreign language. A teacher is not adequately qualified to teach a language merely because it is his mother tongue.
18. Where there are several languages in a country, it is an advantage if they are written as uniformly as possible.
19. For convenience of printing, languages should as far as possible be written with a limited set of symbols which are written in a single line.
20. For the needs of a polygot state which is developing a national language, the materials for teaching the language should be simplified for instructional purposes, so that pupils may progress towards full mastery without having anything to unlearn.

(This sense of 'vernacular' contrasts with the two senses identified in modern sociolinguistics in Chapter 3; with the sense of 'any unofficial language' in colonial parlance; and with another popular modern sense of 'an unwritten language'.) 'Mother tongue' is another elusive term that the Committee tried to pin down for their purposes. They stressed that it need not be the language which the parents of a particular child use, nor need it be the language the child first learns to speak, since circumstances may cause him or her to abandon it early in life (Fishman 1968: 689–90).

In his discussion of the report, Ralph Fasold (1984: 293–307) focuses on the objections of its critics. Many criticisms are mainly of a practical nature, stressing problems in connection with a lack of trained teachers in particular languages, lack of reading materials and so on. Of greater concern is the perceived inadequacy of vernacular languages to cope as adequate media of instruction. This objection is frequently raised in connection with scientific and technical vocabulary (e.g. W. Bull 1964: 530). Some sociolinguists point out optimistically that many of today's 'developed' languages, including German and English, were themselves once believed to be inadequate for educational purposes (see Coulmas 1989b). Vernacular languages can be expected to undergo a vocabulary expansion if the need arises, in the same way as English and German had expanded. The report makes recommendations about the most effective means of vocabulary expansion (Fishman 1968: 707–8). Since this topic usually falls under 'language planning', we postpone discussing it until Chapter 12.

Choosing a localised medium of instruction is not a purely linguistic issue. Educational choices are frequently subject to the interests of the economy and those who control it. A stringent reviewer of the Unesco document, William Bull (1964: 528 – originally written in 1955), has this to say:

> The Committee, rather obviously, strongly believes that what is best for the child psychologically and pedagogically should be the prime point of departure in planning for universal education. This proposition appears, however, to be somewhat unrealistic. What is best for the child psychologically may not be what is best for the adult socially, economically or politically and, what is even more significant, what is best for both the child and the adult may not be the best or even possible for the society.

This position is often echoed by parents of children who wish their children to be educated in the most prestigious language, typically associated with economic success. In addition, parents may cite a cognitive reason: a belief that learning one language restricts the capacity for learning other languages. More proficiency in one language is held to imply fewer skills in the others. Macnamara (1966) formulated this as the 'balance hypothesis'. This hypothesis has been contested by the Canadian sociolinguist James Cummins (1979), who studied the academic successes and failures of children in bilingual educational programmes in Canada and elsewhere. In these programmes, more than one language was used by the school as a medium of instruction. Children from middle-class backgrounds who spoke English at home could opt for an education which would enable them to be functionally bilingual in English and French. In this model, called **immersion education,** they would be taught all subjects from an early age in French, their weaker language. English, however, would be taught as a subject (in English). This model fits the description of **additive bilingualism** (Lambert 1978: 217), in which a child adds 'a second, socially relevant language to his [or her] repertory of skills' without losing fluency and skills in the first language. The successes of this programme (in terms of learning of content as well as of language) contrasted with the relative failure of the bilingual education programmes offered to children of immigrants and minorities. In the latter case, the home language was used initially to build up skills in the societally dominant language, which soon took over as medium of instruction. This is sometimes called a model of 'transitional bilingualism'. It often results in what Lambert called **subtractive bilingualism,** in which the learning of a societally dominant language leads to a loss of skills (or even a complete loss) of the home language. In addressing the claims of Macnamara's 'balance hypothesis', Cummins argued that studies which pointed to an apparent negative effect of bilingualism in education were all conducted in settings involving subtractive bilingualism. On the other hand, immersion education and other types of bilingual education that were fully supportive of both languages (rather than using one as a transitional route into the other) reported a high degree of success.

Cummins proposed that children can attain educational success in a second language provided that first-language development is also heeded, particularly in developing vocabulary and concepts relevant to the school. This attention to first-language development may be done in the home, as in the case of immersion education, where the children's first language (the dominant language of the society) was fully supported in the home and neighbourhood, in terms of books, media coverage and so on. On the other hand, children in immigrant communities often speak a home language that has little of the support that dominant languages enjoy. Cummins argues that in such cases the home/school mismatch leads to a delay in the acquisition and development of the second language. This will result in educational failure, unless the school intervenes to provide support in the minority language. To summarise the argument, second-language acquisition benefits from the development of first-language skills, and a child's first language must be developed in school as a basis for successful acquisition of the second language and – hence – for success in education. This argument has come to be known as the **interdependence hypothesis**: first- and second-language development are closely tied together. As Appel and Muysken (1987: 107) point out, Cummins' hypothesis is attractive since it explains many phenomena related to language and school success in multilingual environments. However, it remains a hypothesis, and has not been easy to verify in settings outside the somewhat special Canadian case. Critics argue that success in bilingual education is dependent on many more factors than the relationship between first- and second-language development. For example, motivational, emotional, financial and sociopolitical factors are also involved.

The next two case studies are concerned with the joint efforts of linguists and communities to bridge the gap between home language and classroom language. Although they did not involve immigrant minorities, these studies show the strengths of some of Cummins' ideas. They also show some of the practical and ideological problems surrounding the use of minority languages in primary education.

Building Language Interdependence: A Case Study on the Northern Ute Reservation

Language-related educational problems have been a visible part of the school experiences of American Indian students on the northern Ute reservation (described in section 8.5). The low achievement profiles, disciplinary problems and high drop-out rates reported for minority children in many countries are also reported for Indian students in the northern Ute schools (Leap 1993: 265–79). You might recall from section 8.5 that Ute students enter school fluent in the tribe's ancestral language and/or a Tribally specific variety of English, but not familiar with standard English at all. Ute parents regard home/school language discontinuities as one of the primary causes of their children's educational problems. On the other hand, teachers assume that since most Ute students are 'speakers of English', they are coming to school already familiar with the standard code. To resolve this problem, Leap (1991, 1993) describes how a small group of Ute women, working closely with Ute parents and tribal officials, proposed a bilingual education programme at one of the on-reservation elementary schools. The aim was that Ute students (and interested non-Indian students as well) could receive language arts instruction in the Ute language as well as in standard English. None of the women had received formal training in language teaching or curriculum development, but they spoke their ancestral language fluently, understood its importance and saw how Ute instruction could enrich school experiences for Ute children. Before proceeding with this plan, the women discussed their proposal with several Ute parent groups. The groups' reactions were consistent: Ute language instruction could be an asset to Ute student education. But the instruction had to be exclusively oral in basis – the Ute language could not, and should not, be written. Parent groups could not endorse Ute-language instruction if the instructional plan made use of writing in any form. The women agreed to comply with this restriction, and in September 1981 the *Wykoopah* ('two-paths') bilingual education programme began providing Ute language and culture instruction to Ute and non-Indian students at Todd Elementary School.

Ute objections to written information in the ancestral language could not be attributed to 'primitive superstition', 'conservative Tribal attitudes' or 'Tribal resistance to change'. Their comments, which are summarised below, showed that members of the Tribe had given serious thought to the mechanics of writing Ute and to the broader effects which written Ute would have on Tribal life.

- The Ute language was a gift to the Ute people from the Creator, and the Creator had not provided a written form of the language to the people. Therefore, it would be highly inappropriate for anyone to propose alterations or improvements to the Creator's generosity.
- Formalising a written Ute language on the reservation would create a new distinction– 'literate' vs 'illiterate' – within the Tribal membership. This distinction could reshape the age-based hierarchies traditionally basic to northern Ute social organisation dramatically.

- What would people do with literacy skills, since there were no written materials for people to read?
- How could a spelling system for Ute be created, given that each of the northern Ute bands has its own way of speaking, and individual Utes find additional ways to impose their own, personalised style onto their sentences and texts?
- Since presentation of meaning in spoken Ute relies heavily on inference, contextual cues and other forms of speaker-related background information, would written Ute texts would be able to communicate their messages through equally indirect means?

For the first six months, instruction was entirely based on the spoken language. But in March and April of the following year, the Ute language teachers noticed that the Ute students were making notes on new vocabulary and other facts about the Ute language, using the 'word-attack' skills they had acquired in English-language arts classes as the guidelines for making decisions about spelling. The Ute language staff reported this discovery to the Wykoopah parents' advisory group and to other Tribal and community leaders. They were deeply concerned about the emergence of written language. They agreed to withhold any objections to the practice, because writing the Ute language was something that the Ute children had created, and something which the children felt was important to their Ute language development and to their classroom education. Parents also noted that if the children were going to write the Ute language, they needed to do so 'correctly'. So they asked the Ute language staff to develop a practical spelling system for the Ute language and to include training in the use of that writing system in the Wykoopah curriculum. The dramatic reversal was quite pleasing to the Wykoopah staff, who had been struggling to develop meaningful lesson plans for Ute language instruction which made no use of written Ute.

Mindful of the Ute language's already fluid rules of sentence and text construction, Wykoopah staff decided not to create a 'standard spelling' for Ute. Instead, children were encouraged to spell Ute words in the form that they found appropriate. Students were reminded, however, that they had to be able to read what they wrote; reading personal spellings aloud became the Wykoopah equivalent of the English language-based 'spelling test'. Next, Wykoopah staff invited parents and community members to sit in on any of the Ute language classes at the school. Children were encouraged to take their worksheets and other products home to share with family members and friends. Wykoopah students gave language-related presentations at school assemblies, community meetings, meetings of Tribal government, pow-wows and other public occasions. Through these means, Wykoopah staff made clear that Ute literacy was to be public knowledge, and not a skill restricted to a Tribal 'elite'. The public presentations also addressed Tribal concerns about the mechanics of writing Ute, by modelling various alternative spellings, and written forms, for different words, phrases and sentences. Wykoopah staff reminded their audience that it was the students who began these innovations, and that the spelling conventions which Wykoopah was using were those which the students themselves had proposed. This argument was an attempt to draw parallels between the highly valued practice of speaking Ute in individualised fashions, and the equally individualised innovations in spelling which the students had developed under their own initiative.

None of these efforts was able to assuage Tribal concerns about written Ute language completely. But these efforts did make written Ute literacy a more attractive linguistic skill for Ute students, and encouraged Ute parents to become less resistant when they saw how important writing the language became to their children. Even though the bilingual programme ended officially in 1989, members of the Tribe have retained their writing skills and still produce poetry and other written texts for their own enjoyment and the enjoyment of their friends. Written Ute also appears, along with English, on posters and other public advertising on the reservation. The Tribal newspaper now includes written Ute in some of its articles and advertising.

Building Dialect Interdependence: The Ebonics Debate in the USA

A parallel to the development of northern Ute as a language of formal education is the status of AAVE and the possibility of its becoming more visible in schools in which black students are in a majority. We review two proposals which directly address discontinuities between the language of these students and the language of the classroom. These proposals were concerned with improving opportunities for classroom learning by providing students with more effective language arts instruction. The poor performance of African-American students in the absence of such opportunities was at the root of community concerns in two well-publicised areas: Ann Arbor, Michigan, and the Oakland schools in California.

The Ann Arbor Trial

Labov (1982) discusses a court case (28 July 1979) in which a group of parents and community activists (the plaintiffs) in Ann Arbor, Michigan, brought suit in the Federal District court against the Martin Luther King Junior Elementary School, the Ann Arbor School District and the State of Michigan Board of Education (the defendants). The plaintiffs charged that the educational opportunities provided to African-American children enrolled in King Elementary School did not address the cultural, social and economic factors which were limiting their educational experiences at this school. To support their claim, the plaintiffs argued that the African-American students at King Elementary School were fluent in a variety of English which was different from the standard English used in the classroom. By ignoring these differences, the school was unfairly limiting these students' opportunities for learning. Sociolinguists like Geneva Smitherman and William Labov were called to testify on behalf of the plaintiffs. In addition, the research of creolists like Joseph Dillard, and social dialectologists like Ralph Fasold and Walt Wolfram was cited during the trial. Geneva Smitherman, a consulting linguist for the plaintiff in the Ann Arbor case, used comparisons of the African-American students' speech with samples of African-American English from Detroit, Washington DC and other cities, to show that the features of student English which teachers considered to be defective were, in fact, widely attested features of African-American English and were part of the linguistic norm within the students' home speech community.

The presiding judge decided in favour of the plaintiffs (on 12 July 1979). He found that children's home language 'is not in itself a barrier', but it becomes one 'when the teachers do not take it into account in teaching standard English' (cited by Finegan 1997: 430). He directed the Ann Arbor School Board to prepare a plan which would help teachers at all Ann Arbor schools to identify the children who spoke 'Black English' and use the students' fluency in this variety as a foundation for developing standard English skills.

While parent groups expressed satisfaction with the judge's decision, many educators were uncertain about ways to implement the ruling's requirements: how exactly should teachers use African-American English as a basis for teaching standard English skills? Some critics assumed that the teachers were now expected to become fluent speakers of the students' English. Others assumed that classroom time would now be spent 'teaching' rules of African-American grammar and discourse to students who had no connections to these codes. Parents of African-American students, particularly parents from middle-class backgrounds, objected to any attempt to bring 'the language of the ghetto' into the classroom. The Ann Arbor school district created a training programme designed to familiarise teachers with details of African-American language. However, the district ended the training programme after two years because teachers were still uncertain about ways to make the information relevant to classroom instruction.

Ebonics

A decade and a half later, the problems in US education had not improved. Teachers were still regularly assigning African-American students to classes for the mentally handicapped or learning-disabled, or refused to promote them to the next grade level at the end of the academic year. Particular features of the students' English were still considered to be evidence of their handicap, disability or failure to acquire knowledge expected for their grade level. On 19 December 1996, the Oakland (California) school board suggested a policy in language arts instruction for their schools that resembled the Ann Arbor proposals. Again, the school board cited the uniqueness of African-American student English, arguing that this was not a substandard, defective variety of standard English, but a completely different linguistic system. Given these linguistic differences, the school board found it necessary to propose a programme of English-based 'bilingual education' for the Oakland schools. Under this programme, language arts instruction would begin in the language which the children already know (African-American English), and shift into standard English instruction only after the students have received sufficient second-language training in that language.

The Oakland school board went further with this argument, by tracing the origin of many AAVE norms to West African-languages. It argued that the students' English is part of a separate and unique African-American linguistic tradition – what the board termed Ebonics (that is, *Ebony* + *phonics*), and not really 'English' at all. Public reactions to the Oakland proposals were quite mixed, and the Ebonics debate received a great deal of publicity in the media. Views for and against a bilingual programme involving Ebonics and standard English from linguists, teachers and pupils are given in the accompanying box.

While the Oakland proposals reflected efforts on the part of some community members and educators to expand educational opportunities for African-American students, these proposals quickly became the targets of criticism from other parties. And neither of these efforts was ever fully implemented. The Oakland school district never had a chance to implement their proposal for Ebonics–English bilingual education. The extent of local and national objection to the bilingual plan prompted the school board to revise its position. Rather than requiring instruction in English as a second language, the school board decided simply to call for 'a general recognition of language differences among Black students in order to improve their proficiency in English' (*New York Times*, 14 January 1997). To do this, the board asked the superintendent to develop a course of study which will facilitate 'the acquisition and mastery of English language skills, while respecting and embracing the legitimacy and richness of the [students'] language patterns'.

The Linguistic Society of America took a very strong stance in support of the Oakland school board's decision to recognise the vernacular of African-American students in teaching them standard English. Their document is reminiscent of the UNESCO document in many ways (see accompanying box).

Reactions to the Oakland proposals reported in the New York Times in 1997

'It's the same words, we just say them in a different away. We just cut the words short' (16-year-old Black student, disclaiming AAVE as a special language).

'You can talk like that if you want to, but it's your grade. It won't work in a job interview' (high-school junior, recognising the low status of AAVE).

'Sometimes, especially in English, I want to talk to where the teacher will understand me, but the teacher will get confused. I'll end up saying nothing' (sophomore, claiming fluency in AAVE over classroom English).

'For some, this might help their understanding . . . . These kids can speak black vernacular or jive, and then be very articulate in standard English. I can understand them either way' (white Oakland teacher/gym coach, claiming to be bidialectal).

'If a student uses broken English, I'm going to correct the student, not send him to a special class. If you're born in America, you should speak English' (black mathematics teacher at Oakland, dismissing AAVE as a legitimate code).

'It would be misleading for the public to equate the language of the descendants of slaves with the linguistic problems of new immigrants from Russia . . . . [However] there are very few instances where school districts have adequately tried to address the linguistic consequences of slavery. The people involved here have the best interests of the students at heart, so I think it's unfair to be exceedingly critical on linguistic grounds when they're trying to help' (John Baugh, professor of education and linguistics).

'This is an unacceptable surrender, bordering on disgrace. It's teaching down to our children . . . . They cannot get a job at NBC or CBS or ABC [national television networks] unless they can master the language, and I'll tell you they can master the language if they are challenged to do so' (Jesse Jackson, civil rights activist).

'Elevating Black English to the status of a language is not the way to raise standards of achievement in our schools and for our students. The [Clinton] administration's policy is that Ebonics is a nonstandard form of English and not a foreign language' (Richard Riley, US Secretary of Education).

Linguistic Society of America Resolution on the 'Ebonics' issue

Whereas there has been a great deal of discussion in the media and among the American public about the 18 December 1996 decision of the Oakland School Board to recognize the language variety spoken by many African American students and to take it into account in teaching Standard English, the Linguistic Society of America (LSA), as a society of scholars engaged in the scientific study of language, hereby resolves to make it known that:

a. The variety known as 'Ebonics', 'African American Vernacular English' (AAVE), and 'Vernacular Black English' and by other names is systematic and rule-governed like all natural speech varieties. In fact, all human linguistic systems – spoken, signed, and written – are fundamentally regular. The systematic and expressive nature of the grammar and pronunciation patterns of the African American vernacular has been established by numerous scientific studies over the past thirty years. Characterizations of Ebonics as 'slang', 'mutant', 'lazy', 'defective', 'ungrammatical', or 'broken English' are incorrect and demeaning.

b. The distinction between 'languages' and 'dialects' is usually made more on social and political grounds than on purely linguistic ones. For example, different varieties of Chinese are popularly regarded as 'dialects', though their speakers cannot understand each other, but speakers of Swedish and Norwegian, which are regarded as separate 'languages', generally understand each other. What is important from a linguistic and educational point of view is not whether AAVE is called a 'language' or a 'dialect' but rather that its systematicity be recognized.

c. As affirmed in the LSA Statement of Language Rights (June 1996), there are individual and group benefits to maintaining vernacular speech varieties and there are scientific and human advantages to linguistic diversity. For those living in the United States there are also benefits in acquiring Standard English and resources should be made available to all who aspire to mastery of Standard English. The Oakland School Board's commitment to helping students master Standard English is commendable.

d. There is evidence from Sweden, the US, and other countries that speakers of other varieties can be aided in their learning of the standard variety by pedagogical approaches which recognize the legitimacy of the other varieties of a language. From this perspective, the Oakland School Board's decision to recognize the vernacular of African American students in teaching them Standard English is linguistically and pedagogically sound.

Chicago, Illinois   January 1997

11.5 CONCLUSION

This chapter described the contributions of sociolinguistics to an understanding of language in education. Classroom talk is seen as a special register with conventions of its own, especially IRE sequences. Analyses of pupils' responses in class shows that pupils from a minority background might employ different strategies which reflect the norms of their culture, but which clash with classroom expectations. A key theme in educational linguistics is the role of language in school success or failure. Bernstein conceptualised two different orientations towards language, the restricted and elaborated codes. He saw each of these as more characteristic of one social class than another. Since classroom discourse favoured the elaborated code, pupils with little previous access to it were at a disadvantage compared to those from a middle-class background whose primary socialisation, according to Bernstein, included the elaborated code. The notion of the two opposing codes has been severely criticised by sociolinguists. Nevertheless, Bernstein's work is important, at least in revealing the gap between children's experience and school's expectations.

Another important theme in educational linguistics is the choice of the most appropriate language for pupils in multilingual schools. The UNESCO team of specialists favours the use of vernacular languages wherever practically possible, seeing them as the most viable way into early cognition. Their document also stresses the complementary responsibility of the school in making a more widely spoken language eventually accessible to children. Cummin's interdependence hypothesis stresses the symbiotic relationship between learning in a first language and in a second language. Success in learning in the second language comes only after a threshold has been reached in the first. Under these circumstances, learning in a second language may well help to sustain the first language.

We cited two case studies concerned with bringing the language of the home into the classroom, in an attempt to address educational failure. The 'language problems' in the first example grew out of Tribal objections to the creation of a written form of the ancestral language, and their insistence that classroom instruction in that language be confined exclusively to speaking and listening skills. The 'language problems' in the second example stem from teacher, community and outsider resistance to using African-American English and standard English as languages of instruction in the classroom. Sociolinguistic research, and the informed commentaries of sociolinguistic researchers, were heavily involved in events surrounding both of these cases. Taken together, these examples show how the findings from sociolinguistic research can influence educational policy and be useful to educational change. They also show how the concerns of the students' home/community, public opinion and other 'non-linguistic factors' (re)shape the usefulness of such research and its findings. Chapter 12 looks more explicitly at the contributions of linguists to state planning and policy issues in which language plays a key role.

Notes

1. Bernstein denies that this was a valid interpretation of his work (see J. R. Edwards 1979a: 33, 44).
2. The term 'copula' usually refers to the verb *be* in its linking function between a subject and a predicate like a noun or adjective: for example, in *She is well*, the verb *is* functions as a copula. Copular *be* contrasts with another function of *be* in AAVE: invariant *be*, denoting habitual activity, as in *She be playing* (where standard English speakers might say 'She usually plays').

12
LANGUAGE PLANNING AND POLICY

12.1   INTRODUCTION

Societal attention to, and interference in, questions of language use is a common phenomenon: complaints about slippery grammar in letters to newspaper editors, spelling reforms, questions of 'political correctness', advocacy of 'plain language' use in insurance policies, the role of minority languages in education, interpreter training for the courtroom, the development of international terminologies, the selection of official languages – the list seems endless. In sociolinguistics, all these examples are increasingly being treated as part of a more unified field known as **language planning**.

The term 'language planning' was introduced by the American linguist Einar Haugen in the late 1950s and refers to all conscious efforts that aim at changing the linguistic behaviour of a speech community. It can include anything 'from proposing a new word to a new language' (Haugen 1987: 627). **Language policy** is sometimes used as a synonym for language planning. However, more precisely, language policy refers to the more general linguistic, political and social goals underlying the actual language planning process. Although language planning is a widespread and long-standing practice, only in the 1960s, when a large number of newly independent nations in Africa and Asia faced the question of the selection and implementation of a national language, did language policy and planning emerge as an area of sociolinguistic enquiry.

However, the very concept of language planning as 'deliberate language change' (Rubin and Jernudd 1971b: xvi), initiated by human actors, remained questionable for many linguists until well into the 1970s. This is reflected, for example, in the title of a collection which has become a classic of language-planning literature: *Can Language Be Planned?* (Rubin and Jernudd 1971a). Although nowadays linguists accept that deliberate language change is possible, this does not mean that they consider language planning advisable: *It can be done, but it should not be done* remains a common attitude (Fishman 1983). Emphasising the descriptive nature of linguistics as a science, linguists have often approached language planning and its essentially prescriptive nature with some degree of suspicion and left its execution to politicians and lay people.

12.2 DIMENSIONS OF LANGUAGE PLANNING

Based on the distinction between language as an autonomous linguistic system and as a social institution, the German linguist, Heinz Kloss (1967, 1969), distinguished two basic types of language planning: **corpus planning**, which is concerned with the internal structure of the language, and **status planning**, which refers to all efforts undertaken to change the use and function of a language (or language variety) within a given society.[1]

Typical activities of corpus planning include devising a writing system for a spoken language, initiating spelling reforms, coining new terms and publishing grammar books. A central aspect of corpus planning (and language planning *per se*) is **language standardisation,** which can be understood as the creation and establishment of a uniform linguistic norm. Not all languages show the same degree of standardisation, and different types or stages of standardisation have been distinguished:

> **Unstandardised oral language,** for which no writing system has been devised. Examples: Gallah (Ethiopia), Phuthi (Lesotho), and so on.
> **Partly standardised or unstandardised written language** used mainly in primary education. The language is characterised by high degrees of linguistic variation in the morphological and syntactic system.
> Examples: most of the American Indian languages.
> **Young standard language,** used in education and administration, but not felt to be fit for use in science and technology at a tertiary or research level.
> Examples: Luganda (Uganda), Xhosa (South Africa), Basque (France/Spain) and so on.
> **Archaic standard language,** which was used widely in pre-industrial times but lacks vocabulary and registers for modern science and technology.
> Examples: classical Greek, classical Hebrew, Latin and so on.
> **Mature modern standard language,** employed in all areas of communication, including science and technology at a tertiary level.
> Examples: English, French, German, Danish, modern Hebrew and so on.
>
> (based on Cobarrubias 1983: 43–4)

Status planning, which refers to the allocation of new functions to a language (such as using the language as medium of instruction or as an official language), affects the role a language plays within a given society. The decision to use Hebrew as a medium of instruction in Jewish schools in Palestine from the end of the nineteenth century is an example of status planning. Previously, classical Hebrew had not been used in everyday communication, and its use had been restricted to prayers and religious as well as scholarly writings. The introduction of Hebrew-medium schools created the conditions for the revival of Hebrew as a common language used in everyday communication. Language-planners distinguish many possible functions a language can occupy in society.

Official: the use of a language 'as legally appropriate language for all politically and culturally representative purposes on a nationwide basis. In many cases, the official function of a language is specified constitutionally' (Stewart 1968).
Example: in Ireland both Irish and English have official status.

Provincial: the use of a language 'as a provincial or regional official language. In this case, the official function of the language is not nationwide, but is limited to a smaller geographic area' (Stewart 1968).
Example: in the Canadian province of Quebec, French is the only official language (since 1974), while both English and French have official status in the other provinces of Canada.

Wider communication: the use of a language 'as a medium of communication across language boundaries within the nation (*lingua franca*)' (Stewart 1968).
Examples: Swahili in Kenya and Tanzania, Hindi and English in India.

International: the use of a language 'as a major medium of communication which is international in scope, e.g. for diplomatic relations, foreign trade, tourism, etc.' (Stewart 1968).
Example: in medieval Europe, Latin was the major medium of international communication. Today it is English.

Capital: the use of a language 'as a major medium of communication in the vicinity of the national capital. The function is especially important in countries where political power, social prestige, and economic activity is centred in the capital' (Stewart 1968).
Example: the provinces in Belgium have either Dutch or French as a provincial official language. The capital Brussels, however, is bilingual.

Group: the use of a language 'primarily as the normal medium for communication among the members of a single group, such as a tribe, settled group of foreign immigrants, etc.' (Stewart 1968).
Example: Jamaican Creole functions as a group language among Afro-Caribean immigrants in Britain.

Educational: the use of a language 'as a medium of primary or secondary education, either regionally or nationally' (Stewart 1968).
Example: in Norway, the local dialects are widely used in primary education.

School subject: the language 'is commonly taught as a subject in secondary and/or higher education' (Stewart 1968).
Example: French is taught as a school subject in most German high schools.

Literary: 'The use of a language primarily for literary or scholarly purposes' (Stewart 1968).
Example: Latin was used as the main language of literary and particularly scientific writing in Europe until the early eighteenth century.

Religious: 'The use of a language primarily in connection with the ritual of a particular religion' (Stewart 1968).
Example: religions such as Islam and Judaism require the use of a sacred language (Arabic and Hebrew repectively) for the recitation of religious texts and prayers.

Mass media: the use of a language in the print media and on radio and television.

Example: in Israel, the government determines how many hours should be broadcast in Hebrew, Arabic and foreign languages.

Work place: the use of a language as a medium of communication in the workplace.

Example: although German is the main language used in German factories, Turkish, Greek, Italian and other immigrant languages dominate in certain areas of production-line work.

(based on Cooper 1989: 99–119)

Although language planners separate corpus and status planning conceptually, it is necessary to understand that the two dimensions interact closely with each other (Cobarrubias 1983). The allocation of new language functions (status planning) often requires changes in the linguistic system (corpus planning) such as the development of new styles and lexical items. A good example of the interaction of status and corpus planning is the above-mentioned adoption of Hebrew as medium of instruction in Palestine. The change in language status made it necessary to expand the vocabulary of classical Hebrew in order to provide terms for the teaching of modern school subjects such as chemistry, physics and biology (Rabin 1989).

Subsequently, two more dimensions of language planning have been identified: **prestige planning** and **acquisition planning**. Prestige planning is directed towards creating a favourable psychological background which is crucial for the long-term success of language planning activities (Haarmann 1990). The high prestige which Hebrew commanded as the traditional religious language made explicit prestige planning unnecessary. Prestige planning, however, is vital when the promoted language has previously been limited to low-culture functions (as in the case of diglossia, see Chapter 1). In order to make the promoted status changes socially acceptable, it is necessary to improve the prestige of the respective language. Thus, prestige planning often becomes a prerequisite for status planning.

Efforts to spread and promote the learning of a language are described as instances of acquisition planning. For example, cultural institutions such as the British Council or the Goethe Institute are set up and supported by their respective governments to promote the learning of English and German as a second language in other countries. Another example of acquisition planning is the activities by the Maori community in New Zealand to promote the acquisition of Maori. In the early 1980s, most Maori children had no knowledge of their ancestral language, and linguists identified Maori as an endangered language. In a response to the decline of Maori, so-called 'language nests' (*kohunga reo*) were established by the Maori community. In these pre-schools, older Maori-speaking members of the community worked voluntarily as caretakers and taught the Maori language to the children (Cooper 1989: 157–9).

12.3   THE PROCESS OF LANGUAGE PLANNING

Haugen (1966, 1987) developed a useful framework for the description of the process of language planning. According to Haugen, language planning typically consists of four stages, which can (but need not) be sequential:

1. Selection
2. Codification
3. Implementation
4. Elaboration.

Language planning begins with the possibility of choosing between a number of **linguistic alternatives** (Haugen 1987). To choose certain linguistic forms or language varieties over others, and promote them as being 'the norm', is the basis of most language-planning activities. Language planning can thus be understood as a normative response to linguistic diversity.

Selection is the term used to refer to the choice of a language or language variety to fulfil certain functions in a given society: for example, official language, medium of instruction, religious language and so on. Often this means that the most prestigious dialect or language is chosen, as in the case of modern French, which is based on the prestigious dialect spoken in the region around Paris (*Île-de-France*). This is sometimes called monocentric selection. However, sometimes language planners have deliberately created a composite of several dialects. A good example of this is the recent standardisation of Basque, a language spoken in the south-west of France and north-west of Spain. Unified Basque (*Euskara batua*) was created from the late 1960s as an amalgam of the four main Basque dialects (Mahlau 1991). Standard Basque is an example of polycentric selection.

Codification refers to the creation of a linguistic standard or norm for a selected linguistic code and is commonly divided into three stages: graphisation (developing a writing system), grammatication (deciding on the rules/norms of grammar) and lexicalisation (identifying the vocabulary) (Haugen 1987: 627). Codification is often administered by language academies, as in the cases of French and Basque; however, the examples given below show that codification has just as frequently been the achievement of individuals.

Graphisation of a previously oral language with no written tradition involves many important decisions regarding the selection of a writing system. Should it be logographic (based on words and morphemes), syllabic (based on syllables) or alphabetic (based on the vowels and consonants as individual units)? Should one adopt an existing writing system or create a new one?

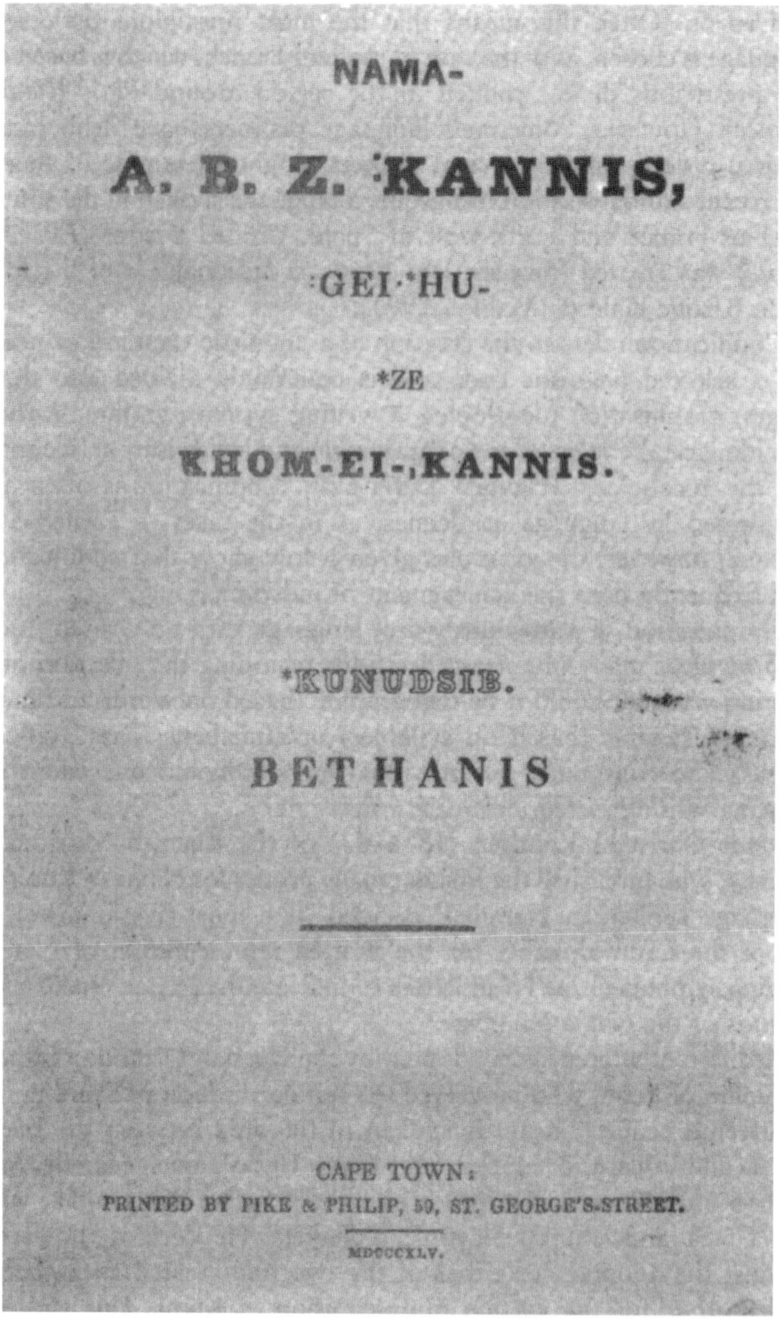

NAMA-

A. B. Z. ǀKANNIS,

ǀGEI·ǀHU-

*ZE

KHOM-EI-ǀKANNIS.

*KUNUDSIB.

BETHANIS

CAPE TOWN:
PRINTED BY PIKE & PHILIP, 59, ST. GEORGE'S STREET.

MDCCCXLV.

Figure 12.1   Nama Primer published by H. C. Knudsen in 1845
(Moritz 1978: 4)

Hans Christian Knudsen (1816–63) of the Rhenish Missionary Society, who published the first language primer for Nama, a Khoisan language spoken in Namibia, decided (like most missionaries) to adopt the Latin alphabet for the written representation of Nama, adding symbols to the Latin letters to indicate the characteristic click sounds of the Nama language (see Figure 12.1).

A different strategy was adopted by the Russian Orthodox bishop St Stefan of Perm, who pioneered the standardisation of Komi in the fourteenth century. Komi is spoken in the area between the rivers Kama and Volga and belongs to the Finno-Ugric language family. As a bishop of the Russian Orthodox church, St Stefan was familiar with the Greek and Church Slavonic alphabets. He decided, however, against the adoption of either of the two and created an alphabet called *Abur* for the written representation of Komi. This strategy allowed the Komi people to see their alphabet as distinctively theirs, enhancing their separate group identity (Ferguson 1967).

Graphisation can also involve the revision of an existing writing system. For example, the writing systems for non-Russian languages in the former Soviet Union were devised in the 1930s on the basis of the Russian Cyrillic alphabet. This was done to promote a common writing system in the country and facilitate the acquisition of Russian as a second language (Lewis 1983: 321–3). Many eastern European countries have, however, returned to the Latin script since the disintegration of the Soviet Union after 1990 (see Figure 12.2).

Figure 12.2 The 'Language Festival' in Moldavia celebrating the reintroduction of the Roman alphabet for the writing of Moldavian (August 1990, photo: Mark Sebba)

Another aspect of the language-planning process is the normative formulation of the rules of grammar. In other words, one decides which forms will belong to the new standard, thus reducing syntactic and morphological variation (Haugen calls this process '**grammatication**'). In many spoken varieties of English, for example, the verbal ending *-s* is variable in the third-person singular (*she likes him* versus *she like him*). In standard English, however, the ending *-s* was made obligatory, and variation is not acceptable.

Lexicalisation refers to the selection and publication of an appropriate vocabulary for the selected variety. Lexicalisation is frequently characterised by puristic tendencies which aim at the exclusion of words of foreign origin. This was the case in the standardisation of Hindi in India, where many commonly used loanwords from Persian, English and other languages were replaced with borrowings and adaptations from classical Sanskrit (Coulmas 1989a: 11). The typical products of the codification process are orthography, grammar books and dictionaries.

The sociopolitical realisation of the decisions made in the stages of selection and codification is called **implementation**. This includes the production of books, pamphlets, newspapers and textbooks in the newly codified standard as well as its introduction into new domains, especially the education system. While linguistically trained people often dominate the processes of selection and codification, implementation is typically conducted by the state. The implementation of a new standard variety or language can involve marketing techniques to promote its use, including awards for authors who publish texts in the new standard, language bonuses for civil servants, and even advertisements (Haugen 1983; Cooper 1989: 75–6). For example, in the Nunavut Territory in Canada the Nunavut Literary Price has been established to encourage writing in Inuit – one of

---

Language marketing in Israel

Posters with the (Hebrew) injunction 'Hebrew [person] speak Hebrew' appeared in Palestine in the early part of the twentieth century, long before the establishment of the state. The Academy of the Hebrew Language publishes and distributes lists of approved terms for various specialized fields. For many years the Israeli radio broadcast a one-minute skit, twice daily, in which one speaker criticized another for using a given expression (in many cases used by everyone in everyday speech) and then supplied a normative alternative (in many cases used only in writing or only on the most formal public occasions if at all), sometimes justifying the preferred variation by citing its appearance in the Bible.

(Cooper 1989: 63)

Canada's indigenous languages – and every year an Inuit Language Week takes place to promote the use of this minority language.

Implementation can mean vigorous legal enforcement of a language policy as in Quebec, where the Charter of the French Language (Bill 101) demands the use of French in all areas of public life. Implementation can also mean encouragement as in the Spanish province Catalonia, where the use of Catalan is encouraged and actively supported, but not legally enforced (O'Donnell 1993).

Elaboration (sometimes referred to as **modernisation**) involves the terminological and stylistic development of a codified language to meet the continuing communicative demands of modern life and technology. The main area of language elaboration is the production and dissemination of new terms, and often different strategies of lexical enrichment are used simultaneously. This is the case with Hausa, an Afro-Asiatic language spoken by approximately 50 million people in West Africa. In Hausa, three strategies are used for lexical modernisation:

1. Borrowing (from Arabic or English)
2. Extension of the meaning of a native term
3. Creation of new terms (neologisms).

Strategies for lexical modernisation in Hausa

1. Borrowing (from Arabic or English):
   (Engl.) *government*   > *gwamnatì*
   (Ar.) al qali (to judge)   > *àlkaalii*
2. Extension of the meaning of a native term:
   Ambassador   *jàkaadàa* (important palace messenger)
   development   *cîi gàba* (getting ahead, continuing)
3. Creation of new terms (neologisms):
   helicopter   *jirgin samà mài sàukař ūngūlu* (lit.vehicle-of above with landing-of vulture)
   United Nations   *Màjàlisař Dikìn Duuniyàa* (council-of sewing (up)-of world)

N.B. These neologisms may appear unusually long, but are fully accepted by Hausa speakers.

(McIntyre 1991)

Like lexicalisation, terminological modernisation is often characterised by puristic tendencies. The *Academy of the Hebrew Language* in Israel, for example, prefers Hebrew and Semitic roots (Aramaic, Cana'anite, Egyptian or Arabic) for the creation of new Hebrew words. Borrowing from non-Semitic languages is strongly discouraged (Fainberg 1983). Elaboration is an ongoing process in every language, as there is a never-ending need to develop new terms to talk and write about new ideas, concepts and inventions.

It is not easy to relate the four dimensions of language planning (corpus, status, prestige and acquisition planning) directly and unambiguously to the four stages of language planning (selection, codification, implementation and elaboration). Following Haugen (1987), codification and elaboration can be identified as aspects of corpus planning, while the dimensions of status, prestige and acquisition planning underlie the practices of selection and implementation. The aim of both models is to describe 'what' language planners do, and little attention is paid to the 'how', that is, how do language planners arrive at their descisons. To approach this question in a more systematic manner, a framework called the 'Rational Choice Model' was developed.

12.4   THE RATIONAL CHOICE MODEL AND ITS CRITICS

The logic of language planning is rooted in the recognition of language as a societal resource. Some language-planning theorists argue that in a similar way to the use of natural resources (water, gold, coal and so on), the use of language(s) in society can be rationally and systematically planned (Jernudd and Das Gupta 1971). As in economic planning, goals are identified, means through which to achieve these goals are determined and outcomes and consequences are predicted and monitored. Within this general planning model, language planning can be characterised as a method of decision-making in which a rational choice between alternative solutions is made. Five important steps guide the decision procedure:

1. Identification of the problem and fact-finding.
2. Specification of goals (development of a language policy).
3. Production of possible solutions, cost-benefit analysis of the alternative solutions and rational choice of one solution (decision-making stage).
4. Implementation of the solution.
5. Evaluation of the solution, that is, comparing predicted and actual outcomes.

(based on Rubin 1971; Jernudd 1971)

According to this model, language planning is applied to solve language problems, and the identification of the problem forms, therefore, the first important step. Lack of graphisation, codification and/or modernisation are often identified as problems by language planners (Jernudd and das Gupta 1971).

Ideally, language planning should take place against the background of an in-depth sociolinguistic profile of a country. Fact-finding as a prerequisite for rational decision-making includes, for example, the carrying-out of national censuses and/or large-scale sociolinguistic surveys to investigate the number of mother-tongue speakers, number of second-language speakers, degree of bilingualism and patterns of language choice and maintenance, as well as language attitudes in a given society. However, sociolinguistic fact-finding, typically conducted with the help of questionnaires, is not an easy enterprise. Language planners often operate under financial constraints and have neither the time nor the money to conduct extensive fieldwork to establish patterns and facts of language use in a country. In addition, the way in which questions are phrased not only determines the answers one gets, but in many communities there is no straightforward answer to apparently simple questions such as 'what is your mother tongue?' Is your mother tongue the language(s) you learned first, the language(s) you know best or the language(s) you use most? Or does the concept of mother tongue transcend all these definitions based on origin, function and competence? Is it rather to be understood in terms of identity, that is, is your mother tongue the language you identify with (Skutnabb-Kangas and Phillipson 1989)?

What is your mother tongue?
My father's home language was Swazi, and my mother's home language was Tswana. But as I grew up in a Zulu-speaking area we used mainly Zulu and Swazi at home. But from my mother's side I also learned Tswana well. In my high school I came into contact with lots of Sotho and Tswana students, so I can speak these two languages well. And of course I know English and Afrikaans. With my friends I also use Tsotsitaal.
(23-year-old male student from Germiston, South Africa)
(quoted in Mesthrie 1995: xvi)

Different questions will elicit different answers and in some cases national census questionnaires have changed through time, making it difficult to obtain a clear picture of changing patterns of language use within a society for policy purposes. This can be seen with respect to the Australian Census where language-related questions have changed significantly throughout the twentieth century:

- In 1921 respondents were asked if they could read and write;
- In 1933 respondents were asked if they could read and write a foreign language *if* they are unable to read and write English (many of Australia's residents are migrants from non-English speaking countries, cf. Chapter 4);
- Between 1947 and 1971 there were no language-related questions in the census;

- In 1976 respondents were asked to list 'all languages regularly used';
- In 1981 a question on the ability to speak English was introduced;
- Since 1986 the census includes two language-related questions: (a) language used in the home, and (b) self-assessed ability to speak English.

A further complication arises from the fact that similar and even identical questions can be answered quite differently depending on the sociohistorical context. A good example of this is the census data collected in the USA between 1960 and 1970 (Fishman et al. 1985). During this period, non-English mother-tongue claims increased dramatically. While the general population rose by only some 13 per cent, the increase in non-English mother-tongue claiming amounted to over 70 per cent. This has been interpreted as a result of the widespread discussion of ethnopolitical issues and the formation of strong ethnic identities in America during the 1960s.

An Example of Census Language Questions: Canada
The Canadian Census has included language questions since 1901. The census data provides important information for understanding the multilingual nature of Canadian society, where the percentage of those speaking a language other than English in the home is growing due to international migration. Canada also has many indigenous minority languages (such as, for example, Inuit and Cree), and recognizes two official languages: English and French. In 2006 the census asked the following questions:

Question 13. Can this person speak English or French well enough to conduct a conversation?
 English only/ French only/ Both English and French/ Neither English nor French.

Question 14. What language(s), **other than English or French**, can this person speak well enough to conduct a conversation?
 None/ Specify _____

Question 15a. What language does this person speak **most often** at home?
 English/ French/ Other, Specify _____

Question 15b. Does this person speak any other languages **on a regular basis** at home?
 None/ Yes, English/ Yes, French/ Yes, Other, Specify

_____

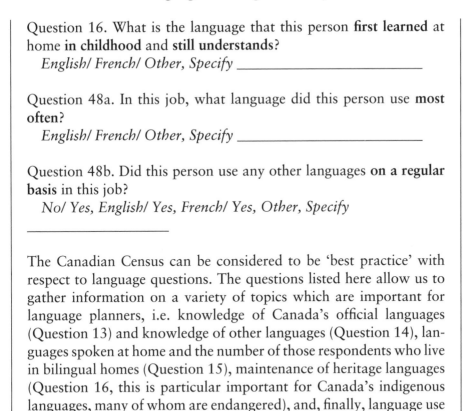

Question 16. What is the language that this person **first learned** at home **in childhood** and **still understands?**
English/ French/ Other, Specify _____

Question 48a. In this job, what language did this person use **most often?**
English/ French/ Other, Specify _____

Question 48b. Did this person use any other languages **on a regular basis** in this job?
No/ Yes, English/ Yes, French/ Yes, Other, Specify

_____

The Canadian Census can be considered to be 'best practice' with respect to language questions. The questions listed here allow us to gather information on a variety of topics which are important for language planners, i.e. knowledge of Canada's official languages (Question 13) and knowledge of other languages (Question 14), languages spoken at home and the number of those respondents who live in bilingual homes (Question 15), maintenance of heritage languages (Question 16, this is particular important for Canada's indigenous languages, many of whom are endangered), and, finally, language use in the workplace (Question 48).

Cost-benefit analysis (CBA) is used widely by economists and aims at identifying, quantifying and evaluating the monetary consequences of different business alternatives (Thorburn 1971). CBA as applied to fields of governmental decision-making (such as social policy, health policy and language policy) differs considerably from strictly economic CBA, in that non-material consequences need to be considered. Cost-benefit analysis can play a useful role in language planning. It not only forces the language planner to specify goals, identify problems and clarify consequences, but also provides an extra piece of information that can be taken into account for the decision making process. The application of cost-benefit analysis in language planning is difficult for two reasons. First, the long time-frame of many language-planning decisions (often stretching over several decades) makes it difficult to calculate costs and benefits accurately. Secondly, and more importantly, benefits of language planning are generally not calculable in monetary terms (Thorburn 1971; Coulmas 1992: 140–1; Grin 1996). For example, official bilingualism in Belgium (French/Dutch) is a rather costly enterprise. The alternative (French only or Dutch only) could, however, lead to social unrest and political conflict, as the nexus between

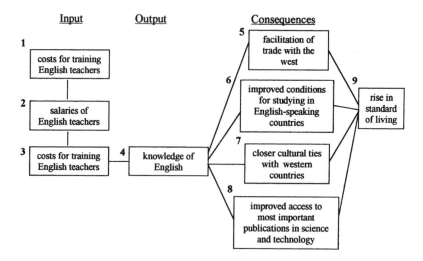

The costs are listed in boxes 1–3 and the main benefit of the alternative is given in box 4 ('knowledge of English'). The direct and indirect consequences of the alternative are summarised in boxes 5–9.

Figure 12.3   Cost-benefit analysis for the adoption of English as first foreign language in Poland (from Coulmas 1992: 143)

linguistic and cultural identity is particularly strong in Belgium. Figure 12.3 gives a hypothetical example of the use of CBA in language planning. The question of whether Russian, taught traditionally in Poland as the first foreign language, should be replaced by English was a very real problem facing many eastern European countries in the early 1990s (Coulmas 1992: 143–5). In the terminology of CBA, two alternatives are considered in this case: the *zero alternative* of leaving the curricula unchanged, and the *main alternative* of replacing Russian with English. The costs and benefits resulting from the introduction of English as the first foreign language are listed in the graphic model.

The rational-choice model assumes that language planning is conducted by a central authority, which controls and coordinates the steps required for reaching an informed and rational decision. Many definitions of language planning, therefore, identify governments and government-authorised agencies as the main agents of language-planning activities (see Cooper 1989: 30–1). This approach to language planning has been criticised by, for example, African academics who view it as Eurocentric, idealistic and alien to African experiences of language planning (Bamgbose 1987; Chumbow 1987; Alexander 1992). While language planning in the developed countries has often been initiated and implemented at government level, much language-planning work in Africa is done by non-governmental institutions. Furthermore, few African governments have specified explicit language policies. In most cases, language-planning decisions are not rationally based on sociolinguistic fact-finding, and implementation strategies are often determined on an *ad hoc* basis.

Some language planners have therefore argued that it is too narrow to adopt a definition of language planning which centres around planning activities conducted formally and rationally by a central authority. In reality, language planning rarely conforms to this ideal, and more often than not language planning is 'a messy affair, *ad hoc,* haphazard, and emotionally driven' (Cooper 1989: 41). It can be conducted by a wide range of institutions apart from governments, including language academies, ministries of education, churches, language societies, pressure groups and

---

The Ethnologue

In addition to specialized national surveys and census data, the *Ethnologue* – a publication of the Summer Institute of Linguistics (a non-governmental, non-profit organization focusing on issues of language documentation and development) – provides important information for those interested in language policy and planning (and linguistic diversity more generally). The *Ethnologue* is currently in its 15th edition (Gordon 2005) and has an on-line version which is publicly available (www.ethnologue.com). The aim of the Ethnologue is to provide a full catalogue of the world's languages, to indicate their linguistic relationships (by giving information on language families), and to describe linguistic profiles at state level.

Generally, the *Ethnologue* is considered to be fairly reliable, due to its large network of professional linguists which supply most of the data updates. However, the *Ethnologue* has been criticized for its occasional reliance on old sources. Paolillo (2006) notes, for example, that the reported number of 120 speakers for the Nigerian language Beele is based on a source from 1920. He concludes, "It is unclear whether [this language] would have survived to the present day with such small numbers of speakers." Due to capacity constraints (a staff of only three), data updates are slow, especially with regard to language endangerment and population figures. Many languages still listed on the *Ethnologue* are believed to be extinct by linguists. Paolillo (2006) provides the following overall assessment regarding the reliability of the *Ethnologue*: "[T]he language statistics available today in the form of the *Ethnologue* population counts are already good enough to be useful, and to guide us in learning about the global situation of language diversity. Many areas of improvement remain, however, and the overall order of the task of improving the state of language statistics remains very large."

even individuals (Haugen 1966: 168). The efforts of the feminist movement to combat instances of linguistic sexism (such as the use of generic *he* and *men* as well as the use of *man* in compounds; see section 10.5) are an example of such a non-governmental, decentralised language-planning process. The fragmented nature of the feminist movement made it impossible to conduct language planning within the rational-choice model (including procedures such as fact-finding, cost-benefit analysis and systematic evaluation). Despite its haphazard nature, the feminist movement was exceptionally successful. An analysis of half a million words of running text from a wide range of American publications carried out by Robert L. Cooper in the early 1980s shows a dramatic decline in the use of masculine generic forms between 1971 and 1979. Style guides used in the publishing industry have also adopted many of the suggestions made by feminist organisations (Cooper 1984; see also Fasold et al. 1990). In order to include non-governmental strategies of deliberate language change under the term 'language planning' Cooper has suggested the following definition: 'Language planning refers to deliberate efforts to influence the behaviour of others with respect to the acquisition, structure and functional allocation of their language codes' (Cooper 1989: 45).

12.5   THE QUESTION OF ACCEPTANCE

In an important article entitled *'Linguistics and language planning'* (1966), Haugen identified the 'acceptability criterion' as a hallmark of 'good' language planning. The 'acceptability criterion' simply refers to the probability that the proposed corpus and/or status changes will be accepted by the society concerned. Two approaches to language planning in general and the question of acceptability in particular are commonly distinguished in the literature on language planning: the **instrumental approach** and the **sociolinguistic approach** (Haugen 1971; Fasold 1984).

The instrumental approach, as expressed in the work of Punya Sloka Ray (1963) and Valter Tauli (1968), views languages as mere tools for communication, necessarily imperfect in their natural state. The central aim of language planning is the methodological improvement of the linguistic system based on a language ideal which is characterised not only by linguistic efficiency (i.e. easy to learn and use) and communicative adequacy, but also by uniformity and 'beauty' (Tauli 1968: 29–42). The possible symbolic value of a language or language variety as an expression of group solidarity and identity is largely ignored, and language attitudes which might run counter to the acceptance of proposed linguistic 'improvements' or status changes are believed to be easily changeable by propaganda and the exercise of political power and authority (ibid.: 152–3). **Linguistic**

engineering is sometimes used to refer to this approach, which often focuses on changes affecting the language corpus and perceives language planning as a mere technical, linguistic exercise.

However, the fact that acceptability does not depend on linguistic criteria alone becomes clear when one takes a look at the attempts to establish an artificial language as medium for international communication. The linguistic structure of artificial languages, such as Esperanto, has been constructed according to a linguistic ideal similar to the one expressed by Tauli: an international language should be clear, easy to learn, regular, 'aesthetic' and highly standardised. Yet, despite their claims to linguistic efficiency, uniformity and communicative adequacy, none of the over 600 artificial languages that have been developed has succeeded as a language for international communication (Sakaguchi 1989). It seems that other criteria than narrowly linguistic ones are to blame for this failure of implementation (lack of political and economic power as well as negative attitudes to the 'unnatural' character of artificial languages might be some of those non-linguistic reasons).

The **sociolinguistic approach** to language planning stresses the social and symbolic context of language use and the importance of language attitudes. Since languages are embedded in the social life of their users, language planning cannot proceed successfully by considering purely linguistic questions alone. Effective planning depends on the understanding of the relevant social, cultural, political and historical variables, knowledge of language attitudes and the direction of social change in a given society. From this, it follows that linguists are not the only one whose expertise is needed in language planning. Political scientists, economists, sociologists, educationists and anthropologists also have important roles to play. Yet, it appears that sociolinguists are particularly well equipped for participation in language-planning activities. Knowledge about the interrelationship between language and society, as well as expertise in the more narrowly linguistic questions such as mutual intelligibility, seems to be the mixture of skills needed (Christian 1988).

12.6 LANGUAGE PLANNING, POWER AND IDEOLOGY

The need to develop a sociolinguistic approach to language planning is emphasised by the fact that language-planning activities often form part of a wider social engineering and are employed to achieve non-linguistic goals, such as socioeconomic modernisation or national integration (Rabin 1971; Cooper 1989). In such cases, linguistic choices are made for purposes other than narrowly linguistic ones, and language planning becomes central to the attainment of more general political goals. For example, at the beginning of the twentieth century, some Chinese intellectuals attributed the perceived backwardness of their country (when compared to the technically advanced western nations) to a large degree to the nature of the Chinese character script. Written Chinese was believed to be difficult to learn and use, and to contribute to high levels of illiteracy. Widespread literacy, however, was seen as the necessary prerequisite for the spread of technology and science, which turn would facilitate the effective modernisation of China's society. One of the advocates for script reform, Lu Zhuanzhang, wrote in 1892:

> Chinese characters are probably the most difficult script in the world . . . I believe that the strength and prosperity of the country depends upon the physical sciences which can grow and flourish only if all people – men and women, old and young – are eager to learn and sensible. To them to be eager to learn and sensible depends upon the phonetization of the script . . . it depends upon having a simple script that is easy to learn and write. As a result, this will save more than ten years time. If all that time is applied to the study of mathematics, physical sciences, chemistry and other practical studies, how can there be any fear that our country will not be rich and strong.
>
> (quoted in P. Chen 1996: 17)

Thus, script reform was believed to contribute directly to social change (see S. R. Ramsey 1987; P. Chen 1993, 1996). Proposals for script reform focused on two areas: development of a simplified, phonemic script based on the spoken standard language,[2] and simplification and standardisation of the complex Chinese character script. More than 1,000 systems for the phonemic representation of Chinese have been proposed during the last 100 years. Of these, only *Pínyín*, which uses the Roman alphabet and assumes phonemic representation, has received full government support (since 1958) and is currently used in literacy programmes and the teaching of Chinese as a second language. Simplification and standardisation of the character script is carried out by the Committee on *Language Reform*. In 1964, the committee published a list of over 2,000 simplified characters.

Figure 12.4 Simplified Chinese characters (based on S. R. Ramsey 1987: 148–9) (top left: complex form for *yin*; top right: complex form for *yang*; bottom row: simplified equivalent characters)

However, as this is only about a third of the over 7,000 characters required to write modern Chinese, one still has to master a large number of complex characters to be fully literate.

Young Chinese intellectuals were the leading figures in the promotion of the Chinese script reform. Descriptions of language-planning cases have shown repeatedly how social and political elites regularly take the leading role in language-planning activities. It is typically the politically or economically powerful groups in society who identify the existence of a language problem and establish the goals to be achieved. Without their support, success is unlikely (Haugen 1966; Cooper 1989).

The role of elites in language planning
Language planning may be initiated at any level of the social hierarchy, but it is unlikely to succeed unless it is embraced and promoted by elites and counterelites . . . . Neither elites nor counterelites are likely to embrace the language planning initiatives by others unless they perceive it to be in their own interest to do so . . . . Whereas it is in the interest of established elites to promote acceptance of a standard, it is in the interest of counterelites to promote acceptance of a counterstandard . . . . When counterelites seek to detach a periphery from a center and when existing elites try to keep the periphery from falling away, they promote collective symbols of affiliation.

(Cooper 1989: 183–4)

Assumptions and beliefs about what kind of linguistic order is beneficial for a community or nation influence the formulation of language-planning goals. Juan Cobarrubias (1983: 63–6) has identified four major ideologies that underlie the development of language policies: linguistic assimilation, linguistic pluralism, vernacularisation and internationalisation. The ideology of **linguistic assimilation** is based on the belief that everyone should be able to speak and function in the dominant language of the community or nation. Examples of this approach are numerous, and it is safe to say that linguistic assimilation has been the most common model for language planning. Statistical correlations between national multilingualism, poverty and lack of industrialisation have occasionally been interpreted as forming a causal relationship, and monolingualism was promoted as the cost-efficient way to development and economic progress (for a critical summary, see Coulmas 1992). Linguistic as well as cultural or ethnic variation was believed not only to obstruct communication, but also to generate social and political conflict which in turn would hinder economic progress. We have already mentioned the case of France, where the dialect spoken

Language policy and language rights

In the 1990s the notion of language rights (or linguistic human rights) became influential in language policy research and practice, and challenged existing ideologies of linguistic assimilation. Language rights can be considered to form a subset of cultural rights, and in 1996 the Universal Declaration on Linguistic Rights was signed by UNESCO and a number of non-governmental organisations in Barcelona, Spain. The most fundamental rights are stated in Article 3: the right to be recognised as a member of a language community, the right to use one's own language in private and public, and the right to use one's own name. Article 3 also recognises collective language rights: the right to education in one's own language, the right to have access to media in one's own language, the right to interact with the government in one's own language. Whether these collective rights can be met usually depends on the size of the speech community in a given territory, i.e. only if there are sufficient numbers of speakers will it be feasible for governments to offer mother tongue education.

In 1996 the Linguistic Society of American published a detailed list of language rights, applicable to the United States. This list constitutes a good starting point for discussion:

'At a minimum, all residents of the United States should be guaranteed the following linguistic rights:

A. To be allowed to express themselves, publicly or privately, in the language of their choice.
B. To maintain their native language and, should they so desire, to pass it on to their children.
C. When their facility in English is inadequate, to be provided a qualified interpreter in any proceeding in which the government endeavors to deprive them of life, liberty or property. Moreover, where there is a substantial linguistic minority in a community, interpretation ought to be provided by courts and other state agencies in any matter that significantly affects the public.
D. To have their children educated in a manner that affirmatively acknowledges their native language abilities as well as ensures their acquisition of English. Children can learn only when they understand their teachers. As a consequence, some use of children's native language in the classroom is often desirable if they are to be educated successfully.

E. To conduct business in the language of their choice.
F. To use their preferred language for private conversations in the workplace.
G. To have the opportunity to learn to speak, read and write English.'

Sociolinguists specialising in the area of language rights and language policy include Tove Skutnabb-Kangas (2000) and Stephen May (2001).

---

in the north was identified as the 'national language' and speakers of other dialects and languages were expected to adopt this 'national language'. Policies of linguistic assimilation are also regularly applied to immigrants, who are expected to learn the language of the majority culture while the use of their native language is restricted to private functions.[3]

In contrast to the ideology of linguistic assimilation, **linguistic pluralism** stresses the multilingual reality of societies and involves the 'coexistence of different language groups and their right to maintain and cultivate their languages on an equitable basis' (Cobarrubias 1983: 65). A well-known example of a pluralistic language policy is that of India where sixteen languages are officially recognised. Most of these languages are used on a regional basis, with only English and Hindi being used nationwide. Today, many language-planning theorists view cultural pluralism and multilingualism as sociolinguistic facts which have to be seen positively

---

The cost-efficiency of multilingual policies
A further instance that comes to mind readily is of a Melbourne construction firm with a large number of Mediterranean-origin workers. For some time the management laboured under the monolingual myth, the misapprehension that it was simpler, cheaper etc. to deal with all their workers, the Greeks, Italians, Portuguese, Spanish and Maltese labourers in English. Elaborate safety information was, as a result, imperfectly communicated, safety jeopardised, and accidents, miscommunication and conflict resulted. A change in strategy, using the naturally occurring affinity groups among the workers and utilising management with knowledge of the relevant languages, or work-leaders in language groups, as well as workplace English classes with some classroom focus on relevant occupational as well as general English, was judged by the management to be more effective and less costly than the denying of the diversity that existed. (LoBianco 1996: 38)

as resources upon which language planning must built, and not just as obstacles on the way to national unity and socioeconomic advancement. Language planners, such as the Australian Joseph LoBianco (1995, 1996), argue that linguistic pluralism in fact facilitates economic development. Pluralism has been identified as a central issue in the global economy, where increasing attention is also given to multi-skilling, consumerism, negotiation and communication. Accordingly, verbal mastery and discursive power in many different languages and language varieties are important for economic success.

Although today's language planners view multilingualism positively and are sensitive to the rights and needs of linguistic minorities, it is often difficult to justify pluralistic policies (especially in developing countries), as such policies are initially rather costly for the state. The training of teachers, translators and interpreters, the development of materials and the provision of multilingual broadcasting services can impose a considerable strain on the national budget. Language-related expenses are often hard to justify in the face of more pressing social problems such as severe unemployment, housing and health (on language and economy see Grin 2003).

The ideologies of internationalisation and vernacularisation refer to the status which a language policy assigns to the indigenous languages of the country. **Vernacularisation** involves the selection and restoration of an indigenous language or languages as main vehicles of communication and official language(s). An example is Papua New Guinea, where two pidgin-based indigenous languages (Tok Pisin and Hiri Motu) have official status alongside English. The ideology of **internationalisation** refers to the selection of a non-indigenous language of wider communication (often abbreviated to 'LWC' in language planning studies) as an official language or language of instruction. Just as with the ideology of linguistic assimilation, internationalisation is based on the paradigm of modernisation through westernisation and goes hand in hand with strategies of linguistic assimilation. The adoption of a non-indigenous language of wider communication, typically the language of the former colonial power, has characterised language planning in many postcolonial countries.

In the early days of language planning Western sociolinguists argued that the ethnic neutrality of a European language will help to prevent ethnic segregation and facilitate national integration. Choosing a foreign language was believed to be 'uniformly unfair' to all citizens, while choosing an indigenous language would give advantage to one ethnic group (Scotton 1978: 730). The consensus recommendation to the newly independent nations of Africa and Asia was to select a major European language for official use, while indigenous languages could serve other, more local, functions: "The result – stable diglossia – had the (perhaps unintended) effect of lowering the status . . . of indigenous languages . . . while elevating the status . . . of the former colonial language, [thus] helping to perpetuate the stratified, class-based structures of the colonial era" (Ricento 2006: 13). The educated upper and middle classes are often the only groups who are proficient in the former colonial language which was granted official status. As a result, social boundaries are erected and political power is distributed on the basis of knowledge of and access to the official language. Carol Myers-Scotton (1990) referred to this process as 'elite closure'. Internationalisation is perhaps most evident in Africa where, according to the 2007 edition of the *CIA World Factbook* English remains an official language in 52 countries/territories, French in 29 countries, Spanish and Arabic in 24 countries, and Portuguese in eight countries (the total number of countries/territories is 61).

However, policies of internationalisation have on the whole been unsuccessful in Africa. Bernd Heine reports that 'according to conservative estimates less than twenty percent of the African people are able to make use of their official language' (Heine 1992: 27). An example of internationalisation is Namibia's adoption of English as the only official language. Although more than twenty different languages are spoken in Namibia, the constitution of 1990 recognises only English as the official language. The official language policy for Namibia was laid down in 1981 in a document drafted by the liberation movement SWAPO (South West African People's Organisation) in cooperation with the *United Nations Institute for Namibia*. The document shows how the selection of an international language was seen as an instrument to create national loyalty and unity in Namibia: 'The aim of introducing English is to introduce an official language that will steer the people away from lingo-tribal affiliations and differences and create conditions conducive to national unity in the realm of language.' The constitutional provision for 'English only' is problematic in view of the fact that English is known by less than 10 per cent of the Namibian population. Furthermore, the necessary spread of English is hindered considerably by a shortage of competent teachers and a lack of suitable teaching material. Afrikaans, on the other hand, which is widely known especially in the south, stood no chance of being introduced as an official language in the newly independent Namibia because of its association with South Africa's policy of apartheid (Cluver 1993).

12.7 TWO CASE STUDIES: NORWAY AND SOUTH AFRICA

The deliberate development of two different written standard languages in Norway from the mid-nineteenth century is probably the best-known example in the research literature on language planning. Norwegian language planning started when the country gained its independence after more than four centuries of Danish domination (1380–1814). For over 400 years, Danish had been the language of administration and public life. By the time of independence, no common Norwegian language was spoken in Norway. Most members of the educated urban classes used a variety of Danish as their colloquial standard. This variety was strongly influenced by Norwegian pronunciation and, to a lesser extent, by Norwegian grammar and vocabulary. Artisans and working-class people, on the other hand, used language varieties which were closely related to the rural dialects but also showed some Danish influence. Finally, the dialects spoken by the farming community showed no influence from Danish, and differed greatly from one another (Haugen 1968). Norwegian nationalists soon identified this lack of a common Norwegian language as a problem and put the question of a national language on their agenda. In the 1850s, two opposing responses to the question of a national language, one revolutionary, one reformist, were formulated. The dialectologist Ivar Aasen (1813–96) promoted the creation of a common Norwegian language as a composite of the rural local dialects, while the schoolteacher Knud Knudsen (1812–95) advocated the gradual revision of Norwegian Danish in the direction of the prestigious speech varieties used by the educated urban classes (Haugen 1968).

Ivar Aasen: Concerning our written language (1836)
Now that our native land has again become what it once was, namely free and independent, it must be urgent for us to use an independent and national language, inasmuch as this is the foremost hall mark of a nation: . . .

   We do not need ever to go outside our borders for a language; we should search in our hiding places to find out what we ourselves possess before we go off to borrow from others . . . . While time and circumstances made the Copenhagen dialect dominant among us, our national language was nevertheless preserved and cultivated in the peasants' cottages in our valleys and along our coast . . . . The peasant has the honor of being the savior of our language; therefore one should listen to his speech.

(quoted in Haugen 1972: 295–8)

Both Aasen and Knudsen quickly engaged in the codification process and published grammatical descriptions and dictionaries. Aasen named his linguistic project *Landsmål* (Language of the Country). *Dansk-Norsk*

Codification of Landsmål and Dansk-Norsk/Riksmål in the nine-teenth century

1853	First sample of texts in Aasen's Proto-Norwegian 'Prøver af det norske Landsmål'
1856	Grammar of Riksmål
1864	Grammar of Landsmål
1873	Dictionary of Landsmål
1881	Dictionary of Riksmål

(Dano-Norwegian) and *Riksmål* (Language of the State) were the names used to refer to the variety promoted by Knudsen. Despite their difference in social basis (lower-class rural dialects versus urban upper-class speech), both proposals answered to the nationalist sentiments of the time. In 1885, the Norwegian parliament recognised both languages as official languages of Norway. This resolution formed the basis for the implementation of *Landsmål* and *Riksmål* in administration and the educational system, where the two standards have been in competition ever since *Landsmål* (since 1929 called *Nynorsk*, 'New Norwegian') and *Riksmål* (since 1929 called *Bokmål*, 'Book Language') are structurally similar and mutually comprehensible. The main linguistic difference lies in the area of morphology.

From the 1880s, the role of the government became increasingly prominent in Norwegian language planning. Official language committees were set up to deal with the linguistic modernisation of both standard languages, and to coordinate implementation strategies. The continuing competition between the two standards was soon felt to be awkward and impractical by many, and the idea of deliberately fusing the two languages in one gained popularity in the early twentieth century. Between 1917 and 1981, a language policy aiming at a future amalgamation of the two varieties into one written standard (*Samnorsk*, 'United Norwegian') was followed by the government. The procedure adopted was to gradually incorporate more Nynorsk forms into Bokmål and to replace the archaic dialectal forms found in Nynorsk with the more modern forms found in contemporary dialects. This procedure, however, implied that forms typical of working-class and rural speech (Nynorsk forms) had to be pushed into the prestigious standard of Bokmål, according to Jahr and Janicki a 'unique sociolinguistic experiment' (1995: 40). Ideologically, the government promoted these reforms within the framework of socialism. The envisaged new standard was referred to as the true *Folkemålet* ('People's Language'), uniting the Norwegian population and transcending the barriers of social class (Jahr 1989). However, the reforms failed ultimately because of the

Nynorsk/Bokmål

Nynorsk

Det rette heimelege mål i landet er det som landets folk har arva ifrå forfedrene, frå den eine ætta til den andre, og som no om stunder, trass i all fortrengsle og vanvørnad, enno har grunnlag og emne til eit bokmål, like så godt som noko av grannfolk-måla.

Bokmål

Det rette heimlige mål i landet er det som landets folk har arvet ifra forfedrene, fra den ene ætt til den andre, of som nå om stunder, trassi all fortrengsle og vanvørnad, ennå har grunnlag og emne til et bokmål, like så godt som noe av nabomålene.

English

The right native tongue in this country is the one that the people of the country have inherited from their ancestors, from one generation to the next, and which nowadays, in spite of all displacement and contempt, still has the basis and material for a written language just as good as any of the neighbours' languages.

(from Ivar Aasen: Minningar fraa Maalstriden (1859), in Haugen 1968)

strong resistance among Bokmål users. In 1981, a new official reform of Bokmål resulted in the acceptance of most conservative non-Nynorsk forms back into Bokmål.

Today, the *Norsk Språkråd* (Norwegian Language Council), founded in 1971, functions as the government's advisory body regarding the Norwegian languages. Amalgamation of Nynorsk and Bokmål has been abandoned in favour of a 'policy of dual cultivation' (Haugen 1983: 285). The Council also gives advice on general questions of language use, as for example in the case of non-sexist language (T. Bull 1992). Private persons and enterprise are not compelled to follow the advice of the Council, but its language recommendations are implemented in governmental and educational publications (Haugen 1983).

Since the end of the Second World War, Nynorsk has lost much of its formerly strong position in Norway. Over one-third of schoolchildren received their education in Nynorsk in 1944, compared to only 17 per cent today (Wiggen 1995). Because it is the preferred language only for a minority of Norwegians, Nynorsk is occasionally described as a minority language which enjoys equal rights with Bokmål only in its core area, the rural districts of north-western Norway (Oftedal 1990). Although the equality of Nynorsk and Bokmål is recognised by law, little is done to enforce these legal provisions (Vikør 1993).

Two standards – many standard forms
It is important to understand that (compared to many other European standard languages) the two Norwegian standard languages exhibit a great deal of intra-standard variation. Both standards allow a multitude of parallel morphological and lexical forms, the choice of which is left to the individual writer. The phrase *She takes the book out herself*, for example, allows the following optional forms:

Bokmål	*Hun/Ho*	*tar*	*fram/frem*	*boka/boken*	*selv/sjøl.*
Nynorsk	*Ho*	*tek/tar*	*fram*	*boka/boki*	*sjølv.*
	she	takes	out	book-the	herself.

This means that writers can, for example, exaggerate the differences between Bokmål and Nynorsk by selecting the following forms:

| **Bokmål** | *Hun tar frem boken selv.* |
| **Nynorsk** | *Ho tek fram boki sjølv.* |

Or writers can aim at minimising the differences by choosing the forms common to both Nynorsk and Bokmål: *Ho tar fram boka sjøl(v)*. Often the selection of certain linguistic forms has political-ideological implications. Thus, to write *sjøl* is to indicate a progressive and left-wing position, while selv is used by conservatives.

(based on Jahr and Janicki 1995; Hansen 1997)

Questions concerning the status of minority languages have played an increasingly important role in the literature on language planning in recent years. In Norway, the positions of the Sámi languages and Finnish raise important issues of minority rights.

Equal rights for Nynorsk?
Post offices and other government services are required to provide forms in both languages. But in most such offices only Bokmål forms are in sight. If you want a Nynorsk form you have to ask for it, and as often as not it cannot be found. (Oftedal 1990: 129)

The *Sámi* (also known as 'Lapps') are the indigenous people of Arctic Scandinavia and north-west Russia. At least three different Sámi languages, all of them belonging to the Finno-Ugric language family, are spoken by the approximately 30,000 Sámi who live in Norway: *Northern*

Sámi, *Southern Sámi* and *Lule Sámi* (Bull 1995). In 1990, the Norwegian parliament recognised the linguistic rights of the Sámi people and guaranteed Sámi equal status with Norwegian. Between 80 and 90 per cent of Norwegian Sámi live in northern Norway. This core area is called the *Sámpi*, and the linguistic rights guaranteed to the Sámi people are largely restricted to this area. In the Sámpi, all laws, regulations, official announcements and forms have to be offered in Sámi, and Sámi is used as a medium of instruction until the ninth school grade. The latter provision (mother-tongue education) also applies to Sámi people who live outside the core area; implementation is, however, still dependent on the availability of teachers (Corson 1995). The official recognition of Sámi in 1990 stands in sharp contrast to the policies of oppression and assimilation which dominated in Norway until the late 1960s, when Sámi was first introduced into the school system. Although the full implementation of the act from 1990 has been delayed by a lack of educational resources and trained Sámi teachers, the overall picture is positive, as the Canadian linguist David Corson (ibid.: 506) emphasises: 'In summary, only two years after the enforcement of the act, the language programs are reaching between 90% and 100% of Sámi children in Norway, who have identified themselves as candidates under the act'.

The future of the Sámi languages remains, nevertheless, uncertain. The use of Sámi is still decreasing and language shift towards Norwegian monolingualism continues, especially among Sámi people who live outside the core area (see Wiggen 1995; Bull 1995).

In contrast to Sámi, the language of the Norwegian Finns, who immigrated to Norway from the eighteenth century and speak a variety of Finnish called *Kven*, has no official position in Norway. The position of Kven is similar to other immigrant languages in Norway, in that it is taught in elementary schools but its use is generally restricted to the private sphere, and complete language shift to Norwegian monolingualism seems inevitable (Wiggen 1995).

South Africa does not have a single main language that could function as a likely candidate for an official language. More than twenty different languages are spoken throughout the country. Apart from the members of the four major African language groups Nguni (Ndebele, Swati, Xhosa, Zulu), Sotho (Northern Sotho, Southern Sotho, Tswana), Tsonga and Venda, there are the former official languages English and Afrikaans, as well as at least six European immigrant languages (Dutch, German, Greek, Italian, Portuguese and French), five Indian languages (Tamil, Hindi-Bhojpuri, Telugu, Gujarati and Urdu), several African languages from neighbouring countries, a minimum of three Chinese languages as well as South African Sign Language. Furthermore, there are small numbers of speakers of the indigenous Khoisan languages. The census data show that over 75 per cent

South Africa's home languages (2001)

	Number of speakers	Percentage of the population
Zulu	10 677 305	23.8
Xhosa	7 907 153	17.6
Afrikaans	5 983 426	13.4
Northern Sotho	4 208 980	9.3
Tswana	3 677 016	8.2
English	3 673 203	8.2
Southern Sotho	3 555 186	7.9
Tsonga	1 992 207	4.4
Swati	1 194 430	2.7
Venda	1 021 757	2.3
Ndebele	711 821	1.6
Other	217 000	0.5

South African Census 2001

of all South Africans use an African language as their home language, and less than 25 per cent use either English or Afrikaans.[4]

During the apartheid era (1948–94), South Africa had only two official languages, English and Afrikaans. The nine indigenous African languages, however, had regional co-official status in the respective self-governing or independent territories (the so-called 'homelands'). In 1990, negotiations between the apartheid government and the liberation movement the *African National Congress* (ANC) opened the path for a new political order. The ANC had by the early 1990s identified language as an area in need of planning for post-apartheid South Africa, and it was evident that the former state bilingualism with Afrikaans and English as official languages would not survive. English as the language of liberation and national unity had been a dominant theme in the ANC's language policy for a long time. Since the late 1980s, however, a pluralist approach has surfaced in the debate. The original view of English as the language of liberation has yielded to a new principle of promoting the indigenous languages (Crawhall 1993: 19–20). Although individual multilingualism is widespread in South Africa, it typically involves proficiency in African languages. Levels of proficiency in English, on the other hand, are low, and recent research has shown that one-third of the South African population has no understanding of English at all (Webb 1995: 17, 33). The adoption of English as the only official language would have thus excluded more than one-third of the population from meaningful political participation, and would have disadvantaged them in the education system and labour market.

An interesting contribution to the debate over a new South African language policy came in the late 1980s from the educationist and language-planner Neville Alexander (1989). Drawing on suggestions made in the 1940s by the ANC member Jacob Nhlapo, Alexander proposed creating a *Standard Nguni* based on Ndebele, Swazi, Xhosa, and Zulu, and a *Standard Sotho* based on Pedi, South Sotho and Tswana. According to Alexander, both language groups are essentially clusters of mutually intelligible dialects. Alexander's proposal is similar to Ivar Aasen's construction of Landsmål as an amalgamation of features found in the rural Norwegian dialects. Linguistic unification was also relatively successful in Zimbabwe, where Standard Shona was developed from five Shona dialects (Cluver 1994). However, the dialects which were used as the basis for the new standards in Norway and Zimbabwe were unstandardised. Acceptance of the new unified standard languages, therefore, did not clash with existing sociolinguistic norms and identities, which are strong in South Africa.

South Africa's new constitution was tabled and introduced in April 1996. In article 6 of the constitution, all eleven languages which had official or regional co-official status under the former regime are recognised

---

Constitutional multilingualism

(1) The official languages of the Republic are Sepedi [Northern Sotho], Sesotho [Southern Sotho], Setswana, siSwati, Tshivenda, Xitsonga, Afrikaans, English, isiNdebele, isiXhosa and isiZulu.

(2) Recognising the historically diminished use and status of the indigenous languages of our people, the state must take practical and positive measures to elevate the status and advance the use of these languages . . .

(4) The Pan South African Language Board must –
   a. promote and create conditions for the development and use of
      i. all official languages;
      ii. the Khoi, Nama and San languages; and
      iii. sign language.
   b. promote and ensure respect for languages, including German, Greek, Gujarati, Hindi, Portuguese, Tamil, Telugu, Urdu, and others commonly used by communities in South Africa, and Arabic, Hebrew, Sanskrit and others used for religious purposes.

(Constitution of South Africa 1996)[5]

as official languages throughout the country. Furthermore, community languages such as the Indian languages and South African Sign Language are guaranteed government support.

Clearly, a range of problems emanates from these provisions when it comes to the crucial step of implementation. The *Curriculum Framework for General and Further Education and Training* (December 1995) and the *Curriculum 2005* (March 1997) promote multilingualism as a guiding principle of the national curriculum and advocate the development of multilingual skills at school. So far, schools have been single-medium and have taught additional languages only as second languages. Language-planners like Neville Alexander have thus called repeatedly for a definite commitment to the establishment of multilingual schools (schools which use more than one medium of instruction) to fulfil the constitutional provisions (Alexander 1997). However, so far there are few teachers adequately prepared for the teaching practice in such multilingual schools, and teaching materials are not yet available for the higher grades. Financial constraints on the school budget often make it difficult for state-aided schools to hire new teachers for the African languages which are now being promoted in the schools. Furthermore, many parents, whose home language is a language other than English, prefer their children to receive their schooling in English and not in their first language (L1).

Although English is *de jure* only one of the official languages of the country, its position as a medium of international communication and its dominant position in South African public life (politics, media and economy) leads many parents to assume that knowledge of English is a guarantee for success and a better life (DeKlerk 2000; De Kadt 2002, 2005). Another area which highlights the problems associated with the implementation of the multilingual provisions and the recognition of language rights is the communication in South African courts. Article 35 (3h) of the constitution states: 'Every accused has a right to a fair trial which includes the right to be tried in a language that the accused person understands, or if that is not practicable, to have the proceedings interpreted in that language.' Usually this right is ensured with the help of interpreters. However, the constitutional guarantee to a fair trial can be undermined by poor translations. In a study of court communication in the province KwaZulu-Natal, N. C. Steytler (1993) has shown that inaccurate translations have been a common phenomenon in South African courts, often to the disadvantage of the accused.

Similar problems have been reported for the health sector, where diagnosis and adequate treatment depend on effective communication. Interpreting in hospitals is typically done by nurses, who mostly have an

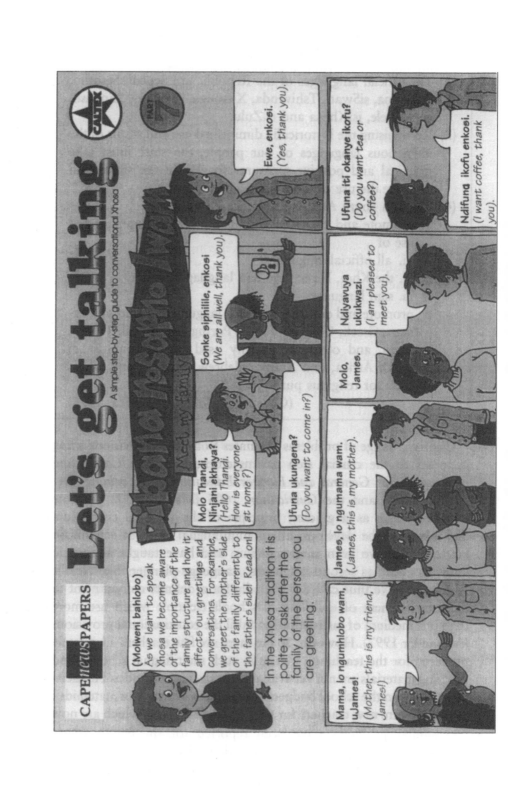

Promoting the learning of African languages: 'Let's get talking', sponsored by Caltex.

African language as their L1. They are, however, not trained as interpreters and receive no recognition for their services.

To ensure the implementation of the constitutional provisions, an independent body, the *Pan South African Language Board* (PANSALB), was created in 1996. The Language Board is expected to play a crucial role in the realisation of South Africa's language policy. It will advise national and provincial governments on language legislation, develop and support the official and non-official languages of the country and ensure the protection of language rights. In short, its brief is the promotion and realisation of the constitutional provisions for a multilingual South Africa. In addition, non-governmental organisations have always played an important role in South African language planning and will continue to do so. An example of a non-governmental activity regarding the promotion and spread of African languages is a language course for Xhosa as a second language, which has been published in community newspapers in the Western Cape in the 1990s and was financed by a major oil company. However, whether these comic strips will actually get people to learn Xhosa is questionable.

Examples of court communication in South Africa

(a) *The accused tries to initiate bail.*

Accused (Zulu): Please ask for payment so that I will be out.

Interpreter (Zulu): That is not my business. Go down! (*indicating towards the cells*)

This conversation was not translated and the magistrate did not instruct the interpreter to interpret it.

(b) *The prosecutor read out the following charge.*

Prosecutor (English): The charge against the accused is that he contravened section 2(b) of act 41 of 1971 read with section 10(3) in that on [date] at or near Warwick avenue in the district of Durban he had wrongfully and unlawfully in his possession a prohibited dependence-producing substance to wit a small quantity of dagga (marijuana). How do you plead?

Interpreter (Zulu): Do you find yourself guilty?

Accused (Zulu): I do have a case against me.

Interpreter (English): I plead guilty.

Steytler's study shows that in a large number of cases the charge was not interpreted for the accused.

(from Steytler 1993: 42, 45)

12.8 CONCLUSION

The more recent language-planning activities in Norway and South Africa illustrate some of the topics which have become prominent in language-planning research in the 1990s, for example the maintenance and support of minority languages (such as the protection of *Sámi* in Norway or the Indian languages in South Africa) and the implementation of pluralistic language policies (as exemplified in South Africa's constitution and the promotion of two standard languages in Norway).

Language planning has come a long way since its early days. Taxonomies such as Kloss's distinction between status and corpus planning or Haugen's processes of language planning have been useful for the description of language-planning case studies which form the bulk of language-planning research. However, language planning is still far from being able to offer explanations and guidelines for the development of language policies. The interdisciplinary nature of the field, which involves not only linguistic matters but also social, political and historical factors, makes the development of a comprehensive theory of language planning difficult.

Notes

1. Usually the term 'status' is used to mean 'rank', '(social) position' or even 'prestige'. Kloss, however, uses the term as a synonym for 'function' or 'domain'.
2. What is called the 'Chinese language' is in reality a cluster of extremely diverse and mutually unintelligible regional varieties which are best described as separate languages. Based on the grammar of Northern Mandarin and the Beijing pronunciation, a lingua franca had been used in China since the fifteenth century, mainly for the administration of the empire. A common version of this lingua franca (called *pŭtōngua*) functions as the spoken standard in modern China.
3. Linguists estimate that between 5,000 and 7,000 languages are spoken worldwide. However, in the 1990s only 104 languages were granted official state in the then 195 political states (Daoust 1997: 451–2).
4. It is difficult to obtain accurate figures on language use in South Africa. The linguistic data given by the last population census of 2001 refer only to the language used at home. Proficiency in other languages, which is widespread among many black South Africans, is not reflected in the census data.
5. The constitution refers to South Africa's African languages with their noun class prefixes, i.e. *isiZulu* rather than *Zulu*. In Nguni *isi-* is a prefix which is used when referring to the language, *ama-* is used when referring to the people (i.e. *isiZulu*, the Zulu language; *amaZulu*, the Zulu people). In current usage both forms (*isiZulu and Zulu*) are found. In this book we have used the languages names without prefixes as this remains the norm in most

international publications on African languages. For a useful discussion of the pros and cons of using prefixes (and the political implications of language naming in the South African context) see: http://translate.org.za/content/view/1591/63/lang.en-za.

13

THE SOCIOLINGUISTICS OF SIGN LANGUAGE

13.1 INTRODUCTION

Sign languages are used by Deaf people as their primary means of communication. Unlike spoken languages which rely on sound and hearing, sign
languages are visual-gestural languages perceived through the eyes, not the
ears and using body movement instead of sound (Baker-Shenk and Cokely
1991: 47–8). From early on linguists have paid attention to social and
cultural factors which have shaped the use of sign languages (e.g. Stokoe
1969–70; Woodward 1972). Linguists have studied, for example, aspects
of sociolinguistic variation in sign languages (e.g. Battison et al. 1975;
Woodward 1974, 1975; Shroyer and Shroyer 1984), language contact
(between sign languages and spoken languages; see Chapter 8), language
attitudes (e.g. Kannapell 1989; Valli et al. 1992; Burns et al. 2001), and
language policy and planning (e.g. Ramsey 1989; Reagan 2001). Two
important anthologies of sign sociolinguistics have been edited by Ceil
Lucas (1989; 2001), who is also the series editor for the 'Sociolinguistics in
Deaf Communities' series published by Gallaudet University Press.

Presenting the sociolinguistics of sign languages in a separate chapter
is not intended to suggest that sign languages are in any meaningful way
different from spoken languages. Sign languages are ordinary human languages and are used to communicate about the same things hearing people
communicate about using spoken language. However, as many people
know relatively little about sign languages, we thought it useful to describe
this group of languages in some detail.

To follow the discussion presented in this chapter, it is necessary to
have an understanding of some of the linguistic aspects of sign languages.
An overview of structural aspects of sign languages is, therefore, given in
section 13.2. In writing down sign language we have followed the conventions used by Lucas (1989): sign translations into English are represented
in capital letters (GIVE), while fingerspellings are separated by hyphens
(G-I-V-E).

13.2   SOME ASPECTS OF THE STRUCTURE OF SIGN LANGUAGES AND OTHER SIGN SYSTEMS

Contrary to common beliefs among hearing people, sign languages are not pantomine-like systems of gestures, universally understood and restricted in content and expression. They are autonomous natural languages with the same degree of linguistic complexity and expressive range as spoken languages. Although the sign languages used in different countries by different communities show some lexical and grammatical similarities, they are not mutually intelligible: Australian Sign Language cannot be understood by users of Chinese Sign Language, nor can Swedish Sign Language be understood by users of Russian Sign Language and so forth. Sign languages are also independent from the majority spoken languages in the countries in which they are used: for example the dominant spoken language in the USA and the UK is English, but the sign languages used in the two countries are mutually unintelligible. At the same time, however, research has shown that the different national sign languages use similar mechanisms to express grammatical structures.

Like spoken languages, sign languages are rule-governed and structured at different levels of analysis: semantics, syntax, morphology and phonology. And just as spoken words are combinations of different sounds, signs are also made up of individual components. Sign-language research has shown that four components are important for the identification and distinction of individual signs:

1. the **location** of the sign in space
2. the **handshape** used to make the sign
3. the type of **movement** made by the hands
4. the **orientation** of the palms of the hands. (Kyle and Woll 1985: 28)

In spoken language, it is possible to arrange pairs of words which differ by just one unit of sound but have an entirely different meaning (*real* versus *zeal*, *cat* versus *mat* and so on). Such pairs of words are called **minimal pairs** and provide important information about the phonemic contrasts in a language. In sign languages, a change in any one of the four components listed above can also result in a change of meaning. Signs can, therefore, be arranged in pairs just as with words in spoken languages. The signs for MAKE and TALK in British Sign Language (BSL), given in Figure 13.1, are an example of such a minimal pair.

Sign languages involve not only (manual) signs made by the hands; other parts of the body also participate in the language production. **Non-manual features** (such as facial expressions, lip movements, posture, orientation and movement of head or body) are frequently used to indicate morphological and grammatical categories in natural sign languages. In American

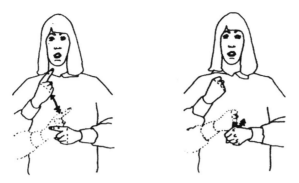

Figure 13.1 BSL signs for TALK/MAKE. Both signs are made in front of the chest (location) with the same movement (right hand taps left hand) and orientation (palm facing signer); only the handshape used to make the signs is different (index finger extended from a closed fist vs closed fist) (Kyle and Woll 1985: 91)

Sign Language (ASL), for example, two different types of questions are distinguished merely by facial signals: questions that can be answered simply by responding *yes* or *no* (such as *Would you like some coffee?*) are indicated by raised eyebrows, wide open eyes with the head and shoulders leaning slightly forward, while questions which seek information (i.e. questions beginning with *who*, *what*, *why*, *when* and so on in English) show squinted eyebrows with only the head moving slightly forward (Baker-Shenk and Cokely 1991). Other grammatical categories indicated by facial expressions include the relative clause marker, which is signalled in Swedish Sign Language by the following non-manual features: raised eyebrows, raised cheeks and the chin drawn back.

Figure 13.2 Non-manual encoding of grammatical categories in Swedish Sign Language: the relative clause marker (Bergman and Wallin 1991: 201)

Sign languages make use of a three-dimensional or **spatial grammar** to encode the grammatical relations between subject and object in a sentence. The space in front of the signer (roughly stretching from just below the waist to above the head, from elbow to elbow and stretching outwards in front of the signer) is used to indicate subject and object of the phrase which is being signed.

Nominal referents or pronouns are assigned positions in the signing space. The pronoun *you*, for example, is located in front of the chest, the third-person singular (*he* or *she*) slightly to the right and the first-person singular (*I*) is indicated by touching the chest (Figure 13.3).

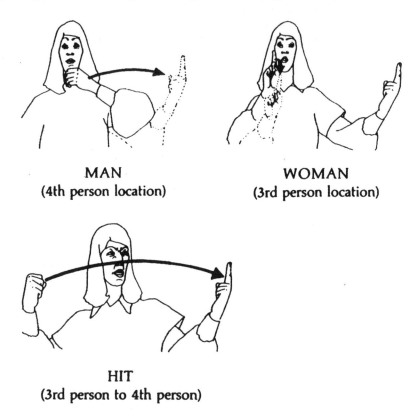

MAN
(4th person location)

WOMAN
(3rd person location)

HIT
(3rd person to 4th person)

WOMAN-HIT-MAN

First the sign for MAN (object) is made with the left hand in the appropriate location (in front of the chin), then the position of the object referent is established in the signing space (using the index finger held upright). The left hand (which indicates the object) is held stationary while the right hand signs the subject WOMAN (index finger extended from fist, palm facing away from signer, held beside the cheek and quick downward movement). Finally the right hand, now signing HIT (closed fist), moves sharply to the left hand (the object of the sentence).

Figure 13.3   Subject/Object encoding for the sentence *The woman hit the man* in BSL (Kyle and Woll 1985: 141)

Apart from natural sign languages, two other systems of signing are frequently used for communication with deaf people, and are often confused with natural sign languages by hearing people: fingerspelling and manual (artificial) sign codes.

Fingerspelling simply represents the letters of a written language directly, and different national alphabets exist. Fingerspelling is often used in sign languages to spell out the names of individuals (P-A-U-L-A) or place names, for which there are no established signs.

While sign languages have developed naturally in contexts where deaf

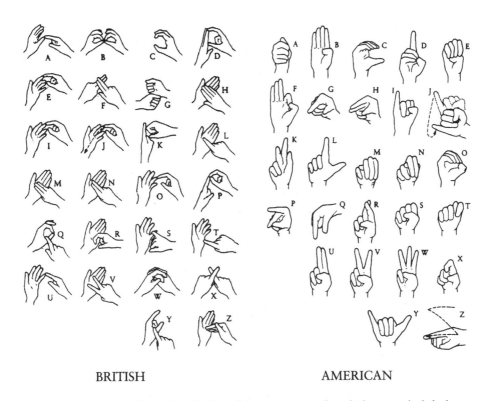

BRITISH   AMERICAN

Figure 13.4   British two-handed and American one-handed manual alphabet
(Crystal 1987: 225)

people interact with one another, **manual sign codes** (such as 'Seeing Exact English' [SEE-1], 'Signing Exact English' [SEE-2] or the Paget–Gorman System) have been artificially designed to represent the structure of a spoken language (English, German, Swedish, Russian and so on) in a visual modality, and are used predominantly in education. In these codes, signs from the national sign language (for example BSL) are borrowed, but arranged according to the word order of the spoken language (in this case English), and invented signs for inflections (such as -s for the third-person singular of verbs) are added. The resulting code is called signed or manually coded English (or Russian or German, depending on the spoken language that is represented manually). While sign languages have remained largely unstandardised, manual sign codes are highly standardised linguistic systems, artificially constructed and taught prescriptively (C. L. Ramsey 1989).

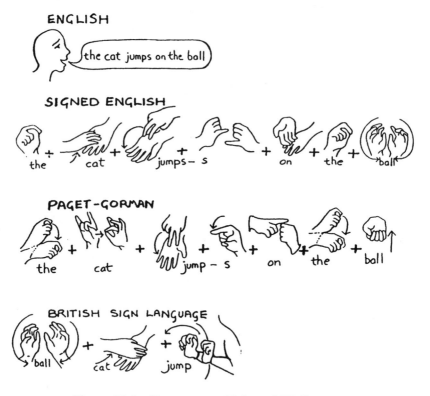

Figure 13.5   Sign systems (Kyle and Woll 1985: 248)

13.3   THE DEAF COMMUNITY AS A LINGUISTIC MINORITY

In contemporary industrial societies, medical deafness is a rather rare phenomenon, with fewer than 1,000 children born deaf or becoming deaf soon after birth. However, many more children lose their hearing in their early school period as a result of infectious diseases (such as rubella, meningitis or measles) which to date remain untreated in many Third World countries. Furthermore, people can lose their hearing in adulthood as a result of regular exposure to loud noise.

Clinical-pathological and audiological definitions of deafness, however, are only of limited use for understanding Deaf communities. Unlike the majority of hearing people, members of Deaf communities rarely view deafness simply or exclusively as a medical deficiency and disability. Rather it is also – if not primarily – viewed as a form of positive social and cultural identity, defined by shared beliefs and experiences, rules of inter-action, cultural narratives and, most centrally, the use of sign language (Baker-Shenk and Cokely 1991: 55–6). Linguists, anthropologists and sociologists therefore describe the various national Deaf communities as linguistic and cultural minorities which exist within a dominant hearing culture (Lane et al. 1996; Baker 1999).

Like other social-cultural groups Deaf communities show layers of mem-bership. Among the most important criteria for membership are the use of sign language as one's primary language, a positive attitude towards Deaf culture ('attitudinal Deafness') and active participation in Deaf social life and organisational networks (clubs, national organisations, schools etc.; cf. Baker-Shenk and Cokely 1991). Core members of these communities are typically Deaf children of Deaf parents, who have acquired sign language as their first language and who have been socialised into the Deaf com-munity from infancy. Audiologically deaf people, however, who have been acculturated into the hearing world and make no use of sign language are generally not considered to be part of Deaf communities. In addition, there are many states of partial or peripheral belonging, including, for example, the hard of hearing who use both sign language and spoken language, or the hearing children of Deaf parents who have acquired sign language as their first language, but who are also full members of the majority hearing group (cf. Senghas and Monaghan 2002: 73; Grushkin 2003).

The semantic and cultural distinction between physiological deafness and cultural/linguistic identity is captured symbolically by the Deaf/deaf convention: *Deaf* (with a capital letter) refers to those deaf individuals who identify themselves as members of Deaf communities; *deaf* (with a lower-case letter), on the other hand, describes individuals who are audiologically deaf, but do not identify with Deaf culture.[1] The in-group/out-group dis-tinction is further marked by a range of terms which are used within these communities to describe out-group members. In American Sign Language (ASL), for example, the sign ORAL can be used pejoratively to refer to deaf people who use speech and lip-reading as their primary means of commu-nication; the signs THINK-HEARING or HEARING-IN-THE-HEAD are used to describe deaf people who think and behave like hearing people, and who have not adopted Deaf culture (Humphries 1990: 222; Senghas and Monaghan 2002: 72). The cohesiveness of Deaf communities as separate sociocultural and linguistic groups is further strengthened by the existence of strong pattern of endogamous marriages (between 80 and 90 per cent of Deaf people marry within the Deaf community; cf. Marcowicz and Woodward 1978).

As minority groups within the majority hearing culture, Deaf communities are multilingual groups whose members make regular use not only of sign language, but also (to varying degrees) of the language(s) of the majority hearing culture (in its spoken, signed and written forms). While members of Deaf communities are typically bilingual in sign language and the majority (or spoken) language(s), knowledge of sign language(s) is extremely low among the hearing majority. Exceptions are individuals with Deaf family members and professional sign-language interpreters. Like other minority groups, the various national Deaf communities thus experience forms of societal marginalization and discrimination on the basis of language.

'Deaf fakes'?

Extract from an interview which Jennifer Harris conducted with Richard, who was born to hearing parents and became deaf as a child (through meningitis), in the early 1990s.

Richard: Now the Deaf saying instead of using; 'I am a strong sign language user' (say) 'I'm BSL' and it has become a real cultural obsession – a thing of great pride for the Deaf community. In fact the BDA (British Deaf Association) has become a BSL organisation, but if you look at history the people at the very beginning of the BDA were people like myself – deafened people, and now it is changing, and people like myself are in fact being pushed out.

J. Harris: Yes. Yes.

Richard: You see people like me are becoming called 'Not the Real Deaf'.

J. Harris: How does that make you feel?

Richard: Well. *I spoke to a born Deaf person, she said I was a fake* – that feeling was not there ten or fifteen years ago.

J. Harris: You were more sort of looked up to? Now you are sailing downwards?

Richard: Yes. Well it doesn't hurt me much. But what hurts me is – what disappoints me is the fear that the *BDA* could become an organisation of the *'True Deaf – the Real Deaf'* and people who could contribute enormously would be pushed out. I would like to see an organisation of ALL Deaf People.

(quoted in Harris 1995: 154–5)

Children born to Deaf parents enjoy the advantage of learning sign language as their first and natural language from an early age. Research has shown that sign-language acquisition by children of Deaf parents proceeds through developmental stages similar to those known for the acquisition of spoken languages by hearing children. Such children are known to 'babble' spontaneously (with their hands) and to acquire lexical and grammatical features of sign languages progressively by making errors almost identical to those made in spoken language acquisition (Deuchar and James 1985). Over 90 per cent of Deaf children, however, are born to hearing parents and, thus, grow up in a linguistic environment dominated by the spoken language with little exposure to sign language. Basic communication in hearing families with Deaf children is maintained by using **home-signs**, which are created spontaneously in communication and form a highly context-dependent and variable type of rudimentary sign language used primarily between family members (Mylander and Goldwin-Meadow 1991).

Home signs

I expressed my ideas by manual signs or gestures. At that time the signs I used to express my ideas to my family were quite different from the signs of educated deaf-mutes. Strangers did not understand us when we expressed our ideas with signs, but the neighbours did.

(from the autobiography of Jean Massieu (d. 1846), in Lane 1984b: 76)

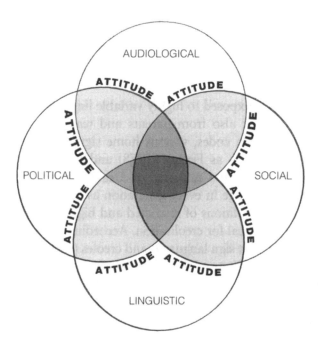

Figure 13.6 Avenues to membership in the Deaf community (Baker-Shenk and Cokely 1991: 56)

Deaf children of hearing parents acquire proficiency in sign language, therefore, outside the parent–child relationship, typically after enrolment in a residential school for the Deaf where they come into regular contact with Deaf children of Deaf parents or older Deaf children. An important difference between the Deaf community and other cultural and linguistic minorities is, thus, that in the Deaf community language and culture are not passed on intergenerationally from parent to child, but rather from child to child in the residential school environment (Meadow 1972).

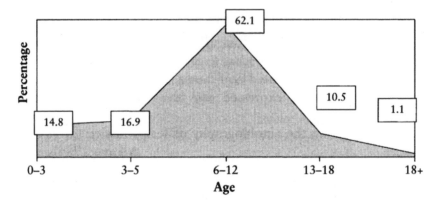

Figure 13.7   Age during which sign language is learned (Penn 1992: 278). Distribution of sign users by period of acquisition of sign language

Deaf children are exposed to highly variable linguistic input not only from their peers, but also from parents and teachers, including sign language, manual sign codes, various home sign systems and spoken language. Authors such as Fischer (1978) and Deuchar (1987) have, therefore, argued that the majority of Deaf children are forced to (re)creolise sign language in every generation as acquisition necessarily takes place under conditions of restricted and highly variable linguistic input, a situation typical for creolisation. Accordingly, structural similarities between different sign languages and creoles (such as, for example, the lack of the copula (*be*) and the use of FINISH as a perfective marker) have been interpreted as a result of the innate language faculty (see section 9.4) being called into play because of restricted linguistic input. However, the creole status of sign languages has been questioned by Lupton and Salmons (1996), who argue that the linguistic structures that have been described for languages such as ASL are unlike the linguistic structures known for most creole languages.

The delayed L1 acquisition of sign language for the majority of Deaf children can result in limited proficiency. Thus, only a small number of individuals (mainly Deaf children of Deaf parents) are considered fluent native signers, while most children arrive at school with minimal communication skills in both sign language and spoken language (Loncke et al. 1990).

13.4   SIGN LANGUAGE AND EDUCATION

The history of Deaf education, controlled for the most part by hearing people, has been characterised by continuing and often dogmatic debates. Some educators have supported the use of sign language in Deaf education (the manual approach), while others have advocated the use of spoken language (the oral approach). A manual approach combining signing (primarily manual sign codes) and speech was used by the so-called 'manualists' in the eighteenth century. This system of teaching was developed in Paris by the Abbé Charles-Michel de l'Epée (1712–89) and his successor Abbé Roch-Ambroise Sicard (1742–1822). The oral approach to Deaf education, initially propagated by Samuel Heinicke (1727–90) in Leipzig and Hamburg, emphasised the advantages of lip-reading and speech, while signing was often entirely banned from the classroom. Aiming at integration into the majority hearing culture at all costs, oralist approaches have been supported by many hearing educators, but are opposed by most Deaf people.

The oralist approach gained strength in the course of the late nineteenth century, and the victory was complete when, in 1880 at the International Congress on the Education of the Deaf in Milan, hearing participants voted for the implementation of oralism in all schools for the Deaf. The effects of this vote were dramatic: while in 1867 every American school for the Deaf utilised and taught ASL and manual sign codes to varying degrees, not one school did so in 1907 (Dolnick 1993). Deaf education became reduced to speech training, and little time and effort was left for the teaching of the normal school curriculum.

It is extremely difficult for people who are Deaf from infancy to learn to use oral language. Deaf people have to try to mimic sounds they have never heard, and being unable to monitor their own speech production it remains difficult to correct and control pitch, volume and phonetic correctness of the spoken utterance. As a result, the speech production of most Deaf people is largely unintelligible to the unaccustomed listener (Prillwitz 1991). Lip-reading remains equally difficult for someone who has never heard a language spoken. Many words look very much alike on the lips although they sound different and mean different things. The sentences *go to Texas* and *no new taxes*, for example, are indistinguishable if one has to rely on lip-reading only – you can try this out by looking in the mirror (Dolnick 1993).

Growing concern about the educational performance of Deaf children in the 1960s (with illiteracy rates of over 30 per cent among Deaf adults), and first results from early sign-language research, led to a reconsideration of the oral approach, and as a result a method termed Total Communication was widely propagated in the late 1970s and early 1980s. Total Communication makes simultaneous use of spoken language and

Learning to speak
The abbé would pull his chair up to my stool so close that our knees were touching and I could see the fine network of veins on his bulbous red-blue nose. He held my left hand firmly to his voice box and my right hand on my own throat, and glowered down at me through beady, rheumy eyes. Then his warm garlic-laden breath would wash over my head and fill my nostrils to suffocating.

'*Daa*,' he wailed, exposing the wet pink cavern of his mouth, his tongue obscenely writhing on its floor, barely contained by the picket fence of little brown-and-yellow teeth.

'*Taa*,' he exploded and the glistening pendant of tissue in the back of his mouth flicked toward the roof, opening the floodgates to the miasma that rose from the roiling contents of his stomach below.

'*Taa, daa, tee, dee*,' he made me screech again and again, but contort my face as I would, fighting back the tears, search as I would desperately, in panic, for the place in my mouth *accurately* to put my tongue, convulse as I would my breathing – I succeeded no better.

(Lane 1984a: 15–16)

different sign systems including fingerspelling, manual sign codes (such as the Paget–Gorman system) and to some extent sign languages.[2] It was believed that the use of manual sign codes whose grammatical and syntactic structure represented the oral language would ease the acquisition of literacy in the majority hearing language among Deaf children. This seemingly logical assumption, however, proved to be problematic. Research has shown that the production of a proposition (a unit of meaning) in manual sign codes takes on average twice as long as the production of a proposition in spoken language. The proposition rate between sign languages and spoken languages is, however, equivalent. The reason for this is that the spatial organisation of sign-language grammar allows for the simultaneous production of lexical signs as well as grammatical and morphological indicators. An illustration of the almost simultaneous arrangement of information is the ASL representation of the English sentence *A person is running zigzag uphill* in Figure 13.8.

The human subject of the sentence is represented by the two index fingers extended downwards in front of the human body. The movement of the hands (hands pushing forward in alternation) then represents the verb RUN. A second sign is performed (one-handed but same handshape), moving across the three-dimensional space to show path and direction of the event. The partially simultaneous arrangement of signs is not possible in the sequentially organised manual codes, where the production rate is

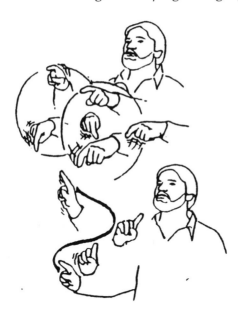

Figure 13.8 ASL representation for *A person is running zigzag uphill*
(T. Supalla 1991: 135)

slow and exceeds the temporal constraints for cognitive processing (Bellugi and Fischer 1972). Understanding manual codes is, therefore, extremely tiresome, and most Deaf people reject these systems as being unnatural and awkward (Reagan 1995).[3] A second problem resulting from the slower production rate is that teachers using speech and manual sign codes simultaneously have to slow down their speech rate. This can lead to the deletion of grammatical and morphological units as well as prosodic features, thus exposing pupils to an ungrammatical and unnatural oral language model (Hyde and Power 1991).

Patterns of age variation in sign language production can be a consequence of changing educational policies (cf. Sutton-Spence and Woll 1999: 24–5 for BSL; Lucas et al. 2001b: 35–6 for ASL). In Japan compulsory education for the Deaf was only introduced after the Second World War and the 1970s saw the mainstreaming of the majority of Deaf children into hearing schools (Nakamura 2003). Three main age groups can be distinguished in contemporary Japan with regard to their educational experiences: (a) the pre-compulsory-education group; (b) the compulsory-education, pre-mainstreaming group; and (c) the compulsory-education, mainstreaming group. Table 13.1 summarises the distinct social and linguistic characteristics of the three groups. Whereas members of the oldest group only acquired Japanese Sign Language (JSL) during adulthood, the middle group (b) acquired JSL in the residential school environment. However, oralism, signed Japanese and fingerspelling dominated

Age Group	Social and Linguistic Characteristics
(a) pre-compulsory education (born during the 1900s and 1930s)	high levels of illiteracy; localised home signs; acquisition of Japanese Sign Language (JSL) only during adulthood (through national organisation for the Deaf); no fingerspelling and no voicing
(b) compulsory education, pre-mainstreaming (born during the 1940s and 1950s)	identify themselves as 'Deaf' (*roua*); use of JSL but also of signed Japanese, fingerspelling, voicing
(c) compulsory education, mainstreaming (born 1960–1980)	identify themselves mostly as hard-of-hearing (*nanchousha*), hearing-disabled (*choukakushougaisha*) or not-Deaf (*roudewa*); use of spoken language, signed Japanese, JSL, fingerspelling, full voicing

Table 13.1   Age variation and school policies in Japan (based on Nakamura 2003)

in the classrooms and are part of the **linguistic repertoire** of this group. A complex linguistic repertoire is also characteristic of the youngest age group. However, they differ from the middle group in their self-identification (*roudewa*, 'not-deaf') and the frequency with which they employ linguistic forms other than JSL in everyday interactions.

However, according to Karen Nakamura (2003) two recent sociocultural developments have contributed to changes in the linguistic repertoire of youngest age group. These are described as 'U-Turn Deaf' and 'Deaf Shock'. 'U-turn Deaf' describes children who move from hearing schools back into schools for the Deaf where JSL functions as the primary language of peer-group interaction. 'Deaf Shock' refers to the discovery of Deaf identity by mainstreamed Deaf students as they become adults. These young adults refer to themselves neither as *roua* ('deaf') nor *choukakushougaisha* ('hearing-disabled'), but as *defu* (an American loanword; they also use the Roman character *D* to indicate their identification with Deaf culture). Their use of JSL, however, differs significantly from that of age group (b) as they avoid any voicing or fingerspelling and, moreover, borrow extensively from ASL.

Contemporary approaches to Deaf education are generally rooted in the recognition of Deaf people as a minority group with distinctive educational and linguistic needs (Reagan 1985). Sign languages, although not 'mother tongues' in the orthodox sense, are nevertheless seen as the natural first language for Deaf people (Deuchar and James 1985) and are used as the initial medium of instruction. Spoken languages (in their oral and written form) are then taught as second languages. Such **bilingual education** programmes have now been introduced in several schools for the Deaf in Europe and

Sign language oppression in Deaf education
Extracts from interviews which Jennifer Harris conducted with Deaf informants in Britain during the early 1990s. The age of the informants ranged between 17 and 67 years. All informants had been educated via oralist methods.

(1)
J. Harris: What happened if you signed at school – what did the teacher do to you? If they saw you signing?
Steven: Oh they would smack you – smack you round the head or throw the chalk at you – or make you write lines 'I must not sign'.
J. Harris: Oh that's hard isn't it?
Steven: Yes – that's cruel. It's cruel.

(2)
J. Harris: Right, so what happened to you if you used to sign in the classroom – what happened?
Barry: It was very serious . . . so we signed in secret and we never let the teachers see we were signing.
. . .
J. Harris: But the teacher was she very angry if you signed?
Barry: They made you sit on your hands, they put you in the corner sometimes, they put a hat on you with a D on the top.
(quoted in Harris 1995: 59–70)

America, and have shown positive results regarding the cognitive and social development of Deaf children (Hansen 1991). In Sweden, for example, where Deaf people are legally recognised as a linguistic and cultural minority, and are entitled to certain linguistic rights such as mother-tongue education and interpreters. Furthermore, hearing parents of Deaf children are required to take classes in Swedish Sign Language (Ahlgren 1991; Bergman and Wallin 1991). Although much practical work (such as interpreter and teacher training, the development of teaching materials and resources) remains to be done, bilingual approaches have so far proven successful.

13.5 LANGUAGE CONTACT, DIGLOSSIA AND CODE-SWITCHING

As a subculture within the majority hearing culture, the Deaf community has been described as a multilingual group, whose members make regular use not only of natural sign languages but also (to varying degrees) of the language(s) of the majority hearing culture, in their spoken, signed and written forms (Davis 1989). Early and intense exposure to the spoken language in its various forms takes place at school, and is reinforced by the constant confrontation with hearing people in everyday interactions. Sign languages are, thus, in continuous **language contact** with spoken varieties. Linguistic interference is, however, limited by differences in modality and sociolinguistic factors such as attitudes towards the majority language and hearing culture in general.

A result of the language-contact situation is the occasional borrowing of fingerspelled words from spoken languages into sign languages, where they become subject to linguistic constraints typical for sign languages (such as hand symmetry), so that their origin may ultimately become unrecognisable. For example, the BSL loan sign for *kitchen* is based on the fingerspelling K-I-T-C-H-E-N, but reduced to the mere representation of the repeated initial letter *K* (see Figure 13.9).

KITCHEN (-k-k-)

Figure 13.9   BSL initialised loan sign for *kitchen* (Kyle and Woll 1985: 126)

The assimilation of entire spoken words into some sign languages is another result of language contact. German Sign Language, for example, makes extensive use of spoken word material, which accompanies the production of manual signs (Ebbinghaus and Hessmann 1990). Oral and manual units are used together to modify and elaborate on semantic concepts (ibid.: 110). This reciprocal relationship is highlighted in the example given in the box, when the signer mouths the word *living-room* (*Wohnzimmer*) while simply signing ROOM, thus using spoken language material to elaborate on the meaning of the manual sign. The mouthing of German words in German Sign Language should not be regarded as an attempt to speak German while signing, as no effort is made to use the spoken-word material according to the syntactic and grammatical rules of German.

An important result of the contact between sign languages, manual sign codes and spoken languages is the development of a wide range of **contact varieties**, such as **Pidgin Sign English** (PSE), which has been described as showing linguistic features of both ASL and English, and is

Oral units in German Sign Language

	increasingly intense	frustrated ----------		
SIT ROOM SIGN ++---------		STUCK HEAR BELL INFORM ME?	ME	DOWN
living-room				must	down

Translation:
We sat down in the living-room and were wrapped up in our signing until suddenly we were interrupted by the doorbell ringing, letting me know that I had to stop and go down.
Non-manual, manual and oral units are transcribed in separate lines: top line = non-manual behaviour, middle line = manual signs, bottom line = oral units (spoken words). Dotted lines indicate temporal extension of a unit, and [+] stands for repetition of a sign.

(from Ebbinghaus and Hessmann 1990: 107–8)

said to occur typically in interactions between Deaf and hearing people (Woodward 1973; Reilly and McIntire 1980). It is not entirely clear if what has been labelled PSE is really a pidgin (that is, a result of language contact under conditions of restricted input) or the outcome of imperfect second-language acquisition and/or strategies of linguistic accommodation (Bochner and Albertini 1988; Lucas and Valli 1989). The more general label 'contact signing' has been suggested by Lucas and Valli. However, the term PSE is still used widely by members of the Deaf community as well as some researchers (Lucas and Valli 1989, 1991).[4]

Some linguistic characteristics of PSE/'contact signing' in the USA

- ASL signs accompanied by the mouthing of corresponding English lexical items
- semantic change of some ASL lexical items
- English word order
- no English or ASL inflectional or derivational morphology

(Lucas and Valli 1989)

It is important to distinguish between native (L1) and non-native (L2) sign production, namely PSE (or 'contact signing') as produced by Deaf signers and PSE (or 'contact signing') as produced by hearing signers. The former typically shows more aspects of ASL and is linguistically stable, while the latter is strongly influenced by English grammar and is highly variable (Erting and Woodward 1979; Lee 1982). The linguistic boundary between ASL and PSE is difficult to establish, and variation is conceptualised on a continuum. Since ASL and English constitute two independent languages and are not linguistically related, the situation is best represented by using two overlapping but distinctive continua (see Figure 13.10).

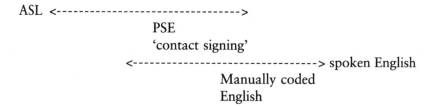

Figure 13.10   The American Sign Language Continuum (based on Reagan 1985: 270)[5]

In the 1970s, William Stokoe and others (e.g. Stokoe 1969–70; Woodward 1973; Washabaugh 1981) have argued that the American Deaf community is best described as diglossic, with various forms of signed, spoken and written English functioning as a prestigious H language (and are used in formal contexts), whereas ASL can be described the as L language (and is used only in informal contexts; cf. also Deuchar 1987 for an interpretation of the BSL community as diglossic).

The usefulness of the concept of diglossia for the description of variation in today's American Deaf community has, however, been questioned. The alternate use of ASL and English/manually coded English does not seem to be tied to domain or register (Lee 1982; Johnson and Erting 1989). For many members of the American Deaf community the situation appears to be one of extensive bilingualism (English, ASL). This gives rise to a variety of contact phenomena in formal as well as informal contexts (including code-switching, nonce-borrowings, calquing etc.; cf. Kuntze 2000), as signers shift between different segments of the continuum according to familiar sociolinguistic categories such as addressee, topic, situation and the desire to establish one's social identity (Lucas and Valli 1989, 1991).

This research, however, is almost entirely based on the situation in the USA where the status of ASL has undergone revolutionary changes since the early 1970s, and significant differences exist between countries regarding the functional allocation of sign systems (Lee 1982). In Italy, for example, the situation still appeared to be one of diglossia in the early 1990s when it was reported that Italian Sign Language is used only in private, informal settings, while Italian (spoken and manually coded) is used in all public settings (Tessarolo 1990). Similarly, Lenore Grenoble (1992: 323) described a largely diglossic situation in the early 1990s for Russia with (signed) Russian as the High language and Russian Sign Language (RSL, *Russkii Zhestovyi Iazyk*) as the Low language. The prestige difference is linked to educational attainment: signers who are competent in (signed) Russian are called *gramotnye* ('literate'), while those who only used RSL are labelled *negramotnye* ('illiterate'). However, the social and political changes in Russia during the last ten years have also affected the status of sign languages. Michael Pursglove and Anna Komarova (2003) note that bilingual programmes have started in Russia and that there is an increased awareness for Deaf history and cultural traditions. It is likely that this will support a more positive evaluation of RSL.

Overt prestige of Pidgin Sign English
I started to sign English sentences. People began to say that I always talked in sentences. I thought I always signed right while those who used ASL were wrong. Why? because I observed that the teachers called ASL users names like 'stupid' or 'dumb' while they praise me. I was their pet, just because I used English sentences. That's how I thought my signs were right and ASL signs were wrong. I was smarter than they were, etcetera. Too bad. All my life, I rarely saw deaf students using PSE. Whenever they used PSE, I identified with them and became good friends. We thought we were better than others. We were high class.

(quoted in Kannapell 1989: 208)

Although ASL commands a great deal of prestige in today's American Deaf community, research has shown that varieties approaching the English end of the continuum still enjoy overt prestige among some Deaf people. This has been explained by the fact that many teachers still equate language with English (spoken and signed), and negative attitudes towards sign languages have been fostered in the educational setting (Edwards and Ladd 1983; Lane 1995).

Code-switching, including alternation in channel (from oral to manual) as well as switching across the sign continuum (from sign language to manual sign codes), is a pervasive feature of Deaf–hearing and Deaf–Deaf communication. Examples of situational code-switching between ASL and manually coded English have been described by Robert E. Johnson and Carol Erting in their study of linguistic and social interaction in an American Deaf school. At this particular school, a situation closely tied to the use of varieties of manually coded English is the serving of food. The example given in the box below shows how the 'food-serving situation' is redefined by the five-year-old J's breach of etiquette (touching the food). D, the Deaf aide at the school, switches to ASL to reprimand J and instruct him about proper cultural values (in this case table manners). Then D re-establishes the 'food-serving situation' by turning to T, and signing the sentence *Do you want bread?* in careful English word order with clearly articulated signs.

Situational code-switching in ASL

D to J   #D-O YOU WANT (one-handed) # BREAD (loan sign from fingerspelling)

J   (touches three pieces before deciding on his choice)

D   (sets plate down and grabs J's arm)

NOT TOUCH (one-handed, high)
(*Don't touch it!*)

 NOT TOUCH (distributive, over bread) NO ONE PICK
(*Don't touch every one. No! Pick one*)

NOT TOUCH (distributive, one hand) NOT
(*Don't touch them all.*)

(hands J a slice of bread)

THAT ONE
(*Take that one.*)

(turns to T)

#D-O YOU WANT (two-handed) BREAD (citation form)

English translation in italics, ASL signing in bold caps, manually coded English in caps. # indicates that a sign has been lexicalised from fingerspelling; upper-case letters separated by hyphens represent fingerspelling.

    The **citation form** of a sign is the form one finds in dictionaries. In the actual production of sign sequences, signers typically simplify the full citation form.

                         (from Johnson and Erting 1989: 75–6)

Although speech and lip-reading are used as primary means of communication only by a minority of Deaf people, code-switching in the Deaf community does occasionally involve the use of the spoken language. Deaf mothers, for example, have been observed to use both sign language and spoken language with their hearing infants. Preliminary research indicates that in some Deaf communities, situations typically associated with the affective and emotional function of language tend to be associated with spoken language, while sign language dominates in object-oriented communication (Mills and Coerts 1990).

13.6   SOCIOLINGUISTIC VARIATION IN SIGN LANGUAGE

Since sign languages have been largely excluded from the educational setting and are learned in informal situations typically without access to an adult language model, it is not surprising that they form highly variable linguistic systems. Although a number of notation systems have been developed for linguistic research, the absence of a commonly recognised writing system for sign languages is another factor contributing to the lack of linguistic stability. It can be expected that contemporary bilingual educational models for the Deaf which will make it necessary to provide models and norms for sign-language teaching (including sign-language dictionaries and textbooks) will lead to increasing linguistic uniformity and standardisation (Swisher and McKee 1989).

The main forces towards uniformity have been residential schools for the Deaf and the intergenerational transmission of sign languages from Deaf parents to Deaf children. That regular contact between Deaf people is a major force for the development of uniform sign languages can be seen from the situation in India. A relatively standardised sign language has developed in the urban centres, where interaction between Deaf people is easy and regular, not only in schools for the Deaf but also in social clubs and other organisations. Rural Indian Sign Language, on the other hand, is highly idiosyncratic, reflecting the fact that Deaf people in the rural areas are geographically scattered and have little opportunity for interaction with each other (Jepson 1991). Similar developments have been described for South Africa (Aarons and Akach 2002), The Netherlands (Schermer 2003), Kenya (Okombo 1994), Nicaragua (Kegel et al. 1999).

Like all natural languages sign languages show variation according to language-internal and language-external factors.

Regional Variation: Regional differences have been described for many countries. Local residential schools for Deaf children have played an important role in the formation of regional dialects. This was noted by Carl Croneberg (1976: 314; in Stokoe et al.) for the American Deaf community: "The school for the deaf is of central importance in the dissemination of dialect. At such a school, the young deaf learn ASL in the particular variety characteristic of the local region". Swiss German Sign Language (*Deutschschweizerische Gebärdensprache*), for example, has five regional dialects each associated with a different residential school (Boyes Braem et al. 2003). The situation is similar in the Netherlands where patterns of variation are moreover influenced by the educational histories of these schools. Thus, the sign language variety used in the south (the region around Eindhoven) shows strong influences from a sign system which was developed by Martinus Van Beek, who founded the Institute for the Deaf in Sint Michielsgestel in 1910. Many of the signs used around Eindhoven still resemble the initialised signs typical of the Van Beek system (Schermer 2003). The signs used in the north, on the other hand, have been influenced by French Sign Language (LSF, *Langue des Signes Française*). Different regional sign languages have been described for Viet Nam. Each of the languages is connected to an urban centre: Ho Chi Min City Sign Language, Ha Noi Sign Language and Hai Phong Sign Language. All three sign languages show strong influence from LSF which was used in the schools for the Deaf during the time of French colonisation. However, signers in Hai Phong have maintained considerably more original Southeast Asian signs and shows less influence from LSF than signers in the other cities (Woodward 2000).

Geographical variation in sign language use can also be a consequence of different social group identities linked to the spoken languages of a given geographical or political area (cf. Sutton-Spence and Woll 1999: 29). Thus, in Switzerland the marked cultural and political boundaries between the German-, French- and Italian-speaking cantons have supported the development of three different sign languages (Boyes Braem et al. 2003). In Belgium, there are also important differences between the sign languages used in Wallonia and Flanders. These linguistic differences reflect the split of Deaf clubs and associations along the linguistic and cultural boundaries which divide Belgium into a French-speaking and a Flemish-speaking territory (De Weerdt and Vanhecke 2004).

Gender variation: As discussed in Chapters 3 and 7, sociolinguistic studies of modern Western societies have found a pattern of women favouring the prestige (or standard) variants and men favouring non-standard variants. A similar pattern was observed for ASL by Alyssa Wulf and her colleagues (2002; also Lucas et al. 2001b: 158–75) in a study of the use of subject pronouns with plain verbs. Plain verbs are represented by signs which do not indicate the acting subject through sign location or palm orientation. The verb 'know', for example, is a plain verb in ASL and the signer would need to sign I, KNOW and YOU separately if he or she wanted to indicate the subject and object of the sentence. This, however, is not obligatory: null pronouns are possible in ASL and signers vary in their performance (i.e. they sometimes sign the subject pronouns, sometimes their omit it). Use of subject pronouns in Wulf et al.'s corpus of narratives was clearly affected by the sex of the signer: women frequently signed subject pronouns separately (41 per cent), whereas men showed a strong tendency to omit subject pronouns (29 per cent). Wulf et al. (2002: 70) explained the higher production of subject pronouns by women as a consequence of the social prestige which is still attached to English in the American Deaf community (i.e. a language which does not allow the omission of subject pronouns, a non-pro-drop language):

> It may be that women produce more pronouns than men because overt pronouns represent a prestige variant . . . . ASL has made great strides in the last thirty-five years in gaining recognition as a natural human language. Nevertheless, English, which is not a pro-drop language, enjoys a certain prestige in the Deaf community in recognition of the fact that access to power and resources is still very restricted for people who do not have a working command of English.

In countries were Deaf girls and boys were educated at separate institutions, gender differences can be quite pronounced. In Dublin, different sign vocabularies developed in two residential schools for the Deaf (St Mary's School for Deaf Girls and St Joseph's School for Deaf Boys) between 1846 and 1957. In the early 1990s sign variation could still be observed between middle-aged and elderly male and female signers (different male/female variants were found for more than two-thirds of signs). Some of these signs were unrelated in form, while others showed phonological variation. Communication between the sexes was, however, guaranteed as most women knew a large number of male signs and used these in conversations which involved both male and female participants. Female signs were used only in single-sex conversations with other women and were rarely understood by male signers (LeMaster and Dwyer 1991; LeMaster 2003).

In Chapter 7 we discussed work by Jennifer Coates which showed that overlaps are common in informal conversations among women friends. Male friendship groups, on the other hand, prefer a no-overlap conversational style. In a subsequent study Jennifer Coates and Rachel Sutton-Spence (2001) found a similar pattern of turn-taking in sign language (BSL) conversations with overlapping signing being a characteristic feature of all-female conversations. The all-male groups, like their hearing counterparts, preferred the no-overlap mode of conversation.

Age variation: With regard to ASL, Ceil Lucas and her colleagues (2001b) found that location variation was not only conditioned by linguistic factors (assimilation and grammatical category of the sign), but also by age differences (extralinguistic factor). As shown in Figure 13.11, innovative, non-citation forms were favoured by younger signers; older signers (55 years and older), on the other hand, favoured the more conservative citation forms.

Ethnic variation: Sign-language variation also exists with respect to ethnic group membership, as for example in the USA. A history of segregated educational facilities and residential areas, separate Deaf clubs and other social institutions has led to the isolation of the Deaf Black community

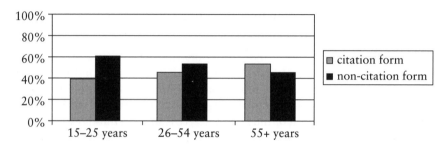

Figure 13.11   Location variation by age (based on Lucas et al. 2001b: 138)

in the USA, a separation emphasised linguistically by the development of different varieties of signing.

In the *Dictionary of American Sign Language* (1976), Stokoe et al. acknowledged that American Sign Language varies according to ethnic group. However, they explicitly avoided collecting data from Black informants, thus enforcing the perception that Black signing was non-standard.

Non-standard signing in the USA
I once asked a Black woman receiving vocational training when she learned signs. She replied that her interpreter just taught her. Being surprised by her fluency, I asked if she hadn't attended a residential school. She said yes. I then continued with 'You mean you didn't use signs at the residential school?' She answered, 'Yes, but now I am learning correct signs.'

(Woodward 1976: 217)

Differences between Black and White signing were described first by James Woodward (1976), who showed that variation existed not only on the lexical but also on the phonological level. For example, ASL has shown historically a trend towards centralisation: that is, signs are increasingly articulated in the central area in front of the chest. Woodward's study, carried out in the 1970s in Georgia and Lousiana, showed that this development had not yet affected Black signing. Black informants still articulated most signs around the waist.

During the 1960s and 1970s, the politics of racial integration led to a radical change in the social and educational structure in USA. As a result, Black Deaf pupils, now being educated together with White Deaf pupils, show a more ASL-like signing than Black adults who had attended segregated schools (Maxwell and Smith-Todd 1986).

However, differences remain between the two groups and Woodward's interpretation of African-American signing as relatively conservative has been supported by more recent studies. Ceil Lucas and her colleagues (2001b: 135–6) found that with regard to location variation, African-American Deaf signers disfavour the lowered non-citation sign location and preferably use the more conservative citation form (forehead/temple location).

Linguists have also described lexical variation between white and African-American signing. Anthony Aramburo (1989) studied two African Americans signing together and then each signing with a white signer. Although the African-American signers used ASL in all situations, there were significant differences between their lexical choices, when signing together, and when signing with the white signer (see Figure 13.12).

Ceil Lucas and her colleagues (2001a) used thirty-four sign stimuli to investigate lexical differences in a sample of 140 signers (about two-thirds

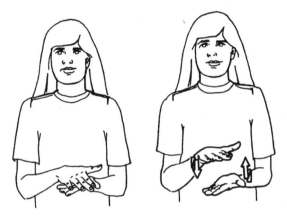

SCHOOL, citation form

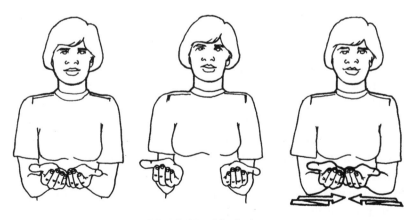

SCHOOL, Black form

Figure 13.12 Citation form (used with white interlocutor) and Black form (used with black interlocutor) of SCHOOL (Aramburo 1989: 116–17)

of these were African Americans). For twenty-eight of these signs African-American signers had separate lexical variants. For example, while white signers had two different sign variants for RABBIT, African-American signers had four variants.

Sometimes the degree of variation between different ethnic groups is rather difficult to assess, as is the case in South African Sign Language (SASL). Deaf education in South Africa started with the arrival of a group of Irish nuns who established the first school for the Deaf in Cape Town (1863). Irish Sign Language did not, however, remain the only one used: other schools for the Deaf used BSL as well as different manual sign codes. Today, South African Sign Language, which has developed from these different roots (including a possible indigenous sign language), is used in television programmes, interpreter training and national events for the Deaf community. More recently, ASL has also gained some importance in South Africa, especially among younger Deaf people, some of whom have been educated at the only liberal arts college for the Deaf, at Gallaudet University in the USA (Penn 1995).

Linguistic variation resulting from the existence of different sign languages and different manual sign codes in the educational system has been complicated by policies of apartheid, which separated the population on the basis of 'race'. Ironically, the advent of apartheid and the Separate Education Bill in 1948 created a situation in which Deaf education at Black schools was educationally superior to education at White schools. While a manual sign code based on the Paget–Gorman system was used in Black schools, White (and to a lesser extent Indian and Coloured) Deaf children were subjected to an uncompromising oralism which was at that time seen as being more prestigious than the use of manual codes (Penn 1992, 1993).

Before the political and social transformation of South Africa, little contact existed between the 'racially' segregated Deaf communities, leading to considerable lexical diversity in SASL. Based primarily on ethnicity, eleven historically and linguistically distinct Deaf communities have been distinguished by the authors of the *Dictionary of South African Signs* (Penn et al. 1992–4). Sign variation as recorded in the dictionary is impressive, with an average of six lexical variants per entry.

However, the dictionary has been criticised for not recognising the possibility that much of the lexical variation described may actually be the result of contextual or stylistic rather than ethnic variation (Aarons and Akach 1998). Preliminary research has also shown that, for example, the syntax (and possibly the morphology) of SASL is far more cohesive than the lexicon (Ogilvy-Foreman et al. 1994; Aarons and Akach 1998, 2002). Deaf South Africans are generally accustomed to strategies of accommodation and are often able to understand unfamiliar signs, especially when they occur in familiar grammatical structures (Aarons 1995). More research is needed to assess the degree of linguistic variation in SASL and to answer the question of the extent to which different ethnic sign-language communities developed during the years of apartheid and whether these communities still exist.

In South Africa, many things are still in a state of transition; attitudes towards Deafness and sign language are two of these. Although Deafness is still predominantly perceived as a medical condition, Deaf culture and Deaf pride are becoming increasingly visible, often transcending the diverse ethnic identities which were fostered by apartheid policies. The government's commitment to a multilingual policy of linguistic empowerment which led to the recognition of SASL in the constitution (see Chapter 12) will certainly influence the future status and use of sign language in South Africa, especially in educational settings (Penn 1993).

Figure 13.13   Deaf Pride in South Africa (courtesy of Bastion of the Deaf, Cape Town)

Social variation: Membership in religious groups can also affect language use and religion has therefore been included as a social variable in sociolinguistics studies. In the case of Ireland, for example, Catholicism has been shown to be a central marker of group identity and an important extralinguistic variable for the study of variation in Irish English. In British Sign Language (BSL) differences between Roman Catholic and Protestant signers have been reported, and Roman Catholic signing is strongly influenced by Irish Sign Language (Sutton-Spence and Woll 1999: 28). Religion also accounts for some of the variation in Australian Sign Language (Auslan) and interacts with generational differences. Auslan like BSL – to which it is closely related – generally uses the two-handed alphabet. However, older

Catholic signers in Australia regularly use the Irish one-handed manual alphabet with each other. This pattern is much less common among younger Catholic signers (Johnston 1998: 561–2, 564).

We still know comparatively little about social class differences in sign language use. With regard to ASL linguists have repeatedly commented on what one might call the Gallaudet élite, that is, graduates from Gallaudet University who are in professional employment and who are financially relatively prosperous. Croneberg (1976: 318; in Stokoe et al.) described the language of this group as highly prestigious: "People with these attributes tend to seek each other out and form a group. Frequently they use certain signs that are considered superior to the signs used locally for the same thing" (see also Stokoe et al. 1976). Educational opportunities still shape linguistic variation in ASL: Ceil Lucas and her colleagues (2001b: 187) found that middle-class signers used more fingerspelling than working-class signers, possibly as a result of their greater educational exposure to and proficiency in the majority hearing language.

Register variation: Language varies not only according to characteristics of the language user (regional origin, gender, age, ethnicity), but also according to contexts of use (register variation, see Chapter 2). Register variation was described by Charlotte Baker-Shenk and Dennis Cokely (1991: 94) for ASL: in formal contexts ASL signers often use both hands for signs which also have an informal one-handed variant. In addition, signing space tends to be more restricted in formal contexts (Sutton-Spence and Woll 1999: 31; also Zimmer 1989).

Informal and colloquial registers often include slang and taboo words which are used within a particular social group, and which are avoided in more formal registers as well as in out-group communication. William Rudner and Rochelle Butowsky (1981) studied signs which are used by members of the Deaf gay community. Their research showed that Deaf gay signers make use of in-group signs. For example, the sign GAY, made by tugging at one's right earlobe with thumb and forefinger, was understood by less than half of the heterosexual informants, and about half of the gay informants indicated that they would use the sign only in conversations with other gay people.

Figure 13.14   The sign for 'gay' (Rudner and Butowsky 1981: 40)

Rudner and Butowsky also identified some phrases which are used exclusively by and within the Deaf gay community. The signed phrase 'Are you one of us?' is typically signed YOU ONE? by Deaf gay people. Many heterosexuals, however, interpreted the sign as meaning 'Are you alone?' Another clandestine sign is the sign for 'my lover' used mainly by Deaf lesbians. It is signed as WE TWO, and is often used in situations where heterosexuals are present and discretion is required. An important part of this subculture sign is body movement: when signing TWO, the body is turned to hide the signing hand.

Figure 13.15   The sign for 'my lover' (Rudner and Butowsky 1981: 46)

Kleinfeld and Warner (1997) report further examples of group-specific signs. For example, the conventional ASL sign for *drag* is the initialised sign D+GIRL. However, this sign is not accepted by the Deaf gay community. Gay signers prefer an alternative sign which has been borrowed from German Sign Language (*Deutsche Gebärdensprache*).

Political correctness is a type of taboo or euphemistic language behaviour which has been an important force in lexical change since the 1970s (see Chapter 10). In sign languages politically or ideologically charged signs also have been replaced with more neutral signs. Thus, the original ASL sign for JAPAN (produced on the outer corner of the eye with a J handshape thus emphasising anatomical difference) has been replaced by a sign borrowed from JSL (an iconic sign representing the shape of Japan). This newer sign has recently been borrowed into BSL, Auslan and NZSL.

In addition to borrowing, fingerspelling is frequently used to avoid potentially offensive signs. Kleinfeld and Warner (1997) found that hearing informants, sensitive to the gay community's objection to the conventional ASL sign for *drag*, would often use fingerspelling (D-R-A-G). Sign euphemisms generally avoid visual explicitness (which is a characteristic feature of taboo signs and insults), are more contained in terms of movement and signing space, and facial expressions tend to be neutral. Sutton-Spence and Woll (1999: 249) describe a continuum of BSL variants for 'abortion' from euphemistic to taboo: usually the sign is made in a neutral place, however, it can also be made in front of the abdomen, or it can be "made deliberately shocking (called a 'dysphemism'), by a representation of stabbing the abdomen" (ibid.).

Acquisition variation: Although there are many parallels across modalities, James C. Woodward has been careful to observe that in addition to the well-known social variables employed in most sociolinguistic studies (region, age, gender, social class and ethnic group), variables important for socialisation into the Deaf community (being Deaf, having Deaf parents, having learned signs before the age of six) play a significant role in sign-language variation (Woodward 1973). Woodward has shown that positive correlations exist between these variables and a typical feature of ASL morphology called 'verb reduplication'. This term refers to the repetition of the movement component of a sign which can specify the temporal dimensions of an action (whether for example an action is continuous as in *he waited for ages and ages*, or habitual: *she always reads*). Correlations with the extralinguistic variables listed above demonstrated that varieties close to the ASL end of the scale (allow verb reduplication in most environments) correlated significantly with the variables of being Deaf, having Deaf parents and having learned signs before the age of six (Woodward 1973).

Lucas and her colleagues (2001b) also found differences between native signers (sign-language acquisition in the family) and near-native signers (sign-language acquisition before the age of six in a residential school context). Native signers generally prefer the more conservative citation forms, whereas near-native signers made use of a range of innovative variants. According to Lucas et al. (ibid.: 187) this difference is probably a consequence of the different contexts in which near-native acquisition takes place: because of their diverse language background (involving home-signs systems as well as different forms of ASL in the educational setting) near-native signers show a high tolerance towards variation and a lower awareness of formal linguistic norms (ibid.: 187).

13.7 'EVERYONE HERE SPOKE SIGN LANGUAGE': MARTHA'S VINEYARD REVISITED

For centuries, Deaf people have been marginalised in society and labelled not only as medically but also as linguistically and socially pathological. The inability of Deaf people to acquire spoken language was seen as an indicator of their lack of intelligence, and the existence of visual-gestural communication systems as the natural languages of Deaf people was ignored. This perception of Deaf people as 'deficient' led to a long tradition of discriminatory legal and social practices all over the world, often placing Deaf people in the same category as children and the mentally ill.

Nora E. Groce's anthropological study (1985) of social responses to hereditary deafness on the island of Martha's Vineyard (see Chapter 3) shows that marginalisation, discrimination and social inequality need not be the necessary consequence of being Deaf. While social restriction and isolation structured the experience of Deafness on the American mainland, Deaf people on the island were fully integrated into the social life of the island.[6] The integration of Deaf people in the island's society was possible because of the existence of societal bilingualism: the inhabitants of Martha's Vineyard were bilingual in English and the island's sign language. Similar patterns of societal bilingualism have been described by Schmaling (2000) for Nigeria where Deaf people appear to fully integrated into the social and economic life of the local villages and hearing people frequently acquire knowledge of the local sign language (called *maganar hannu* 'the language of the hands'). Societal bilingualism has also been described for the island of Grand Cayman in the Caribbean (Washabaugh 1981), the Yucatan peninsula of Mexico (Johnson 1994), and a village in Bali called *Desa Kolok* (lit. 'deaf village'; Branson et al. 1996).

A complex pattern of intermarriage among a particular group of English settlers on Martha's Vineyard led to the spread of a recessive gene for deafness, and incidences of hereditary deafness were strikingly high on the island in the eighteenth and nineteenth centuries, when one in every 155 islanders was born deaf, as opposed to one in over 2,000 on the American mainland (Groce 1985: 3). When immigration to the island ceased in 1710, the island's society became socially and genetically isolated from the American mainland. Groce has calculated that by the late 1700s over 96 per cent of island marriages took place between individuals who were already related to each other (ibid.: 41). This pattern of intermarriage and genetic isolation was most prominent in the up-island towns of West Tisbury and Chilmark, where one in twenty-five inhabitants was born deaf. The island's response to this pattern of hereditary deafness was characterised not by exclusion of the Deaf islanders, but by the existence of an extensive societal bilingualism (English/local sign language) which made it possible for Deaf individuals to participate fully in all aspects of society. Deaf islanders grew up, married, took part in the island's social life and local affairs, earned their living and died – just like anyone else. That Deafness was clearly not perceived as a severe disability and personal tragedy, but as just one of a person's characteristics, becomes visible in many of Groce's interviews.

I asked, "Do you remember anything similar about Isaiah and David?"
"Oh yes!", she replied. "Both were very good fishermen, very good indeed."

"Weren't they born deaf?" I prodded.

"Yes, come to think of it, I guess they both were," she replied. "I'd forgotten about that."

(Groce 1985: 4)

Sign language was used by both the Deaf and the hearing, it was casually learned from an early age, and fluency was reinforced by continuous use. To get by in the up-island towns of Chilmark and West Tisbury and to participate in community activities, a good knowledge of sign language was essential.

> We would sit around and wait for the mail to come in and just talk. And the deaf would be there, everyone would be there. And they were part of the crowd, and they were accepted. They were fishermen and farmers and everything else. And they wanted to find out the news just as much as the rest of us. And oftentimes people would tell stories and make signs at the   same time so everyone could follow him together. Of course, sometimes, if there were more deaf than hearing people there, everyone would speak sign language – just to be polite you know. (Groce 1985: 60)

Hearing signers used sign language not only in the presence of Deaf people but also among themselves, which shows that societal bilingualism was deeply entrenched in everyday communicative behaviour. Signing was used by children at school or in church when speaking was out of place, by fishermen on the open water and by couples and families to communicate messages over distances. And as in other bilingual communities, code-switching between the two varieties was common and often determined by stylistic and situational factors.

> People would start off a sentence speaking and then finish it in sign language, especially if they were saying something dirty. The punch line would often be in sign language. If there was a bunch of guys standing around the general store telling a [dirty] story and a woman walked in, they'd turn away from her and finish the story in sign language. (Groce 1985: 67)

Bilingualism in sign language and English became an important marker of community identity, when mainland holidaymakers came to Martha's Vineyard from the late nineteenth century onwards. Sign language was not only used to ridicule the ignorant visitor but also to maintain social distance (Groce 1985: 66).

The demographics of deafness changed dramatically in the early twentieth century, when more and more marriages took place between islanders and off-islanders, leading to a rapid decrease in the number of children born deaf. However, old habits die hard. Although the last Deaf islander died in 1952, O. Sacks (1989) reports that when he visited the island during the late 1980s he still witnessed bilingual communication practices among the old (hearing) inhabitants.

13.8   CONCLUSION

This chapter has shown in some detail that sign languages are subject to many of the same sociolinguistic influences as spoken languages. Sociolinguistic variation, language contact, bilingualism and language standardisation can be observed across modalities (sign versus speech). Communities that use sign language also display a range of attitudes towards their own language and the language of the majority hearing culture, including what Labov termed overt and covert prestige (see Chapter 3).

Issues of power and inequality surface in the 'misrecognition' (see Chapter 10) and sidelining of sign languages by educational authorities in favour of other communication systems oriented towards socially dominant languages. Issues of power and social domination are also visible in the perception of many older Black signers in the USA that their variety of signing is non-standard, as well as in the willingness with which Dublin Deaf women accommodate towards dominant male varieties of signing.

Notes

1. Similarly, one does not write of the Spanish or English (and so on) using a lower-case letter.
2. It should be clear from the brief discussion of the structure of sign languages in section 13.2 that Total Communication cannot include the simultaneous use of a natural sign language and spoken language, as facial signals (including mouth movements) have grammatical and morphological meaning in sign language. The simultaneous use of sign language and spoken language would thus violate the rules of sign language and result in the production of ungrammatical and sometimes incomprehensible signed utterances (Vogt-Svendson 1983).
3. It has been shown that children who are exclusively exposed to manual sign codes and have no natural sign-language will still develop linguistic structures which make grammatical use of space and are sturcturally similar to natural sign languages (S. J. Supalla 1991).
4. The linguistic description of such contact varieties is further complicated by the fact that there are significant differences between sign languages of different countries. For example, mouthing has been described above as an integral part of German Sign Language, but is seen as an indicator for contact signing in ASL.
5. Fischer (1978) has described the sign situation in the USA as analogous to that of a post-creole continuum (see Chapter 9). In this case, manual English forms the acrolect, PSE is used as a cover term for the intermediate varieties (mesolects), and ASL, which is seen as being the result of a creolisation process, forms the basilect.
6. It seems that the situation on Martha's Vineyard was not unusual for a society with high instances of deafness. Washabaugh (1980) has described a similar situation for Providence Island (Columbia), and Sacks (1989: 60–1) also mentions some examples.

EPILOGUE

In writing this book, one immediate problem was what to include and what to exclude under the umbrella of 'sociolinguistics'. Sociolinguistics is a large and rapidly expanding academic field, and while there are certain agreed 'core' areas (such as the quantitative study of language variation and change) it is not at all obvious where the subject ends. Furthermore, many topics studied by sociolinguists (such as language and gender, or language and education) are also informed by other, related disciplines. We have covered what we believe are the key areas of study that constitute sociolinguistics but, inevitably, the selection of topics and issues is influenced by our own interests and experience.

We have tried to show how important it is to look not simply at the results of sociolinguistic enquiry (for instance, aspects of geographical, social or stylistic variation) but also at how these results were obtained – how sociolinguists have gone about their work and, more specifically, the research methods employed by different sociolinguists. Evidence about language use is never simply 'discovered': different methods affect both what counts as evidence and how this is interpreted (you may remember the contrast drawn in Chapter 5 between qualitative and quantitative studies of speaking style). Paying attention to research methods has the immediate practical benefit of helping you evaluate individual studies but also provides more general insights into how sociolinguists construct their subject.

Different approaches to sociolinguistic research, and the detail of research methods in individual studies, are discussed where relevant in earlier chapters, but there are some general issues that run across chapters and that will confront any new researcher.

Models of society

Sociolinguistic research always implies a model of society, and different approaches to sociolinguistics are often characterised by competing views of society and how it works. Chapter 1 contrasted three views of society: functionalism (underlying much of the variationist work discussed in Chapters 3 and 4), Marxism (drawn on, often explicitly, by some researchers with an interest in language and power discussed in Chapter 10) and interactionism (underlying, or at least consistent with, much of the research on language in interaction discussed in Chapter 6). Functionalism and Marxism give rise to radically different conceptions of social class, often taken as a key social dimension in sociolinguistic research. However, the priority accorded to class has itself been questioned – by, for instance, feminist researchers, whose work on language and gender was discussed in Chapter 7. Other studies have highlighted aspects of social identity that may interact with class, or that may assume greater importance in certain contexts (e.g. age, discussed in Chapters 3 and 4, and ethnic group, the focus of many studies discussed in Chapter 5).

Chapter 7 also highlighted changing perceptions of social identity: from a relatively fixed set of attributes (gender, class, ethnicity, age) to a more fluid model in which identities are negotiated as speakers interact, and different identities may be played up, or played down in different contexts. This relatively fluid model is consistent with many studies of interaction discussed in Chapter 6, and with studies of code-switching and style-shifting discussed in Chapter 5, but it seems harder to reconcile with approaches to dialectology (Chapter 2) and large-scale variationist studies (Chapters 3 and 4).

Models of language

All sociolinguistic studies see language as dynamic and are concerned to document patterns of variation and change. At a less general level, however, different approaches to sociolinguistic enquiry may be characterised by different views of language and how it works. We mentioned in Chapter 1 that sociolinguistics has, until recently, focused largely on the analysis of speech rather than writing. The variationist studies discussed in Chapters 3 and 4 identified discrete linguistic forms (e.g. pronunciation and sometimes grammatical features) and charted their distribution across social groups and across contexts. A number of social meanings were suggested on the basis of this distribution (e.g. the overt prestige attached to pronunciations associated with high social status, in contrast to the covert prestige attached to certain vernacular forms). Interactional studies, such as those discussed in Chapters 5 and 6, have taken a more holistic view of language: they have also placed much more emphasis on the functions which language fulfils and how it is used to achieve certain ends in an interaction. Interactional studies tend to see the meanings of language forms as relatively fluid and context-dependent, the subject of negotiation between participants in an interaction.

The relationship between language and society

Language has sometimes been seen as reflecting pre-existing social divisions and social values (a position implied by variationist studies that look at the broad distribution of linguistic features across social groups). This may suggest a kind of social determinism: that people speak as they do *because* they are working-class, or male, and so on. Alternatively, language has been seen as relatively powerful, constraining its speakers' thoughts and beliefs (a position taken in some early studies of language and power). In their extreme forms, neither position would allow much scope for individual agency or creativity. The creativity of individual speakers is, however, emphasised in much interactional research (e.g. studies of code-switching discussed in Chapter 5). Recent research acknowledges the complexity of the process by which individuals not only are constrained by, but also help to construct more general social structures. The precise nature of the relationship between the 'micro' (individual, contextualised interactions) and the 'macro' (large-scale social divisions and social processes) is the subject of continuing debate within sociolinguistics.

Sociolinguists and their subject matter

Sociolinguists' relationship with their subject matter can be characterised as either 'dispassionate' or 'engaged', and Chapter 1 emphasised the descriptive nature of sociolinguistic enquiry (drawing a distinction between linguistic *de*scriptivism and *pre*scriptivism). It would not be going too far to say that descriptivism is one of the tenets of sociolinguistics, and in fact of linguistics more generally. Sociolinguists have, traditionally, tried to act as impartial observers, describers and analysts of language use. Sociolinguistic enquiry cannot, however, be entirely neutral: we suggested above that different sociolinguistic approaches implied different models of society, and sociolinguists' values and beliefs will inevitably affect what they choose to study and how they carry out their research. Sociolinguists not only study but also tend to favour diversity over homogeneity; they have lamented language 'death' and supported endangered languages (as discussed in Chapter 8). Sociolinguists have also made a point of studying stigmatised languages like pidgins and creoles to establish their rule-governed structure and historicity (see Chapter 9); and they have been preoccupied with documenting vernacular language use: rather less is known about the variable language use of high-status speakers.

Many sociolinguists engage more directly with social policy and practice: in Chapters 3 and 6 we discussed the applications of sociolinguistic research in institutional contexts such as industry and the law. Chapters 11 (education) and 12 (policy and planning) focused in more detail on contexts in which sociolinguists have been particularly concerned not simply to describe, but also to have an effect on how language is used. Some sociolinguists have criticised attempts by others to maintain a detached stance. Researchers who take a critical approach to language study (many of those interested in language and gender (Chapter 7) and language and power (Chapter 10), for instance) frequently acknowledge the social and political beliefs that influence their work, and their engagement in social/political action.

Sociolinguistics and ethics

Because it is a social science, involving the study of people, ethical considerations are highly important in sociolinguistic research – these are bound up with the approaches and specific research methods which sociolinguists adopt. Chapter 3, for instance, discussed the 'observer's paradox', according to which any language data collected cannot help but be influenced by the presence of the observer. Those who strive for relatively 'uncontaminated' data have adopted various forms of deception – ranging from concealing the true purpose of the research to recording people surreptitiously – to minimise the effects on speakers of being observed or recorded. Surreptitious recordings are now generally regarded as unacceptable, but researchers vary in the amount and type of information which they divulge to their informants.

Other aspects of data collection have ethical implications. Research using traditional sociolinguistic interviews (discussed in Chapters 3 to 5) allows the researcher to collect similar types of data from each speaker and to draw systematic comparisons between certain groups of speakers. However, this approach may also distance researchers from their informants: research is carried out 'on' people, who may themselves derive very little benefit from the study. Other researchers (discussed in Chapters 4 to 6) have tried to collect relatively 'naturalistic' data, away from the contrived setting of the traditional interview. Many have drawn on 'participant observation', in which they take on some sort of role in the community under investigation. This could have certain ethical benefits – researchers may take on a socially useful role, and may form continuing relationships with community members. However, the blurring of the researcher's role introduces new ethical dilemmas: to what extent should the research be acknowledged, for instance? Is there a danger of data being gathered under false pretences? Is it harder to 'decommit' from a relationship based on friendship than from a more distant professional relationship (a problem encountered by Lesley Milroy in her Belfast study, discussed in Chapter 4)?

Researchers with an interest in language and power tend to acknowledge the interests of research participants, and may explicitly set out to 'empower' participants. This may seem to pose fewer ethical problems, but there remains the issue of who decides what participants' interests are, and what happens if participants' beliefs and social values conflict with those of the researcher.

These are continuing issues in sociolinguistics, none of which is likely to have an easy resolution. If you have become interested in sociolinguistic research and the issues raised by different approaches, the list which follows provides a starting point for further reading.

FURTHER READING

Full references to these texts are given in the Bibliography.

General
For definitions and discussion of key terms in sociolinguistics, see *A Dictionary of Sociolinguistics* (Swann, Deumert, Lillis and Mesthrie, 2004).

Chapter 1
Introductions to linguistics: V. Fromkin, R. Rodman, and N. Hyams (2007), *An Introduction to Language* is a detailed introductory textbook. A shorter introduction is R. A. Hudson (1985), *Invitation to Linguistics*. A compelling book on generative grammar and the mind aimed at the general reader is S. Pinker (1994), *The Language Instinct*.

Linguistic terms: a comprehensive reference book is D. Crystal (2003), *A Dictionary of Linguistics and Phonetics*. For definitions and discussion of key terms in sociolinguistics, see Swann, Deumert, Lillis and Mesthrie (2004), *A Dictionary of Sociolinguistics*.

On prescriptivism: D. Cameron (1995b), *Verbal Hygiene*, and J. Milroy and L. Milroy (1985a), *Authority in Language*.

On society: A. Giddens (1987), *Sociology* and M. Haralambos, R. Heald and M. Holborn (2000), *Sociology: Themes and Perspectives*.

On standard English and RP: D. Leith (1997), *A Social History of English*.

Chapter 2
P. Trudgill and J. K. Chambers (1999), *Dialectology*; K. M. Petyt (1980), *The Study of Dialect*.

Chapter 3
On variationist linguistics: W. Labov (1972a), *Sociolinguistic Patterns*, and J. K. Chambers (2003), *Sociolinguistic Theory*.

On field methods: W. Labov's chapter in J. Baugh and J. Sherzer (eds) (1984), *Language in Use*, pp. 28–53, and C. Feagin's chapter in J. K. Chambers, N. Schilling-Estes and P. Trudgill (eds), *The Handbook of Language Variation and Change*.

On language and the law: J. Gibbons (ed.) (1994), *Language and the Law*.

Chapter 4

On social networks: L. Milroy (1980), *Language and Social Networks*, is the pioneering classic.

On language change: J. Aitchison (1991), *Language Change: Progress or Decay?* is a lively introduction to the field.

On principal components analysis: B. Horvath (1985), *Variation in Australian English*, is the most useful.

For students with a good background in linguistics, W. Labov's *Principles of Linguistic Change* is expected to cover three volumes. To date, vol. 1 (1994) and vol. 2 (2000) have appeared.

The Atlas of North American English (Labov, Ash and Boberg) was published in 2006 and includes a CD of illustrations.

Chapter 5

Myers-Scotton (1993) provides a good discussion of the social motivations for code-switching, based on evidence from Africa. The papers in Auer (ed.) (1998) illustrate conversational approaches to code-switching, and Milroy and Muysken (eds) (1995) include a wider range of disciplinary perspectives. Woolard (2004) provides a critical overview of code-switching research.

Eckert and Rickford (eds) (2001) include a range of studies of speaking style, and Coupland (2007) provides an overview of this aspect of sociolinguistics.

While most studies of language choice and code-switching in interaction focus on spoken language, Danet and Herring (eds) (2007) bring together a range of studies of multilingual language use on the internet.

Chapter 6

Albert (1972), Basso (1972), Frake (1964) and other papers in these collections are good examples of early 'classic' ethnographic studies. Duranti and Goodwin (1992) contains some interesting, more recent studies, and Duranti (ed.) (2004) provides an exploration of key concepts in linguistic anthropology that are relevant to this and other chapters. Saville-Troike (2003) is the third edition of a long-established introduction to the ethnography of communication. Cameron (2001) outlines different approaches to the analysis of spoken interaction.

Chapter 7

General overviews of gender and language can be found in several recent text books, including Coates (2004, 3rd edn); Eckert and McConnell-Ginet (2003), Talbot (1998) and Litosseliti (2006). Coates (1998) is a useful reader and Sunderland (2006) includes key edited readings and activities. Cameron and Kulick (2006) is a reader on language and sexuality.

There are several edited collections that contain useful selections from contemporary research. Examples include: Bergvall et al. (1995); Hall and Bucholtz (1995); Harrington et al. (2008); Holmes and Meyerhoff (2003); Johnson and Meinhof (1997); Litosseliti and Sunderland (2002); and Wodak (1997). Papers in these collections adopt diverse methodologies, but most take a broadly qualitative approach. Hultgren (2008), however, provides a strong argument in favour of quantitative research.

Chapter 8

On language contact, a clear and informative textbook is *Language Contact and Bilingualism* by R. Appel and P. Muysken (1987). More recent accounts can be found in Winford (2003) *An Introduction to Contact Linguistics* and Thomason (2001) *Language Contact: An Introduction*.

The classics on language shift are N. C. Dorian (1981), *Language Death: The Life Cycle of a Scottish Gaelic Dialect*, and S. Gal (1979), *Language Shift: Social Determinants of Linguistic Change in Bilingual Austria*.

The most readable book on endangered languages is *Vanishing Voices: the Extinction of the World's Languages* by Nettle and Romaine (2000); see also the volume *Endangered Languages: Current Issues and Future Prospects* edited by Grenoble and Whaley (1998). J. Fishman's (1991), *Reversing Language Shift*, is subtitled *Theoretical and Empirical Foundations of Assistance to Threatened Languages*.

Chapter 9

Of the many introductory books on pidgins and creoles, we recommend *Contact Languages: Pidgins and Creoles* by M. Sebba (1997), and *Pidgins and Creoles: An Introduction*, edited by J. Arends, P. Muysken and N. Smith (1995). An excellent reference set is formed by the two-volume *Pidgins and Creoles* by J. Holm (1998, 1989).

On new varieties of English, B. B. Kachru (1986), *The Alchemy of English*, and a collection edited by him (1992a), *The Other Tongue: English across Cultures*, are essential reading. See also his book *Asian Englishes: Beyond the Canon* (2005) and Kingsley Bolton's (2005) *Chinese Englishes: A Sociolinguistic History*.

Chapter 10

On discourse: N. Fairclough (1992), *Discourse and Social Change,* and J. Blommaert's (2005) more explicitly sociolinguistic book *Discourse*.

On various aspects of power and language: R. Andersen (1988), *The Power and the Word*, R. Phillipson (1992), *Linguistic Imperialism*, and A. Pennycook (1994), *The Cultural Politics of English as an International Language*.

On symbolic power: P. Bourdieu (1991), *Language and Symbolic Power*.

On propaganda: R. Jackall (ed.) (1995), *Propaganda* is a comprehensive collection of articles.

Chapter 11

On ethnography, language and education: S. B. Heath (1983), *Ways with Words*.

On Bernstein and other approaches to language variation and the school: J. R. Edwards (1979a), *Language and Disadvantage*.

On bilingual education in social perspective: W. Leap (1993), *American Indian English*.

A comprehensive and up-to-date overview of the field is provided by Spolsky and Hult (eds) (2008) *The Handbook of Educational Linguistics*.

Chapter 12

R. L. Cooper (1989), *Language Planning and Social Change* was long the standard reference. A more recent highly readable account is *Language Policy* by B. Spolsky (2004).

J. A. Fishman (1991), *Reversing Language Shift: Theoretical and Empirical Foundations of Assistance to Threatened Languages*, contains an 'action-oriented' approach to language planning for minorities.

I. Fodor and C. Hagége (eds) (1983–9), *Language Reform: History and Future*, is a five-volume collection of case studies on language planning.

D. Cameron (1995b), *Verbal Hygiene*, is concerned with processes of language regulation.

A good internet site for language planning and policy is that of the Language Policy Research Centre (Israel): http://www.biu.ac.il/hu/lprc/

Chapter 13

H. Lane (1984a), *When the Mind Hears*, is a historical novel about the French Deaf teacher Laurent Clerc (1786–1869), who went to the USA with Thomas Gallaudet to teach sign language.

O. Sacks (1989), *Seeing Voices: A Journey into the World of the Deaf*, contains three essays dealing with, inter alia, the structure of sign languages, the psychology of Deafness, sign-language acquisition, and Deaf culture. E. Klima and U. Bellugi (1979), *The Signs of Language* is an encyclopaedic and well-illustrated overview.

NEXT STEPS

If you wish to pursue sociolinguistics after this introductory course, more special-ised courses and textbooks can be found in the areas covered in this book. Many universities offer courses on language planning, gender, variation theory, pidgins and creoles and so on. Further courses in linguistics and sociology are important for a strong foundation in sociolinguistics. Allied subjects which could profitably be studied include another language, anthropology, social psychology and intro-ductory courses in statistics and computer use. Applied linguistics and corpus linguistics also overlap with the concerns of sociolinguists.

The major journals of sociolinguistics with (abbreviations used in the Bibliography) are *Language Variation and Change* (*LVC*) (Cambridge University Press), *Language in Society* (*LiS*) (Cambridge University Press), *Journal of Sociolinguistics* (Blackwell) and *International Journal of the Sociology of Language* (*IJSL*) (Mouton de Gruyter).

Statistics textbooks
Ehrenberg (1986), *A Primer in Data Reduction*, is an introductory textbook which is particularly useful as a reference book. Mathematical formulas for sta-tistical procedures are given, but the procedures themselves are explained in lay language. A list of definitions of important statistical terms can be found at the end of each chapter.

Reid (1987), *Working with Statistics*, is a clear and accessible description of statistical methods which contains hardly any mathematical equations. Reading this book might convince you that doing statistics can be fun.

Sociolinguistics and ethics
Many professional groups have their own guidelines on research ethics, which are useful to sociolinguists:

The British Association for Applied Linguistics (BAAL) has a sixteen-page booklet entitled 'Recommendations on Good Practice in Applied Linguistics' (1994).

The American Anthropological Association has a set of guidelines of relevance to sociolinguists.

The book *Research in Language: Issues of Power and Method* by D. Cameron et al. (1992) contains a specifically sociolinguistic perspective of the topic.

BIBLIOGRAPHY

AEQ   *Anthropology and Education Quarterly*
AnthL   *Anthropological Linguistics*
ARA   *Annual Review of Anthropology*
IJAL   *International Journal of American Linguistics*
IJSL   *International Journal of the Sociology of Language*
LC   *Language and Communication*
LiS   *Language in Society*
SLS   *Sign Language Studies*

Aarons, D. (1995), 'Hands full of meaning'. *Bua!* 10 (1) (December): 8–10.

Aarons, D. and P. Akach (1998), 'South African Sign Language: one language or many? A sociolinguistic question'. *Stellenbosch Papers in Linguistics* 31: 1–28.

Aarons, D. and P. Akach (2002), 'South African Sign Language: one language or many?', in R. Mesthrie (ed.), *Language in South Africa*. Cambridge: Cambridge University Press, pp. 127–47.

Abercrombie, D. (1967), *Elements of General Phonetics*. Edinburgh: Edinburgh University Press.

Achebe, C. (1962), *Things Fall Apart*. London: Heinemann.

Agar, M. (1981), 'Stories, background knowledge and themes: problems in the analysis of life story narratives'. *American Ethnologist* 7: 223–39.

Agard, J. (1985), *Mangoes and Bullets*. London: Pluto.

Ahlgren, I. (1991), 'Swedish conditions: Sign Language in Deaf education', in Prillwitz and Vollhaber (eds), pp. 91–4.

Aitchison, J. (1976), *The Articulate Mammal: An Introduction to Psycholinguistics*. London: Hutchinson.

Aitchison, J. (1991), *Language Change: Progress or Decay?*, 2nd edn. Cambridge: Cambridge University Press.

Aitchison, J. (1994), 'Pidgins, creoles and change', in R. Asher (ed.), *The Encyclopedia of Language and Linguistics*. Oxford: Pergamon, vol. 6: 3, pp. 181–6.

Albert, E. M. (1972), 'Culture patterning of speech behavior in Burundi', in J. J. Gumperz and D. Hymes (eds) (1972, rev. edn 1986), *Directions in Sociolinguistics: The Ethnography of Communication*. New York and Oxford: Basil Blackwell, pp. 72–105.

Alexander, N. (1989), *Language Policy and National Unity in South Africa/ Azania*. Cape Town: Buchu.

Alexander, N. (1992), 'Language planning from below', in Herbert (ed.), pp. 143–9.

Alexander, N. (1997), 'Language policy and planning in the new South Africa'. *African Sociological Review* 1 (1): 82–98.

Althusser, L. (1971), 'Ideology and ideological state apparatuses', in Althusser (ed.), *Lenin and Philosophy and Other Essays*. London: New Left Books, pp. 121–73.

Andersen, R. (1988), *The Power and the Word: Language, Power and Change*. London: Paladin.

Angermeyer, P. and J.V. Singler (2003), 'The Case for Politeness: Pronoun Variation in Co-ordinate NPs in Object Position in English'. *Language Variation and Change* 15: 171–209.

Ansre, G. (1971), 'Language standardisation in sub-Saharan Africa', in T. A. Sebeok (ed.), *Current Trends in Linguistics*, vol. 7: *Linguistics in Sub-Saharan Africa*. The Hague: Mouton, pp. 680–98.

Appel R. and P. Muysken (1987), *Language Contact and Bilingualism*. London: Arnold.

Aramburo, A. J. (1989), 'Sociolinguistic aspects of the Black Deaf community', in Lucas (ed.), pp. 103–22.

Arends, J. (1995), 'The socio-historical background of creoles', in Arends et al. (eds), pp. 15–24.

Arends, J., P. Muysken and N. Smith (eds) (1995), *Pidgins and Creoles: An Introduction*. Amsterdam: Benjamins.

Auer, P. (1998), 'Introduction: *Bilingual Conversation* Revisited', in P. Auer (ed.), *Code-Switching in Conversation: Language, Interaction and Identity*. London: Routledge, pp. 10–11.

Auer, P. (2003), '"Türkenslang" – Ein jugendsprachlicher Ethnolekt des Deutschen und seine Transformationen', in A. Häcki-Buhofer (ed.), *Spracherwerb und Lebensalter*. Tübingen/Basel: Francke, pp. 255–64.

Austin, J. L. (1962), *How to Do Things with Words*. Oxford: Oxford University Press.

Bailey, C. J. (1973), *Variation and Linguistic Theory*. Arlington, VA: Center for Applied Linguistics.

Bailey, G. (2002), 'Real and apparent time', in J. K. Chambers, N. Schilling-Estes and P. Trudgill (eds), *The Handbook of Language Variation and Change*. Oxford: Blackwell, pp. 312–32.

Bailey, R. W. (1991), *Images of English: A Cultural History of the Language*. Ann Arbor: University of Michigan Press.

Baker, C. (1999), 'Sign language and the Deaf community', in J. A. Fishman (ed.), *Handbook of Language and Ethnic Identity*. Oxford and New York: Oxford University Press, pp. 122–39.

Baker, P. (1995), 'Motivation in creole genesis', in Baker (ed.), *From Contact to Creole and Beyond*. London: University of Westminster Press, pp. 3–15.

Baker-Shenk, C. and D. Cokely (1991), *American Sign Language: A Teacher's Resource Text on Grammar and Culture*. Washington, DC: Clerc Books, Gallaudet University Press.

Bakhtin, M. M. (1981), *The Dialogic Imagination,* trans. C. Emerson and M. Holquist, ed. M. Holquist. Austin: University of Texas Press.

Bakhtin, M. M. (1984 [1929]), *Problems of Dostoevsky's Poetics*, ed. and trans. by C. Emerson. Minneapolis: University of Minnesota Press.

Bakhtin, M. M. (1986), *Speech Genres and Other Late Essays*, trans. V. W. McGee, ed. C. Emerson and M. Holquist. Austin: University of Texas Press.

Bakker, P. (1995), 'Pidgins', in Arends et al. (eds), pp. 25–39.

Bakker, P. (2003), 'The absence of reduplication in pidgins', in S. Kouwenberg (ed.), *Twice as Meaningful: Reduplication in Pidgins, Creoles and other Contact Languages*. London: Battlebridge, pp. 37–46.

Bakker, P. and P. Muysken (1995), 'Mixed languages and language intertwining', in Arends et al. (eds), pp. 41–52.

Ball, P., C. Gallois and V. Callan (1989), 'Language attitudes: a perspective from social psychology', in P. Collins and D. Blair (eds), *Australian English: The Language of a New Society*. Queensland: University of Queensland Press.

Bamgbose, A. (1987), 'When is language planning not planning?' *Journal of West African Languages* 17 (1): 6–14.

Barbour, S. and P. Stevenson (1990), *Variation in German: A Critical Approach to German Sociolinguistics*. Cambridge: Cambridge University Press.

Barraclough, G. (ed.) (1982), *The Times Concise Atlas of World History*. London: Times Books.

Barrett, R. (1999), 'Indexing polyphonous identity in the speech of African American drag queens', in M. Bucholtz, A. C. Laing and L. A. Sutton (eds), *Reinventing Identities: The Gendered Self in Discourse*. New York: Oxford University Press, pp. 313–31.

Basso, K. (1967), 'Semantic aspects of linguistic acculturation'. *American Anthropologist* 69 (5): 471–7.

Basso, K. H. (1972), '"To give up on words": silence in Western Apache culture', in P. P. Giglioli (ed.), *Language and Social Context*. Harmondsworth: Penguin, pp. 67–86.

Basso, K. H. (1990), *Western Apache Language and Culture: Essays in Linguistic Anthropology*. Tucson: University of Arizona Press.

Batidzirai, B. (1996), 'The significance of the ALLEX project in the modernization and development of African languages in Zimbabwe: experience from the monolingual Shona dictionary'. Paper presented at the International Seminar on Language and Education in Africa, University of Cape Town.

Battison, R. M., H. Markowicz and J. C. Woodward (1975), 'A good rule of thumb: variable phonology in American Sign Language', in R. W. Fasold and R. Shuy (eds), *Analyzing Variation in Language*. Washington, DC: Georgetown University Press, pp. 291–302.

Baugh, J. (1980), 'A re-examination of the Black English copula', in W. Labov (ed.), *Locating Language in Time and Space: Quantitative Analyses of Linguistic Structure*. New York: Academic Press, vol. 1, pp. 83–106.

Baugh J. and J. Sherzer (1984), *Language in Use: Readings in Sociolinguistics*. Englewood Cliffs, NJ: Prentice Hall.

Baumann, M. (1979), 'Two features of "women's speech"?', in B. L. Dubois and I. Crouch (eds), *The Sociology of the Languages of American Women*. Papers in Southwest English IV. San Antonio: Trinity University.

Bell, A. (1984), 'Language style as audience design'. *LiS* 13 (2): 145–204.

Bell, A. (2001), 'Back in style: reworking audience design', in P. Eckert and J. Rickford (eds), *Style and Sociolinguistic Variation*. New York: Cambridge University Press.

Bellugi, U. and S. D. Fischer (1972), 'A comparison of sign language and spoken language'. *Cognition* 1: 173–200.

Benally, A. and D. Viri (2005), 'Dine Bizaad [Navajo language] at a crossroads: extinction or renewal?' *Bilingual Research Journal* 29 (1): 85–108.

Benson, R. W. (1985), 'The end of legalese: the game is over'. *Review of Law and Social Change* 13: 519–73.

Bereiter, C. and S. Engelmann (1966), *Teaching Disadvantaged Children in the Pre-school*. Englewood Cliffs, NJ: Prentice-Hall.

Berg, C., F. Hult and K. King (2003), 'Shaping the climate for language shift? English in Sweden's elite domains'. *World Englishes* 20 (3): 305–20.

Bergman, B. and L. Wallin (1991), 'Sign language research and the Deaf community', in Prillwitz and Vollhaber (eds), pp. 187–214.

Bergwall, V. L., J. M. Bing and A. F. Freed (eds) (1995), *Rethinking Language and Gender Research*. New York: Longman.

Bernstein, B. (1960), 'Language and social class'. *British Journal of Sociology* 10: 311–26.

Bernstein, B. (1974), *Class, Codes and Control,* vol. 1. London: Routledge.

Bertelsen, E. (1997), 'Ads and amnesia: black advertising in the new South Africa', in S. Nuttall and C. Coetzee (eds), *Negotiating the Past: The Making of Memory in South Africa*. Cape Town: Oxford University Press, pp. 221–41.

Besnier, N. (2003), 'Crossing genders, mixing languages: the linguistic construction of transgenderism in Tonga', in J. Holmes and M. Meyerhoff (eds), *The Handbook of Language and Gender*. Oxford: Blackwell Publishing, pp. 289–301.

Bickerton, D. (1975), *The Dynamics of a Creole System*. Cambridge: Cambridge University Press.

Bickerton, D. (1977), 'Pidginisation and creolisation: language acquisition and language universals', in A. Valdman (ed.), *Pidgin and Creole Linguistics*. Bloomington: Indiana University Press, pp. 49–60.

Bickerton, D. (1981), *Roots of Language*. Ann Arbor: Karoma.

Bickerton, D. (1990), *Language and Species*. Chicago: University of Chicago Press.

Blackshire-Belay, C. (1993), 'Foreign workers' German: is it a pidgin?', in F. Byrne and J. Holm (eds), *Atlantic Meets Pacific: A Global View of Pidginization and Creolization*. Amsterdam and Philadelphia: John Benjamins, pp. 431–40.

Blake, R. and M. Josey (2004), 'The /ay/ diphthong in a Martha's Vineyard community: what can we say 40 years after Labov?', *Language in Society* 32 (4): 451–85.

Blanc H. (1968), 'The Israeli Koine as an emergent national standard', in J. A. Fishman, C. A. Ferguson and J. Das Gupta (eds), *Language Problems in Developing Nations*. New York: John Wiley, pp. 237–51.

Blom, J. P. and J. J. Gumperz (1972), 'Social meaning in linguistic structures: code-switching in Norway', in J. J. Gumperz and D. Hymes (eds) (1972, rev. edn 1986), *Directions in Sociolinguistics: The Ethnography of Communication*. New York and Oxford: Basil Blackwell, pp. 407–34.

Blommaert, J. (2005), *Discourse*. Cambridge: Cambridge University Press.

Bloomfield, L. W. (1933), *Language*. New York: Holt, Rinehart and Winston.

Bochner, J. H. and J. A. Albertini (1988), 'Language varieties in the deaf population and their acquisition by children and adults', in M. Strong (ed.), *Language Learning and Deafness*. Cambridge: Cambridge University Press, pp. 3–39.

Bolinger, D. (1980), *Language: The Loaded Weapon*. London and New York: Longman.

Bolton, K. (2005), *Chinese Englishes: A Sociolinguistic History*. Cambridge: Cambridge University Press.

Bourdieu, P. (1977a), *Outline of a Theory of Practice*, trans. R. Nice. Cambridge: Cambridge University Press.

Bourdieu, P. (1977b), 'The economics of linguistic exchanges', trans. R. Nice. *Social Sciences Information* 16 (6): 645–68.

Bourdieu, P. (1984), *Distinction: A Social Critique of the Judgement of Taste*. London: Routledge & Kegan Paul.

Bourdieu, P. (1991), *Language and Symbolic Power*, ed. J. B. Thompson, trans. G. Raymond and M. Adamson. Cambridge, MA: Harvard University Press.

Boyes Braem, P., B. Caramore, R. Hermann and P. Shores Hermann (2003), 'Romance and reality: sociolinguistics similarities and differences between Swiss German Sign Language and Rhaeto-Romansh', in L. Monaghan, C. Schmaling, K. Nakamura and G. H. Turner (eds), *Many Ways to be Deaf. International Variation in Deaf Communities*. Washington, DC: Gallaudet University Press, pp. 89–113.

Branson, J., D. Miller and I. G. Marsaja, with the assistance of I. W. Negara (1996), 'Everyone here speaks sign language, too: a deaf village in Bali, Indonesia', in C. Lucas (ed.), *Multicultural Aspects of Sociolinguistics in Deaf Communities*. Washington, DC: Gallaudet University Press, pp. 39–57.

Brenzinger, M. (1992), 'Patterns of language shift in East Africa', in Herbert (ed.), pp. 287–303.

Brenzinger, M., B. Heine and G. Sommer (1991), 'Language death in Africa', in Robins and Uhlenbeck (eds).

Britain, D. (1997), 'Dialect contact, focusing and phonological rule complexity: "Canadian Raising" in the English Fens'. *LiS* 26 (1): 15–46.

Britto, F. (1986) *Diglossia: A Study of the Theory with Application to Tamil*. Washington, DC: Georgetown University Press.

Brown, G. and G. Yule (1983), *Discourse Analysis*. Cambridge: Cambridge University Press.

Brown, P. (1980), 'How and why are women more polite?: some evidence from a Mayan community', in S. McConnell-Ginet, R. Borker and N. Furman (eds), *Women and Language in Literature and Society*. New York: Praeger. Repr. in J. Coates (ed.) (1998), *Language and Gender: A Reader*. Oxford: Blackwell Publishers, pp. 81–99

Brown, P. (1990), 'Gender, politeness and confrontation in Tenejapa'. *Discourse Processes* 13: 123–41.

Brown, P. and S. Levinson (1987), *Politeness: Some Universals in Language*. Cambridge: Cambridge University Press.

Brown, R. and A. Gilman (1960), 'The pronouns of power and solidarity', in T. A. Sebeok (ed.), *Style in Language*. Cambridge, MA: MIT Press, pp. 253–76.

Browne, J. R. (1868), *Adventures in the Apache Country*. New York: Harper.

Bull, T. (1992), 'Male power and language planning: the role of women in Norwegian language planning'. *IJSL* 94: 155–71.

Bull, T. (1995), 'Language maintenance and loss in an originally trilingual area in North Norway'. *IJSL* 115: 125–34.

Bull, W. (1964) 'The use of vernacular languages in education', in D. Hymes (ed.), *Language in Culture and Society*. New York: Harper and Row, pp. 527–33. (Originally in *IJAL* 21: 288–94.)

Burns, S., P. Matthews and E. Nolan-Conroy (2001), 'Language attitudes', in C. Lucas (ed.), *The Sociolinguistics of Sign Language*. Cambridge: Cambridge University Press, pp. 181–216.

Butler, J. (1990), *Gender Trouble: Feminism and the Subversion of Identity*. New York: Routledge.

Cameron, D. (1992), *Feminism and Linguistic Theory*, 2nd edn. Basingstoke: Macmillan.

Cameron, D. (1995a), 'Rethinking language and gender studies: some issues for the 1990s', in S. Mills (ed.) (1995), *Language and Gender: Interdisciplinary Perspectives*. Harlow: Longman, pp. 31–44.

Cameron, D. (1995b), *Verbal Hygiene*. London and New York: Routledge.

Cameron, D. (1997), 'Performing gender identity: young men's talk and the construction of heterosexual masculinity', in S. Johnson and U. H. Meinhof (eds), *Language and Masculinity*. Oxford: Blackwell Publishers.

Cameron, D. (2001), *Working with Spoken Discourse*. London: Sage Publications.

Cameron, D. (2005), 'Language, gender and sexuality: current issues and new directions'. *Applied Linguistics* 26 (4): 482–502.

Cameron, D. (2007), *The Myth of Mars and Venus*. Oxford: Oxford University Press.

Cameron. D. and D. Kulick (eds) (2006), *The Language and Sexuality Reader*. Abingdon: Routledge.

Cameron, D., E. Fraser, P. Harvey, M. B. H. Rampton and K Richardson (1992), *Researching Language: Issues of Power and Method*. London: Routledge.

Cameron, D., F. McAlinden and K. O'Leary (1988), 'Lakoff in context: the social and linguistic functions of tag questions', in J. Coates and D. Cameron (eds), *Women in their Speech Communities*. London and New York: Longman, pp. 74–93.

Campbell, L. and M. C. Muntzel (1989), 'The structural consequences of language death', in Dorian (ed.), pp. 181–96.

Casagrande, J. B. (1954), 'Comanche linguistic acculturation'. *IJAL* 20: 140–57, 217–37.

Cassidy, F. G. and J. H. Hall (eds) (1985–2002), *Dictionary of American Regional English*. 4 vols. Cambridge, MA: Harvard University Press.

Cazden, C. B. (1988), *Classroom Discourse: The Language of Teaching and Learning*. Portsmouth, NH: Heinemann.

Chambers, J. K. (2003), *Sociolinguistic Theory*, 2nd edn. Oxford: Blackwell.

Chen M. (1972), 'The time dimension: contribution toward a theory of sound change'. *Foundations of Language* 8: 457–98.

Chen, M. (1976), 'Relative chronology: three methods of reconstruction'. *Journal of Linguistics* 12: 209–58.

Chen, P. (1993), 'Modern written Chinese in development'. *LiS* 22: 505–37.

Chen, P. (1996), 'Toward a phonographic writing system of Chinese: a case study in writing reform'. *IJSL* 122: 1–46.

Cheshire, J., V. Edwards, H. Munstermann and B. Weltens (eds) (1989), *Dialect and Education: Some European Perspectives*. Clevedon: Multilingual Matters.

Chew, P. G. L. (1995), 'Lectal power in Singapore English'. *World Englishes* 14 (2): 163–80.

Chomsky, N. (1957), *Syntactic Structures*. The Hague: Mouton.

Chomsky, N. (1965), *Aspects of the Theory of Syntax*. Cambridge, MA: MIT Press.

Christian, D. (1988), 'Language planning: the view from linguistics', in F. J. Newmeyer (ed.), *Linguistics: The Cambridge Survey*, vol. 4: *Language: The Socio-cultural Context*. Cambridge: Cambridge University Press, pp. 193–209.

Chumbow, B. A. (1987), 'Towards a language planning model for Africa'. *Journal of West African Languages* 17 (1): 15–22.

CIA World Factbook 2007. Available at (last accessed 9 December 2007): https://www.cia.gov/library/publications/the-world-factbook/index.html

Cicourel, A. V. (1981), 'Language and medicine', in C. Ferguson and S. B. Heath (eds), *Language in the USA*. Cambridge: Cambridge University Press.

Cicourel, A. V. (1985), 'Doctor–patient discourse', in T. A. van Dijk (ed.), *Handbook of Discourse Analysis*, vol. 4. New York: Academic Press.

Cluver, A. D. de V. (1993), 'Namibians: linguistic foreigners in their own country', in K. Prinsloo, Y. Peeters, J. Turi and C. van Rensburg (eds), *Language, Law and Equality*. Proceedings of the Third International Conference of the International Academy of Language Law (IALL) held in South Africa, April 1992. Pretoria: University of South Africa, pp. 261–76.

Cluver, A. D. de V. (1994), 'Preconditions for language unification'. *South African Journal of Linguistics* (Supplement 20): 168–94.

Clyne, M., E. Eisokovits and L. Tollfree (2000), 'Ethnic varieties of Australian English', in D. Blair and P. Collins (eds), *English in Australia*. Philadelphia and Amsterdam: John Benjamins, pp. 223–38.

Coates, J. (1988), 'Gossip revisited: language in all-female groups', in J. Coates and D. Cameron (eds), *Women in Their Speech Communities*. London and New York: Longman, pp. 94–122.

Coates, J. (2004), *Women, Men and Language*, 3rd edn. London: Longman. (1st edn 1986; 2nd edn 1993.)

Coates, J. (1994), 'No gap, lots of overlap: turn-taking patterns in the talk of women friends', in D. Graddol, J. Maybin and B. Stierer (eds), *Researching Language and Literacy in Social Context*. Clevedon: Multilingual Matters, pp. 177–92.

Coates, J. (1996), *Women Talk*. Oxford: Basil Blackwell.

Coates, J. (1997), 'One-at-a-time: the organization of men's talk', in S. Johnson and U. H. Meinhof (eds), *Language and Masculinity*. Oxford: Blackwell Publishers, pp. 107–43.

Coates, J. (1998), *Language and Gender: A Reader*. Oxford: Blackwell Publishers.

Coates, J. and R. Sutton-Spence (2001), 'Turn-taking patterns in Deaf conversation'. *Journal of Sociolinguistics* 5: 507–29.

Cobarrubias, J. (1983), 'Ethical issues in status planning', in Cobarrubias and Fishman (eds), pp. 41–86.

Cobarrubias, J. and J. A. Fishman (eds) (1983), *Progress in Language Planning: International Perspectives*. Berlin: Mouton Publishers.

Coles, R. (1977), *Privileged Ones: The Well-Off and Rich in America*. Boston, MA: Brown.

Constitution of South Africa (1996), available at: http://www.info.gov.za/documents/constitution/index.htm (last accessed 17 Nov. 2008).

Cooper, R. L. (1982) *Language Spread: Studies in Diffusion and Social Change*. Bloomington: Indiana University Press.

Cooper, R. L. (1984), 'The avoidance of androcentric generics'. *IJSL* 50: 5–20.

Cooper, R. L. (1989), *Language Planning and Social Change*. Cambridge: Cambridge University Press.

Corson, D. (1995), 'Norway's "Sámi Language Act": emancipatory implications for the world's aboriginal people'. *LiS* 24: 493–514.

Coulmas, F. (1989a), 'Language adaptation', in Coulmas (ed.), *Language Adaptation*. Cambridge: Cambridge University Press, pp. 1–25.

Coulmas, F. (1989b), 'The crisis of normative linguistics', in Coulmas (ed.), *Language Adaptation*. Cambridge: Cambridge University Press, pp. 177–93.

Coulmas, F. (ed.) (1992), *Language and Economy*. Oxford and Cambridge, MA: Blackwell.

Coupland, N. (1984), 'Accommodation at work'. *IJSL* 4–6: 49–70.

Coupland, N. (1985), '"Hark, Hark the Lark": social motivations for phonological style-shifting'. *LC* 5 (3): 153–71.

Coupland, N. (2001), 'Dialect stylisation in radio talk'. *LiS* 30 (3): 345–75.

Coupland, N. (2001), 'Stylisation, authenticity and TV news review'. *Discourse Studies* 3 (4): 13–442.

Coupland, N. (2001), 'Language, situation, and the relational self: theorizing dialect style in sociolinguistics,' in P. Eckert and J. Rickford (eds), *Style and Sociolinguistic Variation*. Cambridge: Cambridge University Press.

Coupland, N. (2003), 'Sociolinguistics and Globalisation'. *Journal of Sociolinguistics* 7(4): 465–73.

Coupland, N. (2007), *Style: Language Variation and Identity*. Cambridge: Cambridge University Press.

Coupland, N. (forthcoming), 'The discursive framing of phonological acts of identity: Welshness through English', in C. Evans Davies and J. Brutt-Griffler (eds), *English and Ethnicity*. London: Palgrave.

Coupland, N. and J. Coupland (1997), 'Discourses of the unsayable: death implicative talk in geriatric medical consultations', in A. Jaworski (ed.), *Silence: Interdisciplinary perspectives*. Berlin/New York: Mouton de Gruyter.

Coupland, N. (submitted) (with H. Bishop, A. Williams, B. Evans and P. Garrett), 'Affiliation, engagement, language use and vitality: Secondary school students' subjective orientations to Welsh and Welshness'. *International Journal of Bilingual Education and Bilingualism*.

Crawford, J. M. (1978), *The Mobilian Trade Languages*. Knoxville: University of Tennessee Press.

Crawford, M. (1995), *Talking Difference: On Gender and Language*. London: Sage Publications.

Crawhall, N. (1993), Negotiations and Language Policy Options in South Africa: A National Language Project Report to the National Education Policy Investigation Sub-committee on Articulating Language Policy. Cape Town: National Language Project.

Crawhall, N. (1995), 'Sign of the times: Deaf rights in South Africa'. *Bua!* 10 (1) (December): 4–7.

Croneberg, C. G. (1976), 'The linguistic community', in W. C. Stokoe, D. C. Casterline and C. G. Croneberg (eds), *A Dictionary of American Sign Language on Linguistic Principles*. Silver Spring, MD: Linstok Press, pp. 297–311.

Crowley, T. (1992), *An Introduction to Historical Linguistics*, 2nd edn. Auckland: Oxford University Press.

Crystal, D. (ed.) (1987), *The Cambridge Encyclopedia of Language*. Cambridge: Cambridge University Press.

Crystal, D. (1988), *Rediscover Grammar*. Harlow: Longman.

Crystal, D. (1991), *A Dictionary of Linguistics and Phonetics*, 3rd edn. Oxford: Basil Blackwell.

Crystal, D. (1995), *The Cambridge Encyclopedia of the English Language*. Cambridge: Cambridge University Press.

Crystal, D. (2003), *A Dictionary of Linguistics and Phonetics*, 5th edn. Oxford: Blackwell.

Cummins, J. (1979), 'Linguistic interdependence and the educational development of bilingual children'. *Review of Educational Research* 49: 221–51.

Currie, C. H. (1952), 'A projection of socio-linguistics: the relationship of speech to social status'. *The Southern Speech Journal* 18: 28–37.

Dailey-O'Cain, J. (2000), 'The sociolinguistic distribution and attitudes towards focuser *like* and quotative *like*'. *Journal of Sociolinguistics* 4: 60–80.

Danet, B. and S. A. Herring (eds) (2007), *The Multilingual Internet: Language, Culture, and Communication Online*. New York: Oxford University Press.

Daoust, D. (1997), 'Language planning and language reform', in F. Coulmas (ed.), *The Handbook of Sociolinguistics*. Oxford: Basil Blackwell, pp. 436–532.

Dasgupta, P. (1993), *The Otherness of English: India's Auntie Tongue Syndrome*. New Delhi: Sage Publications.

Davis, J. (1989), 'Distinguishing language contact phenomena in ASL interpretation', in Lucas (ed.), pp. 85–102.

De Kadt, E. (2002), 'Gender and usage patterns of English in South African urban and rural contexts'. *World Englishes* 21 (1): 83–97.

De Kadt, E. (2005), 'English, language shift and identities: a comparison between "Zulu-dominant" and "multicultural" students on a South African university campus'. *Southern African Linguistics and Applied Language Studies* 23 (1): 19–37.

De Klerk, V. (2000), 'To be Xhosa or not to be Xhosa: that is the question'. *Journal of Multilingual and Multicultural Development* 21 (3): 198–215.

De Weerdt, K. and E. Vanhecke (2004), 'Regional variation in Flemish Sign Language', in M. Van Herreweghe and M. Vermeerbergen (eds), *The Lexicon and Beyond. Sociolinguistics in European Deaf Communities* (Sociolinguistics in Deaf Communities, vol. 10). Washington, DC: Gallaudet University Press, pp. 27–38.

De Weerdt, K. and E. Vanhecke (2004), 'Regional variation in Flemish Sign Language', in M. Van Herreweghe and M. Vermeerbergen (eds), (Sociolinguistics in Deaf Communities, vol. 10). Washington, DC: Gallaudet University Press, 27-38.

DeGraff, M. (2003), 'Against Creole exceptionalism'. *Language* 79 (2): 391–410.

den Besten, H., P. Muysken and N. Smith (1995). 'Theories focusing on the European input', in Arends et al. (eds), pp. 87–98.

Dentith, S. (1995), *Bakhtinian Thought: An Introductory Reader*. London: Routledge.

Deuchar, M. (1987), 'Sign languages as creoles and Chomsky's notion of Universal Grammar', in S. Modgil and C. Modgil (eds), *Noam Chomsky: Consensus and Controversy*. New York: Falmer Press, pp. 81–91.

Deuchar, M. and H. James (1985), 'English as the second language of the Deaf'. *LC* 5 (1): 45–51.

Dirven, R. (1993), 'The use of languages and language policies in Africa: goals of the LiCCA program'. *IJSL* 100/101: 179–89.

Dittmar, N. and P. Schlobinski (eds) (1988), *The Sociolinguistics of Urban Vernaculars: Case Studies and their Evaluation* (Sociolinguistics and Language Contact, vol. 1). Berlin and New York: de Gruyter.

Dittmar, N., P. Schlobinski and I. Wachs (1988a), 'Variation in a divided speech community: the urban vernacular of Berlin', in Dittmar and Schlobinski (eds), pp. 3–18.

Dittmar, N., P. Schlobinski and I. Wachs (1988b), 'The social significance of the Berlin Urban Vernacular', in Dittmar and Schlobinski (eds), pp. 19–43.

Dolnick, E. (1993), 'Deafness as Culture'. *Atlantic Monthly* 272 (3): 37–53.

Donnan E. (1965), *Documents Illustrative of the History of the Slave Trade to America,* vol. 2: *The Eighteenth Century*. New York: Octagon Books.

Dorian, N. C. (1978), 'The fate of morphological complexity in language death'. *Language* 54: 590–609.

Dorian, N. C. (1981), *Language Death: The Life Cycle of a Scottish Gaelic Dialect*. Philadelphia: University of Pennsylvania Press.

Dorian, N. C. (ed.) (1989), *Investigating Obsolescence: Studies in Language Contraction and Death*. Cambridge: Cambridge University Press.

Dorr-Bremme, G. (1984), 'Aspects of teacher/student talk in elementary school classrooms'. Unpublished PhD dissertation, University of California (San Diego).

Downing, J. (1980), *The Media Machine*. London: Pluto Press.

Dozier (1956) 'Two examples of linguistic acculturation'. *Language* 32: 146–57.

Dubois, B. L. and I. Crouch (1975), 'The question of tag questions in women's speech: they don't really use more of them, do they?' *LiS* 4: 289–94.

Duranti, A. (1992), 'Language in context and language as context: the Samoan respect vocabulary', in Duranti and Goodwin.

Duranti, A. (1994), *From Grammar to Politics: Linguistic Anthropology in a Western Samoan Village*. Berkeley: University of California Press.

Duranti. A. (ed.) (2004), *A Companion to Linguistic Anthropology*. Malden, MA and Oxford: Blackwell Publishing.

Duranti, A. and C. Goodwin (eds) (1992), *Rethinking Context: Language as an Interactive Phenomenon*. Cambridge: Cambridge University Press.

Eades, D. (1991), 'Communicative strategies in Aboriginal English', in Romaine (ed.), pp. 84–93.

Eades, D. (1992), *Aboriginal English and the Law: Communicating with Aboriginal English Speaking Clients: A Handbook for Legal Practitioners*. Brisbane: Queensland Law Society, pp. 234–65

Eades, D. (1994), 'A case of communicative clash: Aboriginal English and the legal system', in Gibbons (ed.).

Eades, D (1996), 'Legal recognition of cultural differences in communication: the case of Robyn Kina', *Language and Communication* 16 (3): 215–27.

Eades, D. (2004), 'Understanding Aboriginal English in the legal system: A critical sociolinguistics approach'. *Applied Linguistics* 25 (4): 491–512.

Ebbinghaus, H. and J. Hessmann (1990), 'German words in German Sign Language', in Prillwitz and Vollhaber (eds), pp. 97–112.

Eckert, P. (1988), 'Adolescent social structure and the spread of linguistic change'. *LiS* 17: 183–207.

Eckert, P. (1989a), *Jocks and Burnouts: Social Categories and Identity in the High School*. New York: Teachers College Press.

Eckert, P. (1989b), 'The whole woman: sex and gender differences in variation'. *Language Variation and Change* 1 (3): 245–68.

Eckert, P. (1991), 'Social polarization and the choice of linguistic variants', in Eckert (ed.), *New Ways of Analyzing Sound Change*. New York: Academic Press, pp. 213–32.

Eckert, P. (1998), 'Gender and sociolinguistic variation', in J. Coates (ed.), *Language and Gender: A Reader*. Oxford: Blackwell Publishers, pp. 64–75.

Eckert, P. (2000), *Language Variation as Social Practice*. Oxford: Blackwell.

Eckert, P. (2004), 'The meaning of style', in W.-F. Chiang, E. Chun, L. Mahalingappa and S. Mehus (eds), *Salsa 11*. Texas Linguistics Forum, 47.

Eckert, P. (2005), 'Variation, convention, and social meaning'. Plenary talk. Linguistic Society of America, San Francisco.

Eckert, P. (2006), 'Messing with style', in J. Maybin and J. Swann (eds), *The Art of English: Everyday Creativity*. Basingstoke: Palgrave Macmillan.

Eckert, P. and S. McConnell-Ginet (2003), *Language and Gender*. Cambridge: Cambridge University Press.

Eckert, P. and J. Rickford (eds) (2001), *Style and Sociolinguistic Variation*. New York: Cambridge University Press.

Edley, N. (2001), 'Analysing masculinity: interpretative repertoires, ideological dilemmas and subject positions', in M. Wetherell, S. Taylor and S. J. Yates (eds), *Discourse as Data: A Guide for Analysis*. London: Sage Publications.

Edwards, J. (1992), 'Sociopolitical aspects of language maintenance and loss: towards a typology of minority language situations', in W. Fase, K. Jaspert and S. Kroon (eds), *Maintenance and Loss of Minority Languages*. Amsterdam: John Benjamins, pp. 37–54.

Edwards, J. (1995), *Multilingualism*. London: Routledge.

Edwards, J. R. (1979a), *Language and Disadvantage*. London: Arnold.

Edwards, J. R. (1979b), 'Social class differences and the identification of sex in children's speech'. *Journal of Child Language* 6: 121–7.

Edwards, V. and P. Ladd (1983), 'British Sign Language and West Indian Creole', in Kyle and Woll (eds), *Language in Sign*, pp. 147–58.

Eelen, G. (2001), *A Critique of Politeness Theories*. Manchester: St Jerome.

Ehlich, K. (ed.) (1989), *Sprache im Faschismus*. Frankfurt am Main: Suhrkamp.

Ehrenberg, A. S. C. (1986), *A Primer in Data Reduction*. Chichester: John Wiley & Sons.

Eidheim, H. (1969), 'When ethnic identity is a social stigma', in F. Barth (ed.), *Ethnic Groups and Boundaries*. London: George Allen and Unwin, pp. 39–57.

Errington, J. (1988), *Structure and Style in Javanese*. Philadelphia: University of Pennsylvania Press.

Erting, C. and J. Woodward (1979), 'Sign language and the Deaf community: a sociolinguistic profile'. *Discourse Processes* 2: 283–300.

Fainberg, Y. A. (1983), 'Linguistic and sociodemographic factors influencing the acceptance of Hebrew neologisms'. *IJSL* 4: 9–40.

Fairclough, N. (1989), *Language and Power*. London: Longman.

Fairclough, N. (1992), *Discourse and Social Change*. Cambridge: Polity Press.

Fairclough, N. (1994), 'Power and language', in R. Asher (ed.), *The Encyclopedia of Language and Linguistics*. Oxford: Pergamon, vol. 6: 3: 246–50.

Fasold, R. (1975), Review of J. R. Dillard's 'Black English'. *LiS* 4: 198–221.

Fasold, R. (1984), *The Sociolinguistics of Society*. Oxford and Cambridge, MA: Blackwell.

Fasold, R. (1990), *The Sociolinguistics of Language*. Oxford: Basil Blackwell.

Fasold, R., H. Yamada, D. Robinson and S. Barish (1990), 'The language-planning effect of editorial policy: gender differences in *The Washington Post*'. *LiS* 19: 521–39.

Feagin, C. (2002), 'Entering the community', in J. K. Chambers, N. Schilling-Estes and P. Trudgill (eds), *The Handbook of Language Variation and Change*. Oxford: Blackwell.

Feldgate, W. (1982), *The Tembe Thonga of Natal and Mozambique: An Ecological Approach*. Occasional Publications 1, Dept of African Studies, University of Natal, Durban.

Ferguson, C. A. (1959), 'Diglossia'. *Word* 15: 325–40.

Ferguson, C. A. (1967), 'St Stefan of Perm and applied linguistics', in *To Honor Roman Jacobson: Essays on the Occasion of his Seventieth Birthday, 11 October 1966*. The Hague: Mouton, vol. 1, pp. 309–24.

Finegan, E. (1997), 'Sociolinguistics and the law', in F. Coulmas (ed.), *The Handbook of Sociolinguistics*. Oxford: Basil Blackwell, pp. 421–35.

Finlayson, R. (1995), 'Women's language of respect: isihlonipho sabafazi', in R. Mesthrie (ed.), *Language and Social History: Studies in South African Sociolinguistics*. Cape Town: David Philip, pp. 140–53.

Fischer, J. (1958), 'Social influences on the choice of a linguistic variant'. *Word* 14: 47–56.

Fischer, S. D. (1978), 'Sign languages as creoles', in P. Siple (ed.), *Understanding Language through Sign Language Research*. New York: Academic Press, pp. 309–32.

Fischer, S. and A. D. Todd (1983), *The Social Organization of Doctor–Patient Communication*. Washington, DC: Center for Applied Linguistics.

Fishman, J. (1964), 'Language maintenance and language shift as a field of enquiry: a definition of the field and suggestions for its further development'. *Linguistics* 9: 32–70.

Fishman, J. (1965), 'Who speaks what language to whom and when'. *La Linguistique* 2: 67–88.

Fishman, J. (1966), *Language Loyalty in the United States*. The Hague: Mouton.

Fishman, J. A. (1967), 'Bilingualism with and without diglossia; diglossia with and without bilingualism'. *Journal of Social Issues* 23 (2): 29–38.

Fishman, J. A. (ed.) (1968), *Readings in the Sociology of Language*. The Hague: Mouton.

Fishman, J. (1972a), 'Domains and the relationship between micro- and macrosociolinguistics', in J. J. Gumperz and D. Hymes (eds) (1972, rev. edn 1986), *Directions in Sociolinguistics: The Ethnography of Communication*. New York and Oxford: Basil Blackwell, pp. 435–53.

Fishman, J. (1972b), 'Language maintenance and shift as a field of enquiry (revisited)', in *Language in Sociocultural Change: Essays by J. A. Fishman, selected and introduced by A. S. Dil*. Stanford: Stanford University Press, pp. 76–134.

Fishman, J. (1983), 'Modeling rationales in corpus planning: modernity and tradition in images of the good corpus', in Cobarrubias and Fishman (eds), pp. 107–18.

Fishman, J. (1991), *Reversing Language Shift: Theoretical and Empirical Foundations of Assistance to Threatened Languages*. Clevedon: Multilingual Matters.

Fishman, J., M. H. Gertner, E. G. Lowy and W. G. Mitan (eds) (1985), *The Rise and Fall of the Ethnic Revival*. Berlin: Mouton.

Fishman, J. A. (1971), 'The links between micro- and macro-sociolinguistics in the study of who speaks what language to whom and when', in J. A. Fishman, R. L. Cooper and R. Ma (eds), *Bilingualism in the Barrio*. Bloomington: Indiana University Language Science Monograph Series, N. 7, pp. 583–604.

Fishman, P. (1983), 'Interaction: the work women do', in B. Thorne, C. Kramarae and N. Henley (eds), *Language, Gender and Society*. Rowley, MA: Newbury House, pp. 89–101.

Fodor, I. and C. Hagége (eds) (1983–9), *Language Reform: History and Future*, 5 vols. Hamburg: Buske Verlag.

Foucault, M. (1972), *The Archaeology of Knowledge*. London: Tavistock.

Foucault, M. (1981), 'The order of discourse', in R. Young (ed.), *Untying the Text: A Post-Structuralist Reader*. Boston, MA: Routledge & Kegan Paul, pp. 48–68.

Fowler, J. (1986), 'The social stratification of (r) in New York City department stores, 24 years after Labov'. Unpublished MS, New York University.

Fowler, R. (1985), 'Power', in T. van Dijk (ed.), *The Handbook of Discourse Analysis,* vol. 4: *Discourse Analysis in Society*. London: Academic Press, pp. 61–82.

Fowler, R., B. Hodge, G. Kress, and T. Trew (1979), *Language and Control*. Routledge: London.

Frake, C. O. (1964), 'How to ask for a drink in Subanun'. *American Anthropologist* 66 (2): 127–32. Rep. in J. B. Pride and J. Holmes (eds) (1972), *Sociolinguistics*. Harmondsworth: Penguin, pp. 260–6.

Frings, Theodor (1950), *Grundlegung einer Geschichte der deutschen Sprache*. Halle: Niemeyer.

Fromkin, V, R. Rodman and N. Hyams (2007), *An Introduction to Language,* 8th edn, International Student edition. Boston, MA: Wadsworth.

Furfey, P. H. (1944), 'Men's and women's language'. *The American Catholic Sociological Review* 5: 218–23.

Gal, S. (1978), 'Peasant men can't get wives: language change and sex roles in a bilingual community'. *LiS* 77 (1): 1–16.

Gal, S. (1979), *Language Shift: Social Determinants of Linguistic Change in Bilingual Austria*. New York: Academic Press.

Gal, S. (1989), 'Language and political economy'. *ARA* 18: 345–67.

Garrett, P., N. Coupland and A. Williams (1999), 'Evaluating dialect in discourse: teachers' and teenagers' responses to young English speakers in Wales', *Language in Society* 28 (3): 321–54.

Garvin, P. L. and M. Mathiot (1960), 'The urbanization of the Guarani language: a problem in language and culture', in A. C. Wallace (ed.), *Men and Cultures*. Philadelphia: University of Pennsylvania Press, pp. 783–90.

Gee, J. (1990), *Social Linguistics and Literacies: Ideology in Discourses*. Basingstoke: Falmer Press.

Gibbons, J. (ed.) (1994), *Language and the Law*. London: Longman.

Giddens, A. (1987, 3rd edn 1997), *Sociology*. Cambridge: Polity Press.

Giles, H., R. Y. Bourhis and D. M. Taylor (1977), 'Toward a theory of language in ethnic group relations', in H. Giles (ed.), *Language and Intergroup Relations*. London: Academic Press.

Giles, H., N. Coupland and J. Coupland (1991), 'Accommodation Theory: communication, context and consequence', in H. Giles, J. Coupland and N. Coupland (eds), *Contexts of Accommodation: Developments in Applied Sociolinguistics*. Cambridge: Cambridge University Press.

Giles, H. and P. F. Powesland (1975), *Speech Style and Social Evaluation*. London: Academic Press in association with the European Association of Experimental Social Psychology.

Giles, H., D. M. Taylor and R. Y. Bourhis (1973), 'Towards a theory of interpersonal accommodation'. *LiS* 2: 177–92.

Gilliéron, J. (1902–10), *Atlas Linguistique de la France*, 13 vols. Paris: Champion.

Gimson, A. C. (1989), *An Introduction to the Pronunciation of English*, 4th edn, rev. by S. Ramsaran. London: Arnold.

Goffman, E. (1967), *Interaction Ritual*. Harmondsworth: Penguin.

Goke-Pariola, A. (1993), 'Language and symbolic power: Bourdieu and the legacy of Euro-American colonialism in an African society'. *LC* 13 (3): 219–34.

Gordon, R. G. (2005), *Ethnologue. Languages of the World*, 15th edn. Dallas, TX: SIL International.

Graddol, D. and J. Swann (1989), *Gender Voices*. Oxford: Blackwell.

Gramsci, A. (1971), *Selections from the Prison Notebooks*, ed. and trans. Q. Hoare and G. Norwell-Smith. London: Lawrence and Wishart.

Grenoble, L. (1992), 'An overview of Russian Sign Language'. *SLS* 77: 321–38.

Grenoble, L.A. and L.J. Whaley (1998), *Endangered Languages: Current Issues and Future Prospects*. Cambridge: Cambridge University Press.

Grice, H. P. (1975) 'Logic and conversation', in P. Cole and J. L. Morgan (eds), *Syntax and Semantics*, vol. 3: *Speech Acts*. New York City: Academic Press, pp. 41–58.

Grice, H. P. (1978), 'Further notes on logic and conversation', in P. Cole (ed.), *Syntax and Semantics*, vol. 9: *Pragmatics*. New York City: Academic Press, pp. 113–28.

Grierson, G. A. (1903–28), *Linguistic Survey of India*, 11 vols. Calcutta: Government of India.

Grierson, G. A. (1927), *Linguistic Survey of India*, vol. 1, part 1, 'Introductory'. Calcutta: Government of India.

Grierson, G. A. (1975 [1885]), *Bihar Peasant Life*. Delhi: Cosmo (reprint of original)

Grin, F. (1996), 'The economics of language: survey, assessment, and prospects'. *IJSL* 121: 17–44.

Grin, F. (2003), Economics and Language Planning. *Current Issues in Language Planning* 4 (1), 1–66.

Groce, N. E. (1985), *Everyone Here Spoke Sign Language: Hereditary Deafness on Martha's Vineyard*. Cambridge, MA and London: Harvard University Press.

Grosjean, F. (1982), *Life with Two Languages: An Introduction to Bilingualism*. Cambridge, MA: Harvard University Press.

Grushkin, D. A. (2003), 'The dilemma of the hard of hearing within the U.S. Deaf community', in L. Monaghan, C. Schmaling, K. Nakamura and G.H. Turner (eds), *Many Ways to Be Deaf. International Variation in Deaf Communities*. Washington, DC: Gallaudet University Press, pp. 114–40.

Gumperz, J. J. (1962), 'Types of linguistic communities'. *AL* 4 (1): 28–40.

Gumperz, J. J. (1971), 'Some remarks on regional and social language differences in India', in A. S. Dil (ed.), *Language in Social Groups: Essays by John J. Gumperz*. Stanford, CA: Stanford University Press, pp. 1–11.

Gumperz, J. J. (ed.) (1982a), *Language and Social Identity*. Cambridge: Cambridge University Press.

Gumperz, J. J. (ed.) (1982b), *Discourse Strategies*. Cambridge: Cambridge University Press

Guy, G., B. Horvath, J. Vonwiller, E. Daisley and I. Rogers, 1986. 'An intonational change in progress in Australian English.' *LiS* 15 (1): 23–51.

Haarmann, H. (1990), 'Language planning in the light of a general theory of language: a methodological framework'. *IJSL* 86: 103–26.

Haas, M. R. (1944), 'Men's and women's speech in Koasati', *Language* 20: 142–9. Repr. in D. Hymes (ed.) (1964), *Language in Culture and Society*. New York: Harper and Row, pp. 228–33.

Hale, K. (1992), 'Language endangerment and the human value of linguistic endangerment'. *Language* 68: 35–42.

Hall, K. (1994), 'Bodyless pragmatics: feminism on the Internet', in M. Bucholtz, A. C. Liang, L. A. Sutton and C. Hines (eds), *Cultural Performances: Proceedings of the Third Berkeley Women and Language Conference*. Berkeley, CA: Berkeley Women and Language Group, University of California.

Hall, K. (1995), 'Lip service on the fantasy lines', in Hall and Bucholtz, pp. 183–216.

Hall, K. and M. Bucholtz (eds) (1995), *Gender Articulated: Language and the Socially Constructed Self*. New York and London: Routledge.

Hall, R. (1970), *Discovery of Africa*. London: Hamlyn.

Halliday, M. A. K. (1969), 'Relevant models of language'. *Educational Review* 22: 26–37.

Halliday, M. A. K. (1978), *Language as Social Semiotic: The Social Interpretation of Language and Meaning*. London: Edward Arnold.

Halliday, M. A. K. and R. Hasan (1985), *Language, Context, and Text: Aspects of Language in a Social Semiotic Perspective*. Burnwood, Australia: Deakin University.

Halliday, M. A. K., A. Macintosh and P. Strevens (1964), *The Linguistic Sciences and Language Teaching*. London: Longman.

Hancock, I. (1976), 'Nautical sources of Krio vocabulary'. *IJSL* 7: 23–36.

Hancock, I. (1986), 'The domestic hypothesis, diffusion and componentiality: an account of Atlantic Anglophone creole origins', in Muysken and Smith (eds), pp. 71–102.

Hansen, B. (1991), 'Trends in the progress towards bilingual education for Deaf children in Denmark', in Prillwitz and Vollhaber (eds), pp. 51–94.

Hansen, E. F. (1997), 'Babel am Polarkreis'. *Der Spiegel* 27: 187–9.

Haralambos, M. and M. Holborn (1991), *Sociology: Themes and Perspectives*, 3rd edn. London: Collins Educational.

Haralambos, M, R. Heald and M. Holborn (2000), *Sociology: Themes and Perspectives*, 5th edn. London: Collins.

Harrington, K., L. Litosseliti, H. Sauntson and J. Sunderland (eds) (2008), *Gender and Language Research Methodologies*. Basingstoke: Palgrave Macmillan.

Harris, J. (1995), *The Cultural Meaning of Deafness: Language, Identity and Power Relations*. Aldershot, Hants: Avebury.

Haugen, E. (1953), *The Norwegian Language in America: A Study in Bilingual Behaviour*. Philadelphia: University of Pennsylvania Press.

Haugen, E. (1966), 'Linguistics and language planning', in W. Bright (ed.), *Sociolinguistics: Proceedings of the UCLA Sociolinguistics Conference, 1964.* The Hague: Mouton, pp. 50–71.

Haugen, E. (1968), 'Language planning in modern Norway', in Fishman (ed.), pp. 673–87.

Haugen, E. (1971), 'Instrumentalism in language planning', in Rubin and Jernudd (eds) (1974), pp. 281–92.

Haugen, E. (1972), *The Ecology of Language.* Stanford, CA: Stanford University Press.

Haugen, E. (1983), 'The implementation of corpus planning: theory and practice', in Cobarrubias and Fishman (eds), pp. 269–90.

Haugen, E. (1987), 'Language planning', in U. Ammon, N. Dittmer and J. K. Mattheier (eds), *Sociolinguistics. Soziolinguistik. An International Handbook of the Science of Language and Society. Ein internationales Handbuch zur Wissenschaft von Sprache und Gesellschaft* vol. I. Berlin and New York: de Gruyter, pp. 626–37.

Haugen, E., J. D. McClure and D. S. Thomson (eds) (1990), *Minority Languages Today,* rev. edn. Edinburgh: Edinburgh University Press.

Heath, S. B. (1983), *Ways with Words: Language, Life and Work in Communities and Classrooms.* Cambridge: Cambridge University Press.

Heine, B. (1992), 'Language policies in Africa', in Herbert (ed.), pp. 23–35.

Heller, M. (1992), 'The politics of codeswitching and language choice', *Journal of Multilingual and Multicultural Development* 13 (1/2): 123–42.

Herbert R. K. (ed.) (1992), *Language and Society in Africa: The Theory and Practice of Sociolinguistics.* Johannesburg: Witwatersrand University Press.

Herring, S. (1993), 'Gender and democracy in computer-mediated communication'. *Electronic Journal of Communication* 3. Repr. in R. Kling (ed.) (1996), *Computerization and Controversy,* 2nd edn. New York: Academic Press.

Herring, S., D. A. Johnson and T. DiBenedetto (1995), '"This discussion is going too far". Male resistance to female participation on the Internet', in K. Hall and M. Bucholtz (eds).

Hesseling, D. C. (1897), 'Het Hollandsch in Zuid-Afrika'. *De Gids* 60 (1): 138–62.

Hill, J. (1995), 'The voices of Don Gabriel: responsibility and self in a modern Mexicano narrative', in D. Tedlock and B. Mannheim (eds), *The Dialogic Emergence of Culture.* Urbana: University of Illinois Press, pp. 97–147.

Hock, H. (1991), *Principles of Historical Linguistics,* 2nd edn. Berlin: Mouton de Gruyter.

Hockett, C. A. (1958), *A Course in Modern Linguistics.* New York: Macmillan.

Hockett, C. A. (1966), 'The problem of universals in language', in J. Greenberg (ed.), *Universals of Language.* Cambridge, MA: MIT Press, pp. 1–29.

Holm, J. (1988), *Pidgins and Creoles,* vol. 1: *Theory and Structure.* Cambridge: Cambridge University Press.

Holm, J. (1989), *Pidgins and Creoles,* vol. 2: *Reference Survey.* Cambridge: Cambridge University Press.

Holmes, J. (1992), *An Introduction to Sociolinguistics.* London: Longman.

Holmes, J. (1995), *Women, Men and Politeness.* Harlow: Longman.

Holmes, J. (1996), 'Women's role in language change: a place for quantification', in N. Warner, J. Ahlers, L. Bilmes, M. Oliver, S. Wertheim and M. Chen (eds), Gender and Belief Systems: Proceedings of the Fourth Berkeley Women and Language Conference, 19–21 April 1996. Berkeley, CA: Berkeley Women and Language Group, pp. 313–30.

Holmes, J. (2006), *Gendered Talk at Work*. Oxford: Blackwell.

Holmes, J. and M. Meyerhoff (eds) (2003), *The Handbook of Language and Gender*. Oxford: Blackwell Publishing.

Horvath, B. (1985), *Variation in Australian English: The Sociolects of Sydney*. Cambridge: Cambridge University Press.

Houston, A. (1985), 'Continuity and change in English morphology: the variable (ING)'. Unpublished PhD dissertation, University of Pennsylvania.

Hubbell, A. (1950), *The Pronunciation of English in New York City*. New York: Columbia University Press.

Hudson, R. A. (1985), *Invitation to Linguistics*. Oxford: Blackwell.

Hughes, G. (1988), *Words in Time*. Oxford: Blackwell.

Hultgren, A. K. (2008), 'Reconstructing the sex dichotomy in language and gender research: some advantages of using correlational sociolinguistics', in Harrington et al.

Humphries, T. (1990), 'An introduction to the culture of Deaf people in the United States. Content notes and reference material for teachers'. *SLS* 72: 209–40.

Hunter, B. (ed.) (1998), *The Statesman's Yearbook (1997–1998)*. London and Basingstoke: Macmillan.

Hyde, M. B. and D. J. Power (1991), 'Teachers' use of simultaneous communication: effects on the signed and spoken components'. *American Annals of the Deaf* 136 (5): 381–7.

Hymes, D. (1971), *On Communicative Competence*. Philadelphia: University of Pennsylvania Press.

Hymes, D. (1972), 'Models of the interaction of language and social life', in J. J. Gumperz and D. Hymes (eds) (1972, rev. edn 1986), *Directions in Sociolinguistics: The Ethnography of Communication*. New York and Oxford: Basil Blackwell, pp. 35–71.

Hymes, D. (1974a), 'Ways of speaking', in R. Bauman and J. Sherzer (eds), *Explorations in the Ethnography of Speaking*. Cambridge: Cambridge University Press, pp. 433–51.

Hymes, D. (1974b), *Foundations in Sociolinguistics*. Philadelphia: University of Pennsylvania Press.

Ide, S. (1989), 'How and why do women speak more politely in Japanese'. *Studies in English and American Literature* 24. Tokyo: Japan Women's University, 1–19. Repr. in S. Ide and N. H. McGloin (eds) (1990), *Aspects of Japanese Women's Language*. Tokyo: Kurosio Publishers, pp. 63–79.

Ide, S. and M. Yoshida (1999), 'Sociolinguistics: honorifics and gender differences', in N. Tsujimura (ed.), *The Handbook of Japanese Linguistics*. Oxford: Blackwell.

Jaakola, M. (1976), 'Diglossia and bilingualism among two minorities in Sweden'. *Linguistics* 183: 67–84.

Jaberg, K. (1908), *Sprachgeographie*. Aarau: Sauerländer.

Jackall, R. (ed.) (1995), *Propaganda*. Basingstoke: Macmillan.

Jahr, E. H. (1989), 'Limits of language planning? Norwegian language planning revisited'. *IJSL* 80: 33–9.

Jahr, E. H. and K. Janicki (1995), 'The function of the standard variety: a contrastive study of Norwegian and Polish'. *IJSL* 115: 25–45.

James, D. (1996), 'Women, men and prestige forms: a critical review', in V. L. Bergvall, J. M. Bing and A. F. Freed (eds), *Rethinking Language and Gender Research*. New York: Longman, pp. 98–125.

Jenkins, R. (1992), *Pierre Bourdieu*. London: Routledge.

Jepson, J. (1991), 'Urban and rural sign language in India'. *LiS* 20: 37–57.

Jernudd, B. H. (1971), 'Notes on the economic analysis for solving language problems', in Rubin and Jernudd (eds) (1971a), pp. 263–76.

Jernudd, B. H. and J. Das Gupta (1971), 'Towards a theory of language planning', in Rubin and Jernudd (eds) (1971a), pp. 195–215.

Jespersen, O. (1922), *Language: Its Nature, Development and Origins*. London: Allen and Unwin.

Johnson, R. E. (1994), 'Sign language and the concept of deafness in a traditional Yucatec Mayan village', in C. Erting, R. Johnson, D. Smith and B. Snider (eds), *The Deaf Way: Perspectives from the International Conference on Deaf Culture*. Washington, DC: Gallaudet University Press, pp. 102–9.

Johnson, R. E. and C. Erting (1989), 'Ethnicity and socialization in a classroom for Deaf children', in Lucas (ed.), pp. 41–84.

Johnson, S. (1997), 'Theorizing language and masculinity', in S. Johnson and U. H. Meinhof (eds), *Language and Masculinity*. Oxford: Blackwell Publishers, pp. 8–26.

Johnson, S. and U. H. Meinhof (eds) (1997), *Language and Masculinity*. Oxford: Blackwell Publishers.

Johnston, T. (ed.) (1998), *Signs of Australia. A New Dictionary of Auslan (the Sign Language of the Australian Deaf Community)*. North Rocks, Sydney: North Rock Press.

Jones, B. L. (1990), 'Welsh: linguistic conservatism and shifting bilingualism', in Haugen et al. (eds), pp. 40–52.

Jones, C. (1972), *An Introduction to Middle English*. New York: Holt, Rinehart and Winston.

Joos, M. (1959), 'The isolation of styles'. *Georgetown University Monograph Series on Languages and Linguistics* 12: 107–13.

Joos, M. (1962), *The Five Clocks*. Bloomington: Indiana University Research Centre in Anthropology, Folklore and Linguistics.

Joseph, J. E. (1987), *Eloquence and Power: The Rise of Language Standards and Standard Languages*. London: Frances Pinter.

Jourdan, C. (1991), 'Pidgins and creoles: the blurring of categories'. *ARA* 20: 187–209.

Kachru, B. B. (1986), *The Alchemy of English: The Spread, Functions and Models of Non-Native Englishes*. Oxford: Pergamon.

Kachru, B.B. (1988), 'The sacred cows of English'. *English Today* 16: 3–8.

Kachru, B. B. (ed.) (1992a), *The Other Tongue: English Across Cultures*, 2nd edn. Oxford: Pergamon; Urbana and Champaign: University of Illinois Press.

Kachru, B. B. (1992b), 'Models for non-native Englishes', in Kachru (ed.), pp. 48–74.

Kachru, B.B. (2005), *Asian Englishes: Beyond the Canon*. Hong Kong: Hong Kong University Press.

Kannapell, B. (1989), 'An examination of Deaf college students' attitudes toward ASL and English', in Lucas (ed.), pp. 191–210.

Karttunen, F. (1994), *Between Worlds: Interpreters, Guides and Survivors*. New Brunswick, NJ: Rutgers University Press.

Kegl, J., A. Senhas and M. Coppola (1999), 'Creation through contact: sign language emergence and sign language change in Nicaragua', in M. DeGraff (ed.), *Language Creation and Language Change*. Cambridge, MA: MIT Press, pp. 179–238.

Kerswill, P. (1996), 'Milton Keynes and dialect levelling in south-eastern British English', in D. Graddol, D. Leith and J. Swann (eds), *English: History, Diversity and Change*. London and New York: Routledge in association with the Open University, pp. 292–300.

Kiesling, S.F. (2005), 'A variable, a style, a stance: Word-final -*er* and ethnicity in Australian English'. *English World Wide* 26: 1–44.

Klein, W. (1988), 'The unity of a vernacular: some remarks on "Berliner Stadtsprache"', in Dittmar and Schlobinski (eds), pp. 147–53.

Kleinfeld, M. S. and N. Warner (1997), 'Lexical variation in the deaf community relating to gay, lesbian and bisexual signs', in A. Livia, K. Hall and E. Finegan, *Queerly Phrased: Language, Gender and Sexuality*. Oxford: Oxford University Press, pp. 58–84.

Klemperer, V. (1975 [1957]), *LTI – Lingua Tertii Imperii. Die Sprache des Dritten Reiches*. Leipzig: Reclam.

Klima, E. and U. Bellugi (1979), *The Signs of Language*. Cambridge, MA: Harvard University Press.

Kloss, H. (1966), 'German–American language maintenance efforts', in Fishman (ed.), pp. 206–52.

Kloss, H. (1967), '"Abstand Languages" and "Ausbau Languages"'. *AL* 9 (7): 29–41.

Kloss, H. (1969), *Research Possibilities on Group Bilingualism: A Report*. Quebec: International Center for Research on Bilingualism.

Knowles, G. O. (1978), 'The nature of phonological variables in Scouse', in P. Trudgill (ed.), *Sociolinguistic Patterns in British English*. London: Edward Arnold, pp. 80–90.

König, W. (1978), *dtv-Atlas zur deutschen Sprache*. Munich: Deutscher Taschenbuch Verlag.

Kotsinas, U.B. (1988), 'Immigrant children's Swedish – a new variety?' *Journal of Multilingual and Multicultural Development* 9: 129–40.

Krauss, M. (1992), 'The world's languages in crisis'. *Language* 68: 4–10.

Kroch, A. (1978), 'Towards a theory of dialect variation'. *LiS* 7: 17–36.

Kroch, A. (1996), 'Dialect and style in the speech of the upper class of Philadelphia', in G. R. Guy, C. Feagin, D. Schiffrin and J. Baugh (eds), *Towards a Social Science of Language: Essays in Honour of William Labov*. Philadelphia, PA: Benjamins, pp. 23–46.

Kulick, D. (1992), *Language shift and cultural reproduction. Socialization, self, and syncretism in a Papua New Guinean village*. Cambridge: Cambridge University Press.

Kuntze, M. (2000), 'Code-switching in ASL and written English language contact', in K. Emmorey and H. Lane (eds), *The Signs of Language Revisited. An Anthology to Honour Ursula Bellugi and Edward Klima*. Mahwah, NJ and London: Lawrence Erlbaum, pp. 287–302.

Kurath, H. and R. McDavid (1961), *The Pronunciation of English in the Atlantic States*. Ann Arbor: University of Michigan Press.

Kurath, H., M. Hanley, B. Bloch and G. S. Lowman (1939–43), *Linguistic Atlas of New England*, 3 vols. Providence, RI: Brown University Press.

Kyle, J. G. (1991), 'The Deaf community: culture, custom and tradition', in Prillwitz and Vollhaber (eds), pp. 175–185.

Kyle, J. G. and B. Woll (eds) (1983), *Language in Sign: An International Perspective on Sign Language*. London: Croom Helm.

Kyle, J. G. and B. Woll (eds) (1985), *Sign Language: The Study of Deaf People and Their Language*. Cambridge: Cambridge University Press.

Labov, W. (1963), 'The social motivation of a sound change'. *Word* 19: 273–309.

Labov, W. (1966), *The Social Stratification of English in New York City*. Washington, DC: Center for Applied Linguistics.

Labov, W. (1969a), 'The logic of nonstandard English'. *Georgetown Monographs in Languages and Linguistics*, 22. Repr. in Labov (1972b), pp. 201–40.

Labov, W. (1969b), 'Contraction, deletion and inherent variability of the English copula'. *Language* 45 (4): 715–62. Repr. in Labov (1972b), pp. 65–129.

Labov, W. (1972a), *Sociolinguistic Patterns*. Philadelphia: University of Pennsylvania Press.

Labov, W. (1972b), *Language in the Inner City: Studies in the Black English Vernacular*. Philadelphia: University of Pennsylvania Press.

Labov, W. (1972c), 'The transformation of experience in narrative syntax', in Labov (1972b), pp. 354–96.

Labov, W. (1982), 'Objectivity and commitment in linguistic science: the case of the Black English trial in Ann Arbor'. *LiS* 11: 165–201.

Labov, W. (1984), 'Field methods of the project on linguistic change and variation', in J. Baugh and J. Sherzer (eds), *Language in Use*. Englewood Cliffs, NJ: Prentice Hall, pp. 28–53.

Labov, W. (1987), 'Are Black and White vernaculars diverging?' (Section VIII, excerpt from panel discussion). *American Speech* 62 (1): 5–80.

Labov, W. (1988), 'The judicial testing of linguistic theory', in D. Tannen (ed.), *Linguistics in Context: Connecting Observation and Understanding*. Norwood, NJ: Ablex, pp. 159–82.

Labov, W. (1989), 'The child as linguistic historian'. *Language Variation and Change* 1 (1): 85–97.

Labov, W. (1991), 'The three dialects of English', in P. Eckert (ed.), *New Ways of Analyzing Sound Change*. New York: Academic Press, pp. 1–44.

Labov, W. (1994), *Principles of Linguistic Change*, vol. 1. Oxford: Basil Blackwell.

Labov, W. (2000), *Principles of Linguistic Change*, vol. 2: *Social Factors*. Oxford: Blackwell.

Labov, W. (2003), 'Pursuing the cascade model', in D. Britain and J. Cheshire (eds), *Social Dialectology: In Honor of Peter Trudgill*. Amsterdam: Benjamins, pp. 9–22.

Labov, W. and W. Harris (1986), 'De facto segregation of black and white vernaculars', in D. Sankoff (ed.), *Diversity and Diachrony*. Amsterdam: Benjamins, pp. 1–24.

Labov, W., S. Ash and C. Boberg (2006), *The Atlas of North American English: Phonetics, Phonology and Sound Change*. Berlin: Mouton de Gruyter.

Ladefoged, P. (1992), 'Another view of endangered languages'. *Language* 68: 809–11.

Ladefoged, P. (1993), *A Course in Phonetics*, 3rd edn. New York: Harcourt Brace.

Lakoff, R. (1975), *Language and Woman's Place*. New York: Harper and Row.

Lakoff, R. T. (2004), *Language and Woman's Place: Text and Commentaries*, ed. M. Bucholtz. Oxford and New York: Oxford University Press.

Lambert, W. E. (1978), 'Some cognitive and sociocultural consequences of being bilingual', in J. C. Alatis (ed.), *Georgetown Round Table on Languages and Linguistics 1978*. Washington, DC: Georgetown University Press, pp. 214–29.

Lambert, W. E., Hodgson, R. C. Gardner and S. Fillenbaum (1960), 'Evaluational reactions to spoken languages'. *Journal of Abnormal and Social Psychology* 60: 44–51.

Lane, H. (1984a), *When the Mind Hears*. New York: Random House.

Lane, H. (ed.) (1984b), *The Deaf Experience: Classics in Language and Education*, trans. F. Philip. Cambridge, MA and London: Harvard University Press.

Lane, H. (1995), 'Constructions of Deafness'. *Disability and Society* 10 (2): 171–89.

Lane, H., R. Hoffmeister and B. Bahan (1996), *A Journey into the DEAF-WORLD*. San Diego, CA: DawnSignPress.

Lanham, L. W. and C. Macdonald (1979), *The Standard in South African English and its Social History*. Heidelberg: Julius Groos.

Lass, R. (1987), *The Shape of English: Structure and History*. London: Dent.

Lass, R. (1997), *Historical Linguistics and Language Change*. Cambridge: Cambridge University Press.

Lass, R. and Wright, S. (1986), 'Endogeny versus contact: "Afrikaans influence" on South African English'. *English World-Wide* 7: 201–24.

Laycock, D.C. (1982), 'Melanesian linguistic diversity: a Melanesian choice?', in R. M. May and H. Nelson (eds), *Melanesia: Beyond Diversity*. Canberra: Australian National University Press, pp. 33–8.

Le Page, R. B. and A. Tabouret-Keller (1985), *Acts of Identity: Creole-based Approaches to Language and Ethnicity*. Cambridge: Cambridge University Press.

Leap, W. (1978), 'American Indian English and its implications for bilingual education', in J. Alatis (ed.), *International Dimenstions of Bilingual Education*. Washington, DC: Georgetown University Press, pp. 657–69.

Leap, W. (1981), 'American Indian languages', in C. A. Ferguson and S. B.

Heath (eds), *Language in the USA*. Cambridge: Cambridge University Press, pp. 116–44.

Leap, W. (1991), 'Pathways and barriers to ancestral language literacy-building on the Northern Ute reservation'. *AEQ* 22: 21–41.

Leap, W. (1993), *American Indian English*. Salt Lake City: University of Utah Press.

Leap, W. L. (ed.) (1995), *Beyond the Lavender Lexicon*. Newark, NJ: Gordon and Breach.

Leap, W. L. (1996), *Word's Out: Gay Men's English*. Minneapolis: University of Minnesota Press.

Lee, D. M. (1982), 'Are there really signs of diglossia? Reexamining the situation'. *SLS* 35: 127–52.

Lehtonen, J. and K. Sajavaara (1985), 'The silent Finn', in D. Tannen and M. Saville-Troike (eds), *Perspectives on Silence*. Norwood, NJ: Ablex.

Leith, D. (1983), *A Social History of English*. London: Routledge.

Leith, D. (1997), *A Social History of English*, 2nd edn. London: Routledge.

LeMaster, B. C. (2003), 'School language and shifts in Irish Deaf identity', in L. Monaghan, C. Schmaling, K. Nakamura and G. H. Turner (eds), *Many Ways to Be Deaf. International Variation in Deaf Communities*. Washington, DC: Gallaudet University Press, pp. 153–72.

LeMaster, B. C. and J. Dwyer (1991), 'Knowing and using female and male signs in Dublin'. *SLS* 73: 361–73.

Levine, L. and H. J. Crockett (1966), 'Speech variation in a Piedmont community: postvocalic *r*', in S. Lieberson (ed.), *Explorations in Sociolinguistics*. Special issue of *Sociological Inquiry* 36 (2): 76–98.

Lewis, G. (1983), 'Implementation of language planning in the Soviet Union', in Cobarrubias and Fishman (eds), 309–26.

Lewis, I. (1991), *Sahibs, Nabobs and Boxwallahs*. Delhi: Oxford University Press.

Li, W. L. (1982), 'The language of Chinese-Americans'. *IJSL* 38: 109–24.

Li Wei (1998), 'Banana split? Variations in language choice and code-switching patterns of two groups of British-born Chinese in Tyneside', in R. Jacobson (ed.), *Codeswitching Worldwide*. Trends in Linguistics: Studies and Monographs 106. Berlin and New York: Mouton de Gruyter.

Liddell, S. K. (1980), *American Sign Language Syntax*. The Hague: Mouton de Gruyter.

Linde, C. (1993), *Life Stories: The Creation of Coherence*. London: Oxford University Press.

Linton, R. (1945), 'Present world conditions in cultural perspective', in Linton (ed.), *The Science of Man in World Crisis*. New York: Columbia University Press, pp. 201–21.

Lippi-Green, R. (1989), 'Social network integration and language change in progress in a rural Alpine village'. *LiS* 18: 213–34.

Litosseliti, L. (2006), *Gender and Language: Theory and Practice*. London: Hodder Arnold.

Litosseliti, L. and J. Sunderland (eds) (2002), *Gender Identity and Discourse Analysis*. Amsterdam: Benjamins.

Livia, A. and K. Hall (eds) (1997), *Queerly Phrased*. Oxford: Oxford University Press.

LoBianco, J. (1995), 'Multilingualism, education and the new notion of nation', in *Constitutionally Enshrined Multilingualism: Challenges and Responses. Proceedings of the 15th Annual Conference of the Southern African Applied Linguistics Association, Stellenbosch 1995*. Stellenbosch, pp. 1–33.

LoBianco, J. (1996), *Language as an Economic Resource*, Language Planning Report No. 5.1. Pretoria: Department of Arts, Culture, Science and Technology.

Lockwood, D. (1973), 'The distribution of power in industrial society: a comment', in J. Urry and J. Wakeford (eds), *Power in Britain: Sociological Readings*. London: Heinemann, pp. 266–72.

Lockwood, W. B. (1972), *A Panorama of Indo-European Languages*. London: Hutchinson.

Loncke, F., S. Quertinmont and P. Ferreyra (1990), 'Deaf children in schools: more or less Native signers?', in Prillwitz and Vollhaber (eds), pp. 163–76.

Lucas, C. (ed.) (1989), *The Sociolinguistics of the Deaf Community*. San Diego, CA: Academic Press.

Lucas, C. (ed.) (2001), *The Sociolinguistics of Sign Languages*. Cambridge: Cambridge University Press.

Lucas, C. and C. Valli (1989), 'Language contact in the American Deaf community', in Lucas (ed.), pp. 11–40.

Lucas, C. and C. Valli (1991), 'ASL or contact signing: issues of judgement'. *LiS* 20: 201–16.

Lucas, C., R. Bayley, R. Reed and A. Wulf (2001a), 'Lexical variation in African American and White signing'. *American Speech* 76: 339–60.

Lucas, C., R. Bayley and C. Valli (2001b), *Sociolinguistic Variation in American Sign Language*. Washington, DC: Gallaudet University Press, p. 138.

Lupton, L. J. Salmons (1996), 'A re-analysis of the creole status of American Sign Language'. *SLS* 90: 80–94.

Lyons, J. (1970), *New Horizons in Linguistics*. Penguin: Harmondsworth.

McAdams, M. (1996), 'Gender without bodies'. *CMC Magazine*, 1 March.

McAfee, C. (1983), *Varieties of English around the World – Glasgow*. Amsterdam: Benjamins.

Macaulay, R. (1988), 'The rise and fall of the vernacular', in C. Duncan-Rose and T. Venneman (eds), *On Language: Rhetorica, Phonologica, Syntactica – A Festschrift for Robert P. Stockwell*. London: Routledge, pp. 106–15.

Macaulay, R. K. (1991), *Locating Dialect in Discourse: The Language of Honest Men and Bonnie Lasses in Ayr*. Oxford: Oxford University Press.

Macaulay, R. K. S. (1978), 'Variation and consistency in Glaswegian English', in P. Trudgill (ed.), *Sociolinguistic Patterns in British English*. London: Edward Arnold, pp. 132–43.

McCourt, F. (1999). *'Tis*. New York: Harper Collins, p. 53.

Macdonald, J. (1984), 'The social stratification of (r) in New York City department stores revisited'. Manuscript (cited in Labov 1994).

McIntyre, J. A. (1991), 'Lexical innovation in Hausa (Niger, Nigeria)', in von Gleich and Wolff (eds), pp. 11–20.

McMahon, A. (1994), *Understanding Language Change*. Cambridge: Cambridge University Press.

Macnamara, J. (1966), *Bilingualism and Primary Education*. Edinburgh: University of Edinburgh Press.

McWhorter, J. (2002), *The Power of Babel: A Natural History of Language*. London: Heinemann.

Mahlau, A. (1991), 'Some aspects of the standardization of the Basque language', in von Gleich and Wolff (eds), pp. 79–94.

Makhudu, K. D. P. (1995), 'Flaaitaal', in R. Mesthrie (ed.), *Language and Social History: Studies in South African Sociolinguistics*. Cape Town: David Philip, pp. 298–305.

Mallik, B. (1972), *Language of the Underworld of West Bengal*, Research Series 76. Calcutta: Sanskrit College.

Maltz, D. N. and R. A. Borker (1982), 'A cultural approach to male–female miscommunication', in Gumperz (ed.) (1982a).

Marcowicz, H. and J. Woodward (1978), 'Language and the maintenance of ethnic boundaries in the Deaf community'. *Communication and Cognition* 11 (1): 29–38.

Martin, E. (2002), Cultural images and different varieties of English in French television commercials. *English Today* 18 (4): 8–20.

Martinet, A. (1952), 'Function, structure and sound change'. *Word* 8: 1–32.

Maxwell, M. M. and S. Smith-Todd (1986), 'Black sign language and school integration in Texas'. *LiS* 15: 81–94.

May, S. (2001), *Language and Minority Right: Ethnicity, Nationalism and the Politics of Language*. London: Longman.

Maybin, J. (1997), 'Story voices: the use of reported speech in 10–12-year-olds' spontaneous narratives', in L. Thompson (ed.), *Children Talking: The Development of Pragmatic Competence*. Clevedon: Multilingual Matters.

Maybin, J. (2006), *Children's Voices: Talk, Knowledge and Identity*. Basingstoke: Palgrave Macmillan.

Meadow, K. P. (1972), 'Sociolinguistics, sign language and the deaf sub-culture', in T. J. O'Rourke (ed.), *Psycholinguistics and Total Communication: The State of the Art*. Washington, DC: American Annals of the Deaf.

Mehan, H. (1979), *Learning Lessons*. Cambridge, MA: Harvard University Press.

Mesthrie, R. (1989), 'The origins of Fanagalo'. *Journal of Pidgin and Creole Languages* 4 (2): 211–40.

Mesthrie, R. (1992a), *English in Language Shift: The History, Structure and Sociolinguistics of South African Indian English*. Cambridge: Cambridge University Press.

Mesthrie, R. (1992b), *Language in Indenture: A Sociolinguistic History of Bhojpuri-Hindi in South Africa*. London: Routledge.

Mesthrie, R. (1995), 'Introduction', in Mesthrie (ed.), *Language and Social History: Studies in South African Sociolinguistics*. Cape Town: David Philip, pp. xv–xx.

Mills, A. E. and J. Coerts (1990), 'Functions and forms of bilingual input: children learning a sign language as one of their first languages', in Prillwitz and Vollhaber (eds), pp. 151–61.

Mills, S. (2003), *Gender and Politeness*. Cambridge: Cambridge University Press.

Milroy, J. and L. Milroy (1985a), *Authority in Language*. London: Routledge.

Milroy, J. and L. Milroy (1985b), 'Linguistic change, social network and speaker innovation'. *Journal of Linguistics* 21: 339–84.

Milroy, J. and L. Milroy (1992), 'Social network and social class: toward an integrated sociolinguistic model'. *LiS* 21, 1–26.

Milroy L. (1980, 2nd edn 1987), *Language and Social Networks*. Oxford: Basil Blackwell.

Milroy, L. (1992), 'New perspectives in the analysis of sex differentiation in language', in K. Bolton and H. Kwok (eds), *Sociolinguistics Today: International Perspectives*. London and New York: Routledge, pp. 162–79.

Milroy, L. and P. Musken (eds) (1995), *One Speaker, Two Languages: Cross-disciplinary Perspectives on Code-switching*. New York: Cambridge University Press.

Mishler, E. G. (1984), *The Discourse of Medicine: Dialectics of Medical Interviews*. Norwood, NJ: Ablex.

Mitchell, A. G. and A. Delbridge (1965), *The Pronunciation of English in Australia*. Sydney: Angus and Robertson.

Moritz, W. (1978), *Das älteste Schulbuch in Südwestafrika/Namibia: H. C. Knudsen und die Namafibel* (Aus alten Tagen in Südwest, Heft 6). Windhoek, Namibia: John Meinert.

Morley, D. (1980), 'Texts, readers, subjects', in S. Hall, D. Hobson, A. Lowe and P. Willis (eds), *Culture, Media, Language*. London: Hutchinson, pp. 163–73.

Mous, M. (2005), 'Yaaku and Ma'a: an endangered language and the way out', in N. Crawhall and N. Ostler (eds), *Creating Outsiders: Endangered Languages, Migration and Marginalisation*. Proceedings of the Ninth conference of the Foundation for Endangered Languages, Bath, pp. 55–8.

Mufwene, S. (2001), *The Ecology of Language Evolution*. Cambridge: Cambridge University Press.

Mühlhausler, P. (1986), *Pidgin and Creole Linguistics*. Oxford: Basil Blackwell.

Mühlhausler, P. (1991), 'Overview of the pidgin and creole languages of Australia', in Romaine (ed.), pp. 159–73.

Mukherjee, A. (1996), *Language Maintenance and Shift: Punjabis and Bengalis in Delhi*. New Delhi: Bahri.

Muysken, P. and N. Smith (eds) (1986), *Substrata versus Universals in Creole Genesis*. Amsterdam: Benjamins.

Myers-Scotton, C. (1990), 'Elite closure as boundary maintenance: the evidence from Africa', in B. Weinstein (ed.), *Language Policy and Political Development*. Norwood, NJ: Ablex, pp. 25–41.

Myers-Scotton, C. (1993), *Social Motivations for Codeswitching: Evidence from Africa*. Oxford: Clarendon.

Mylander, C. and S. Goldwin-Meadow (1991), 'Home sign systems in Deaf children: the development of morphology without a conventional language model', in Siple and Fischer (eds), pp. 41–63.

Nakamura, K. (2003), 'U-turns, deaf shock and the hard of hearing: Japanese deaf identities at the Borderlands', in L. Monaghan, C. Schmaling, K.

Nakamura and G. H. Turner (eds), *Many Ways to Be Deaf. International Variation in Deaf Communities*. Washington, DC: Gallaudet University Press, pp. 211–29.

Nettle, D. and S. Romaine (2000), *Vanishing Voices: The Extinction of the World's Languages*. Oxford: Oxford University Press.

New Encyclopedia Britannica (Macropaedia, The) (1986), 15th edn. Chicago: Encyclopedia Britannica, vol. 27, pp. 225–38 ('Servitude').

Nichols, P. (1979), 'Black women in the rural south: conservative and innovative', in B. L. Dubois and I. Crouch (eds), *The Sociology of the Languages of American Women*. Papers in Southwest English IV. San Antonio, TX: Trinity University, pp. 103–14.

Niedzielski, N. A. and D. R. Preston (2000), *Folk Linguistics*. Berlin/New York: Mouton de Gruyter.

Norrick, N. R. (1997), 'Twice-told tales: collaborative narration of familiar stories', *Language in Society* 26 (2): 199–220.

Noth, W. (1990), *Handbook of Semiotics*. Bloomington: Indiana University Press.

Nwoye, G. (1985), 'Eloquent silence among the Igbo of Nigeria', in D. Tannen and M. Saville-Troike (eds), *Perspectives on Silence*. Norwood, NJ: Ablex, pp. 185–91.

Ochs, E. (1992), 'Indexing gender', in A. Duranti and C. Goodwin (eds), *Rethinking Context: Language as an Interactive Phenomenon*. Cambridge: Cambridge University Press.

Ochs, E., R. Smith and C. Taylor (1996) (first pubd 1989), 'Detective stories and dinnertime: problem-solving through co-narration', in D. Brenneis and R. K. S. Macaulay (eds), *The Matrix of Language: Contemporary Linguistic Anthropology*. Boulder, CO: Westview Press, pp. 39–55 (Cultural Dynamics 2. Los Angeles: Sage Publications).

O'Donnell, P. E. (1993), 'Francisation, normalization and bilingual education: advantages and disadvantages of "heavy" and "light" language planning', in *Proceedings of the XVth International Congress of Linguistics. Quebec 9–14 August 1992*, vol. 4. Sainte Foy: Les Presses de l'Université Laval, pp. 73–6.

O'Donnell, W. R. and L. Todd (1980), *Variety in Contemporary English*. London: Allen and Unwin, p. 52.

Oftedal, M. (1990), 'Is Nynorsk a minority language?', in Haugen et al. (eds), pp. 120–9.

Ogilvy-Foreman, D., C. Penn and T. Reagan (1994), 'Selected syntactic features of South African sign language: a preliminary analysis'. *South African Journal of Linguistics* 12 (4): 118–23.

Okamoto, S. (1995), '"Tasteless Japanese": less "feminine" speech among young Japanese women', in K. Hall and M. Bucholtz (eds).

Okamoto, S. and J. Shibamoto Smith (eds) (2004), *Japanese Language, Gender and Ideology*. Oxford: Oxford University Press.

Okombo, O. (1994), 'Kenyan Sign Language (KSL). Some attitudinal and cognitive issues in the evolution of a language community', in I. Ahlgren and K. Hyltenstam (eds), *Bilingualism and Deaf Education*. Hamburg: Signum, pp. 37–54.

Orton, H. and N. Wright (1974), *A Word Geography of England*. London: Seminar Press.

Pandit, P. B. (1972), *India as a Sociolinguistic Area* (Gune Memorial Lectures 1968). Ganeshkind, India: University of Poona.

Paolillo, J. C. (2006), *Evaluating Language Statistics: The Ethnologue and Beyond*. A Report prepared for the UNESCO Institute for Statististics. Available at: http://ella.slis.indiana.edu/~paolillo/research/u_lg_rept.pdf (last accessed 9 December 2007).

Patrick, P. (2002), 'The Speech Community', in J. K. Chambers, P. Trudgill and N. Schilling-Estes (eds), *The Handbook of Language Variation and Change*. Malden, MA: Blackwell.

Paulsen, F. (1990), 'The recent situation of the Ferring language, the North-Frisian language of the islands Föhr and Amrum', in Haugen et al. (eds), pp. 182–8.

Penn, C. (1992), 'The sociolinguistics of South African Sign Language,' in Herbert (ed.), pp. 277–84.

Penn, C. (1993), 'Signs of the times: Deaf language and culture in South Africa'. *South African Journal of Communication Disorders* 40: 11–23.

Penn, C. assisted by D. Ogilvy-Foreman, D. Simmons and M. Anderson-Forbes (1992–4), *Dictionary of Southern African Signs*. Pretoria: Human Science Research Council.

Penn, C. (1995), 'On the other hand: implications of the study of South African sign language for the education of the deaf in South Africa'. *South African Journal for Education* 15 (2): 92–6.

Pennycook, A. (1994), *The Cultural Politics of English as an International Language*. London: Longman.

Pennycook, A. (2003) 'Global Englishes, Rip Slyme and performativity'. *Journal of Sociolinguistics* 7 (4): 513–15.

Petyt, K. M. (1980), *The Study of Dialect*. London: André Deutsch.

Peukert, D. J. K. (1987), *Inside Nazi-Germany: Conformity, Opposition and Racism in Everyday Life*. London: Penguin.

Philips, S. (1972), 'Participant structures and communicative competence: Warm Springs children in community and classroom', in D. Hymes, C. Cazden and V. John (eds), *Functions of Language in the Classroom*. New York: Teachers College Press, pp. 370–94.

Philips, S. (1983), *The Invisible Culture: Communication in Community and Classroom on the Warm Springs Indian Reservation*. New York: Longmans.

Phillipson, R. (1992), *Linguistic Imperialism*. Oxford: Oxford University Press.

Pickford, G. (1956), 'American linguistic geography: a sociological appraisal'. *Word* 12: 211–33.

Piller, I. (2001), 'Identity constructions in multilingual advertising'. *Language in Society* 30: 153–86.

Pinker, S. (1994), *The Language Instinct*. London: Penguin.

Platt, J. T. (1975), 'The Singapore English speech centinuum and its basilect "Singlish" as a creoloid'. *AnthL* 17 (7): 363–74.

Platt, J. T. (1983), 'English in Singapore, Malaysia and Hong Kong', in R. Bailey and M. Görlach (eds), *English as a World Language*. Ann Arbor: University of Michigan Press, pp. 384–414.

Platt, J. T., H. Weber and M. L. Ho (1984), *The New Englishes*. London: Routledge.

Plummer, K. (1995), *Telling Sexual Stories: Power, Change and Social Worlds*. London: Routledge.

Polyani, L. (1989). *Telling the American Story: A Structural and Cultural Analysis of Conversation Story-telling*. Cambridge, MA: MIT Press.

Pope, J., M. Meyerhoff and D. R. Ladd (2007), 'Forty years of language change on Martha's Vineyard'. *Language* 83 (3): 615–27.

Population Census (1996), *Census in Brief: The People of South Africa*. Pretoria: Statistics South Africa.

Potter, J. and M. Wetherell (1987), *Discourse and Social Psychology: Beyond Attitudes and Behaviour*. London: Sage Publications.

Poulantzas, N. (1973), 'The problem of the capitalist state', in J. Urry and J. Wakeford (eds), *Power in Britain: Sociological Readings*. London: Heinemann, pp. 291–305.

Pratkanis, A. R. and E. Aronson (1991), *Age of Propaganda: The Everyday Use and Abuse of Persuasion*. New York: W. H. Freeman.

Preisler, B. (1986), *Linguistic Sex Roles in Conversation: Social Variation in the Expression of Tentativeness in English*. Berlin: Mouton de Gruyter.

Preston, D. (1989) *Perceptual Dialectology*. Dordrecht: Foris.

Prillwitz, S. (1991), 'The long road towards bilingualism of the Deaf in the German-speaking area', in Prillwitz and Vollhaber (eds), pp. 13–25.

Prillwitz, S. and T. Vollhaber (eds) (1990), *Current Trends in European Sign Language Research. Proceedings of the 3rd European Congress on Sign Language Research, Hamburg, July 26–29, 1989*. Hamburg: Signum Verlag.

Prillwitz, S. and T. Vollhaber (1991), *Sign Language Research and Application. Proceedings of the International Congress, Hamburg, March 23–25, 1990*. Hamburg: Signum Verlag.

Pursglove, M. and A. Komarova (2003), 'The changing world of the Russian Deaf community', in L. Monaghan, C. Schmaling, K. Nakamura and G. H. Turner (eds), *Many Ways to Be Deaf. International Variation in Deaf Communities*. Washington, DC: Gallaudet University Press, pp. 249–59.

Rabin, C. (1971), 'A tentative classification of language-planning aims', in Rubin and Jernudd (eds) (1971a), pp. 277–9.

Rabin, C. (1989), 'Terminology development in the revival of a language: the case of contemporary Hebrew', in Coulmas (1989a), pp. 26–38.

Rampton, B. (1998), 'Language crossing and the redefinition of reality', in P. Auer (ed.), *Code-Switching in Conversation: Language, Interaction and Identity*. London: Taylor and Francis, pp. 295–7.

Rampton, B. (1999), 'Styling the other: introduction'. *Journal of Sociolinguistics* 3/4: 421–7.

Rampton, B. (2005), *Crossing: Language and Ethnicity among Adolescents*, 2nd edn. Manchester: St Jerome Press.

Ramsey, C. L. (1989), 'Language planning in Deaf education', in Lucas (ed.), pp. 123–46.

Ramsey, S. R. (1987), *The Languages of China*. Princeton, NJ: Princeton University Press.

Ray, P. S. (1963), *Language Standardization: Studies in Prescriptive Linguistics*. The Hague: Mouton de Gruyter.

Ray, P. S. (1968), 'Language standardization', in Fishman (ed.), pp. 754–65.

Reagan, T. (1985), 'The Deaf as a linguistic minority: educational considerations'. *Harvard Educational Review* 55 (3): 265–77.

Reagan, T. (1995), 'Neither easy to understand nor pleasing to see: the development of manual sign codes as language planning activity'. *Language Problems and Language Planning* 19 (2): 133–50.

Reagan, T. (2001), 'Language planning and policy', in C. Lucas (ed.), *The Sociolinguistics of Sign Languages*. Cambridge: Cambridge University Press, pp. 145–80.

Reid, S. (1987), *Working with Statistics*. Cambridge: Polity Press.

Reilly, J. M. L. McIntire (1980), 'American Sign Language and pidgin Sign English: what's the difference?' *SLS* 27: 151–92.

Reisman, K. (1974), 'Contrapuntal conversation in an Antiguan village', in R. Baumann and J. Scherzer (eds), *Explorations in the Ethnography of Speaking*. Cambridge: Cambridge University Press, pp. 110–24.

Rew, G. (1990), 'Wa'er'. *The Scots Magazine* (February): 497–501.

Reynolds, K. A. (1986), 'Female speakers of Japanese in transition', in S. Bremner, N. Caskey and B. Moonwomon (eds), *Proceedings of the First Berkeley Women and Language Conference*. Berkeley, CA: Berkeley Women and Language Group, University of California. Repr. in S. Ide and N. H. McGloin (eds) (1990), *Aspects of Japanese Women's Language*. Tokyo: Kurosio Publishers, pp. 129–46.

Ricento, T. (2006), 'Language policy: theory and practice – an introduction', in T. Ricento (ed.), *An Introduction to Language Policy*. Oxford: Blackwell.

Rickford, J. (1986), 'The need for new approaches to social class analysis in sociolinguistics'. *LC* 6 (3): 215–21.

Rickford, J. (1987), *Dimensions of a Creole Continuum: History, Texts and Linguistic Analysis of Guyanese Creole*. Stanford, CA: Stanford University Press.

Roberts, C., E. Davies and T. Jupp (1992), *Language and Discrimination*. London: Longman.

Roberts, J. M. (1976), *The Hutchinson History of the World*. London: Hutchinson.

Robins, R. H. and E. M. Uhlenbeck (eds) (1991), *Endangered Languages*. Oxford: Berg.

Robinson, F. N. (1974), *The Complete Works of Geoffrey Chaucer*, 2nd edn. Oxford: Oxford University Press.

Rogers, E. M. (1995), *Diffusion of Innovations*, 4th edn. New York: The Free Press.

Romaine, S. (1988), *Pidgin and Creole Languages*. London: Longman.

Romaine, S. (1989a), 'English and Tok Pisin (New Guinea Pidgin English) in Papua New Guinea'. *World Englishes* 8 (1): 5–23.

Romaine, S. (1989b), *Bilingualism*. Oxford: Basil Blackwell.

Romaine, S. (ed.) (1991), *Language in Australia*. Cambridge: Cambridge University Press.

Romaine, S. (1994), *Language in Society: An Introduction to Sociolinguistics*. Oxford: Oxford University Press.

Romaine, S. (2003), 'Variation in language and gender', in J. Holmes and M.

Meyerhoff (eds), *The Handbook of Language and Gender*. Oxford: Blackwell Publishing.

Ross, A. (1959), 'U and non-U: an essay in sociological linguistics', in N. Mitford (ed.), *Noblesse Oblige*. Harmondsworth: Penguin, pp. 9–32.

Rubin, J. (1971), 'Evaluation and language planning', in Rubin and Jernudd (eds) (1971a), pp. 217–41.

Rubin, J. and B. H. Jernudd (eds) (1971a), *Can Language Be Planned? Sociolinguistic Theory and Practice for Developing Nations*. Honolulu: Hawaii.

Rubin, J. and B. H. Jernudd (1971b), 'Introduction: language planning as an element in modernization', in Rubin and Jernudd (eds) (1971a), pp. xiii–xxiv.

Rudner, W. A. and R. Butowsky (1981), 'Signs used in the Deaf gay community'. *SLS* 30: 36–48.

Sacks, H., E. Schegloff and G. Jefferson (1974), 'A simplest systematics for the organization of turn-taking in conversation'. *Language* 50 (4): 696–735.

Sacks, O. (1989), *Seeing Voices: A Journey into the World of the Deaf*. Berkeley and Los Angeles: University of California Press.

Sajavaara, K. and J. Lehtonen (1997), 'The silent Finn revisited', in A. Jaworski (ed.), *Silence: Interdisciplinary Perspectives*. Berlin/New York: Mouton de Gruyter.

Sakaguchi, A. (1989), 'Towards a clarification of the function and status of international planned languages', in U. Ammon (ed.), *Status and Function of Languages and Language Varieties*. Berlin and New York: Mouton de Gruyter, pp. 399–440.

Sandburg, D. (1989), *The Legal Guide to Mother Goose*. New York: Price, Stern & Sloan, a member of the Penguin Group.

Sankoff, G. (1979), 'The genesis of a language', in K. C. Hill (ed.), *The Genesis of Language*. Ann Arbor: Karema, pp. 23–47.

Sankoff, G. (1986), *The Social Life of Language*. Philadelphia: University of Pennsylvania Press.

Sapir, E. (1921), *Language*. New York: Harcourt, Brace, World.

Sapir, E. (1929), 'Male and female forms of speech in Yana', in St W. J. Teeuwen (ed.), *Donum Natalicium Schrijnen*. Nijmegen and Utrecht. Repr. in D. G. Mandelbaum (ed.) (1964), *Selected Writings of Edward Sapir in Language, Culture and Personality*. Berkeley and Los Angeles: University of California Press; London: Cambridge University Press.

Sarup, M. (1993), *An Introductory Guide to Post-Structuralism and Postmodernism*, 2nd edn. New York: Harvester Wheatsheaf.

Saussure, F. de (1959), *Course in General Linguistics*, C. Bally and A. Sechehaye with A. Riedlinger, trans. W. Baskin (original notes of 1907–11). New York: McGraw Hill.

Saville-Troike, M. (1985), 'The place of silence in an integrated theory of communication', in D. Tannen and M. Saville-Troike (eds), *Perspectives on Silence*. Norwood, NJ: Ablex, pp. 3–18.

Saville-Troike, M. (2003), *The Ethnography of Communication: An Introduction*, 3rd edn. Malden, MA: Blackwell Publishing.

Schermer, T. (2003), 'From variant to standard: an overview of the standardization process of the lexicon of sign language of The Netherlands over two decades'. *Sign Language Studies* 3: 469–86.

Schlobinski, P. (1987), 'Berlin', in U. Ammon, N. Dittmar and J. K. Mattheier (eds), *Sociolinguistics. Soziolinguistik. An International Handbook of the Science of Language and Society. Ein internationales Handbuch zur Wissenschaft von Sprache und Gesellschaft*, vol. 2. Berlin and New York: de Gruyter, pp. 1,258–63.

Schmaling, C. (2000), *Maganar Hannu: Language of the Hands. A Descriptive Analysis of Hausa Sign Language*. Hamburg: Signum Press.

Schmidt, J. (1872), *Die Verwandtschaftsverhältnisse der Indogermanischen Sprachen*. Weimar: Bohlä.

Schönfeld, H. and P. Schlobinski (1995), 'Language and social change in Berlin', in P. Stevenson (ed.), *The German Language and the Real World: Sociolinguistic, Cultural, and Pragmatic Perspectives on Contemporary German*. Oxford: Clarendon Press, pp. 117–34.

Schuchardt, H. (1882), 'Kreolische Studien I: Über das Negerportugiesische von San Thome (Westafrika)'. *Sitzungsberichte der Kaiserlichen Akademie der Wissenschaften zu Wien* 101 (2): 889–917.

Schumann, J. H. (1974), 'Implications of pidginization and creolization for the study of adult second language acquisition', in R. C. Gingras (ed.), *Second Language Acquisition and Foreign Language Teaching*. Arlington, VA: Center for Applied Linguistics, pp. 137–51.

Scott J. C. (1985), *Weapons of the Weak: Everyday Forms of Peasant Resistance*. New Haven, CT: Yale University Press.

Scotton, C. M. [Myers-Scotton] (1978), 'Language in East Africa: linguistic patterns and political ideologies', in J. A. Fishman (ed.), *Advances in the Study of Societal Multilingualism*. The Hague: Mouton de Gruyter, pp. 719–59.

Searle, J. R. (1969), *Speech Acts: An Essay in the Philosophy of Language*. Cambridge: Cambridge University Press.

Sebba, M. (1984), 'Serial verbs: something new out of Africa', in M. Sebba and L. Todd (eds), *Papers from the York Creole Conference*, 24–27 September 1983, York Papers in Linguistics 11. York: York University, pp. 271–8.

Sebba, M. (1997), *Contact Languages: Pidgins and Creoles*. London: Longmans.

Seidel, E. and I. Seidel-Slotty (1961), *Sprachwandel im Dritten Reich. Eine kritische Untersuchung faschistischer Einflüsse*. Halle (Saale): VEB Verlag Sprache und Literatur.

Senghas, R. J. and L. Monaghan (2002), 'Signs of their times: Deaf communities and the culture of language'. *Annual Review of Anthropology* 31: 69–97.

Sherzer, J. (1977), 'The ethnography of speaking: a critical appraisal', in M. Saville-Troike (ed.), *Linguistics and Anthropology*. Washington, DC: Georgetown University Press, pp. 43–58.

Shroyer, E. and S. Shroyer (1984), *Signs Across America: A Look at Regional Differences in American Sign Language*. Washington, DC: Gallaudet University Press.

Shuy, R. (1970), 'Sociolinguistic research at the Centre for Applied Linguistics: the correlation of language and sex', in *International Days of Sociolinguistics*. Rome: Istituto Luigi Sturzo.

Siegel, J. (1996), 'Bislama pronouns', in D. Graddol, D. Leith and J. Swann (eds), *English: History, Diversity and Change*. London: Routledge.

Singh, R. (1995), 'On new/non-native Englishes: a quartet'. *Journal of Pragmatics* 24: 283–94.

Singler, J. (2001), 'Why you can't do a VARBRUL study of quotatives and what such a study can show us'. *Pennsylvania Working Papers in Linguistics* 7: 257–78.

Siple, P. and Fischer (eds) (1991), *Theoretical Issues in Sign Language Research*, 2 vols. Chicago and London: University of Chicago Press.

Skutnabb-Kangas, T. and R. Phillipson (1989), '"Mother Tongue": the theoretical and sociopolitical construction of a concept', in U. Ammon (ed.), *Status and Function of Languages and Language Varieties*. Berlin and New York: Mouton de Gruyter, pp. 450–77.

Skutnabb-Kangas, T. (2000), *Linguistic Genocide in Education – or Worldwide Diversity and Human Rights*. Mahwah, NJ: Lawrence Erlbaum.

Solomon, J. L. (1995), 'The negotiation of academic language stylistic registers in three elementary school classrooms'. Unpublished PhD dissertation, Department of Anthropology, American University, Washington, DC.

South African Census (2001), Pretoria: Statistics South Africa.

Southworth, F. (1974), 'Linguistic masks for power: some relationships between semantic and social change'. *AnthL* 16: 177–91.

Spencer, J. and M. Gregory (1964), 'An approach to the study of style', in N. E. Enkvist, J. Spencer and M. Gregory (eds), *Linguistics and Style*. London: Oxford University Press, pp. 57–105.

Spender, D. (1990), *Man Made Language*. London: Pandora.

Spender, D. (1995), *Nattering on the Net: Women, Power and Cyberspace*. Melbourne: Spinitex.

Spolsky, B. (2004), *Language Policy*. Cambridge: Cambridge University Press.

Spolsky, B. and F. Hult (2008), *The Handbook of Educational Linguistics*. Oxford: Blackwell.

Spolsky, B. and E. Shohamy (1999), *The Languages of Israel: Policy, Ideology and Practice*. Clevedon: Multilingual Matters.

Sreedhar, M. V. (1974), *Naga Pidgin: A Sociolinguistic Study on Interlingual Communication Pattern in Nagaland*. Mysore: Central Institute of Indian Languages.

Stewart, W. (1968), 'A sociolinguistic typology for describing national multilingualism', in Fishman (ed.), pp. 531–45.

Steytler, N. C. (1993), 'Implementing language rights in court: the role of the court interpreter in South Africa', in K. Prinsloo, Y. Peeters, J. Turi and C. van Rensburg (eds), *Language, Law and Equality. Proceedings of the Third International Conference of the International Academy of Language Law (IALL) held in South Africa, April 1992*. Pretoria: University of South Africa, pp. 38–56.

Stokoe, W. C. (1960), *Sign Language Structure: An Outline of the Visual Communications Systems of the American Deaf*. University of Buffalo, Occasional Papers 8.

Stokoe, W. C. (1969–70), 'Sign language diglossia'. *Studies in Linguistics* 21: 27–41.

Stokoe, W. C., H. R. Bernard and C. Padden (1976), 'An elite group in Deaf society'. *Sign Language Studies* 12: 189–210.

Stokoe, W. C., D. C. Casterline and C. G. Cronenberg (1976), *A Dictionary of American Sign Language on Linguistic Principles*. Washington, DC: Gallaudet College Press.

Street, B. (1993), *Cross-cultural Approaches to Literacy*. Cambridge: Cambridge University Press.

Stubbs, M. (1986), *Educational Linguistics*. Cambridge: Cambridge University Press.

Sunderland, J. (1995), '"We're boys, miss!": finding gendered identities and looking for gendering of identities in the foreign language classroom', in S. Mills (ed.), *Language and Gender: Interdisciplinary Perspectives*. Harlow: Longman, pp. 160–78

Sunderland, J. (2006), *Language and Gender: An Advanced Resource Book*. Abingdon: Routledge.

Supalla, S. J. (1991), 'Manually coded English: the modality question in signed language development', in Siple and Fischer (eds), pp. 85–109.

Supalla, T. (1991), 'Serial verb motion in ASL', in Siple and Fischer (eds), pp. 127–52.

Sutton-Spence, R. and B. Woll (1999), *The Linguistics of British Sign Language. An Introduction*. Cambridge: Cambridge University Press.

Swadesh, M. (1948), 'Sociologic notes on obsolescent languages'. *IJAL* 14: 226–35.

Swann, J. (2002), 'Yes, but is it gender?', in Litosseliti and Sunderland.

Swann, J. (2003), 'Schooled language: language and gender in educational settings', in Holmes and Meyerhoff.

Swann, J. and J. Maybin (2008), 'Sociolinguistic and ethnographic approaches to language and gender', in Harrington et al.

Swann, J., A. Deumert, T. Lillis and R. Mesthrie (2004), *A Dictionary of Sociolinguistics*. Edinburgh: Edinburgh University Press.

Swisher, M. V. and D. McKee (1989), 'The sociolinguistic situation of natural sign languages'. *Applied Linguistics* 10 (3): 294–312.

Tagliamonte, S. and A. D'Arcy (2004), '*He's like, She's like* – The quotative system of Canadian Youth'. *Journal of Sociolinguistics* 8: 493–594.

Talbot, M. M. (1998), *Language and Gender: An Introduction*. Cambridge: Polity Press.

Tannen, D. (1985), 'Silence: anything but', in D. Tannen and M. Saville-Troike (eds), *Perspectives on Silence*. Norwood, NJ: Ablex, pp. 93–111.

Tannen, D. (1990, UK 1991), *You Just Don't Understand: Women and Men in Conversation*. New York: William Morrow; London: Virago.

Tauli, V. (1968), *Introduction to a Theory of Language Planning*. Uppsala: Almqvist and Wiksell.

Taylor, A. (1981) 'Indian lingua francas', in C. A. Ferguson and S. B. Heath (eds), *Language in the USA*. Cambridge: Cambridge University Press, pp. 175–95.

Taylor, D. (1961), 'New languages for old in the West Indies'. *Comparative Studies in Society and History* 3: 277–88.

Tessarolo, M. (1990), 'Deaf people's bilingualism as pseudo-bilingualism', in Prillwitz and Vollhaber (eds), pp. 89–94.

Thomas, B. (1988), 'Differences of sex and sects: linguistic variation and social networks in a Welsh mining village', in J. Coates and D. Cameron (eds), *Women in their Speech Communities*. London and New York: Longman, pp. 51–60.

Thomason, S. (2001), *Language Contact. An Introduction*. Edinburgh: Edinburgh University Press.

Thompson, J. B. (1991), 'Introduction', in Bourdieu, pp. 1–31.

Thomson, D. (1990), 'Gaelic in Scotland: assessment and prognosis', in Haugen et al. (eds), pp. 10–20.

Thorburn, T. (1971), 'Cost–benefit analysis in language planning', in Rubin and Jernudd (eds), pp. 253–62.

Thurston, W. (1987), *Processes of Change in the Language of North-Western New Britain*. Pacific Linguists B-99. Canberra: Australian National University.

Todd, L. (1984), *Modern Englishes: Pidgins and Creoles*. Oxford: Blackwell.

Todd, L. (1990), *Pidgins and Creoles*. London: Routledge.

Todd, L. (1994), 'Pidgins and creoles', in R. Asher (ed.), *The Encyclopedia of Language and Linguistics*. Oxford: Pergamon, vol. 6: 3,177–81.

Treichler, P. A., R. M. Frankel, C. Kramarae, K. Zoppi and H. B. Beckman (1984), 'Problems and *problems*: power relationships in a medical encounter', in C. Kramarae, M. Schulz and W. M. O'Barr (eds), *Language and Power*. New York: Sage Publications.

Troemel-Ploetz, S. (1991), 'Selling the apolitical'. *Discourse and Society* 2: 489–502.

Trudgill, P. (1974), *The Social Differentiation of English in Norwich*. Cambridge: Cambridge University Press.

Trudgill, P. (1975), *Accent, Dialect and the School*. London: Edward Arnold.

Trudgill, P. (1978), 'Sex, covert prestige, and linguistic change in the urban British English of Norwich'. *LiS* 1: 179–96.

Trudgill, P. (1983a), *Sociolinguistics: An Introduction to Language and Society*, 2nd edn. Harmondsworth: Penguin.

Trudgill, P. (1983b), *On Dialect: Social and Geographical Perspectives*. Oxford: Basil Blackwell.

Trudgill, P. (1986), *Dialects in Contact*. Oxford: Basil Blackwell.

Trudgill, P. and J. K. Chambers (1980), *Dialectology*. Cambridge: Cambridge University Press.

Trudgill, P. and J. K Chambers (1999), *Dialectology*. Cambridge: Cambridge University Press.

Tsujimura, N. (2007), *An Introduction to Japanese Linguistics*, 2nd edn. Oxford: Blackwell Publishing.

Turkle, S. (1995), *Life on the Screen: Identity in the Age of the Internet*. New York: Simon and Schuster.

Uchida, A. (1992), 'When "difference" is "dominance": a critique of the "anti-power-based" cultural approach to sex differences'. *LiS* 21: 547–68.

UNESCO (1953), *The Use of Vernacular Languages in Education* (Monographs of Fundamental Education No. 8). Paris: UNESCO. Repr. in Fishman (ed.)

(1968), pp. 688–716.

Upton, C. and J. D. A. Widdowson (2006), *An Atlas of English Dialects*, 2nd edn. London: Routledge.

Van Name, A. (1869–70), 'Contributions to creole grammar'. *Transactions of the American Philological Association* 1: 123–67.

Vikør, L. S. (1993), *The Nordic Languages: Their Status and Interrelations*. Oslo: Novus Press (Nordic Language Secretariat Publications no. 14).

Vogt-Svendsen, M. (1983), 'Position and movement of the mouth in Norwegian Sign Language', in Kyle and Woll (eds), pp. 85–95.

Voloshinov, V. N. (1973 [1929]), *Marxism and the Philosophy of Language*, trans. L. Matejka and I. R. Titunik. Cambridge, MA: Harvard University Press.

von Gleich, U. and E. Wolff (eds) (1991), *Standardization of National Languages*. Symposium on Language Standardization, 2–3 February 1991. Hamburg: UNESCO Institute for Education.

Wallwork, J. F. (1969), *Language and Linguistics: An Introduction to the Study of Language*. London: Heinemann.

Ward, M. (1971), *Them Children: A Study in Language Learning*. Prospect Heights, IL: Waveland Press.

Wardhaugh, R. (1978), *Introduction to Linguistics*, 2nd edn. New York: McGraw-Hill.

Warren, J. 1999. '"Wogspeak". Transformations of Australian English'. *Journal of Australian Studies* 62: 86–94.

Washabaugh, W. (1980), 'The manu-facturing of a language'. *Semiotica* 29 (1/2): 1–37.

Washabaugh, W. (1981), 'Sign Language in its social context'. *ARA* 10: 237–52.

Watzinger-Tharp, J. (2004), 'Turkish-German language: An innovative style of communication and its implications for citizenship and identity'. *Journal of Muslim Minority Affairs* 24: 285–94.

Webb, V. N. (1995), 'A sociolinguistic profile of South Africa: a brief overview', in Webb (ed.), *Language in South Africa: An Input into Language Planning for a Post-apartheid South Africa*. Pretoria: University of Pretoria, pp. 15–40.

Weber, M. (1947), *The Theory of Social and Economic Organisation*, trans. A. M. Henderson and T. Parsons, ed. T. Parsons. New York: Free Press.

Weber, M. (1956), *Wirtschaft und Gesellschaft: Grundriss der verstehenden Soziologie*, 4th edn. Tübingen: J. C. B. Mohr (Paul Siebeck).

Weinreich, U. (1968), *Languages in Contact: Findings and Problems*. The Hague: Mouton de Gruyter. (First pub'd as Publications of the Linguistic Circle of New York, No. 1, 1953.)

Weinreich, U., W. Labov and M. Herzog (1968), 'Empirical foundations for a theory of language change', in W. P. Lehmann and Y. Malkiel (eds), *Directions for Historical Linguistics*. Austin: University of Texas Press, pp. 95–189.

Wells, C. J. (1987), *German: A Linguistic History to 1945*. Oxford: Clarendon Press.

Wells, J. C. (1982), *Accents of English*, vol. 1. Cambridge: Cambridge University Press.

Wenker, G. (1895–1925), *Der Sprachatlas des Deutschen Reichs*. Marburg: Elwert.

West, C. (1984), 'When the doctor is a "lady": power, status and gender in physician–patient encounters'. *Symbolic Interaction* 7: 87–106.

West, C. and D. H. Zimmerman (1983), 'Small insults: a study of interruptions in cross-sex conversations between unacquainted persons', in B. Thorne, C. Kramarae and N. Henley (eds), *Language, Gender and Society*. Rowley, MA: Newbury House.

Whinnom, K. (1956), *Spanish Contact Vernaculars In the Philippine Islands*. Hong Kong: Hong Kong University Press.

Whinnom, K. (1965), 'The origin of European-based pidgins and creoles'. *Orbis* 14: 509–27.

Whinnom, K. (1971), 'Linguistic hybridization and the "special case" of pidgins and creoles', in D. Hymes (ed.), *Pidginization and Creolization of Languages*. Cambridge: Cambridge University Press, pp. 91–115.

Whorf, B. L. (1956), *Language, Thought and Reality: Selected Writings*, ed. J. B. Carroll. Cambridge, MA: MIT Press.

Widdowson, H. (1995), 'Discourse analysis: a critical view'. *Language and Literature* 4: 157–72.

Wiggen, G. (1995), 'Norway in the 1990s: a sociolinguistic profile'. *IJSL* 115: 47–83.

Williams, J. (1987), 'Non-native varieties of English: a special case of language acquisition'. *English World-Wide* 8 (2): 161–99.

Winford, D. (2003), *An Introduction to Contact Linguistics*. Oxford: Blackwell.

Wodak, R. (ed.) (1997), *Gender and Discourse*. London: Sage Publications.

Wolfram, W. (1969), *A Sociolinguistic Description of Detroit Negro Speech*. Washington, DC: Center for Applied Linguistics.

Woods, H. B. (1991), 'Social differentiation in Ottawa English', in J. Cheshire (ed.), *English Around the World*. Cambridge: Cambridge University Press, pp. 134–49.

Woodward, J. (1972), 'Implications for sociolinguistics research among the Deaf'. *Sign Language Studies* 1: 1–7.

Woodward, J. C. (1973), 'Some observations on sociolinguistic variation and American Sign Language'. *Kansas Journal of Sociology* 9: 191–200.

Woodward, J. (1974), 'Implicational variation in American Sign Language: negative incorporation'. *Sign Language Studies* 39: 20–30.

Woodward, J. C. (1976), 'Black southern signing'. *LiS* 5: 211–18.

Woodward, J. (2000), 'Sign language and sign language families in Thailand and Viet Nam', in K. Emmorey and H. Lane (eds), *The Signs of Language Revisited. An Anthology to Honor Ursula Bellugi and Edward Klima*. Mahwah, NJ: Lawrence Erlbaum, pp. 23–47.

Woolard, K. A. (2004), 'Codeswitching', in A. Duranti (ed.), *A Companion to Linguistic Anthropology*. Malden, MA and Oxford: Blackwell Publishing.

Wright, F. (1984), 'A sociolinguistic study of passivisation amongst Black adolescents in Britain'. Unpublished PhD dissertation, University of Birmingham.

Wulf, A. P. Dudis, R. Bayley and C. Lucas (2002), 'Variable subject presence in ASL narratives'. *SLS* 3: 54–76.

Wylie, M. (1995), 'No place for women'. *Digital Media* 4 (January).

Yates, S. (1996), 'Computer-mediated English: sociolinguistic aspects of computer-mediated communication', in J. Maybin and N. Mercer (eds), *Using English: From Conversation to Canon*. London: Routledge in association with the Open University, pp. 76–83.

Zenter, K. (1983), *Illustrierte Geschichte des Widerstandes in Deutschland und Europa 1933–45*, 2nd edn. Munich: Südwest Verlag.

Zimmer, J. (1989), 'Toward a description of register variation in American Sign Language', in C. Lucas (ed.), *The Sociolinguistics of the Deaf Community*. San Diego: Academic Press, pp. 253–72.

Zimmerman, D. H. and C. West (1975), 'Sex roles, interruptions and silences in conversation', in B. Thorne and N. Henley (eds), *Language and Sex: Difference and Dominance*. Rowley, MA: Newbury House.

GLOSSARY

This glossary contains only general linguistic terms (and some sociological terms) that are used in several parts of the text. Sociolinguistic terms and concepts defined and explained at some length in the book are excluded; you should refer to the index if you wish to look these up. An asterisk (*) indicates the use of a term that is itself explained elsewhere in the glossary.

affricate a sound that is a combination of a stop* and a fricative*. The initial sound in the word _chin_ is an affricate, a combination of the stop [t] and the fricative 'sh' (the initial sound in _shed_).

backed vowel a vowel which occupies a back position in the vowel space in a particular dialect, rather than the front or central position which it occupies in most other dialects. See Figure B (p. xxv).

centralised vowel a vowel which occupies a central position in the vowel space in a particular dialect, rather than the front or back position which it occupies in most other dialects. See Figure B (p. xxv).

coda a linguistic unit that rounds off a larger unit. For example, the line 'and that was the worst moment of my life' may act as a coda, rounding off a narrative.

code a term for any variety of language, usually stressing the linguistic rules that underpin the variety. (Bernstein's notion of elaborated and restricted codes involves a different meaning of 'code' – see index.)

copula the verb _be_ (and its variants like _am_, _is_, _are_, _was_, _were_) used before a noun or adjective, to denote membership of a set. For example, in the sentence _She is my aunt_, the verb _is_ denotes membership of the set of aunts. Copular _be_ contrasts with auxiliary _be_ which modifies a verb (for example _She is playing outside_), though some sociolinguists do not observe this distinction in terminology.

diphthong a vowel sound made up of two vowels. For example, the vowel in _my_ is in most varieties of English a diphthong made up of the simpler vowels [a] and [ɪ], the first of which glides into the second, forming one phonetic unit – the diphthong.

endogamy a customary practice of marrying within one's social group.

epistemic modal an auxiliary verb that expresses the speaker's belief or confidence in the main verb which it qualifies. (**Modal** typically refers to the 'mood' or 'mindset' expressed by auxiliary verbs like *will, may, might, must, can.* **Epistemic** is a philosophical term meaning 'knowledge or degree of acceptance of a proposition'. It includes grammatical categories like 'probability', 'possibility' and 'necessity', expressed by the modal verbs.)

exogamy   a customary practice of marrying outside one's social group.

fricative   a consonant which is produced when one articulator approaches another so closely as to produce audible friction. For example, [f] is a fricative produced by the slight contact made between lower teeth and upper lip. Other fricatives are [s], [v], [z] and so on.

fronted vowel   a vowel which occupies a front position in the vowel space in a particular dialect, rather than the central or back position which it occupies in most other dialects. See Figure B (p. xxv).

icon   a sign* in which the signifier* has a 'natural' relationship with a signified*. For example, the English word *cock-a-doodle-do* is meant to imitate the actual sound made by the cockerel.

index   a sign* which stands in some kind of logical relationship with another sign. E.g. in the pair of signs *smoke* and *fire*, the first is an index of the second.

lingua franca   a language that is used to facilitate communication between two communities which have different first languages. A lingua franca could be a simple pidgin or a fully developed language like English (as when a person from Saudi Arabia might communicate with a person from Japan).

marked   a linguistic unit that is a special case, or is rare or contains an extra feature compared to a related unit. For example, *This book, I love* is marked in comparison with the more usual *I love this book.* (The former contains two extra features compared to the latter: movement of the phrase *this book* to initial position, and special intonation.) The latter sentence is said to be **unmarked** in relation to the first.

matched guise   a technique in social psychology that elicits listeners' judgements of the social characteristics associated with what they assume are different speaking voices on tape. Since listeners are unaware that it is the same speaker assuming different language varieties, researchers are able to draw conclusions about attitudes to these language varieties in a particular society.

minimal pair   see **phonemic contrast**

morpheme   the smallest unit that conveys meaning in a language. For example, the word *players* has three morphemes which convey the meanings of 'play', 'doer of action' (*-er*) and 'plural' (*-s*). The first is a **lexical morpheme**, which conveys the basic meaning of the word, while the last two are **grammatical morphemes**, which convey grammatical meanings pertaining to tense, number, negation and so on. (Morpheme is not to be confused with syllable, which is a unit of sound having a vowel as its nucleus. A syllable need not have a meaning.)

morphology   the study of the structure of words, especially the way in which meaningful sub-units of words are put together (see **morpheme**).

participant observation   a technique used in research where a researcher becomes part of the group which he or she wishes to study for an extended period.

phoneme a sound that is basic to a language insofar as it can change the meaning of words. In English, [p] and [b] are separate phonemes since they differentiate between, for example, *pat* and *bat*. In Tamil, these two sounds cannot change the meanings of words; rather, they occur in different positions in words and are thus not separate phonemes in Tamil.

phonemic contrast the difference between /p/ and /b/ in English exemplifies phonemic contrast (see phoneme*). *Pat* and *bat* are an example of a **minimal pair**, that is, a pair of words which differ by just one phoneme*.

phonology the study of the systematic way in which sounds are arranged to form syllables, words and other units of language, as well as the study of the relationships between different sets of sounds in language. See **phoneme**.

postvocalic a phonetic term referring to a consonant occurring after a vowel. For example, the word *sold* contains a postvocalic 'l'; the word *palm* does not (since the 'l' is not pronounced). The term 'non-prevocalic' is sometimes also used.

sign a sign is a linguistic unit which comprises either sounds (in spoken language), a series of letters (in written language) or handshapes and other movements (in sign language) **and** the meaning conveyed by them. A linguistic sign like *dog* consists of both the form of the word and its meaning. See **signifier, signified.**

signified meaning conveyed by the units of a language. In the above example, the concept 'dog' conveyed by the pronunciation (or spelling or signing) is the signified.

signifier element which in itself has no meaning, but which is used to convey meaning within the language system. In the above example, the sequence pronounced (or spelt or signed) 'd-o-g' is a signifier in English.

stop a sound produced when the air flow in the mouth is cut off by contact between one articulator and another. For example, the sound [t] is a stop produced by the temporary obstruction of air made when the tongue makes contact with the area just behind the upper teeth (the alveolar or gum ridge). Other stops include [d], [p], [b], [k] and [g].

symbol a sign* in which the relationship between signifier* and signified* is arbitrary.

tag question a linguistic construction whose first part resembles a statement, and whose second part resembles a reduced question. In a sentence like *Jane will be going, won't she?*, the tag is the phrase *won't she?*

Universal Grammar the approach to language advocated by Chomsky, who seeks to describe the abstract rules that underlie all human languages. In this way, he hopes to characterise the 'linguistic competence' common to all humans.

unmarked see **marked**

INDEX